HxR

THE FIRST WORLD WAR:
THE ESSENTIAL GUIDE TO SOURCES
IN THE UK NATIONAL ARCHIVES

The First World War

The Essential Guide to Sources in the UK National Archives

Ian F. W. Beckett

PUBLIC RECORD OFFICE

First published in 2002 by

Public Record Office
Kew
Richmond
Surrey
TW9 4DU
www.pro.gov.uk/

A catalogue record for this book is available from the British Library

ISBN 1 903365 41 4

Jacket illustrations, from top:
Ministry of Munitions poster, 1918 (EXT 1/315/1); Richard Leonard
Atkinson, awarded the Military Cross, 1917 (PRO 8/55);
stretcher-bearers collecting wounded under fire, *Illustrated London
News*, 25 September 1916 (ZPER 34/149); peace celebrations, 1919
(WORK 21/74); Navy Recruitment Poster, RNVR Signal Branch, 1917
(ADM 1/8331)
Back: Ministry of Munitions poster, 1914–18 (EXT 1/315/17)

Typeset by Carnegie Publishing, Lancaster, Lancashire
Printed in Great Britain by Cromwell Press, Trowbridge, Wiltshire

Contents

The plate section falls between pages 144 and 145

Introduction		vii
Acknowledgements		ix
List of Abbreviations		xi
List of Department Codes		xiii
Using the PRO		xv
1.	*The Higher Direction of the War*	1
	Cabinet Government and War	2
	War, Strategy and International Politics	8
	Dominions and Colonies	22
	The Peace Settlements	25
2.	*New Ways of War*	39
	Science and War	39
	The War on Land	51
	The War at Sea	83
	The War in the Air	105
	Absorbing the Lessons	117
3.	*The Nation in Arms*	121
	Recruitment	121
	War Service	130
	Losses, Veterans and Dependants	150
	Commemoration	165
4.	*War, State and Society*	173
	The Growth of Government	173
	War Finance	181
	War and Industrial Mobilisation	187
	Labour	199
	Women	203
	Food Supply	212
	Social Values and Leisure	218
	State Welfare	222

The Management of Morale   231
Aliens and the Enemy Within   239

Appendix: Other First World War Record Sources in the UK   253

Further Reading   256
Index   261

Introduction

The great war was an event of immense significance, shaping the twentieth-century world. Four empires were destroyed – those of Imperial Germany, Austria-Hungary, Tsarist Russia, and Ottoman Turkey. The consequences were profound, not least in the Middle East, whose politics still reflect the events between 1914 and 1918 as well as the post-war settlement effected by Britain and France. Without the Great War, communism arguably would not have triumphed in Russia, nor fascism been given its opportunity in Germany and Italy. At the same time, the war gravely weakened Europe's influence generally, even if the United States chose to wield its new-found power in financial rather than military or diplomatic terms until after the Second World War. In innumerable ways, the world created by the war's causes, course, and consequences endured at least until the collapse of communism in Europe in 1989.

In Britain, too, the effects and impact of the Great War are evident to this day. At one level, it is recalled by such annual rituals as British Summer Time while popular linguistic use still echoes soldiers' slang such as Blighty, conchie, and so on. There is an enduring artistic and literary legacy, even if much of it is by no means representative of actual wartime experience and, if anything, actually profoundly misleading. Of course, there are also the annual rituals of remembrance and the physical evidence of commemoration in terms of national and local war memorials. Indeed, there remains a wholly mythic collective British popular memory of the war with an emphasis upon a lost generation slaughtered in a futile war, leaving its survivors disillusioned and embittered.

In part, the myth of the Great War in Britain was created by its early historiography, in which memoirs by leading politicians and soldiers were invariably selective and self-serving and official histories designed more to obscure the past than to elucidate it. The particular interpretations advanced in the 'battle of the memoirs' in the 1920s and 1930s could not be readily challenged by historians who possessed neither firsthand knowledge of events at the higher level nor access to primary sources. Indeed, the public accessibility of corrective documents is of crucial importance and it must be borne in mind that, even when the 50 Year Rule was introduced by the Public Records Act of 1958, it was by no means clear that this would apply to Cabinet papers and memoranda although, in practice, the constraints that the Cabinet secretariat wished to maintain could not be sustained. In effect, some papers also became available under an informal 30 Year Rule prior to its actual introduction under the Public Records Act of 1967, but most official records relating to the Great War were not open to historians until the mid 1960s. Some, of course, remained closed for a period of 75 years, and it was only in the 1990s that surviving personnel records of Great War servicemen and women began to be released. Some documents closed for 100 years still remain unavailable. Nonetheless, the overwhelming majority of surviving public collections relating to the Great War are now readily accessible in the Public Record Office, enabling all – historians, postgraduate students, genealogists or simply those interested in the past – to discover the reality that lies behind the received myth of the war.

The immensity and variety of the global conflict is well represented in the collections of the Public Record Office, and it is the intention of this new guide to introduce the reader to the wealth of source material available, so much of which remains unexplored and unexploited. The collections are not simply confined to the higher direction of the war at the level of Cabinet government and to military, naval and diplomatic events though, even here, there is much scope for further work on such neglected aspects of the conduct of war as the implementation of the economic blockade on the Central Powers of Germany and Austria-Hungary, or the pursuit of war criminals in terms of the post-war settlement. Indeed, there is much of importance in terms of the effect of the war on state and society ranging from the introduction of the one pound note or 'Bradbury' to the role of women in agriculture and industry, labour disputes, questions of morale and welfare, and the treatment of the 'enemy within'. Genealogists have already discovered the value of the personnel records of Great War servicemen, but there is much more available in terms of medals and awards, and the post-war provision for widows and other dependants. Commemoration itself is another area richly represented in largely unused series. Indeed, there have been constant surprises in compiling the guide.

Rather than simply listing documents by series and departments, the guide is arranged thematically with sub-sections drawing together relevant sources across the whole spectrum of the Public Record Office collections. It is hoped that this will enable readers to make appropriate connections for the subjects in which they are interested rather than having to search the whole catalogue. This should prove particularly useful for readers in terms of some of the larger series such as ADM 1, AIR 1, HO 45, and WO 32, and those for which detailed catalogues do not as yet exist such as LAB 2 and T 1. Of course, it has not been possible to list the contents of each and every file and there has been a degree of selection in some cases in choosing illustrative examples of the material available. In such cases, however, the examples chosen are representative of the contents of the particular series and, therefore, a valuable starting point for the reader. Indeed, the guide can be claimed as comprehensive in its scope and content and, therefore, an essential working tool for all readers researching aspects of the Great War.

The Public Record Office has by far the largest national archive relating to the Great War as it affected Britain. Its holdings, however, can be supplemented by the collections of other, mainly personal, papers in other national repositories. Such repositories are listed in the Appendix.

Acknowledgements

I WOULD like to thank Sheila Knight, Anne Kilminster and Aidan Lawes for their encouragement of the project, and Paul Carter and David Matthews for sharing their knowledge of the Ministry of Labour and Treasury series respectively. My thanks also go to Sue Breakell of the Imperial War Museum for assistance with the contents of those PRO series retained at the museum. A special debt is owed to William Spencer, the Military Specialist at the PRO, for assisting in the compilation of this guide, drawing my attention to series that I might otherwise have missed, commenting on the manuscript, and giving me the benefit of his great knowledge on the war, not least with regard to the Royal Navy. None of the foregoing, of course, is responsible for those errors that remain.

List of Abbreviations

AIF	Australian Imperial Force
ASC	Army Service Corps
ATS	Auxiliary Territorial Service
BET	British Expeditionary Force
CEF	Canadian Expeditionary Force
CGW	Comrades of the Great War
CID	Committee of Imperial Defence
CIGS	Chief of the Imperial General Staff
CinC	Commander in Chief
CTA	County Territorial Association
DMI	Director of Military Intelligence
DMO	Director of Military Operations
DORA	Defence of the Realm Act
DSIR	Department of Scientific and Industrial Research
FANY	First Aid Nursing Yeomanry
GHQ	General Headquarters
GOC	General Officer Commanding
GWDP	German War Documents Project
ILP	Independent Labour Party
INV	Irish National Volunteers
IUX	International Union of Ex-servicemen
IWGC	Imperial War Graves Commission
IWM	Imperial War Museum
KRRC	King's Royal Rifle Corps
LOC	Lines of Communication
MEF	Mediterranean Expeditionary Force
MID	Munitions Inventions Department
NAAFI	Navy, Army and Air Force Institute
NADSS	National Association of Discharged and Demobilised Sailors and Soldiers
NCF	No Conscription Fellowship
NFDSS	National Federation of Discharged and Demobilised Sailors and Soldiers
NUX	National Union of Ex-servicemen
OTC	Officers' Training Corps
PID	Political Intelligence Department
PUS	Parliamentary Under Secretary
QAIMNS	Queen Alexandra's Imperial Military Nursing Service
QARNNS	Queen Alexandra's Royal Naval Nursing Service

QMAAC	Queen Mary's Army Auxiliary Corps
RAMC	Royal Army Medical Corps
RAOC	Royal Army Ordnance Corps
RAVC	Royal Army Veterinary Corps
RE	Royal Engineers
RFA	Royal Field Artillery
RFC	Royal Flying Corps
RGA	Royal Garrison Artillery
RIC	Royal Irish Constabulary
RM	Royal Marines
RMA	Royal Marine Artillery
RMLI	Royal Marine Light Infantry
RN	Royal Navy
RNAS	Royal Naval Air Service
RNR	Royal Naval Reserve
RNR(T)	Royal Naval Reserve Trawler Section
RNVR	Royal Naval Volunteer Reserve
SSAU	Soldiers, Sailors and Airmens' Union
SWC	Supreme War Council
TC	Tigris Corps
TFNS	Territorial Force Nursing Service
UVF	Ulster Volunteer Force
VADs	Voluntary Aid Detachments
VTC	Volunteer Training Corps
WAAC	Women's Army Auxiliary Corps
WEWNC	War Emergency Workers' National Committee
WI	Women's Institute
WRAF	Women's Royal Air Force
WRNS	Women's Royal Naval Service
YMCA	Young Men's Christian Association
YWCA	Young Women's Christian Association

List of Department Codes

ACT	Government Actuary's Department
ADM	Admiralty
AIR	Air Ministry
AN	British Railways Board
AO	Audit Office
AP	Irish Soldiers and Sailors Land Trust
AR	The Wallace Collection
AVIA	Ministry of Aviation
BT	Board of Trade
CAB	Cabinet Office
CHAR	Charity Commission
CM	Department of Defence Services
CN	Photographs
CO	Colonial Office
CSC	Civil Service Commission
CUST	Board of Customs and Excise
DEFE	Ministry of Defence
DO	Dominion Office
DPP	Director of Public Prosecutions
DSIR	Department of Scientific and Industrial Research
DV	Central Midwives Board
ED	Board of Education
EF	Health and Safety Commission
EN	Imperial War Museum
FD	Medical Research Council
FO	Foreign Office
GFM	German Foreign Ministry
HCA	High Court of Judicature
HLG	Ministry of Housing and Local Government
HO	Home Office
HW	Government Communications Headquarters
INF	Ministry of Information
IR	Inland Revenue
J	Supreme Court of Judicature
KB	King's Bench

KV	Security Service
LAB	Ministry of Labour
LCO	Lord Chancellor's Office
MAF	Ministry of Agriculture and Fisheries
MEPO	Commissioner of the Metropolitan Police
MH	Ministry of Health
MT	Ministry of Transport
MUN	Ministry of Munitions
NATS	Ministry of National Service
NSC	National Savings Committee
PCOM	Prison Commission
PIN	Ministry of Pensions
PMG	Paymaster-General
POWE	Ministry of Power
PREM	Prime Minister's Office
PRO	Public Record Office
PT	Public Trustee Office
RECO	Ministry of Reconstruction
RG	Registrar General
SUPP	Ministry of Supply
T	Treasury
TS	Treasury Solicitor
WO	War Office
WORK	Ministry of Works
ZJ	The London Gazette
ZLIB	British Transport Historical Records

Using the PRO

THE Public Record Office (PRO) at Kew, in south-west London, houses one of the finest, most complete archives in the world, running from the Domesday Book in 1086 to the present century. It holds the records for the central government of the United Kingdom (primarily of England and Wales, as Scotland and Northern Ireland have their own central record offices), as well as the records of the law courts of England. In addition, it is also a major international archive, because of its vast holdings on the former British colonies, and on foreign relations over eight centuries.

Public Record Office
Kew, Surrey
TW9 4DU
Tel: 020 8392 5200
Fax: 020 8392 5286
Email: enquiry@pro.gov.uk
Web site: www.pro.gov.uk
PROCAT: catalogue.pro.gov.uk

Opening hours:

Monday	9 a.m. to 5 p.m.
Tuesday	10 a.m. to 7 p.m.
Wednesday	9 a.m. to 5 p.m.
Thursday	9 a.m. to 7 p.m.
Friday	9 a.m. to 5 p.m.
Saturday	9.30 a.m. to 5 p.m.

The PRO is closed on public holidays, on Saturdays preceding a public holiday and for annual stocktaking (usually one week in December).

Documents may be ordered until 4 p.m. on Mondays, Wednesdays and Fridays; till 4.30 p.m. on Tuesdays and Thursdays; from 9.30 a.m. to 12 noon and from 1.30 p.m. to 3 p.m. on Saturdays.

The PRO also offers an extensive Library and Resource Centre, a bookshop, and an Education and Visitor Centre. You do not need an appointment to visit but you will need to obtain a reader's ticket. To do so when you first visit, please bring formal documentary proof of identity. Citizens of Britain and the Republic of Ireland should provide a valid cheque card or driver's licence. If you are not a British citizen bring your passport or national identity card.

If you do not have any of these forms of identity, please contact the PRO for advice before visiting. Without a valid reader's ticket you cannot order documents.

To protect the documents, each one of which is unique, security in the reading rooms is tight, and eating, drinking and smoking are not permitted. You may use personal computers, typewriters and tape recorders in most of the reading rooms, but pens of any kind are not allowed, and you may only write with graphite pencils. The rules are available at www.pro.gov.uk/about/access/rules.htm.

In general the records are arranged firstly by the department which transferred the records to the PRO and secondly by the series, which often represents the type of document, e.g. musters or government correspondence, or records of an internal division. The records are then usually arranged chronologically or sequentially by former departmental file references.

Each document has a unique three-part reference. The first part is the **department** code, for example WO for the War Office, according to the department which created it. The second part (before the /) is the **series** number, which represents the series within the department code. The third and final part (after the /) is the **piece** number, which represents the individual document.

These references can be discovered from the various finding aids on site, and by using the online catalogue.

The *PRO Guide* gives an overview of the history and content of all the records in the care of the PRO. The *Guide* occupies several loose-leaf volumes, and is divided into three parts. Part 1 contains the history of government. Part 2 contains series descriptions in alphabetical order by series code. Part 3 is the index to the other two parts. Several printed copies are available on site, so you can sit and browse at leisure.

PROCAT, the PRO online catalogue, is accessible over the web and on site at Kew. It is a multilevel catalogue containing over 9 million entries, with a powerful search engine which allows you to search all catalogue descriptions by key word(s). Once registered as a PRO reader you can bookmark entries of interest and save your searches.

1. The Higher Direction of the War

I T IS SOMETIMES SUGGESTED that Britain could have averted the Great War by an early declaration of firm support for France and Russia in the July crisis of 1914 but it is doubtful whether this would have made any real difference to events. The British Foreign Secretary, Sir Edward Grey, had not done so in anticipation of a British role in attempted mediation, which displayed a wholly misplaced confidence in Berlin's good intentions. In any case, Grey's denial of Anglo-Russian naval talks, which had been going on through July, robbed him of credibility in German eyes. In many respects, however, the crucial decisions that led to involvement in the war were not taken by the Cabinet as a whole but largely by the Prime Minister, Herbert Asquith, and Grey and, to a lesser extent, the First Lord of the Admiralty, Winston Churchill.

That raises the problem of the unity of the Liberal Cabinet in 1914 and the increasingly fashionable view that British entry to the war was unnecessary, even if the intervention of the British Expeditionary Force (BEF) probably did prevent a German victory. It was the case that the Foreign Office had concluded that the 1839 Treaty of London, guaranteeing Belgian neutrality, did not require Britain to go to Belgium's assistance in all circumstances and some British military and naval planners had themselves contemplated violating Belgian neutrality, if necessary to do so in order to take the war to Germany. There is also no doubt that the extent of Britain's 'moral commitment' to France since the initiation of staff talks between the British and French general staffs in 1905 had been concealed. Most ministers remained unaware of the talks until 1911 and the German invasion of Belgium was a gift to Asquith in terms of preserving his government: he lost only two Cabinet ministers and a junior minister by resignation.

Nevertheless, it was not in Britain's long-term strategic interests to allow Germany either to dominate the Low Countries and the Channel ports, or to upset the balance of power in Europe. Nor is it likely that, even if Germany's immediate war aims had been limited by a need to ensure British neutrality, a victorious Germany would not have soon threatened British interests. Unpleasant though the far-reaching consequences were for Britain, it was a necessary war.

Cabinet Government and War

It was not a war, however, for which Britain was really prepared. Certainly, the machinery required for waging war on an unprecedented scale was wholly lacking, as epitomised by the ad hoc meetings of ministers, chiefs of staff and other senior military and naval officers as a 'War Council' on 5 and 6 August 1914. In Britain, the pre-war Committee of Imperial Defence (CID) had been a relatively useful mechanism for strategic decision-making but the new War Council, which emerged from it in November 1914, proved unsatisfactory. No memoranda were circulated, there was no regular agenda, meetings were infrequent, and there was no proper record kept of decisions. In theory, the 13-man War Council's decisions were not binding on the 19-man Cabinet, but the latter was effectively bypassed by Asquith's reliance upon Churchill, the Chancellor of the Exchequer, David Lloyd George, and the autocratic Field Marshal Lord Kitchener, who had been appointed Secretary of State for War on 5 August 1914. The War Council was a parallel decision-making body but, as one junior minister remarked in March 1915, the only real difference between it and the Cabinet was Kitchener, Churchill and Lloyd George dominating proceedings in front of 'a different set of spectators'. Indeed, while some issues were discussed in both Cabinet and War Council, others were discussed in only one and others informally settled outside both bodies.

Asquith did not have sufficient confidence to judge between conflicting military and naval experts. Indeed, Asquith was too used to seeking compromise and consensus to be an effective war leader, largely counting upon the desire of his Liberal colleagues to cling to office and upon the desire of the Unionist leader, Andrew Bonar Law, to avoid an election for fear of losing control over the Unionists. Such a situation left the initiative within the War Council in the hands of 'strategic entrepreneurs', namely Churchill, Lloyd George and the increasingly influential secretary to the CID and now the War Council, Maurice Hankey. The result of the memoranda circulated by Churchill, Lloyd George and Hankey in December 1914 was the Dardanelles expedition.

The failure of the naval and military campaigns at the Dardanelles, coupled with Admiral Fisher's resignation as First Sea Lord; the impact of the publicity given the BEF's shortage of shells on the Western Front; and other domestic political events resulted in Asquith forming a coalition government in May 1915. For Asquith, preservation of the party truce and of his own position were probably uppermost, but the principal beneficiaries appeared Unionists, with both Bonar Law and the former prime minister, Arthur Balfour, entering the government, though the Labour Party also secured three minor posts, its leader, Arthur Henderson, becoming President of the Board of Education. Asquith was not able to remove Kitchener as he wished but, despite the removal from the Cabinet of Richard Burdon Haldane and Churchill, who retained a seat on the War Council as Chancellor of the Duchy of Lancaster, the Liberals retained the more important ministries.

The War Council now gave way to the Dardanelles Committee, originally comprising in May 1915 six former members of the War Council and five

Unionists, but without serving officers other than Kitchener. In theory, its responsibilities were confined to strategy and diplomacy in the eastern Mediterranean. It met less frequently than the Cabinet and, since it recommended continuing the Dardanelles campaign, its decisions were challenged in Cabinet. In November 1915, following Unionist pressure on Asquith to refine the machinery further, the Dardanelles Committee begat the five-man War Committee, comprising Asquith, Lloyd George, Reginald McKenna, Balfour and Bonar Law. The CIGS and First Sea Lord customarily attended and minutes, produced by Hankey in the form of 'conclusions', were circulated.

In December, consequent upon declining confidence in both Kitchener and the CinC of the BEF, Sir John French, French was succeeded by Sir Douglas Haig, and Sir William Robertson became CIGS. Robertson's terms were that the CIGS should be regarded as sole military adviser to the War Committee. This proved a considerable disadvantage as the committee was given no alternatives for the most important strategic decisions which had to be made. Kitchener, already shorn of responsibility for munitions by the creation of a new ministry under Lloyd George in May 1915, was confined to administrative matters until his death by drowning in June 1916, when HMS *Hampshire*, carrying him on a mission to Russia, struck a German mine off the Orkneys.

Disputes between Unionists and Liberals over possible reform of the franchise opened new wounds in the coalition in the early summer of 1916. The failure of the Somme offensive and the suggestion within the Cabinet by Lord Lansdowne in November 1916 for serious peace negotiations led to demands by the Unionists for a more vigorous prosecution of the war. Manoeuvring by Bonar Law, Sir Edward Carson and Lloyd George forced Asquith's resignation in December 1916, although it would appear he believed that no one else could form an administration. Lacking sufficient support from his own party and unable to command the support of the Liberal majority, Bonar Law declined to form a government, but Lloyd George accepted the invitation to construct a new coalition. Lloyd George succeeded in doing so although, with all the previous Liberal ministers standing by Asquith, the key appointments now went to the Unionists. Labour participation, however, also increased with the number in government going up from three to eight, Henderson joining the new War Cabinet.

Unionist back-bench pressure had pushed Law into supporting Asquith's removal and Lloyd George's survival depended upon a degree of military success. Ironically, the same back-benchers would not countenance the change in the high command Lloyd George deemed necessary to secure that success. The extent of Robertson's power over strategy had become clear to Lloyd George when he succeeded to the War Office on Kitchener's death. As prime minister, Lloyd George's ability to impose his own strategic views was further circumscribed through the weakness of his political position and lack of any majority support within parliament. This was despite the establishment of a five-man War Cabinet, which theoretically offered him far more influence over decision-making. The War Cabinet had a permanent secretariat under Hankey and, eventually, increased to seven members. In addition, Lloyd George established his own secretariat – the 'Garden Suburb' – which provided a further independent source of advice. In practice, however, Lloyd George often scrapped the War Cabinet's agenda at short notice and, despite Hankey's efforts, its meetings were far from businesslike. Thus, it strongly resembled the War Committee, albeit with clearer overall authority.

As is well known, Lloyd George resorted to subterfuge in attempting to outmanoeuvre Robertson and Haig and to force one or both to resign. At Calais on 27 February 1917, Lloyd George proposed subordinating Haig to the French general, Robert Nivelle. The resulting crisis was resolved by Haig being considered to be under Nivelle's command only for the limited period of Nivelle's proposed offensive and retaining tactical control of British forces. The disastrous failure of Nivelle's offensive in April 1917, and the collapse of much of the French army into mutiny, greatly weakened Lloyd George's hand. The War Cabinet established a War Policy Committee in June to assess the plans advanced by Haig for a British offensive in Flanders. Half-hearted approval was eventually given for what became Passchendaele but the War Policy Committee did not reconvene until September. The War Cabinet itself then proved unwilling to halt operations, which had manifestly failed to meet the criteria for continuation laid down in June.

The collapse of the Italian army at Caporetto in October 1917 finally enabled Lloyd George to divert troops from France and in November the Entente conference at Rapallo agreed on the establishment of a Supreme War Council (SWC) at Versailles. As British representative, Lloyd George proposed Sir Henry Wilson, who had suggested the council in the first place and who, like Sir John French, had been invited by the prime minister to offer unofficial strategic advice. Through the SWC, Wilson could now provide a formal counterweight to the CIGS. In February 1918 a dispute over the control of an allied reserve enabled Lloyd George to trap Robertson into either remaining CIGS with reduced powers or going to Versailles as British representative. Refusing both posts, Robertson resigned and was replaced by Wilson, although Haig and Nivelle's successor, Philippe Pétain, were able to block the creation of a general reserve.

The prospect of the British and French armies being split apart by the German offensive of March 1918 finally forced Haig to accept the appointment of Ferdinand Foch as allied supreme commander at the Doullens conference, though Haig and Pétain retained tactical control over their own troops. Moreover, the offensive enabled Lloyd George to establish a new 'X' committee consisting of himself, Wilson and Lord Milner, now Secretary of State for War, to discuss strategy prior to meetings of the War Cabinet. Like the War Policy Committee before it, the 'X' committee took decisions without reference to the War Cabinet. Lloyd George himself, however, had to deflect criticism of holding back troops from France in the so-called Maurice affair in May 1918. Haig's position remained insecure but there was no acceptable alternative and, by the summer, the Entente was on the offensive, although no one expected the war to be won in 1918.

ADM 116 contains Admiralty memoranda for the War Cabinet, 1917–22 (ADM 116/1768–76), as well as some of Admiral Lord Fisher's personal papers for 1914–17 (ADM 116/3454).

AIR 1, Records of the Air Historical Branch, includes material relating to the deliberations of the War Cabinet including War Cabinet papers and reports, 1918–19 (AIR 1/2313/221/41 and 47); committee reports relating to air policy, 1917–18 (AIR 1/678/21/13/2102, 818/204/4/1310, 2312/221/38, 43 and 53); and discussions and decisions by the War Cabinet relating to air policy issues (AIR 1/724/78/2 and 2422/305/18/12).

AIR 8/3 contains War Cabinet conclusions, 1917–21, among the papers of the Chief of the Air Staff.

CAB 1/10–29, miscellaneous Cabinet Office papers collected by Sir James Masterton-Smith, include notes on Lloyd George's meeting with Haig in September 1917 (CAB 1/25), and material of the Committee on War Policy, June 1918 (CAB 1/27). In addition, there is a note by Hankey of a conversation with Asquith on the progress of the war dating from October 1917 (CAB 1/42).

CAB 2/3 comprise the minutes of the Committee of Imperial Defence, 1912–23. The series is available on microfilm, in the Microfilm Reading Room.

CAB 4/5–7 comprise miscellaneous printed memoranda of the Committee of Imperial Defence, 1912–22. The series is available on microfilm in the Microfilm Reading Room.

CAB 15 has the papers of the Committee of Imperial Defence's Committee on the Co-ordination of Departmental Action on the Outbreak of War, 1911–14 (CAB 15/1–2), which resulted in the production of three successive editions of the *War Book* in 1912, 1913 and 1914 (CAB 15/3–5).

CAB 17, miscellaneous correspondence and papers of the Committee of Imperial Defence, includes assorted material from the War Council, Dardanelles Committee and War Committee, 1915–16 (CAB 17/114); miscellaneous memoranda by the secretariat of the Committee of Imperial Defence, 1915 (CAB 17/130); papers on proposed Councils of War, 1915 and 1916 (CAB 17/115 and 134); and material on the supply of information to the War Committee, 1916 (CAB 17/150).

CAB 21, registered files of the Cabinet Office, includes correspondence and papers on the reporting of War Cabinet minutes, 1917–18 (CAB 21/18 and 97); the circulation of War Cabinet papers, 1918 (CAB 21/100); the organisation and functions of the War Cabinet, 1918 (CAB 21/101–2); and giving Asquith access to papers after he had left office (CAB 21/19). There are papers on the Calais Conference coupled with later papers on Robertson's resignation and the Doullens Conference (CAB 21/41); the functions of the CIGS following Robertson's resignation (CAB 21/105); and the Committee on War Policy (CAB 21/88).

CAB 22 contains minutes and papers of the War Council, 1914–15 (CAB 22/1) and its successors, the Dardanelles Committee, 1915 (CAB 22/2), and War Committee 1915–16 (CAB 22/3). Minutes are effectively the manuscript notes made by Hankey as secretary subsequently printed for record purposes in 1916. In the case of the War Committee, however, notes were only kept between November 1915 and January 1916. The remaining 10 months of the War Committee's deliberations are represented by files, in which manuscript or typescript minutes are accompanied by agenda, circulated papers and other notes and correspondence (CAB 22/4–79), with additional unnumbered memoranda (CAB 22/80–81). However, a short summary of conclusions of meetings was printed as the 'WC' (War Committee) series (CAB 22/82).

CAB 23 contains minutes of the Cabinet from December 1916 to December 1918 (CAB 23/1–8); the secret 'A' minutes, 1917–18 (CAB 23/13–16); minutes of the X Committee, 1918 (CAB 23/17); minutes of the Prime Minister's Committee, 1918 (CAB 23/44A); and papers of the War Cabinet, 1917–19 (CAB 23/44B). The minutes reflect the purposes for which they were created, namely for current administration. They were prepared objectively and impersonally so as to record agreement and consensus rather than promote any of the controversies which may have surrounded the actual discussions. While they contain much of the information available to the War Cabinet, the speed of events could mean that the written record fell into arrears or was not fully prepared, and that the final stages are missing. Moreover, a wide range of matters were settled outside the War Cabinet by direct discussion.

CAB 24 contains the 'G War' and 'GT' series of Cabinet papers. Apart from the small number of printed papers of the 'G War' Series, which were circulated to the War Council from January 1915 and continued for the Dardanelles and War Committees (CAB 24/1–5), and the papers of the 'GT' series as circulated to the War Cabinet, 1917–18 (CAB 24/6–37), there are also other reports prepared by the Cabinet Office summarising the political and general situation abroad. These comprise Eastern Reports, 1917–19 (CAB 24/143–5); Western and General Reports, 1917 (CAB 24/146–7); Foreign Reports, 1918–19 (CAB 24/148–50); and Empire and Africa Reports, 1918–19 (CAB 24/151–3). There are indices to the main series of G War and GT papers and a microfilm copy is available on open access for some (CAB 24/1–3).

CAB 27 has papers of the War Policy Committee, 1915 (CAB 27/2); and minutes, reports and memoranda of the War Policy Committee, which studied the naval and military situation prior to the opening of the Passchendaele offensive, 1917 (CAB 27/6–8 and 88).

CAB 37, Cabinet Papers, 1880–1916, contains photographic copies of printed Cabinet papers for 1914–16 (CAB 37/120–62), including copies of letters written by the Prime Minister to the King and copies of reports by the War Policy Committee, 1915 (CAB 37/132/22, and 134/9 and 23) and by the Cabinet Committee on Elections, November 1915 (CAB 37/137/18). They are also available on microfilm and there is a full index in the publications, *List of Cabinet Papers, 1880–1914* and *List of Cabinet Papers, 1915 and 1916*.

CAB 38, Papers of the Committee of Imperial Defence to 1914, contains photographic copies of printed papers from 1888 to 1914. They are available on microfilm and there is a full index in *List of the Papers of the Committee of Imperial Defence to 1914*.

CAB 41/35–7 are copies of Cabinet papers in the Royal Archives, 1914–16, consisting of the letters written to the King by the Prime Minister after each Cabinet meeting. These were the only record of discussions prior to the establishment of the War Cabinet secretariat in December 1916. A number of Cabinet committees are mentioned in the Prime Minister's letters for which no reports or other papers survive, including Food Prices, January 1915; Prevention and Relief of Distress, March 1915; Drink, April 1915; Food Supplies, March 1915; Belgian Imports and Exports, August 1915; Control of Industry, September 1915; Retrenchment, September 1915; Registration, June 1916; Ireland, January 1916; Meat Supplies After the War (July 1916); Proxy Voting (November 1916); Domestic Questions of National Organisation, November 1916; and South Wales Coal Mines, November 1916.

CAB 42/1–26 contains photocopies of printed papers in the 'G War' Series including reports of the War Council (CAB 42/1–2), Dardanelles Committee (CAB 42/3–4), and War Committee (CAB 42/5–26). They include reports and memoranda of other committees such as the War Policy Committee, 1915 (CAB 42/4/8). They are available on microfilm and there is a full index in the publication, *List of Cabinet Papers, 1915 and 1916*.

CAB 63, the papers of Maurice Hankey, includes his 'Magnus opus' files for the war period (CAB 63/1–24), including correspondence and appreciations of Kitchener, May 1915 (CAB 63/4); memoranda for the Committee of Imperial Defence, the War Committee and the Prime Minister (CAB 63/12–16); and memoranda and papers for the War Cabinet, 1917–18 (CAB 63/19–24). They are available on microfilm.

CAB 132 has reports of the Cabinet Committee on War Policy, 1915 (CAB 132/21 and 28).

CAB 133 also has reports of the War Policy Committee, 1915 (CAB 133/1, 5, 9 and 10).

PRO 30/30, the papers of Lord Milner, includes the British and French agreement on the appointment of Foch, a confidential memorandum on Doullens, and Milner's diary for 23–26 March 1918 (PRO 30/30/1–3).

PRO 30/57, the papers of Field Marshal Lord Kitchener, includes his correspondence with Asquith (PRO 30/57/76); Robertson (PRO 30/57/55); and the influential Lord Esher (PRO 30/57/59). There is also correspondence with the Admiralty, 1914–15 (PRO 30/57/72); Cabinet colleagues (PRO 30/57/77–8); miscellaneous correspondence (PRO 30/57/80 and 83); Kitchener's own drafts and notes, 1914–16 (PRO 30/57/81); press cuttings, photographs, wartime songs and verses about him (PRO 30/57/87–8); and his appointment as a Privy Councillor in 1914 (PRO 30/57/86). There is also material on Kitchener's fatal journey to Russia (PRO 30/57/85); official and unofficial letters of condolence, and tributes (PRO 30/57/89, 113–15 and 124); and details of the memorial service (PRO 30/57/118). Sir George Arthur was appointed trustee of Kitchener's papers (PRO 30/57/90), and was his biographer (PRO 30/57/91 and 93–5).

PRO 30/67/25 includes some general wartime material of the former Unionist Secretary of State for War, St John Brodrick, now Earl of Midleton, including notes on Haldane and Lloyd George and correspondence with the Marquess of Salisbury.

RECO 1/853–61 contains general material relating to the War Cabinet.

WO 32 deals with the Maurice affair, 1918 (WO 32/10085), while there is also material on the co-ordination of the allied armies under Foch's direction following Doullens (WO 32/5595–6 and 5598).

WO 106 includes, among papers of the Directorate of Military Operations, General Staff appreciations of the military situation, 1915–16 and 1918 and General Staff memoranda for the Cabinet, 1915–19 (WO 106/310–20, 982, and 1447); as well as reports on general war policy, 1918 (WO 106/327). There are minutes of a conference held by Wilson as CIGS in July 1918 (WO 106/1448).

WO 158, correspondence and papers of Military Headquarters, includes correspondence between Haig as CinC of the BEF, Robertson as CIGS and successive Secretaries of State for War (WO 158/21–5); minutes of the War Cabinet, 1917–18 (WO 158/45); the agenda and notes for the notorious Calais conference, 1917 (WO 158/41); and a memorandum for the War Cabinet on the future conduct of the war by Lloyd George's unofficial strategic advisers, Sir John French and Sir Henry Wilson, October 1917 (WO 158/46).

WO 159, papers of Kitchener's Private Office, 1914–16, include strategic and political papers, 1914–16 (WO 159/2–8); telegrams to Kitchener, 1914–15 (WO 159/13–14); Kitchener's memorandum to the Cabinet in May 1915 on the progress of the war since August 1914 (WO 159/21); and a paper on the war from the Committee of Imperial Defence, January 1915 (WO 159/22).

WO 256 contains copies of the wartime diaries of Sir Douglas Haig, covering the period from 29 July 1914 to 11 November 1918 (WO 256/1–25 and 27–37), and his final report on operations on the Western Front, 1916–18 (WO 256/38). There is no actual break in the narrative despite the apparent omission of one section (WO 256/26). Access is given only to those readers who give an undertaking in respect of the use made of the information contained in the diaries, the originals of which are held in the National Library of Scotland.

ZLIB 10/43–4 are War Cabinet reports on the years 1917–18.

War, Strategy and International Politics

Given the origins of the Dardanelles campaign and the subsequent struggle between Lloyd George and his military advisers, the traditional view of wartime strategic decision-making in Britain has been that of the clash between 'Westerners' and the 'Easterners'. In Britain it was an image that was relentlessly cultivated in the so-called 'battle of the memoirs' in the 1920s and 1930s. Briefly stated, the traditional argument is that, once deadlock occurred on the Western Front in the autumn of 1914, politicians in Britain were motivated to seek a new strategy to break that deadlock. However, their earlier easy transference of control over strategy in August 1914 to the soldiers now rebounded since the latter were unwilling to divert manpower from the Western Front to other theatres. Soldiers regarded the latter as 'side-shows' irrelevant to the main effort. Indeed, to use the oft-repeated phrase of defenders of Haig's strategy, the war could not be won without 'engaging the main body of the main enemy in a continental war'.

Soldiers like Haig and Robertson, therefore, were 'Westerners'. Politicians like Churchill and Lloyd George were 'Easterners', convinced of the desirability of finding an 'indirect approach' through such campaigns as that of the Dardanelles against the Turks between February 1915 and January 1916, and that at Salonika in Macedonia against the Bulgarians between October 1915 and September 1918. In fact, the supposed division between 'Westerners' and 'Easterners' is somewhat artificial since there was much common ground between them, particularly with respect to the position of Britain within the Entente. Kitchener, Robertson, and Lloyd George could happily agree on the need to raise and deploy a large British army in order to demonstrate to France and Russia that Britain intended to stand by them. Both soldiers and politicians recognised the importance of holding the Entente together in order to defeat Germany. They also intended to ensure that Britain would become the strongest partner in the coalition in order to be able to impose its own terms on enemies and allies alike.

The real alternative strategy in British policy circles was one associated principally with Lloyd George's successor as Chancellor of the Exchequer, Reginald McKenna, and the President of the Board of Trade, Walter Runciman, who wished to avoid raising a large army, believing that the best way to sustain the Entente would be by continuing to bankroll it and to maintain an economic blockade through capitalising on Britain's maritime strength. A strategy of 'limited liability', however, was increasingly untenable. Naval blockade could not result in any swift German economic collapse and intensification of the blockade would risk alienating the United States. Moreover, the very heavy losses suffered by the French and Russians in 1914–15 made it increasingly clear that the future of the Entente depended upon Britain's readiness to play a major role in the continental land war. By early 1916, therefore, most British policy-makers were reluctantly convinced that the war might end either in an indecisive peace, or possibly even a German victory, if the British did not participate fully in the continental war. In any case, such participation offered the best opportunity for Britain to realise its own objectives.

Every belligerent fought in order to win or, at least, not to lose and, therefore, there was an essential unity of purpose between coalition partners. Thus, Britain, France and Russia adopted the joint Declaration of London in September 1914, which rejected concluding a separate peace and accepted the need for consensus in formulating peace terms. Each state, however, had its own reasons for entering the war and would have, or develop during the conflict, its own particular objectives, serving its own national interests. Consequently, war aims within a coalition could conflict with those of allies. Moreover, by 1918 the Entente had swelled. Britain, Belgium, France, Russia, Serbia were the initial partners, joined by Montenegro and Japan in 1914, Italy in 1915, Portugal, Albania and Romania in 1916, Greece, the United States, China, Siam, Brazil, Cuba, Panama, and Liberia in 1917, and Guatemala, Nicaragua, Costa Rica, Honduras and Haiti in 1918. The initial Central Powers of Germany and Austria-Hungary were joined by Turkey in 1914 and Bulgaria in 1915. Not all of the Entente partners, of course, were significant and the

United States also chose to regard itself as an 'associated power' rather than an ally of the Entente.

The most obvious early British war aim was the restitution of Belgium, although adherence to the Entente also implied acquiescence in general French and Russian aims, which served British interests less well than safeguarding the Channel ports. In terms of wider aims, however, it was soon clear that the rather vague expression of a war being fought to destroy 'Prussian militarism', a theme used by Asquith in a speech on war aims at the Guildhall in November 1914, masked differences of perception.

On the part of the soldiers, there was a determination to inflict a sufficiently clear military victory on Germany to deter future aggression. At the same time, there was a certain ambivalence towards what might be termed total victory since the British military leadership as a whole believed that nothing would be gained by stripping Germany of her colonies or imposing crippling economic indemnities in view of the need to re-establish an effective post-war balance of power in Europe. On the other hand, both the Colonial Office and Admiralty were keen to take German colonies to ensure the future security of the empire. The Foreign Office shared some of the army's views with respect to Germany but favoured a degree of self-determination and was generally more favourable towards comprehensive German disarmament. Generally, politicians sought a more total victory in order to be able to restructure Germany. Nonetheless, most British policy-makers recognised that, after the war, Germany would be required to balance France and, especially, Russia. The Russian collapse in 1917 saw a modification of attitudes towards the balance of power, with a renewed sense of the need to strengthen France, since Russian defeat suggested greater opportunities for Germany to increase its own post-war power.

Austria-Hungary was hardly regarded as an opponent at all and, while no one was especially committed to its preservation, it was seen as a useful barrier to Germany's eastern ambitions. Thus, it was only very belatedly, with the failure to detach Vienna from Berlin, that Britain came round to the view of allowing self-determination to prevail although some elements within the Foreign Office had been hostile to Austria-Hungary from the beginning. If Austria-Hungary did not arouse much passion outside the Foreign Office, there was similarly little animosity towards Bulgaria. Of greater importance was the future security of the empire and, in this context, the break up of the Ottoman Turkish Empire was increasingly seen as desirable. In the process of encouraging Arabs and Zionists to fight against the Turks, as Sir Henry Wilson remarked, the British made so many contradictory promises that 'I cannot for the life of me see how we can get out of our present mess without breaking our word to somebody'. Fighting alongside the French and Russians did not automatically extinguish older imperial rivalries and winning the war for Britain therefore meant increasing security against both current enemies and current allies. Some policy-makers even conceived of acting on the defensive in the west and seizing the initiative in the east, expanding British influence to the Caucasus, Armenia and the Caspian as an appropriate buffer zone between a German-dominated eastern Europe and a British-dominated Asia and Middle East.

In its attempts to effect some degree of co-operation, the Entente developed a relatively elaborate system of inter-allied committees by the end of the war, numbering 25 in total. However, these were entirely absent initially and there was no formal machinery for strategic or political co-ordination. Asquith and his French counterpart, for example, did not meet until July 1915 while Kitchener met his opposite number only five times in the first 12 months of war. Coinciding with the first meeting of the British and French prime ministers, the first inter-allied military conference was held at Chantilly in July 1915.

Other conferences followed such as those at Calais in September 1915 and, again, at Chantilly in both December 1915 and December 1916. Often, however, there was little co-ordination between the decisions reached at the military conferences and those at the political conferences. The entry of the United States into the war brought new measures for inter-allied co-operation such as an Inter-Allied Council for War Purchases and Finance working through an Allied Purchasing Commission. Similarly, after March 1918, blockade policy was co-ordinated by an Allied Blockade Committee and the Inter-Allied Trade Committees established in five European neutral capitals. The Supreme War Council, of course, brought together British, French and Italian representatives in November 1917 and they were later joined by American and Japanese representatives. The Council met eight times in its first year, mainly at Versailles. Representatives received all proposals, information and documents relating to the war from their respective governments and tendered advice to the Council in the form of joint notes. Inter-allied Committees were also created by the Military Representatives for Naval Liaison, Aviation, Tanks, and Transportation. After Foch's appointment as allied supremo in April 1918, however, the work of the Supreme War Council was largely confined to matters relating to the Balkans and Russia.

ADM 1, papers of the Admiralty Secretariat, deals with the British, French and Italian Naval Convention, May 1915 (ADM 1/8420/125); the Admiralty role in Inter-allied organizations, July 1918 (ADM 1/8530/192); and the policy to be adopted in 1914 if Greece joined the Central Powers (ADM 1/8393/301) and towards the Netherlands as either ally or enemy (ADM 1/8407/494).

ADM 116, Admiralty 'case files', deals with the Declaration of London, 1914 (ADM 116/1233–5); the pre-war agreements with France for naval co-operation, 1912–14 (ADM 116/3109); the British Naval Mission to Greece, 1915–17 (ADM 116/1457 and 1574); Japanese naval assistance in the Pacific and Mediterranean, 1916–19 (ADM 116/1702); the Allied Naval Council, 1918 (ADM 116/1635); and command of the allied fleets in the Mediterranean, 1918 (ADM 116/1649).

ADM 137, 'case files' assembled by the Historical Section of the Committee of Imperial Defence for use in compiling the post-war Official History, has papers of the Allied Naval Council, 1918 (ADM 137/1786–94).

AIR 1, Air Historical Branch records, contains cable messages received from the British Air Mission in Washington, 1918 (AIR 1/680/21/13/2205), and papers of the Supreme War Council relating to air operations, 1917–18 (AIR 1/2295–2300).

CAB 1/10–29, miscellaneous Cabinet papers collected by Sir James Masterton-Smith, have much material on British war aims and strategy, relations with allies, and diplomatic manoeuvres. As might be expected, there is periodic consideration of the general war situation (CAB 1/13, 22, 25–6 and 29). There is a copy of the Declaration of London (CAB 1/15); relations with Japan (CAB 1/23–4); relations with Italy (CAB 1/20–21 and 28), including the Treaty of London of April 1915 (CAB 1/12); relations with the United States (CAB 1/11 and 25); and attitudes towards German, Austro-Hungarian and Turkish peace offers (CAB 1/21–2 and 24–5).

CAB 16/36 contains papers from the ad hoc committee of the Committee of Imperial Defence on Territorial Changes, 1916–17.

CAB 17/160–61, among miscellaneous papers of the Committee of Imperial Defence, have memoranda and notes on conditions for possible peace negotiations, 1916, including a review of past schemes for securing perpetual peace.

CAB 21, registered files of the Cabinet Office, includes notes on a conference attended by Lord Milner in Rome (CAB 21/40); the minutes of the Munitions Sub-committee of the allied conference held in Petrograd in early 1917 (CAB 21/42); material on the situation in the Balkans and, particularly, Greece, 1917 (CAB 21/47–50 and 52); relations with the United States (CAB 21/55–7); the Balfour Declaration of November 1917, by which Britain promised to establish a Jewish national home in Palestine (CAB 21/58); possible peace terms including reports of the Cabinet Committees on Terms of Peace (Desiderata) and Terms of Peace (Economic and Other Non-territorial Desiderata) from April 1917 (CAB 21/59, 52, 71, 77–8); the Cabinet Committee appointed in April 1917 to consider exchanging Gibraltar for Ceuta (CAB 27/51); the Belgian Relief Commission (CAB 21/63); allied military policy (CAB 21/90 and 121); and Anglo-French relations on immediate post-war affairs in Turkey and Russia, 1919 (CAB 21/158). There is also material on the creation of the Supreme War Council (CAB 21/91); reports of the British secretariat at the Supreme War Council, 1917 (CAB 21/4); minutes of the Supreme War Council from 1919 (CAB 21/29–37); and minutes of the Inter-allied Tanks and Anti-aircraft Committees, 1918 (CAB 21/103–4).

CAB 25 contains papers of the Supreme War Council including general papers (CAB 25/1–118), and (indexed) circulated papers received by the Council and the Permanent Military Representative (CAB 25/120–27). Among the circulated papers are copies of minutes of sessions of the Council between November 1917 and March 1919, and minutes of the meetings of Military Representatives to November 1919. In addition, there are minutes of the Executive War Board (CAB 25/119).

CAB 27 has papers of the Cabinet Committee on the Inter-Ally Council and Inter-Ally Executive, established in April 1918 to consider certain questions raised by the Italians (CAB 27/45); and papers of the Cabinet Committee on British Desiderata (war aims) in Turkey in Asia, 1915 (CAB 27/1).

CAB 28/1–9 are microfilmed papers ('IC' Series) on Anglo-French and other Allied War Conferences, 1915–20.

CAB 29/1–5 has memoranda of the Cabinet Committee on Peace, 1916–20.

FO 115, general correspondence relating to the United States, covers general wartime subjects (FO 115/1999–2001, 2159–60, 2348 and 2473), as well as containing memoranda by the Political Intelligence Department on the United States, 1918 (FO 115/2431).

FO 146/4368–4604 cover communications with the French government through the British Embassy in Paris and other Consular Offices, 1914–15.

FO 147/101–4 are the Registers of Correspondence of the British Embassy and Consular Offices in France, 1914–15.

FO 170, the records of the British Embassy and Consular Offices in Italy, including communications between the Foreign Office and the Italian government among the general files for 1915 (FO 170/832–913), 1916 (FO 170/914–93), 1917 (FO 170/995–1077), and 1918 (FO 170/1080–1159). There is material, for example, on the British Military Mission in Rome, 1917 (FO 170/1040).

FO 262/1156–1376 has correspondence concerning Japan, 1914–18, though primarily of a commercial and consular nature.

FO 286/572–687, wartime records of the British Embassy and Consular Offices in Greece, has miscellaneous unlisted material for the period 1914–16 but is more detailed from 1916 onwards, including coverage of the Salonika Mission to the anti-German Greek Provisional Government on Crete in January–April 1917 (FO 286/617); the Allied landings at Piraeus and the abdication of the pro-German King Constantine in June 1917 (FO 286/631); the French deployment of Senegalese troops in Greece (FO 286/633); the Allied blockade of Greece (FO 286/636); the arrival of the head of the Provisional Government, Eleutherios Venizelos, in Athens and the Greek declaration of war on Germany in June 1917 (FO 286/638); and the work of the British Naval Mission (FO 286/639 and 645).

FO 345/52 contains correspondence, telegrams and minutes relating to the role of Japan in the First World War among the Foreign Office's Japan Miscellanea class.

FO 350 has the papers of Sir John Newell Jordan, 1901–19, Envoy Extraordinary and Minister Plenipotentiary to Peking from 1906–20. There is Jordan's correspondence with the Foreign Office, 1913–15 (FO 350/12–14) and 1916–17 (FO 350/16); as well as corresponded with Sir W. Langley, Assistant Under Secretary of State, 1916 (FO 350/15).

FO 368/921–2048 contain the correspondence of the Foreign Office's Commercial Department, 1914–18, arranged by alphabetical order of country by year, with general miscellaneous material at the end of each year. Foreign Office correspondence generally for 1910–19 is included on the Foreign Office Card Index, 1910–19 available at the PRO, which embraces that of the Commercial, Consular and Political Departments. Individual papers are identified by a country code, a paper number and a file number. These, however, have to be translated to modern PRO references by using the Series Lists arranged by country, date and file number.

FO 369/658–1058 contain the correspondence of the Foreign Office's Consular Department, 1914–18, arranged in the same way as that for the Commercial Department.

FO 371/1878–4351, the papers of the Foreign Office's Political and War Departments, are similarly organised but with specific prefix references in many cases to the war. Thus, there are files for War (FO 371/2158–76, 2190–2207, 2503–10, 2514–50, 2802–6, 2809–23, 3075–86, 3090–3106, 3434–51, and 4255–4308); News (General) War (FO 371/2208–21); America General War (FO 371/2223–6, 2581–3, 2584–92, 2846–52, 3108–24, 3486–93, and 4335); Austria-Hungary War (FO 371/2602 and 2862–4); Balkans War (FO 371/2241–82, 2602–34, 2865–95, 3140–60, and 3563–3608); Belgium War (FO 371/2283–93, 2635–8, and 2896–9); France War (FO 371/2360–26, 2678, and 2934–8); Germany War (FO 371/2367–8, 2678–80, and 2939–42); Italy War (FO 371/2374–80, 2684–7, and 2945–8); Morocco War (FO 371/2415); Netherlands War (FO 371/2418–19, 2716 and 2973); Persia War (FO 371/2427–38, 2724–38, and 1981–9); Scandinavia War (FO 371/2458–60, 2753–5, and 3021–5); Spain and Portugal War (FO 371/2469–72, 2759–62, and 3031–7); Switzerland War (FO 371/2474, 2764–66A, and 3039–40); and Turkey War (FO 371/2477–92, 2767–83, and 3042–62).

FO 438/1–12 has the Foreign Office Confidential Print, covering correspondence and further correspondence, 1914–18.

FO 794/3 among Private Office individual files, contains the correspondence of Sir Herbert Dering as Minister at Athens, 1915–18.

FO 800, collections of the private correspondence of Foreign Office ministers and prominent civil servants, includes that of Sir Edward Grey as PUS, 1892–5, and Foreign Secretary, 1905–16 (FO 800/35–113). Grey's collection has papers on Austria-Hungary, 1909–14 (FO 800/41); Belgium, 1906–15 (FO 800/42); France, 1905–16 (FO 800/49–560); Germany, 1906–14 (FO 800/61–2); Italy and the Vatican, 1914–16 (FO 800/65–7); Portugal and Romania (FO 800/71); Turkey, 1910–15 (FO 800/80); and the United States, 1914–16 (FO 800/84–6). In addition, there are Admiralty and War Office papers, 1906–16 (FO 800/88 and 102), and correspondence with Asquith, 1906–16 (FO 800/100). The papers of Sir Francis Bertie (FO 800/159–91) cover relations with France, 1914–18 (FO 800/166–9); Romania, 1914–16 (FO 800/176); Turkey, 1914–16, and the United States, 1905–18 (FO 800/181); as well as general wartime issues (FO 800/188–91). The papers of Viscount Cecil as PUS, 1915 and Assistant Secretary of State, 1918, include correspondence on the Balkans, Belgium, France and various neutrals, 1915–17 (FO 800/195–6), as well as miscellaneous wartime correspondence, 1915–19 (FO 800/197–8). The papers of Arthur Balfour as Foreign Secretary, 1916–19 (FO 800/199–217) include his correspondence with the King and Lloyd George, 1917–18 (FO 800/199); general correspondence arranged by country in alphabetical order, 1916–22 (FO 800/200–6, 210–11, and 213); and miscellaneous correspondence, 1917–19 (FO 800/207 and 214–17). The papers of Sir Mark Sykes (FO 800/221) cover events in 1918, while the correspondence of Sir Cecil Spring Rice (FO 800/241–2) covers his successive postings to Tehran, Stockholm and Washington, 1903–18.

FO 1011 contains the papers of Sir Percy Lorraine, Bt., who served in the British embassies in Paris and then Madrid before working for the Admiralty War Staff in intelligence work. There is correspondence between Lorraine and the Under Secretary of State at the Foreign Office, Lancelot Oliphant, 1916–19 (FO 1011/1–5); correspondence from France, 1912–16 (FO 1011/114); and correspondence from Madrid, 1916–19 (FO 1011/116–17).

German Foreign Ministry

Microfilms of the records of the German Foreign Ministry, captured by the Allies in 1945, were made as part of the German War Documents Project (GWDP). Various additional selections were made by institutions before the files were returned to Germany. While the majority were concerned with the conduct of German foreign affairs after 1920, some selections covered the archives back to 1867. There is a printed *Catalogue of Files and Microfilms of the German Foreign Ministry Archives, 1867–1920* available in the Reader Services Department, which gives the file titles alphabetically by registry series with an index of subjects, though it covers all files and not just those that were filmed. Those which were filmed have a serial number and a code letter representing the institution responsible for the filming. There is a key to the code in the catalogue and the Readers Service Department copy has a further key in the table of contents to indicate those institutions whose selections have been retained in the PRO and to show which PRO series should be consulted. Those series most relevant to the pre-1920 period are the selections of the GWDP Projects K and L (**GFM 3** and **4**); GWDP Project M, covering 1916–18 (**GFM 5**); the St Anthony's College selection, 1880–1920 (**GFM 6**); the London School of Economics selection on Italy and the Balkans, 1868–1921 (**GFM 7**); the South African Government selection, 1869–1914 (**GFM 8**); the University of California selection, 1867–1920, which has much on pre-1914 German relations with Austria-Hungary and Turkey (**GFM 10–11**); the Florida State University selection on the Eastern Question, 1865–1919 (**GFM 13**); the University of Michigan selection on the Balkans, 1866–1919 (**GFM 14**); the French Foreign Affairs Ministry selection on Franco-German relations, 1867–1919 (**GFM 16**); the American Committee for the Study of War Documents selection covering the United States, 1855–1920 (**GFM 21**); the University of London selection on Italy and the Papal States, 1867–1919 (**GFM 22**); and the American Historical Association selection of diplomatic archives, 1839–1927 (**GFM 25**). There are various additional means of reference and lists (**GFM 1**); various assorted copies and photocopies, 1867–1945 (**GFM 19** and **33**); and also microfilms of some of the photocopies (**GFM 34**).

HW 7, Official Histories of Intelligence Organisations and papers relating to the operation of the Admiralty's Room 40, include Admiralty and War Cabinet intelligence papers relating to Austro-Hungarian and Papal peace proposals, 1917–18 (HW 7/18); and Room 40 decrypts of German, Greek, Spanish and United States diplomatic telegrams relating to peace initiatives, 1917–18 (HW 7/22).

MT 25/32 has minutes of the Allied Supreme Council of Supply and Relief, 1919.

POWE 33/8–9 has material on the Allied Petroleum Conference, 1918.

PRO 30/57/57, among the papers of Field Marshal Lord Kitchener, contains correspondence with the French, 1914–16.

WO 32 deals with the military agreement between Britain, France and Russia in 1915 (WO 32/5088); the creation of the Supreme War Council (WO 32/10692–4); the British Military Mission in the United States, 1917 (WO 32/5403); the transportation of the American Expeditionary Force to France and arrangements for training it alongside British troops, 1917–18 (WO 32/5165–7 and 5764); exchanges of British and French divisions in 1918 (WO 32/5599–600); and the

Portuguese Expeditionary Force, 1917–18 and the desire to have contingents serve in the occupation of the Rhineland (WO 32/5661–2). There is also the formal thanks of the Belgian government for the British army's wartime services, 1919 (WO 32/5568).

WO 33/884 deals with the supply of the Greek army, 1918.

WO 95, War Diaries, 1914–18, includes those of the British Military Missions to the Portuguese Expeditionary Force (WO 95/60 and 5488–9), to the Allied Armies of the Orient (WO 95/5492); and in Washington (WO 95/5490–91), Bucharest (WO 95/5493) and Makran (WO 95/5418).

WO 106, papers of the Directorate of Military Operations, includes the original scheme for placing the BEF on the left flank of the French army as worked out by Sir Henry Wilson as DMO, 1910–14 and subsequent mobilisation schemes (WO 106/49A/1–51). There is material on the allied conferences at Chantilly in December 1915 and May 1916, and at Boulogne in October 1916 (WO 106/391, 394–5 and 1454); reports of other wartime conferences with the French, including on the extension of the British line in 1916 and 1917 (WO 106/393, 396–8, and 1455); reports of the British Military Mission with the French army in 1917 and 1918 (WO 106/404–5 and 1456); assorted minutes of the Supreme War Council, 1917–19, and notes on Clemenceau's appearance at the Council in December 1917 (WO 106/324–6 and 729); and Foch's request for British co-operation in 1918 (WO 106/410). There is material on Siam, 1915–17, including the Siamese entry into the war on the side of the Entente in July 1917 (WO 106/62). There is also material on the British Military Missions in Washington, April–May 1917 (WO 106/351), and the Adriatic (WO 106/1344 and 1346–7). Other material is included on the British Military Missions in Italy (WO 106/758, 761–2 and 772), Serbia (WO 106/1350) and at Salonika (WO 106/1353, 1379 and 1388), together with a report on the wartime role of British military missions generally (WO 106/6190).

Additionally, there is a considerable amount of material on the American Expeditionary Force (WO 106/464–543), including its training (WO 106/466); its progress (WO 106/475, 478, 490, and 513); its commanders (WO 106/526); and its operations (WO 106/529–30). There is also material on the Portuguese Expeditionary Force (WO 106/544–55), including Portuguese entry to the war in March 1916 (WO 106/544). Post-war British Military Missions in Czechoslovakia and Romania are also covered (WO 106/702–3), as is the role of Czechs in the wartime British army (WO 106/678). Other material on the Czechs (WO 106/678–703) includes the proclamation of the Czech Republic in October 1918 (WO 106/695). There is material on Poland, 1916–20 (WO 106/963–74) including the German and French raising of Polish units (WO 106/963–4), and the post-war British Military Mission in Poland, 1919–20 (WO 106/967–74). Additionally, there is material on the Anglo-French-Russian agreement on the Near East in July 1917 (WO 106/719), and on US relations with Germany, 1915–16 (WO 106/6072). There is also a report of a Cabinet Committee appointed by Asquith in 1915 to consider British Desiderata with respect to Turkey in Asia (WO 106/6286).

WO 107/59 includes a letter giving general impressions formed by the Adriatic Mission in January 1916.

WO 158, Military Headquarters papers, includes Haig's correspondence with Joffre, Nivelle, Pétain and Foch (WO 158/13–15, 26–30, 37, and 48); material on a conference at French GQG (General Headquarters) in December 1915 (WO 158/33); reports of the British liaison officers at GQG, 1917–19 (WO 158/43–4); correspondence on the extension of the British line in France, 1917–18 (WO 158/51); notes on and reports from the Supreme War Council 1917–18 (WO 158/57–63); reports of Anglo-French conferences on the conduct of the war, 1918 (WO 158/72); material on the interchange of British and French formations (WO 158/74); correspondence and notes of the British Military Representatives liaising with Foch as supreme commander, 1918 (WO 158/84, 98 and 101); and Foch's directives and telegrams (WO 158/105–6). There is further material on the British Military Mission to the Portuguese forces (WO 158/112 and 469).

It was not just German influence that increasingly encouraged some British policy-makers to push towards the east for the rise of the Bolsheviks in 1917 also challenged British interests. The British extended some assistance to those within Russia likely to continue the war against the Germans at the end of 1917 in order to keep the Ukraine out of German hands and thus blunt the threat to British interests elsewhere. With the negotiation of the Treaty of Brest Litovsk between Germany and the Bolsheviks in March 1918, matters looked blacker still. Neither Britain nor France had many troops to spare, however, and they therefore pressed the United States and the Japanese to intervene in Russia, it being anticipated that the latter would advance along the Trans-Siberian railway. The revolt against the Bolsheviks in May 1918 by the Czech Legion, recruited by the Russians from former Austro-Hungarian prisoners of war, provided a useful opportunity, since the Czechs were distributed along the Trans-Siberian railway and had seized the port of Vladivostock. The Americans were apprehensive of such an enterprise but were persuaded by July 1918 that the Germans must be forced to retain large numbers of troops inside Russia for fear of tilting the balance in the West against the British and French before the Americans could arrive in force. As a result, US troops were landed at Vladivostock in August 1918, together with Japanese. British troops had earlier landed at Murmansk in March 1918 and had also penetrated Transcaspia from Mesopotamia and Persia. British, French and American troops also landed at Archangel in August 1918. With the exception of the Japanese, who remained until October 1922, the allied contingents had all withdrawn from Russia by 1920, the British leaving the Trans-caspia in September 1918, Archangel and Murmansk in North Russia in September and October 1919 respectively, and Novorossiisk in South Russia in March 1920.

ADM 1, Admiralty In-Letters, includes material on the British naval and military mission to Russia, March 1915 (ADM 1/8415/81); a report by Colonel Knox on the military situation in Russia, 1915 (ADM 1/8434/280); consideration of the effect of Russian withdrawal from the Entente in April 1917 (ADM 1/8484/64); a report on the British Naval Mission in Russia by Major David Davies, MP, 1917 (ADM 1/8485/75); and a request to the Admiralty in 1922 to issue a formal denial of the existence of the Anglo-Russian Naval Entente in 1914 (ADM 1/8627/110).

ADM 137, Admiralty Historical Section 'Packs', includes the telegrams passing between the Admiralty and Russia in 1917 (ADM 137/4640–44); papers on the Allied Mission to Russia, 1917 (ADM 137/1947); digests of information on the situation in Russia, 1918 (ADM 137/4183); and reports on the immediate post-war situation in the Baltic and in the Black Sea and Caspian Sea, on the Danube and at Archangel and Murmansk (ADM 137/1663–796).

AIR 1, Records of the Air Historical Branch, includes reports on operations in North Russia, 1919 (AIR 1/9/15/1/33/1, and 472–4); the Caspian (AIR 1/32/15/1/187 and 344/15/226/288); and on the Dvina River Force operating out of Archangel (AIR 1/438). There is also correspondence between the War Office and the British Military Mission at Vladivostock, 1919 (AIR 1/451/15/312/14), and HQ papers of the RAF in South Russia (AIR 1/1956–63). There is an overall summary of the work of the RAF in North Russia (AIR 1/2295/209/76/2).

AIR 2, Registered Files of the Air Ministry, includes material on the organisation of the British forces sent to North Russia, 1918–19 (AIR 2/89/B 7797); reports on operations at Archangel and Vladivostock (AIR 2/80/B 3487, 81/B 3497 and 86/B 6742); reports on the assistance rendered to the White Russian leader in South Russia, General Denikin (AIR 2/89/B 8028 and 129/C 92250); and Treasury correspondence and returns on the cost of operations against the Bolsheviks and British financial claims upon anti-Bolshevik governments in Russia and the Baltic, 1919–21 (AIR 2/10112–16).

BT 62/1 and **3** deal with supplies to Siberia, 1918.

CAB 1, among miscellaneous Cabinet papers collected by Sir James Masterton-Smith, includes material on relations with Russia, the deteriorating situation inside Russia, and ultimate intervention (CAB 1/11, 21, 24–5, and 27–9).

CAB 17 contains assorted correspondence on Russia, 1916, including a Committee on the Revision of the Anglo-Russian Convention of 1907, and correspondence on munitions (CAB 17/180–83). There is also miscellaneous correspondence from 1917 (CAB 17/197).

CAB 21 has reports on the situation in Russia, 1917–18, including those by Professor Bernard Pares (CAB 21/12, 44 and 114).

CAB 27/189 contains papers of the Russian Supplies Committee, 1915–18, collected by Colonel F. Byrne. The papers are sub-divided into 24 parts, which need to be ordered separately. Included are reports of the allied conference at Petrograd in January–February 1917; general correspondence; reports by Byrne on the situation in Russia; the shipment of materials to Russia by the Commission Internationale de Revitaillement; reports of visits to Russian factories; telegrams; and memoranda on Archangel. The committee was dissolved in March 1918 but the material extends to November 1918.

CAB 45, correspondence relating to the Official Histories of the War, has material on Russia (CAB 45/101–9), including a diary of events in Trans-caucasia (CAB 45/105).

CN 1/27 is a photograph of an allied parade in Vladivostock, 1919.

CN 5/25 includes a photograph of a seaplane of the Dvina River Force, 1919.

FO 141/640, papers of the British Embassy and Consular Offices in Egypt, includes material on Bolshevik activities in the Middle East, 1917–27.

FO 175/1–29 are the papers of the Allied High Commission in Archangel, 1918–19, including reports by Captain H. E. Lee (FO 175/11); material on the British Supply Mission (FO 175/18); an inter-departmental conference on Russian affairs (FO 175/19); and wireless intercepts (FO 175/21). The series has an index (FO 175/29).

FO 176/1–2 are the Registers of Correspondence of the Allied High Commission in Archangel, covering general correspondence, telegrams, journals and account books, 1918–19.

FO 181/937–41, among records of the British Embassy and Consular Offices in Russia, 1914–18, include miscellaneous communications to and from Consuls. They also deal with Bolshevik seizures of British commercial interests in 1918 (FO 181/941).

FO 371, records of the Foreign Office Political and War Departments, includes files on 'Russia War' (FO 371/2445–57, 2742–52, and 2995–3020).

FO 538/1–4 has papers of the Allied High Commission in Vladivostock, 1918–21, including correspondence on the murder of the Tsar and Bolshevik atrocities in Siberia (FO 358/1); documents illustrating Bolshevik policies and events in Siberia (FO 538/2); miscellaneous correspondence on the situation in Siberia, 1918–21 (FO 358/3); and a memorandum on the political and military situation by the British Consul in Ekaterinburg, together with correspondence on operations against the Bolsheviks in Siberia, 1919 (FO 538/4).

FO 794/4 contains the correspondence of Sir Francis Lindley as counsellor at the British embassy in Petrograd, 1915.

FO 800, private correspondence collections of ministers and prominent civil servants, includes Sir Edward Grey's papers on Russia, 1905–16 (FO 800/72–5); Sir Francis Bertie's papers on Russia, 1916–18 (FO 800/178); and material on Sir Halford Mackinder's mission to South Russia, 1919–20 (FO 800/251).

MT 25, correspondence of the Ministry of Shipping, deals with supplies to Russia, 1917 (MT 25/2), and has a report on the activities of the German peace delegation in Petrograd in December 1917 (MT 25/10).

PRO 30/57/67, among Kitchener's papers, contains his correspondence on Russia, 1914–16.

WO 32 has much material on the British intervention in Russia including the instructions of the British Military Mission at Murmansk under Major-General F. C. Poole (WO 32/5643); reports on operations at Murmansk and on the situation in North Russia, 1918–19 (WO 32/5675, 5677, 5682, 5687–8, 5691, 5693, 5698, 5700, and 5703–5); the mutiny in the locally raised 1st Battalion, Slavo British Legion in North Russia (WO 32/9545); the possible use of gas against the Bolsheviks in North Russia (WO 32/5749); reports on the situation in Siberia, 1918–19, including those of the British Military Mission there under General Sir Alfred Knox and by Lieutenant Colonel John Ward, MP of the 25th Battalion, Middlesex Regiment

(WO 32/5676, 5707, 5720, and 5747); reports from the Caspian, 1918–19 (WO 32/5671–2, 5696, and 9567); a report from the British Military Mission in the Baltic under Brigadier-General A. J. Turner (WO 32/5717); the situation in the Caucasus, 1919 (WO 32/5691); General Sir Hubert Gough's mission to the Baltic (WO 32/5751); a report on operations in South Persia, 1918 (WO 32/5208 and 5221); reports from the British and RAF Missions in South Russia (WO 32/5710–12); and a report on the activities of Lieutenant Colonel J. W. Boyle in South Russia and Romania (WO 32/21671). More general matters covered include reports of the request by Sir Ernest Shackleton to go to Russia to assist with transport and supply problems, 1917 (WO 32/5664); German withdrawal from Russia, 1918–19 (WO 32/5670); the German evacuation of the Baltic states, 1919–20 (WO 32/5701, 5706, and 5708); interviews with the German military on the Bolshevik threat, 1920–21 (WO 32/5783); provision of supplies for British forces (WO 32/5683); the raising of loyalist Russian forces (WO 32/5666); the cost of operations against the Bolsheviks (WO 32/5684); and a possible exchange of POWs (WO 32/5699). There are also reports concerning the murder of the Tsar (WO 32/5721) and the Bolshevik capture and execution of Admiral Kolchak, the White Russian Supreme Leader, in Siberia in February 1920 (WO 32/5720 and 5723). An earlier file concerns a Russian request for heavy artillery in 1915 (WO 32/5663).

WO 33, Confidential Printed Papers, includes a report on the Russian military situation, February–March 1915 (WO 33/712); the order of battle of British units in North Russia, 1918 (WO 33/911); a report from North Russia, 1919 (WO 33/950); telegrams from Russia, 1919 (WO 33/962, 966–7, and 975); and a narrative of events in Siberia with reference to British efforts to support Kolchak, 1918–20 (WO 33/977A).

WO 79, Miscellaneous Private Collections, includes maps of the Caucasus and Russia, 1918 (WO 79/98–101) among the papers of Major-General Sir William Thomson, who commanded the North Persian Force. There are also proposals for carrying out the civil administration in the Caucasus, 1919 (WO 79/102).

WO 95, War Diaries, 1914–18, includes those of the British units serving in Persia (WO 95/5042–51 and 5415–18); North Russia and Siberia (WO 95/5419–32); South Russia and the Caucasus (WO 95/4958–60); and the Black Sea (WO 95/4950–57).

WO 106 includes a short history of events in Russia, 1917–19 (WO 106/1470); minutes of the Russia Committee, 1918 (WO 106/1560); and papers and reports on the situation in Russia, 1914–20 and operations against the Bolsheviks, 1918–20 (WO 106/60–61, 983–1348, 1559–65, and 5930), including those by Generals Knox and Hanbury-Williams, Colonel Blair, Captain Neilson and Professor Pares (WO 106/987–1140). Other reports cover events at Murmansk and Archangel, (WO 106/1153–84), including reports from General Poole's mission (WO 106/1150 and 1161); the Caucasus and South Russia (WO 106/1190–1205 and 6240–41); the Caspian (WO 106/1206); and Siberia (WO 106/1215–31, 1233–50, 1284–317, and 5724–6); the Black Sea (WO 106/1563); and the withdrawal from Persia (WO 106/188). There are also reports from Persia, 1916–19 (WO 106/55, and 925–62); reports of the British Military Missions in Russia and Poland, 1919 (WO 106/352); and situation and other reports from Finland and the Baltic states, 1919–20 (WO 106/596–632 and 6046), including Sir Hubert Gough's mission (WO 106/615). The Czech Legion and the British Military Mission serving with it in Siberia are also covered (WO 106/680, 682–7 and 691), and there is an 'historical sketch' of the Japanese role in Siberia, 1917–21 (WO 106/6144–5). Brigadier-General Spears reported on events in Russia to the French government and also reported on Central and Eastern Europe generally (WO 106/1251–4 and 1521).

WO 153, Maps and Plans, includes situation maps for the Eastern Front, 1914–20 (WO 153/785–803), the great majority of which relate to the period of allied intervention (WO 153/794–803). In addition, there are maps for the operations of Dunster Force in Persia (WO 153/1031–2), and other maps for North and South Russia (WO 153/1205–8).

WO 154, Supplementary War Diaries, being those unit war diaries previously extracted from WO 95 due to their sensitive content, includes those for the Deputy Adjutant General at HQ, Black Sea (WO 154/234–6); the British Military Mission in Siberia, 1920 (WO 154/237–9 and 341); the British Military Agent in the Caucasus, 1918–19 (WO 154/328); and HQ and units of the Elope, Syren and Dvina forces (WO 154/329–40 and 342), including that of the 2nd Battalion, Slavo British Legion (WO 154/339).

WO 157, Intelligence Summaries, includes those for Dunster Force and the North Persia Force 1918–19 (WO 157/854–67); South Russia and the Caucasus, 1919–20 (WO 157/765–75); and North Russia, 1918–20 (WO 157/1201–16, and 1218–33), including those for the Dvina Force (WO 157/1209–15). There are also summaries from the British Intelligence Mission in Petrograd in 1916 (WO 157/1217).

WO 158, Military Headquarters papers, has material on operations in Russia (WO 158/711–53), including general policy issues in North Russia, 1918–19 (WO 158/712–13); the amphibious operations of the Syren Lake and Dvina River forces (WO 158/719–20, 724, 727–8); RAF operations in North Russia (WO 158/735); correspondence and reports of Knox as head of the British Military Mission in Siberia (WO 158/737, 739–40, and 742); reports of the British Military Missions in Romania and South Russia (WO 158/748–53); and reports from the Black Sea (WO 158/746–7). In addition, there are further reports on the situation in Russia and the British Military Mission with Denikin (WO 158/964–5); more reports from North Russia and Siberia, 1919–21 (WO 158/970–72); and an account by Commander B. Fraser and Major C. Rowan of their release from captivity at Baku, November 1920 (WO 158/934).

WO 160, the 1914–18 Special Series, has intelligence material from operations in Russia (WO 160/7–21) including reports from the Dvina and Syren Forces (WO 160/9, and 18–20); other appreciations and reports from North Russia, 1918–19 (WO 160/11–12, and 14–17); a report from Estonia, December 1919 (WO 160/13); an Intelligence War Diary from Sorlavala, 1920 (WO 158/8); an operational report from Plesetskaya, 1919 (WO 158/21); and a report on the mutiny in the Slavo British Legion, July 1919 (WO 160/10). In addition, there is a report on an alleged German–Japanese understanding on spheres of influence in Russia, 1918 (WO 160/3); and an early dispatch from Petrograd on Russian manpower, September 1916 (WO 160/4). In addition, there is material on the Bermondt affair, the defeat by Latvian and Anglo-French forces of an invasion of Latvia by the German-sponsored, supposedly anti-Bolshevik 'West Russian Army' of the White Russian Colonel, Pavel Bermondt-Avalov, 1919–20 (WO 160/2).

WO 161/5, among Miscellaneous Unregistered Papers, is a short history of events in Russia, 1917–19.

Dominions and Colonies

Colonial empires represented a manpower reserve and an economic resource to be employed in the interests of the metropolitan power. In the event, however, the war not only further stimulated the development of distinctive national identities in the case of Britain's white dominions, but also generally encouraged limited degrees of indigenous nationalism and economic independence.

Britain had by far the largest empire in 1914 and some 2.8 million men from the empire fought during the war, of whom over 1.4 million were from the Indian Army. The imperial effort also embraced a high percentage of the white male populations of the dominions, amounting to 19.3 per cent from New Zealand, 13.4 per cent from Canada, 13.4 per cent from Australia and 11.1 per cent from South Africa. This compares favourably with the 22.1 per cent of the British male population who served in the wartime army.

By and large, government and opposition in the dominions vied to demonstrate imperial loyalty. In fact, there was more resistance to recruitment efforts than sometimes supposed, both the Australian Imperial Force (AIF) and Canadian Expeditionary Force (CEF) having a disproportionate number of British-born, as opposed to locally born, initial recruits. Underlying divisions within Australian society became pronounced during referenda on conscription in October 1916 and December 1917 and, on both occasions, conscription was rejected. In Canada, French Canadians were particularly resistant to enlistment and the introduction of conscription in May 1917 led to a bitterly contested election. New Zealand's level of mobilisation was the highest of the dominions and its manpower policy sounder than most but here, too, conscription was introduced in August 1916 and, as in Australia, it was opposed by the labour movement, Catholics and those of Irish extraction. In the case of South Africa, there was an Afrikaner rebellion in 1914 led by two Boer veterans of the South African War, Koos De la Rey and Christiaan De Wet. Nevertheless, Australians, New Zealanders, Canadians, South Africans, Rhodesians and Newfoundlanders all made valuable contributions to the war effort.

Initially, an Indian corps was despatched to France but it was not a success on the Western Front. The extension of the war, not least the entry of Ottoman Turkey, however, opened up new theatres of direct concern to India. Indeed, the campaign against the Turks in Mesopotamia was to be directed from India. Indian troops also served in Egypt and German East Africa, greatly increasing the manpower demands in India itself. Britain also raised about 56,000 troops from Black Africa and, after some reluctance, even 15,000 from the West Indies. In addition, non-combatant labour corps were raised from the empire, providing much needed logistic support for the British army. On the Western Front alone by 1916, there were 193,500 native labourers serving the British army drawn from China, India, South Africa, Egypt, the West Indies, Malta, Mauritius, the Seychelles and Fiji, with similar labour corps in Mesopotamia, East Africa, Egypt, Italy and at Salonika. In addition, just over a million Africans were employed by the British as labourers or carriers during the war, the prevalence of tsetse fly making the use of baggage animals impossible in German South West and, especially, German East Africa.

At the same time that the colonial empires were proving a manpower quarry, they also represented an economic resource. The British empire's financial contributions to the war effort were considerable. Similarly, colonial production of both raw materials and manufactured goods was increased to assist the British war effort.

Given the overall contribution to the war effort and the way in which military participation of the Anzacs at Gallipoli in 1915 or the Canadians at Vimy in 1917 raised the national consciousness of the dominions, it was not surprising that there was a degree of increased recognition for their political significance. Australian and Canadian prime ministers on occasions attended Cabinet meetings when in London. Australian and Canadian representatives also attended the allied economic conference at Paris in June 1916. Above all, there was the establishment of an Imperial War Cabinet in December 1916, although the consultation process amounted to little in real terms and the British saw it mainly as a means by which more manpower might be obtained. There was also an Imperial War Conference in 1917, which included two Indians in the three-man Indian delegation. The South African prime minister, Jan Smuts, joined the War Cabinet itself. Moreover, Australia, Canada and New Zealand all insisted on separate representation at the post-war peace conference and were represented both within a British Empire Delegation and by their own delegates, as well as being recognised as separate signatories of the Versailles treaty.

ADM 1/8520/103 deals with preparations for the discussion of the naval defence of the empire at the Imperial War Conference.

AIR 1/2313/221/46 has minutes of the Imperial War Cabinet, 1918.

CAB 17 has memoranda on Imperial Co-ordination penned by Leopold Amery in 1917 (CAB 17/190 and 199).

CAB 21 has notes on meetings of the Imperial War Cabinet, 1918 (CAB 21/98) There are also papers on the British Empire Delegation at the Paris conference, 1919 (CAB 21/140 and 142–3).

CAB 23 contains minutes of the meetings of the Imperial War Cabinet for March to May 1917 (CAB 23/40), and from June to December 1918 (CAB 23/41–2), with notes in shorthand from the meetings of March 1917 and June and July 1918 (CAB 23/43).

CAB 29 has a record of meetings of the British Empire Delegation during the peace conferences, 1919–22 (CAB 29/28); and an historical account by Clement Jones on 'The Dominions and the Peace Conference' compiled in 1920 (CAB 29/80).

CAB 32/1 are the minutes and papers of the Imperial War Conference, March 1917 to July 1918.

Colonial Office

Wartime material for the Colonies can be found in Colonial Office Registers of Correspondence, the Government Gazettes published in each territory and the proceedings of local assemblies. The Colonial Office Registers are the daily registers of correspondence arranged by colony and date and divided into three tranches of 'despatches', 'offices' and 'individuals' though often containing references to documents which no longer survive. The registers record the date of receipt of correspondence, the number allocated, the name of sender, the date of despatch, the sender's reference number, the subject matter, references to previous and subsequent papers on the same subject, and the action taken. The Government Gazettes, which were sent to the Colonial Office twice annually, were primarily intended to publicise new legislation and a variety of legal transactions within a specific colony, and they provide a wealth of detail on social, economic and administrative matters.

Wartime material can be found for Australia (CO 418/123–75 and CO 562/53–71); South Australia (CO 15/196–210 and CO 16/113–21); Western Australia (CO 20/66–70 and CO 21/57–62); the Bahamas (CO 23/274–83, CO 25/33, and CO 26/64–71); Barbados (CO 28/283–94, CO 31/101–5, and CO 32/51–9); Bermuda (CO 37255–62 and CO 40/80–83); Canada (CO 42/980–1010, CO 44/203–11, CO 45/1156–314, and CO 47/204–5); the Cape of Good Hope (CO 51/410–14); Ceylon (CO 54/773–817, CO 57/190–97, and CO 58/176–93); Cyprus (CO 67/173–90, CO 69/30–34, and CO 70/9–10); the Falklands (CO 78/131–49 and CO 80/8–9); Fiji (CO 83/121–43); Gibraltar (CO 91/456–69 and CO 94/103–7); the Gold Coast (CO 96/547–95, CO 98/24–30, and CO 99/27–33); Hong Kong (CO 129/412–52 and CO 131/49–55); Jamaica (CO 137/704–29 and CO 140/244–54); Kenya (CO 533/139–205 and CO 542/8–12); Malta (CO 158/386–407 and CO 161/108–15); Natal (CO 181/69–70); Newfoundland (CO 194/288–95, CO 196/1697–8, and CO 198/11–12); New South Wales (CO 204/538–81 and CO 205/264–81); New Zealand (CO 209/280–99, CO 211/294–315, and CO 212/83–94); Nigeria (CO 583/17–71); Nyasaland (CO 525/57–81); Queensland (CO 236/245–63); Somaliland (CO 535/35–54); South Africa (CO 417/542–615, CO 551/59–110, and CO 552/19–29); the Straits Settlements (CO 273/408–81 and CO 275/93–100); the Transvaal (CO 293/61–5 and CO 294/50–54); Uganda (CO 536/70–92); Victoria (CO 311/278–95); West Africa (CO 554/17–40); the Western Pacific (CO 225/128–63); and the West Indies (CO 318/332–47). There is also general correspondence on the Colonies (CO 323/624–791), and the Dominions (CO 532/67–129).

CO 537, Confidential Correspondence, includes a paper for the Imperial War Conference, 1917, on British Honduras (CO 537/728). General material relating to the Dominions, 1914–18 (CO 537/985–1019) includes South African views on the Imperial War Conference and considerations for the conference relating to the Pacific (CO 537/987 and 989); reports on possible post-war territorial changes (CO 537/988, 990 and 993), especially relating to German colonies (CO 537/1016–17 and 1020); competing Japanese claims in the Pacific (CO 537/1019); and Dominion representation at the Paris conference (CO 537/1018). There is also earlier information on New Zealand views of Japanese Pacific claims, 1915 (CO 537/1173).

CO 616/1–82 is Dominions War Correspondence, 1914–18, subdivided like the Colonial Office Registers into 'despatches', 'offices', and 'individuals'.

CO 687/1–68 is Dominions War Trade Correspondence, 1914–18, again subdivided into despatches, offices and individuals.

CO 752/1–8 contain the register of general wartime correspondence (In-letters) from the Dominions, 1914–19. As with all Colonial Office Registers, the daily registers of correspondence are arranged by dominion and date and divided into three tranches of 'despatches', 'offices' and 'individuals' and often contain references to documents which no longer survive. The registers record the date of receipt of correspondence, the number allocated, the name of sender, the date of despatch, the sender's reference number, the subject matter, references to previous and subsequent papers on the same subject, and the action taken.

CO 753/1–5 contain the register of wartime Out-letters to the Dominions, 1914–19.

CO 756/1–4 contain the register of wartime correspondence received from the Dominions relating to trade, 1916–19.

CO 757/1–4 contain the register of wartime Out-letters to the Dominions regarding trade, 1916–19.

FO 374/22, among the printed Acts of the Peace Conference, has the *Minutes of the Meetings of the British Empire Delegation*, published in 1919.

RECO 1/839–46 contain records of proceedings and associated memoranda of the Imperial War Conference, 1917–18.

WO 32 contains reports by the Inspector General of Overseas Forces on the Australian forces, 1914–15 (WO 32/4818); the organisation and preparation of the Australian Imperial Force (AIF) for service in Europe, 1914–15 (WO 32/5138 and 5256); the conferment of the Royal title on the Newfoundland Regiment, 1917–18 (WO 32/5012); and control of the Canadian Expeditionary Force (CEF) in Europe, 1917–18 (WO 32/5139).

WO 106/430 is a report on raising additional Canadian forces in 1918.

The Peace Settlements

There had been little expectation that the war would end quite as it did. Bulgaria collapsed first as British and French forces launched an offensive from Salonika on 15 September 1918, the Bulgarian King requesting an armistice on 26 September and hostilities ceasing on 30 October 1918. The British meanwhile were also advancing up the Tigris towards Mosul and had taken Damascus on 1 October and Aleppo on 23 October. The Turks opened negotiations on 26 October and concluded an armistice on 30 October. In Italy, the allies broke through the Austro-Hungarian lines at Vittorio Veneto on 24 October. Austria-Hungary, already breaking under the demands of its constituent nationalities for independence, requested an armistice on 28 October though it was only signed on 3 November and did not come into effect until 11 November, with Emperor Karl abdicating political power though not formally renouncing the throne. In Hungary, a new government had been established on 31 October and, though initially declining to accept that the armistice applied to Hungary, the Hungarians signed their own officially on 13 November, Hungary becoming a republic three days later. The German military leadership, meanwhile, had concluded in late September that an armistice was necessary though only conceiving this as a means of acquiring a breathing space as the allied armies pushed the German field army back towards the German western frontier. With the Kaiser persuaded to abdicate, a republic was proclaimed on 9 November, the day following the beginning of armistice negotiations. The German representative then signed the armistice agreement at 0510 hours on 11 November 1918, it coming into effect at 1100 hours for a period of 36 days. Normally an armistice implied simply cessation of hostilities but the Entente had imposed conditions designed to ensure that Germany could not renew the struggle. Remaining German forces evacuated France and Belgium by 18 and 26 November respectively, the U-boat fleet sailing into Harwich on 20 November and the remainder of the High Seas Fleet reached Scapa Flow on the following day.

ADM 1 has naval views on any armistice as formulated in April 1918 (ADM 1/8522/117); the Admiralty letter to the Fleet on the actual armistice (ADM 1/8542/288); the armistice terms and naval conditions (ADM 1/8542/290 and 299); instructions to the allied naval armistice commission (ADM 1/8545/309); an unofficial account of the negotiations by Commander W. T. Bagot and an official report of the first meeting with the German Naval Commission on 5 December 1918 (ADM 1/8546/319–20); and a report of the Air Section of the Allied Naval Armistice Commission, December 1918 (ADM 1/8547/342).

ADM 116 contains the Private Office papers on the armistice, 1918 (ADM 116/1651); papers on the armistices with Austria and Turkey (ADM 116/1816–17 and 1823); the handing over of German submarines at Harwich and the internment of the High Seas Fleet at Scapa (ADM 116/1825–7); and the armistice terms (ADM 116/1931).

ADM 137 deals with the armistice (ADM 137/3891), and also includes decrypted messages bearing on the armistice negotiations (ADM 137/4184–5).

AIR 1 deals with the surrender of German aircraft upon the armistice (AIR 1/34/15/1/208/2), and has general instructions for the implementation of the armistice (AIR 1/1156/204/5/2442). There is also a list from October 1918 of German towns in range of artillery or aircraft in the event of the German army withdrawing to the Rhine (AIR 1/2297/209/77/22).

FO 141, papers of the British Embassy and Consular Offices in Egypt, includes information on the armistice with Turkey and its application to Tripolitania, where the Turks had encouraged the Senussi tribes to revolt against Italian control, and against whom British forces had also been deployed in 1916 (FO 141/431, 670, and 794).

HW 7/22 has material on the Bulgarian request for an armistice, September 1918.

WO 32 has material on the suggested armistice terms for both Germany (WO 32/5374) and Turkey (WO 32/5761).

WO 106 has material on the terms of the armistices with Germany, 1918 (WO 106/412), Hungary (WO 106/1393), and Turkey (WO 106/1433–5 and 1571).

WO 144 contains the Papers of the Chief of the British Delegation, Inter-allied Armistice Commission, 1918–20. Formed by Foch on 12 November 1918 with representatives of the American, Belgian, British and French armies, the commission was intended to investigate and resolve details of the armistice agreement not settled at the time the instrument was signed. The subjects involved were repatriation of POWs, surrender of war materiel, taking over of depots and stores, and the handing over of locomotives, wagons and motor lorries. Subsequently, the administrative functions were extended to cover not only the Western Front, but also Alsace-Lorraine and the Eastern Front. The series consists of the War Diary of the British Representative, Lieutenant General Sir Richard Haking, 1918–20 (WO 144/1–2), and Haking's dispatches (WO 144/3–35). An index to the latter is available. It was decided in July 1919 that the commission would remain the machinery of communication between allied governments and Germany until the ratification of the peace treaty, at which time communication would revert to normal diplomatic channels. Accordingly, the commission was dissolved in January 1920, three days after ratification of the Treaty of Versailles.

WO 158/848 deals with the possibility of the Germans continuing to fight into 1919.

There were to be six separate peace treaties, of which five were negotiated at Paris. The Treaty of Versailles was signed on 28 June 1919 to conclude the war with Germany, followed by the Treaty of St Germain concluded with Austria on 10 September 1919, and the Treaty of Neuilly with Bulgaria on 27 November 1919. Delayed by the Hungarian revolution, the Treaty of Trianon concluded the war with Hungary on 4 June 1920. The Treaty of Sèvres concluded the war with Turkey on 10 August 1920 and a further Treaty of Lausanne was then signed with Turkey on 24 July 1923 following the overthrow of the Sultan, and of the previous settlement, by a resurgent Turkish nationalist movement headed by Mustapha Kemal.

Once the conference convened at Paris on 18 January 1919 with some 27 states represented – the defeated were not represented – the decision-making process was initially conducted by the so-called 'Council of Ten', comprising the heads of government and foreign ministers of Britain, France, Italy, Japan and the United States. In March 1919, as a means of resolving the many outstanding issues, decisions were made by the 'Council of Four', namely Lloyd George; the French prime minister, Georges Clemenceau; the President of the United States, Woodrow Wilson; and the Italian prime minister, Vittorio Orlando. The latter, however, withdrew from the conference between 21 April and 7 May. After the end of the main negotiations in July 1919, subsequent decisions were made between governments and various agencies of the Entente. The terms imposed on Turkey, negotiations for which were not completed at Paris, were then settled in London between February and April 1920 and finalised at San Remo in April, leading to the signing of the Sèvres treaty four months later.

The peace settlements proved an unhappy compromise between the French desire for a punitive settlement, the British desire for stability, and the American desire to create a better world based on principles of internationalism, democracy and self-determination. In any case, the 'Big Four' could not of themselves necessarily enforce even their collective will over some parts of Europe. The break-up of Austria-Hungary (and of Tsarist Russia) was established fact before the conference convened and the situation created thereby was irreversible. In most cases achieving an economic and strategic frontier was simply incompatible with the geographical spread of nationalities on the ground, rendering self-determination all but impossible. The arrangements made at Sèvres were also soon rendered void by events in Turkey.

It was also the case that, technically, none of the Central Powers had actually surrendered unconditionally, all having accepted military armistices. Moreover, in the case of Germany, Wilson had offered his 'Fourteen Points' of January 1918 in reply to the German approach for terms prior to the armistice. The Fourteen Points themselves were sufficiently vague to allow several interpretations while the Entente had made widely contradictory wartime promises to allies, which were frequently incompatible with the underlying principles of the Fourteen Points. Each Entente delegation at Paris also had to satisfy a public still imbued with the promises made them in return for their wartime sacrifices.

Britain had prepared carefully for the peace settlement. Indeed, the Foreign Office had established a Political Intelligence Department (PID) expressly for this purpose in March 1918. Lloyd George, however, distrusted traditional diplomacy and looked beyond Foreign Office advisers. He also had to consider pressure groups in Britain such as the Union of Democratic Control and the 'New Europe Group', whose advocacy of self-determination was well represented within the PID. More significantly, however, despite his overwhelming electoral victory in December 1918, Lloyd George was boxed in by election pledges to a public and press baying for retribution, and by a need to satisfy similar demands from his own back-benchers. A consummate politician, Lloyd George was a liberal realist on the needs of any peace settlement but this was tempered by British interests and his own parliamentary position.

Immediate British security requirements had been satisfied by the surrender of the German High Seas Fleet but there was a need to compensate for the possible failure of the proposed League of Nations. Thus, the British stressed the necessity for a balance of power in Europe and were hostile to exaggerated Italian territorial claims and to French gains beyond Alsace-Lorraine, although there was a desire to strengthen Belgium. In eastern Europe, stability required a settlement based on largely ethnic lines. There was some support in the Foreign Office for recognition of Czechoslovakia, but wide divergences of opinion of the desirability of a greater Greece or a greater Poland. Generally, there was a determination to avoid any obligation requiring Britain to uphold the settlement in central or eastern Europe and the British would have favoured some kind of federation of former Habsburg states without the Habsburgs.

Beyond Europe, there was a need to juggle self-determination with imperial needs and to reconcile contradictory wartime promises, not least those made to Arabs and Zionists. There was less preparation on economic and legal questions and, in the event, political considerations led to deviation from prepared negotiating positions, notably on the issue of reparations. Nonetheless, Britain achieved most of its essential aims in addressing the six principle issues which informed the formulation of the treaties relating to Europe, namely the acceptance by Germany of its responsibility for the war; the imposition of reparations; a territorial settlement, including the re-distribution of the German colonies; a measure of arms control; the establishment of a League of Nations; and provision of safeguards against Bolshevism.

In terms of the Ottoman Empire, Britain received the mandates for Palestine, Transjordan and Iraq, and a protectorate over Arabia. Britain also received German East Africa, which it had hoped to annexe outright to achieve a closer East African union, while South Africa received German SouthWest Africa. France took most of Togo and Cameroon, but with boundaries adjusted so that the whole of certain tribes already partly within neighbouring British territories now came under British control.

Britain, however, was to face nationalist unrest in Ireland (1919–21), India (1919), Egypt (1919–23), Palestine (1920–21) and Iraq (1920) at a moment when financial pressures and the need for demobilisation severely stretched resources. By 1921, therefore, Britain was forced to withdraw troops from Russia, the Caucasus, Transcaspia, Persia and Afghanistan, where it had briefly fought the Third Afghan War between May and August 1919 to deter the new Amir, Amanulla, from encouraging Muslim nationalists in the North-West Frontier Province. Moreover, the dominions were less willing to support imperial ventures, all declining to send troops to Iraq in 1920 or to support Britain in a serious confrontation with Mustapha Kemal's Turkish nationalist government at Chanak in 1922. British forces withdrew from Constantinople following the Treaty of Lausanne in 1923 but they remained in the Rhineland until 1930. Technically, indeed, Britain's war itself did not end until the Order of Council of 31 August 1921.

ADM 1 deals with the Admiralty's representatives at Paris (ADM 1/8542/284); the Admiralty's views on the issue of freedom of the seas (ADM 1/8545/312); and has notes on the peace terms as affecting naval interests (ADM 1/8546/329). There is also a memorandum by the First Sea Lord on the question of German naval war criminals, March 1919 (ADM 1/8553/72).

ADM 116/1931–2048 contain papers of the Inter-allied Naval Commission of Control, 1919–24, for the implementation of the peace treaties with respect to naval matters.

ADM 137 contains the letters of Commander Lucas, a member of the British Delegation at Paris, 1918–19 (ADM 137/4187); and also records of the naval base established at Constantinople, 1919–23 (ADSM137/2497–512).

AIR 1 deals with RAF requirements from the peace conference as regards both Germany and Austria-Hungary (AIR 1/35/15/1/220 and 344/15/226/291–2), and has reports from the RAF members of the British Delegation at Paris (AIR 1/463/15/312/128). General papers on the peace conference (AIR 1/2325) includes reports of the meetings of British and French representatives, telegrams to the British delegation, and a report on a convention prolonging the armistice in January 1919.

AIR 2 deals with the disposal of German aircraft surrendered in fulfilment of the peace terms, 1918–19 (AIR 2/125/B 11426); the work of the Aeronautical Control Committee with regard to the peace terms imposed upon Austria (AIR 2/126/A 22101 Pt I. II); and the air clauses of the peace treaties with Bulgaria and Turkey (AIR 2/126/B 11515).

BT 62 deals with the collection of outstanding war accounts for supplies and services due or against allied governments, 1918–26 (BT 62/21 and 25); and with British claims on the Greek government for wartime supplies and services, 1922–6 (BT 62/16).

BT 69 comprises minutes and papers of the Royal Commission on Compensation for Suffering and Damage by Enemy Action. Established by Royal Warrant in August 1921, the commission was to consider cases in which there was a moral claim by British nationals for compensation as a result of enemy action within Annexe 1 to Part 8 of the Treaty of Versailles and to make recommendations as to the distribution of some £5 million. Chaired by Lord Sumner, the commission began by drawing up a body of principles, reporting first in January 1923 and then finally in February 1924. The series includes minutes, 1921–2 (BT 69/1–2); decisions on claims, 1921–4 (BT 69/3–4); and general papers, parliamentary questions and related claims, 1922–4 (BT 69/5).

BT 102 are the records of the Board of Trade's Reparation Claims Department, 1920–26. The Department was established in January 1920 to work in conjunction with the Royal Commission on Compensation for Suffering and Damage by Enemy Action preparing British claims against Germany and also administering the release of Turkish property in the United Kingdom. Policy papers (BT 102/1–17, 19–20, 22, 25–6, 32, 35–7, 41–2, and 47) include notes on meetings (BT 102/1, 3 and 10); reparations claims procedures in other states such as Belgium and Japan (BT 102/32 and 41); consideration of various categories of civilian claims (BT 102/4, 6, 8, 15, and 17); property claims (BT 102/11, 13, 16, and 26); claims by companies (BT 102/7 and 22); procedural issues (BT 102/5, 14, 20, and 37); and specimen forms (BT 102/47). Files on actual claims (BT 102/18, 22–4, 29–30, 34, 38–40, and 43–6) include summaries of total British claims (BT 102/23); total claims against Turkey (BT 102/29); British claims relating to losses in Belgium and France (BT 102/38, 40 and 46); and representations by associations such as the Mercantile Marine Service Association, the British Fishing Vessels War Risks Insurance Association and the British Chamber of Commerce in Belgium (BT 102/34, 39, and 46). There are also papers of the British Restitution Service, 1920–26 (BT 102/33).

BT 203 contains the papers of the Enemy Debts Clearing Office, 1920–36. In January 1920 the Enemy Debts Clearing Office was established under the Treaty of Peace Order to administer claims by British nationals on such ex-enemy property, and claims by ex-enemies on property held by British nationals left in abeyance during the war. Having already taken over the duties of the Trading with the Enemy Department of the Public Trustee Office with respect to Austrian and Bulgarian property in 1920, the Office absorbed the Trading with the Enemy Department as a whole in January 1925 and the Russian Claims Department, formerly of the Foreign Office, in April 1927. The series comprises the minutes of the Treaty Execution and Marine Insurance Advisory Committees (BT 203/1–8); papers of the British, Belgian, Maltese, German, Austrian and Hungarian Clearing Offices (BT 203/9–28, and 57–84); material on matters affecting Ireland and Scotland (BT 203/54–6); papers on the Reparations Commission and the National Bank of Egypt (BT 203/45–8); and papers relating to arbitration tribunals and patents (BT 203/29–44 and 85–8). The Office ceased to exist in March 1936, when it was replaced by an Enemy Property Branch of the Solicitor's Department.

CAB 1, miscellaneous Cabinet papers collected by Sir James Masterton-Smith, has material on wartime preparations for the future peace conference in December 1917 (CAB 1/25); as well as the deliberations of the Committee on the League of Nations, May 1918 (CAB 1/26); consideration of French proposals, October 1918 (CAB 1/27); the peace conferences themselves (CAB 1/28); and particular issues such as the future of Upper Silesia (CAB 1/29).

CAB 21, registered files of the Cabinet Office, includes papers prepared for the War Cabinet by the Political Intelligence Department, 1918 (CAB 21/99); arrangements by the War Cabinet secretariat for the peace conference (CAB 21/124); material on the peace conference secretariat (CAB 21/141); reports on the progress in the conference (CAB 21/144 and 149); and various papers on aspects of the conference deliberations such as the recognition of Finnish independence, the future of Constantinople, the occupation of the Rhineland, the possible transfer of Cyprus to Greece, the situation in Hungary, Belgian proposals, the future of Syria, and the relief of Europe following the cessation of the allied economic blockade (CAB 21/138–9, 145, 148, 150, and 152–5).

CAB 23/25 has the report of the Cabinet Committee on German Reparations, April 1921.

CAB 27 has minutes of the Imperial War Cabinet Committee on Indemnity, set up in November 1918 under the chairmanship of the Australian prime minister, W. M. Hughes, to consider the payment of an indemnity or reparations by Germany (CAB 27/43). There are also minutes of a meeting of the subsequent Cabinet Committee on German Reparations, April 1921 (CAB 27/109). In addition, there are minutes and reports of the Cabinet Committee on the Pay of the Army of Occupation, January 1919 (CAB 27/55).

CAB 29 are microfilmed papers relating to the Peace Conference and other related International Conferences. There are memoranda of the 'P' (Peace) Series, 1916–20, the 'WCP' (War Cabinet Paris) Series, 1919–20, the 'M' (War Cabinet Paris) Series, 1919; and the 'AJ' (Peace Conference) Series, 1920–22 (CAB 29/1–5, 7–27, and 29–35). In addition, there are minutes and other records of the proceedings of the meetings of the Council of Heads of Government (The Big Four), 1919, the Ministers of Foreign Affairs, 1920–22, the Council of Ambassadors, 1920–22, and the Heads of Delegation of the Five Powers ('HD' Series), 1919–20 (CAB 29/37–79). There are also draft resolutions and other papers submitted to the Peace Conference ('PB' Series), 1919 (CAB 29/36); papers on the Ottoman Empire and the financial conditions of peace, 1916–20 (CAB 29/6); minutes of the Allied and International Conferences on the Terms of Peace and Related Subjects ('ICP' Series), 1919–22 (CAB 29/81–99); and papers of the London Conference on reparations, July–August 1924 (CAB 29/103–6).

CAB 29 has the report of the Imperial War Cabinet Committee on Indemnity, December 1918 (CAB 29/2), as well as Appendices to the Conclusions of the Cabinet Committee on German Reparations, 1921 (CAB 29/21). There are also memoranda relating to the peace conferences, 1920–22 (CAB 29/7–20, 22 and 29–35); draft resolutions submitted to the conference, 1919 (CAB 29/36); papers relating to the deliberations of the Council of Four (CAB 29/37–9); and minutes of the meetings of the Heads of Delegation, 1919–20 (CAB 29/69–77).

CAB 44/38 has the despatches of General Harington, British CinC in the Army of Occupation at Constantinople, 1920–23, among military narratives and other material collected for the Official History of the War.

DO 140, papers of the British Phosphate Commissioners, deals with the administration of the former German Pacific island colony of Nauru. Occupied by Australian troops in November 1914, it was acquired for the empire under the Treaty of Versailles, a Board of Commissioners being established by Britain, Australia and New Zealand to hold and manage the phosphate deposits. Wartime material mainly consists of deeds and leaseholds (DO140/417–19 and 423), but there are reports of wartime visits to Ocean Island and Nauru by an official in 1915 and 1918 (DO140/835–6).

FO 93, material relating to protocols and treaties, includes details of various protocols relating to amendments of the Treaty of Versailles, 1921–4 (FO 93/1/86 and 88, 93/14/101, 93/33/285, 93/36/82 and 92), and a declaration from 1919 regarding provisions of the German Weimar constitution in contradiction to the treaty (FO 93/36/94). There are also agreements on financial matters relating to the Treaty of Trianon from 1930 (FO 93/122/11 and 16); protocols relating to the Treaty of Neuilly, 1932–8 (FO 93/21/17 and 19); and material relating to Egyptian nationality as defined by the Treaty of Lausanne in 1923, and a verbal agreement on ratification of Lausanne, 1932 (FO 93/33/291 and 93/36/125).

FO 115/2542 contains material on the United States and the peace conference, 1919.

FO 141, papers of the British Embassy and Consular Offices in Egypt, deals with both the peace arrangements relating to Austria-Hungary (FO 141/436), and the effect of the Treaty of Versailles on subsequent Egyptian relations with Germany, 1923–8 (FO 141/446).

FO 286/684 deals with the establishment of the Political Intelligence Department.

FO 324/1 has the records of the Anglo-Austrian Mixed Arbitration Tribunal, 1921–31, as established by the Treaty of St Germain. The series consists of the minutes and decisions of the tribunal with a printed copy of the rules of procedure from August 1921, and a copy of the agreement provisionally dissolving the tribunal in July 1931.

FO 325/1–4 are the records of the Anglo-Bulgarian Mixed Arbitration Tribunal, 1921–7 as established by the Treaty of Neuilly. The series comprises the minutes

1921–7, and a printed document of the agreement dissolving the tribunal in June 1927 (FO 325/1); and a record of decisions, May 1922 to January 1927 (FO 325/2–4).

FO 326/1–19 are the records of the Anglo-German Mixed Arbitration Tribunal, 1921–31 as constituted under the Treaty of Versailles. There are minutes, 1921–31 together with printed copies of the rules of procedure (FO 326/1–5); rules, orders and decisions, 1920–31 (FO 326/6); and a record of decisions, 1922–8 (FO 326/7–19).

FO 327/1 has the records of the Anglo-Hungarian Mixed Arbitration Tribunal, 1921–35 as constituted under the Treaty of Trianon. There are minutes, an index to the register and decisions, with a printed copy of the rules of procedure, and the provisional agreement to dissolve the tribunal in January 1935.

FO 328/1 records the decisions of the Clause Four Arbitration Mixed Arbitration Tribunal, 1922–30, being a form of arbitral procedure established by the Treaties of Versailles, St Germain and Trianon.

FO 371, records of the Foreign Office Political Department, includes those of the Political Intelligence Department Peace Conference Series, 1919 (FO 371/4352–6), and of the Political Intelligence Department generally for 1919 (FO 371/4357–87).

FO 373/1–7, Peace Conference Handbooks, contain 167 separate handbooks prepared between November 1918 and April 1919 on various states, contested areas and issues for the guidance of the British Delegation and the government. There are, for example, ethnographic maps of Central and South-east Europe and western Asia (FO 373/1/1); and handbooks on Dalmatia (FO 373/1/14); Luxemburg and Limburg (FO 371/2/10); Galicia (FO 373/3/10); Kiachow (FO 371/4/5); Togoland (FO 373/6/11); and the New Hebrides (FO 373/7/20). Subjects included are the rise of Islam and the Pan-Islamic Movement (FO 373/5/7); freedom of the seas (FO 373/7/21); indemnities of war (FO 373/7/32); Zionism (FO 373/7/35); Woodrow Wilson's policies (FO 373/7/39); German utterances before the war on territorial and political questions and ambitions (FO 373/7/28–9); and British wartime subsidies and loans to foreign powers (FO 373/7/33).

FO 374 are the published *Acts of the Peace Conference, 1919–20*. The series includes *Acts of the Supreme Council*, published in 1934–5 (FO 374/1); proceedings of *Plenary Sessions of the Conference and Commissions of the Conference* as published in 1922–3 (FO 374/2–11); *Negotiations and Signature Treaties with Enemy Powers*, as published in 1924 (FO 3374/12–13); *Putting into Force Treaties with Enemy Powers*, published in 1934 (FO 374/14–15); *Preparation and Signature of Divers Treaties and Conventions*, published 1922–3 (FO 374/15–17A); *The Putting into Force Collection of Resolutions of the Conference of Ambassadors*, published in 1932 (FO 374/17B–18); *Correspondence with the German Delegation* (FO 374/19); *Miscellaneous Papers of the British Delegation*, published in 1919 (FO 374/20–21); *Secretary's Notes of Conversations and Précis of Meetings of the Supreme War Council*, published in 1919 (FO 374/23–5); *Protocols of Plenary Sessions and Minutes of the Representatives of the Powers with Special Interests*, 1919 (FO 374/26); *The Peace Conference Drafting Committee Instructions and Decisions*, 1919 (FO 374/27–8); and *Conclusions of the Council of Four*, 1919 (FO 374/29–34).

FO 608, correspondence relating to the Peace Conference, 1919–20, includes general files (FO 608/2–270); files of the Eastern Mission (Turkey) (FO 608/

271–8); and private papers of Sir P. Waterlow of the British Delegation on the Supreme Economic Council, 1919 (FO 608/279–81). The British Delegation papers of Lord Sumner (FO 608/282–311) include papers on the cost of the war (FO 608/284); the draft treaty amendment drawn up by J. M. Keynes (FO 608/296); reparations schemes (FO 608/293–4); reparations relating to Austria and Bulgaria (FO 608/ 297–300 and 302); German objections to reparations (FO 608/303–5); minutes of the Council of Four (FO 608/306); letters from the Armenian, Italian, Japanese, Portuguese and Serbo-Croat-Slovene delegations (FO 608/307–8); and correspondence from Hankey (FO 608/311–12). There is a large and comprehensive subject index to the general files (FO 608/1) in the Public Search Room.

FO 801, archives of the Reparation Commission, covers the work of the Commission as established in June 1919 to settle those issues concerning reparations not agreed in the peace conference. It was intended to assess the damage done and to lay down the method and schedule of payments by May 1921. There are papers of the Committee on the Organisation of the Reparation Commission, 1919–20 (FO 801/1–3); minutes of the Reparations Commission, 1920–31 (FO 894/4–12); minutes of proceedings, 1924–31 (FO 801/115–17); annexes to minutes of proceedings, 1920–30 (FO 801/13–87 and 118–26); minutes and decisions of the Permanent Managing Committee of the Commission, 1925–6 (FO 801/91–2); a record of decisions of the Commission, 1925–31 (FO 801/90); Out-letter books, 1920–29 (FO 801/96–114); details of the Commission's administrative expenditure, 1924–9 (FO 801/88–9); and the report of the Committee of Experts on German Reparations, 1929 (FO 801/93–5). For all practical purposes, the Committee of Experts, which was established in 1923, and chaired by the American representative, Charles Dawes, put an end to reparations through the inauguration of the Dawes Scheme in 1924. Ultimately reparations were terminated entirely by the Lausanne Conference in 1932.

FO 839/1–49 are papers connected to the Lausanne Conference, 1922–3, leading to the Treaty of Lausanne which amended that of Sèvres, Lausanne being the only peace settlement that was negotiated rather than imposed. There is material on such issues as the administration of Constantinople, 1922–3 (FO 839/2); the allied command in Turkey (FO 839/3); the expulsion of Greeks from Turkey following the Greek defeat in the Greco-Turkish War of 1920–21 (FO 839/11); the Armenian question (FO 839/12); the naval demilitarisation of the Black Sea (FO 839/20); Italian territorial demands (FO 839/32); and British wartime promises to the Arabs (FO 839/37). There is also a draft of the treaty (FO 839/48); and bound volumes of day to day reports on the conference (FO 839/50–53).

FO 893/1–33 contain the minutes of proceedings of the Conference of Ambassadors, 1920–30 as established at the peace conference, many in French (FO 893/11–32). There is an index (FO 893/33) to some of the minutes (FO 893/1–8).

FO 894/1–33 are minutes of the Inter-allied Rhineland High Commission, 1920–30.

FO 895/1–3 is the correspondence of the Klagenfurt Plebiscite Commission (British Section), July–November 1920, covering the administration of plebiscites for the former Austrian territories of Sopron and Slovenia. Plebiscites were also held to determine the future of Marienwerder, Allenstein, Upper Silesia and Schleswig in Germany.

FO 896/1–3 are the papers of the Inter-allied Commission of Control for Austria. There are reports on industry, 1926 (FO 896/1) and the final report on the Commission's work, 1928 (FO 896/2–3).

FO 1011/118 contains correspondence and papers relating to the Paris peace conference from the collection of Sir Percy Lorraine, Bt., who was attached to the British delegation.

MT 9, correspondence and papers of the Board of Trade Marine Department, has a body of material on reparations (MT 9/1291, 1321, 1356, and 1425), including notes on a Chamber of Commerce deputation on the issue in 1917 (MT 9/1097).

MT 25, correspondence of the Ministry of Shipping, has minutes of the Armistice Shipping Commission meeting in Rotterdam in April 1919 (MT 25/26); material on the compensation to be demanded for the scuttling of the High Seas Fleet at Scapa Flow in June 1919 (MT 25/33); details of the agreement between Lloyd George and Woodrow Wilson on the retention and distribution of seized German vessels (MT 25/35B); and drafts of the penultimate paragraph of the Treaty of St Germain with Austria (MT 25/75A).

PIN 15/338–42 deal with German reparations, 1918–31, as relating to payment of British war pensions.

PREM 1/12 deals with the progress of negotiations for the trial of alleged German war criminals, 1920. The Treaty of Versailles allowed for war crimes trials but an attempt to extradite the Kaiser from the Netherlands failed and only a few individuals were brought to trial by the Weimar Supreme Court in Leipzig, receiving derisory sentences. The pursuit of Turkish war criminals was similarly fruitless.

PRO 30/30, Milner's papers as Secretary of State for War, includes a General Staff confidential memorandum on political questions in Europe, November 1918 to January 1919 (PRO 30/30/7), and papers on the future of Syria, 1919–20 (PRO 30/30/10–11).

PRO 30/66, papers of Brigadier-General Sir Henry Osborne Mance, covers his role as a communications expert in the British Delegation at the Paris peace conference. They include a memorandum on the post-war rehabilitation of European transport systems (RO30/66/11); papers and a later lecture on port, waterway and railway issues at Paris (PRO 30/66/12 and 18); his visits to Europe as President of the Communications Section of the Supreme Economic Council, 1919 (PRO 30/66/13); and a census of European rolling stock, 1920–22 (PRO 30/66/14).

RECO 1/335–6 deal with the consideration of the post-war reconstruction of the German mercantile marine.

T 194 contains papers of the British Delegation to the Reparation Commission, 1919–30, which was established under the auspices of the Treaty of Versailles to determine the scale of reparations and to oversee their implementation. Initially, the London Committee co-ordinated the British work of the Commission before the appointment of Sir John Bradbury as principal British Delegate. Thereafter, the London Committee prepared information and advice for the British Delegate. Two sub-committees of the London Committee dealt with damage to civilians and property, and compensation due to military and naval forces. In terms of proceedings and processes, the series comprises minutes, papers and memoranda of the

London Committee, 1919–29 (T 194/1–3); Bradbury's official and semi-official correspondence, 1919–24 (T 194/4–13); legal opinions prepared for the London Committee, 1920–29 (T 194/14–33); minutes of meetings between the Treasury and Dominions representatives, 1926 (T 194/264); Bradbury's own scheme for a comprehensive settlement, 1922–4 (T 194/262); a memorandum by Bradbury, 1920 (T 194/272); miscellaneous papers of Sir Otto Niemeyer on reparations, 1924–8 (T 194/259–60); reparations schemes suggested by the South African prime minister, Smuts, and the Czech prime minister, Eduard Beneš, in 1924 (T 194/278–9); papers on the United States' withdrawal from the Commission, 1921 (T 194/274); details of the American-sponsored Dawes Plan of 1924 (T 194/266); reports on the Hague Conference, 1929–30 (T 194/248–52); and general accounts, 1930 (T 194/144–5). On reparation claims for damage done by Germany, there are papers on British claims (T 194/34–66), including estimates of damages suffered by civilians (T 194/38), of damage to British property in France and Belgium (T 194/46), of claims by the empire (T 194/35, 50–52, 54, 56–7 and 59), of the particular cost of the New Zealand occupation of German Samoa (T 194/61), of the costs of servicemen's wartime separation allowances (T 194/37) and of disability pensions (T 194/45).

There are also details of other claims on Germany (T 194/67–111) including those of the French (T 194/76), Italians (T 194/78), Greeks (T 194/68, 75, 88, 96, and 165), Cubans (T 194/94), Brazilians (T 194/87 and 89), and Liberians (T 194/97). There is also material on particular categories of reparations relating to Germany including deliveries in kind of commodities such as coal, timber and cattle (T 194/193–200); shipping losses (T 194/201–6); loss and capture of river craft (T 194/207–19); the value of German tank steamers (T 194/220–22), which were claimed by the Standard Oil Company; the value of German submarine cables (T 194/223–31); the value of German war materiel (T 194/232–7), including that delivered in compensation for the scuttling of the High Seas Fleet (T 194/234); and the value of shares in the Baghdad railway (T 194/238–47).

Claims on Austria (T 194/142–5 and 168–92) particularly emphasise those on art treasures such as the Belgian claim to the Triptych of St Ildephonse (T 194/142), while claims on Hungary (T 194/112–28) are supplemented by papers on Hungarian bonds and loans, 1924–8 (T 194/129–36). There is also material on claims on Bulgaria under the Treaty of Neuilly (T 194/147 and 149–62), including minutes of the Inter-allied Commission for Bulgaria (T 194/147 and 149–51), and the agreement between Bulgaria and Romania settling claims in 1925 (T 194/159). Czech claims were also considered in the light of the recognition of Czechoslovakia as an independent power in 1921 (T 194/137–41). There is also material on ceded property in Memel, which was seized by Lithuania in 1923 (T 194/253–6).

TS 26 contains correspondence of HM Procurator General's Department, 1919–24, relating to war crimes (TS 26/1–61 and 907–8). Correspondence includes a memorandum on the Kaiser's overall responsibility (TS 26/1); preparations for the Leipzig trial in 1921 (TS 26/7); daily reports from Leipzig (TS 26/16); a draft report on Leipzig for Parliament (TS 26/17); naval cases (TS 26/15); and reports on alleged Bulgarian and Hungarian war criminals (TS 26/4–5). There are files on 39 separate individuals, 1920–21 (TS 26/24–61); and further files and supplementary statements on the responsibility of two U-boat commanders, Helmut Patsig and Karl Neumann, for sinking hospital ships (TS 26/907–8).

TS 27 deals with the legal niceties of the precise end of the war (TS 27/91); and with claims between 1923 and 1927 with respect to the destruction of Romanian oilfields by a British agent to prevent them falling into German hands in 1916.

WO 32 deals with the state of execution of the peace treaty with Germany up to December 1920 (WO 32/5787); a memorandum on gas warfare issues for the Paris conference (WO 32/5190); the question of raising the economic blockade against Hungary on the conclusion of the peace negotiations with Germany (WO 32/5695); the food situation in Germany in 1919 (WO 32/5375); alleged war crimes and the decision to prosecute alleged war criminals (WO 32/5425 and 5607); the possible culpability of the German general, Liman von Sanders, in war crimes committed by the Turks (WO 32/5385); the application of the Versailles treaty to the disclosure by the Germans of the Haber process for production of gas (WO 32/5786); aspects of the peace negotiations relating to Hungary (WO 32/5559–60); aspects of the peace negotiations relating to Turkey, 1920–22 (WO 32/5735, 5376–7, and 5774); the assistance provided by the British army in Belgian post-war reconstruction, 1919 (WO 32/5566); the disposal of British and German ammunition in France and Belgium, 1919–20 (WO 32/5576); and the destruction of German war materiel (WO 32/5759).

WO 93/30–32 among miscellaneous papers of the Judge Advocate General, are the proclamations of martial law issued for the occupation of the German Rhineland, 1918.

WO 95/4961–4 are the War Diaries of British units serving in the post-war army of occupation at Constantinople.

WO 106 includes material on the British Military Mission based at Klagenfurt in post-war Austria, 1919 (WO 106/353); reports on conditions in post-war Germany and Bavaria (WO 106/434 and 1397); telegrams on the progress of the Paris conference (WO 106/435); and material on German compliance with the peace terms, 1920 (WO 106/437). There is also material on the army of occupation in the Rhineland (WO 106/439–63) and the mission to Bulgaria in October 1918 (WO 106/765). Other issues include the question of the futures of Silesia (WO 106/975–81) and of Fiume, intended for the new Kingdom of the Serbs, Croats and Slovenes (Yugoslavia from 1929), but seized by the Italian nationalist, Gabriele D'Annunzio, in September 1919 (WO 106/853, and 857–65). There is also coverage of the Greco-Turkish War (WO 106/1437–8 and 1446).

WO 153, Maps and Plans, covers the area of occupation of the British Army of the Rhine (WO 153/38–41); and maps of the British positions at Chanak in 1922 (WO 153/1340).

WO 155/1–64 are papers of the Allied Military Committee of Versailles, and its commissions established to oversee the implementation of the military aspects of the peace treaties. There are telegrams to and from the British Delegation at Paris (WO 155/1); reports on the situation in Germany, 1919–25 (WO 155/2–4); material on the transformation of German and Austrian war factories and plant and on their legal and illegal activities (WO 155/7–8, 11, 14, 16, and 19–22); lists of correspondence between the German government and the Inter-allied Commission of Control, 1920–27 (WO 155/44–5); details of arms and ammunition authorised for use by the new German army and police (WO 155/46–8); and the final report of the Commission of Control on Germany in February 1927 (WO 155/63). With regard to Hungary, there is material on the composition and work of the Inter-allied Military Commission of Control, 1920–26 (WO 155/25–8), and minutes of the meetings of the Conseil de Presidence and Conseil des Délégués of the Council of the Inter-allied Military Commission of Control, 1922–5 (WO 155/29–43). There are also minutes of the Conseil des Délégués of the Liquidation Organisation of the Inter-allied Commission of Control in Bulgaria, 1922–4 (WO 155/57–62). In addition, there are minutes of the Financial Administration Committee and other material on the financial affairs of the Inter-allied Commission of Control, 1924–7 (WO 155/50–56), and a progress report on the British Section, February 1921 (WO 155/64).

WO 158, Military Headquarters Papers, includes correspondence on the Army of Occupation in the Rhineland, 1919–29 (WO 158/109–10). There is also material on the post-war situation in Turkey (WO 158/766–91), including papers of the Allied Commission of Control and Organisation (WO 158/768–71); reports by the Commission's British Military Representative (WO 158/772); minutes and correspondence of the Mixed Military Railway Mission, 1922–3 (WO 158/776); correspondence of the Directing Committee of Generals of the Inter-allied Commission (WO 158/782 and 791); details of the peace terms with Turkey (WO 158/787–90); and a history of the Turkish nationalist movement, 1919–20 (WO 158/766). In addition, there are Intelligence Summaries from Constantinople, 1918–21 (WO 158/933); and a report on the capture of a defence vessel by insurgents in Iraq, August 1920 (WO 158/967).

WO 160 has material on the recruitment of the new German army, 1919 (WO 160/1); and Italian and Turkish post-war intrigues in the Balkans (WO 160/6).

WO 190, Appreciation Files prepared for the Imperial General Staff by the Director of Military Intelligence, has some material on attitudes towards post-war Germany, including the Allied note to the German government on the future military control of Germany, October 1922 (WO 190/1); a draft on the subject of surrendered German war material, May 1923 (WO 190/7); and matters in respect of which the Inter-allied Military Commission of Control for Germany had had reason to complain in 1923 (WO 190/9).

WORK 6/362/8 deals with the reconstruction problems facing Belgium as a result of wartime damage, 1919.

2. New Ways of War

I T HAD BECOME APPARENT by the end of 1914 that deadlock on the Western Front confronted belligerents with new problems. Asquith's reaction to various suggestions made by Maurice Hankey, in his 'Boxing Day' memorandum in December 1914, for developing new technological means for breaking the deadlock was to find it curious that there might be a reversion to what he called medieval forms of warfare. In reality, science and technology were to be harnessed to the war effort to an extent that, not only was the destructive impact of weaponry greatly increased, but it became possible to more effectively target civilian populations. Indeed, Churchill was to write after the war that, 'When all was over, Torture and Cannibalism were the only two expedients that the civilised, scientific Christian societies had been able to deny themselves: and these were of doubtful utility.'

Science and War

From the beginning of the war, the scientific communities within belligerent states became involved in their respective war efforts in one way or another. In Britain, scientific involvement was somewhat slower to develop despite the existence of pre-war scientific advisory commissions such as that at the Royal Arsenal at Woolwich and the Royal Aircraft Factory at Farnborough. Neither army nor Royal Navy responded with any great alacrity to the offer by the Royal Society in October 1914 to establish advisory committees, primarily from the assumption that the war would be short. Indeed, it was not until July 1915 that the Admiralty Board of Invention and Research was established under Lord Fisher, Third Lord of the Admiralty and Controller of the Admiralty, while, in August 1915, Lloyd George set up the Munitions Inventions Department (MID). A third board, the Air Inventions Committee, became operational in May 1917. The boards were really established to shift the burden of dealing with unsolicited ideas for new weapons from the Admiralty and Ministry of Munitions, although it was also recognised that they would place research and development on a sounder basis.

The ideas themselves were often quite ludicrous, such as the suggestion that cormorants with explosives fastened to them be trained to swoop on surfaced submarines, and others trained to peck away the mortar on the chimneys of the Krupps armaments factory in Essen. Consequently, a shift in emphasis was soon made to initiating worthwhile scientific research, such as the development of underwater detection methods from November 1915 onwards. This laid the basis for the emergence of what was to become known as ASDIC or sonar. Similarly, research into anti-aircraft defence was to result in the development of some early prototypes of height and range finders by 1917.

The difficulty was that invention and development was not a rapid process and, in fact, sonar was not developed in time to be used on active service during the war itself. Thus, actual practical wartime developments tended to be on the smaller scale, such as the Stokes trench mortar developed by the Trench Warfare Department of the MID. However, with the encouragement of the Ministry of Munitions, advances were also made by industrial scientists in areas such as munitions production, synthetic substitution and new industrial processes. The Zionist, Dr Chaim Weizmann, made an invaluable contribution to British munitions output with a new production method for acetone. Moreover, a new department of state, the Department of Scientific and Industrial Research (DSIR) was established in 1916 to provide a more co-ordinated and coherent approach towards the integration of government and science: it was to survive into the post-war period.

ADM 1 has some material of relevance including the collaboration of scientists and naval officers on patenting and publication of ideas, August 1915 (ADM 1/8431/246); co-operation with the French Ministry of Inventions, November 1916 and the US Naval Consulting Board, November 1917 (ADM 1/8473/263, and 8505/260); use of the City and Guilds College laboratory by the Admiralty Engineering Laboratory (ADM 1/8428/45); the relationship of the Board of Invention and Research to other Admiralty departments ASDM 1/8484/66); the organisation of invention and research (ADM 1/8493/167B); and the report of the Awards Committee on Inventions, 1917 (ADM 1/8508/284). Specific inventions covered include a new bomb sight by the Air Department; Percy Scott's mechanical ciphering machine (ADM 1/8435/299 and 302); George Clarke's method of camouflage (ADM 1/8482/50); and Engineer Commander Gush's mounting for boiler electrodes (ADM 1/8542/282). Trials were carried out on P. Tudor-Hart's camouflage method in April 1917 (ADM 1/8485/77) and Major Coates's hot-air balloons in the following month (ADM 1/8489/112). Patents and claims included are the patents on the Dreyer and other fire control devices as well as gun and bomb sights (ADM 1/8464/181 and 8488/101); patents of Dr Chaim Weizmann (ADM 1/8451/65); and the claims by Rear Admiral E. C. Villiers to have developed 'Otter' protection against mines, and by J. M. Campbell to have invented blister or bulge protection of warships against torpedoes (ADM 1/8525/138, and 9598). There are also reports on trials of long distance wireless in submarines and destroyers from October 1916 (ADM 1/8471/241)

ADM 116 has 'case' files of the Board of Invention and Research, 1917–18 (ADM 116/1601B) and of the Board's sub-committees, including the Airship, Aeroplane and Seaplane sub-committees, 1915–18 (ADM 116/1430–31). In addition, there is material on trials of smoke screens in 1915 (ADM 116/1435).

ADM 137 has some material on wartime inventions (ADM 137/2092, 2098, and 2711).

ADM 212 comprises papers of the Admiralty Research Laboratory, which originated as the Admiralty Experimental Station at Hawkcraig, near Aberdour in Fife in 1915, transferring to Parkeston Quay, Harwich in 1917. Reports on underwater experiments (ADM 212/1–15) include minutes of the Clyde Anti-submarine Committee (ADM 212/5 and 13); and correspondence of the Lancashire Anti-Submarine Committee and the experimental station at Shandon, 1918–19 (ADM 212/12). There are also minutes and memoranda of the Board of Invention and Research (ADM 212/156, and 158–9); weekly reports from Parkeston Quay, 1917–18 (ADM 212/160–64); and a file on the work of Sir Ernest Rutherford, 1915–16 (ADM 212/157). In addition, there is material on range and direction finding and early electrical research (ADM 212/42–4, and 178).

ADM 218 comprises the papers of Albert Beaumont Wood of the Board of Invention and Research. Wood, a physicist from the University of Liverpool, and H. Gerrard, an electrical engineer, were the first scientists attached to the Admiralty. Initially, Wood set up the station at Hawkcraig before transferring to Parkeston Quay. Wood's personal papers include his recollections and notes (ADM 218/1–4). Papers of the Board of Invention and Research, 1915–19, include material on hydrophones and sound waves, including reports by Sir Oliver Lodge and Sir Ernest Rutherford (ADM 218/8–23), while there are also papers and reports from Hawkcraig (ADM 218/74–82), and more of the weekly reports from Parkeston Quay (ADM 218/83). Those from Hawkcraig include material on the formation of the Board's committees (ADM 218/76). Apart from work on hydrophones and other means of detecting submarines under water (ADM 218/69, 103–5, 177, and 304), there is also material on mine warfare (ADM 218/189–91, and 295); on depth charges (ADM 21/24); and pressure logs (ADM 218/264). The series also contains patents obtained by Wood and Gerrard, including those for electrical firing of mines (ADM 218/92–7). Wood continued to work for the Admiralty and the Royal Naval Scientific Service until 1964.

ADM 226/17–21 contains reports of the Admiralty Experimental Works, 1913–19. First established in 1871, it had moved to Haslar, Gosport in 1886. Its work during the war included design of cruisers, patrol vessels, and monitors; experiments on rudders, bilge keels, and hydrophones; and work on the screw dimensions and wave profile of battlecruisers, leading to a major report in March 1917.

ADM 229/97–9 consist of reports from Stanley Goodall on American naval production and development, 1917–20.

ADM 245 has records on the Admiralty Awards for Inventions, including summaries of the recommendations of the Admiralty Awards Council, 1894–1925 (ADM 245/1–3); papers of the committee of inquiry investigating conflicting claims on the dazzle painting of ships (ADM 245/4); and patent applications, 1915–21, such as those for bomb sights, sound detection, and ejecting signal cartridges from submarines (ADM 245/5–11).

ADM 265, containing unregistered papers of the Engineer in Chief, includes material on the hydraulic propulsion of ships and submarines, 1915–23 (ADM 265/16–17); propeller design, 1916–20 (ADM 265/40); and turbine blading, 1917–28 (ADM 265/67).

ADM 293 contains records of the Admiralty Board of Invention and Research. Though the secretariat of the board remained naval, the board itself was mostly civilian, involving prominent scientists like Sir Ernest Rutherford, Sir Oliver Lodge and Sir William Crookes on the Scientific Panel. Sub-committees were divided into six main sections, dealing with research into such areas as aeronautics, submarines, naval construction, anti-aircraft devices, ordnance, gases, aerial photography, and armament. There are minutes of general meetings and of Central Committee meetings, reports of proceedings, and memoranda of meetings, 1915–18 (ADM 293/7, and 11); lists of the principal reports received and later reports arising from them (ADM 293/21); and a report on the organisation of the board, 1917 (ADM 293/8–9). There are reports from three of the board's sections, covering aeronautics, 1914–17 (ADM 293/1), submarines, mine warfare and electrical and acoustic issues, 1915–17 (ADM 293/2–3, 5, and 10); and on naval construction and marine engineering, 1915–17 (ADM 293/6). There are also other sectional weekly reports from 1918 (ADM 293/20); reports from the Hawkcraig and Harwich stations (ADM 293/4); and those of the Director of Experiments and Research in 1918 on such areas as conductivity, loop circuits and mine warfare (ADM 293/12–19).

AIR 1 has material on Sir William Weir's work on technical developments (AIR 1/6A/4/39 and 41); the testing of armoured seats and bullet proof sheets, 1914–15 (AIR 1/140/15/40/300); self-sealing fire-proof petrol tanks (AIR 1/2002/204/276/1); hydrophone towing trials (AIR 1/645/17/122/300); the development of the Buckingham incendiary bullet, 1914–16 (AIR 1/719/35/8, and 1081/204/5/1696); Uxbridge Armament School, 1917–18 (AIR 1/723); balloon experiments, 1915–17 (AIR 1/933–9); and waterproofing and treatment of canvas, 1917–18 (AIR 1/946–7). There are reports on technical subjects and by the Air Ministry Technical Branch and Advisory Committee for Aeronautics (AIR 1/697–710, and 2089–95); technical information from Air Council reports, 1918 (AIR 1/2130); reports by the Directorate of Aircraft Equipment, 1915–19 (AIR 1/2429–30); minutes of the Aircraft Development Committee, March 1918 (AIR 1/2418/305/3); technical publications (AIR 1/2426–7); and research documents of the Canadian Air Force (AIR 1/721). Air diagrams of aircraft and equipment include some photographs (AIR 1/710–17). There is a report by the Aeroplane Sub-committee of the Admiralty Board of Invention and Research, 1916 (AIR 1/2101/207/28/15), and minutes of the Air Inventions Committee, 1917–18 (AIR 1/2423/305/18/38).

AIR 2, registered files of the Air Ministry, offers much information on technical developments including Weir's proposal for a single seater armoured machine, 1917 (AIR 2/731); experimental Tarrant fuselages and bombers (AIR 2/963–4, and 1030–36); propeller designs (AIR 2/1038–42); engine specifications (AIR 2/1024–6, and 1043); transmission systems (AIR 2/1009–10); stabilisation devices (AIR 2/1042); turn indicators (AIR 2/1536–59); gunsights (AIR 2/53/AB 275/7553); flame-proof petrol tanks (AIR 2/52/AB 275/2800/ENC 5); wireless (AIR 2/8/87/6373, 18/MA, and 125/B 11207); incendiary thermite bombs (AIR 2/49/AB 275/754); and aviation spirit (AIR 2/167/RU 8886). The institution, membership and terms of reference of the Air Inventions Committee, 1916, are also covered, and there is also the report of the Committee of Awards to Inventors, 1918–22 (AIR 2/47/AB 203/14, and 72/A 6886). The series also contains a wartime Royal proclamation prohibiting the export of aero designs (AIR 2/84/B 5615).

AIR 11, papers of the Royal Airship Works, Cardington, includes plans of the 'Neale aerial warship' considered by the Ministry of Munitions Inventions Department, 1917 (AIR 11/1); and the *Experimental Bulletins* of the Naval Airship Department, 1916–18 (AIR 11/4). Instituted by Short Brothers as the Naval Aircraft Works in 1917, Cardington was taken over by the Air Ministry in 1919.

AVIA 1/1 contains Flight Log Books, 1914–18, of the Royal Aircraft Factory. Established as the Balloon Equipment Store at Woolwich Arsenal in 1878, what was by now the Balloon Factory moved to Farnborough in 1905. Renamed the Royal Aircraft Factory in 1912, the establishment was confined to research and development in 1916 after criticism of its aircraft designs.

AVIA 6 contains reports of the Royal Aircraft Factory, including those on experiments in aerodynamics, 1917–18 (AVIA 6/1148–305); notes on wind channels, 1916–18 (AVIA 6/2459–73); experiments in physics, 1916–18, including doped aircraft fabric (AVIA 6/2698–878); experimental flying, including engine tests, 1917–18 (AVIA 6/4691–717, 4816–49, and 5135–57); and mechanical tests, 1918 (AVIA 6/5870–83).

AVIA 8 includes material on the Air Inventions Committee, including its formation (AVIA 8/7), its co-operation with the Society of British Aircraft Constructors, 1917–18 (AVIA 8/8), and scientific co-operation with the United States (AVIA 8/3). There are also minutes of the Anti-Aircraft and Parachute Committees (AVIA 8/4, and 11), and reports from the Imber Court and Orfordness experimental stations (AVIA 8/5–6). In addition, there is correspondence on various aspects of royalties and rewards for air inventions (AVIA 8/1–2, 9, and 12–13), and on the prohibition of publication regarding inventions, 1918 (AVIA 8/10). Most of the material relating to the war, however, concerns individual aviation developments and inventions, ranging from strut and spar improvements to propeller design, balloon improvements, aircraft controls, armaments, engines, fire-proof petrol tanks, tinted goggles, sound ranging, night vision, and windscreens (AVIA 8/52–7, 84–6, 97–8, 100–11, 123, 201–2, 213–27, 264–71, 360–62, 450, 468–9, 473–80, 491, 504, 507–9, 523, and 526–8). Included are reports by the Advisory Committee on Aeronautics regarding straight flying in fog and cloud, 1917–18 (AVIA 8/219–21); the Lancaster Illumination Scheme trials, 1916–18, to detect enemy aircraft (AVIA 8/473, 475, and 477); and proceedings of a conference on night vision in 1918 (AVIA 8/491).

AVIA 20 contains reports of the Research and Development Establishment of the Royal Airship Works, Cardington. There are reports of the Advisory Committee on Aeronautics regarding fabric strength, stability and balloon design, 1916–18 (AVIA 20/468, 477, 486, and 499); and reports of the National Physical laboratory, 1916 (AVIA 20/472).

AVIA 46 has historical narratives on a number of research establishments covering wide periods and embracing both world wars, including the Radio Research Establishment (AVIA 46/220); Admiralty Experimental Works (AVIA 46/222); Admiralty Compass Observatory (AVIA 46/225); Admiralty Engineering Laboratory (AVIA 46/226), established in 1917; and Aeronautical Research Council (AVIA 46/227). There are also narratives on the development of bombs and weapons (AVIA 46/285 and 303); and on the lessons of British war production, 1914–39 (AVIA 46/312).

CAB 2/4 has minutes and papers of the Cabinet Committee on Research, established in September 1918 to consider an Admiralty proposal for a Physical

Research Institution for the Royal Navy. Until March 1919, however the committee investigated general facilities for military and civil scientific research.

CAB 17, miscellaneous papers of the Committee of Imperial Defence, include correspondence on the co-ordination of the inventions committees in 1915 (CAB 17/120); on the control of long range firing (CAB 17/121); and on camouflage, 1917 (CAB 17/188).

CAB 21/26 has a file on the Neale 'aerial warship' as considered by the MID, 1917.

DEFE 15 contains papers of the Research Department at the Woolwich Arsenal, later the Royal Armament Research and Development Establishment. The series includes a history of the Proof and Experimental Establishment at Woolwich, 1913–18 (DEFE 15/4); a report by the Ordnance Branch on shells, 1915 (DEFE 15/35); papers on the development of TNT and amatol (DEFE 15/78–9); and a memorandum on explosives research, 1918 (DEFE 15/92).

DSIR 1/1 contains the minutes of the Advisory Council of the Privy Council, 1915–18, which was established in July 1915 at the suggestion of the President of the Board of Education, under the same Order in Council that also established the Privy Council's Committee for Scientific and Industrial Research. A separate Department of Scientific and Industrial Research was then established in December 1916 with its own parliamentary vote, and responsible to Parliament through the Lord President of the Council.

DSIR 2/329–31 are the papers of the Applications Committee, 1917–19, one of the sub-committees which advised the Advisory Council on awards and scholarships.

DSIR 3 contains papers of various Research Boards and Committees set up by the Department of Scientific and Industrial Research as occasion arose to supervise investigations into particular problems. Those dating from the war years concern research into abrasives and polishing powders, brass and copper castings, building materials, copper and zinc, metal corrosion, electrical engineering, gas cylinders, illuminating engineering, industrial fatigue, mine rescue, oxygen, glass and optical instruments, metallurgy, steam plant, timber, tin and tungsten, vitreous compounds, and lubricants (DSIR 3/1, 26, 50–51, 57–61, 66, 95–7, 144, 156, 178–81, 233–4, 250, 307–8, 310, 312–20, 323, 325, 331–2, and 392).

DSIR 15 has papers of the Imperial Trust for the Encouragement of Scientific and Industrial Research, established in November 1916 to administer the 'Million Fund', by which Parliament voted £1 million to finance research and award grants to industrial research organisations. Apart from the constitution and seal (DSIR 15/1–2), there are agenda and minutes of meetings, 1916–19 (DSIR 15/4–5); details of the holding of the Fund by Trust, 1916–19 (DSIR 15/42); commitments, estimates and financial statements, 1917–19 (DSIR 43); and transfers of funds from the National Physical Laboratory to the Trust and the Froude Tank Fund for a ship model testing tank (DSIR 15/45). The original fund was exhausted by 1932 but was used for other purposes such as holding superannuation funds and monies for research. It was finally abolished in 1956.

DSIR 16 covers the work of industrial research associations supported by the 'Million Fund' and the Imperial Trust. There is material on the original scheme to encourage groups of firms to set up co-operative research associations in individual industries in 1916 (DSIR 16/1), and on bringing inventors into touch with research associations in 1917 (DSIR 16/6). Those associations for which wartime papers exist dealt with the cotton industry (DSIR 16/44–8); iron (DSIR 16/76); motor and motor cycle manufacturers (DSIR 16/93 and 95); photography (DSIR 16/105); portland cement (DSIR 16/106); scientific instruments (DSIR 16/119); woollen and worsted manufacturing (DSIR 16/129); and manufacturers of X-ray apparatus (DSIR 16/139).

DSIR 17 comprises registered files of the Department of Scientific and Industrial Research. They cover, however, the early wartime efforts to encourage scientific and industrial research in 1915 through the agency of the Privy Council Committee for Scientific and Industrial Research (DSIR 17/1–2); the appointment and work of the Advisory Council, 1915–17 (DSIR 17/3, 34–5, 81–2, and 103); the establishment of the Million Fund and other grants and scholarships, 1915–19 (DSIR 17/36, 54, 63, 132, 134, 136, and 137–46); proposals to extend the scheme to the empire and co-operation with the Imperial Institute, 1915–17 (DSIR 17/113 and 126); and optical glass research at the National Physical Laboratory, 1915–17 (DSIR 17/131).

DSIR 22 deals with the Advisory Committee for Aeronautics, later the Aeronautical Research Council, which undertook experiments at the National Physical Laboratory and the Royal Aircraft Factory. There are minutes of the Advisory Committee, 1909–20 (DSIR 22/1) and its Aerodynamics Sub-committee, 1917–19 (DSIR 22/38); together with minutes of additional wartime sub-committees on internal combustion engines, scale effect and light alloys (DSIR 22/14–17).

DSIR 23/341–1276, comprising reports and papers of the Advisory Committee for Aeronautics, 1914–18, include material on the additional expenditure on staff and scientific equipment arising from demands of the Admiralty and War Office to double the output of work, 1915 (DSIR 23/594); and the work of the Royal Aircraft Factory, 1914–18, as laid down in reports to Parliament (DSIR 23/500, 714, 949, and 1147).

DSIR 24/3–4 deal with the reorganisation of the Advisory Committee for Aeronautics in 1917, the formation of the Air Inventions Committee, and the proposed Timber sub-committee.

DSIR 26 contains reports by the Laboratory of the Government Chemist, which undertook sampling analyses. During the war, the laboratory undertook sampling of War Office food supplies such as jam and flour (DSIR 26/378, 46, and 364); inspection of food at bases and depots such as Newhaven (DSIR 26/365 and 367); experiments on the suitability of cardboard containers for condensed milk and other supplies (DSIR 26/366, and 368); and even examination of captured German rations (DSIR 369).

DSIR 36, containing files of the Records Bureau of the Department of Scientific and Industrial Research Library, includes details of Admiralty and Air Board specifications for aluminium alloy castings, 1917 (DSIR 36/310); and MID reports on physical data in relation to the use of liquid air and oxygen, 1918–20 (DSIR 36/397), and fuse slags and fuse filling composition, 1918 (DSIR 36/1978–9). There are also reports on optical glass research including the improvement of optical instruments for the armed forces, 1917–20 (DSIR 36/3328, and 3709–11); and papers of the Non Ferrous Section of the Standing Committee on Metallurgy, 1915–18 (DSIR 36/3358–61, 3363, and 3365–76).

DSIR 37 comprises the registered files of the Munitions Inventions Department together with those of some of its committees, as well as papers of the Ministry's Explosives Supply Department. Established in August 1915 under Ernest Moir to evaluate ideas from external inventors, the MID became responsible in November 1915 for accepting, testing and developing all War Office and Ministry of Munitions stores. Apart from ideas received for evaluation by the Department, mostly on the manufacture of fuel from peat, (DSIR 37/1–14), there are also papers of its Nitrogen Products Committee (DSIR 37/23–141), established in June 1916 to make a detailed examination of British and imperial nitrogen requirements for military, agricultural and industrial purposes. The reports include details of synthetic production, including the German Haber process for ammonia production (DSIR 37/23, and 68); patents (DSIR 37/119–39); and reports of visits to French and American factories (DSIR 37/111–18). There is also material on the Chemical Waste Products Committee, established in 1918 to deal with the question of unutilised chemical waste products (DSIR 37/224–75).

In addition, there are the technical records of the Ministry's Explosives Supply Department (DSIR 37/15–22). Formed in June 1915 under Lord Moulton as Director General, the department was responsible for the supervision of all contracts for high explosives and their ingredients, state manufacture through national factories, storeholding, accounting and transit arrangements for explosives. Also included in the class are the research files of Dr J. A. Harker, formerly Chief Assistant at the National Physical Laboratory, who became Director of Research for the MID, tasked particularly with investigating the fixation of nitrogen (DSIR 37/142–215). The material includes details of Harker's visits to the United States (DSIR 37/174), and his correspondence with the Permanent Under Secretary of the Ministry of Munitions, Sir W. Graham Greene (DSIR 37/177).

DSIR 53/1 are the annual reports of the Privy Council Committee for Scientific and Industrial Research and the subsequent Department of Scientific and Industrial Research, 1915–23.

FO 115/1833–4 deal with war inventions in 1914 among general correspondence relating to the United States.

MUN 10/1–37 contain the technical bulletins of the Department of Aircraft Production, 1918.

SUPP 28 are the records of the Director of Experiments and Research of the Research Department (later Armament Research Department) at Woolwich. Consisting largely of reference abstract cards, they are filed either under scientific or technological headings, or under 'Foreign' or by name of country. Under the former, they include amatol, bombs, chemical ammunition, cordite, explosives, fuses, gas, and propellants (SUPP 28/4, 9–11, 14–15, 19–22, 26–9, 35–40, and 66–7). Under the latter, cards include Germany (SUPP 28/31–3, and 100–101) and America (SUPP 28/95–9). In addition, however, there are miscellaneous wartime research reports (SUPP 28/71–94, 330–33, and 356–7), including one on TNT production (SUPP 28/93); a variety of loose papers relating to the war years (SUPP 28/234, 236, 239, 243, 251–3, 257, 260, 263–6, 268–9, 271, 276–7, 280,

282–3, and 286); and correspondence between Woolwich and Messrs Curtis and Harvey Ltd, 1917–18 (SUPP 28/355).

T 173 comprises the papers of the Royal Commission on Awards for Inventors, 1919–37, intended to evaluate the claims relating to all inventions used during the war. As well as files on the principles for determining awards (T 173/1–34C), there are claims files (T 173/72–543), and transcripts of proceedings (T 173/544–828). In particular, there are files on hydrophones (T 173/829), and smoke generators (T 173/830).

TS 21 covers assignment of patents for Major G. Hazelton's device for firing machine guns through aircraft propellers, 1916–18 (TS 21/68); the agreement reached with Major P. N. Nissen for the army's use of his Nissen hut (TS 21/70); and that reached with Sopwith Aviation for purchase of designs and drawings in 1918 (TS 21/71).

TS 28, comprising files relating to the Air Ministry, includes further claims for improvements to Lewis guns and machine guns by Hazelton (TS 28/62, 74, and 112). In addition, there is material on the claim to the Royal Commission on Awards to Inventors by Ernest Willows in connection with kite balloons' apron defences against aircraft (TS 28/2); a petition of right against the Admiralty by Isaac Taylor for its failure to honour an agreement on an anti-aircraft device in November 1915 (TS 28/5); and a claim by the British Aeroplane Company regarding a fighter (TS 28/65).

TS 32/7 deals with a claim to the Royal Commission on Awards to Inventors by the Poulsen Wireless Telegraph Company.

WO 32/9281 has details of an inter-departmental conference on the co-ordination of inventions committees and the creation of the MID, 1915.

WO 313/1 covers the proceedings of the Committee of Awards to Inventors, 1920–30. Originally established in 1867, the work of assessing claims was taken over by the Ministry of Munitions during the war but re-established under the auspices of the Master General of the Ordnance in December 1920.

One area where technology particularly contributed to development was in intelligence. Human sources of intelligence were regarded as the most import-ant and considerable effort continued to be put into obtaining intelligence from trench raids, the capture of documents such as paybooks and the interrogation of prisoners. Signals intelligence, however, became increasingly significant. Wireless telegraphy in itself was a significant advance but it was not secure and, in any case, for speed of communication, messages were frequently sent in clear rather than in cipher. Armies in the western theatre therefore turned to telegraph or telephone at the end of 1914. Electrical currents from the cables, however, could be intercepted through the earth. By 1916, armies in the west had reverted to radio. Consequently, there was a constant struggle between encryptors and code breakers and no codes remained safe for long, especially as carelessness was commonplace.

At sea, the Admiralty's celebrated Room 40 played a major role by de-ciphering German naval codes, although the Admiralty did not always make best use of its intelligence. Established by the Director of Naval Education, Sir Alfred Ewing, in 1914, Room 40 – so named after the room within the Admiralty in which it was located from November 1914 – was transferred to the Naval Intelligence Division of the Naval Staff in May 1917. Its work was greatly assisted by the Russian capture of code books from the German light cruiser *Magdeburg* in August 1914; the Australian discovery of the German merchant marine code in a seized steamer; and the unexpected recovery in a fishing net of the German flag officers' code from a weighted chest thrown overboard from a sinking torpedo boat in October 1914. In addition, the cable ship, *Telconia*, had lifted the German overseas telegraph cables from the North Sea on 5 August 1914, forcing the Germans to rely upon wireless. Room 40 also contributed to the wider accumulation of intelligence, especially through the interception of enemy and allied diplomatic messages.

ACT 1/72 contains calculations by the Committee of Imperial Defence on German casualties, 1914–16.

ADM 1/8411/45 is a report of a committee on the leakage or compromise of cipher codes, February 1915.

ADM 7/997–8 consist of indices (in German) to the German Admiralty, and to German charts, both dating from 1914.

ADM 137 includes material on the working of Room 40 including decrypts of German diplomatic signals between Berlin and Washington, 1915 (ADM 137/3956–63, and 4047); messages received, dispatched or intercepted by the Admiralty and Naval Intelligence on the movements of enemy and allied ships (ADM 137/4057–97), including intercepts of German messages concerning the bombardment of the north east coast (ADM 137/4067); and the war diary of the senior intelligence officer in the Far East (ADM 137/4079–82). Room 40's accumulation of material on the German navy includes captured papers (ADM 137/4157–8); histories of German senior naval officers and submarine officers (ADM 137/4161–7); and the original German codebook captured from the *Magdeburg*, which reached the Admiralty in October 1914 (ADM 137/4156). There are a variety of other captured German and Austro-Hungarian army and naval codebooks, cipher keys, ships' log books, and documents (ADM 137/4217–463, 4493–518, 4650–71, and 4712–87); registers of intercepts (ADM 137/4464–92); registers of enemy call signs (ADM 137/4519–35); and direction finding plots (ADM 137/4536–61).

Papers associated with Captain Herbert Hope of Room 40 (ADM 137/4168–71, and 4678–711) include notes on German naval movements (ADM 137/4168 and 4170); a diary of information derived from decrypts (ADM 137/4169 and 4171), German charts (ADM 137/4683); notes on the naval situation (ADM 137/4686), agents' reports on enemy fleets (ADM 137/4697); correspondence and notes on intelligence and signals interception (ADM 137/4699); material from the BEF's Intelligence Branch (ADM 137/4700–701); intercepts at the time of Jutland (ADM 137/4710–11); and Hope's own card index to the High Seas Fleet (ADM 137/4687). In addition, there are other papers on decrypted cipher traffic, 1915–18 (ADM 137/4562–636), copies of *Weekly Direction Finding Bulletins*, 1917–18 (ADM 137/4672–7); abstracts of information on suspicious merchant ships by country (ADM 137/4190–216); shipping intelligence officers' memoranda, 1917–19 (ADM 137/2881–6); and early copies of Room 40's *Wireless News* (ADM 137/4797–8).

ADM 156/176 deals with breaches of the Navy's own security through the loss of secret documents and confidential books on HMS *Cardiff*, the temporary loss of others from HMS *Commonwealth*, though the salvage of others from submarine *G11*.

ADM 223 contains records of the Naval Intelligence Division, including its message logs, 1915–17 (ADM 223/646–60, 662–70, and 673); and diplomatic intercepts and decrypts by Room 40 between Berlin and German embassies in Argentina, Brazil, Chile, Mexico, Spain, Sweden, Turkey, the United States, and the Balkans (ADM 223/638–45, 661, 672, 735–73, and 774–89). Also included in the series are the Director of Naval Intelligence's secret telegrams (ADM 223/58–9); intercepts of French Mediterranean signals (ADM 223/761); *Bulletins of Adriatic Intelligence*, 1918 (ADM 223/790); code lists (ADM 223/788); and correspondence of the Intelligence Section of GHQ, Mesopotamia, 1917–18 (ADM 223/791). In addition, there is Room 40's war diary, 1914–15; a memorandum on its Political Branch; and its staff records (ADM 223/767, 769, and 773).

ADM 233 consists of copies of *Wireless News*, established by Room 40 in December 1918, with summaries of messages from Germany, Russia and so on. The publication passed to the new Government Code and Cipher School in November 1919.

AIR 1 has some intelligence material, including *Air Intelligence Summaries*, 1918–19 (AIR 1/6B/4/56/2A-F, and 2666–9); *Technical Air Intelligence Summaries*, 1918–19 (AIR 1/2083–4); *Aeronautical Intelligence Circulars*, 1918 (AIR 1/2663–5); intelligence reports from GHQ, BEF drawn from RFC material, 1914–18 (AIR 1/2135–41); daily summaries of intelligence, 1917–18 (AIR 1/78/15/9/1/189–91, and 79/15/9/192–5); and intelligence reports on enemy aviation, 1918 (AIR 1/2670–76). There are also files on wireless interception, 1916–17 (AIR 1/996), and reports and papers on naval intelligence by Lieutenant P. M. C. O'Caffrey, RNVR, 1914–18 (AIR 1/305/15/226/157). In addition, there is information on the dropping of agents by the RFC in September 1915 (AIR 1/675/21/13/1726).

CAB 42/19/4 has the report of the Enemy Personnel Sub-committee of the Committee of Imperial Defence, September 1916.

DEFE 15/101 contains notes on German artillery, compiled in 1914.

FO 115, general correspondence relating to the United States, has naval intelligence reports, 1914–17 (FO 115/1805–10, 1937–50, 2104–8, and 2284–8), and files on the Secret Service from 1918 (FO 115/2452–4).

FO 141/473 deals with intelligence in Egypt, 1915–18.

FO 1011/278, among the papers of Sir Percy Lorraine, Bt., has correspondence between Lorraine and Lord Herschell at the Admiralty Intelligence Division, 1917–18. Posted to the British embassy in Madrid as First Secretary in 1916, Lorraine was then employed in intelligence work for the Admiralty War Staff.

HW 3 contains personal and other papers relating to the Government Code and Cipher School and its predecessors. Material relating to the Naval Section as collected by W. F. Clarke covers the early years of Room 40; Churchill's original charter for Room 40; pen portraits of Room 40 personnel by Clarke; the annual salary list of the Admiralty Intelligence Division; and a poem on Room 40 confidential waste by Lady Hambro (HW 3/1, 4, and 6). In addition, there is a chapter entitled 'Intelligence' written by Frank Birch in 1919 for inclusion in a projected history of the war by Clarke and himself (HW 3/8). Operational material includes comments on the signals intelligence (sigint) log maintained by HMS *Glasgow* in the South Atlantic, where it survived the engagement at Coronel in November 1914 before participating in the battle off the Falklands in the following month (HC 3/7); papers aimed at improving dissemination of naval intelligence, 1917–18 (HW 3/9); Admiralty sigint related files on various subjects, 1917–20 (HW 3/36); and information on German military and naval monitoring of diplomatic communications between March and August 1917 to ascertain if they were vulnerable to interception (HW 3/181). A number of signals interception and direction finding sites supporting Room 40 were closed in 1918–19 (HW 3/10), while the new Government Code and Cipher School was opened in 1919 (HW 3/34–5), passing from Admiralty to Foreign Office control in November 1921.

HW 7 comprises official histories of intelligence activities written by various officers. Included is a three volume work by W. F. Clarke and Frank Birch, *Contribution to the History of German Naval Warfare, 1914–18* subtitled *The Fleet in Action, The Fleet in Being,* and *Authorities* (HW 7/1–4). Private papers contributed by Clarke deal with the sinking of HMS *Hampshire*, which struck a mine while carrying Kitchener to Russia in June 1916 (HW 7/23), and correspondence between Admiralty and War Office on the operational use of signals intelligence derived from Zeppelins, 1915–17 (HW 7/24). In addition, there are Room 40 decrypts of Chilean, German, Greek, Spanish, Swiss and United States diplomatic telegrams, 1916–17 (HW 7/5–7, 16–17, 21, and 34). In particular, there are decrypts of German and American telegrams relating to the German introduction of unrestricted submarine warfare in February 1917 and the subsequent break of diplomatic relations between Germany and the United States in March 1917 (HW 7/19–20). Other issues covered are attempted German and Turkish subversion in Morocco and Egypt (HW 7/32), and intelligence reports on vessels in Spanish ports, May–June 1916 (HW 7/33). There are also reports to the First Lord by the Deputy Director of the Intelligence Division, September–October 1917 (HW 7/22).

WO 32 includes a history of the wartime Directorate of Military Intelligence and material on intelligence work in Egypt and Salonika (WO 32/10776–7). There is also a translation of a German document on the experience gained in winter battles against the French in Champagne, 1915 (WO 32/5323).

WO 33 containing confidential printed papers includes copies of *The Index to German Foot Artillery Forces in the Field* (WO 33/751, 803, and 857); *The Index to German Forces in the Field* (WO 33/752, 762, 790, 810, 818–19, 841–2, and 860); *The Index to German Infantry Regiments* (WO 33/826); *Austro-Hungarian Forces in the Field* (WO 33/759, 798, 825, 864, and 907); *Provisional Notes on Balkan Armies, 1915* (WO 33/709); and *The Handbook of the French Army, 1914* (WO 33/2829). Publications in the *Intelligence Series* cover Belgium (WO 33/613, and 690–91); and German Home Defences (WO 33/693).

WO 106 deals with the dropping of information to agents from the air and also contains a history of intelligence and secret service operations, 1917–19 (WO 106/45); and schemes for the creation and reorganisation of secret service activities in the War Office (WO 106/6147, and 6292). In addition, a small collection of papers made by Lieutenant M. R. K. Burge of MI1a includes a general history of British wartime intelligence, a history of British secret service activities in the Netherlands,

1914–17, and intelligence papers on various countries (WO 106/6189–91). Similarly, there are a list of honours and awards to named French, Belgian and Dutch wartime agents in British pay (WO 106/6192), while other intelligence papers concern Iraq and the Sudan (WO 106/6055 and 6225–6). There is also a copy of the weekly pamphlet, *Matters Relating to the Central Powers*, for October–November 1917 (WO 106/322), and summaries of intelligence, 1916–18 (WO 106/346–8).

There are also miscellaneous papers of the Director of Military Intelligence, George MacDonogh, 1916–18 (WO 106/1510–17); an account of the work of the DMI in the war, compiled in 1921 (WO 106/6146); out-going correspondence of MI2, 1917–19 (WO 106/5130–33); and correspondence with British military attachés in Athens, Madrid, Peking, Petrograd, Rome, Tiflis, Tokyo and Washington (WO 106/5128). In addition, there is an explanation for the War Cabinet of the perceived failure of the Intelligence Branch of the General Staff, December 1917 (WO 106/727).

WO 158, Military Headquarters Papers, includes papers on the reorganisation of GHQ Intelligence Branch, 1917 (WO 158/961–2); and correspondence between MacDonogh and the Branch, 1916–17 (WO 158/897–8). Material from the Intelligence Branch (WO 158/975–84) includes papers on the control of the French and Belgian civil population, January 1916 (WO 158/982); a lecture on the prevention of leakage of information by Lieutenant Colonel Walter Kirke, May 1916 (WO 158/981); notes on the French field intelligence system, 1916 (WO 158/983); and instructions on the collection and transmission of intelligence in Britain (WO 158/984). In addition, there are *Intelligence Circulars* (WO 158/989–94).

WO 160/24 deals with the Italian army's counter-espionage branch.

WO 161/88–94 contain reports, assessments, summaries and analyses of German casualties, 1914–16, and material on German manpower resources, including minutes of a sub-committee of the Committee of Imperial Defence on the issue in 1916.

WO 208/3196 is a history of the MI6L Section of the Directorate of Military Intelligence, 1917–19.

WO 900/43–4 contains, among specimens of documents later destroyed, particulars and effects of deceased Germans found on the field of battle, 1914–15 and 1918.

The War on Land

That deadlock had occurred on the Western Front was not altogether surprising given the impact of industrialisation upon warfare, not least in terms of weapons development, the growth in the size of armies, the inability of soldiers to predict what would occur on the future battlefield, and the greater acceptance of war and the prolongation of conflict as an appropriate test of nationhood and national virility. Initially a junior military partner of France and Russia though the strongest economic and naval power in the Entente, Britain was increasingly forced by heavy French and Russian losses and the ability of the Germans to remain on the defensive in the west to play an ever greater role in the continental land war.

Having helped blunt the opening German advance at Mons and Le Cateau in August 1914, the British Expeditionary Force (BEF) had encountered entrenched German forces on the Aisne in September 1914 and had then fought desperately to hold Ypres in October and November 1914 before the front stabilised. The major British offensive at Loos in September 1915, which followed some experimental attacks earlier in the year at Neuve Chapelle, Festubert, Aubers Ridge and Givenchy, was mounted primarily for the political purpose of sustaining French and Russian morale. By early 1916, most British policy-makers were reluctantly convinced that the war might be lost unless the British participated fully in the offensive planned for the summer of 1916, the Somme being chosen as the battlefield because this was where the British and French sectors of the front lines met.

The hopes dashed in 1916 gave way to a further British offensive at Ypres – commonly called the Passchendaele offensive – in 1917, again partly launched in the belief that, if the British stood idle, the spectre of defeat would spread through the alliance. Moreover, Russia had already suffered the first of its revolutions and the French army had all but broken in a series of mutinies. Indeed, from holding just 24 miles of the length of the Western Front in November 1914, the BEF's frontage had increased to 123 miles by February 1918. With the failure of the offensive, Lloyd George determined to husband remaining manpower resources. In the event, the failure of the Germans' own spring offensives in 1918 enabled the Entente to counter-attack in the summer of 1918, the British army achieving an impressive number of major victories during the 'Hundred Days' of August to November 1918.

The Western Front thus remained the major theatre for the British army, accounting for 1.9 million of the 3.2 million British, Dominion and imperial forces in the field in November 1918 (59.3 per cent). Similarly, France and Flanders accounted for 611,000 of the 722,000 military deaths recorded for the army between August 1914 and November 1918 (84.6 per cent).

ADM 1 has material on the formation and employment of the naval brigade in August 1914 (ADM 1/8391/267 and 278), and the operations at Antwerp in October 1914 (ADM 1/8397/362). There is also information on transport arrangements for the Australian Imperial Force in November 1914 (ADM 1/8403/426); and on the provision of armed barges on Belgian canals (ADM 1/8418/94). There is also material on the employment of the Portuguese on the Western Front (ADM 1/8481/41).

ADM 116 has material among its case files on the naval contribution to the Western Front, including the formation of Naval Brigades and Special Service Squadrons in 1914 (ADM 116/1322 and 1323); and the formation and operations of the Royal Naval Division, including its depot at the Crystal Palace (AM116/1337–8, 1352–3, and 1411–13). The series also covers the division's initial commitment to Antwerp, after the fall of which large numbers of men were interned in the Netherlands, and into which there was an official enquiry in 1918–19 (ADM 116/1438–9, 1458, and 1814). There is also material on the committees dealing with the dispatch of the BEF to France in 1914 (ADM 116/1324 and 1331–3).

ADM 137 also deals with the interment and enquiry into the internment of the 1st

Royal Naval Brigade in the Netherlands (ADM 137/1010 and 3926–7); and the fall of Antwerp (ADM 137/1943). It also contains the war diaries, operational reports and other papers of the 63rd (Royal Naval) Division (ADM 137/3087–8A, and 3929–42); the 63rd Division's Transport and Medical services (ADM 137/3066 and 3071); papers of the Royal Marine Artillery Siege and Anti-aircraft Brigades (ADM 137/3924–5); and reports on the Anglo-Russian Armoured Car Unit, 1917–18 (ADM 137/3943B).

ADM 201/16 deals with the formation of the Royal Marine Special Service Brigade in 1914.

AIR 1 deals with inundations of the Flanders coast, 1916–18 (AIR 1/105/15/9/275); and German defences on the same coast (AIR 1/673/17/141/1); while papers of Lieutenant H. A. Jones, RFC, include a sketch of the mine craters blown under the German lines at La Boiselle on 1 July 1916 (AIR 1/719/35/4). There is also information on RNAS Armoured Trains, 1914–15 (AIR 1/2099/207/21). There is the record of conferences between Haig as CinC and his army commanders, 1916–18 (AIR 1/978/204/5/1137), and miscellaneous reports on the European war include material on the movements of the BEF in 1914 (AIR 1/2098–9, and 2182). In addition, there is material from GHQ and papers relating to First Army (AIR 1/2066–8, and 2280–82).

CAB 1 includes a discussion of a possible attack on Ostend and Zeebrugge in November 1916 (CAB 1/20), and the possible repercussions of the fall of the Channel ports to the Germans during their 1918 spring offensives (CAB 1/26).

CAB 17, containing miscellaneous correspondence of the Committee of Imperial Defence, includes a memorandum by Haig from 1915 on the possibility of a German western offensive (CAB 17/129); material on locomotives and rolling stock for the British armies in France, 1916 (CAB 17/155); discussion of the Belgian army in 1916 and 1917 (CAB 17/172 and 187); and consideration of operations on the Western Front, 1917 (CAB 17/195).

CAB 20/1–4 contain copies of German documents on the Schlieffen Plan, 1905–12 including various versions of the celebrated *denkschrift* (study) of December 1905 including comments by von Moltke in 1911 and the 'final' version of December 1912 (CAB 20/1–2); a memorandum by Schlieffen from 1902 and some papers from 1911 on the presumed opening French deployment in any war (CAB 20/3); and maps (CAB 20/4). Doubt has now been thrown on the whole concept of the *denkschrift* as the culmination of Schlieffen's planning as Chief of the German General Staff from 1896 to January 1906. Indeed, it may date to after his retirement.

CAB 21, containing registered files of the Cabinet Office, has material from the Joint Naval and Military Committee on Combined Operations, 1916 (CAB 21/3); and a report on the operations of the Canadian Cavalry Brigade in 1917 (CAB 21/17). There is also a memorandum by Haig on Western Front operations, the file also containing original documents from the enquiry into the ultimate failure of the Cambrai offensive in November 1917 (CAB 21/22). In addition, there are reports by Foch and other French generals on their 1917 offensives (CAB 21/122).

CAB 45 has a considerable amount of material on operations on the Western Front gathered for use in the compilation of the Official History (CAB 45/114–206, and

289–90). It includes correspondence, accounts and diary extracts arranged by battle, covering the Aisne, Arras, The Bluff, Cambrai, La Becqe, Le Cateau, Loos, the Lys, the Marne, Messines, Meteren, Mons, St Eloi, Soissons, the Somme, Vimy and Ypres (CAB 45/114–45); battles with Canadian participation, namely Mount Sorrel, St Eloi, the Somme, and Ypres (CAB 45/146–56); and expeditions, principally that to Antwerp in 1914 (CAB 45/157–8). In addition, there are accounts covering the operations of the Third, Fourth and Fifth Armies (CAB 45/184–93); French and German accounts (CAB 45/159–76); the diaries of General Clive, Captain Chadwych-Healey, Cyril Falls, Major G. Goodwin Whiffen, Lieutenant Colonel G. Holland, and General Sir Horace Smith-Dorrien (CAB 45/201–6); and miscellaneous material (CAB 45/177–83, 194–9, and 289–90), including coverage of the Chantilly and Doullens conferences (CAB 45/177–8); and the movements of German corps on the Marne, 1914 (CAB 45/290). Papers of Gershom Stewart MP include correspondence on Canadian troops (CAB 45/210), and an account of a visit to the Western Front in May 1915 (CAB 45/207).

CN 4/1 has photographs of French and Belgian railway stations, 1918.

MT 23, containing the correspondence and papers of the Admiralty Transport Department, includes material on the transportation of the 4th Division to France, the 6th Division to England from Ireland, and Territorials to Egypt in August and September 1914 (MT 23/305 and 313); movement of ambulance ships supporting the BEF in 1914 (MT 23/307); and arrangements as to sending more heavy guns to France in 1916 (MT 23/641).

PRO 10/99–100 consists of samples of War Office documents, later destroyed, relating to army units and formations.

PRO 30/30/6, among the papers of Lord Milner as Secretary of State for War, has material relating to the repercussions of the collapse of the Fifth Army in March 1918.

PRO 30/57, comprising Kitchener's papers, has considerable information on the conduct of the war on the Western Front between 1914 and 1916 including general correspondence (PRO 30/57/49–50 and 53); reports and memoranda (PRO 30/57/58); correspondence with Sir Henry Rawlinson, who commanded successively 7th Division, IV Corps and Fourth Army (PRO 30/57/51); correspondence on the Indian and Canadian troops serving in France and Flanders (PRO 30/57/52 and 56); and Kitchener's own visits to the front (PRO 30/57/54).

PRO 30/66/9–10 contain correspondence on rail movements and other wartime correspondence of Brigadier-General Sir H. Osborne Mance, RE, Director of Railways, Light Railways and Roads in the BEF.

PRO 30/67/25 contains a diary of the visit of the former Secretary of State for War, Lord Midleton, to France in December 1914.

WO 32, as might be expected, contains a large amount of material on the war on the Western Front. Operational material includes a report on the fall of Antwerp in 1914 (WO 32/5086); other aspects of the 1914 campaigns and the situation in Belgium (WO 32/5561–4); the instructions of both French and Haig as CinC of the BEF (WO 32/5590–92); Haig's reactions to the Cambrai enquiry in 1917 (WO 32/5095B); and his report on the collapse of the Fifth Army in March 1918

(WO 32/5097). From the same crucial period, there is also material on the collapse of Portuguese units on the Lys; the possible flooding of northern France to protect Calais and Dunkirk from further German advances; and Haig's request for the return of the Second Army from the nominal command of King Albert of the Belgians (WO 32/5099–5100 and 5102–3). Logistics is represented by reports on railways and inland waterways, including reports by Sir Percy Girouard in 1914 and General Nash in 1916, and the appointment of Sir Eric Geddes as Director of Transportation in 1916 (WO 32/5144–7, and 5162–4). Other support functions are also covered such as engineering and the Army Service Corps (WO 32/4802, 4810, 5090–91, 5104, and 11374), and the report of the Debenham Committee on the Royal Army Clothing Department (WO 32/5540). Other miscellaneous material includes the issue of dismounting cavalry for infantry (WO 32/11355), and a war history of the Directorate of Military Operations (WO 32/10775).

WO 33, comprising confidential printed papers, has railway timetables and other printed material on the mobilisation of the BEF in August 1914 (WO 33/611, 657, 660–61, 665, 668, 670, 672–3, 676, 679–80, 684–8); printed telegrams relating to the war on the Western Front (WO 33/713–14, 739, 747–8, 768, 806, 809, 856, 913, 920, 945, 982, and 991); telegrams on the general war situation (WO 33/832, 924, 931, 947, 956, 958, and 963); general programmes for the sea movement of troops, including British, Dominion and Indian forces (WO 33/708, 716, 736, 740, 753, 763, 780, 784–6, 805, 821, 836, 847, 852, 863, 886, 896, 915, and 926); allotment of ASC units (WO 33/730, 744, and 893); and war establishments of formations in France and Flanders (WO 33/673, 778, and 900–902). There are also minutes of the Army Council for 1915–16 (WO 33/881).

WO 73/97–109 comprise the general monthly returns on the distribution of the army for the war years.

WO 79, miscellaneous private collections, includes papers of Sir Archibald Murray, initially Chief of Staff to the BEF and then briefly CIGS, relating to the Western Front, 1914–15 (WO 79/62–3), and German defences on the Flanders coast (WO 79/65). The papers of Lieutenant-General the Earl of Cavan cover the formation of the Guards Division in 1915 (WO 79/71), and his command of XIV Corps on the Western Front (WO 79/66).

WO 95 consists of War Diaries, 1914–22, containing daily records of operations, intelligence reports and other events as recorded in each unit by an appointed junior officer. Some record little more than daily losses and map references and, in many cases, are scribbled hastily in pencil or sometime after the events, or are a second carbon copy of the original, the PRO copies being those sent to the War Office rather than the original retained by the unit in question. Some, however, are more descriptive. For the Western Front, covering France, Belgium and the immediate post-war occupation of the Rhineland, they are arranged by those of GHQ and its branches (WO 95/1–85); GHQ troops (WO 95/86–153); GHQs and troops of the BEF's five armies (WO 95/154–571); Corps GHQs, branches and troops (WO 95/572–1095), including the Anzac (WO 95/980–1044), Canadian (WO 95/1045–87), and Indian corps (WO 95/1088–95); Cavalry Divisions (WO 95/1096–189); Infantry Divisions (WO 95/1190–3948), including again Anzac, Canadian and Indian divisions (WO 95/3155–948); and LOC units and troops (WO 95/3949–4193). In addition, there are Orders of Battle (WO 95/5467–87); a guide to the location of army units, 1914–19 (WO 95/5494); and to the deployment of units of the Labour Corps, Royal Military Police, RAOC, RAVC, RE and Army Postal Services (WO 95/5495–500). There is a supplementary finding aid index in the Catalogue Room for units.

WO 106 contains the instructions issued to British CinCs, 1914–18 (WO 106/298), while there is also the *Summaries of Events in the European War* (WO 106/299–308), and the *Monthly Diary of Military and Political Events, 1916–18* (WO 106/5129). There is also material on army reorganisation in 1917 (WO 106/355–6 and 358–61), and the reorganisation of the General Staff in 1918 (WO 106/328). Operational material (WO 106/380–438) includes reports on the defences of the Channel ports, 1914 (WO 106/380–86); the Indian Corps at Neuve Chapelle in March 1915 (WO 106/388B); the contentious issue of the reserves at Loos in September 1915, which ultimately led to Sir John French's dismissal (WO 106/390); general situation reports and other material from 1915 (WO 106/1519–20 and 1524–9); the Vimy operations in 1917 (WO 106/399 and 402); the collapse of the Portuguese in April 1918 (WO 106/1530); the 1918 operations, including those at Rheims and Soissons (WO 106/418–25 and 1458–9); and possible operations inside Germany for 1918–19 (WO 106/433). There is also a report on the army's veterinary services (WO 106/388A), and on the role of the Works Directorate behind the lines in France and Flanders (WO 106/1476–89).

WO 107, consisting of the papers of the Quartermaster-General's Department at the War Office, includes correspondence with the Inspector-General of Communications, 1914–17 (WO 107/13–25); material relating to the Western Front, 1915–18 (WO 107/29–37); and other miscellaneous matters, 1917–18 (WO 107/66–8).

WO 111/13 is the Royal Ordnance Corps' Record of Important Events, 1915–19.

WO 123 contains Army Orders, 1914–18 (WO 123/56–60); Army Council Orders, 1916–23 (WO 123/191–2); and General Routine Orders for the BEF in France and Flanders, including those of the Inspector-General of Communications (WO 123/199–201).

WO 153 consists of maps and plans, drawn mostly from unit war diaries. There is a very large number relating to the Western Front covering all the major campaigns including Mons and First Ypres in 1914 (WO 153/114, 116–23, and 1283); Neuve Chapelle, Aubers Ridge, Festubert, Second Ypres and Loos in 1915 (WO 153/124–52); the Somme in 1916 (WO 153/153–209); Vimy, Arras, Messines, Passchendaele and Cambrai in 1917 (WO 153/210–82); and the German spring offensives, Amiens and the Hundred Days in 1918 (WO 153/283–353). In addition, there are assorted trench maps (WO 153/334–8); and GHQ situation maps, 1914–18 (WO 153/339–95, and 426–31). Various Orders of Battle of British, French, German and American forces are also to be found (WO 153/1–114, 396–401, 403, 406–8, 410–12, 417–21, 432–38, and 440). Material is also arranged by the BEF's five armies (WO 153/439, 441–620, 1061–2, 1096–102, and 1111–29); by Corps (WO 153/636–733, 735–54, 1137–61, and 1276–81); and by Divisions (WO 153/1162).

Miscellaneous material includes general maps of France, Belgium and Germany (WO 153/822–72); maps illustrating coastal operations (WO 153/875–8, 881–7, 889, and 1349); maps of water supplies and inundations (WO 153/890–93); communications and signals maps (WO 153/995–7, 1080–89, and 1170–73); RE mining maps (WO 153/904–14, and 920); and billetting maps (WO 153/1167). There are also the maps used to illustrate Haig's dispatches (WO 153/1091); and those later prepared by the Cabinet Office Historical Section (WO 153/1295–318). There are also German maps illustrating organisation and defences such as trenches and artillery positions (WO 153/930–54, 959–61, and 965–77, 1063–72, 1196, and 1127–30). Non-map material includes artillery, gun and ammunition charts and statements (WO 153/1216–26); railway graphs and charts (WO 153/1244–8); other assorted graphs and tables (WO 153/1249–57, and 1265–7); panoramas of the Western Front, some being pencil or coloured sketches (WO 153/1268–75); and a photographic mosaic of the German defences in Belgium, 1917 (WO 153/1350).

WO 154 contains Supplementary War Diaries, being those originally extracted from WO 95 as containing more sensitive material, including, for example, the few surviving provost diaries. For the Western Front, the diaries are arranged by Corps (WO 154/1–16), and Divisions (WO 154/17–114).

WO 157 comprises *Intelligence Summaries*, 1914–18, arranged by theatre of operations. Those covering the war on the Western Front (WO 157/1–631) are broken down into GHQ summaries (WO 157/1–47); Army summaries (WO 154/48–223); and Corps summaries (WO 157/224–631), including those for the Anzac, Canadian and Indian Corps (WO 157/550–608) and the New Zealand Division (WO 157/609–31).

WO 158 contains the correspondence and papers of Military Headquarters. Those for the BEF's GHQ (WO 158/1–79) include an account of the death and funeral of Field Marshal Lord Roberts, who died while visiting the Indian Corps in December 1914 (WO 158/1); reports by the Director of Supplies (WO 158/2–3); the daily war diary of MO2(c) on intelligence matters, 1915 (WO 158/4–7); an account of the visit of the King to the front in December 1914 (WO 158/12); notes on operations, 1915–18 (WO 158/17–20); a report on the 24th Division, one of the crucial reserve divisions, at Loos in September 1915 (WO 158/32); coastal operations, 1916–18 (WO 158/36); plans relating to Aubers Ridge, 1917 (WO 157/40); the Cambrai enquiry (WO 157/52–6); and plans for retreat in 1918 (WO 158/64–71). In addition, there is correspondence on the Portuguese Expeditionary Force, including its collapse on the Lys in April 1918 (WO 158/111–21).

The correspondence of the Inspector of Mines (WO 158/129–65) includes information on the formation of specialised mining units (WO 158/129); mining notes (WO 158/130–31); reports by the Australian Electrical and Mining Company, 1917–19 (WO 158/133–4); weekly mining summaries, 1917–19 (WO 158/135); mining diaries and tunnelling company reports (WO 158/137, and 140–42); and technical details of the mining operation at Messines in June 1917 (WO 158/139). Papers of the Engineer in Chief include conference proceedings, 1916–18 (WO 158/166–80). Army GHQ papers (WO 158/181–344) include much on Neuve Chapelle and Loos in 1915 (WO 158/258–9, 261–4, and 272–3); the Somme in 1916 (WO 158/321–44); and Messines and Cambrai in 1917 (WO 158/299–308, and 314–20). Corps HQ papers (WO 158/345–432) include material on Passchendaele and Cambrai (WO 158/379–96, and 425–32). There is a small selection of Divisional GHQ material (WO 158/433–7).

In addition, miscellaneous material includes records of the army commanders conferences, February to July 1918 (WO 158/864); histories of inland water transport and light railways (WO 158/851–2); a report on the Vimy operation in 1917 (WO 158/900); and more on the Portuguese (WO 158/850, and 870–71). There are also papers of the HQ of the British Military Mission with the Portuguese (WO 158/709–10), which include the convention for the employment of the Portuguese on the Western Front.

WO 159, comprising Kitchener's Private Office papers, includes correspondence received from Brigadier-General H. Yarde-Buller, 1914–15 (WO 159/9–12), and correspondence between the Master-General of the Ordnance, Stanley von Donop, and officers of the BEF, 1914 (WO 159/15).

WO 160/22 contains semi-official correspondence of GHQ, BEF, July 1918.

WO 161, miscellaneous unregistered papers, includes accounts of mine rescue work on the Western Front, and a report on the role of the Geographical Section of the General Staff compiled in 1920 (WO 161/86 and 113). There are also copies of engagements, commanders and signs of British armies, corps and divisions, 1914–18 (WO 161/87). In addition, there is the official French account of the battle of the Somme, 1916 (WO 161/79).

WO 163 contains minutes and précis of the Army Council, 1914–18 (WO 163/21–3), and minutes of the meetings of its Military Members, 1914–16 (WO 163/44–6).

WO 293 contains War Office Instructions, 1914–15 (WO 293/1–3), and Army Council Instructions, 1915–18 (WO 293/4–9).

WO 293 consists of topographical maps of the Western Front produced by survey mapping and printing units in the field and the United Kingdom – principally the British Geographical Section, General Staff and the Field Survey Companies – together with French, Belgian and German maps and some specially produced for use by the Indian Corps and Portuguese contingent. The main purpose was to depict ground positions of the opposing enemy trench lines (shown in the catalogues as 'G') and, often in skeletal form, those of the allies ('A'). This information on trenches formed the main overprint on the base topographical map although some other thematic overprints were sometimes included. They mostly cover the area of operations of the British forces, lines of communication and forward areas into Germany with some significant adjacent areas of Belgian and French interest. Although the majority were produced during the war, some such as those on a smaller scale, predate the war. A very few were produced after the war. The maps are arranged by scale, nationality and by origin. There is no comprehensive index, but there are a few contemporary indices and some later manuscript indices (WO 297/1–56), together with guides to figures, diagrams and conventional signs (WO 297/57–79). Following British town plans (WO 297/80–135) and miscellaneous British maps (WO 297/136–209), there are British, French and Belgian maps in 1:5 000 scale (WO 297/210–443); British, French and Belgian maps in 1:10 000 scale (WO 297/513–2750, and 6543–649); British, French and Belgian maps in 1:20 000 scale (WO 297/2751–5334); British maps in 1:40 000 scale (WO 297/5363–949); French maps in 1:50 000 scale (WO 297/5950–81); British maps in 1:80 000 scale (WO 297/5982–6087); British maps in 1:100 000 scale (WO 297/6088–503); British maps in other scales (WO 297/6514–42); and French, Belgian and German maps in other scales (WO 297/444–512, 5335–62, and 6504–13).

WO 316 are photographs of the Western Front, mostly taken from aircraft for the purposes of intelligence, reconnaissance and mapping and covering Belgian coast defences, 1917–18 (WO 316/1–16); battlefields, 1914–18, but mostly from 1917 (WO 316/40–53); and the Second Army's operations, 1917 (WO 316/55). However, there are also photographs taken by Canadian Corps photographers, 1916–18 (WO 316/17–23); artillery panoramas (WO 316/24–39); undated photographs taken to gauge the effectiveness of artillery barrages (WO 316/57); and aerial photographs taken by Major Moore-Brabazon, 1915–18, to illustrate a book (WO 316/58). In addition, there is a contact print of negatives taken by Lt Towell, RA at Mons (WO 316/54).

The harnessing of science and technology to the war effort promised potentially some solution to the problems of the Western Front. Soldiers in all armies were confronted with both new technical and managerial problems in coming to terms with the practical difficulties of trench warfare, the enormous increase in the size of armies and the scale of conflict. In every case, it required a considerable process of adjustment and learning on the part of commanders.

For all the popular emphasis upon the machine gun, the really significant developments in the Great War were in artillery for it was the key to protecting infantry as it crossed what soon became known as 'No Man's Land' and enabling it to 'break in' the opposing defences. Unfortunately, the ability to protect the attackers was limited to the range of the artillery, which could not be readily brought forward from its fixed positions behind the lines in order to extend any break made by the infantry. Even if a 'break in' was achieved, however, a 'break through' presented just as many difficulties of recognising and reinforcing success.

By 1917 the Royal Artillery had improved immeasurably in terms of the development of more sophisticated methods such as sound ranging, flash spotting, survey work and aerial reconnaissance and photography, which enabled a new accuracy in indirect and predicted fire and far more refined creeping barrages and counter-battery fire. Equally, by the end of 1917, British infantry tactics were steadily refined, with men trained to fight their own way forward in specialised platoons with increased firepower of their own such as Lewis guns, Stokes mortars and rifle grenades while the Machine Gun Corps had been created as a kind of light artillery. At the same time, the ability to communicate with infantry beyond its own front line was also improving.

What needs to be emphasised, however, is that no one actually solved the problem of converting a break-in into a break-through because the technical means to do so were never actually available for all the developments in artillery and communications. Indeed, the only arm of exploitation available remained cavalry.

The absence of a technical means of breaking deadlock did not mean that technical solutions were not attempted. Thus, the *flammenwerfer* (flame-thrower) was first used by the Germans at a tactical level. They also introduced gas as an intended breakthrough weapon although, in military parlance, its real function was as a 'force multiplier'. Its first significant usage was in the form of chlorine gas released from cylinders between Pilckem and Langemarck on 22 April 1915 to initiate the Second Battle of Ypres. Increasingly, however, gas was put into shells. Some 63 different types were used during the war on all fronts, from acute lung irritants such as chlorine, to paralysants such as hydrocyanic acid, and vesicants such as dichlordiethyl sulphide (mustard gas).

For all its apparently devastating impact, soldiers were better protected from gas than from any other weapon during the war, provided masks were put on promptly and properly. The one exception was mustard gas, which attacked all moist parts of the body. Gas on its own, therefore, was not a decisive weapon and rare indeed in being invented in one war and discarded in the next.

More promising, in theory, was the tank. The idea of utilising pre-war agricultural caterpillar-tracked tractors as a means of overcoming barbed wire occurred to a number of individuals including the secretary to the War Council, Maurice Hankey, and the British official war correspondent in France, Colonel Ernest Swinton, whom Hankey credited with first alerting him to the potential in October 1914. Churchill took up Hankey's idea in February 1915 by establishing an Admiralty Landships Committee, the Royal Naval Air Service (RNAS) having operated armoured cars from its first base at Ostend in August 1914 and, thereafter, from Dunkirk. Subsequently, the first Mark I or 'Mother' tanks reached France in August 1916, being used for the first time in a renewed attack on the Somme at Flers-Courcelette on 15 September 1916.

Unfortunately, both on the Somme and in later actions such as Cambrai in November 1917 and Amiens in August 1918, the tank proved to have chronic technical limitations. Not only were tanks vulnerable to mechanical problems, but also to artillery and anti-tank rifles, which the Germans soon introduced. In addition, crews suffered greatly from heat exhaustion and carbon monoxide poisoning. Tanks, therefore, during the war remained what GHQ concluded in August 1918, a 'mechanical contrivance' with potential usefulness only as an adjunct to combined infantry and artillery assault.

ADM 1 has material on the employment of RNAS armoured cars, including the offer of O. Locker-Lampson, later a Lieutenant Commander, to raise an armoured car squadron in November 1914 and his subsequent request for 10,000 armoured cars in April 1917 which he would arm from private funds (ADM 1/8403/428 and 8484/69); action reports from June and September 1915 (ADM 1/8424/13 and 8433/267); the collision of an armoured car with a public house in July 1915 (ADM 1/8426/190); the suggested use of armoured cars in Romania, November 1916 and additional needs and policy for armoured cars in Russia (ADM 1/8473/259, 8518/76, and 8530/201).

ADM 116/1339 deals with the Admiralty's part in the inception and evolution of 'Landships'.

AIR 1 has reports on RN Armoured Cars in Russia and East Africa (AIR 1/16/147/15/4), and in Russia (AIR 1/662/17/122/667, and 664/17/122/702).

AIR 2 has a file on rewards granted to former RFC officers in connection with the development of the tank (AIR 2/93/C 65300); weekly reports of the British Armoured Car Division, July 1917 (AIR 2/37/AIR 02278/1917); and correspondence between Squadron Commander Gregory, RN and Locker-Lampson regarding the Armoured Car Squadron in Romania, 1916 (AIR 2/36/AIR 0404/1917).

AIR 11/218 has material on gas experiments by the Naval Aircraft Works, Cardington, 1917–20.

AVIA 8 contains some material on artillery experiments among papers of the Air Inventions Committee, including sound location trials in France, 1917 (AVIA 8/474); progress reports on range finders, 1917–18 (AVIA 8/476); trials of the artillery spotting device designed by Lt Power at Orfordness, 1918 (AVIA 8/478); and the flash spotting device developed by Captain W. C. Gardiner in 1918 (AVIA 8/479–80).

CAB 1 has some material on the changing needs of land warfare including reports from December 1915 on the amount of ammunition required to attack a fortified line, and on the future conduct of war including trench warfare and chemical warfare (CAB 1/14); reports on machine gun purchases in January 1916 and on Madsen machine guns (CAB 1/15); the supply of tanks, flame throwers, howitzers, gas, anti-tank guns and trench mortars in March 1916 (CAB 1/16); and body armour (CAB 1/19). There is also material on reprisals to be taken against enemy officers found in possession of soft-nosed or dum-dum bullets (CAB 1/23).

CAB 17 contains papers among the miscellaneous correspondence of the Committee of Imperial Defence on the development of tanks, 1915–16 (CAB 17/120B), and tank policy, 1916 (CAB 17/167).

CAB 21/83 has material from Cabinet Office registered files on gas and smoke screens, 1917.

CAB 45 deals with gas attacks on the Western Front, 1914–18 (CAB 45/289), and there is also material on the Tank Corps (CAB 45/200).

CN 4/4 has photographs of casualties of a German gas attack on 24 May 1915.

DSIR 36 has a number of files on chemical warfare among those of the Records Bureau of the Departmental Library. There are reports on captured German breathing apparatus, 1916–18 (DSIR 36/405); a report on French gas cylinders, 1918 (DSIR 36/424); and on the post-war recovery of glycerine from anti-gas helmets, 1920 (DSIR 36/2654). In addition, there are reports of the visit by the British Mission appointed to inspect German chemical factories in the allied occupied zone that had been engaged in the wartime production of munitions, February 1919, and of the similar visit by the British Chemical Mission of the Association of British Chemical Manufacturers in June 1919 (DSIR 36/1966–7).

DSIR 37, containing papers of the Munitions Inventions Department, includes those of the Chemical Inventions Committee, 1915–18 (DSIR 37/215–23), which was appointed in August 1915 as an Advisory Panel of the MID, operating through a sub-committee intended to report on all cases dealing with chemical inventions before they were submitted to the main committee. There are the committee's minutes (DSIR 37/215–22), and its reports (DSIR 37/223). In addition, there is also a list of staff working in the MID Chemical Research Section, 1914–18 (DSIR 37/174).

FO 115/1960 deals with President Woodrow Wilson's attitudes towards the use of poison gas, 1915.

WO 32 includes useful material on the new developments. On gas warfare, there is information on the formation of the original Special Gas Companies of the Royal Engineers and of a Reserve Company of the subsequent Special Brigade to carry out experiments at Porton Down (WO 32/5173 and 11375); the establishment of the Chemical Warfare Department (WO 32/9287); and proposals to reorganise the chemical warfare service to increase production in 1918 (WO 32/5179). There is also correspondence and reports on both the use of gas and also anti-gas measures in the field (WO 32/5170–171, 5174, 5178, 5183, and 11376). There is also correspondence on the alleged use of gas by the allies at the Dardanelles and the provision of gas respirators for the Mediterranean Expeditionary Force (WO 32/5117, 5121, and 5172). Consideration was given in 1917 to the protection of the British population against the use of air-dropped gas (WO 32/5191 and 5275), while in 1918 the International Red Cross appealed to both sides to stop using gas when the Germans threatened to develop yet new gases (WO 32/5177).

Equally controversial was the use of explosive (dum-dum) bullets, allegations of which were often made by both sides (WO 32/4904, 5085, 5157–8, 5186–7, and 5555–6). Machine Gun Companies and the creation of the Machine Gun Corps (MGC) are covered (WO 32/5185, 11293, 11392 and 11394), as well as the Heavy Branch of the MGC (WO 32/11393), from which the Tank Corps eventually emerged (WO 32/5185 and 5754). In addition, there is a report from a conference on the tactical employment of tanks in 1917 and a memorandum on the possible formation of tank armies (WO 32/5154 and 5933); and papers of Major-General Hickman's Siege Committee, 1914 and 1918–19 (WO 32/5151 and 5153).

WO 33, comprising confidential printed reports, includes material on improved armaments and other technical developments such as in machine guns and artillery (WO 33/683, 705, 718, 723, 734–5, 756, 807, 829, 831, and 874); handbooks on chemical, incendiary and smoke shells, bombs and grenades (WO 33/933–4); tactical notes and manuals (WO 33/717, 721, and 725), including notes on recent cavalry fighting from April 1917 (WO 33/816); the report of Major-General Hickman's Siege Committee, 1914 (WO 33/699–702); and reports on German artillery (WO 33/703, and 770). Among printed war establishments are those of the RE Experimental (Chemical Warfare) Stations at Wembley and Porton (WO 33/850–51), and the Tank Corps in France (WO 33/912), while there are also copies of *Weekly Tank Notes* for 1918–19 (WO 33/2850–51).

WO 95/91–118 contain the war diaries of the Tank Corps and its units, 1914–22.

WO 106 has material on the duties of the GOC, Machine Gun Corps (WO 106/374); and on tanks, including armament (WO 106/375–7). There is also information on a conference on a mobile army held in 1918 (WO 106/343). Other developments are covered including mining operations, 1914–17 (WO 106/587), and gas warfare (WO 106/389 and 392).

WO 140/14–15 contain reports of trials of arms and ammunition at the School of Musketry, Hythe, 1914–16.

WO 142 comprises the papers and reports of the Chemical Warfare Department of the Ministry of Munitions, 1915–20. Analytical work to identify gases used by the Germans was initially carried out at a Central Laboratory of GHQ in France but it was soon appreciated that there was a need for an experimental site. After some trials on Cannock Chase, the War Department Experimental Ground was established at Porton, Wiltshire, in March 1916 with an Experimental Company of the Royal Engineers attached from existing Special Brigade personnel in France. In addition, there was a Royal Artillery Experimental Battery and RAMC personnel, all supporting a Field Trials Department, Chemical, Physiological and Anti-Gas Laboratories, and a Meteorological Section. An Anti-Gas Department was also located at the Royal Army Medical College, Millbank, but increasingly, all work was centred upon Porton, research into smoke weapons being added to the remit in due course. Meanwhile, the Ministry of Munitions had created a Design Department in December 1915, subsequently made part of the Design Group in August 1917 and, in turn, incorporated into the Trench Warfare (Research) Department. In October 1917 responsibility for all gas and anti-gas research passed to the Ministry from the War Office and the Ministry's new Chemical Warfare Department also incorporated the Design Department's Chemical Advisory Committee. In April 1918, the Chemical Warfare Department was transferred from the Design Group to the Explosives Group.

This extensive series includes the minute books of the Trench Warfare Research Department's numerous committees and sub-committees, 1915–19, including the Chemical Advisory and Chemical Warfare Committees (WO 142/52–75); technical and other reports of these committees (WO 142/76–7); research and liaison files of the Chemical Warfare Department, including both chemical weapons and smoke (WO 142/110–52); and minutes of the Trench Warfare Committee, 1917–18 (WO 142/206–8). Other files include those of the Director of Gas Services with the BEF, 1915–18 (WO 142/90–109); the Central Laboratory in France (WO 142/153–71); the Anti-Gas Department (WO 142/183–92); the Director of Explosive Supplies, 1916–18, including some dealing with the manufacture of mustard gas and phosgene (WO 142/196–201); the Wembley Pyrotechnics Laboratory, 1917–18 (WO 142/202–5); the Colonel Commandant at Porton, reporting trials and experiments, 1916–19 (WO 142/209–11); and a report of the Physiology War Committee of the Royal Society, 1916 (WO 142/299). There are also reports on French, Italian and Russian gas experience, 1915–18 (WO 142/172–82, and 193–5); and a collection of documents on the United States chemical warfare services, 1917–18, including the Chemical Warfare Service of the US Bureau of Mines, the Chemical Warfare Laboratory, the American Chemical Warfare Experimental Station at Hanlon Field in France, and the Chemical Warfare Services Research Division (WO 142/1–51), as well as a file on the British Gas Warfare Mission to the United States (WO 142/9).

Technical material includes drawings and specifications of British respirators (WO 142/78–81); tests and data on chemical compounds (WO 142/82–9); information on German ammunition and fuses (WO 142/212); and medical investigations of gas effects (WO 142/220–24, and 238). Other miscellaneous material (WO 142/330–33) includes reports on the medical aspects of mustard gas production (WO 142/330). Files from the Porton Historical Collection (WO 142/239–767) deal with the evolution of British chemical warfare organisation (WO 142/239, 240, and 242), and include correspondence on the subject of gas between Kitchener and Sir John French in 1915 (WO 142/241). They also deal with German gas organisation (WO 142/243, and 267–8); the work of the Chemical and Scientific Advisory Committees (WO 142/245–7, and 276); the RE establishments at Porton, Wembley and University College, London (WO 142/277); experimental work on chemical and smoke weapons (WO 142/249, and 251–2); and anti-gas measures, including the problem posed by mustard gas (WO 142/254–5, 258, 263, 267–72, and 284). There are more copies of the report by the British Chemical Mission in Germany in 1919 (WO 142/244 and 273); and also an undated paper by Captain Hay on the subject of the Trench Warfare Tank (WO 142/250).

Miscellaneous personal material includes notes on mustard gas and other lecture notes by Lieutenant C. (later Sir Charles) Lovatt Evans, and his notebooks of experiments, 1916–18 (WO 142/279, 298, and 301); papers of Colonel A. E. Kent, including his message pad recording the wind direction for an operation in 1915 (WO 142/280 and 283); Professor H. B. Baker's diary of his visit with Dr J. S. Haldane to view the effects of the first German use of gas in 1915 (WO 142/281); the first laboratory notebook of Dr L. H. Parker of the Anti-Gas Department at Millbank, 1915 (WO 142/282); laboratory notebooks of O. C. M. Davies, R. A. M. Cole and the Assistant Superintendent of the Anti-Gas Department, Captain W. C. Balls (WO 142/302–7, and 327–9); and other laboratory notes from Porton and from field tests at Boscombe, 1916–18 (WO 142/308–11). The work of the RE Special Brigade in France is reflected in maps illustrating its operations (WO 142/285–97); operational orders (WO 142/300); war diaries and other miscellaneous material (WO 142/312–16); lists of its officers (WO 142/334, and 338–9); and a report on the Special Brigade by its commander, Brigadier-General C. H. Foulkes, 1918 (WO 142/336–7). With the run down of the Ministry of Munitions after the war, responsibility for chemical warfare passed back to the War Office as a responsibility of the Master General of the Ordnance.

WO 153 contains some maps relating to Tank Corps operations (WO 153/1166) and Tank Corps ranges, 1917–18 (WO 153/978), as well as maps relating to gas operations, 1915–18 (WO 153/988).

WO 157/239–44 contain the *Tank Corps Intelligence Summaries, 1917–18*.

WO 158, Military Headquarters Papers, has the correspondence of the Director of Gas Services (WO 158/122–8), including discussion of gases used by the Germans in 1915 (WO 158/122); British gas casualties, 1915–18 (WO 158/123); gas shells used at Messines (WO 158/126); and the gas shell activity report for the Hundred Days (WO 158/128). Material on tanks includes Tank Corps HQ papers for Cambrai (WO 158/430–32), but also a range of other papers (WO 158/798–830). These include histories of the Heavy Branch, Machine Gun Corps and the Central Ordnance Workshops (WO 158/798 and 809); material on tank production and supply (WO 158/801, 813); training in infantry–tank co-operation (WO 158/803); correspondence between Generals Anley and Elles, April to May 1917 (WO 158/814); correspondence of Tank Corps HQ in France, 1917–18 (WO 158/816–17); conferences on tank policy (WO 158/81–19 and 830); a note on the origin of the Tank Committee (WO 158/812); and correspondence on the work of Lieutenant Colonel S. Stern as Controller of the Mechanical Warfare Department and as British Commissioner for Mechanical Warfare, May to July 1918 (WO 158/826). There are also GHQ papers on the employment of tanks (WO 158/831–45 and 854–69), which include general correspondence (WO 158/833 and 835); tactical evaluations (WO 158/831–2, 834, and 854); reports on tank operations (WO 158/839); records of conferences on various aspects of tank policy (WO 158/840–41, and 861); co-operation with other arms (WO 158/855–6); a memorandum by the CIGS in July 1918 on a planned tank offensive for 1919 (WO 158/842); and minutes of the Tank Committee, 1917–18, and of the Tank Board, 1918–19 (WO 158/859 and 867).

Papers of GHQ Mesopotamia include some on anti-gas measures, 1917–18 (WO 158/659–60).

WO 161, miscellaneous unregistered wartime papers, includes the record of chemical supplies for offensive purposes, 1915–16 (WO 161/1); and a history of military mechanical transport, 1914–18 (WO 161/7). Various papers generated by the Master-General of the Ordnance (WO 161/22–7) include the supply of arms and ammunition to the New Armies, 1914–15 (WO 161/22); and material on tanks, including reports on Whippet tanks, tank output and conferences (WO 161/24–7). Papers of the Works Directorate include a list of hospitals, depots and camps constructed (WO 161/2).

WO 162/8 contains papers on Lord Dundonald's invention of a combustible compound, 1914.

WO 186/4 has trial reports from the Royal Artillery Establishment at Shoeburyness, 1914–18.

WO 188 has papers of the Chemical Defence Establishment. Initially established in 1916 as the War Department Experimental Ground, it moved to Porton after the war. Most relate to developments after 1918, but there is some wartime material including improvements to respirators (WO 188/1); research reports on chemical weapons and compounds (WO 188/143, 156–9, and 191); and chemical weapons intelligence reports (WO 188/767).

Of course, an alternative to the deadlock on the Western Front was bypassing it through another theatre. The origin of the Gallipoli campaign was the decision by the War Council on 15 January 1915 to knock Turkey out of the war and open up the supply route to Russia through the Dardanelles initially through a naval expedition. After an abortive attempt to force a passage of the Straits with capital ships on 18 March 1915, a military expedition was mounted on only six weeks' notice in order to land British and Anzac forces at Helles and Suvla on the Gallipoli peninsula and French forces on the Asiatic coast on 25 April 1915. These and subsequent landings in the Suvla and Anzac sectors in August 1915 failed to achieve their objectives, the catalogue of operational failures leading to the evacuation of allied forces in December 1915 and January 1916.

Turkish entry to the war had been of particular concern since the Turks could pose a threat to Britain's Middle Eastern oil interests, centred on the operations of the Anglo-Persian Oil Company in the Persian Gulf, and to control of the Suez Canal. In the event, a Turkish attempt on the Canal was thrown back in February 1915 and, by March 1916, Britain had also contained the Senussi in the Western Desert, these long-term opponents of Italian control of Libya having been persuaded by the Turks to harass allied forces. With the threat to Egypt at an end, the British launched their own offensive into the Sinai and Palestine in March 1917, the British advance being supported by a second front against the Turks resulting from encouragement by T. E. Lawrence and others of an Arab revolt in the Hejaz since June 1916. Ultimately, British forces took Jerusalem in December 1917 and Damascus in October 1918.

The Government of India, meanwhile, had committed Indian army forces to Mesopotamia in November 1914, capturing Basra. Initial success encouraged advances along both the Tigris and Euphrates and, ultimately, an attempt on Baghdad. Forced back, a British and Indian force was besieged in Kut in December 1915 and compelled to surrender in April 1916. Following reorganisation, British and Indian forces renewed their advance in December 1916, taking Baghdad in March 1917.

The failures at the Dardanelles and in Mesopotamia both resulted in official enquiries by Royal Commissions under the Special Commissions (Dardanelles and Mesopotamia) Act, 1916. Designed by Asquith to ward off criticism, their reports in 1917 were a damning indictment of his government.

ADM 1 has operational orders for the Royal Naval Division at the Dardanelles in July 1915 (ADM 1/8427/197); gunnery reports on firing and indication methods at the Dardanelles (ADM 1/8440/335); naval dispatches on the Dardanelles (ADM 1/8553/76); and information on the use of small river gunboats in Mesopotamia, December 1915 (ADM 1/8441/354).

ADM 116 has material on the Dardanelles Commission (ADM 116/1437B and C, and 1713–14); reports on the operations at the Dardanelles (ADM 116/1432–4); and technical reports on ships' firing during the campaign (ADM 116/1451).

ADM 137/2168 deals with the landing at Suvla in August 1915.

ADM 238/16 contains information on prize bounties in the Mesopotamia campaign, 1914–15.

AIR 1 includes an account of Commander G. R. Samson's experiences at Gallipoli, June 1915 (AIR 1/7/6/172); a report on the date of Turkish mine laying at the Dardanelles, March 1915 (AIR 1/2327/223/76/1); other material on the Dardanelles campaign (AIR 1/681/21/13/2209); material on the work of the RNAS Armoured Car Division in Egypt (AIR 1/11/15/1/41–4); papers of HQ, RFC in the Middle East and of the Alexandria Seaplane Squadron (AIR 1/1638–49, and 1971); operational files of the Egyptian Expeditionary Force, 1915–18 (AIR 1/2283–94); a resumé of Middle Eastern air operations, April–August 1917 (AIR 1/36/15/1/244–7); the RNAS contribution to operations aimed at neutralising the *Goeben* and *Breslau* in January 1918 (AIR 1/271/15/226/121, and 661/17/122/659); reports and photographs from Mesopotamia, 1916 (AIR 1/121/15/40/110, 432/15/260/26, and 439–41); an aerial photograph of Kut (AIR 1/733/186/1); a report and photographs from Egypt, 1916 (AIR 1/449/15/307/1); unit material from the Middle East (AIR 1/2328–84); and correspondence on the Arab revolt (AIR 1/2413/303/9). There are also copies of the reports of the Dardanelles and Mesopotamia Commissions (AIR 1/232/223/53/1 and 4).

AIR 2 has RFC communiqués from Mesopotamia, 1916–18 (AIR 2/940), and photographs and reports from Palestine, 1918–19 (AIR 2/98/D 12917).

CAB 1 has some material on the Dardanelles (CAB 1/12, 14, and 33/6) among the Cabinet papers collected by Sir James Masterton-Smith. There is also a report on Mesopotamia in July 1916 (CAB 1/19), and material on the Mesopotamia Commission (CAB 1/24–5). In addition, there is a paper on the defence of Mecca from December 1916 (CAB 1/21), and on Turkish war finance from July 1918 (CAB 1/27).

CAB 17, miscellaneous papers of the Committee of Imperial Defence, has correspondence on the Dardanelles campaign (CAB 17/123–8); on the publication of reports on the campaign (CAB 17/132); and on the Dardanelles Commission (CAB 17/184). There is also material on the Mesopotamia Commission (CAB 17/173 and 191). In addition, there are papers on Middle Eastern policy including the Arab Revolt; copies of the *Arab Bulletin*; and proceedings of the sub-committee on the control of operations in the Hejaz, 1917 (CAB 17/174–9, and 192–3).

CAB 19 contains the reports and supporting correspondence of the Dardanelles and Mesopotamia Commissions. The first, supplementary and final reports of the Dardanelles Commission (CAB 19/1) are supported by statements and documents produced by witnesses before giving evidence, arranged alphabetically (CAB 19/28–31); additional statements and documents from witnesses after giving evidence (CAB 19/32); and a record of the 89 days of proceedings (CAB 19/33). The report and proceedings of the Mesopotamia Commission (CAB 19/2–27) include the actual report and a minority report by Commander Josiah Wedgwood MP (CAB 19/26); a record of the proceedings of the first 43 days in manuscript (CAB 19/2–7); printed statements of evidence and appendices as submitted on the 44th day, of which no detailed record was made (CAB 19/8); the secretary's minute book recording proceedings of days 45–60 of the enquiry (CAB 19/9); correspondence with principal figures such as Generals Sir John Nixon, Sir Edmund Barrow and Sir Beauchamp Duff (CAB 19/10–20); and statements to the House of Commons in manuscript form (CAB 19/21–5).

CAB 21 contains registered files of the Cabinet Office dealing with naval and military measures for the support of the Arab Revolt and a report on the Hejaz operations (CAB 21/10 and 75); plans for operations in Syria (CAB 21/13); a memorandum by Captain Orsmby-Gore on the campaigns in Palestine and Syria (CAB 21/15); policy in Mesopotamia and Egypt (CAB 21/60–61 and 76); reforms in the Indian army as a result of the failures in Mesopotamia (CAB 21/64–5); and the reports of the Dardanelles and Mesopotamia Commissions (CAB 21/69–70).

CAB 24/143–5, the 'Eastern' reports to the War Cabinet, 1917–19, include copies of the *Arab Bulletin* of the Arab Bureau.

CAB 27 contains papers of the Cabinet Committees on Egyptian administration, 1917 (CAB 27/12), Mesopotamia Administration, 1917 (CAB 27/22), and the Middle East, 1918 (CAB 27/23). The latter absorbed the Mesopotamia Administration Committee in July 1917 and then merged in March 1918 with the Russia Committee (from the Foreign Office) and the Persia Committee (an inter-departmental committee) as the Eastern Committee, whose minutes and memoranda for 1918–19 are also included in the series (CAB 27/24–39). The Eastern Committee, which combined discussion of Middle Eastern and Central Asian affairs was dissolved in January 1919. There is also material from the Asiatic Turkey sub-committee of the Committee of Imperial Defence, July 1915 (CAB 27/1).

CAB 42 has the report of the sub-committee of the Committee of Imperial Defence on the strategic situation in Mesopotamia, October 1915 (CAB 42/4/7) and papers of the Asiatic Turkey sub-committee, 1915 (CAB 42/3/12).

CAB 44, containing various narratives utilised in the compilation of the Official Histories, includes a translation of the memoirs of the German commander of the Turkish Fifth Army at the Dardanelles, Liman von Sanders, 1920 (CAB 44/13); Turkish accounts of the campaign in Mesopotamia (CAB 44/32–6); a printed copy of *The Advance of the Egyptian Expeditionary Force*, 1919 (CAB 44/12); correspondence between the CIGS, Sir William Robertson, and the GOC in Egypt, Sir Archibald Murray, 1916–17 as printed in 1932 (CAB 44/15); and a 1927 paper by the Foreign Office on relations between Britain, Italy and the Senussi, 1912–24 (CAB 44/14).

CAB 45, correspondence and papers relating to the compilation of the Official Histories, has material on Egypt and Palestine (CAB 45/75–80), including extracts from a report on T. E. Lawrence's journey from Wejh to Nekl selected by Sir Reginald Wingate (CAB 45/76); and original correspondence (CAB 45/78–80). Material on Mesopotamia (CAB 45/85–99) includes extracts from Townshend's diary and that of T. Fraser (CAB 45/86 and 96–8); original correspondence (CAB 45/90–91); and Turkish accounts (CAB 45/87). On the Dardanelles (CAB 45/215–17, and 219–61), there is an account of the landing on Y Beach in April 1915 by Commander Adrian Keyes (CAB 45/216); diaries of Major Generals Cunliffe-Owen and Egerton (CAB 45/246 and 249); original correspondence (CAB 45/241–5); and coverage of a temporary armistice in May 1915 for the burial of the dead (CAB 45/239). Amongst miscellaneous material is a Turkish account on the fall of Baghdad (CAB 45/291).

CAB 63, the so-called 'Magnus opus' files of Sir Maurice Hankey as secretary successively to the War Council, Dardanelles Committee, War Committee and War Cabinet, includes correspondence between Churchill and Fisher on the Dardanelles, January–May 1915 (CAB 63/4); correspondence between Asquith and Hankey and others on the Dardanelles, July–August 1915 (CAB 63/7); other Dardanelles correspondence and memoranda, including on supplies and stores (CAB 63/8–11); and memoranda and minutes produced by Hankey as evidence to the Dardanelles Commission (CAB 63/17–18).

CN 5/2 has aerial photographs taken by the RFC in Palestine and Mesopotamia, 1917–19.

FO 141, papers of the British Embassy and Consulates in Egypt, has much on Arab affairs and the Arab Revolt (FO 141/453, 456, 460–2, 464, 516, 545, 668, 736, 738, 746, 749, and 825), including reports of the Arab Bureau (FO 141/738), files on T. E. Lawrence (FO 141/453 and 516), and the role of the French Military Mission in the Hejaz (FO 141/609). There is also coverage of the operations against the Senussi in the Western Desert (FO 141/652–3, and 746), and the wider war against Turkey (FO 141/527, 732, 735 and 803), including movements of enemy aircraft (FO 141/796), and the work of the Egyptian Labour Corps (FO 141/667 and 797–8).

FO 170/987–8 also contain material on the threat of the Senussi from the perspective of the British embassy in Rome, 1916.

FO 371, the correspondence and papers of the Foreign Office's Political Departments, including the War Department, 1914–20, includes general material on political, trade and other relations under the heading of Egypt – War (FO 3712353–7, 2668–72, and 2929–32).

FO 686/1–149 contain the papers of the Jeddah Agency, 1916–25. There are papers on the origins of the Arab Revolt, including the proclamation of Hussein, the Sherif of Mecca, announcing the reasons for his revolt (FO 686/7); material on Hussein and his sons (FO 686/33–49); Hussein's views on his future status (FO 686/11); the raising of Arab forces (FO 686/52, 58); tribal operations against the Turks (FO 686/10, 54–6); and intelligence reports (FO 686/6). There is also correspondence with the Sirdar, Sir Reginald Wingate, from 1916 (FO 686/66).

FO 882 contains bound volumes of miscellaneous correspondence of the Arab Bureau, 1914–20, arranged as the A, B and C series (FO 882/2–24) and copies of numbers 1–114 of the *Arab Bulletin*, 1916–19 (FO 882/25–8). There are integral indices to Series B and C in the bound volumes (FO 882/19–20), and a separate index to Series A (FO 882/1).

HO 45/331607 contains the reports of both the Dardanelles and Mesopotamia Commissions.

HO 139/23 is concerned, in part, with the Official Press Bureau's treatment of the Dardanelles campaign (HO 139/23), and the surrender of Kut (HO 139/40).

MT 23 deals with the appointment of a naval transport officer to supervise the Dardanelles landing operations in April 1915 (MT 23/355), and the question of priorities regarding the conveyance of reinforcements to, and the evacuation of, wounded from the Dardanelles (MT 23/427).

PRO 30/30/20 contains general correspondence on Mesopotamia from the papers of Lord Milner as Secretary of State for War, including a map marked as 'Lawrence's map'.

PRO 30/57 contains Kitchener's correspondence and papers relating to the Dardanelles campaign, including his own visit to Gallipoli (PRO 30/57/61–6), and those relating to the affairs of Egypt, 1914–16 (PRO 30/57/45–8). In addition, there are papers by Kitchener's biographer, Sir George Arthur, on the Dardanelles Commission (PRO 30/57/92).

WO 32 includes material on the Dardanelles, including an appreciation of the situation in the Mediterranean by Sir Ian Hamilton in 1915 (WO 32/5605); Hamilton's instructions (WO 32/5594); possible Greek co-operation (WO 32/5654); and reports on operations (WO 32/5118–19 and 5123). There were allegations of atrocities on both sides (WO 32/5116 and 5603–4). From Mesopotamia, there are a large number of dispatches and reports (WO 32/5197, 5200–202, 5206, 5210–14, 5217, and 5220), and details of the financial assistance provided to Russian forces in Persia to enable them to co-operate with the British in Mesopotamia, 1917–20 (WO 32/5619). The fall of Kut was an embarrassment (WO 32/5192, 5204 and 5207), and publication of material on it posed a particular problem (WO 32/5193–6, and 5198–9). From the Hejaz are reports by the Sirdar of the Egyptian army, Sir Reginald Wingate, and others (WO 32/5327 and 5577–9), and the request by T. E. Lawrence and Emir Faisal for tanks and other equipment in 1918 (WO 32/5729). There are also dispatches and reports from Egypt and Palestine (WO 32/5131 and 5134), and consideration of the forces to be retained in Egypt, Palestine and the Middle East after the war (WO 32/3514).

WO 33 has printed telegrams on the war in the Mediterranean (WO 33/731, 747–8, 760, and 820); a report on Ayas Bay in Syria (WO 33/738); dispatches from the

GOC in Egypt, Sir John Maxwell, 1915 (WO 33/796); the war establishment for Egypt, 1917 (WO 33/838); and printed telegrams on Egypt and Constantinople, 1916–17 (WO 33/887, 905, 935, 946, 952, 960, 965, and 974).

WO 79, miscellaneous private papers, includes correspondence of Sir Archibald Murray as CIGS relating to the Dardanelles (WO 79/53) and to Murray's tenure of the command in Egypt and Palestine (WO 79/64). Those of Lieutenant-General the Earl of Cavan, commanding XIV Corps, also have reference to the Middle East, 1916–17 (WO 79/66). Papers of Major-General Sir William Thomson include maps of Mesopotamia and Turkey, 1915–17, and the order in battle of the Mesopotamia Expeditionary Force in January 1919 (WO 79/91–5). In addition, there are field notes on Mesopotamia compiled in 1917 by Lieutenant Ockleford, RFA (WO 79/86).

WO 95 has the unit war diaries for GHQ, Mediterranean Expeditionary Force, its branches and troops, and those of Corps and Divisions under command (WO 95/4263–4359), including the Anzacs (WO 95/4326–54), and Royal Naval Division units on Mudros, 1916 (WO 95/4949). Those for the Middle East embrace Egypt, Palestine, Syria, including within Egypt those of the Suez Canal defences; Delta, Western, Eastern and North Forces; and the Alexandria, Cairo and Kantara Districts (WO 95/4360–755). There are also the diaries for units serving in Mesopotamia and post-war Iraq (WO 95/4965–5041 and 5052–288).

WO 106 has material on the Dardanelles (WO 106/704–9, 1462–7, 1534–41, and 1558), including the initial concept (WO 106/1463 and 1539); the naval operations (WO 106/1465); naval orders for the landing in April 1915 (WO 106/705); an account of signal work (WO 106/704); appreciations of future prospects, October–November 1915 (WO 106/1467); and evacuation (WO 106/1541). Mesopotamia is also covered (WO 106/52–5, 877–924, 944–5, and 1554–7), including a report on the genesis of the campaign and a critical study undertaken in 1925 (WO 106/877 and 923–4); a diary of operations (WO 106/883); dispatches (WO 106/914–17); material on the decision to advance on Baghdad and the resulting failure at Kut (WO 106/893–4, 903, 907, and 947); and a copy of the report of the Mesopotamia Commission (WO 106/911). From Egypt, there are daily diaries of Major E. M. Woodward, 1915–16, and telegrams between the War Office and the Egyptian Expeditionary Force (WO 106/14 and 43). There is also other material on Egypt and Palestine (WO 106/710–31 and 1542–5) including the defence of the Suez Canal (WO 106/712); and naval co-operation with Allenby's forces (WO 106/724). There is also material on operations in South Arabia and against the Senussi in Cyrenaica (WO 106/591, and 672–7).

There is consideration of the future of Egypt and the Middle East generally, including Arab and Zionist aims (WO 106/189–209, and 321), and reports, including maps and sketches, of Turkey in Asia Minor and the lines of communication between Turkey and Persia (WO 106/63–5, and 173). Other material on Turkey (WO 106/1415–46, 1469, 1472–5, 1568–9, and 5978–81) includes consideration of Turkish war aims (WO 106/1415), consideration in November 1914 of possible offensive operations that could be taken against Turkey (WO 106/1469); possibilities of attacking Constantinople (WO 106/1473); notes on the Turkish army (WO 106/1472); military and political reports (WO 106/1417–32); Turkish forces in the Lebanon (WO 106/1568–9); and military reports on the Marara region (WO 106/5978–81). There is also material on the proposed attack on Alexandretta in Syria, one of the alternative strategies considered alongside that of the Darda-nelles campaign (WO 106/1570).

WO 107/38–44 contain papers of the Quartermaster-General's Department at the War Office relating to the Dardanelles campaign, 1915–16 (WO 107/38–44), and Mesopotamia (WO 107/47–52).

WO 123 has General Routine Orders for Egypt and the Mediterranean, 1915–20 (WO 123/280–82), and for Mesopotamia, 1916–18 (WO 123/290).

WO 153 contains situation, operational and extracted war diary maps for Mesopo-tamia, 1914–18 (WO 153/998–1004, 1031–2, 1204, 1214–15, and 1342–3); situation, operational and extracted war diary maps for Egypt and Palestine, 1916–18 (WO 153/1033–48, 1200, and 1211); and operational maps including artillery maps for the Dardanelles (WO 153/1049–61, and 1199), as well as panoramas and sketches (WO 153/1335–40).

WO 154, Supplementary War Diaries, originally extracted from WO 95 due to their sensitive material, cover GHQ and LOC units for Gallipoli (WO 154/115–20). For Egypt and Palestine they cover GHQ Branches and Services (WO 154/121–52), Divisions (WO 154/153–77), and LOC (WO 154/178). For Mesopotamia, they include that of the Provost Marshal (WO 154/239), and also cover Corps and Divisions (WO 154/240–87).

WO 157, Intelligence Summaries, covers the Dardanelles campaigns (WO 157/647–86). Those for Egypt and Palestine include *Political, Economic and Intelligence Summaries*, 1918 (WO 157/735); intelligence papers, 1915–18 (WO 157/736–8), in-cluding part of a dispatch by T. E. Lawrence; and telegrams between the British ambassador in Athens and the GOC, Egypt, August–October 1915 (WO 157/739). There are also summaries for the Eastern Force covering the defence of the Suez Canal, 1916–17 (WO 157/740–47); and for Mesopotamia (WO 157/776–1111), which include weekly intelligence reports to the GOC on Indian and Middle Eastern affairs, 1916–17 (WO 157/776–824), and Corps and Division summaries (WO 157/868–1111).

WO 158, Military Headquarters Papers, has papers of GHQ Mediterranean dealing with the Dardanelles campaign (WO 158/573–600), many of which concern the evacuation of the British and Dominion forces in December 1915 and January 1916 (WO 158/575, 578, 580–81, 584–95, and 598–9). In addition, there are papers on the landings at Suvla in August 1915 (WO 158/889); on the armistice for burial of the dead in May 1915 (WO 158/921); and on a post-war examination of the Turkish defences of the Dardanelles (WO 158/796). Papers for Egypt, Palestine and the Middle East (WO 158/601–45) include minutes of CinC's conferences, August–October 1917 (WO 158/612); consideration of political questions, 1918–19 (WO 158/619); and material on the Arab Revolt (WO 158/624–42), including the supply of arms, equipment and finance to the Hejaz (WO 158/628 and 630); RFC co-operation with the Arab forces (WO 158/644); the recruitment of the Arab legion (WO 158/631–3); and reports, notes and sketch maps by T. E. Lawrence (WO 158/640B).

There are also further reports including those relating to the defence of the Suez Canal (WO 158/890–91, and 922–6); correspondence on the Zion Mule Corps, 1915–16 (WO 158/966); and handbooks and reports on routes in Egypt and the Hejaz (WO 158/985–8). Papers of GHQ Mesopotamia (WO 158/655–708) include a report from Kut by Townshend, September 1915 (WO 158/656); the Turkish dispositions at Ctesiphon in November and December 1915 (WO 158/663A); operations after the fall of Kut (WO 158/675); aviation questions, 1915–16 (WO 158/682–4); and reports by Tigris Corps, 1915–16 (WO 158/693–5). There are also additional Mesopotamia reports (WO 158/893–4).

WO 160/23 has printed assessments of various personalities in southern Syria, May 1917.

WO 161 contains a short undated account of the Dardanelles campaign (WO 161/4); a letter of Sir William Birdwood dating from 1924 on the dispatch of the Anzacs to Gallipoli (WO 161/84); material on transport services in Mesopotamia (WO 161/14–16); and correspondence of the Director of Fortifications and Works in Egypt and Palestine, 1916–18 (WO 161/32–72), including memoranda of the Engineer in Chief (WO 161/63), and material on water supplies (WO 161/65–72). In addition, there is a copy of the printed account, *The Advance of the Egyptian Expeditionary Force*, 1918 (WO 161/81).

WO 301 consists of maps of the Dardanelles Campaign, with additional maps prepared for the Dardanelles Commission and the Official History, and post-war maps of Turkey. In some cases, the failures at the Dardanelles originated in poor topographical intelligence and allegedly inaccurate and inadequate maps. Such British maps of the area as existed before the campaign were either legacies from the Crimean War or derived from obsolete Turkish sources. Advantage was taken of the fortuitous capture of more reliable modern Turkish maps since ground survey was impossible and, in any case, there was a lack of trained survey and mapping staff in GHQ, MEF and an initial lack of suitable aircraft, photographic equipment and trained observers. Some panoramas were made from naval vessels.

Included are reports on British, Anzac and Turkish mapping (WO 301/45–9); general British, French and Turkish topographical maps (WO 301/50–471); maps and diagrams from the Official History, *Military Operations: Gallipoli* (WO 301/655–67); and maps for the Dardanelles Commission (WO 301/635). Among the British, French, and Turco-German operational material (WO 301/472–634) are intelligence and planning maps, photographs and diagrams (WO 301/472–515); sketches and panoramas (WO 301/516–28); position diagrams and trench maps (WO 301/529–618), including one set of photographic reproductions of maps supposedly marked up by Liman von Sanders (WO 301/618); naval operational material, mostly at 1:24 000 and 1:26 000 scale and including boat loading and towing diagrams (WO 301/619–27); and signal communications and air operations diagrams, including aircraft silhouettes and aiming diagrams (WO 301/628–34). There are a series of graphical and textual indices (WO 301/1–44).

WO 302 comprises maps of the Mesopotamia campaign, many produced by the Survey of India and bearing Tigris Corps (TC) numbers, a label which continued to be used after the corps had lost its unique mapping functions. Maps were also produced by the War Office Geographical Section, General Staff, and General Staff India, often using the civil map production organisations of the Ordnance Survey and the Survey of India, but with a wide variety of scales. The class is variously arranged by scales, origin of maps and area, including TC maps (WO 302/38–538); maps issued by GHQ without TC numbers (WO 302/539–44); general maps and surveys of Mesopotamia and Persia (WO 302/574–666); town maps and surveys, including a photographic mosaic of Baghdad (WO 302/545–55); maps of Basra (WO 302/556–73); maps of the Tigris (WO 302/667–85); general maps of eastern Turkey (WO 302/686–98, and 777–85); degree sheets (WO 302/699–750); German maps to the 1:400 000 scale (WO 302/751–74); and maps extracted from printed reports (WO 302/786–826). There are various graphic indices including contents list, an explanation of abbreviations used on the maps and in the catalogues, and a table of Imperial scales with their equivalent representative fractions (WO 302/1–37).

WO 303 contains maps of the Palestine campaign, mostly produced by the Survey of Egypt, using such sources as those of the Palestine Exploration Fund, the work of the 7th Field Survey Company RE, and Turkish and German maps. Many new techniques of exploiting aerial photographs were developed in producing these maps. The series includes a report on the publication history of the maps of both the Palestine Exploration Fund and the Survey of Egypt (WO 303/17). The series is mostly arranged by region. There are small-scale topographical maps (WO 303/18–39); maps of the Western Desert (WO 303/40–70); topographical maps of Egypt (WO 303/71–119); topographical maps of the Canal Zone and Sinai (WO 303/120–99), including a folder of maps captured from the Turkish VIII Corps (WO 303/133); topographical maps of Palestine (WO 303/200–320); and topographical maps of Syria, Transjordan and the Hejaz (WO 303/434–84). Operational maps (WO 303/321–433) are on various scales, while there are also special maps including those of British front line positions and battle sites (WO 303/485–94), and maps of towns, railways and water supplies (WO 303/495–514). There are various indices (WO 303/1–16).

WO 317 consists of photographs of the Dardanelles campaign. There is a general album (WO 317/1); photographs of 'Brighton', Ocean Beach and V Beaches (WO 317/2, 4 and 7); photographs of the SS *River Clyde* (WO 317/3); views of Suvla, the Straits and Gallipoli from the sea (WO 317/5, 8, and 10–12); various panoramas (WO 317/6 and 9); and a list of photographs taken by Captain J. J. Ball (WO 317/14).

Failure at the Dardanelles shifted Anglo-French hopes in the Mediterranean to Salonika, whence another allied expedition was dispatched as a means of assisting Serbia, already facing defeat at the hands of Austro-Hungarian and German forces and which had come under even greater pressure when Bulgaria joined the Central Powers in October 1915. In the event, the allied forces were confined at Salonika until breaking out in September 1918, hence the German gibe that it had represented their largest internment camp. Bulgaria had been encouraged to enter the war by the allied failure at the Dardanelles. Elsewhere in the Mediterranean, the Italian entry to the war on the allied side in May 1915 had been one consequence of the high expectations of the beginning of the same campaign. It was not until the major Italian defeat at the hands of German and Austro-Hungarian forces at Caporetto in October 1917, however, that British forces were transferred to the Italian theatre, staging a major offensive in October 1918.

ADM 137 has material on the supply and then evacuation to Corfu of the Serbian army (ADM 137/1153); and a paper on the situation in the Balkans, 1915–22, by Admiral Lord Mark Kerr (ADM 137/4178).

AIR 1 includes papers on the RFC at Salonika, 1916–18 (AIR 1/129/15/40/198, and 1686–94); and a report on the Italian war effort, 1915–18 (AIR 1/684/21/13/2237).

AIR 2/5/87/1782 has details of a bomb used to bring down a German plane attacking a balloon at Salonika in November 1917.

CAB 17, miscellaneous papers of the Committee of Imperial Defence, includes correspondence on Salonika and the Balkans (CAB 17/113, 131, 168, and 186) as well as on the situation in Romania in 1916 (CAB 17/163–4). There is also consideration of combined operations on the Italian front, 1916 (CAB 17/151).

CAB 21 includes, among registered files of the Cabinet Office, more proposals for combined operations on the Italian front, 1917 (CAB 21/11); reports on the situation at Salonika and the Italian military contribution there (CAB 21/16, 46 and 51); papers on military support for Italy, 1917 (CAB 21/89); and supplies for the Serbian army at Salonika, 1918 (CAB 21/117).

CAB 45 has some material on the Italian Front (CAB 45/83–4) used in the compilation of the Official History, including the official report of the convention on Anglo-Italian military co-operation, 1917 (CAB 45/83). There are also accounts and narratives of the war in the Balkans (CAB 45/2–5).

DSIR 23/821 and **854** deal with winds over Macedonia as observed from balloons, 1916.

FO 141 includes information of the Italian high command, 1916–17 (FO 141/796) and on Italy and the war, 1914–16 (FO 141/636) among papers of the British embassy in Cairo. There is also information on Greece and the war, 1915–18 (FO 141/746), and on the treatment of Greek civilians in Egypt in the event of war (FO 141/817).

FO 195/2459 and **3084** deal with the Austro-Serbian war in 1914 as seen from the perspective of the British embassy in Constantinople prior to Turkey's entry into the war.

PRO 30/57/84 contains Kitchener's correspondence relating to Italy, 1915–16.

WO 32 contains various reports on the situation in the Balkans, 1915–18 (WO 32/5120, 5122, 5124, 5130, 5593, 5836, and 10695). There is the final report on the Salonika campaign by Sir George Milne (WO 32/5127). There is also a file on the dispatch of British troops to Italy in 1917 (WO 32/4999), and dispatches and field returns from the Italian theatre, 1917–18 (WO 32/5000–5003).

WO 33 has a report on the Salonika to Uskub railway, 1915 (WO 33/707); Salonika war establishments (WO 33/787, 849 and 922); Italy telegrams (WO 33/951); and a military report on Anatolia, 1918 (WO 33/2849).

WO 79, containing miscellaneous private papers, has papers of Lieutenant-General the Earl of Cavan relating to his command of British troops in Italy, 1917–19 (WO 79/67–8) and his draft account of the campaign (WO 79/79). There are also maps and plans of telegraph and telephone lines and signals stations at Salonika in 1916 among the papers of Major-General Sir William Thomson (WO 79/103–4).

WO 95 has the unit war diaries for formations serving at Salonika and in Macedonia generally including the immediate post-war occupation of Turkey (WO 95/4756–949 and 4961–4).

WO 106 covers Austro-Hungarian operations in Albania, 1917–18 (WO 106/592–4), and there is much material on Italy (WO 106/746–865, and 1548–50). This includes reports by the British Military Mission (WO 106/761–2 and 772); reports and impressions of the Italian army (WO 106/757 and 773); the dispatch of British artillery and troops in 1917 (WO 106/781, 784–5, 798, and 1548–50); unrest and poor morale in Italy after Caporetto (WO 106/807 and 813–14); and operational reports on the British and allied victory at Vittorio Veneto (WO 106/937 and 846). Salonika is also represented (WO 106/1334–97, and 1566), including secret telegrams on the campaign (WO 106/1336–41, and 1364–70); reports of the British Adriatic Mission and of the British Mission to the Serbian army (WO 106/1344, 1346–7, and 1350); correspondence with the French (WO 106/1355 and 1387); and consideration of Salonika's possible evacuation in 1918 WO 106/1383). There is additional material on Serbia (WO 106/1398–1410, and 1567), including the withdrawal of the Serbian army to Corfu (WO 106/1407).

WO 107/53–62 deal with aspects of the Salonika campaign, 1915–16, concerning the Quartermaster-General's Department at the War Office.

WO 123 contains General Routine Orders for Italy, 1917–20 (WO 123/279), and Salonika, 1915–20 (WO 123/293).

WO 153 contains general and operational maps for the Italian front, 1915–18 (WO 153/734, 755–84, 1198 and 1210); and situation and war diary maps for Salonika, 1915–18 (WO 153/1005–30, 1202, and 1212–13). There are also diagrams of the carriage of troops in Italy by water and rail in 1918 (WO 153/1341); and charts and panoramas of Salonika (WO 153/1344–7).

WO 154 contains Supplementary War Diaries for the Salonika campaign arranged by GHQ Branches and Services (WO 154/179–218), Divisions (WO 154/219–24), and LOC (WO 154/225–33).

WO 157, Intelligence Summaries, cover both the Italian campaign (WO 157/632–46), and Salonika (WO 157/748–64), including Corps and Divisional summaries (WO 157/756–64).

WO 158, Military Headquarters Papers, includes a report on the Italian front, 1915–16, among those of GHQ in France and Flanders (WO 158/31) together with correspondence on the possible transfer of heavy artillery there in the autumn of 1917 (WO 158/50). Material from GHQ Italy (WO 158/646–54) includes papers on the reorganisation of the signals service (WO 158/646), and operational orders (WO 158/647–50). Papers of GHQ at Salonika (WO 158/754–65) include a history of the British 'Salonika Army' (WO 158/756); correspondence on Greek railways (WO 158/762); and a report on a special mission to Bulgaria in October 1918 (WO 158/765). In addition, there is a report from Salonika, May 1918 (WO 158/895); and letters and telegrams from GHQ, Salonika, December 1915 (WO 158/973).

WO 161 includes material on transport and supply at Salonika (WO 161/20–21); correspondence of the Director of Army Priority on the utilisation of munitions ordered by the Serbian government, 1917–18 (WO 161/31); and a report by the Director of Works of wartime work in Italy, 1919 (WO 161/73)

WO 162/70 contains minutes of the meetings of the military members of the Army Council on Italy, 1917.

WO 298 consists of Salonika Campaign Maps, including British, French, Italian, Serbian, Bulgarian and German maps arranged by scale, nationality and origin. There is no overall index. The maps comprise British, French and Serbians maps in 1:10 000 scale (WO 298/1–65); British, French and Italian maps in 1:20 000 scale (WO 298/66–411); Serbian maps in 1:25 000 scale (WO 298/412–69); British, French and Serbian maps in 1:50 000 scale (WO 298/470–701); British and French maps in 1:100 000 scale (WO 298/702–23); British maps in 1:200 000 scale (WO 198/724–59); British maps in 1:250 000 and 1:400 000 scale (WO 298/769–813); Serbian maps in other scales (WO 298/760–68); British triangulation diagrams (WO 298/814–31); and assorted German and Bulgarian maps (WO 298/832–5).

WO 323/1–11 consist of photographs of the Italian front, mostly panoramas and some undated.

WO 369 contains maps of the Italian campaign, initially for the support of the British Military Mission but then produced by 6th Field Survey Company RE once British forces were introduced in late 1917. The whole theatre was covered by overlapping Italian and Austro-Hungarian pre-war maps, which were adapted and enhanced to meet British requirements. Allied maps are arranged in groups of topographical, intelligence and operations/trench maps for each front, irrespective of the nationality of the producer. Austro-Hungarian maps are arranged topographically whether they bear military overprints or not. There is a report on the work of 6th Field Survey Company (WO 369/29); and photographic and drawn panoramas (WO 369/79–107). The maps themselves include large maps of the theatre of operations (WO 369/108–229); maps of Italian sections of the front (WO 369/230–314); British sectors of the Asiago and Piave fronts (WO 369/315–426); and maps of medical service sites from the papers of Professor Miles Coplans (WO 369/427–39). There are also a large number of Austro-Hungarian maps in various scales (WO 369/457–836). There are a variety of graphic and indices to British, Italian and Austro-Hungarian maps (WO 369/1–28, 440–49), together with technical instructions for the use of British and Austro-Hungarian maps (WO 369/30–78, and 450–56).

Beyond Europe and the Middle East, British forces were also engaged in the occupation of German colonies. Australian and New Zealand forces were engaged in overrunning Germany's Pacific possessions and South African forces took German South-West Africa. British forces assisted in the conquest of Togoland as early as August 1914 and in that of the German port in China, Tsingtau, in November 1914. Kamerun (Cameroon), however, did not fall until March 1916 and German forces in German East Africa only surrendered after the armistice in November 1918.

ADM 1/8467/224 contains RNAS operational reports from East Africa, September 1916.

ADM 116/1711 deals with enemy vessels captured on the African Great Lakes.

ADM 123, containing records of the Africa Station, includes material on the campaign in German South-West Africa (ADM 123/144); that in German East Africa (ADM 123/138–40); the activities of the German surface raider, *Königsberg*, sunk in the Rufigi delta in July 1915 (ADM 123/141); and operations on the Great Lakes (ADM 123/142). General material includes diaries of the Senior Naval Officer at Simonstown, sailing orders, correspondence with the Admiralty, and administrative records (ADM 123/136–7, 143, and 146–57).

ADM 125/62–6 contains the correspondence of the China Station, 1914–18.

AIR 1 has material on the supply and reinforcement of the RNAS contingent serving in East Africa, 1915 (AIR 1/148/15/77) as well as RN armoured cars there ((AIR 1/147/15/64). There is also a file on role of aircraft in the destruction of the *Königsberg* (AIR 1/674/21/6/86), and papers of the immediate post-war RAF GHQ at Dar es Salaam (AIR 1749).

AIR 2 has RFC communiqués from East Africa, 1916–17 (AIR 2/997), a report on RN Armoured Car operations there, March–April 1916 (AIR 2/35/AIR 01160/1916).

CAB 5/3 has memoranda of the Committee of Imperial Defence regarding colonial defence, 1912–21.

CAB 6/4 contains memoranda of the Committee of Imperial Defence on the defence of India, 1908–23.

CAB 7/8 contains the minutes of the Committee of Imperial Defence's Colonial and Overseas Defence Committees, 1900–16, the Colonial Defence Committee being renamed the Overseas Defence Committee in 1911.

CAB 8/6 contains 'Series M' memoranda of the Overseas Defence Committee, 1913–22.

CAB 9/19 contains 'Series R' memoranda of the Overseas Defence Committee, 1913–29, these being remarks on memoranda and on defence schemes prepared by the colonies.

CAB 11 comprises memoranda or instructions by the Colonial/Overseas Defence Committee of the Committee of Imperial Defence to Colonial Governors and GOCs concerning the preparation of local defence schemes. Pre-war consideration was given to the status of defence schemes in time of war and wartime food supplies for the Dominions (CAB 11/77 and 120). There is material on special measures taken in the Seychelles during the war and the war's impact on the islands (CAB 11/164–5); as well as special measures in the Straits Settlement (CAB 11/166). There are also reports on the Ceylon Defence Force, 1915–17, and on the Singapore and Penang Volunteer Force, 1915 (CAB 11/160–62, and 167).

CAB 17, miscellaneous papers of the Committee of Imperial Defence, includes correspondence on East Africa, 1916 (CAB 17/143), and the defence of the North-West Frontier, 1916 (CAB 17/149).

CAB 18/94–7 are returns of resources of the colonies, 1914–18.

CAB 42 has a paper and the report of the Future Operations in East Africa sub-committee of the Committee of Imperial Defence, October to November 1915 (CAB 42/4/5 and 5/15).

CAB 44 has a narrative of events in South Africa and German South-West Africa, 1914–15 (CAB 44/2), and Japanese accounts of the Tsingtau expedition (CAB 44/11).

CAB 45 contains material on African campaigns used in the compilation of the Official History (CAB 45/6–74, 110–13, and 218), including photographs of East Africa (CAB 45/11); a memorandum on the general lessons of the East African campaign (CAB 45/27); original correspondence (CAB 45/30–37); diaries, including that of Colonel R. E. Murray (CAB 45/44, and 49–56); and accounts of RNAS operations and the sinking of the *Königsberg* (CAB 45/218).

CO 445/34–45 contain dispatches on offices and individuals connected to the West African Frontier Force, 1914–18.

CO 534/18–29 contain similar material for the King's African Rifles, 1914–18.

CO 537 has material on military operations from Northern Rhodesia, and against German East Africa generally (CO 537/525–6, 592, 772); the occupation of the Caprivi strip (CO 537/580); the situation in South Africa in 1914 (CO 537/581); and a post-war report on expenditure in the King's African Rifles in relation to the campaign in East Africa (CO 537/784). There is also consideration of the administration of occupied German territories (CO 537/589–90). In addition, there are the measures to be taken on receipt of the telegrams announcing hostilities at Wei hai Wei in China (CO 537/583).

CO 649/1–6 contain Colonial Office correspondence concerning Cameroon, 1915–18.

CO 687/1–20 contain Colonial Office correspondence concerning German East Africa, 1916–18.

DO 119, correspondence of the British High Commissioner in South Africa, includes material on the operations in the Caprivi strip (DO 119/891, 897, and 904); operations against German South-West Africa (DO 119/893–5, and 910); co-operation with Belgian forces (DO 119/898 and 901); military affairs in the Rhodesias (DO 119/892, 906–7, 909, and 916); the Tanganyika Motorboat expedition intended to wrest control of Lake Tanganyika from the German lake flotilla (DO 119/908, 915, and 918–19); the administration of occupied territories (DO 119/896); the establishment of POW camps (DO 119/890); and local defence in South Africa (DO 119/889).

FO 141 deals with the political and military situation in Aden, 1915–19 (FO 141/523–4), and war measures taken in the Sudan (FO 141/587).

FO 371, correspondence of the Foreign Office Political Departments, including the War Department, 1914–20, includes files under the heading of Contract Labour (FO 371/2344–5, 2600, 2922, and 3192), dealing with native labour corps; and Africa – War (FO 371/2596–600, 2856–60, 3128–9, and 3501–2).

MT 23, papers of the Admiralty Transport Department, deals with the shipping arrangements for the transportation of the expedition to Tsingtau in 1914 (MT 23/306); that to West Africa in 1914 (MT 23/309); a Portuguese expeditionary force to Angola in 1914 (MT 23/336); and of British colonial forces from West Africa to German East Africa in 1916 (MT 23/579).

MT 25 has some material on the campaign in German East Africa among the general files of the Ministry of Shipping, 1917–18 (MT 15/1–25).

PRO 30/57/68–71 contain Kitchener's wartime correspondence relating to Indian and Far Eastern affairs, 1914–16.

WO 32 has material on the occupation of the German colonies in the Pacific (WO 32/4997), on the Tsingtau expedition (WO 32/4996B); on German seditious activities in the Far East, 1915–16 (WO 32/5347), and on British interests in Persia, 1914–16 (WO 32/5805). In terms of the African campaigns, there are reports from Cameroon, including co-operation with Belgian forces (WO 32/5320–22, 5326–7, and 5353); from Togoland (WO 32/5627 and 5788–9); from the continuing campaign against the 'Mad Mullah' in Somaliland, 1914–16 (WO 32/5809 and 5828); and from the campaign in German East Africa (WO 32/5027, 5324, 5627, 5810, 5813–17, 5819 5822–6, and 5829), including an appreciation by Sir Horace Smith-Dorrien in 1915 (WO 32/5325), information on co-operation with Belgian forces (WO 32/5811–12 and 5818) and the question of whether to publish Jan Smuts's report on the campaign in 1916 (WO 32/5820–21). There is also the consideration given to a proposed neutral zone in Central Africa in 1915 (WO 32/5204). In addition, there is a history with photographs of the East African Frontier Force's Railway Corps, 1914–19 (WO 32/5830).

WO 33 has a printed report on German South-West Africa in 1914 (WO 33/666); the West African Expeditionary Force, 1914–16 (WO 33/781); telegrams from the German East Africa campaign (WO 33/858 and 953); the Straits Settlement, 1915 (WO 33/715); the situation in the Darfur region of the Sudan, 1916 (WO 33/757).

WO 95 contains unit war diaries for all the African campaigns (WO 95/5289–5388). Even further afield are those covering India (WO 95/5389–5414), and colonies and protectorates, including Aden, Bermuda, Ceylon, Hong Kong, Gibraltar, Malta, Mauritius and Singapore (WO 95/5434–51). There is also a war diary of New Zealand's West Pacific Expeditionary Force on Samoa (WO 95/5452).

WO 106 covers continuing pacification operations on the North-West Frontier, in Burma and in Aden (WO 106/56, 58, 558–69, 636, and 732–45). On the major campaigns, there is material on German East Africa (WO 106/571–87) including on co-operation with the Belgians and Portuguese in East Africa and Belgian operations generally (WO 106/257, 580, 582, and 585); a general history of the British East African Expeditionary Force (WO 106/1490); a translation of the diary of the German Governor (WO 106/1460); the threat of Pan-Islamism in East and Central Africa (WO 106/259); monthly intelligence reports from the Sudan, 1913–18 (WO 106/6225–6); and the performance of the King's African Rifles (WO 106/273–9). Operations in German South-West Africa are also covered (WO 106/588–9), as well as Togoland (WO 106/1533); Cameroon (WO 106/638–56), and Tsingtau (WO 106/660–68). There is also wartime coverage of British colonies and protectorates (WO 106/633–5, 657–9, 669–71, 866–8, 871–6, and 1411–14), and problems facing the Indian army (WO 106/1449).

WO 107/45–6 contains papers of the Quartermaster-General's Department at the War Office relating to the campaign in German East Africa, 1915–17.

WO 123/288–9 contain General Routine Orders for East Africa, 1916–20.

WO 153 contains situation and operational maps for the East African campaign, 1914–18 (WO 153/804–12, and 1205–6).

WO 154 contains Supplementary War Diaries for the East African campaign, arranged by GHQ Branches and Services (WO 154/288–97), Divisions (WO 154/298–300), and LOC (WO 154/301–7). There are also some diaries for

Cameroon (WO 154/308–9); India (WO 154/310–11); Aden (WO 154/312–15); Hong Kong (WO 154/316–24); Malta (WO 154/325); the Straits Settlement (WO 154/326); and the New Zealand Western Pacific Expeditionary Force on Samoa, 1914 (WO 154/327).

WO 157, Intelligence Summaries, include those for East Africa (WO 157/1112–82); Cameroon (WO 157/1183–1200); India (WO 157/1234–46); Persia (WO 157/1247–64); Aden, 1916–18 (WO 157/1265–97); and Hong Kong, 1914–15 (WO 157/1298).

WO 158, Military Headquarters Papers, has those of GHQ East Africa (WO 158/439–513) including patrol and road reports 1914–16 (WO 158/445–58); reports on Portuguese East Africa and reports and telegrams on the Portuguese forces (WO 158/468–79); preparations for the defence of Entebbe, Mombassa and Nairobi (WO 158/483, 485–94, and 505–6); and operational reports, which include investigation of an alleged atrocity involving the 2nd East African Division and 1st South African Mounted Brigade in 1916 (WO 158/513). Additional material (WO 158/872–88, and 903–7) includes arrangements for treating Belgian troops and native porters (WO 158/877); more on the defence of Mombassa and Nairobi (WO 158/885 and 888); and the eventual surrender of the German commander, Paul von Lettow Vorbeck (WO 158/905–7). Material from Cameroon (WO 158/514–66) includes correspondence with the War Office, 1914–16 (WO 158/514–16); routine orders (WO 158/529–33); reports on French operations (WO 158/555–61); lists of German casualties and POWs (WO 158/553); and correspondence on the murder of two Germans at Azameken in 1915 (WO 158/525). Additional papers (WO 158/908–20) include details of the original campaign plan from August 1914 (WO 158/908). There are a few papers from GHQ Aden (WO 158/438 and 974).

WO 159/20 has material on Cameroon among Kitchener's Private Office Papers, 1915.

WO 160/5 deals with the breakdown of the Indian army's organisation, August 1916.

WO 300 comprises maps of West, South-West and East African Campaigns. Mapping in Africa was still at a primitive stage in 1914. The German Colonial Ministry, however, had reasonably good medium scale maps of its territories and these were reproduced by the War Office. Due to the mobile nature of the campaigns, little new mapping occurred and, for many purposes, time and distance diagrams were utilised. There are general maps of Africa (WO 300/13–51); maps of various British and other territories (WO 300/52–82, 234–67, and 419–41); maps of Togo and Cameroon (WO 300/83–192); maps of German South West Africa (WO 300/193–217); and maps of German East Africa (WO 300/218–33, and 268–418), including some relating to naval and military operations for the capture and occupation of Dar es Salaam in September 1916 (WO 300/403–6). There are various indices to both British and German maps (WO 300/1–12).

It was not actually until late 1917 that there were more British troops in France and Flanders than in Britain. Partly, this was a matter of training the New Armies but home defence was also a concern. Indeed, Kitchener's fear that the Germans might invade East Anglia led to the initial holding back in Britain of two of the original six infantry divisions of the BEF, a recommendation arising from the three pre-war invasion enquiries by the Committee of Imperial Defence. The German capture of Antwerp in the autumn of 1914 increased fears, as did the German naval bombardment of east coast towns in December 1914. As late as January 1916 the official estimate was that the Germans might be able to land 160,000 men compared to the pre-war calculation of a risk of raids up to only 70,000 men. The potential threat renewed public concerns, echoing earlier invasion scares in the nineteenth century, and led to increasing pressure on government to accept the formation of new auxiliary forces for home defence. Accordingly, in November 1914, the government somewhat reluctantly recognised those units prepared to affiliate to the Central Association of Volunteer Training Corps, a body which had emerged in September. New volunteer legislation was then passed in December 1916. The scale of expected attack was only reduced to 30,000 in December 1917 and, finally, to 5,000 in September 1918.

ADM 1/8466/211 deals with the suspension in August 1916 of any Channel Tunnel scheme for the duration.

ADM 131, correspondence of the Plymouth Station, includes operational orders for dealing with enemy raids, 1914 (ADM 131/86), and the Plymouth Defence Scheme (ADM 131/91–2).

ADM 137 contains a number of files on anti-invasion measures from 1914 onwards (ADM 137/865–6, and 965–7).

ADM 183, comprising correspondence of the Royal Marines Chatham Division includes the Order Book for 1916 (ADM 183/33), the Deal Defence Orders, 1917–18 (ADM 183/40), and the Letter Book of the 5th RM Battalion, 1918–19 (ADM 183/130).

ADM 184, records of the Royal Marines Plymouth Division, includes Divisional Orders, 1914–18 (ADM 184/20 and 72–6), and General Weekly Returns, 1914–19 (ADM 184/33–4).

ADM 185/34 has the Order Book for the Royal Marines Portsmouth Division, 1916–17.

ADM 193/6 and **10** are the Order and Orderly Books of the Royal Marine Artillery, Portsmouth Division, 1917–18.

AIR 1 deals with RNAS co-operation with home defence troops in anti-invasion duties, 1917 (AIR 1/94/15/9/253); and there are also home defence notes (AIR 1/727/149/1 and 3).

AIR 9/4 has material from the papers of the Director of Air Plans on coast and port defence, 1917–34.

BT 13/59 deals with the role of wartime coast guard stations, 1914.

CAB 1/22 includes a discussion of the Channel Tunnel project in January 1917.

CAB 3/2–3 contains memoranda of the Committee of Imperial Defence on home defence, 1906–22.

CAB 12/1 has the minutes of the Home Ports Defence Committee of the Committee of Imperial Defence, 1909–23. The committee was tasked with dealing with the armament of coast defences and home ports.

CAB 13/1 contains memoranda of the Home Ports Defence Committee, 1909–21.

CAB 16/34 has papers from the ad hoc committee of the Committee of Imperial Defence on London in War, 1914.

CAB 17, miscellaneous correspondence and papers of the Committee of Imperial Defence, has material on defence against invasion, 1913–14, including consideration of the resources and economic position of London in wartime (CAB 17/32–7). In 1916 there was consideration once more of the Channel Tunnel (CAB 17/139) and, from the same year, correspondence of the Emergency Committee (CAB 17/144).

CAB 18/28 has a progress report from the Cromarty Defence Committee, 1914.

CAB 21/14 contains Sir John French's reflections on lessons for home defence as derived from the Gallipoli campaign, 1917.

CAB 42/1/41 has a paper of the Civil Population and Hostile Landing Sub-committee of the Committee of Imperial Defence, February 1915.

CUST 49/352 deals with coast watching in 1915.

WO 32 has material on the dispatch of the 6th and 8th Divisions of the BEF to France (WO 32/5082 and 5278). There are reports and memoranda on the requirements for home defence (WO 32/5266–8 and 5273), and on the protection of railways, bridges and other vulnerable points (WO 32/5271, 5279, and 9967–8). In addition, there is a report on a conference to consider the continuing possibilities of invasion in 1917 (WO 32/5274).

WO 33 contains a large amount of printed material on home forces and home defence including defence schemes (WO 33/662, 671, 694, 722, 726, 728–9, 745, 773–4, 776–7, 788–9, 794, 801–2, 813, 830, 834, 844–5, 848, 853, 862, 867, 872, 875, 877–8, 880, 885, 888–9, 891–2, 897–9, and 906), including that for use of tank companies from the Tank Training Centres at Wool and Wareham in 1918 (WO 33/899); distribution, composition and establishment of home forces (WO 33/692, 710, 719, 724, 733, 741, 749, 754, 765, 767, 772, 779, 782, 795, 797, 800, 810, 812, 814–15, 817, 823–4, 833, 835, 837, 843, 854–5, 865–6, 868–70, 876, 879, 883, 890, 894, 903–4, 909, and 929); instructions (WO 33/664, and 771); conferences (WO 33/681, and 742); and vulnerable points (WO 33/758, 792–3, and 871). In addition, there is the report of the Committee on Coast Defence Range Finding, 1918 (WO 33/910).

WO 95 contains war diaries for home forces (WO 95/5453–66), including some hospitals and depots (WO 95/6465–6).

WO 153 has orders of battle and distribution charts of Home Forces, 1914–18 (WO 153/115 and 425).

WO 107/26–8 contains correspondence of the Quartermaster-General's Department at the War Office relating to home forces, 1915–18.

WO 158, Military Headquarters Papers, has some material from GHQ Home Forces (WO 158/792–5, and 927–32) including information on the formation of cyclist battalions in August 1914 and the 2nd Mounted Division in September 1914

(WO 158/792–3); and the composition of the Central and Local Force, October 1914 (WO 158/927–9).

WO 161 includes material of the Director of Supplies and Transport, Home Forces (WO 161/6–13), including a chart of the reserve supply depot at Deptford (WO 161/11); and material on training areas by the Director of Mechanical Transport (WO 161/29–30).

WO 192, Fort Record Books, includes short histories of particular wartime coast defence batteries established at Hartlepool, South Shields, Stevenston, Tynemouth, Dover, Barry, Milford Haven, the Firth of Forth, and on the Orkneys (WO 192/87, 90, 103, 108, 195, 227B, 241–2, 254, 256, 263, 321, and 323).

The War at Sea

Some of those in Britain who opposed the commitment of large British forces to the continent believed that it would be better to use British financial muscle to bankroll allies such as France and Russia while utilising British naval power to impose an economic blockade on Germany and her allies.

Naval blockade risked alienating neutrals, not least the United States, the Anglo-American War of 1812 having centred on the issue of the rights of neutral shipping. There had been further tensions during the American Civil War (1861–5) when Britain had built Confederate commerce raiders and, more recently, during the British attempts to impose economic blockade on the Boer republics during the South African War. In February 1909, the Declaration of London saw a measure of agreement on the definition of contraband. In the event, however, fears that too much was being conceded persuaded the House of Lords to reject legislation ratifying the declaration in December 1911.

By the Order in Council of 20 August 1914 and, without formally announcing it as such, Britain thus imposed an economic blockade on the Central Powers which clearly repudiated the restrictions of belligerent rights implicit in the Declaration of London. The definition of contraband was steadily extended with the Royal Navy not only stopping shipping on the high seas, but forcing vessels into port for examination. Shipping was also impeded by British mining of the North Sea, which was declared a military area on 3 November 1914.

Generally, agreements, whether formal or on the basis of trust, were reached between the Entente and neutrals like the Netherlands, Norway, Denmark, Sweden and Switzerland whereby imported goods would not be re-exported to the Central Powers enforced, if necessary, by threats. With the intensification of the blockade in March 1915, new agreements were reached with Denmark, the Netherlands, and Switzerland, extending allied control not only over neutral imports but also exports of neutral products to the Central Powers containing more than 25 per cent imported raw materials or semi-manufactures. With Norway and, particularly, Sweden, agreements were reached on particular commodities. Where commodities were not covered by the agreements, the Entente purchased the export surplus. With the entry of the United States into the war, there was an attempt to restrict virtually all exports to the European neutrals and the blockade became far more effective.

As a result of the blockade and organisational failures within the Central Powers, food supply clearly declined though the effect was variable depending upon the proximity of a given location to agricultural areas. It is often claimed that over 762,000 Germans died from malnutrition, but there is little evidence to support this contention. Indeed, despite the difficulties and the undoubted fact that they were often hungry, Germans did not starve and while the blockade continued until July 1919 to ensure Germany's compliance with the armistice and peace terms, conditions did not markedly deteriorate further. It was essentially the psychological perception of starvation that made the greatest impact, contributing to the collapse of the military and home fronts in Germany in October and November 1918.

ADM 1, consisting of Admiralty In-letters, has some material on the blockade, including procedures for requisitioning cargoes (ADM 1/8391/265); consequences of the abolition of prize money (ADM 1/8391/284–5); seizure of German reservists on a Dutch vessel (ADM 1/8393/314); Baltic states' neutrality laws (ADM 1/8396/350); seizures of German vessels in Cameroon and of Norwegian vessels (ADM 1/8407/474–5); a paper of the Committee on the Restriction of Enemy Supplies, January 1915 (ADM 1/8408/1); the Order in Council of March 1915 (ADM 1/8414/65); compensation claims in the Prize Courts (ADM 1/8426/188); an American complaint of a patrol too close to its territorial waters in November 1915 (ADM 1/8440/338); appointment of a new secretary for Lord Peel's Committee on the Detention of Neutral Shipping, 1916 (ADM 1/8454/84); the blockade of Red Sea ports (ADM 1/8460/147); naval attaché reports on the blockade from neural states (ADM 1/8468/225); a memorandum on the work of the Trade Division, March 1918 (ADM 1/8518/74); and a report on neutral merchant shipping during the war from December 1918 (ADM 1/8547/341). A report on the work of the Marshal of the Prize Court, 1914–23, is also included (ADM 1/8693/261).

ADM 116 has a number of 'case' files of relevance to the blockade, including those dealing with enemy and neutral shipping, 1914 (ADM 116/1276–7); prize money (ADM 116/1319B–C and 1715); appeals to and decisions by the Alien Masters Committee, 1915–18 (ADM 116/1391–2); contraband traffic between Cameroon and Spain, 1915 (ADM 116/1399); the removal of enemy subjects from neutral vessels (ADM 116/1537 and 1563); the Netherlands and neutrality, 1918 (ADM 116/1628); the Overseas Prize Disposal Committee, 1914–19 (ADM 116/1687A); and the neutrality of the Panama Canal (ADM 116/1721).

ADM 123, containing records of the Africa Station, includes material on the seizure of the German merchantman, *Kamerun* (ADM 123/145), and proceedings of prize courts in South Africa, 1914–18 (ADM/158).

ADM 131/97 contains material on contraband and detention from the correspondence of the Plymouth Division.

ADM 137, which includes records of the Admiralty Trade Division (ADM 137/2733–2928) in its HSB series, has material on the Restriction of Enemy Supplies Committee, 1914–15 (ADM 137/2988–9); the Enemy Exports Committee, 1915–19 (ADM 137/2990–93); the Contraband Committee, 1915–18 (ADM 137/3000–3005);

the War Trade Advisory Committee, 19151–16 (ADM 137/2921); the Allied Blockade Committee, 1918–19 (ADM 137/2285–98, and 3011–24); the Superior Blockade Council, 1919 (ADM 137/3026–7); and the Supreme Economic Council, 1919 (ADM 137/3028–31). In addition, there are copies of proclamations (ADM 137/ 2878–80); *Shipping Black Lists*, 1915–19 (ADM 137/2979), and the *Who's Who in War Trade*, 1915–17 (ADM 137/2969–78). General blockade policy is also covered (ADM 137/1910–18), and there is material on instructions regarding contraband, traffic instructions and fishing regulations (ADM 137/2816–17).

ADM 238, comprising records of the Accounting Department's Prize Branch, includes the *Prize Branch Journal*, 1894–1935 (ADM 238/1–2), and the *Prize Branch Ledger*, 1915–21 (ADM 238/8).

ADM 268/34 has papers of the Committee on the Distribution of Prize Money, 1917.

BT 8 contains the papers of the Enemy Debts Committee, established under the chairmanship of Sir Henry Babington Smith in November 1916 to report on the arrangements for the liquidation of commercial, banking and other financial transactions between British and enemy persons, the completion of which had been prevented by the outbreak of war. The committee received oral and written evidence as well as returns of property held or managed on behalf of aliens by the Public Trustee under the Trading with the Enemy (Amendment) Act, 1914, and of debts and bank balances due to British firms or persons and of property held by enemies for British firms and persons.

Alongside the committee minutes (BT 8/10), draft reports (BT 8/12), transcripts and précis of evidence (BT 8/11, and 13–16), and the returns of the Public Trustee (BT 8/17–26), there is extensive correspondence. This includes that with government departments (BT 8/28–9, 31, 44–5, 59, 64, 88–9, 91, 114, 121, 125–6, and 130); between the secretary and members of the committee (BT 8/32–8); with banks and insurance companies (BT 8/51–5, 74, 101, and 112); with exchanges, commercial associations and firms such as the Stock Exchange, Calico Printers Association, Liverpool Cotton Association, Asiatic Petroleum Co., and British American Tobacco (BT 8/27, 42–3, 56–8, 61, 66, 68–71, 75, 79, 81–2, 84–5, 87, and 99); and with allies including the FBI and the French ambassador (BT 8/115, 132, and 134). In addition, miscellaneous material includes a report on the Egyptian War Trade Department (BT 8/100), and a copy of DORA trade regulations, 1914 (BT 8/136). The committee presented its report in January 1918, but remained in existence to complete business and present supplementary recommendations, being finally dissolved in June 1920.

BT 13 has some material of relevance, including papers on import and export controls (BT 13/69); a report by the Merchants' Committee of the London Chamber of Commerce on government control of trade, 1917 (BT 13/78); and a report on the Board of Trade's activities in 1917–18 (BT 13/91).

BT 15 contains one of the Orders in Council for enforcing the blockade, 1915 (BT 15/66); papers on British property left at the Leipzig exhibition on the outbreak of the war (BT 15/68); and post-war claims dealt with by the Enemy Property Branch (BT 15/101, 103, 115, 134, and 136).

BT 73 comprises the papers of the War Trade Department, which originated in the Inter-departmental Committee on Trade with the Enemy appointed by the Treasury in August 1914. Charged with consideration of questions regarding trade with the enemy and neutrals, the committee's work predominantly consisted of granting import and export licences for goods on prohibited lists through the Privy Council Office. With the increase in the volume of work, the committee was replaced by the War Trade Department in February 1915. Apart from licences, it advised on changes in proclamations prohibiting exports and maintained a consolidated *Black List* though other functions of the former committee relating to the movement of funds were transferred to the Treasury and its overall work co-ordinated with other departments through the War Trade Advisory Committee until January 1917. The department operated through a main licensing committee and a number of sub-committees with a Trade Clearing House as its intelligence branch, though the latter became a separate War Trade Intelligence Department under the Ministry of Blockade in March 1916. A separate statistics section was also subsequently transferred to the Ministry of Blockade as the War Trade Statistical Department in January 1917. The War Trade Department was itself absorbed into the Board of Trade in April 1919 as the Export Licensing Department. Most of the surviving files date from this post-war manifestation of the department, but there are general papers on export licensing for 1916 (BT 73/1), and on restrictions applying to the Channel Islands, also in 1916 (BT 73/2).

BT 103, containing papers of the Board of Trade Solicitor's Department, includes draft proclamations, 1914–18 (BT 103/38); copies of the legislation on trading with the enemy, 1914–16 (BT 103/454–5); and general minute books, 1913–20 (BT 103/357–9).

CAB 1, comprising Cabinet papers collected by Sir James Masterton-Smith, includes a variety of material on the blockade of the Central Powers, 1915–18 (CAB 1/11–12, 15, 22–5, and 28); its impact on Germany (CAB 1/20–21); and also upon neutrals (CAB 1/21–2 and 25). There was also consideration of the disposal of enemy property in allied states in October 1916 (CAB 1/20).

CAB 16, comprising papers of Ad-hoc committees of the Committee of Imperial Defence, includes that on seizing enemy vessels in neutral ports, 1915 (CAB 16/35), and on the arms traffic from 1917 (CAB 16/44). In addition, there are papers of two 1914 committees on Instructions for Shipping, and Supplies in War (CAB 16/29–30).

CAB 17, miscellaneous correspondence and papers of the Committee of Imperial Defence, covers the pre-war consideration of the treatment of enemy and neutral vessels, 1911–14, and the immediate imposition of wartime controls in 1914 (CAB 17/84–9). There is further material on the gradual extension of the blockade, 1914–17, and its possible effect on Germany and her allies (CAB 17/104, 111A and B, 116–18, 122, 133, 142, 147, 162, and 189).

CAB 21, comprising registered files of the Cabinet Office, includes a number on aspects of the blockade (CAB 21/2, 6, 31, and 108–9) including papers of the Cabinet Committee on the Economic Offensive and its successor in June 1918, the Economic Defence and Development Committee (CAB 21/108–9); and correspondence of the Committee on Prohibited and Restricted Imports, which was established under Lord Milner's chairmanship in November 1917 (CAB 21/74).

CAB 24 has reports of the Cabinet Committee on Restrictions of Imports for January–February 1917 (CAB 24/3); and minutes of the Cabinet Committee on Northern Neutrals, established in July 1917 to investigate the position of Norway and other northern neutrals in relation to the war (CAB 24/4).

CAB 27 has minutes and memoranda of the Cabinet Committee on the Economic Offensive, 1917–18 (CAB 27/15–16), which met under Sir Edward Carson's chairmanship to consider recommendations as a basis for discussion with France and the United States; minutes and papers of the Committee on Prohibition of Imports, 1917–18 (CAB 27/20); on Northern Neutrals, 1918 (CAB 27/40); and on Economic Defence and Development, 1918 (CAB 27/44). There are also papers of the Cabinet Committee on the Dutch Agricultural Agreement, set up in November 1917 to examine the advisability of denouncing the agreement (CAB 27/11).

CAB 39 has the minutes and memoranda of the War Trade Advisory Committee, appointed by the Treasury in September 1915 to advise on the restriction of enemy supplies, and to co-ordinate the administration of the War Trade Department and other committees controlling exports. Chaired by Lord Crewe, it also advised the Cabinet on policy arising from these activities. The series consists of minutes and agenda, 1915–17 (CAB 39/1–57), and papers of sub-committees, 1916–18 (CAB 39/58–114). In January 1917 some of the committee's work was taken over by the Ministry of Blockade but it continued in theory to advise the War Cabinet on inter-departmental questions relating to supplies and trade. Few papers, however, survive after June 1917.

CAB 42 contains papers of a number of sub-committees of the Committee of Imperial Defence and War Committee, including Trade Co-ordination, January 1915 (CAB 42/1/15 and 17); Questions of Principle Raised by the War Trade Department, April 1915 (CAB 42/2/18); and Transfer of Enemy Vessels lying in Neutral Ports to Allied or Neutral Flags, August 1916 (CAB 42/3/21)

CO 537 contains material on the pre-war consideration of the treatment of enemy and neutral ships in wartime, 1911–14 (CO 537/361, 368, 371, 374, 381, 592, and 595); and on the prohibition of exports of warlike stores, 1914 (CO 537/585). There are also minutes of the Economic Offensive Committee, 1917–18 (CO 537/997–8, and 1000–1002); and the Orders in Council on Control of Supplies in September and November 1918 (CO 537/615 and 617).

CUST 106/59 deals with the detention of a German trawler, the *Sophie Busse*, in 1914.

FO 115, general correspondence relating to the United States, 1915–17, deals with such issues as the Orders in Council and policy on the blockade (FO 115/1857–65, 2023–4, and 2178–82); contraband (FO 115/1880–81, 1887–8, 2038–40, and 2199–2201); enemy arms purchases (FO 115/1895–8); interned and requisitioned vessels (FO 115/1912 and 2132); trading with the enemy (FO 115/1991–3, and 2152–3); and shipping certificates (FO 115/1978–83).

FO 170/1048 deals with contraband from the perspective of the British embassy in Rome, 1917.

FO 286/672 deals with the distribution of the *Weekly Bulletin of the War Trade Intelligence Department* from the perspective of the British embassy in Athens.

FO 382/1–2523 contain the general correspondence of the Foreign Office Contraband Department and the Ministry of Blockade, 1915–19. The series is arranged by country, area or commodity under the headings of America (FO 382/1–24, 492–541, 1223–43, 1781–95, and 2114–23); America Jute (FO 382/1244–50); Balkans (FO 382/25–54, 542–64, 1251–64, 1796–1804, and 2124–7); Denmark Navicerts (FO 382/1265); Denmark Ships (FO 382/565–612, 1266–75, and 1805–9); Exports to Denmark (FO 382/54–83, 613–25, 1276–83, 1810–14, and 2128–9); Exports to Italy (FO 382/84–102); Exports to the Netherlands (FO 382/103–24); Exports to Norway (FO 382/125–53, 626–47, 1284–98, 1815–26, and 2130–34); Exports to Sweden (FO 382/154–77, 648–76, 1299–1307, 1827–31, and 2135–7); France (FO 382/178–83, 677–81, 1308–10, 1832–5, and 2138–9); Germany (FO 382/184–8, 682–4, 1311–14, 1836–7, and 2140–41); Italy (FO 382/189–202, 685–94, 1315–20, 1838–44, and 2142–6); Netherlands (FO 382/203–52, 695–797, 1321–81, 1845–76, and 2147–79); Netherlands Ships (FO 382/798–811, 1382–94, 1877–8, and 2180–81); Northern Europe (FO 382/1879–96); North and West Europe (FO 382/1395–1404); Norway Navicerts (FO 382/1405–6); Norway Ships (FO 382/812–40, 1407–19, and 1897–1900); Russia (FO 382/253–6, 841–4, 1420–21, 1901–9, and 2182–2201); Scandinavia (FO 382/257–342, 845–949, 1422–1505, 1910–49, and 2202–64); Scandinavia Fish and Oil (FO 382/950–93, 1506–27, and 1950–57); Scandinavia Navicerts (FO 382/1528); Scandinavia Ships (FO 382/343–84, 994–1033, 1529–36, 1958–9, and 2265–72); Spain and Portugal (FO 382/385–402, 1034–54, 1537–56, 1960–66, and 2273–5); Switzerland (FO 382/403–31, 1055–95, 1557–98, 1967–99, and 2276–2303); Miscellaneous General (FO 382/432–74, 1096–1162, 1599–1635, 2000–2023, and 2304–56); Miscellaneous Relief and Relief (FO 382/1163–76, 1636–53, 2024–35, and 2357–89); Coal (FO 382/475–91, 1177–1222, and 1654–84); Tonnage (FO 382/1685–1750); Coal and Tonnage Denmark (FO 382/1751–2, 2036–44, and 2390–99); Coal and Tonnage Netherlands (FO 382/1753, 2045–56, and 2400–2406); Coal and Tonnage Norway (FO 382/1754–6, 2056–63, and 2407–12); Coal and Tonnage Sweden (FO 382/1757–8, 2064–73, and 2413–8); and Coal and Tonnage General (FO 382/1759–65, 2074–2105, and 2149–2504).

FO 551, material on Contraband and Trading with the Enemy, 1915–17, covers contraband correspondence, 1915–18 (FO 551/1–9), and further correspondence on trading with the enemy, 1916–17 (FO 551/10–11).

FO 800/250 has correspondence of Cecil Harmsworth as Under Secretary of State on the Blockade, 1919.

FO 833 contains correspondence of the Foreign Trade Department, comprising reports and memoranda on the formation of the department in January 1916 as well as material on the *Statutory Black List* (FO 833/16–18); and registers of correspondence, 1916–19 (FO 833/4–15).

FO 902 comprises the papers of the War Trade Intelligence Department. Established in February 1915 as the Intelligence Branch of the War Trade Department under the title, Trade Clearing House, the department was transferred to the Ministry of Blockade in March 1916 as the War Trade Intelligence Department. It acted as a clearing house for the collection, collation and distribution of information from other departments, the censors, the foreign press and British traders, as well as making evaluations of the policy and operation of the blockade and its impact. The series contains copies of three of the Department's publications, *Weekly Bulletin of Trade Information*, 1915–19 (FO 902/1–33), *Contraband Herald*, 1915–18

(FO 902/34–5), and *Summary of Blockade Intelligence* (FO 902/40–41). Other publications were *Daily Notes from the Foreign Press*, *Who's Who in War Trade*, and *Transit Letter Bulletin*. There are also minutes of the Ministry of Blockade, 1917 (FO 902/36), and some papers of the Ministry's Finance Section (FO 902/37–9). Though still retaining its connection to the Ministry of Blockade, the department was attached for administrative purposes to the Department of Overseas Trade in 1918. It was dissolved in October 1919.

HCA 57 comprises the minute books of the Probate, Divorce and Admiralty Division of the High Court of Justice while sitting as a Prize Court. Entered under the reference number of the originating writ, they contain brief details on the progress of prize cases. Of the minute books for 1914–25 (HCA 57/1–11), the first four have indices of ships. Until August 1916 retaliatory prize cases, which provided for the seizure and detention of enemy cargo, whether in British, allied or neutral ships, were entered separately (HCA 57/12).

HCA 59 contains the Commission issued by King George V on 6 August 1914 under the Great Seal to the Lords of Admiralty to authorise Vice Admiralty Courts to proceed upon captures and prizes and to hear and determine prize cases, thus effectively authorising the seizure of German vessels and goods as a state of war existed between Britain and Germany (HCA 59/2). There is also the accompanying Warrant of the same date from the Commissioners of Admiralty to the Judges of the High Court of Justice requiring them to proceed likewise (HCA 59/3).

HCA 61, miscellaneous files of the Admiralty Registrar, contains general correspondence with various government departments on wartime prize work including Admiralty, Colonial Office, Foreign Office, and Treasury (HCA 61/3–4, and 7–10); correspondence on American and Norwegian claims (HCA 61/6 and 14); material on various staff matters (HCA 61/5, and 11–12); correspondence on Droits of Admiralty, 1914–15 (HCA 61/1); and settlement of appeals and accounts to 1921 (HCA 61/13 and 15).

HO 45 has a number of files on the prevention of trading with the enemy (HO 45/254895, 265402, 268597, 269001, 272100, 274473, 275411, and 276059). In addition, there is a circular to justices' clerks on the penalties of trading with the enemy, 1915 (HO 45/TE 5324); papers on the prohibition of diamond imports, 1915–16 (HO 45/TE 3333); the position of enemy shareholders in English companies (HO 45/256000); and arbitration of enemy salvage claims, 1915 (HO 45/273531). Some papers relate to the Home Office's own Trading with the Enemy Department, 1915–16 (HO 45/273933).

MT 9, comprising correspondence and papers of the Board of Trade Marine Department has some material of relevance to the blockade, including a copy of the *Statutory Black List*, 1916 (MT 9/1062); papers on prize courts (MT 9/975, 983, 1282); the transfer of enemy vessels to British or other flags (MT 9/972, and 990); and the issue of neutral vessels in British ports (MT 9/1117). There is also material on the chartering of German and Dutch vessels for the Belgian Relief Commission in 1915 (MT 9/1024–5).

MT 25 has papers on the work of the Overseas Prize Dispersal Committee, 1914–19 (MT 25/78–82), and copies of the *War Trade Board Journal*, 1918 (MT 25/11). There is also correspondence on negotiations over Spanish tonnage in 1918 (MT 25/10).

PRO 10 contains, among samples of documents destroyed, material relating to the work of the War Trade Intelligence Department, 1915–19 (PRO 10/108, 284 and 326). In addition, papers deposited by the Official Press Bureau include the *Shipping Black List* of the Admiralty War Staff Trade Department for October 1917 (PRO 10/502).

PT 1 contains papers relating to the wartime role of the Public Trustee as Custodian of Enemy Property in England and Wales. Established in January 1908 to provide the public with the services of a perpetual trustee guaranteed to administer funds with integrity and impartiality at cost price, the Office was tasked with acting as custodian of enemy property by the Board of Trade under the Trading with the Enemy Amendment Act, 1914. This involved the registration of enemy property, the collection of income or capital sums deriving from such property, and the administration and disposition of enemy property or enemy subjects vested in the Public Trustee by orders of the High Court or the Board of Trade. In addition, by proclamations of September 1916 and November 1917, the Public Trustee was required to register claims by British subjects against enemies in respect of debts or property owing in enemy or enemy occupied territory. A new Trading with the Enemy Department was created, mirroring the organisation of the main office on a smaller scale with secretariat and administrative, property adviser's, accountants' and investment divisions.

General work of the Trading with the Enemy Department is covered (PT 1/21 and 44), together with the liaison between the Department and the Public Trustee's Investment Advisory Committee (PT 1/33). There is also general wartime correspondence of the Public Trustee's Office, 1916–19 (PT 1/54–8); correspondence relating to a particular French enquiry to the Office in 1917 (PT 1/29); and a memorandum on the wartime work of the Trading with the Enemy Department compiled as guidance for a future War Book in 1919 (PT 1/24). After the war, the Department worked in association with the Enemy Debts Clearing Office of the Board of Trade in connection with the release of enemy property in England and Wales and of British property in enemy territories. In 1920 its duties as custodian of Austrian and Bulgarian property were transferred to the Clearing Office and in January 1925 the Trading with the Enemy Department was absorbed within the Clearing Office.

T 198 contains the papers of the Committee on Trading with the Enemy, 1914–17. At the suggestion of a sub-committee of the Committee of Imperial Defence, the committee was established by Treasury minute on 4 August 1914 to consider the co-ordination of departmental action. It consisted of representatives from the Treasury, Home Office, Foreign Office, Admiralty, War Office, Colonial Office, India Office, Board of Trade, Board of Customs and Excise, and the Privy Council. No policy files survive, the series consisting of case papers referred to it by the Office of Parliamentary Counsel. The general files (T 198/1–21) deal with matters such as the committee's terms of reference (T 198/1); a Norwegian request to allow grain ships to proceed in August 1914 (T 198/2); the legality of paying German firms for goods bought before the declaration of war (T 198/5); the refusal to allow stock-brokers to communicate with enemy clients concerning the sale of shares, 1915 (T 198/13); and individual claims to be allowed to continue to trade (T 198/8–9, and 12).

'A' files (T 198/22–89), mostly dating from 1915, include measures taken to prevent export of prohibited goods (T 198/25); the refusal to allow import of Belgian

raw material (T 198/30); the refusal to allow money to be sent to German manufacturers (T 198/37); the refusal to allow British banks in Japan to purchase bills
of exchange drawn by enemy firms on British firms (T 198/58); the proceedings
of a conference on trading with enemy firms in China (T 198/65); approval for
an increased remittance for an ailing Scottish woman in Germany (T 198/71);
dividends to be paid to firms originally operating in Turkey but moved to Greece
(T 198/76); the sale of Brazilian coffee in Rotterdam (T 198/84); and the transfer
of shares to an interned German subject (T 198/89).

TS 13 consists of papers of the King's Proctor when acting for the Crown in matters
relating to prize and prize bounty cases, including affidavits, briefs, ships' papers,
and correspondence. Case files for the Great War are arranged in alphabetical
order of ships (TS 13/1–791), as are the registers of goods claimed (TS 13/792–
796C) though these lack the volumes for A–M. Similarly arranged by alphabetical order of ships are notices of motion, briefs and claims (TS 13/797–8);
decrees of court (TS 13/799–810); and affidavits (TS 13/811–50, and 852–7). There
is an index to affidavits giving the names of ships and traders (TS 13/851), and
indexed registers of correspondence giving brief details of business covered and
its disposal (TS 13/3989–97). In addition, there are reports on the work of the
Prize Department, 1914–18 and the Marshal of the Prize Court, 1914–24 (TS 13/858
and 3985).

TS 14 represents blockade records generated by the Foreign Office Contraband
Committee and Enemy Exports Committee, the Trade Clearing House section and
the War Trade Statistical Department of the Ministry of Blockade. The papers were
transferred to the custody of the Procurator General following the disbandment of
the Ministry of Blockade in May 1919 and the dissolution of the War Trade
Intelligence Department in October 1919. The class comprises primarily of the
minutes of the Contraband Committee, 1914–18, including monthly indices of
ships, subjects and persons (TS 14/1–19); supplementary minutes of the Allied
Blockade Committee, 1918 (TS 14/20); minutes of the General Black List Committee, 1915–17, and its sub-committee, 1916–18 (TS 14/21–32); and minutes of the
Enemy Exports Committee, 1915–18 (TS 14/33–6). In addition, there is a set of the
Trade Clearing House and War Trade Intelligence Department's *Transit Letter
Bulletins*, 1915–19, giving information about the activities of traders obtained from
intercepted mail with index (TS 14/37–50); and war trade statistics compiled by
the War Trade Statistical Department, 1915–19, regarding imports into neutral
countries adjacent to enemy territories, principally Scandinavia (including Iceland
and the Faroes), the Netherlands and Switzerland (TS 14/51–5).

TS 27/106 deals with the claims of the Dutch government regarding Dutch vessels
requisitioned after detention.

WO 32 deals with the allocation of prize money for German vessels seized on the
African Great Lakes and in German South-West Africa (WO 32/5830). In addition,
there is consideration of the food situation in Germany and the prolongation of
the blockade into 1919 (WO 32/5375 and 5383).

The naval blockade on the Central Powers was primarily enforced by means
of patrols and mines but, in response, the Imperial German Navy resorted to
submarine warfare. The German submarine *U-21* became the first submarine

to sink a ship in action at sea when sinking HMS *Pathfinder* in the Firth of Forth on 3 September 1914, the only previously successful submarine attack in the American Civil War having been inside a harbour. The first merchantman to fall victim was the SS *Glitra* to *U-17* on 20 October, while HMS *Birmingham* became the first vessel to sink a submarine by ramming *U-15* in the North Sea on 9 August 1914.

It should be noted, however, that the first submarine campaign was largely waged using surface gunfire, since U-boats carried few torpedoes and submerged in order to approach vessels undetected and then to evade detection themselves. Indeed, only 10 British merchantmen were lost to submarine attack prior to the introduction of 'unrestricted' submarine warfare in February 1915, compared to 14 to mines and 51 to surface raiders.

Unrestricted submarine warfare implied attacking vessels without prior warning. Though this was suspended in the Channel and Atlantic in August 1915 as a result of American pressure, submarines continued to attack vessels in the Mediterranean with impressive results and, therefore, full unrestricted submarine warfare was revived by the Germans in February 1917. A dramatic increase in Entente shipping losses resulted, rising from 464,599 tons in February 1917 to 507,001 tons in March and 834,549 tons in April 1917.

A number of methods were initially utilised against the submarine such as decoy ships or Q-ships – heavily armed vessels disguised as harmless merchantmen. Minefields and nets were also used, as in the Dover Barrage, to try and close off the U-boat route into the Channel. However, the solution to unrestricted submarine warfare was a revival of the method well known to the age of sail, namely the convoy. Convoys had been used from the beginning of the war to protect troop ships and, in February 1917, were successfully introduced for the coal trade between Britain and France and, in April 1917, for the Scandinavian trade.

After initial resistance from the Admiralty, an experimental convoy was run from Gibraltar to Plymouth on 10 May 1917 without loss. By October 1917, a total of 99 homeward bound convoys had reached harbour safely and only ten vessels had been lost. In all, British shipping losses in the last quarter of 1917 of 702,779 tons (235 ships) were only just over half the peak figure of 1,315,496 tons (413 ships) lost in the second quarter of the year. By November 1917, the convoy system was fully operational and U-boats were forced to attack underwater and largely in coastal waters.

Escorts were now more successful using prototype hydrophones to detect submarines and equally newly developed depth charges. Airships, flying boats and towed balloons had also all been introduced in anti-submarine roles. Submarine successes had also spurred development of bulges added to ships as underwater protection and, by 1917, it was possible for naval vessels to survive torpedo attack. Paravanes also reduced the effectiveness of mines, an area of warfare in which the Royal Navy was itself generally somewhat deficient.

ADM 1, containing Admiralty In-Letters, has considerable material on the threats from submarine and mine and counter-measures to them. Losses of particular vessels to mine or U-boat are covered (ADM 1/8388/25, 8393/308, and 8429/222 and 230), including the enquiries into the loss of the old cruisers, HMS *Aboukir*, *Cressy* and *Hogue*, to *U-9* off the Broad Fourteens in September 1914 (ADM 1/8396/356), and of HMS *Hampshire* (ADM 1/8470/238), there also being allegations of delays in sending help to the latter vessel (ADM 1/8468/226). The loss of the *Lusitania* brought a legal action against Messrs Cunard for the disclosure of Admiralty instructions (ADM 1/8451/56). More general material on submarine warfare includes various anti-submarine measures (ADM 1/8405/463, 8406/469, 8407/490, 8409/15, 8428/216, 8441/352, 8478/2, 8480/36, 8497/191, 8498/208, and 8529/191), and calculations of losses of ships and tonnage 1914–17 and to February 1918 (ADM 1/8509/1 and 8515/52). Specific anti-submarine measures included camouflage and dazzle painting (ADM 1/8412/50, and 8533/215) and the use of paravanes and otters (ADM 1/8566/240). The navy's own submarine construction programme is also covered (ADM 1/8428/209), as are anti-mine measures (ADM 1/8392/291, 8393/317, and 8420/123) including post-war clearance (ADM 1/8518/81). A Director of Torpedoes and Mines was appointed in January 1917 and an Operational Planning Section for Hydrophones in the Admiralty's Anti-Submarine Warfare Department in June 1917 (ADM 1/8478/3 and 8490/131).

ADM 111/1526 has material on the loss of HMS *Hampshire*.

ADM 116, comprising 'case' files, includes a number on submarine warfare, including war navigational instructions for merchantmen, 1915–18 (ADM 116/1389–90); the loss of the *Lusitania* (ADM 116/1416); the loss of HMS *Hampshire* (ADM 116/5976); treatment of German POWs from *U-8* and *U-12*, and German submariners generally (ADM 116/1418 and 1513); enemy submarine activity in the Mediterranean, and in home waters (ADM 116/1429 and 1601A); Mediterranean anti-submarine reports and statistics (ADM 116/1610); defence against torpedoes (ADM 116/1428); defensively armed merchant ships (ADM 116/1463–6 and 1536); bi-monthly mine sweeping reports, 1916–18 (ADM 116/1515–18); protection of Norwegian shipping against submarines, 1916–17 (ADM 116/1552); proceedings of the Committee on Mercantile Marine Vessels, 1917 (ADM 116/1579–81); returns of the merchant vessels sunk, damaged or attacked, 1917–18, and losses from submarine activity in 1918 (ADM 116/1600 and 1647); the attack on the SS *April* in June 1917 (ADM 116/1648); and post-war mine clearance (ADM 116/1725). There is also a file on the sinking of the German merchant vessel, *Ems*, by the British submarine, *G4*, in 1916 (ADM 116/1542).

ADM 131, containing correspondence of the Plymouth Station, includes material on Q-ships and other special service ships (ADM 131/84–5); mine sweeping reports (ADM 131/87–90); warnings to merchant ships and information on defensively-employed merchantmen (ADM 131/95–6); convoy statistics and other convoy material (ADM 131/98–102); reports on British and enemy submarine patrols (ADM 131/104–7); and reports on British and foreign merchant vessels attacked, 1915–18 (ADM 131/113–18).

ADM 136/11–12 contains the ships' books of the Materials Department relating to a number of wartime K, M, N and W class submarines.

ADM 137, containing 'packs' and other miscellaneous records of the Admiralty Historical Section, has reports on all homeward convoys, 1917–18 (ADM 137/2523–2604), and outward convoys (ADM 137/2605–43); together with précis of the reports (ADM 137/2656–7, and 2660). There are also other convoy, trading and shipping reports among papers of the Trade Division (ADM 137/2776–88, and 2838–42). There is miscellaneous material on convoys, including those in the Mediterranean with anti-submarine reports, tonnage losses and papers of the Anti-Submarine Division (ADM 137/2645–50, 2653, and 2655). Reports compiled in 1918 on the convoy system for historical purposes are also included (ADM 137/2658–9, and 2664); and there are monthly statements on the employ-ment of British merchant vessels, 1916–18 (ADM 137/2661).

Other material includes information on the loss of HMS *Aboukir, Cressy* and *Hogue* (ADM 137/47 and 2232); the German seizure of a Danish vessel in 1916 (ADM 137/3212); the accidental sinking of the British submarine *G9* by HMS *Pasley* and of an Italian submarine by a British submarine in April 1918 (ADM 137/3302 and 3745); the capture of *U-48* (ADM 137/3327); the loss of HMS *Hampshire* (ADM 137/3621); and the premature explosion of depth charges (ADM 137/3755 and 3766). Anti-submarine measures covered include the movement of Q-ships, 1916–18 (ADM 137/4056); anti-submarine equipment (ADM 137/4172–3); paravanes (ADM 137/1889, 1930, 1967–8, 1995, 2087, and 2141); defensively armed merchant ships (ADM 137/2859–61, and 2900–908); and assessments of the results of attacks on German U-boats (ADM 137/4137–50 and 4152–5).

There is much material on German submarine operations including interro-gation reports (ADM 137/3060, 3865–6, 3870–76, 3883–8, 3897–3903, 3912–20, 3965–4046, and 4048); original history sheets for individual U-boats (ADM 137/3899–3900, 3912–18, and 4151); and the log book of *U-20* covering the period of the sinking of the *Lusitania* (ADM 137/3923), which is also dealt with in general terms (ADM 137/1058). In addition, there are reports on attacks on shipping, 1915–16 (ADM 137/3061); and the diary of an officer on board the German surface raider, *Karlsruhe*, 1914–16 (ADM 137/3062). The class also has reports on German submarine activity received by the Naval Intelligence Division, 1917–18 (ADM 137/4098–4122).

ADM 156, papers of courts martial and boards of enquiry, deals with the loss or abandonment of a number of merchantmen (ADM 156/114–15, 118, 121–2, 124–5, 127–8, 130, and 140), many lost to torpedoes or mines (ADM 156/29, 133, and 141–4), including some in convoy (ADM 156/138–9). Naval vessels were also lost to, or damaged by, submarines or mines (ADM 156/31, 40, 42, 120, 129, 145, and 170), including HMS *Formidable* in January 1915 (ADM 156/183–5). There were also enquiries into particular submarine encounters involving negligence or unverified claims of sinkings (ADM 156/123, 126, 134, 146, 160, 164, and 168–9), including the failure to prevent *U-39* from sinking after its capture in March 1917 (ADM 156/28).

ADM 173 contains submarine logs from 1914 onwards, recording all wheel, tele-graph and depth keeping orders with information on battery charges, torpedo firing and navigation. Unlike ships' logs, which were kept on a monthly basis, submarine logs were continuously kept by those engaged in steering or depth keeping. They contain abbreviated references and some are enhanced by cryptic drawings, car-toons and other embellishments. The logs are arranged by class of submarine. Class A-G submarines all saw wartime service in their entirety (ADM 173/1–2533). Some H-N, R-S and V-W class submarines also saw war service (ADM 173/2534–8,

2761, 2872–9, 3040–46, 3223–7, 3322–31, 3573–7, 3762–3, 3835–6, 5830–85, 5986–6008, 6092–6110, 6118–38, 6164–80, 6265–80, 6290–307, 6339–54, 6386–98, 6410–26, 6455–70, 6554–61, 6627–35, 6659–66, 6676–81, 6858–70, 6998–7007, 7125–33, 7250–58, 7380–86, 7506–10, 7675–86, 7785–92, 7886–90, 7951–9, 8095–9, 8214–15, 8364–72, 8511–16, 8670–72, 11205–12, 11543–57, 12418–20, 12440, 12624–8, 12640–43, 12655, 12949–56, and 13096–218).

ADM 178, comprising supplementary case files and mostly the proceedings of courts martial or boards of enquiry, include the enquiries relating to the loss of HMS *Aboukir*, *Cressy* and *Hogue*, and of HMS *Formidable* (ADM 178/13 and 33). There is also consideration of the status of gun crews of the defensively armed merchantmen, SS *Boldwell*, lost to a submarine in 1917 (ADM 178/25).

ADM 186 includes, among official Admiralty publications, interrogation reports of U-boat survivors (ADM 186/37–8); and material on torpedoes and anti-submarine warfare (ADM 186/367–426).

ADM 189, the reports of the Torpedo and Anti-submarine School at HMS *Vernon*, Portchester, covers the war in general (ADM 189/34–8), but also mines and mine sweeping (ADM 189/73–4 and 82), and research into torpedo firing, 1915–18 (ADM 189/100).

ADM 236/54 contains reports on war experience, 1914–18, compiled by the Captain of Submarine Flotillas in 1939 for the guidance of submariners.

ADM 244/1 contains photographs of the boom defences of the Firth of Forth bridge.

AIR 1 deals with the Northern Barrage, 1918 (AIR 1/30/15/226/171, and 308/15/226/161).

BT 15/69 deals with a series of ship explosions at Archangel in 1916.

CAB 1 has some material on the German submarine threat in February 1915 (CAB 1/11); effects on merchant shipping and the restrictions placed on women and children travelling by sea in 1917 (CAB 1/14 and 23); the submarine threat to Italy in 1916 (CAB 1/21); Dutch vessels taken by German submarines, and the arming of merchant vessels in 1917 (CAB 1/22).

CAB 21 has memoranda by both Admiral Sir John Fisher and Maurice Hankey on the submarine threat (CAB 21/7–8, and 95), as well as related files on the shipping situation (CAB 21/9, 43 and 156).

CAB 45, correspondence and papers relating to the Official History, includes material on the sinking of the *Lusitania* (CAB 45/267), and the loss of HMS *Hampshire* (CAB 45/276). There is also coverage of escort operations (CAB 45/271).

CN 1/25 has photographs of the Tudor-Hart method of camouflage, 1917.

FO 115, general correspondence relating to the United States, has material on armed merchantmen (FO 115/1825, and 2017–18); German submarines (FO 115/2062–4); and submarine bases (FO 115/2326).

FO 141/731 deals with submarine intelligence collected in Egypt, 1917–18.

FO 286/682 deals with mine clearance in the Aegean, 1918–19.

HO 139/20 includes material on the Official Press Bureau's treatment of the loss of HMS *Audacious* to a mine in October 1914, a fact kept secret from the public until the end of the war.

MT 9, correspondence of the Board of Trade Marine Department, includes some material relating to submarine warfare, including the arming of merchant ships (MT 9/994, 1004, and 1128). The effect of the war on the merchant marine is reflected in notification of the general hazards to trade routes in August 1914 (MT 9/961); an assessment of the effect of the war on trade by the Liverpool Steamship Owners Association, 1915 (MT 9/991); transfers of British vessels to foreign flags (MT 9/1010); returns of losses (MT 9/1014, 1099, 1178, 1270, and 1292), tonnage comparisons in October 1915 and October 1916 (MT 9/1080); Dutch protective measures in the North Sea and Channel, 1916 (MT 9/1038); the loss of vessels to explosion at Archangel in 1916 (MT 9/1189); and depositions on submarine attacks, 1918 (MT 9/1194). In addition, there is a memorandum on services rendered the allies by British shipping (MT 9/1042); overall statistics for British merchant shipping, 1914–18 (MT 9/1221); and a war history of the merchant marine (MT 9/1360). In 1917 the Admiralty organised a conference on the supply of wireless operators to the merchant marine (MT 9/1121).

MT 23 contains Admiralty orders for British fishing vessels in 1914 (MT 23/338); the Admiralty's responsibility for the cost of a collier taken by the German surface raider, *Emden*, in 1914 (MT 23/319); the escort and protection of troops and horses being transported overseas, 1915 (MT 23/356); and a review of oil fuel tonnage in 1917 (MT 23/737).

MT 25 has much material relating to submarine and mine warfare amid the general correspondence files of the Ministry of Shipping, 1917–18, including reports for owners and masters on the effects of mines and torpedoes (MT 25/1); returns of losses at various dates (MT 25/2–3, 5, 53 and 58); British merchant and fishing vessel losses for the war as a whole (MT 25/23 and 83–5); total British cargo losses as stated for the benefit of the post-war Reparations Commission (MT 25/26); the internment of British vessels in Germany (MT 25/75A); losses of other belligerents (MT 25/30–31, and 36); insurance of Greek vessels sunk by German submarines (MT 25/88); the use of merchant ships for mine laying, 1918 (MT 25/13); dazzle painting of merchantmen (MT 25/16 and 67); post-war mine sweeping (MT 25/21); a memorandum by the Shipping Controller on tonnage available in June 1918 (MT 25/22); supply to Russia (MT 25/33 and 38–41); minutes of the International Shipping Committee, 1916–17 (MT 25/44); and correspondence and returns on Atlantic, Gibraltar and Russia convoys (MT 25/47–9).

WO 158, Military Headquarters Papers, has material on the blockade of Cameroon (WO 158/547–57); and the searching and detention of Spanish vessels, 1915 (WO 158/547–50).

The appearance of the submarine, mine and torpedo boat ensured that the Great War was the last in which the battleship would be regarded as the main instrument of seapower. The vulnerability of the capital ship contradicted prevailing contemporary belief, encompassed in the work of the American naval theorist, Alfred Thayer Mahan, that a culminating fleet action would alone confer the command of the sea.

In terms of capital ships themselves, the Royal Navy's launching of the revolutionary HMS *Dreadnought* in 1906, combining big guns with oil-burning turbine engines, had forced technological change but technical advances in one field were often offset by both teething problems and continuing limitations in other fields. Indeed, in certain areas such as range finding, fire direction and control, Germany rather than Britain held the lead, the Royal Navy assuming that ships would engage in battle in long, relatively static parallel lines. German range finding and fire control was certainly superior at Coronel in November 1914 and it was perhaps fortunate that the German cruisers, *Goeben* and *Breslau*, successfully evaded the pursuing British Mediterranean squadron in October 1914. Notwithstanding its reversal of the defeat at Coronel, British shooting was poor at the Falklands in December 1914 and again at the Dogger Bank in January 1915.

The only sustained clash between the Grand and High Seas Fleets came at Jutland on 31 May–1 June 1916. Overall, the High Seas Fleet fired 3,597 shells during the action as a whole and achieved 120 hits (3.33 per cent) compared to the Grand Fleet's discharge of 4,598 shells, of which 100 hit (2.17 per cent). Subsequent investigation attributed the British failures largely to poor shells but, while this was a factor, German gunners were better trained and the Dreyer fire control system proved incapable of dealing with rapid changes of range. It was also the case that the British battlecruisers were inadequately armoured, three being lost. The British also lost three cruisers and eight destroyers. German losses were one battleship, another old pre-dreadnought battleship, four cruisers and five destroyers.

Nevertheless, while Jutland was inconclusive on the relative merits of British and German naval construction, in the wider context, it made no significant difference to the Royal Navy's strategic advantage: as one journalist famously remarked, the High Seas Fleet had succeeded only in assaulting its gaoler before returning to gaol.

ADM 1, comprising Admiralty In-letters and material not generally used in the compilation of the Official History, has reports on some actions including a cruiser engagement off the Heligoland Bight in August 1914 (ADM 1/8391/286); HMAS *Sydney*'s destruction of the *Emden* in November 1914 (ADM 1/8402/412); the Falklands action in December 1914 (ADM 1/8404/); the Dogger Bank in January 1915 (ADM 1/8413/54); the capture of enemy trawlers in October 1915 (ADM 1/8435/295); Jutland (ADM 1/840/149, 8461/153, 8463/176, 8463/178, and 8477/308); and that of HMS *Strongbow* and *Mary Rose* against superior forces in October 1918 (ADM 1/8541/267).

Aspects of naval construction and armament programmes are also covered (ADM 1/8390/25, 8424/171, 8435/297, 8446/17, 8488/100, 8500/225, and 8507/280), including overall records of wartime warship construction (ADM 1/8547/340). There are enquiry and courts martial reports on the loss of various vessels (ADM 1/8445/9, 8452/69, 8463/179, 8485/79, 8500/223, and 8527/161). General aspects of naval policy are also reflected, including the report of a conference between the CinC Home Fleet and the Third Sea Lord in October 1916 (ADM 1/8470/236), a general review of the naval situation for the War Cabinet in March 1917 (ADM 1/8483/58); deputations to and conferences held by the First

Lord, 1917–18 (ADM 1/8512/28A); and the granting of Vice Admiral's rank to Eric Geddes as Controller of the Navy (ADM 1/8489/122). There is also a summary of British naval wartime effort (ADM 1/8547/336), and an unidentified commodore's diary of events, 1914–16 (ADM 1/8640/118). The series is in chronological order, but there is no direct index.

ADM 12 comprises indices and digests to Admiralty In-Letters (ADM 1), Admiralty Out-Letters (ADM 2), and the minutes of the Board of Admiralty, as well as to the HS Series (ADM 137) and Admiralty case files (ADM 116). The indices for 1914–18 (ADM 12/1519–24, 1513A–38B, 1548A–60B, 1569A–81B, and 1590A–1602B) give references to individuals and ships in alphabetical order. The digests for 1914–18 (ADM 12/1525–30, 1539A–47B, 1561A–68B, 1582A–89B, and 1603A–1608B) combine a summary of papers and a subject index, following a system of numbered cuts which is explained in successive editions of the Table of Heads and Sections under which the correspondence of the Admiralty Board is digested. The volumes provide cross-references to each other and to the location of the original documents. The means of translating these references into modern PRO form is explained by a Guide in the Reference Room. Between 1915 and 1919 the increase in work made it necessary to employ two clerks simultaneously in indexing and digesting, each with a separate set of volumes. Consequently, each section of the index and digest is in two parts and both may have to be consulted.

ADM 53/32493–69772 comprise Ships' Logs, 1914–20. Kept by the Officer of the Watch for all naval vessels, they record standard navigational information as well as wheel and telegraph orders, deaths on board and visits by dignitaries. Inspected weekly by the Captain, they were passed to the appropriate administrative authority and on to the Admiralty. Some were retained separately as exhibits for enquiries or courts martial and these are listed at the beginning of each section of the series list. Naval vessels did not keep war diaries. The logs are arranged primarily in alphabetical order, but with all monitors and motor launches by number under M, patrol boats by number under P, Q-ships by number under Q, special service squadrons by number under S, and torpedo boats by number under T. There is also an addendum section (ADM 53/69446–69772).

ADM 116 has much material on naval operations in general among its 'case files', including the Grand Fleet Battle Orders and Grand Fleet Orders, 1914–18 (ADM 116/1341–3 and 1663–74); reports on naval vessels lost, including those at Coronel, the Dardanelles and Jutland, HMS *Pathfinder*, and HMS *Formidable* (ADM 116/1354–8, 1370, 1437A, 1440–46, 1521–35, 1553, 1613–17, and 1625); naval and military policy, 1914–18 (ADM 116/1348–51); the printed dispatches on Jutland (ADM 116/1482–92); the First Lord of the Admiralty's alphabetical files, 1917–18 (ADM 116/1602–5); naval weekly appreciations, 1917–18 (ADM 116/11612B); records of the Admiralty War Department, 1917–20 (ADM 116/1763–6); minutes of the Maintenance Committee, 1917–19 (ADM 116/1777–99); salvage cases, 1916–17 (ADM 116/1500–512); coastal motor boats, torpedo boat destroyers and the yacht patrol (ADM 116/1479, 1567 and 1685); the Royal Australian Navy, 1914–19 (ADM 116/1686); and the capture of the German hospital ship, *Ophelia*, in 1915 (ADM 116/1384–8). The series is not arranged in any particular order but there is a rough index following the system of the Admiralty digest (ADM 12).

ADM 130/23–7 contain records of the Plymouth Station, including standing orders, and general orders of the CinC, Plymouth.

ADM 131, the correspondence of the Plymouth Station, includes material on allied warships using the port (ADM 131/65–6); sailing and movement orders (ADM 131/78–9); the Auxiliary Patrol (ADM 131/67–76); various types of naval vessels such as destroyers, minesweepers, and cable ships (ADM 131/80–5); shipping intelligence (ADM 131/93–4); fishing fleet reports (ADM 131/103); reports of sightings of and actions with enemy vessels (ADM 131/108–12); signals and communications (ADM 131/121); various classified telegrams and memoranda (ADM 131/122–3); and miscellaneous material including General Orders for Devonport, 1917 (ADM 131/77 and 124).

ADM 136, comprising selected samples of ships' books from the collection of the Materials Department, include those of the battleship HMS *Queen Elizabeth*, launched in 1913 (ADM 136/10); the battlecruiser HMS *Invincible*, launched in 1907 and lost at Jutland (ADM 136/8); the monitor, HMS *Terror*, launched in 1916 (ADM 136/23); and the destroyer, HMS *Zubian*, constructed in 1917 from the remains of HMS *Zulu* and HMS *Nubian* (ADM 136/9).

ADM 137 are 'packs' and miscellaneous records of the Admiralty Historical Branch mostly extracted from ADM 1 and ADM 116 during the compilation of the post-war Official History and arranged in a form reflecting the contents of the history in three series, known as the HS, HSA and HSB series. The HS series are mostly telegrams, signals and operational reports extracted from the Admiralty Secretariat files. The HSA series is similar but represents papers generated by the Grand Fleet and other naval commands, though not all overseas commands are represented. The HSB series derived from the Naval War Staff, particularly the Trade Division. A key is included (ADM 137/3059) which lists all title papers, though primarily by year and by government department. This enables anyone working from entries in the Admiralty Digest and Index (ADM 12) to find the HS volume series in which the papers have been placed. Checking the HS reference against ADM 137 also reveals the modern piece number, but this excludes references to the HSA and HSB series. However, a number of other indices are provided to the HS, HSA and HSB series (ADM 137/3058), while a smaller index covers the records of the Trade Division (ADM 137/2733–928) and Plans Division (ADM 137/2706–12) in the HSB series. An index to ships mentioned covers only part of the series (ADM 137/3053–4046). The indices are necessary as the first part of the series lists give only the piece numbers without further explanation for the HS series (ADM 137/1–1798), HSA series (ADM 137/1799–2522), and HSB series (ADM 137/2665–3056). A fuller description appears in the series list for some of the HSA series (ADM 137/2523–2664), and the remainder of the series as a whole (ADM 137/3060–4836).

Subject headings indexed in the HSA and HSB series, for example, include Auxiliary Patrol Areas Weekly Reports, Channel Barrage, Collisions, Cruiser Force, Destroyer Flotillas, Grand Fleet Policy, Mine laying Operations, Neutrality Questions, Policy, Shell Hits in Action, and Zeebrugge. In terms of the Royal Navy's operations, there are miscellaneous charts (ADM 137/3057); Grand Fleet orders, battle orders and battle instructions (ADM 137/4049–55); and reports on the losses of various vessels from varying causes (ADM 137/3089–3839). Some of the latter reports touch on other issues such as the pursuit of the *Goeben* and *Breslau* (ADM 137/3105 and 4176); a German destroyer raid on the Dover Patrol, March 1917 (ADM 137/3239); the proceedings of the 5th Destroyer Flotilla,

February–March 1917 (ADM 137/3651); material on Jutland, including damage done to the Germans, British survivors' reports, extracts from logs and signal logs, and post-battle committees investigating the events (ADM 137/2027–33, 3839, 4808–9, and 4825); the Zeebrugge raid, including photographs (ADM 137/2706 and 2708); and the capabilities of, and improvements to, types of projectiles in use with the fleet (ADM 137/3834–8).

German naval operations are also covered (ADM 137/3840–921) such as those by surface raiders, including a survivor's statement from the *Emden* (ADM 137/3850, 3878, and 3910); material on pre-war German naval construction (ADM 137/3858–60); more on damage to German vessels at Jutland (ADM 137/3880–81); the results of the British raid on Zeebrugge and Ostend in April 1918 ADM 137/3894); movement of enemy ships as reported by the Admiralty War Room, 1914–17 (ADM 137/4788–91); and the German naval mutinies in 1918 (ADM 137/3891).

ADM 151/83–4 contain Admiralty correspondence received by the Nore Station, 1914–18.

ADM 156, comprising records of courts martial and courts of enquiry, deals with the loss or damage of particular naval vessels during the war through various causes (ADM 156/14–16, 20, 25, 84, 88, 113, 117, 162, and 175). Many involved collision (ADM 156/18, 22, 37–8, 41, 45, 82, 85–6, 90, 135, 161, 163, 171, and 173–4), grounding or stranding (ADM 156/44, 83, 111–12, 148, and 154), or accidental identification as hostile (ADM 156/131, 147 and 172). There is also material on the German destroyer attack on the Grisney patrol in June 1918 (ADM 156/137); and the supposed interception of German raiders by HMS *Avenger* and HMS *Teutonic* in March 1917; (ADM 156/166). In addition, there is the high profile case of the responsibility of Rear Admiral Trowbridge and Admiral Sir Berkeley Milne for the escape of the German cruisers, *Goeben* and *Breslau*, into the Black Sea in September 1914 (ADM 156/12, 76, 110, 159 and 182).

ADM 167/48–55 have the minutes of the Board of Admiralty, 1914–18.

ADM 176 contains photographs of a variety of Royal Navy ships, many relating to the Great War.

ADM 178 deals with enquiries into the loss of HMS *Natal* to an explosion in 1916 (ADM 178/122–3), and that of HMS *Ariadne* in 1917 (ADM 178/30).

ADM 179 comprises correspondence of the Portsmouth Station, including general matters, 1913–23 (ADM 179/36–40); dockyard records, 1914–24 (ADM 179/68–9); and General Orders, 1914–18 (ADM 179/75–9).

ADM 182 contains Admiralty Fleet Orders, both Weekly Orders, 1914–18 (ADM 182/5–13), and Monthly Orders, 1914–18 (ADM 182/21–6).

ADM 186, comprising official Admiralty publications, includes such miscellaneous material as notes on German destroyer tactics (ADM 186/17); entry into defended ports (ADM 186/20–21); identification for allied surface vessels in the Mediterranean (ADM 186/39); half-yearly appropriation lists of technical training instructions (ADM 186/164–9), including reports of the Shell Committee, 1917–18 (ADM 186/167–8); lists of HM ships showing armament (ADM 186/864–6); historical studies (ADM 186/566–86), including reports on the Falklands battle (ADM 186/566), and Jutland (ADM 186/569); area handbooks (ADM 186/570–72

ND 577–8); war light lists for the German Bight (ADM 186/634); and a variety of manuals on signals and wireless (ADM 186/673–750), and on gunnery (ADM 186/191–236).

ADM 189/83–4 are the wireless appendices for 1914–15 to reports by the Torpedo and Anti-Submarine School at HMS *Vernon* in Portchester.

ADM 195 contains photographs of dock construction programmes, those for Dover, Malta, Portsmouth and Rosyth covering the war years (ADM 195/13, 70, 79, and 93–7).

ADM 900/49–68 are Admiralty Branch indices, 1916–18, among specimens of papers preserved from destruction.

CAB 1 includes a report by a captured German naval officer on the Heligoland action, November 1914 (CAB 1/10), and a report on naval affairs since the outbreak of war compiled in January 1915 (CAB 1/11). In addition, there are also papers relating to the period when Sir James Masterton-Smith worked in the Private Office of Churchill as First Lord of the Admiralty, 1911–15, and again in the First Lord's Private Office in 1917 (CAB 1/32–4).

CAB 17/194, among miscellaneous papers of the Committee of Imperial Defence, deals with naval policy, 1917.

CAB 21 includes material on Fisher's idea for an attack on the Baltic (CAB 21/5), and notes and correspondence relating to the first informal meeting of the Cabinet Committee on the Release of Long-range Guns by the Admiralty, August 1917 (CAB 21/81).

CAB 44, material used in the compilation of the Official History, includes an account of the life of the commander of the German East Asian Squadron, Maximilian von Spee (CAB 44/44); and notes on the development of the German Navy, compiled in 1922 (CAB 44/45).

CAB 45, correspondence and papers relating to the Official History, contains material on the naval war (CAB 45/262–81), including correspondence of Admiral Sir Roger Keyes (CAB 45/268); Jutland (CAB 45/269); the Zeebrugge raid (CAB 45/272); and the Dogger Bank (CAB 45/273, and 282–6), the latter including information drawn from Admiral von Pohl's letters (CAB 45/282–8).

CN 20/1 has photographs of the German hospital ship, *Ophelia*, 1915.

FO 115/2357–8 deals with the business of the British naval attaché in the United States, 1918.

Yet another challenge to the capital ship was airpower, a German guard ship being the first sunk from the air when attacked by Japanese aircraft at Tsingtau in October 1914. Mines were also laid from the air in the Baltic and an air torpedo attack attempted at the Dardanelles in March 1915. During the same campaign, HMS *Triumph* became the first ship to fire on another it could not see using aerial spotting.

Despite some opposition to developing airpower within the Royal Navy, on 3 November 1915, a conventional aircraft was successfully flown off an improvised flight deck on HMS *Vindex*. The first to land successfully – a

Sopwith Pup – was flown on to HMS *Furious* on 2 August 1917, although its pilot, Squadron Commander E. H. Dunning, drowned trying to repeat the feat five days later. In July 1918 seven Sopwith Camels successfully flew off *Furious* to bomb a Zeppelin base at Tondern.

Increasingly, too, aircraft were used to escort convoys, albeit within the limitations of range, but dirigibles had a much longer range and were used fairly successfully. HMS *Ark Royal*, a converted steamer, was used as a seaplane carrier at the Dardanelles but, in October 1918, the world's first true aircraft carrier, HMS *Argus*, was commissioned. In fact, it was not to see actual service in the war and was a converted liner. The first vessel specifically designed as an aircraft carrier, HMS *Hermes*, was laid down in 1917 but not put into commission until 1923.

ADM 1 has much material of interest on naval aviation including reports of seaplanes being flown off the decks of the carriers *Campania* and *Vindex* in August 1915, from *Campania* again in December 1917, and other carriers in June 1918 (ADM 1/8430/233, 8432/253, 8507/275, and 8529/181); minutes of a conference from September 1915 (ADM 1/8433/270B); naval and military aerial co-operation (ADM 1/8449/39A); policy on the development of torpedo-carrying aircraft, and the suggested aerial attack on the German fleet at Cuxhaven (ADM 1/8477/307, and 8525/136); the retention of the Kite Balloon Section in naval service in March 1918 (ADM 1/8518/85); and a report of an aerial reconnaissance in June 1918 (ADM 1/8528/170). There is also consideration of the use of seaplanes and dirigibles in anti-submarine patrols (ADM 1/8486/81, 8488/97, and 8490/126).

ADM 116 includes information on the development of the Naval Airship Service, 1914–18 and airship policy, 1917–18 (ADM 116/1335 and 1607).

ADM 131/64 deals with the organisation of aircraft, airships, balloons and kites in the Plymouth Station, 1914–18.

ADM 137 includes reports on a failure to launch seaplanes from HMS *Vindex* in May 1916 (ADM 137/3617); and much material on the operation of kite balloons (ADM 137/1930, 1953, 1957, 2133, 2179, and 2215).

ADM 186/567 deals with seaplane operations against Cuxhaven in December 1914.

AIR 1 has considerable information on naval aviation, including papers of the Admiralty Air Department (AIR 1/185–345), including a précis of daily proceedings, 1914–15 (AIR 1/185/15/226/1); records of the Inspecting Captain of Aircraft Records, 1914–15 (AIR 1/346–60); daily reports of operations, 1915–18 (AIR 1/189–233, and 240–51); weekly reports from stations, 1916–18 (AIR 1/337–41); Air Division files, 1917–18 (AIR 1/273–8, and 280–92); and Air Department folders, 1914–18 (AIR 1/297–305). There are notes by Murray Sueter on the early history of the RNAS and reports on RNAS operations, October 1914 to June 1915 (AIR 1/7/6/1, and 24); correspondence on general policy (AIR 1/69/15/9/112–14); lists of aircraft and engines in use with the RNAS, 1917 (AIR 1/1/4/18 and 6A/4/48); RNAS fortnightly communiqués, 1916–18 (AIR 1/39/15/9/4–5); daily operational reports from RNAS squadrons at Dunkirk, 1916–18 by squadron (AIR 1/40/15/9/7–9, 41/15/9/10–11, 42/15/9/12–14, 43/15/9/15–17, 44/15/9/18–19, 45/15/9/20–22, 46/15/9/23–6, 47/15/9/27–8, 48/15/9/29–31, 49/15/9/32–4, and 629), and by wing (AIR 1/51–6);

flying maps (AIR 1/345/15/22/294); daily reports by RNAS stations, 1917–18 (AIR 1/310–32 and 341); material on the RNAS station at Vendome (AIR 1/2017–20); other RNAS squadrons (AIR 1/423–5); and RNAS memoranda, 1916–17 (AIR 1/2096). Sueter's own papers (AIR 1/2435–662) include papers of the Rigid Airship Committee, 1915–16 (AIR 1/2565–8, 2611–12, and 2618–19).

The airship service is also covered in the series (AIR 1/110–11, and 2314/222/1); and there are records of RNAS Airship Stations at Mullion and Pulham (AIR 1/423/15/252/1–2, and 437–8). The work of seaplane carriers is also represented (AIR 1/305/15/226/161) including the role of HMS *Engadine, Hermes, Glorious* and *Campania* as seaplane carriers (AIR 1/436/15/279/1, 436/15/281/1, 436/15/285/1, 436/15/286/1, 631/17/122/55, 636/17/122/132, and 1507/204/54/1); the performance of *Engadine* and *Campania* at Jutland (AIR 1/9/15/1/32, and 671/171/134/8); and the loss of a large American seaplane in April 1918 (AIR 1/342/15/226/273). There is material on the attempted take off from the turret roof of HMS *Repulse* in October 1917 (AIR 1/641/17/122/218), and on landing trials on HMS *Argus*, October 1918 (AIR 1/667/17/122/748). Details on seaplane raids include plans, proposals and reconnaissance for attacks on Cuxhaven in December 1914 (AIR 1/2099/207/23/4); Kiel, Emden and Borkum in April 1915 (AIR 1/148/15/86 and 88); and for a torpedo attack on the Kaiser Wilhelm Canal in October 1918 (AIR 1/643/17/122/276). There is also a photograph of results of a raid on the seaplane sheds at Ostend, May 1917 (AIR 1/660/17/122/630), and reports on the Tondern raid (AIR 1/455/15/312/44).

The role of aircraft in anti-submarine work is seen in statistics, weekly summaries and charts, 1918 (AIR 1/17/15/1/89 and 309/15/226/192); other anti-submarine patrol reports, 1917–18 (AIR 1/71/15/9/124, 253/15/226/81, 254/15/226/82, 255/15/226/83, 256/15/226/84, 2105, and 2314); and material on air dropped mines (AIR 1/72/15/9/141). Kite balloons are also covered including material on the kite balloon schools at Lydd and Larkhill, and material on the airship *SS40* (AIR 1/136/15/40/264, and 1529); and a short history of kite balloons (AIR 1/1951/204/258/1).

AIR 2 has minutes of a conference on landing aircraft on ships' decks, August 1917 (AIR 2/39/AIR 141757/1917); reports on the Fairey Seaplane, 1917–18 (AIR 2/969); and papers on a request by Murray Sueter to name a torpedo-carrying aircraft as the Sueter-Sopwith (AIR 2/37/AIR 02634/1917). There are reports by Beatty on the co-operation of airships with the Grand Fleet, September 1917 (AIR 2/37/AIR 02626/1917); on the downing of airship *C27* by a German seaplane (AIR 2/41/AIR 606427/1917); and on the co-operation of HMS *Comely Bank* and airship *C5A* in depth charging a U-boat (AIR 2/41/AIR 607058/1917). In addition, there are a number of airship daily reports, route charts and patrol reports (AIR 2/82/B 4627, and 174–190/MR 5241–53), and much on the Burney Scheme (AIR 2/168/MR 906–13 and 1557–8, 169/MR 1559, 1561–2, and 1567, 170/MR 1568, 1571–2, 1574–5, and 1578, 171/MR 1579, and 172/MR 1580–81). There is also material on kite balloons, including a report by Jellicoe in 1916 (AIR 2/77/B 1395, and 127/B 11683).

AIR 3/6–42 are the wartime log books for Airship Nos 2–5, 7–8, *SS17–18*, *SS20*, *SS22–24*, *SS33–34*, *SS36* and *NS11*.

AIR 10 has a general description of the RN Airship Station, Dunkirk, 1915 (AIR 10/502), and the RNAS Kite Balloon Training Manual, 1917 (AIR 10/270).

AIR 11 contains papers of the Royal Airship Works, Cardington. There are airship specifications (AIR 11/2–7); material on kite balloons generally, 1916–18 (AIR 11/211–15); photographs of balloons and balloon equipment, 1916–18 (AIR 11/219–25); and details of tests and experiments with accident reports (AIR 11/203–8).

AIR 12, containing airship and engine drawings of the Royal Airship Works, include details of Beta (AIR 12/2); C or Coastal (AIR 12/7, and 13–18); Delta (AIR 12/4); NS or North Sea (AIR 12/8); R (AIR 12/9–12, 19–24, and 2–104); and SS or Submarine Spotter (AIR 12/6) airship types.

AIR 59/1–10 contain photographs by the Directorate of Works including wartime airship sheds at Bedford, Howden and Pulham (AIR 59/1, and 5–7), wartime airship mooring towers (AIR 59/4), and wartime seaplane bases (AIR 59/8).

AIR 75/129 contains material on seaplanes, 1914–45, among the papers of Marshal of the Royal Air Force, Sir John Slessor.

AVIA 20, reports of the Naval Airship Works at Cardington, includes the so-called B, C and K Series reports on airships and balloons, 1917–19 (AVIA 20/175–236, and 268–467); assorted memoranda, 1916–18 (AVIA 20/469–71, 473–6, 478–85, 487–98, and 500–513); and the OR Series of reports, 1916–18 (AVIA 20/564–616), including a report on the French Balloon Defence Scheme, 1918 (AVIA 20/585).

AVIA 24 contains drawings of various types of balloons and their constructional details from the Naval (and Royal) Airship Works. These include the Italian AP type observation balloon developed in 1916 and employed as barrage balloons around London, 1917–18 (AVIA 24/1–63); B type captive balloons, 1917–18 (AVIA 24/64–88); M type meteorological balloons, 1917–22 (AVIA 24/413–59); models and baskets, 1917–23 (AVIA 24/460–529); Nurse balloons for storing hydrogen, 1917–18 (AVIA 24/530–57); and R type naval observation balloons, developed from a French army design, 1917–18 and later used on the south coast during the Second World War to observe the position of V2 launching sites (AVIA 24/558–605).

CAB 16/33 has papers from the ad-hoc committee of the Committee of Imperial Defence on seaplane and aeroplane stations, 1914.

CN 5 has photographs of metal mooring girders for naval airships, 1916 (CN 5/16), and of flying trials off HMS *Campania*, 1917 (CN 5/17).

DSIR 23 deals with investigations into the flow of air over the landing decks of both HMS *Campania* and *Furious* (DSIR 23/700 and 1094). There is also a report of the flying trials on HMS *Argus*, 1918 (DSIR 23/1273), and of experiments on models of HMS *Vindictive* and *Eagle* (DSIR 1221 and 1231).

Apart from its role in imposing food shortages upon civilians in central Europe, seapower was also used to attack civilians directly, the German High Seas Fleet bombarding West Hartlepool, Scarborough and Whitby on 16 December 1914, causing 133 civilian deaths. Naval bombardment of civilian targets was not repeated on a large scale though U-boats occasionally surfaced and fired shots at coastal targets, but it was the same airpower that so threatened the supremacy of the capital ship that showed even greater potential to strike at the will of a civilian society to wage war.

AIR 1 deals with German naval bombardment of Lowestoft and Yarmouth in April 1916 (AIR 1/577/16/15/167); and also contains details of casualties in all coastal bombardments, December 1914 to June 1918 (AIR 1/604/16/15/235).

BT 102, records of the Board of Trade's Reparation Claims Department, includes estimated figures for the damage to property and civilian casualties on the East Coast compiled in 1920–22 (BT 102/27); an assessment made in 1920 of the damage to property in Scarborough and Margate (BT 102/31); and Scottish police reports compiled in 1920–21 on wartime civilian losses from bombardment (BT 102/28). The Department was established in 1920 to prepare British claims against Germany arising from the terms of the Treaty of Versailles.

CAB 45/262–4 have material on the German raids on Scarborough and Hartlepool among the correspondence and papers relating to the compilation of the Official History of Naval Operations.

MT 9/964 has the proceedings of the Committee on Insurance Claims arising from the German raids on Scarborough, Hartlepool and Whitby, 1914.

WO 32/5261–5 contain reports on the German naval bombardment of coastal towns, 1914–16.

The War in the Air

Aircraft had been used in the Italo-Turkish War (1911–12) and, to a limited extent, in the Balkan Wars (1912–13), at least proving that there was a military potential. Initially, aircraft were regarded only as reconnaissance machines, as in the opening campaign of the war. In fulfilling the reconnaissance function, however, airmen began to experiment with improvised weapons to bring down opponents in the attempt to ensure unimpeded reconnaissance.

Three RFC machines became the first to force down an opponent on 25 August 1914. The RFC also undertook its first aerial spotting for artillery on 13 September, although, at this stage, aircraft were unable to communicate directly with the ground. Aerial wireless carried in a balloon was first used to direct artillery fire at Aubers Ridge on 9 May 1915 and aircraft were utilised to monitor the progress of an attack at St Julien on 25 April 1915 during Second Ypres. Aerial photography was first attempted by the RFC on 15 September 1914, although the first suitable camera was only developed in the following year. By 1918, however, photographic images could be taken as high as 15,000 feet. Arguably, indeed, aerial reconnaissance and observation remained the most important contribution of airpower to the war though, by 1917–18, the ground attack role, in which the RFC in particular had become adept, was of increasing significance.

AIR 1 has material on co-operation between army and RFC, including a complaint by Allenby, then commanding the Cavalry Division, of not getting sufficient air reconnaissance reports in August 1914 (AIR 1/2265/209/68/1); reconnaissance reports, October–November 1914 (AIR 1/751/204/4/8); a report on co-operation between artillery and balloons, December 1914–January 1915 (AIR 1/123/15/40/142);

material on the co-operation of artillery and aircraft at Loos in September 1915 (AIR 1/675/21/13/1322), and generally, 1915–18 (AIR 1/918–19); the use of balloons on the Somme in 1916 and by Third Army in 1918 (AIR 1/444/15/303/13); air operations in support of attack on Messines in June 1917 and Cambrai in November 1917 (AIR 1/676/21/13/1872, and 678/21/13/1942); and papers of Group Captain Ludlow Hewitt and Captain P. H. Sumner on aerial direction of artillery and tanks and aircraft co-operation with tanks (AIR 1/725). There are also reports on aerial observation, 1914–15 (AIR 1/782/204/4/514); notes for observers, June 1915 (AIR 1/128/15/40/178); and on training and grading of RFC observers, 1917–18 (AIR 1/161/15/123/15, and 1025–8).

Aerial photography material includes the proceedings of a conference on photography, July 1915 (AIR 1/127/15/40/147); a report on progress on photography, 1915–16 (AIR 1/123/15/40/144); camera training for pilots, 1915–16 (AIR 1/133/15/40/234); the establishment of the School of Photography at South Farnborough, 1916–18 (AIR 1/17/15/1/86); French and British photographic studies, 1916–18 (AIR 1/82/15/9/204–7); papers of Lieutenant Colonel J. T. C. Moore-Brabazon on photographic work, 1914–18 (AIR 1/724); notes on photography by Captain Campbell, December 1918 (AIR 1/7/6/98/20); and miscellaneous correspondence (AIR 1/538–9, 888–92, and 894). There are a large number of actual photographs, 1916–18 (AIR 1/83/15/9/208, 84–6, 178/15/212/4, 179–80, 181/15/212/4, 182, 499/15/327/1, 895–902, and 2269–79); photographs of Zeebrugge and Ostend after bombardment, May–June 1917 (AIR 1/305/15/226/156); of the Belgian and East African coasts (AIR 1/342/15/226/276–6); photographs before and after air raids (AIR 1/153/15/121/5, and 718/29/6); German photographs (AIR 1/500/15/328/1); reconnaissance photographs (AIR 1/154/122/2, and 155–9); and air survey photographs (AIR 1/2125).

On wireless, there is information on the establishment of the School of Wireless at Farnborough, 1916 (AIR 1/120/15/40/89); wireless telegraphy and directional wireless telegraphy, 1916–18 (AIR 1/71/15/9/126–7); and results of a conference on the tactical use of wireless telegraphy in France, 18 July 1918 (AIR 1/32/15/1/169).

AIR 2 includes reports on tests of ground attack aircraft, 1918 (AIR 2/1530); the design of the RE8 as a reconnaissance aircraft, 1916 (AIR 2/16/MA/AEROS/313); notes on co-operation with troops on the move, 1915 (AIR 2/7/87/4823); the development and design of the Lewis Gun aerial camera, 1916 (AIR 2/8/87/7117); and reports on aerial photography (AIR 2/38/AIR 140497/1917, and 38/AIR 03567/1917).

AIR 9/1 has papers on combined operations, 1914–30, among those of the Director of Air Plans.

AIR 10 includes an album of photographs taken by the RFC in 1917 (AIR 10/200), and also a photographic study of the characteristics of ground and landmarks of the German lines on the British front from the sea to St Quentin, 1918 (AIR 10/61).

AIR 69/2 is an account of the first steps in aerial photography compiled by Wing Commander W. Sholto Douglas in 1925.

AIR 75/131, among papers of Sir John Slessor, deals with air reconnaissance on the Aisne in 1914.

DSIR 23, reports of the Advisory Committee on Aeronautics, includes research into photo shutters for aerial cameras, 1916 (DSIR 23/671); and the effect of rifle fire on petrol tanks, 1917 (DSIR 23/973).

WO 153/1287 is a map showing enemy activity on the Western Front from aerial observations, January 1915.

WO 158 contains air reconnaissance reports from the Hejaz, July–August 1918 (WO 158/645); and reports on co-operation between RFC and artillery in Mesopotamia, 1915 (WO 158/681).

WO 316/56 has instructional photographs of aerial mosaics, 1917.

WO 317/13 has notes on aerial mapping during the Dardanelles campaign.

WO 319/1–6 consists of aerial photographs and panoramas of Palestine taken for survey purposes, inclining coverage of Aqaba and Gaza (WO 319/1–2).

WO 323/12 are undated aerial photographs of the Piave front in Italy.

Air superiority thus became increasingly recognised as a necessary adjunct to ground operations. It was assumed by early airpower theorists such as Frederick Sykes, however, that most air battles would only take place by mutual consent and that aircraft could literally hide in the vast expanse of the sky. Indeed, it appeared difficult to win command of the air without seeking constant battles that an opponent could choose to avoid. Consequently, for much of the war, the RFC's policy, as established by its GOC in the field from August 1915 to December 1917, Hugh Trenchard, was one of 'strategic offensive' to win command of the air over German lines. Trenchard's policy was one of continued standing patrols maintained regardless of the tactical situation on the ground. The Germans, meanwhile, could choose to concentrate aircraft to gain local superiority as desired. Inevitably, this resulted in losses both from German aircraft but also from the failure of damaged machines to make their way back to allied lines against the prevailing westerly winds.

The RFC's difficulties were compounded by the lack of progress made prior to the war in developing a British aviation industry compared to those in France and Germany. Consequently, there was over-reliance on the Royal Aircraft Factory, which trailed behind the Germans in technical efficiency, not least in engine development. Newer models constantly evolved with higher speed and higher rate of climb to present new challenges. The lead times in aircraft production, indeed, were sometimes measured only in weeks.

There was also a refusal by the RFC to adopt parachutes on the grounds that they were unreliable, too bulky and might lead airmen to abandon aircraft too readily – all demonstrably untrue. Indeed, both fixed and free fall parachutes were available before the war, but no British order was placed for free fall parachutes until September 1918, although agents were dropped behind German lines by such means. Attrition rates among aircrew were also increased by accidents.

The war in the air is often portrayed as one of personalised air duels between 'aces' but this was a relatively short-lived phenomenon as formation flying became the norm in 1916 and there was little of the 'knights of the air' chivalry suggested by wartime propaganda. Indeed, aerial warfare became as much a war of attrition and mass as that on the ground.

ADM 116 has material on air policy in 1916–17 and imperial air policy in 1917–18 (ADM 116/1519 and 1606).

ADM 178/833 is the RNAS navigational manual.

AIR 1 is a major source on air operations. Early material includes Henderson's remarks on RFC requirements, September 1914 (AIR 1/118/15/40/36); the establishments of the first four squadrons sent to France (AIR 1/162/15/124/2); semi-official correspondence of Trenchard and Sefton Brancker, the Deputy Director of Military Aeronautics at the War Office, 1914–15 (AIR 1/1283); Brooke-Popham's papers (AIR 1/1–7), with notes on the early history of the RFC, as well as letters written by him, March–August 1918 (AIR 1/1/1 and 11); returns of the number and type of squadrons in France, 1915–18 (AIR 1/1/4/22); and Sefton Brancker's notes on history of RFC compiled in 1915 (AIR 1/408/15/231/49). Policy issues are covered by minutes of Air Progress Committee (AIR 1/270/15/226/113); minutes of the Joint War Air Committee (AIR 1/133/15/40/237, 270/15/226/115, and 2319/223/26–8); minutes of the Progress and Allocation Committee (AIR 1/1144–5); reports from the Air Board to the War Cabinet, 1917–18 and other cabinet memoranda on air policy (AIR 1/500/15/331/2, and 2311–13), including papers on Lord Derby's resignation in 1916 (AIR 1/2312/221/39); minutes of the Committee on Air Organisation, 1917 (AIR 1/500/15/331/1); reports of the Committee on Administration and Command of the RFC, 1916 (AIR 1/2405/303/4/2); a paper by Trenchard on future air policy, 1916–17 (AIR 1/718/29/1); and minutes of the Inter-allied Aviation Committee, 1917–18 (AIR 1/25/15/1/119, and 2298–9).

Operational material includes correspondence of HQ, RFC, including reports and work summaries (AIR 1/750–821); routine orders and the index to them (AIR 1/829–32); the register of correspondence received, 1914–17 (AIR 1/832–3, and 1045–6); records of HQ Administration Wing, RFC (AIR 1/1283–1311); papers of GHQ, BEF RFC (AIR 1/2142–54); papers of the Director of Air Operations, 1914–18 (AIR 1/1951); and papers on the administration and command of the RFC, May–July 1916 (AIR 1/516–37). There are also Air Orders, 1916–18 (AIR 1/2433–4); returns of aircraft dispatched to operational and training units, 1914–18 (AIR 1/162/15/124/1, and 827/204/5/151); a comparison of British and French results on Western Front, 1916–18 (AIR 1/109/15/16); summaries of operations (AIR 1/674/21/6/95 and 106, 838, 2117, 2131); and the overall RFC/RAF War Diary, 1914–18 (AIR 1/1171–87).

A very large collection of assorted unit records, war diaries, log books, papers and histories of RFC, RNAS and RAF balloon sections, balloon companies, flights, wings, squadrons and stations (AIR 1/163–84, 362, 408–18, 433–4, 687–96, 734–49, 1232–46, 1252–82, 1310–2055, 2077–82, 2155–81, and 2183–2265), includes one anonymous diary of 10 Squadron, April 1918 (AIR 1/166/15/149/2). Aerial fighting is represented by fighting notes, 1916–18 (AIR 1/98/15/9/267, 122/15/40/113, 129/15/40/191, and 911); notes on observations of aerial gunfire, March 1916 (AIR 1/625/17/8); and combat reports (AIR 1/1216–28). There are reports on aerodromes and air parks, including Manston (AIR 1/1126, 1190–97, 1968, and 2014); while material on particular aircraft includes details of the BE2c, DH4, FE2, FE8, SE5, Handley Page, Spad and Sopwith models (AIR 1/14/15/1/58, 731/176/6/15–16, 904–5, 907, 1067–70, 1075–7, 1091–2, 1109–10, 1149–51, 1158, and 2608).

Equipment details include engine log books (AIR 1/2056–76); reports on the life of engines and causes of engine failure, 1917 (AIR 1/29/15/1/142); miscellaneous reports of aircraft casualties (AIR 1/822); engine reports (AIR 1/1098–1101, and 1105–6); weekly reports on states of aircraft and engines, and other engine reports (AIR 1/333–6, and 835).

Papers of the Royal Aircraft Factory, Farnborough (AIR 1/728–32) include monthly summaries of work, 1916–18 (AIR 1/732/176/6/23). Armament details are also covered including Lewis and Vickers guns (1086, and 1090–91); and there is a schedule of armament components, 1918 (AIR 1/2406–11). Training material includes files of the Directorate of Training (AIR 1/160–61), with instructions schemes for the Oxford and Reading Schools of Military Aeronautics (AIR 1/160/15/123/8, and 1831); complaints of pilots being sent out to the BEF without sufficient training, 1915–16 (AIR 1/131/15/40/218); night flying training (AIR 1/137/15/40/275); and papers on the Central Flying School (AIR 1/1625). Parachutes are discussed, with papers on the Spencer model, and E. R. Calthrop's 'Guardian Angel' (AIR 1/148/15/84, and 1121/204/5/2073), and supplies of parachutes to balloon crews (AIR 1/868). Support functions covered include the establishment of Schools of Fitters at Netheravon, Navigation and Bomb Dropping at Stonehenge, and Aerial Gunnery and Fighting (AIR 1/120/15/40/86, and 122/15/40/136–7). There are also bound correspondence volumes of the War Office directorates of Military Aeronautics and Air Organisation and other War Office correspondence (AIR 1/362–407, and 2086).

There is coverage of French air operations, including those at Verdun (AIR 1/881, 1283, and 2251); co-operation with the Belgian air force, 1918 (AIR 1/89/15/9/216); a report on the Russian Aviation Corps, 1916 (AIR 1/2002/204/276/3); the Australian Flying Corps and South African Aviation Corps (AIR 1/1044/204/5/1506, and 1247–51); training the US Army Air Service (AIR 1/450/15/312/7); and consideration of aerial violations of Dutch neutrality (AIR 1/65/15/9/94, and 93/15/9/237). Material on the German air force includes Brooke-Popham's notes and reports on captured German aircraft, 1915–18 (AIR 1/4/26/5–6, 9–10, 12–14, 3/4/16–17, 20–22, and 4/4/26/23–9); notes and photographs of German aircraft (AIR 1/7/4/56/12–16); historical reports on German air operations at Mons and on the Marne in 1914 (AIR 1/8/15/1/18, and 2132/207/127/1); statistics of German aircraft driven down by British and French machines, 1916–18 (AIR 1/109/15/22), notes on German war organisation (AIR 1/8/15/1/9, and 2255); and some German accounts (AIR 1/2398).

AIR 2 has material on experiments and trials with parachutes, including Calthrop's 'Guardian Angel' (AIR 2/978–82 and 55/AB 275/8242), and on their use in dropping agents (AIR 2/81/3597). There is a file on the types of aircraft and engines used on active service, 1914–18 (AIR 2/5/87/1860), and also specifications for particular aircraft such as the FE4 and Bristol Fighter (AIR 2/1045, 16/MA/FE4/1, 165/MR 107722–3, 16/MA/Aeroplanes/1230, 2/87/304, 11/87/Aeroplanes/1524, and 12/AS 29578/18). Some operational matters are also covered, including a report on distribution of aircraft and engines, December 1916 to April 1917 (AIR 2/124/B 10984); losses of engines on charge to the BEF, January to June 1917 (AIR 2/47/AB 145/35); and the additional 40 squadrons proposed for the RFC in 1917–18 (AIR 2/59/5324/1918). Other policy matters covered include a statement of the duties of the RNAS for the Joint War Air Committee, February 1916, and a summary of RNAS operations on the Belgian coast, May 1916

(AIR 2/35/AIR 0396/1915, and 35/AIR 01148/1916). There are also reports on the Italian and Russian air services, and on the training of American squadrons in Canada (AIR 2/42/AIR 608614/1917, 89/A 15625, and 944)

AIR 5/1348 has material on tests carried out on the Calthrop parachute, 1917.

AIR 6 contains the minutes of the Air Board, 1916–17 (AIR 6/1–11), originally established in May 1916; and minutes and memoranda of the Air Council, 1918, which succeeded the Air Board in January 1918 upon the creation of the Air Ministry (AIR 6/12–13, and 16–19).

AIR 8, comprising papers of the Chief of the Air Staff, includes more minutes of the Air Council, 1918–19 (AIR 8/5), and a synopsis of the British air effort, 1914–18 (AIR 8/13). There is also material on allegations of false markings on aircraft, 1914–15 (AIR 8/4).

AIR 11/217 deals with parachute experiments at the Naval Aircraft Works, Cardington.

AIR 19/84–6 contain files on the shape of the post-war RAF among private office papers of successive Secretaries of State for Air and their Permanent Under Secretary, J. L. Baird, 1917–19.

AIR 27 are Squadron Operational Record Books, The great majority are from the Second World War, but some cover the Great War (AIR 27/191, 233, 252, 258, 278, 305, 341, 388, 397, 406, 424, 435, 460, 480, 501, 527, 554, 583, 598, 624, 629, 645, 650, 655, 660, 669, 681, 686, 694, 716, 807, 826, 841, 849, 857, 865, 878, 887, 1000, 1089, 1177, 1197, 1214, 1221, 1233, 1239, 1291, 1298, 1332, 1338, 1383, 1412, and 1422).

AIR 69/1 contains lectures on the air war on the Western Front delivered at the RAF Staff College by Air Vice Marshal Brooke-Popham in 1926.

AIR 72/1 comprises the Air Ministry's Weekly Orders, 1918–20.

AVIA 6/13554 deals with head resistance tests on the BE2c in 1917.

AVIA 14 contains tracings of aircraft, engines and ancillary equipment designed and built at the Royal Aircraft Factory, Farnborough, 1911–18, as well as drawings of aircraft and equipment of interest to the factory but not constructed by it. Included are the BE 1–12 models (AVIA 14/1–17); CE1 (AVIA 14/18); FE1–12 models and their derivatives (AVIA 14/19–37); HRE2 (AVIA 14/38); RE1–9 models (AVIA 14/39–48); SE1–5A models (AVIA 14/49–53); and TE1 (AVIA 14/55). Contractor aircraft included are Bristol, Cierva, de Havilland, Hamble, Handley Page, Short, and Sopwith machines (AVIA 14/56). There are additional drawings of engines, ancillary equipment and components such as wireless transmitters, gun sights and speaking tubes (AVIA 14/57–65, and 85–126), as well as drawings of some specific aircraft (AVIA 14/66–84).

CAB 1 includes a report on the number of aircraft available to the RFC in May 1915 (CAB 1/12), and on its work in September 1917 (CAB 1/25).

CAB 14/1 has minutes and memoranda of the Air Committee of the Committee of Imperial Defence, 1912–14, the committee being formed in 1912 to consider all aerial matters referred to it by the CID or by government departments.

CAB 17/152 has correspondence of the Committee of Imperial Defence on the Joint War-Air Committee, 1916.

CAB 21/21 has the reports of the Cabinet Air Organisation Committee. Chaired by Smuts, it was established in August 1917 to examine and report on the arrangements for the amalgamation of the RFC and RNAS.

CAB 27 contains papers of the Cabinet Joint War-Air Committee, February to March 1916 (CAB 27/5), and minutes and papers of the Cabinet Air Policy Committee, established under the chairmanship of Smuts in October 1917 (CAB 27/9).

CAB 45/214 is the diary of a quartermaster with No 4 Squadron, RFC in 1914.

DSIR 23, reports of the Advisory Committee for Aeronautics, includes tests carried out on the BE2 in 1914 (DSIR 23/349–50, 368, 393, and 401) and on mounting a machine gun in front of the propeller of the BE9 in 1915 (DSIR 23/536). There is also information on 'aerial musketry' in 1915 (DSIR 23/568), and attacking aircraft from aircraft in 1917 (DSIR 23/813).

PRO 10 has a variety of samples of Air Ministry documents later destroyed (PRO 10/111, 347–9, 402–17, 435, 448–53, 484–94, 767–8, 775, 785–6, 791, 793–5, 797–9, 821, 823, 959–61, 984, 1056, and 1116–19).

TS 27 includes miscellaneous material on legal aspects of the establishment of the RAF (TS 27/58 and 67).

WO 32 deals with the parliamentary bill authorising the establishment of the RAF and transfer of army personnel to it (WO 32/9289–91, and 9350).

WO 33 has the printed report of the Inter-departmental Committee on Aircraft Landing Places, 1914 (WO 33/678); the provisional training manual for the RFC Military Wing, 1915 (WO 33/737); and the RFC's war establishment, 1917 (WO 33/822).

WO 106/323 has the views of Haig and Pétain on bombing behind enemy lines in support of ground operations, 1917.

WO 153/1231–43 contain maps and charts relating to German air activity over the Western Front, 1914–18, including daily records for 1918.

WO 158/34–5 deal with RFC operations on the Western Front, 1916–17.

At the same time that the effectiveness of airpower was established in relation to ground operations, including the use of tactical bombing, the first wartime experiments also took place with strategic bombing. Technically, aerial attack was prohibited by the Hague conventions of 1899 and 1907 but, since Germany had not signed them, any prohibition was not operative, for it only applied to conflicts between signatories. In any case, since the wording of the conventions was obscure with regard to aerial warfare, most states assumed bombing was legitimate.

On 22 September 1914 the RNAS, which had a more wide-ranging view of the potential of airpower than the RFC, carried out the first really genuine strategic bombing mission on a military target by attacking Zeppelin sheds at

Dusseldorf and Cologne. The first air raids on civilian targets were those by Zeppelins on French and Belgian Channel ports on 21 August 1914 followed by a raid on Paris on 30 August. Great Yarmouth became the first British town attacked on 19 January 1915, with London attacked for the first time on 31 May 1915.

Two years later, on 25 May 1917, the first German strategic air raid using conventional aircraft – Gotha G. IV bombers based at Ghent – rather than dirigibles, was launched on Folkestone. The campaign then extended to London by day and night, one daylight raid on 13 June 1917 by 14 Gothas causing 162 deaths and near panic in the East End. This raid and the appearance of 21 Gothas over London in daylight on 7 July, which resulted in riotous attacks on allegedly German-owned property in the East End, played a decisive role in the establishment of the Smuts Committee. It also persuaded King George V to change his dynastic name from Saxe-Coburg-Gotha to Windsor.

Smuts first recommended a reorganisation of home air defence with more and better aircraft. In a second report on 17 August 1917, Smuts recommended retaliation directed by an authority independent of army and naval rivalries. Following further raids, an air ministry and air staff were established in January 1918 with the Independent Force, Royal Air Force (IAF, RAF), coming into independent existence on 1 April 1918. The RNAS had carried out 13 bombing raids on some German towns from Luxeuil near Belfort between July 1916 and March 1917, but the RAF was tasked on 6 June 1918 with retaliatory attacks on the German homeland. Some 242 raids were carried out on Germany and 543 tons of bombs dropped, at the cost of 109 aircraft lost and 243 wrecked. The tonnage was too small to do much damage and, as early as June 1918, it was concluded that only 23.5 per cent of bombs were falling within the designated target area. The raids resulted in 797 German dead, 380 wounded and an estimated 15 million marks' worth of damage.

German raids resulted in 1,413 of the 1,570 wartime civilian deaths in Britain through enemy action. Little thought had been given to co-ordinating air defence prior to the war and inter-service rivalry continued to bedevil its evolution. A blackout or rather 'dim out' was introduced for defended harbours in August 1914 and was extended to other designated areas. Zeppelin attacks on inland targets such as Burton-on-Trent and Walsall in early 1916 forced a more general extension. The Gotha raids then compelled the introduction of an official air raid warning system in July 1917, policemen on bicycles issuing warnings and Boy Scouts sounding the 'all clear'. The problem was that air defence proved highly ineffective – in 397 sorties the Germans lost only 24 Gothas over England – while tying up over 300 British machines. Moreover, it was calculated that the anti-aircraft guns had needed to fire 14,540 rounds to bring down one aircraft. Improved range finding and sound location devices became available, but the air defence fighters themselves were technically limited.

It was therefore concluded that there was no effective anti-aircraft defence against the bomber though, in reality, neither the Gotha raids nor those of the RAF either proved or disproved the evolving theories of strategic airpower in which both sides had invested so much expectation. Zeppelins, however, could be caught through their slow rate of climb. Flight Sub-Lieutenant Rex Warneford successfully dropped bombs on one on 6 June 1915 over Ghent and Lieutenant W. Leefe Robinson shot down a similar Schütte Lanz dirigible with new incendiary bullets over Cuffley in Hertfordshire on 2/3 September 1915. In all, Germany lost 17 airships in combat.

ADM 1/8425/178 is a report on the anti-aircraft defences of Paris and the use of French 75 mm field guns in an anti-aircraft role, June 1915.

ADM 116 has material on the RNVR Anti-Aircraft Corps and anti-aircraft defences (ADM 116/1344–7 and 1402–8); fire precautions to be taken in dockyards against Zeppelin raids, 1915, and the reduction of ships' lights during air raids (ADM 116/1448 and 1473); and details of air raid casualties at Chatham on 3 September 1917 (ADM 116/1615B).

ADM 137 has a history of German airships, 1915–19 (ADM 137/3964); photographs of German airship bases (ADM 137/4125); material on air raid precautions in East Anglia, 1915 (ADM 137/4174); a report on the death in a flying accident in June 1915 of Flight Sub-Lieutenant Warneford VC just a few days after downing his Zeppelin (ADM 137/4820); and records of the RNVR Anti-Aircraft Corps in defence of London (ADM 137/476 and 4826).

ADM 156/167 is the inquiry into the mistaken bombing of Zierikzee in the Netherlands by No 5 Wing, RFC in July 1917.

ADM 178/559 deals with German rigid airships, 1917.

AIR 1 has a considerable amount of material on bombing, including details of RNAS schemes for repelling both Zeppelins and aircraft (AIR 1/146/15/59, and 361/15/228/11); general reports on German air raids (AIR 1/568–603, 645, 647, and 2123–4); and GHQ communiqués and reports on raids (AIR 1/610/16/15/277, and 2319/223/30/1–27). Early raids are covered by reports on observations made during air raids, January 1915 (AIR 1/818/204/4/1313); police reports on raids, January–June 1915 (AIR 1/552/16/15/38); and correspondence on raids, September–December 1915, and the defence against them (AIR 1/546/16/15/17, 547/15/18 Pts III–IV). There are reports on particular Zeppelin raids on Aldeburgh, Dover, Goole, Hull, Lowestoft, Newcastle, the Tyne, and Ramsgate (AIR 1/549/16/15/19, 564/16/15/78–81, 634/17/122/111–13, 635/17/122/114, and 2576), with photographs of damage to Derby and Burton-on-Trent (AIR 1/943/204/5/984). There was a discovery of a box of incendiaries after a raid on Grimsby, September 1918 (AIR 1/639/17/122/191), while there had been earlier public warnings not to touch bombs in 1915 (AIR 1/657/17/122/571).

Special consideration was given to the defence of the Tyne including the Armstrong and Whitworth works (AIR 1/656/17/122/545). There are minutes of the first meeting of the Air Raids Committee, October 1917 (AIR 1/2423/305/18/44); minutes of the War Cabinet Committee on Air Raid Policy, 1917–18 (AIR 1/678/21/13/2102); and of the Committee on Home Defence against Air Raids, August 1917 (AIR 1/2312/22/43). The defence of London against both Zeppelins and aircraft is covered with reports on its lighting as observed from the air (AIR 1/147/15/70); the effect of bombs dropped (AIR 1/35/15/1/213, 562/16/15/65); the capital's anti-aircraft defence (AIR 1/504/16/3/25, and 512/16/3/62, 513/16/3/75); the allotment of aircraft for home defence (AIR 1/

506/16/3/44 and 507/16/3/46); and plans to obscure the Thames with a smoke screen (AIR 1/618/16/15/339). There is more general material on the method of attacking hostile raiders, 1917 (AIR 1/820/204/4/1319); papers, including a diary and notes on the RNVR Anti-Aircraft Corps, 1914–18 (AIR 1/648/17/122/385); and a general assessment from 1922 on the effect of bombing on British industry (AIR 1/2132).

The Zeppelin threat is also covered by interrogation reports of survivors from Zeppelins brought down (AIR 1/540–42); the burial of deceased German aircrew (AIR 1/565/16/15/93); charges of pilfering from bodies of such dead aircrew (AIR 1/613/16/15/308); and the disposal of wrecked enemy aircraft, 1916 (AIR 1/2609). There are details of the destruction of *L21* and *L31* (AIR 1/721/59/12/1, and 2548); copies of letters removed from *LZ77*, February 1916 (AIR 1/296/15/226/147); and reports on destruction of Zeppelins by Warneford, Leefe Robinson and by Lieutenant S. D. Culley in August 1918 (AIR 1/343/15/226/283, 547/15/18 Pts I–II, 605/16/15/247).

Further afield, there is a report on an enemy raid on Venice, September 1916 (AIR 1/657/17/122/566). Material on retaliatory action by the new IAF, RAF includes much on the formation of, and policy for, the IAF (AIR 1/30/15/1/155/1–3, 109/15/16, 912/204/5/847, 970/204/5/1110); HQ papers of the IAF (AIR 1/1972–2000); IAF communiqués (AIR 1/2085); and correspondence between Trenchard and Lord Weir on the IAF, May–June 1918 (AIR 1/2422/305/18/11). Actual operational material on bombing includes reports of No 3 Wing based at Luxeuil (AIR 1/111–15), with daily aeronautical reports (AIR 1/113/15/39/40–43); a draft history of the Wing and record of its operations (AIR 1/114/15/39/45, and 115/15/39/71); and its officers' qualifications for bombing, July–August 1916 (AIR 1/115/15/39/54). Other bombing unit reports include those of No 9 Wing, March–April 1918 (AIR 1/145/15/41/1–4); other squadron bombing reports (AIR 1/840–42); and reports on the work of the Handley Page night bombing squadron (AIR 1/2684).

General operational material includes Trenchard's reports on IAF operations (AIR 1/458/15/312/69, and 718/29/5); statistical summaries and reports of RNAS bombing raids, 1916–18 (AIR 1/271/15/226/118, and 633); bombing statistics, 1917–18 (AIR 1/61/15/9/72–6); an encyclopedia of bombing missions, 1917–18 (AIR 1/2691); miscellaneous reports on bombing operations, 1916–18 (AIR 1/62/15/9/1, 63/15/9/82–4, 479/15/312/241–3, 955–8, 2104/207/36, and 2428/305/29/1225); and assessments of their effects on German industry (AIR 1/460/15/312/99, and 101–102). There were various suggestions for destroying crops and forests from the air (AIR 1/115/15/39/67, and 2546), including the Houthulst forest in June 1915 (AIR 1/2151/209/3/251).

Reports on individual bombing missions include those by Commander Samson on raids on Brussels and Bruges in November 1914, and on bombing operations on the Western Front, February 1915 (AIR 1/361/15/228/52, and 2545); while other raids described are those on Bruges, Cologne, Dusseldorf, Friedrichshafen, Volklingen, Zeebrugge and the St Ingbert Iron Foundries (AIR 1/361/15/228/19–20, 466/15/312/158, 537/16/12/140, and 2549). Targets in Germany attacked by 8 Brigade, RFC and the IAF, 1917–18 (AIR 1/451/15/312/19–20, 24, 28, and 97, and 2154/209/3/311) are also covered, with reports on the effects of bombing on the Rhenish population (AIR 1/2296/209/77/9). There are also reports on bombing in the Aegean and Adriatic (AIR 1/457/15/312/59 and 83); and a report on a visit to the French Bombardment Group, March 1916 (AIR 1/121/15/40/102).

AIR 2 has much on German bombing raids, including reports of those on Margate, Hull, Derby, Burton-on-Trent, Dover, and Dunkirk (AIR 2/124/B 10904–8, B 10910, and B 10997, 37/AIR 02345/1917, and 18/MA MISC 351); and also details of the meeting between the Air Board and the Parliamentary Air Committee to discuss German air raids on 26 June 1917 (AIR 2/105/A 15920). Air defence measures include consideration of a scheme to display false ground lights to confuse Zeppelins (AIR 2/34/X 8621/1916); the RNAS contribution to home air defence (AIR 2/124/B 10908); aircraft available for the defence of London in June 1916 (AIR 2/124/B 10897); wireless control of home defence fighters (AIR 2/10/87/ 9131); and defences against night bombing (AIR 2/163/MR 1669). There was careful scrutiny of the remains of Zeppelins and Gothas brought down over England (AIR 2/36/AIR 01598/1917, 36/AIR 02129/1916, 40/AIR 602453/1917, 40/ AIR 603521/1917, 41/AIR 605815/1917, and 15/DP(A) 11865/18).

There is material on the creation of the Independent Force (AIR 2/76/B 225, and 78/B 1580); aerial routes for its missions over France (AIR 2/76/B 55), and monthly dispatches on its operations (AIR 2/83/B 4664). On British retaliatory bombing, there are notes by Trenchard on bombing operations, 1915–16 (AIR 2/8/ 87/7042); a report on the British and French bombing raid on Oberdorf (AIR 2/123/B 10827); proposals to bomb Zeebrugge (AIR 2/80/B 2824); notes on multi-engine bombers by the Armament Experimental Station at Orfordness (AIR 2/732); specifications for the Vickers Vimy heavy bomber (AIR 2/948); and general policy on bombing Germany, 1916–18, including charts to illustrate the British bombing effort in 1918 (AIR 2/86/B 6864, 124/B 110880, 129/B 12149, and 197/MR 7119). In addition, there are documents and photographs from the Michelin School of Bombing in France, 1917 (AIR 2/39/AIR 150772/1917).

AIR 9/6 has material from the papers of the Director of Air Plans on bombing land objectives, 1917–37.

AIR 11 contains drawings and plans of Zeppelin *L49* (AIR 11/51); and photographs of components of wrecked Zeppelins (AIR 11/239–40).

AIR 12/25 has drawings of the German LSS airship type.

AIR 69, papers of the RAF Staff College, Andover, include notes made by Air Vice Marshal Brooke-Popham, 1924–7, on the formation of the IAF in 1918 (AIR 69/3), as well as reports of bombing operations by 41st Wing, VIII Brigade, RFC and the IAF, 1917–18, and other miscellaneous papers on the IAF (AIR 69/4–5).

BT 13 has some material on air raid insurance in both 1915 and 1917 (BT 13/64, 78 and 80), and on air raids in general (BT 13/84).

BT 102/21 deals with wartime air raid casualties as part of the post-war calculation by the Board of Trade's Reparation Claims Department of the compensation to be distributed arising from the imposition of reparations upon Germany.

CAB 1, the miscellaneous Cabinet papers collected by Sir Masterton-Smith, reflects the new aerial threat with papers on the defence of Sheffield against air attack in February 1915 (CAB 1/15); Zeppelin attacks on London in 1916 (CAB 1/17); and the possibility of air-delivered germ warfare (CAB 1/23). There is also material on the delivery of anti-aircraft equipment and the use of an Italian field gun in an anti-aircraft role (CAB 1/17–18).

CAB 17/137–8 contain miscellaneous correspondence of the Committee of Imperial Defence on air defence measures, 1916.

CAB 21 deals with air defence, 1917 (CAB 21/27), and the implications of reductions in the size of the London Fire Brigade (CAB 21/106). It also includes the report of the Cabinet Committee on Aerial Operations, established under Lloyd George's chairmanship in July 1917 to examine defensive arrangements against air raids and the general organisation for the study and fighter direction of aerial operations (CAB 21/21).

CAB 27/9 contains minutes and papers of the Cabinet Air Raids Committee, established under the chairmanship of Smuts in October 1917 to consider the replacement of guns and the provision of ammunition for use against air raids, and to consider a retaliatory policy.

CN 5/1 has photographs of bomb damage at Faversham, Kent, 1918.

CSC 5/94 deals with air raid precautions for civil servants.

CUST 49/410 also deals with air raid precautions.

DSIR 23, containing reports of the Advisory Committee for Aeronautics, includes a number on bombing and its problems, 1915–18 (DSIR 23/472–3, 475, 527, 543, 557, 605, 649, 936–8, and 1073). In addition, there is material on the effect of anti-aircraft fire, 1916 (DSIR 23/866), and on equipment recovered from Zeppelins *L15*, *L33*, *L70* and *LZ77* (DSIR 23/708, 734, 748, 769, 884–5, 893, and 1257).

ED 12/23 deals with problems arising from air raids, 1915–17.

ED 24/2033 also deals with the implications of air raids, 1917.

HO 45 has a little material on naval and air bombardment of Britain in general (HO 45/283152); the public's responsibility in the matter of air raid precautions HO 45/344919); and the effects of air raids on buildings (HO 45/346450).

HO 139/20 includes material on the treatment of German aerial and naval bombardment by the Official Press Bureau.

MEPO 2 has material relating to the formation of the RAF (MEPO 2/1622), but also on air raid precautions, including an anti-aircraft poster, 1915 (MEPO 2/1621); material on air raid shelters in the Thames Tunnels and tube stations (MEPO 2/1657 and 1735–9); and reports on the Zeppelins shot down at Cuffley and Potters Bar in 1916 (MEPO 2/1652 and 1654).

MT 6 has some material on air raid precautions in relation to the railways, 1914–16 (MT 6/2428/6); compensation for railwaymen killed in air raids (MT 6/2471/13); and railway raid shelters (MT 6/2489/11).

MT 9 has a little material on insurance claims arising from air raids, including an appeal for rebuilding assistance following incendiary bomb damage in 1915 (MT 9/1005); a claim by J. Smith for bomb damage to a garden fence, 1915 (MT 9/1013); and claims made under the Air Raid Scheme, 1919–20 (MT 9/1424).

NATS 1/237 deals with planning of air raid precautions.

SUPP 5/1052 is a personal record of air raid alarms at the Woolwich Arsenal's Main Factory East, 1915–18, compiled by F. Blythe.

T 172/513 contains, among miscellaneous papers of the Chancellor of the Exchequer's office, a report on special measures taken against air raids in Ramsgate, 1917.

WO 32 has material on precautions against raids by aircraft and airships, including a conference on air defence held in 1914 and the transfer of responsibility for anti-aircraft defence to the Air Ministry (WO 32/5257–8 and 5260). There is also a file on the formation of the Anti-Aircraft Corps in 1917 (WO 32/11514). Trials into the use of rifles and machine guns against aircraft were undertaken at both Hythe and Shoeburyness between 1910 and 1915 (WO 32/9089). There was also a plan in 1918 to manufacture new long-range guns for the bombardment of German towns (WO 32/5161). Inevitably, allegations of war crimes emerged, including the bombing of the British hospital at Etaples in 1918 (WO 32/5189), and there was careful definition of the policy towards bombing Belgian towns (WO 32/5565).

WO 33 has some printed material on anti-aircraft defence methods, equipment, and arrangements (WO 33/720, 727, 746, 775, 828, and 861), including the war establishment for the London anti-aircraft defences and RGA fixed anti-aircraft defences (WO 33/764, 766, 791, 839, 846, 873, and 914).

WO 106 covers anti-aircraft protection at Boulogne, 1915–18 (WO 106/1478), and air raid organisation in Britain, 1918 (WO 106/6288).

WO 153/1325–34 contain 'air packets' of maps including bombing targets for October 1918.

WO 158 includes reports on German airship, aeroplane and seaplane raids on Britain, 1915–18 (WO 158/935–60, 975–80, and 992–4).

WORK 6/362/6 has a report on air raid precautions by the Royal Institute of British Architects, 1916.

Absorbing the Lessons

Looking at the contribution of technology as a whole, the emergence of the aircraft carrier *Argus* at the very end marks the nature of the Great War. It was a new kind of conflict in that tanks, manned aircraft and aircraft carriers all emerged, but their potential really lay all in the future. Indeed, much that occurred was traditional in terms of the line of battle at Jutland or the cavalry charges that took place on the Eastern front and in Palestine. In that sense, therefore, it was a transitional conflict in military terms. Not surprisingly, all belligerents attempted to evaluate the war's lessons through Official Histories.

All belligerents began by publishing their own series of selected documents in the inter-war years to support their version of the war's outbreak. The diplomatic series of volumes, *British Documents on the Origins of the War*, were then supplemented by operational and other narratives. If all the supplementary volumes of maps and appendices are included, the record of *Military Operations* in all theatres ran to 44 volumes, 26 dealing with the Western Front, five with Egypt and Palestine, four with Gallipoli, four with Mesopotamia, two with

Macedonia, one with Italy, one with East Africa, one with Togoland and Cameroon. Even then, the narrative of *Military Operations: East Africa* remained incomplete as its author died before completing the second volume, while three volumes covering operations in Persia and the post-war occupations of the Rhineland and Constantinople were not published until the 1990s. An additional six volumes dealt with Orders of Battle. Including supplementaries, *Naval Operations* consumed nine volumes with three additional volumes on *The Merchant Navy*, four volumes on *Seaborne Trade*, and one volume on *The Blockade of the Central Empires*. *The War in the Air* comprised eight volumes. The Official Medical History, *Medical Services*, and its supplementaries ran to 13 volumes and there were also eight volumes of *The History of the Ministry of Munitions* and a chronological volume listing the war's principal events.

While the official historians had access to papers that would not be made available to the public until after the passing of the Public Record Acts of 1958 and 1967, imposing respectively the 50 and 30 Year Rules, they had little corrective impact in Britain since so much remained deliberately hidden. In the case of the official history of military operations, for example, the last volume of which on Passchendaele only appeared in 1948, criticism tended only to appear in the voluminous appendices and, on occasions, evidence was massaged or twisted by Brigadier Sir James Edmonds. In any case, 'official history' was not the same as objective history.

ADM 1 contains material on proposed war histories from February 1916 and January 1919 (ADM 1/8449/38 and 8548/5), and the abandonment of plans to publish an official narrative of Jutland in September 1920 (ADM 1/8592/125). The Admiralty also made its views known with regard to the introduction and first eight chapters of the first volume of *The War in the Air* in December 1921 (ADM 1/8617/223).

ADM 137/4827–36 consist of drafts of chapters in volume five of *Naval Operations*.

AIR 5/495 deals with the appointment of Dr Hogarth to complete *The War in the Air*, and contains other papers on the history.

CAB 17/119 deals with consideration by the Committee of Imperial Defence in 1915 of the production of a popular history of the war.

CAB 42/1/18 has the report of the Work of the Historical Section Sub-committee of the Committee of Imperial Defence, January 1915.

CAB 44 contains narratives utilised in the compilation of the Official Histories, as well as drafts of the eventual published material. General narrative material includes a paper on the genesis of aviation medicine by C. B. Heald (CAB 44/1); a short history of wars in German East Africa, 1884–1911 (CAB 44/3); a diary of the war with a summary of events, August 1914 to June 1915 (CAB 44/40–41); and notes for guidance for Second World War official historians compiled by Edmonds as a result of his experiences in compiling that for the Great War (CAB 44/428). There are draft chapters from Volumes II-IV of *Military Operations: France and Belgium* (CAB 44/16–30), some with marginal notes by Haig, his head of intelligence, Charteris, and Sir Richard Haking (CAB 44/16–19); draft chapters from the uncompleted second volume of *Military Operations: East Africa*

(CAB 44/4–10); and some draft chapters from *Naval Operations* with extracts from Lloyd George's *War Memoirs* (CAB 44/42–3). In addition, there are the complete manuscripts of the three volumes not published until the 1990s, namely *The Occupation of the Rhineland, Operations in Persia, 1914–19* and *The Occupation of Constantinople, 1918–23* (CAB 44/31, 37, and 39).

CAB 45, correspondence and papers relating to the Official Histories, include draft chapters and comments upon them for *Military Operations: East Africa* (CAB 45/60–70); and correspondence on *The Occupation of the Rhineland* (CAB 45/81–2); *Operations in Persia* (CAB 45/100); and *The Occupation of Constantinople* (CAB 45/108–109). Narratives and drafts related to *Military Operations: France and Belgium* include comments by Haig and Generals Headlam and Jeudwine (CAB 45/182–3).

CAB 103 contains registered files of the Cabinet Office Historical Section. It includes periodical progress reports on the compilation of the Official Histories, 1915–45 (CAB 103/1–21); annual estimates, 1916–46 (CAB 103/22–51); and periodical reports, 1939–50 (CAB 103/63–7). There is correspondence with the French, German and United States official historians (CAB 103/69–71); and papers of the Committee on Official War Histories, 1922–3, and the Sub-committee on Official Histories, 1929–39 (CAB 103/73–5, and 102). There is also correspondence on particular volumes including *Medical Services* (CAB 45/81); *Military Operations: East Africa* (CAB 103/84–94), with comments on drafts by Colonial, Dominion, Foreign and War Offices; *Military Operations: Italy, 1915–19* (CAB 103/114); the 1915 and 1918 volumes of *Military Operations: France and Belgium* (CAB 103/77, 79–80, and 95), with War Office comments; comments on the long delayed Passchendaele volume of *Military Operations: France and Belgium* (CAB 103/111–12); and *Military Operations: Gallipoli* (CAB 103/78) with Foreign Office comments. There is general correspondence from 1939–46 (CAB 103/52–62) including that of Edmonds (CAB 103/53), and on some specific issues such as the disposal of the Haig diaries (CAB 103/55); and gun casualties in 1918 (CAB 103/62). Some specific matters also covered include questions at issue between Britain and the United States, 1914–15 (CAB 103/96), and British and German air strengths in March 1918 (CAB 103/99).

FD 1/5349 contains the Army Medical Service's official history of the war.

MT 25 has some material on the compilation of *Seaborne Trade* (MT 25/24) and upon the collection of statistics for it (MT 25/58).

MUN 5/321B–340 contain schemes for, and correspondence on, the compilation of the official history of the Ministry of Munitions.

TS 46/9 deals with the legal aspects raised, 1935–9, by the custody of copies of Haig's diaries made by the War Office.

WO 32 has papers on the work of the Battle Honours Committee, 1921–5, which allocated battle honours to units, based on the recommended identification of particular actions by the Battle Nomenclature Committee (WO 32/5149 and 5920–22). The work also included allocation of French and Italian decorations to representative units as opposed to individuals (WO 32/5439–43 and 11545). There is material on the recognition of the services rendered by units which had existed only during the war (WO 32/4820), and on the disposal of funds of such units

(WO 32/5449 and 5958). There are papers on aspects of the organisation of the War Cabinet's Historical Section and the collection of War Office data for it (WO 32/9306–8); observations by the War Office on drafts of *Naval Operations* and *The War in the Air* (WO 32/2980 and 4825); and comments on drafts of *Military Operations: Gallipoli* and the first two volumes of *Military Operations: France and Belgium* (WO 32/2979, 2981, and 4826–35). Work was carried out in the archives of the Turkish War Office after the war to illuminate the conduct of the Gallipoli campaign (WO 32/9636). The controversy surrounding the collapse of the British Fifth Army in March 1918 was reflected in formal exchange of historical information with the Germans between 1920 and 1923 on the strength of their forces during the spring offensive (WO 32/5793).

WO 161 has a copy of the third report of the Battle Honours Committee, 1922 (WO 161/83), and reports of the Battle Nomenclature Committee, 1922 (WO 161/95–101).

3. The Nation in Arms

GOVERNMENTS AND ARMED FORCES had anticipated a short war. They were then forced to confront the realities not only of massive casualties, but also of competing demands for manpower between the armed forces, industry and agriculture, as the conflict became one in which it was just as vital to out-produce as to out-fight the enemy. Not surprisingly, the manpower pool available to the armed forces rapidly declined, with ever more desperate efforts to comb out every possible fighting man from the civilian population. Ultimately, in the case of Britain, conscription followed in 1916 from what the Labour leader, Arthur Henderson, characterised as a 'process of exhaustion'.

Recruitment

Between August 1914 and November 1918, 4.9 million men were enlisted in the British army, of whom 2.4 million were volunteers and 2.5 million conscripts. That yielded a wartime total of 5.7 million men in the army at one time or another, approximating to 22.1 per cent of the entire male population of the United Kingdom. It compares to 19.4 per cent of the male population serving in the armed forces as a whole during the Second World War (in which 4.6 million men served). In addition, at a peak in 1917–18, almost 407,000 officers and men were serving in the Royal Navy. Thus, with the possible exception of the almost 23 years of continuous warfare between December 1792 and June 1815, the Great War represents the greatest degree of military participation Britain ever experienced.

Overwhelmingly English in nationality, the pre-war regular army was also largely urban in origin, with unskilled labourers the largest single category of pre-war recruit. There was in effect what Field Marshal Lord Nicholson in 1906 called a 'compulsion of destitution' about recruitment with the burden of military service falling wholly unequally. Behind the regulars stood the small Army Reserve, the Special Reserve and the part-time Territorial Force. While embracing middle-class elements, the Territorials were largely dependent for recruits upon the working class, albeit skilled manual workers in receipt of regular wages rather than the casually employed found in the ranks of the army.

The greater proportion of the BEF would have to be found upon mobilisation from the reserves and these would also make up wastage for the first six months. Thereafter, the Territorials would be the means of expansion, but they were only liable for overseas service if they chose to take the so-called imperial service obligation. In 1914, just over 18,000, or only some 7 per cent, had done so although at least the County Territorial Associations (CTAs) provided a ready-made machinery for wartime expansion.

Whatever assumptions had been made prior to the war, however, all were set aside by the appointment of Kitchener as Secretary of State for War. Kitchener was wholly unfamiliar with any pre-war arrangements and regarded the Territorials as amateurs and a 'town clerk's army'. His attitude effectively spelled the end of any pre-war plans to expand through the CTAs, as Kitchener resolved to raise his 'Kitchener' or 'New' Armies through the War Office.

Nevertheless, there was more to Kitchener's reasoning than simple prejudice. There were no actual practical plans for expansion through the associations and Kitchener believed they would be swamped by having to train and recruit simultaneously. Similarly, Kitchener was reluctant to put pressure on married men to volunteer for service abroad. Most significant of all was his preoccupation with possible German invasion, against which the Territorials were the principal defence. Indeed, two regular divisions were initially kept back from the BEF for home defence. The invasion scare in the autumn of 1914 also brought the creation of the Volunteer Training Corps (VTC), later the Volunteer Force, which was given formal status in November 1914 and recruited initially mostly those over military age or in reserved occupations. Kitchener was eventually reluctantly persuaded to allow Territorials to 'fill the gap' in France and Flanders in the winter of 1914–15.

The Royal Navy, which had almost 143,000 officers and men in 1913–14, had established an efficient reserve system prior to the war so that there was actually a manning surplus of 20–30,000 men once the reserves had been mobilised. These comprised the Royal Naval Reserve (RNR), originally established in 1859 and recruited from merchant seamen and fishermen; the Royal Naval Reserve Trawler Section (RNR(T)), formed in 1911 from trawlermen largely for mine sweeping duties; the Royal Fleet Auxiliaries, also established in 1911, who were usually RNR men; the separate Shetland Royal Naval Reserve, formed in 1914; and the Royal Naval Volunteer Reserve (RNVR), established in 1903 from those not professionally employed at sea in peacetime. Accordingly, naval personnel were made available for military operations, resulting in the creation of the Royal Naval Division, which was redesignated the 63rd (Royal Naval) Division in July 1916 after coming under War Office control. The navy was able to maintain its voluntary nature until the end of the war.

The Royal Flying Corps (RFC), of course, which had 880 officers and men together with 63 aircraft in 1914, was part of the army, having been created in May 1912. The Royal Air Force was not established until 1 April 1918, at which time the RFC numbered just over 31,000 officers and men. It incorporated both the RFC and also the Royal Naval Air Service (RNAS), which had been evolved in July 1914 from the former Naval Wing of the RFC.

The pattern of military participation, as a result of voluntary enlistment, was quite arbitrary and also exceedingly complex with wide regional and local variations. Whatever the reasons for enlistment, the effect of what occurred in August and September 1914 was that certain groups were far more willing to enlist than others. Wales and Scotland certainly increased the proportion of their males under arms to a level largely matching that of England, with Scotland actually producing the largest proportion of recruits under voluntary enlistment within the United Kingdom. In the case of the Welsh and Irish, Kitchener's distrust of the possible politicisation of a proposed 'Welsh Army Corps' and of the offers to raise units from the pre-war Ulster Volunteer Force (UVF) and the rival nationalist Irish Volunteers put something of a blight upon enlistment. There is little evidence, however, to suggest Catholics were reluctant to enlist. Rather similarly, it is difficult to identify any specific Scottish or Welsh service 'experience' substantially different from that of the remainder of the army.

The effective limit of volunteers was reached by December 1915, by which time it was clear that conscription must follow through a process of exhaustion. The first Military Service Act in January 1916 theoretically conscripted all single men and childless widowers between the ages of 18 and 41. The Military Service Act (No 2) then extended conscription to all men between these ages in June 1916, the age range being extended to those between 18 and 50 in April 1918 by a further Military Service (No 2) Act. The same legislation in 1918 also provided for the conscription of men up to the age of 56 if the need arose, and for the extension of conscription to Ireland. Ultimately, the former was deemed unnecessary and the latter politically impossible.

In any case, conscription was applied selectively. The steady evolution of a war economy and of a manpower policy steadily pushed the army to the bottom of the list of priorities. Indeed, in January 1918 the production of timber, iron ore, food, merchant shipping, aeroplanes and tanks all took priority over the army. Moreover, medical boards exempted over a million men in the last 12 months of the war when there was some pressure on doctors to lower rejection rates. Again, while often perceived to be unduly influenced by military demands, the exemption tribunals set up to handle appeals against conscription applied widely differing standards. In October 1918, by which time many exemptions had been removed, there were still 2.5 million men in reserved occupations. Indeed, conscientious objection has received somewhat disproportionate attention considering that only 16,500 claims for exemption were made on such grounds.

ADM 1 has some material of relevance including the arrangements for calling out reserves and extending the service of time-expired men in August 1914 (ADM 1/8388/228); the formation and employment of the Royal Naval Brigade (ADM 1/8391/267 and 278); the RNVR Anti-Aircraft Corps (ADM 1/8409/19); the formation of the Royal Naval Division and its subsequent transfer to War Office control (ADM 1/8410/23 and 8477/309); RNR recruiting in June 1915 (ADM 1/8425/176); exemptions of Admiralty civilians from military service (ADM 1/8479/24); and the establishment of the RAF (ADM 1/8509/7), including the transfer of the RNAS to it (ADM 1/9708). There is also reference to the duties of the National Reserve (ADM 1/8389/246).

ADM 201/94 contains, among papers of the Royal Marine Office, weekly returns and abstracts of the strength of the Corps, 1914–17.

ADM 286/107–21 contains mobilisation returns of the ships' complements, 1914–18, giving not a list of individuals, but of the number of each rank per ship or establishment.

AIR 1 contains statistics for Canadian personnel in the RFC, RNAS and RAF (AIR 1/8/15/1/11). There is also material on the Air Force Constitution Act and the transfer of the RFC and RNAS to the RAF (AIR 1/37/15/1/248/1). The First Lord's returns of the RNAS, 1916–17, are also included (AIR 1/150/15/113/1–3), as are strength returns of pilots and observers on the Western Front in 1918 (AIR 1/476/15/312/216). Files also deal with the expansion of the RFC, 1915–16 (AIR 1/503/16/3/18), its reorganisation in 1916 (AIR 1/1289); and personnel requirements for the RFC with the BEF, 1916–17 (AIR 1/1287–8).

AIR 2 has some relevant material including the RFC and RAF recruitment campaign in South Africa, 1917–18 (AIR 2/197/C 20936); weekly returns of pilots and aircraft with the BEF from July 1916 to February 1918 (AIR 2/939); the Order in Council for the formation of the RAF (AIR 2/75/A 10112); and the transfer of the RFC and RNAS to the RAF (AIR 2/AIR 135587/1917), including the RNAS Laboratory at South Kensington and its Meteorological Service (AIR 2/39/AIR 143308/1917, 108/A 18584, and 168/25206/20).

AIR 8 has material in the papers of the Chief of the Air Staff on the strength of the RFC in France, 1916–18 (AIR 8/1), and the creation of the RAF (AIR 8/2).

AIR 9/5 contains papers on the continuing controversy over a separate air force, 1917–36.

BT 13, containing papers of the Board's Establishment Department, deals with problems arising from the enlistment of its staff in the armed forces (BT 13/59, 66, 67, 68, and 72), as well as the VTC (BT 13/60, 61, and 63).

CAB 1, containing miscellaneous Cabinet material collected by Sir James Masterton-Smith, includes papers from 1915 on the expansion of the army (CAB 1/11); consideration of recruitment options, including the introduction of compulsion (CAB 1/13); a paper from May 1916 on conscientious objectors (CAB 1/18); and the possibility of extending the Military Service Bill to Ireland in 1918 (CAB 1/26). There is also consideration of making more use of coloured troops in February 1917 (CAB 1/23).

CAB 17 considers the existing machinery for enlisting the Territorial Force in 1914 (CAB 17/106), and the return to India of those Indian Army officers hastily employed in the training of the New Armies in 1914 (CAB 17/148). There is also correspondence on the Derby Scheme, 1916 (CAB 17/158).

CAB 21/107 contains material on recruiting among the registered files of the Cabinet Office.

CAB 27/3 contains material from the Cabinet Committee on the size of the Army in April 1916.

CAB 37, containing copies of papers circulated to the Cabinet between 1880 and

1916, includes a report from the Cabinet Recruiting Committee in December 1915 (CAB 37/139/68).

CAB 45/207–12 contain the papers of Gershom Stewart MP, who raised the 13th Battalion, Cheshire Regiment in 1914.

CO 537, comprising confidential papers, has some material on the availability of Dominion and colonial troops and also the raising of native troops in 1915 (CO 537/603–4); material from 1917 on recognition for Australian troops and New Zealand reinforcements (CO 537/1119–20); and on the Dominions' contribution to post-war forces of occupation (CO 537/1122).

CSC 5/85 has the wartime regulations of the Commission, including the treatment of civil servants who enlisted without permission and, later, conscientious objectors.

CUST 49, which comprises various registered papers of the Board, includes material on wartime separation allowances (CUST 49/335); enlistment by employees without permission (CUST 49/369); and the release of men under the Military Service Acts (CUST 49/432).

FO 94/965–6 deal with the Military Service Convention signed between Britain and the United States in June 1918.

FO 115, comprising correspondence relating to the United States, includes material on Americans serving in the British army (FO 115/1848, 2014–15 and 2458–61); British subjects in the United States army (FO 115/2186–7 and 2462–5); recruiting and exemptions (FO 115/2310–13); the Anglo-American Recruiting Convention, 1918 (FO 115/2440–41); and British military imposters in the United States (FO 115/2274).

FO 170, comprising papers of the British embassy and consular offices in Italy, includes material on recruiting officers for the New Armies (FO 170/819); military exemptions (FO 170/977 and 1155–6); and military service (FO 170/1141 and 1157–8).

FO 286, papers of the British embassy and consular offices in Greece, include correspondence on the liability of British subjects resident in Greece to military service as well as the agreements reached on military service with France, Greece and Russia (FO 286/634), and the liability of British legation staff to military service (FO 286/684).

HO 45 contains a number of files relating to wartime recruitment and its implications including issues surrounding the release for military service of police (HO 45/263190, 301945 and 308237); special constables (HO 45/331298); firemen (HO 45/365001); Manx civil servants (HO 45/305212); its own employees (HO 45/255893); and even prisoners (HO 45/325703). Other matters addressed include the extension of the Military Service Acts to the Isle of Man and Jersey (HO 45/306676 and 364571); the issue of war service badges to munitions workers and armlets to those who had volunteered (HO 45/303796 and 308474); exemptions from military service in general (HO 45/321188); call up procedures (HO 45/327880); and the requirement for employers to exhibit lists of employees of military age (HO 45/313165). There is also material on Jersey's Insular Defence Corps (HO 45/360127), and the Central Association of Volunteer Training Corps, which was given formal recognition by the War Office in November 1914 (HO 45/272183).

MAF 39/149 deals with the staff of the Board of Agriculture and Ministry of Food serving with the forces, 1915–17.

MAF 47/1 deals with the exemption of the Board's secretary from military service, 1916.

MH 47 comprises surviving minutes and papers of both the Central Tribunal and the Middlesex Appeals Tribunal, 1915–22, dealing with claims for exemption from military service. The tribunal system was established in October 1915 by local authorities under instruction from the Local Government Board to consider the postponement of the call up of voluntarily attested men. The Central Tribunal was then established in November 1915 as a final appeals body for cases involving claims for occupational exemption, becoming a statutory body with the passing of the Military Service Act. It also acted as an advisory body to the Army Council regarding those sentenced by court martial for breaches of military discipline and who pleaded conscientious objection as a reason for their disobedience. It ceased to meet in January 1919, but its life was prolonged to enable it to issue certificates exempting conscientious objectors from loss of voting rights (for five years) under the provisions of the Representation of the People Act, 1918. The Appeals Tribunals were interim bodies existing between the Central Tribunal and the Local Tribunals while, in addition, there was a Special Tribunal established in 1917 under the Military Service (Conventions with Allied States) Act to deal with Russian, Greek, Italian, French and American citizens residing in London. Other Special Tribunals dealt with claims by doctors, dentists and vets. It was decided to destroy most individual files in 1921, but these documents (originally preserved as PRO 10/162–281, 317–19) survived.

The series includes the minute books and selected papers of the Central Tribunal (MH 47/1–3); selected papers of the Veterinary Tribunal (MH 47/4); and minutes of the Central Medical War Committee, 1916–17 (MH 47/162). Most material, however, relates to the Middlesex Appeal Tribunal consisting of minutes and papers (MH 47/5–6); correspondence, including that with Central Tribunal and local tribunals (MH 47/121–4); letter books (MH 47/145–61); and miscellaneous material such as printed minutes of evidence to the Select Committee on Military Service in 1917 (MH 47/144).

Consideration of individuals is represented by registers and case papers of non-attested men, including exemptions and adjourned cases (MH 47/7–65); registers and case papers of voluntarily attested men, including exemptions and adjourned cases (MH 47/71–111); agricultural cases (MH 47/112); registers and papers on cases involving claims for medical exemption (MH 47/113–17); selected cases raising legal issues (MH 47/118); papers on employers' applications for exemption of employees (MH 47/120); and cases referred to the Central Tribunal (MH 47/119). There are case papers on conscientious objectors (MH 47/66–8); and correspondence on the issue with the Central Tribunal (MH 47/125). Various indices, summary lists and statistical returns are also included, together with blank forms, circulars and pamphlets (MH 47/126–43).

MT 9 deals with the recruitment of merchant seamen into the RNR, 1916 (MT 9/1077), while there was also earlier concern to protect them from enlistment in 1915 (MT 9/1015).

MT 23 covers the issue of an 'On War Service' badge to the Mercantile Marine, 1915 (M23/373); observations on men determined not to sign on for the duration

(MT 23/427); and Admiralty instructions to members of its Transport Department joining the VTC, 1915 (MT 23/324).

NATS 1 contains material on recruitment policies as well as wider manpower issues. Apart from papers of the Irish National Recruiting Committee (NATS 1/245–67), there are the files of the Recruiting Department, 1917–18 (NATS 1/859–916), and on recruiting exemptions (NATS 1/917–1062) and trade exemptions (NATS 1/1115–1266). In addition, there are papers of the Medical Department (NATS 1/711–858). This includes material on medical examinations and, for example, the release of medical staff to assist with the control of the influenza pandemic in 1918 (NATS 1/799), and the exemption of spa staff to further the work of the British Spas War Disablement Committee (NATS 1/835).

There are also policy files on demobilisation (NATS 1/301–25). Among matters included are the recruitment of miners (NATS 1/6); the problem of those who had fled to Ireland to avoid conscription (NATS 1/909 and 935), and of those who attempted to do the same by enrolling as war work volunteers (NATS 1/975); and plans to comb out the hunting and racing establishments (NATS 1/964), and younger men from the aircraft industry (NATS 1/218). There is material on the work of the Glasgow Tribunal (NATS 1/2); recruitment of two translators from the Jewish War Services Committee to help deal with appeals by Russian subjects in Liverpool (NATS 1/917); enrolment of civil servants, teachers and students (NATS 1/86, 273–4, and 956–9); the relationship between the VTC and the tribunal system as well as other problems relating to the VTC (NATS 1/947, 987, 1006, and 1027); the passing of men of inferior physique to the 25th Division (NATS 1/316); the treatment of returned British prisoners of war under military service legislation (NATS 1/1002); the position of British subjects resident in the United States under American conscription legislation (NATS 1/1037–42); and statistical tables with daily summaries of military and naval recruitment between 1914 and 1917 (NATS 1/398–401).

The papers of the Trade Exemptions Department are particularly useful for representations from trade organisations such as the National Organisation of Fish, Poultry, Game and Rabbit Traders (NATS 1/1124); the Leek Silk Manufacturers and Dyers Standing Joint Committee (NATS 1/1128); the Manchester Calico Printers' Association (NATS 1/1148); the British Hay Traders' Association (NATS 1/1159); Messrs Dobson & Crowther, a paper bag and wrapper manufacturer (NATS 1/1167); undertakers (NATS 1/1189); the National Association of Master Bakers and Confectioners (NATS 1/1202); and slaughtermen in the retail meat trade (NATS 1/1236).

PRO 30/57, comprising Kitchener's own papers as Secretary of State for War, includes files on recruiting and manpower issues, 1914–16 (PRO 30/57/73–4). There is also a copy of Alfred Leete's famous recruiting poster featuring Kitchener (PRO 30/57/123).

PRO 30/67 contains correspondence on Kitchener's attitude towards the Territorial Force (PRO 30/67/2) as seen by St John Brodrick, a former Secretary of State for War, as well as papers on recruitment in Ireland (PRO 30/67/29).

RECO 1/217–21 deals with exemptions from military service.

T1 has a number of files dealing with the issue of conscientious objection among civil servants. The Treasury decided in 1917 that cancellation of pension rights was a matter for individual departments (T1/12039/8860). The employment of those unfit for manual labour in the civil service was also discussed (T1/11987/13154, 15292, and 30343). There is an example of a conscientious objector seeking civil service employment (T1/11987/8397, 10779, and 13127), and another of a civil servant court martialled for refusing to obey military orders once conscripted (T1/12076/30228).

T172/541 contains, among the Chancellor of the Exchequer's miscellaneous office papers, material on the financial implications of training new recruits for the army in 1917.

WO 32 also has a number of files dealing with conscientious objection including the issue of altering sentencing procedures for conscientious objectors in 1917 (WO 32/5472); the conditions of service for conscientious objectors serving under military regulations, 1917 (WO 32/18765); discussion of the treatment of those considered to be genuine conscientious objectors (WO 32/5473); the withdrawal of immunity from transfer to combat units of men enlisting in the RAMC from the St John or St Andrew's Ambulance Associations, 1918 (WO 32/18576); general correspondence on exemptions on grounds of conscience (WO 32/5474); and further minutes and memoranda on conscientious objection, 1916–18 (WO 32/5491). There is also material on the proposed extension of the Military Service Act to Ireland (WO 32/9556).

Raising of the New Armies is represented by general papers (WO 32/11342), as well as some on the creation of public schools units (WO 32/11343), and the formation of the divisions of the 'Second New Army' (WO 32/11344). The raising and subsequent development of the Royal Naval Division is also covered by a number of files (WO 32/5074–6, 5084, and 5946). In terms of general recruiting issues, there are papers on manpower (WO 32/9557) and on the age of soldiers (WO 32/3721–2); memoranda by the Adjutant General on prospects in both 1917 and 1918 (WO 32/5917 and 9553–4); and papers on the transfer of labour from agriculture and munitions to the army, 1918 (WO 32/9555 and 11336) though, earlier in 1915–16, it had been a matter of releasing skilled men from the army for munitions work (WO 32/11333) and there was still the need to consider releasing miners as late as 1918 (WO 32/5918). Manpower in the army in France was a particular matter of concern in 1918 and is reflected in the committee chaired by Lieutenant-General H. M. Lawson on the most economic use of the military manpower available (WO 32/5093) and field returns of the BEF for 1918 (WO 32/5096 and 5101). One suggestion was the substitution of coloured for white personnel in many support units (WO 32/5094).

Some rather specific issues include the raising of Princess Patricia's Light Infantry, 1914 (WO 32/5137); the formation of 15th (Overseas) Reserve Battalion from men of the Dominions, 1915–16 (WO 32/18709); the recruitment of the Chinese Labour Corps, 1916–17 (WO 32/11345–6); recruitment of coloured British subjects in the United States, 1917–18 (WO 32/4765); recruitment of 'friendly aliens', 1916 (WO 32/4773); and the possibility raised by M. Jabotinsky of recruiting Jewish units for service in Palestine, 1917–18 (WO 32/11347–52), which found some fruit in the designation of a battalion of the Royal Fusiliers for Jews (WO 32/11353). In addition, files also cover proposed measures against Russian subjects declining to serve in the British forces (WO 32/4774), and the question of the voluntary re-enlistment of previously discharged servicemen in 1918 (WO 32/4766).

The Territorial Force, the VTC and other reserve formations are also well represented. The papers included cover such issues as the proposed raising of a yeomanry mounted brigade in 1914 and Kitchener's appeal to CTAs to help raise the New Armies (WO 32/11341 and 18570); equipping the Territorials, 1914–16 (WO 32/11238); the supply of Territorial cyclists, 1914 (WO 32/2665–6); the wording of attestation forms for the 2nd and 3rd line Territorials, 1915 (WO 32/18560); the establishment of Territorial battalions with the BEF, 1915–16 (WO 32/18564); returns and various organisational schemes from CTAs (WO 32/2695–2701 and 18562); the position of the Territorials with respect to the Military Service Act (WO 32/5452); the reorganisation of the Lovat Scouts and Scottish Horse in 1916 (WO 32/18582); Territorial reservists for the RAMC, 1916–17 (WO 32/18662); the reorganisation of the London Territorials, 1917–19 (WO 32/18625); and the reduction in Territorial units in 1918 (WO 32/18591).

In terms of the VTC, there are files on procedures for calling out the force for active service and its potential role, 1916–17 (WO 32/18552 and 18567); offers by volunteer units to serve, 1916 (WO 32/18554); volunteer conditions of service, 1916 (WO 32/18566); the proceedings of a War Office conference on the volunteers, 1917 (WO 32/5048); the raising of a Motor Volunteer Force, 1916–17 (WO 32/18565 and 18568); special service companies for coastal duties, 1918 (WO 32/5049); and the disbanding of the Volunteer Force, 1919–20 (WO 32/5050). In addition, there is material on the National Reserve, 1914–16 (WO 32/18612, 18617 and 18620); the Royal Defence Corps, 1917–20 (WO 32/18622); and a curious objection on the part of the New Zealand government to a circular on the Inns of Court OTC, 1915 (WO 32/18556). A reflection of the expansion of the army generally was the discussion of temporary military rank, 1915 (WO 32/18633) and the adoption of a rubber stamp bearing the King's signature for wartime commissions (WO 32/18925). There are also copies of the Army Annual Acts for the war years (WO 32/14485–90) and of the Military Service Act, 1916 (WO 32/9348–9).

WO 70, comprising various records of the auxiliary forces, includes the Precedent Books of the Volunteer Force that succeeded the VTC in 1916 (WO 70/41–3); War Office and other miscellaneous correspondence on the Territorial Force, 1914–15 (WO 70/48–9); and a chronological summary of the principal changes in the organisation and administration of the Territorials, 1914–18 (WO 70/50–1).

WO 106 has some material on recruiting (WO 106/364–71 and 373), including the work of the Parliamentary Recruiting Committee and recruiting visits, while there is also coverage of the procedures of tribunals with respect to conscientious objectors (WO 106/372). The increasing manpower shortage is reflected by a report by Lieutenant-General Lawson on the physical categories of men employed out of the fighting area in France, 1917 (WO 106/362–3); and material on the reduction of the strength of British formations in 1918 (WO 106/411 and 427–8).

WO 114 contains Strength Returns for the Army, including weekly returns of the strength of the army at home, 1914–18, which includes Dominion forces in Britain but excludes the Territorial Force (WO 114/25–35 and 57); and returns of the Territorial Force at home and monthly returns of the Territorial Force abroad, 1914–18 (WO 114/43–56).

WO 159, containing papers of Kitchener's private office as Secretary of State, includes material on recruitment, 1914–15 (WO 159/18–19).

WO 161/82 includes statistics on the British army at home and abroad, 1914–18.

WO 162, comprising papers of the Adjutant General's Department, has much material on recruitment, including the supply of officers in 1914 (WO 162/2); the raising and organisation of the New Armies (WO 162/3–4, 20, 22, 24, 26 and 71); the Derby Scheme (WO 162/28); the Military Service Acts (WO 162/27); correspondence with the National Service Department (WO 162/9); the provision of men for the Heavy Branch, Machine Gun Corps in 1917 (WO 162/11); and the results of medical boards in June 1917 (WO 162/12). There are also telegrams of the Mobilisation Branch, 1914–15 (WO 162/25); and material on the mobilisation of the 7th Division from regular units in India (WO 162/19). In addition, there is a file on the strength of the Mediterranean Expeditionary Force, 1915 (WO 162/72).

WO 394/1–20 contain the Statistical Abstracts of the War Office Statistics Branch (C5), established in October 1916 to compile abstracts of information on the army at home and abroad, replacing the pre-war General Annual Reports. The bound volumes include considerable information on the distribution of units, strengths, casualties, recruitment, remounts, munitions supply, embarkation and disembarkation, expenditure, quartering, discipline, and honours and awards. Increasingly, they also include miscellaneous additional information on such subjects as air raids, military railways and demobilisation. There are statistics for the RFC and RAF and the abstracts are by no means limited only to the British army. There is an overall statistical summary for the war as a whole (WO 394/20).

War Service

Conscription had been a major break with pre-war expectations in Britain but, in theory, the wartime experience of military participation as a whole had enormous social and institutional implications. For the first time in a century, very large numbers of troops were permanently visible to British society and, with the delay in providing hutted accommodation in the autumn of 1914, in close proximity to civilians. It was not just a question of becoming aware of one's own country, but of foreign countries as well.

The impact of army life upon those who enlisted would vary as much as the impact upon those civilian communities exposed to a military presence. There were wide differences between service on different fronts and in different sectors. There were divisions between officers in fighting units and staff officers, between officers and men, between the different arms and branches of service, and between specialists such as machine gunners and ordinary infantry. Above all, there were differences between regulars, Territorials and New Army volunteers. As the war continued so the distinctions blurred as units were increasingly fed from the same pool of manpower, but there still remained a distinction between those who had volunteered and those who had been conscripted.

What can be said of the experience of soldiers is that the actual welcome afforded new arrivals in a unit varied widely and the conditioning of men depended almost entirely upon the unit in which they actually served. That might not always be the same unit, for there was a constant change of personalities. Most units would steadily lose any real connection with the particular locality or social group from which they might have been raised. It is apparent that no one British battalion was quite like any other.

As indicated previously, the Royal Navy was not subjected to conscription and its officers and men had customarily committed themselves to a naval career at the age of 13 in the case of officers and 14 or 15 in the case of other ranks. It was as hierarchical as the army, but officers and petty officers had come to recognise that the increasingly sophisticated technical demands of naval warfare required skills and flexibility which would best be encouraged by paternalism. Without necessarily removing all instances of conservatism, such an approach, when coupled with pre-war reforms in pay and conditions, significantly lowered the likelihood of lower deck unrest. This was eminently desirable since many seamen were likely to remain in port for long periods given the nature of the war at sea. Moreover, even when at sea, seamen saw far less action than their military counterparts although naval battle in the Great War was potentially far more deadly for ships and crews than, say, the Napoleonic Wars when it was more common for ships to strike their colours than to be sunk.

ADM 1 contains a considerable amount of relevant material on wartime naval service. There is a list of army prisoners of war held in German camps in July 1915. Approximately 192,800 British servicemen were taken prisoner at some stage during the war (ADM 1/8420/124). In addition, however, there is also material on the opening of the War Office Bureau of Information on POWs in August 1914 (ADM 1/8388/237); the internment of the Naval Brigade in Holland after the fall of Antwerp in October 1914 (ADM 1/8397/367); visits to those interned in Holland by wives (ADM 1/8499/214); payment of British POWs in Germany and Turkey (ADM 1/8423/156); an account of the escape of Signalman Millar from Germany in September 1915 (ADM 1/8434/289); a proposed exchange of British and German POWs in August 1916 (ADM 1/8465/201); and negotiations with Austria-Hungary for the release of merchantmen held as POWs (ADM 1/8493/161). There is also a report on the internment camp at Groningen in May 1915 (ADM 1/8422/142).

General service conditions are represented by material on such issues as allowances for cooks (ADM 1/8404/446); increased pay for chaplains (ADM 1/8414/69); the Naval Marriages Act 1915 (ADM 1/8415/77 and 8419/102); climate pay in the Red Sea (ADM 1/8439/331); the need to confirm Wesleyan sailors before they could participate in Anglican communion (ADM 1/8453/79); the wearing of uniform by hired interpreters (ADM 1/8465/197); and the position of uniformed naval personnel standing for Parliament in 1918 (ADM 1/8537/244), one of whom might conceivably be the Director of Naval Intelligence (ADM 1/8541/279). There are also confidential reports on Rear Admirals serving afloat in June 1916 (ADM 1/8462/166).

Medals and awards are also covered including the award of French, Italian and Japanese decorations (ADM 1/8448/33, 8468/231, 8482/44, and 8484/65); awards for Gallipoli (ADM 1/8450/54) and the recommendation of a VC for Lance Corporal Parker, RMLI for his gallantry at Anzac Cove (ADM 1/8453/77); awards for Jutland (ADM 1/8461/154 and 8474/280) and for Mesopotamia (ADM 1/8493/162); the institution of Bars for the Conspicuous Gallantry Medal and Distinguished Service Medal (ADM 1/8462/162); the institution of the Distinguished Flying Cross, Air Force Cross, Distinguished Flying Medal and Air Force Medal

(ADM 1/8511/15); the institution of the 1914 Star, conditions attached to it and the refusal to award it to merchantmen engaged in military operations (ADM 1/8506/ 269, 8547/338, and 8573/317); posthumous awards (ADM 1/8489/105); suitable recognition for those mentioned in despatches (ADM 1/8489/108 and 8569/275); the consideration of a posthumous VC for the master of SS *Otaki* in May 1918; men decorated when the King visited the Grand Fleet in June 1917 (ADM 1/ 8490/127); the Mercantile Marine Medal (ADM 1/8491/152); perceived obscurities in the regulations for the VC (ADM 1/8528/174); war service badges (ADM 1/ 8549/22); and claims for the award of the medal for post-armistice operations and for civilians (ADM 1/8595/161, 8598/100, and 8614/184). Consideration was given to awarding the Distinguished Service Cross to the towns of Dunkirk, Ramsgate and Margate in 1919 (ADM 1/8501/235). The VC was also awarded to Lieutenant Stuart and Seaman Williams of the Q-ship, HMS *Pargust*, for an action in June 1917 (ADM 1/8584/54 and 8585/59).

ADM 13/200–205 and **207–38** comprise the Passing Certificate for Engineers and Lieutenants, 1868–1902, issued at the point where they qualified in that rank with summaries of career and training to date. Most of those passing in the later years of the nineteenth century were still likely to be serving in 1914.

ADM 104/166–70 contain service records of Surgeons with date of seniority between 1891 and 1914, including short service and temporary wartime appointments (ADM 104/169–70).

ADM 116, containing 'case' papers of the Admiralty Secretariat, includes files on Ratings attached to the RNAS Armoured Car Section in Russia, 1915–17, including individuals' disciplinary conduct and awards received (ADM 116/1626 and 1717). Other matters included are RNAS honours and awards to 1917 (ADM 116/1560); awards to the Torpedo Boat Destroyer and Torpedo Boat flotillas to 1917 (ADM 116/ 1561–2); war medals, 1918–19 (ADM 116/1693–7); honours 1917–18 (ADM 116/ 1575–6 and 1578); honours and awards for the Zeebrugge raid, 1918 (ADM 116/ 1811); and the proceedings of the Naval Clasps Committee, 1919 (ADM 116/481). There is also material on garden parties for winners of the VC at Buckingham Palace, 1914–20 (ADM 116/1683). In addition, there is also material on exchange of British and Turkish POWs, 1917–18 (ADM 116/1565).

ADM 119 contains the papers of the Admiral Commanding Coast Guards and Reserves. In addition to general wartime correspondence on the RNR (ADM 119/120B–3) and RNVR (ADM 119/169); there are returns of RNR officers, 1862–1930 (ADM 119/215); and monthly returns of RNR ratings, 1914–19, which give reasons for discharge (ADM 119/222).

ADM 137 deals with the capture of the Portsmouth Battalion of the Royal Marine Brigade in 1914 (ADM 137/3112 and 4824), and the internment of other members of the brigade in Holland (ADM 137/3926–7 and 4820). There are also honours recommendations for field ambulance units attached to the division (ADM 137/3928).

ADM 157 comprises the attestation forms of Royal Marines enlisted between 1790 and 1925 arranged by Division. For the period of the Great War, these Divisions were based on Chatham, Plymouth and Portsmouth, all representing the Royal Marine Light Infantry (RMLI), in addition to the Royal Marine Artillery (RMA). Forms give details of place of birth, previous occupation, physical description and, often, the record of service. They can be filed either by date of enlistment or date of discharge. Those most likely to cover Great War servicemen are Chatham enlistments to 1883 (ADM 157/1–139); enlistment for ranks without official numbers, 1884–1925 (ADM 157/2058–303); Portsmouth discharges, 1904–23 (ADM 157/2471–847); RMA enlistments, 1861–1928 (ADM 157/2848–9) and 1914–23 (ADM 157/3131–244); RMA discharges, 1860–1923 (ADM 157/2850–3246), and 1899–1925 (ADM 157/3247–69); Royal Marine Labour Corps (Deal) enlistments, 1914–22 (ADM 157/3270–458); Royal Marine Labour Corps (Chatham) enlistments, 1915–19 (ADM 157/3459–66); and Royal Marine Engineers short service attestations, 1914–19 (ADM 157/3467–625). A card index for some files (ADM 157/1–659) is held in the Research Enquiries Room, while there is also a partial index (ADM 313).

ADM 158 contains Royal Marines Description Books, 1755–1940, comprising varying kinds of registers giving such details as date and place of enlistment, age, place of birth, previous occupation, physical description, promotions, and whether injured or killed. They are arranged by Company within Division and then by approximate alphabetical order or rank. Most are for earlier periods, but those for the Deal Depot cover enlistments between 1881 and 1918 (ADM 158/284–98).

ADM 159 consists of Royal Marines Registers of Service, 1842–1936, providing date and place of birth, previous occupation, physical description, religion, date and place of enlistment, and a full record of service including comments on conduct. They are arranged by Division and by service number, which can be located separately (ADM 313). They include both those enlisted for continuous service and those enlisted on wartime short service. Those most likely to be useful for wartime servicemen are for the RMA, 1901–23 (ADM 159/80–102); the Royal Marine Band, 1903–18 (ADM 159/103–12); the Royal Marine Depot, 1866–1920 (ADM 159/113–14); Royal Marine Divisional Train, 1914–18, and Ordnance Company, 1915–16 (ADM 159/116–18); Royal Marine Divisional Engineers (Deal), 1914–16 (ADM 159/119–23); Chatham Division, 1914–19 (ADM 159/130–37 and 143–9); Plymouth Division, 1914–18 (ADM 159/175–80); Portsmouth Division, 1914–18 (ADM 159/191–8); Royal Marine Medical Unit, 1914–18 (ADM 159/209–12); Royal Marine Special Home Coast defence units, 1918 (ADM 159/211); and those Royal Marines transferred to the RNAS, 1912–17 (ADM 159/212).

ADM 171 contains medal rolls for Royal Navy personnel. They include those for the First World War relating to the Royal Navy, Royal Marines, RNAS, RNR, RNVR and Mercantile Marine Reserve covering issue of the 1914 and 1914–15 Stars, the War Medal and the Victory Medal (ADM 171/89–134 and 167–71), with an additional index for the 1914 Star (ADM 171/139). In addition, there are Officers' Honour Sheets for the Great War (ADM 171/78–88); lists of RNR Honours and Awards for 1914–18 (ADM 171/77); the Mention in Despatches Roll, 1914–18 (ADM 171/63); the index for wartime awards of the Conspicuous Gallantry Medal and the Distinguished Service Medal (ADM 171/75); rolls for the Conspicuous Gallantry Medal, Distinguished Service Medal and Naval Meritorious Service Medal (ADM 171/61); foreign orders presented to naval officers (ADM 171/67); lists of foreign officers recommended for British decorations (ADM 171/76); recommendations for post-war honours (ADM 171/138) and the Order of the British Empire (ADM 171/135–7); and a separate list of decorations for the Armoured Car Section in Russia (ADM 171/74).

ADM 175/82A–90 are Coast Guard Records of Service, covering Royal Navy ratings and Royal Marines, 1900–23.

ADM 177/1–18 consist of the confidential wartime version of the Navy List, 1914–18.

ADM 178/44 deals with the question of awarding war medals to lunatics.

ADM 188 contains the Service Records of Royal Navy ratings who enlisted as regulars (i.e., not RNR or RNVR) between 1873 and 1923. They give the dates of birth, ship or shore establishments, and a concise account of service, including successive appointments. The entries are arranged by service number and into Series A and B, these being indexed in name indices available on open access (ADM 188/245–67 and 1132–77) covering enlistments between 1892 and 1912 (ADM 188/1132–54) and between 1913 and 1923 (ADM 188/1155–77). All branches are covered including the RNAS but with the exception of ratings who served with armoured cars in Russia, 1915–17 whose records are to be found elsewhere. The records cover seamen enlisted between 1891 and 1907 (ADM 188/268–559); RNAS enlistments, 1914–18 (ADM 188/560–646); seamen, 1908–18 (ADM 188/647–834); stokers, 1908–18 (ADM 188/867–971); stewards and domestics, 1908–18 (ADM 188/988–1011); miscellaneous enlistments, 1908–18 (ADM 188/1018–86); short service enlistments, 1907–18 (ADM 188/1096–1104); and short service stokers, 1907–19 (ADM 188/1111–25).

ADM 196 comprises microfilmed Officers' Service Records arranged by entry date. In each case, the last date shown is that of the last discharge from the group in question. The records usually include date of birth, wife's name, date and place of marriage, name and profession of father, dates of commission and promotions, details of distinctions, dates for appointment and discharge from each ship, and date of retirement and death. In some cases, there are summaries of confidential reports. The most relevant files are service records for those created Midshipmen between 1912 and 1917 (ADM 196/117–24) and for those who entered as Engineer Officers between 1893 and 1918 (ADM 196/130–36). In addition, there are the confidential reports on Acting Mates and Mates promoted to Lieutenant between 1913 and 1929, which record service up to the rank of Lieutenant Commander (ADM 196/154); confidential reports on Lieutenants and Sub-Lieutenants who entered those ranks between 1885 and 1920 (ADM 196/141–9); confidential reports on those promoted to Commander between 1908 and 1919 (ADM 196/125–6); and confidential reports on those promoted to Captain between 1893 and 1918 (ADM 196/86–90), which also contain reports on those considered for promotion to Flag Rank (Admiral). There are also service records with confidential reports for some categories only for Warrant Officers at date of rank between 1895 and 1922 (ADM 196/156–9); service records and reports for Gunners with date of seniority between 1900 and 1918 (ADM 196/164–6); and service records and confidential reports for Paymasters who entered between 1884 and 1920 (ADM 196/171–4). Other files which may also be relevant to Great War servicemen cover Medical Officers, 1872–1931 (ADM 196/10); Paymasters, 1862–1923 (ADM 196/12); Naval Cadets and Admirals, 1832–1919 (ADM 196/17–20); Engineering Officers, 1869–1922 (ADM 196/25); Warrant Officers, 1851–1922 (ADM 196/31–2); Warrant Officers (Executive) of the Commission and Warrant Branch, 1875–1952 (ADM 196/34–5 and 38–56); Royal Marines, 1863–1954 and 1880–1954 (ADM 196/61–5, 97–102 and 106–14); Royal Marine Warrant Officers, 1904–23 (ADM 196/67); Royal Marine Officers and Warrant Officers, 1884–1914 (ADM 196/106–8); Accountant,

Medical and Navigating Branch, 1872–1922 (ADM 196/80–82); Civil Branch, 1916–22 (ADM 196/85); Executive Officers, 1902–51 (ADM 196/96); and Royal Marine Special Reserve, 1889–1941 (ADM 196/104–5). RNAS Officers are also included (ADM 196/42–56).

Some parts of the series have their own name index while others are indexed separately within the series. An additional index for RM records is available (ADM 313), while there is an alphabetical card index in the Microfilm Room as well as original indices on film (ADM 196/7, 26–8, 33 and 57).

ADM 240 comprises the Officers' Service Records of the RNR, again arranged by entry date with the last date representing the last discharge from the group. They include Lieutenants, 1862–1956 (ADM 240/4–6); Sub-Lieutenants, 1862–1949 (ADM 240/8–12); Senior Engineers, 1865–1947 (ADM 240/29–31); and Honorary Officers, 1862–1960 (ADM 240/36).

ADM 273/1–30 are the Officers' Service Registers for the RNAS, 1914–18, arranged by number. They provide date and place of birth, date of commission and promotions, details of postings and brief notes from confidential reports.

ADM 286/108–21 comprises the Mobilisation Returns, listing the complements of ships for the war period.

ADM 337 are the Service Records for the RNVR, 1903–19. Officers' records (ADM 337/117–28) are accessed by a card index while records of Ratings are arranged by Division and then number. The divisions in question are Anti-Aircraft (ADM 337/93–4); Bristol (ADM 337/1–18); Clyde (ADM 337/19–32); Birmingham Electrical Volunteers (ADM 337/95); London (ADM 337/33–48); Mersey (ADM 337/49–61); Motor Boat Reserve (ADM 337/96–9); Mine Clearance Service (ADM 337/101–8); Crystal Palace (ADM 337/62–7); Sussex (ADM 337/68–9); Tyne (ADM 337/70–84); and Wales (ADM 337/85–91). The service number can be identified from the medal rolls (ADM 171/125–9). Two divisions are not represented in the series, namely the Royal Naval Division and the Shore Wireless Service, while those preserved for Crystal Palace represent those who entered from civil life or the Royal Navy and exclude those who entered from Kitchener's New Armies. There are indices for the Anti-Aircraft Division, Motor Boat Division, and Mine Clearance Service (ADM 337/92, ADM 188/1155–77, and ADM 337/100).

AIR 1, comprising the records of the Air Historical Branch, contains recommendations for RFC and RAF gallantry awards and other honours, 1915–19 (AIR 1/107/15/9/287, AIR 1/163/15/124/10, AIR 1/878/204/5/584, AIR 1/993/204/5/1216, AIR 1/1030–33, AIR 1/1152/204/5/2399, AIR 1/1155/204/5/2441, AIR 1/1169/204/5/2592, AIR 1/1479/204/36/131, AIR 1/1522/204/67/19, AIR 1/1526/204/68/19, and AIR 1/2147/209/3/131). Those for No 5 Group are listed separately (AIR 1/109/15/9/295), as are winners of the VC, 1914–19 (AIR 1/519/16/9/1 and AIR 1/1211/204/5/2). Other information on RFC personnel includes various personnel rolls and returns from 1914 (AIR 1/512/16/3/67, AIR 1/764/204/4/225, AIR 1/765/204/4/237, AIR 1/774/204/4/364, and AIR 1/2442/305/18/8); 1915 (AIR 1/827/204/5/162 and AIR 1/1295–7); 1916 (AIR 1/1288/204/11/48); 1917 (AIR 1/1301); and 1918 (AIR 1/1214/204/5/2).

In addition, there are postings of officers on completion of training at the Central Flying School, 1913–15 (AIR 1/787/204/4/609); classified nominal rolls for individual flying training schools and lists of aviators' certificates granted,

1914–15 (AIR 1/2432/306/1); a chart of Air Service Officers (AIR 1/2530); records of officers' services, 1914–18 (AIR 1/92/15/9/9229 and AIR 1/93/15/9/230); lists of officers' next of kin, 1914–16 (AIR 1/1163/204/5/2534 and AIR 1/1307); officers' particulars (AIR 1/1021); and some confidential reports on officers (AIR 1/1854/204/213/12 and AIR 1/1859/204/214/17).

The RNAS is represented in disposition lists showing where officers were serving between 1914 and 1918 (AIR 1/2108–11); reports and particulars of officers' services, 1915–18 (AIR 1/97/15/9/269, AIR 1/98, AIR 1/99/15/9/270, AIR 1/100, AIR 1/101/15/9/271, and AIR 1/102–3); lists of RNAS officers who served in the Gallipoli campaign (AIR 1/675/21/13/1563); a list of pilots on the Oberdorff raid in October 1916 (AIR 1/112/15/39/10); honours and awards gained by those of the RNAS Dunkirk Command (AIR 1/75/15/9/173); lists of RNAS personnel at Dunkirk, 1914–15 (AIR 1/666/17/122/733); recommendations for honours, awards and promotions, 1916–18 (AIR 1/74/15/9/164–8, AIR 1/75/15/9/169–73 and AIR 1/634/17/122/102); and weekly returns for 1917 of officers and ratings at the RNAS station at Roehampton and in Kite balloon sections overseas (AIR 1/447/15/303/40).

For the RAF, there are also nominal rolls including officers recommended for permanent RAF commissions in 1918 (AIR 1/1161/204/5/2516). Similarly, there are rolls, returns, or reports dealing with American, South African and Canadian officers serving with the RAF including recipients of honours (AIR 1/184/15/223/1, AIR 1/1023/204/5/1403, AIR 1/1035/204/5/1452, AIR 1/1057/24/5/1556, and AIR 1/2418/305/7). There is also a muster roll of the RAF upon its formation, which gives details of name, service number, date of enlistment into the services, trade, period of engagement and rate of pay (AIR 1/819/204/4/1316).

Information on POWs includes lists of RFC officers interned or held prisoner, May 1915 (AIR 1/836/204/5/271); lists of British and Dominion personnel held in Germany, Turkey or Switzerland in 1916 (AIR 1/892/204/5/696–8); records of debriefs of escaped and repatriated airmen (AIR 1/501/15/333/1 and AIR 1/1206/204/5/2); suggested questions to be put in such debriefing sessions (AIR 1/495/15/312/317); general reports on POWs, and officers interned in Denmark and the Netherlands (AIR 1/605/16/15/246, and 462/15/312/117); a report on one particular escape by an airman from Germany (AIR 1/726/129/1); an account of the POW experience of Lieutenant V. S. E. Lindops (AIR 1/733/195/1); and a list of POW camps in Germany (AIR 1/2154/209/3/312).

Issues involving particular individuals covered include the awards of the VC to Sub Lieutenant Warneford and Lieutenant Rhodes Moorhouse (AIR 1/9/15/1/31 and AIR 1/2265/209/64/1); the forced landing of Captain W. Mapplebeck near Lille in 1915 (AIR 1/21/15/1/108); the number of aircraft shot down by Captain J. B. McCudden, 1916–17 (AIR 1/479/15/312/240); the award of the Albert Medal to Lieutenant F. J. Rutland, RNAS 1916 (AIR 1/651/17/122/443); and the combat reports of Captain Albert Ball, VC, 1916–17 (AIR 1/2679). Students at the new post-war RAF Staff College were encouraged to record their war experiences and this material is preserved (AIR 1/2385–9), as are more assorted personal reminiscences (AIR 1/720 and AIR 1/2393–7), which include an account by Captain R. A. Brown of his role in the shooting down of 'The Red Baron', Manfred von Richthofen, in April 1918 (AIR 1/2397/262/1–2). The Air Historical Branch investigated the various claims relating to Richthofen's death after the war (AIR 1/682/21/13/2220), and obtained copies of Richthofen's correspondence and combat reports (AIR 1/675/21/13/1508 and AIR 1/686/21/13/2250). In addition, there are copies of the *London Gazette* and its Supplements, 1914–20 (AIR 1/2318).

AIR 2 includes material on decorations, including those RAF officers awarded Tsarist Russian or Italian decorations (AIR 2/2844–5 and 9366); recommendations for gallantry awards, 1918, including for service on the Western Front and in Mesopotamia (AIR 2/2841 and 2846–7); records of a conference to decide on decorations for Gallipoli, 1918–20 (AIR 2/84/B 5770); the report of a sub-committee on suitable medals and decorations for the new RAF (AIR 2/60/23214/18); authority to confer the Distinguished Service Order and Distinguished Service Cross on RAF officers (AIR 2/2839); the institution of new awards for the RAF in June 1918, namely the Distinguished Flying Cross, Air Force Cross, Distinguished Flying Medal and Air Force Medal (AIR 2/59/21774/1918). In addition, there are papers relating to the 1914–15 Star (AIR 2/92/C 62051), the British War Medal (AIR 2/92/C 59145), and the Silver War Badge (AIR 2/197/C 33296), together with the VC Record for the RFC, RNAS and RAF, 1914–18 (AIR 2/91/C 51021).

Wider war service matters includes proposed revisions to RFC pay and conditions, 1914–16 (AIR 2/6/87/3182); arrangements for RAF officers' pay (AIR 2/12141–3); vision standards for the RAF (AIR 2/59/7049/18); and procedures to register RAF men as absentee voters under the 1918 Representation of the People Act (AIR 2/155/344156/20). There is also a file on the internment of the crew of HM Airship C26 in Holland (AIR 2/42/AIR 607482/1917) and the personal file of Major J. L. Baird, Parliamentary Secretary to the Air Board, 1918–19 (AIR 2/73/A 7964).

AIR 4 contains samples of Aircrews' Flying Log Books. Unlike the situation in the army and navy where war diaries and ships' logs respectively recorded information at a unit level, aircrews maintained individual logs. Most of the sample relate to the Second World War and after but four surviving log books cover aspects of the Great War experience, namely duty at the Central Flying School between June and July 1918 (AIR 4/10); pilot training at home and in the Middle East in 1918 (AIR 4/30 and 47); and operations on the Western Front from October 1916 onwards (AIR 4/26).

AIR 10 has a complete muster list of the RAF on the date the new force came into existence, 1 April 1918 (AIR 10/232–7), and the RAF regulations on pay and allowances (AIR 10/4).

AIR 30 includes the RAF Submission Papers sent to the Sovereign regarding appointments, promotions and medal awards. They include correspondence on the conditions for the award of the Silver War Badge to RAF personnel, 1918 (AIR 30/1); on the institution of decorations for the new force (AIR 30/2); and on 1918 appointments (AIR 30/3–27), awards (AIR 30/34), and commissions (AIR 30/35).

AIR 76/1–567 contain microfilmed Officers' Service Records for those officers of the RFC who subsequently served in the RAF after April 1918, but who relinquished their commissions before the mid 1920s. They are in alphabetical order and include approximately 26,000 of the 27,000 officers serving in 1918. The originals have been destroyed. The records include name, date of birth, home address, next of kin, units in which served and where, appointments and promotions, honours and awards, and medical boards.

AIR 79 contains the Service Records of Airmen and Airwomen who served in the RFC before 1 April 1918 and in the RAF from 1 April 1918. The series includes both RFC and RNAS personnel. They are arranged by service number, for which there is an index available on microfilm (AIR 78/1–177). Some 329,000 enlistments are covered (AIR 79/1–2805) with separate sections for the South African Aviation Corps (AIR 79/2806) and Special Reservists (AIR 79/2807). Generally, records include date and place of birth, physical description, religious denomination, next of kin, spouse and children, date of enlistment, promotions, postings, medal awards, medical and disciplinary history, and date of discharge.

BT 15, consisting of minutes of the Board of Trade, includes material on the relief of distressed seamen in wartime (BT 15/67); a report by survivors of SS *Woodfield* on their escape from internment in 1916 (BT 15/68); and material on the repatriation of men from ships sunk by enemy action (BT 15/70).

BT 103/428, among the papers of the Board's Solicitor's Department, deals with the award of the Mercantile Marine War Medal, the rolls of which, however, are not held by the PRO.

BT 164 comprises a selection of service records for RNR ratings between 1860 and 1913, consisting of volumes and cards with each card or page representing five years' service. An individual, therefore, may be entered in several volumes or cards. Entries are in numerical order of enrolment.

BT 377/1–7 contains an alphabetical index on microfilm for the service numbers of members of the RNR, 1908–55, and records of service in service number order.

CAB 1 contains papers on appropriate reprisals for outrages against POWs and the issue of foreign service for those aged under 19 (CAB 1/22).

CAB 21/94 deals with the establishment of the Order of the British Empire.

CO 537 includes correspondence on decorations for the Gallipoli campaign (CO 537/1008), and material on British POWs held in Turkey in 1917 (CO 537/1123). There is also a file on the gallantry of the Bermuda Contingent, 1918 (CO 537/672).

CO 693 contains correspondence from the Dominions relating to prisoners of war, 1917–18. It comprises despatches for 1917 and 1918 (CO 693/1 and 6); correspondence by the Prisoner of War Department with other ministries, 1917–18 (CO 693/2–5 and 7–9); and despatches and correspondence, 1919 (CO 693/10).

CO 754/1–2 are Registers of Correspondence with the Dominions relating to POWs, 1917–19.

CO 755/1–2 are Registers of Out-letters to the Dominions on POWs, 1917–19.

FO 141 has material on the repatriation and exchange of civilian POWs (FO 141/738); ill treatment of British POWs by the Turks (FO 141/786); British and Italian POWs in the hands of the Senussi, 1915–19, and British POWs in the hands of the Bolsheviks, 1920–21 (FO 141/441 and 472).

FO 286/646–7 deal with awards of Greek decorations to British servicemen.

FO 383/1–547 comprise the records of the Prisoners of War and Aliens Department established within the Foreign Office in 1915 to co-ordinate aspects of work concerning prisoners of war and British civilian internees carried on in other government departments. Files are organised by country or region and year from 1915 until the department ceased to function in 1919. There is correspondence relating to Austria-Hungary (FO 383/1–7, 113–24, 245–51, 359–68, and 476–83); the Balkans (FO 383/8–9, 125–31, 252–4, 369–71, and 484–5); Belgium (FO 383/10–16, 132–7, 255–60, 372–9, and 486–7); Egypt (FO 383/16); France (FO 383/17, 138, 261, 380, and 487); Germany (FO 383/18–81, 139–205, 262–311, 381–420, 430–42, and 488–518); Italy and the Netherlands (FO 383/82, 211, 224, 326, 443–7, and 525–6); Russia and Scandinavia (FO 383/83–5, 212, 327, 448, and 527); Spain and Portugal (FO 383/85, 213–14, 328, and 449); Switzerland (FO 383/86–7, 215–19, 329–31, 450–51, and 527); Turkey (FO 383/88–102, 219–36, 332–45, 452–62, and 525–35); America (FO 383/111–12, 244–5, 476, and 547); and British civilians interned in Germany (FO 383/206–11, 312–24, 421–9, and 519–24). There are also some miscellaneous files (FO 383/103–10, 237–44, 346–58, 463–76, and 536–47). For each year, there is a dedicated prisoner of war index arranged by country and subject.

HO 45 has material on the exchange of POWs (HO 45/365255), and papers of the Committee on the Treatment by the Enemy of British Prisoners of War (HO 45/270829).

LAB 2/426/1 has details of the appointment of the War Workers' Medal Committee, 1918.

MT 9 has considerable material on honours and awards to the Mercantile Marine including awards of the Albert Medal (MT 9/1028, 1093, 1103, 1112, 1118, 1124, 1129, 1140, 1180, 1185, 1222, 1223, 1237, 1311, and 1343); the Silver and Bronze Medals for saving life at sea (MT 9/1287 and 1461); the Silver War Badge (MT 9/1132, 1242, 1404, 1675 and 2110); the Mercantile Marine War Medal (MT 9/1340, 1353, 1371, 1475, 1481, and 1491), including whether it should be awarded to those on Shackleton's ill-fated Antarctic expedition (MT 9/1401); the War Medal (MT 9/1341); the Victory Medal (MT 9/1284); Admiralty awards for incidents involving enemy submarines and mines (MT 9/1230); gallantry on the *Lusitania* (MT 9/1003); and by Captain H. B. Hooper on the Antwerp expedition, 1914 (MT 9/957). There is also general material on the administration of awards (MT 9/1429).

Merchant seamen taken prisoner are also considered (MT 9/962, 1101, 1179, 1182, 1215, and 1240) and listed for 1916–17 (MT 9/1098). In addition, there is material on repatriation including loss of effects of those repatriated from German camps (MT 9/1039, 1127, 1227, 1236, 1238–9, 1243, 1259–60, 1266, 1288, 1307, and 1369). Wages during internment or imprisonment, payments to dependants, and compensation issues are also covered (MT 9/1166, 1253, 1329, and 1427) as well as wages of crews whose vessels had been lost (MT 9/1257). Provision was made for those interned at Ruhleben Camp to study for seagoing certificates of competence (MT 9/1201) and there is coverage of conditions in Holland and Turkey (MT 9/1188 and 1190), reports on camps visited, 1916–18 (MT 9/1249), and a paper on issues to be raised at any peace conference (MT 9/1176). Captured German and Austro-Hungarian merchant marine officers received special consideration (MT 9/1211 and 1245). Curiously, there is also material on RN Division personnel taken prisoner (MT 9/1152). Torpedoed merchant seamen were presented to the King in 1917 (MT 9/1113).

MT 25 deals with the repatriation of British POWs from Germany and of German POWs in England (MT 25/18). In addition, there is information on the disembarkation of Canadian troops at St Nazaire in 1918 (MT 25/13); the general movement of troops to and from France, 1916–18 (MT 25/16–17); embarkation and disembarkation returns and weekly programmes of movements for British troops, 1914–18 (MT 25/29 and 64–5); and records of troopships sent to Mudros during the Dardanelles campaign (MT 25/55).

PRO 30/26, which has miscellaneous collections donated to the PRO, includes the papers of Lieutenant Colonel Harry Hatton Sproule, 2/4th Indian Cavalry, with diaries covering the years 1893–1932 (PRO 30/26/243), and notes on operations in Mesopotamia in 1915 (PRO 30/26/248).

PRO 30/71 contains papers of Lieutenant, later Major, Guy Nightingale, 1st Royal Munster Fusiliers, including wartime letters from Gallipoli in 1915, France in 1918 and North Russia in 1919 (PRO 30/71/3–4) and a diary for 1915 (PRO 30/71/5). There are also some letters to Nightingale's sister from Captain T. W. Filgate, 2nd Royal Munster Fusiliers, 1915 (PRO 30/71/3); and press cuttings on the career of Flight Lieutenant R. A. J. Warneford, VC, a cousin of Nightingale, who brought down a Zeppelin over Ghent in June 1915 (PRO 30/71/7).

WO 25, which contains a variety of miscellaneous material, includes embarkation returns, 1914–18 from home to overseas, between stations abroad, and to home from overseas (WO 25/3533A–78); the corresponding disembarkation returns (WO 25/3696–3732); and records of service for officers of the Royal Engineers, 1873–1935 (WO 25/3915–20), which provide details of campaigns, marriages, children, and names and address of next of kin.

WO 32 has much material relating to aspects of war service including acquisition of training land at Bramshott in Hampshire, 1917–23 (WO 32/21045–8). There is also material on the post-war recognition to be accorded to men and women of the auxiliary voluntary hospitals (WO 32/2937); service on vessels owned by the War Office (WO 32/5542); quartering regulations (WO 32/4075–6); and the issues raised by servicemen's marriages 'within British lines', primarily to French women (WO 32/3180–85). There is a considerable amount on medal awards including the eligibility for awards of Falkland islanders, the British Military Mission in the United States, Lady Fienne's ambulance unit, war correspondents, nurses, Africans, prisoners of war and civilians abroad who helped British POWs to escape (WO 32/4753, 4965, 4977, 5332, 5396, 5398, 5402, 5408, 5571, and 5573–4). In terms of the latter, there are also files on the award of the OBE to Prince and Princess de Croy, as well as an OBE to Mademoiselle de Bettignies for wartime intelligence work (WO 32/5406–7). The swapping of awards with those of other states is also covered (WO 32/5389, 5411 and 5438) including the award of the Military Cross to the towns of Ypres and Verdun (WO 32/4570–71). The question was raised of distinctive decorations for British and Dominion forces engaged at Gallipoli (WO 32/4984–5) as well as the possibility of battle clasps generally (WO 32/5328–9).

Questions relating to particular honours or medals are also covered in the files including the Order of the British Empire (WO 32/5397), Order of St Michael and St George (WO 32/5415–16), Distinguished Service Order (WO 32/5392, 5394, 5400, and 10547), Distinguished Service Cross (WO 32/5388), the Military Cross (WO 32/4912 and 5390), the Military Medal (WO 32/4959–60), the 1914 Star (WO 32/4986 and 5331), and the Victory Medal (WO 32/3444, 4961, 4982, 4987, 5081, and 5412). Some recommendations for the VC are also dealt with, including the bar to the VC for Captain Martin Leake, recommendations from Sir John French, and recommendations for Gallipoli including the 'six VCs before breakfast' won by the 1st Lancashire Fusiliers (WO 32/4912 and 4993–5). War medals were also presented to Asquith and Lloyd George as wartime prime ministers (WO 32/4988); there were parliamentary and other grants to prominent soldiers (WO 32/17845–6); and parliamentary resolutions of thanks to the armed forces in general (WO 32/11488–9). Some miscellaneous issues covered include belated claims for medals (WO 32/2557), procedures for presenting medals to next of kin or to recipients unable to attend presentations (WO 32/5391 and 5393), and the issue of certificates to those mentioned in despatches (WO 32/4296), while there was a general review of all the new decorations and medals arising from the war in 1920 (WO 32/5420).

Issues regarding British prisoners of war and interned civilians are also covered including allegations of ill treatment and employment of POWs close to the front line in violation of the Hague agreements (WO 32/5098, 5188, 5369, 5371, 5381, 5608, and 5610); wartime and post-war arrangements for repatriation of British and other POWs and internees (WO 32/5373, 5377–9, and 5387); the holding of German POWs by the allies (WO 32/5365 and 5367); the parole given by British POWs in Turkey (WO 32/15508); the conditions for British internees in Switzerland (WO 32/5380); and the particular cases of men of the RFC (WO 32/15503–6), and of the Royal Naval Division held in Holland, the latter interned after the fall of Antwerp in 1914 (WO 32/15507). Among other miscellaneous material is the report of the Burnham Committee on the promotion of officers of the Special Reserve, Territorial Force and New Armies, 1917–18 (WO 32/5055), and the report of a committee on promotion convened by Winston Churchill in 1917 (WO 32/5953).

WO 76 contains Returns of the Service of Offices on the active list between 1829 and 1919, with details of date and place of birth, marriage and children. Arranged by regional army record office and, subsequently, by the brigade offices established in the 1950s, it includes those commissioned until early in the First World War for a number of regiments (WO 76/2–3, 9, 24–5, 38, 42, 52, 54, 58, 151, 166, 181, 184, 257, 264, 268, 314–15, 329, 358, 386, 397, 409–10, 417–18, 424, 430, 460, 464, 468, 470, 472, 474, 483, 490, 495, 497, 499, 501, 509, 516, 521, 528, 531, 544, and 552). In addition, however, there are records for a few wartime battalions including the Worcestershire Regiment, 1914–15 (WO 76/267); 2nd and 16th KRRC, 1914–15 (WO 76/293); Sherwood Foresters, 1914–18 (413–16 and 419); 1st Black Watch (WO 76/425–6); 1st Somerset Light Infantry, 1914–19 (WO 76/479); 11th Scottish Rifles, 1915, including Warrant Officers and NCOs (WO 76/491); 3rd Wiltshire Regiment, 1914–18 (WO 76/532–3); and 9th Lancers, 1914–18 (WO 76/553).

WO 79 comprises private collections of papers including a digest of service for the 5th Connaught Rangers, 1914–15 (WO 79/41), and material for a history of the Connaught Rangers, 1915–16, and its war honours (WO 79/42 and 49).

WO 98 contains the Registers for the Award of the Victoria Cross, including the number of awards made to different divisions and units, 1914–18 (WO 98/5), an alphabetical list of recipients, 1914–20 (WO 98/6), and the actual register for 1900–44 (WO 98/409).

WO 100 contains Campaign Medal and Award Rolls. It includes clasps awarded to the Khedive's Sudan Medal (WO 100/407) and the Africa General Service Medal (WO 100/408–9) for wartime operations against insurgents in the Sudan, Nyasaland, the East African Protectorate (Kenya), and Nigeria.

WO 101/2 covers awards of the Meritorious Service Medal, 1855–1919.

WO 103/31 contains appointments in the Volunteer Training Corps and Volunteer Force submitted for Royal approval, 1914–18.

WO 106 has a report by the Directorate of POWs, 1920 (WO 106/1451), as well as a report on British prisoners returned from captivity by the Bolsheviks during the allied intervention in Russia, 1920 (WO 106/1279). In addition, there is material on the captivity of survivors of HMS *Tara*, an armed boarding steamer sunk by *U-35* off the Libyan coast, whose crew were handed over to the Senussi (WO 106/1543).

WO 138 consists of selected personal files previously withdrawn from other service records through the prominence of the individual concerned or some other interesting facet of his career. Those of relevance to the Great War include Brigadier-General C. Fitzclarence, VC, who was killed at Ypres in 1914 (WO 138/25); Major-General B. J. C. Doran (WO 138/26); Major-General the Hon. E. J. Montagu Stuart-Wortley, one of those 'degummed' from wartime command (WO 138/29); Major-General T. D. Pilcher (WO 138/36); Lieutenant-General Sir Frederick Stopford, who manifestly failed at Gallipoli in 1915 (WO 138/40); Major-General Sir W. Douglas (WO 138/42); Field Marshal Lord Kitchener (WO 138/44); Major-General E. C. W. Mackenzie-Kennedy (WO 138/46); Lieutenant-General Sir Stanley Maude, who undertook the successful advance on Baghdad in 1917 (WO 138/47); his unsuccessful predecessor, General Sir John Nixon (WO 138/48); the wartime Quartermaster-General, General Sir John Cowans (WO 138/52); General Sir Charles Townshend, who surrendered at Kut in 1916 (WO 138/64); Captain the Hon. J. R. L. French, on whom a medical board was convened in 1917 (WO 138/65); the poet, Wilfred Owen, killed in 1918 (WO 138/74); and Field Marshal Sir Douglas Haig (WO 138/75–7).

WO 158/968 has statements by officers taken prisoner by the Bolsheviks in North Russia, 1918–20.

WO 161, comprising miscellaneous papers relating to the war, includes interviews with returned prisoners of war conducted by the Committee on the Treatment by the Enemy of British Prisoners of War (WO 161/95–100), for which there is an index (WO 161/101). As well as a narrative, these reports can include details of unit, home address, when and where captured, wounds suffered, transfers between camps, comments on treatment and conditions, and escape attempts. In addition, the class contains narratives and accounts of the Royal Army Service Corps, 1916–19 (WO 161/17–19); war histories of the 1/7th Hampshires, 1/2nd King's African Rifles, 1/2nd Northumberland Fusiliers, and 23rd Sikh Pioneers (WO 161/74–7); wartime services and honours of the Honourable Artillery Company (WO 161/80); and reports on the British and German field postal services (WO 161/114–15). There is also material on the Volunteer Training Corps and Volunteer Force (WO 161/104–12), including correspondence and papers, 1914–17 (WO 161/105 and 107); army orders and Army Council instructions relating to the force (WO 161/106 and 109); training reports on the volunteers in London, 1917 (WO 161/111); and replies by CTAs in 1917–18 to questionnaires on their work with the Volunteer Force since 1914 (WO 161/112).

WO 162, the papers of the Adjutant General's Department, includes embarkation lists of units with dates, 1914–18 (WO 162/7); and papers on the Medals and Clasps Tribunal, 1920 (WO 162/73).

WO 296/1-9 are Notebooks of the War Office Central Department C2 Branch, 1904–23, containing precedents, decisions and policy on general and legal matters. During the war C2 concentrated almost entirely on actuarial questions relating to casualties, including correspondence with enemy countries and eventually it incorporated the Prisoners of War Information Bureau.

WO 329/1-3272 consist of the Medal Award Rolls for the army, RFC and RAF for the 1914 (WO 329/2392–2512) and 1914–15 Stars (WO 329/2513–2956), and the British War Medal and the Victory Medal (WO 329/2–2391), collectively known as 'Pip, Squeak and Wilfred'. In addition, the rolls also cover the Territorial Force War Medal (WO 329/3256–72); the Allied Subjects Medal, awarded for allied personnel who assisted British soldiers behind enemy lines (WO 329/2957); and the Silver War Badge for Services Rendered, for those retired or discharged from wounds or sickness (WO 329/2958–3255). Entries in the rolls need to be located using the former Army Medal Office references for the medal rolls obtained from the card index kept on fiche in the Microfilm Reading Room (WO 372/1–24), the original medal roll index (WO 329/1) also retained in the Microfilm Reading Room, and the current PRO reference from the series list. In many cases, the index card has as much information as the medal roll itself since it gives army number, rank, unit and medal entitlement. Apart from purely British units, the rolls include the awards for more exotic units such as the South Persia Rifles (WO 329/2308), Zanzibar Carrier Corps (WO 329/2342), Zion Mule Corps (WO 329/2346), and Maltese Mining Company (WO 329/2371). It also includes awards to civilian groups in the war zone such as the YMCA (WO 329/2354) and American Ambulance Unit (WO 329/2324).

WO 339 contains the records of approximately 140,000 officers who saw service during the war, but who did not continue in service after 1922. They include pre-war regulars, those given wartime commissions, and those commissioned into the Special Reserve. The files are arranged in so-called Long Number order, the long number of an individual being obtained from the index (WO 338/1–23) held in the Microfilm Reading Room. Apart from forms common to those for enlisted men found in WO 364, there are also likely to be applications for appointment to temporary wartime commissions and to the Special Reserve of Officers.

WO 379/16 has dates of embarkation for units proceeding overseas, 1914–18.

WO 363/1-4915 contain the so-called 'Burnt Collection' or '1914–20 Collation', being those soldiers' service records which survived a German bombing raid on the warehouse in Walworth in which they were stored in September 1940. They comprise about 25 per cent of the original total and cover wartime servicemen who were killed in action, died of wounds or disease, were executed, discharged without pension, or demobilised at the end of the war. Regulars, Territorials, New Army volunteers and conscripts are all represented, including regulars whose service was completed between 1914 and 1920. Currently, the series is being microfilmed as the files are too fragile to be produced, those not yet filmed still being held in the Army Records Office at Hayes. Neither this series nor WO 364 include details of regulars who continued in the army after 1920. The contents of files vary, but may include attestation papers, discharge papers, medical records, disability statements completed on demobilisation, casualty forms, and regimental conduct sheets. Series lists give the range of names as a location for the microfilm, the files not being arranged in strict alphabetical order. The filming programme should be completed by the end of 2002.

WO 364 contains approximately 4,000 microfilms of the so-called 'Unburnt Collection' of soldiers' files, being a supplementary set compiled from those of the Ministry of Pensions after the bombing of the War Office files in September 1940. They deal with those in receipt of war pensions, who had since died or whose claims had been refused, those discharged on medical or associated grounds and regular soldiers discharged at the end of their period of service. They do not include soldiers who signed on for the duration unless they received a pension on medical grounds since such men were entitled only to a gratuity on demobilisation. Two separate alphabetical lists exist for the collection in the Microfilm Reading Room, which will give a reference for the range of names contained in each microfilm. They are generally in better alphabetical order than the Burnt Collection.

WO 374 is a second series of officers' papers with some 70,000 records arranged in alphabetical order. They are primarily officers commissioned in the Territorial Force (the '9 series' so-called after the War Office prefix for Territorial officers) and those with temporary commissions (the so-called 'vowel series' of files arranged by initial letter and first vowel of name).

WO 388/1–5 are the Records of Exchange of Army Decorations between Britain and its Allies, 1914–26, dealing with decorations awarded to and received from 'Arabia' (including awards to the Arab Levy Corps), Belgium, China, Czechoslovakia, Egypt, France, Greece, Italy, Japan, Montenegro, Nepal, Panama, Persia, Poland, Portugal, Russia, Serbia, Siam, Romania and the United States. The series includes a monthly statistical return of medals awarded and received (WO 388/5). Access is under supervision until such time as the series has been microfilmed.

WO 389/1–8 comprise the Military Secretary's Record Books for the Distinguished Service Order and Military Cross, 1914–19, consisting of annotated pasted extracts from the *London Gazette*. In addition, the extracts are from the 'advanced copies' which sometimes had information removed prior to actual publication. Access is under supervision until the series has been microfilmed. There is a nominal index (WO 389/9–24).

WO 390 contains the Military Secretary's Registers for the Distinguished Service Order. The registers cover the war years (WO 390/2–8) as well as honorary appointments of allied officers to the Order (WO 390/13). Access is under supervision until the series has been microfilmed.

WO 391/2–7 are the Military Secretary's Registers for the Distinguished Conduct Medal, comprising annotated pasted extracts from the 'advanced copies' of the *London Gazette*. Access is under supervision until the series is microfilmed.

ZJ 1, which is held in the Microfilm Reading Room together with a microfiche card index, consists of copies of the *London Gazette*. Published since 1665, it contains announcements of gallantry awards and, in some cases, citations, as well as the names of those mentioned in despatches, the latter representing some 2.3 per cent of those who served in the wartime armed forces who were thus entitled to a bronze oak leaf emblem worn on the ribbon of the Victory Medal. Commissions, promotions and appointments were also gazetted.

The SS *River Clyde*, which was run aground on V Beach, Cape Helles, Gallipoli, 23 April 1915. (WO 317/1)

Anti-aircraft emplacement at Konatogani, Dvina River Force, South Russia, 14 September 1919. (CN 5/25, no 48)

The withdrawal of British and Indian forces from Tanga, German East Africa, 5 November 1914 (photograph taken by Lt Colonel E. StG. Kirke, RE). (CAB 45/7)

Men of HMS *Suffolk* at an allied parade in Vladivostock, 15 November 1918. (CN 1/27)

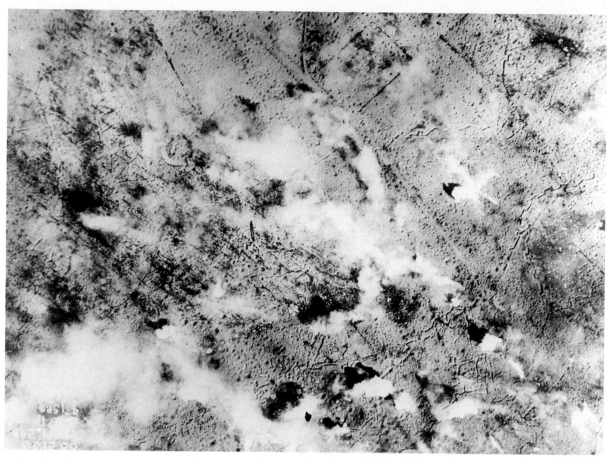

Shell explosions from the British barrage fired during the bombardment prior to the attack on the Messines Ridge on 7 June 1917. (WO 316/55, no 41)

DESTRUCTIVE SHOOT

BEFORE   GB 1731

HOSTILE BATTERY *28 J26D 75.45.   15 Cm H.*
ENGAGED BY *179ʰ S. Bty. Capt: C.V. Stewart M.C.*
OBSERVER *Lieut: Stocks*
DATE *5·5·17*

Before and after: the effect of a British barrage on a German battery position, Messines, 5 May 1917 (photograph taken by No 6 Squadron, RFC). (WO 316/55, no 4)

AFTER.   6B 1804.

David Lloyd George, Minister of Munitions, and Winston Churchill, First Lord of the Admiralty, viewing a wire-cutting experiment at Wormwood Scrubs, 1915. (MUN 5/394, no 10)

British gas casualties, Ypres, April 1915. (CN 4/4, no 1)

Flying trials off HMS *Campania*, 23 April 1917. (CN 5/17, no 1)

The Tudor-Hart method of dazzle camouflage demonstrated on a launch, 12 June 1917. (CN 1/25)

An allied convoy bound for Iceland, 18 October 1918. (AIR 1/419/15/245/1)

The RNAS seaplane station at Otranto in the Adriatic, 1917. (AIR 1/649/17/122/417)

Women police officers chasing boys from the Serpentine, 1918. (MEPO 13/57)

Women workers with a cordite pressing machine, Waltham Abbey, July 1917. (SUPP 5/861, no 313)

Women munitions workers. (MUN 5/297, Pt 4, no 609)

Results of the raid by the German Naval Zeppelin L9 on Hull, 6/7 June 1915. (AIR 1/569/16/15/142)

The wreck of Zeppelin L33 after being crash landed and set on fire by its crew in Essex on the night of 23/24 September 1916. (AIR 1/7/6/98)

German bomb damage at Faversham, 1918. (CN 5/1, no 5)

The peace celebrations in London, June 1919. (WORK 21/74)

Industrialised warfare certainly increased the degree to which men were exposed to concussion and sensory deprivation, derived from heavier and more prolonged artillery bombardment. The battlefield had also become progressively more 'empty' as the range of weapons increased, thus distancing soldiers yet further from a ready identification of the enemy. All armies suffered morale problems. In the British army, military crime invariably rose after heavy casualties and absence without leave and drunkenness remained relatively high throughout the war. There were also some instances of collective indiscipline, the best known being at the Etaples base camp in September 1917, although it has been much exaggerated in popular accounts.

Yet, unlike other armies, the British did not suffer total or near total collapse. Drill and coercion clearly assisted and so, too, did regimental tradition and the local identity of units. Working-class soldiers both accepted and expected the imposition of discipline because, in British society, deference, which was not regarded as subservience, was routinely extended by the working class to social superiors in return for paternalism, which mitigated the harsher aspects of the disciplinary code. There was also the extensive British welfare network of divisional and regimental canteens, YMCA, Church Army and comfort funds: 800,000 parcels were reaching the BEF each week by April 1917. Entertainment was provided by cinemas, concert and bathing parties, the divisional sports meetings, the boxing tournaments, horse shows, football and cricket matches which, incidentally, provided men with an opportunity to embarrass officers without incurring penalties.

Under the provisions of the British Army Act, a total of 361 men were executed during the war, of whom 291 were serving with British regiments. Taking into account all executions up to the suspension of the death penalty in 1924, and including those civilians and prisoners of war executed for various offences, the total comes to 438. It needs to be borne in mind, however, that only 10.8 per cent of death sentences actually imposed by British courts martial on white soldiers were confirmed. Nearly 40 of those executed had previously been sentenced to death and two of them twice previously. Others had previously served, or had had suspended, sentences of imprisonment for capital offences. It should also be noted that standards in the conduct of courts martial differed little from those in pre-war civil courts. In all, there were 305,062 courts martial in the army during the war, with an additional 4,449 cases heard in military courts.

Disproportionate attention has been devoted to the wartime executions, largely through the popular perception that those executed must all have been suffering from 'shell shock', a term first coined in February 1915. However, there was no agreed theory, diagnosis or therapy relating to the condition among medical practitioners, who were divided between physiological and psychological concepts of mental health. Ultimately, shell shock became a usable political issue, which meant different things to different people.

ADM 1 has some material relevant to disciplinary matters including consideration of wartime punishment in October 1914 (ADM 1/8397/360); penalties for desertion

(ADM 1/8485/74); discipline among gun crews on transports (ADM 1/8447/22); and a refusal to do duty by men on HMS *Royal George* in June 1917 (ADM 1/8489/119). Unrest on the lower deck was addressed in September and October 1917 (ADM 1/8498/201, 8501/229). There is also material on the organisation of the Navy and Army Canteen Board, 1916–17 (ADM 1/9743).

ADM 116 concerns postal concessions for naval personnel during the war (ADM 116/3463), and the role of Roman Catholic chaplains with the Fleet, 1914–15 (ADM 116/1373).

ADM 156 comprises the records of naval courts martial and courts of enquiry. Primarily, these deal with naval operations and, particularly, the loss of naval vessels or merchant vessels under Admiralty control. There are, however, some files on other disciplinary offences committed on particular vessels between 1914 and 1918 including drunkenness (ADM 156/13, 43, 81, and 151); disobedience by both officers and seamen (ADM 156/17, 39, 80, and 108); bullying among junior officers (ADM 156/21); fraud (ADM 156/23, 30, and 152); murder (ADM 156/26–7 and 92); desertion (ADM 156/33); lack of discipline (ADM 156/87); looting (ADM 156/78 and 119); and a case of an officer striking a seaman (ADM 156/32). Of particular interest are cases of mutiny on HMS *Teutonic* in 1916 (ADM 156/19), HMS *Amphitrite* in 1917 (ADM 156/34) and HMS *Leviathan* in 1918 (ADM 156/89); the death of an officer and three ratings on HMS *Southampton* in March 1917 (ADM 156/165); and a case of seamen accused of combining to send a petition to the Admiralty (ADM 156/35). There is also a general file on mutinies between 1890 and 1921 (ADM 156/157).

Also included are the papers relating to the controversial court martial of Sub Lieutenant Dyett, RNR, attached to the 63rd (Royal Naval) Division and one of only three British officers to be executed during the war (ADM 156/24). A high profile case is that of Commodore, later Rear Admiral, Murray Sueter, dismissed from his command in Italy in 1917 for writing to the King to complain that the RNAS had not been given sufficient recognition for its pioneering role in the development of the tank (ADM 156/180–81). General operational issues include enquiries into the failures to engage the enemy by HMS *Satellite* in November 1917 (ADM 156/36); action against officers of HMS *Topaze* in the same month (ADM 156/109); the anchoring of HM Trawler *Osiris II* when it should have been on patrol in May 1917 (ADM 156/153); and movements of two motor launches in April 1918 (ADM 156/132).

ADM 178 contains the Supplementary Series of Admiralty Secretariat 'case' papers, primarily courts martial and courts of enquiry previously regarded as sensitive. These include a desertion case in 1915 (ADM 178/15); consideration of the legality of punishment in the Royal Australian Navy in 1915 (ADM 178/16); general procedures for courts martial for the loss of ships (ADM 178/17); discipline in the Trawler Reserve (ADM 178/18); forfeiture of pay as a disciplinary measure for RNR skippers, 1914–15 (ADM 178/19); proceedings against a Tug master (ADM 178/20); the removal of an officer from the RNAS in 1916 (ADM 178/21); consideration of making compassionate allowance for an officer of the RMLI dismissed by court martial, 1917 (ADM 178/23); the trial of a Sub-Lieutenant of a motor launch, 1917 (ADM 178/24); illegal enlistment practices in the RM Submarine Miners, 1917–18 (ADM 178/26); the failure of a Trawler skipper to carry out orders, 1917 (ADM 178/27); and the case of a surrendered deserter, 1919 (ADM 178/34). There is also more material on the Sueter case (ADM 178/29 and 45). In September 1918 there was a review of lower deck benefit societies in the light of grievances and unrest in the fleet (ADM 178/157).

ADM 194 contains the Admiralty Courts Martial Registers. They comprise those for officers and warrant officers of the Royal Navy and Royal Marines between 1857 and 1915 arranged alphabetically (ADM 194/43–5), and a register for the Portsmouth Division of the Royal Marines, 1903–16 (ADM 194/17).

AIR 1 has a little information on disciplinary issues including a confidential report on the failure of four aircraft to take part in a raid in July 1916 (AIR 1/115/15/39/68); and reports of courts of enquiry into accidents and self-inflicted injuries among other ranks, 1915–17 (AIR 1/1035). There is also material on the rest houses for officers at Le Touquet and Paris Plage, 1918 (AIR 1/1042/204/5/1487).

AIR 2 has some material on discipline including consideration of the responsibility for maintaining discipline among RAF personnel attached to the Grand Fleet, 1918 (AIR 2/730); questions put to the Judge Advocate General on the discipline of colonial troops in 1918 (AIR 2/59/20950/18); and rewards for policemen who apprehended deserters (AIR 2/60/24714/18). There is also material on the provision of facilities to RAF stations by the Navy and Army Canteen Board, 1918–19 (AIR 2/96/D 5037), and consideration of accommodation difficulties for RAF servicemen on the converted seaplane carrier, HMS *Eagle* (AIR 2/80/B 2981).

AIR 21/1–10 contains RAF Courts Martial Registers, 1918–65, giving name and rank of prisoners, place of trial, nature of charge and sentence. Those relating to the RAF in 1918 are for District Courts Martial at home and abroad, 1918–38 (AIR 2/1A), Field General Courts Martial abroad, 1918–47 (AIR 2/1B), and General Courts Martial abroad and at home, 1918–60 (AIR 2/2 and 3).

AIR 43/1 contains the RAF Courts Martial Charge Book, 1918–19, arranged in date order.

AIR 44/1 contains Courts Martial Minute Books, 1918–20, representing details sent to the Judge Advocate General concerning legal aspects, precedents and irregularities with regard to RAF courts martial.

AIR 71/1 are the Judge Advocate General's Out-letters, 1918–23, dealing with issues raised by RAF courts martial.

CAB 27/21 contains papers of the Standing Committee on Soldiers' and Sailors' Pay, from August 1917 to May 1919. A Naval, Military and Air Force Pay Committee was subsequently established in June 1919.

CAB 45/213 deals with the work of religious organisations among wartime troops.

CO 537/1192–6 contain material on the issue of pay for South African troops serving on the Western Front, 1916.

CUST 106/99 has material on the supply of goods to the forces overseas and to POWs, 1915–39.

DO 119/912 has papers on the alleged drunkenness of Commander Lee during the motorboat expedition on Lake Tanganyika, 1915.

FO 141/825 contains material on the notorious riot by the Anzacs in Cairo's red light district in April 1915, as well as on the conduct of British troops in Egypt.

HO 45 contains papers on convictions of members of the Australian Imperial Force while in Britain in 1918 (HO 45/349730); the maintenance of discipline on transports engaged in naval and military operations (HO 45/275921); deserters and absentees from the RAF (HO 45/359241); procedures for apprehended deserters and absentees (HO 45/271874); and verifying the veracity of those soldiers who claimed they had been granted leave to visit sick relatives (HO 45/372297).

MT 9 has some material on disciplinary issues raised in respect of merchant seamen under naval orders or brought before naval courts (MT 9/1064, 1068–70, 1090, 1142, 1161, 1195, 1203, 1206, 1209–10, 1216–17, 1220, 1235, and 1258), specific cases including a mutiny on the *Kursk* in 1918 (MT 9/1204) and one of sodomy (MT 9/1172). The master of the *Hare* was censured for failure to rescue torpedoed seamen in 1917 (MT 9/1135).

MT 23/694 covers the erection of shelters and kitchens for troops at Southampton Docks, 1916.

WO 32 contains reports on the mutiny of the 5th (Native) Light Infantry of the Indian army at Singapore in February 1915, which resulted in the deaths of 32 Europeans and the public execution of 37 mutineers. Though blamed on both German and Sikh Ghadarite subversion, internal divisions between Indian officers and men, compounded by poor rations and the strained relationship between British officers, lay at its root (WO 32/9559–60).

Other disciplinary matters covered are the expression of political views by MPs while on active service, 1915 (WO 32/18555); pay and gratuities for temporary wartime officers (WO 32/4858–61); pay and promotion in the RAMC (WO 32/5043–4); an inquiry into discontent among officers and men of the 1/4th Royal Norfolks, 1915 (WO 32/18563); reports on officers of the 201st and 202nd Infantry Brigades, 1916 (WO 32/18581); the appropriate method of reporting deaths to relatives of those executed for disciplinary offences and of announcing such sentences in court (WO 32/3989–90 and 4675); the enforcement of the King's regulations over the handful of Soldiers' and Sailors' Committees that appeared in 1917 (WO 32/5455); the extension of the power of court martial to the GOC, Independent Force, RAF (WO 32/5456); questions of general amnesty and the cessation of the death penalty on the cessation of hostilities (WO 32/5476 and 5479); wartime rules of court procedure (WO 32/5471B); the detention of military prisoners in civil prisons (WO 32/5480); the application of martial law overseas (WO 32/5469); the harbouring of deserters and absentees (WO 32/11663–4); the treatment of Australian troops tried for murder (WO 32/5484); the maintenance of discipline among American and other allied troops in Britain (WO 32/5763 and 5767); and a post-war file on alleged misconduct by wartime military personnel compiled in 1919 (WO 32/18918). The post-war Darling Committee on Courts Martial procedures, 1919–23, is also represented (WO 32/5475, 5477–8 and 5481–2), as is the discussion of the abolition of Field Punishment Number One (WO 32/5460–61).

In terms of issues of morale, there are applications by philanthropic groups for permission to erect recreational huts at camps, 1917–19 (WO 32/20461–4); the King's wartime messages to his troops (WO 32/5083) and, indeed, to American troops on arrival in Britain (WO 32/5768); a narrative of the work of the War Office separation allowances section (WO 32/9316); and material on the creation of the Army Canteen Committee, subsequently the Navy and Army Canteen Board and the forerunner of the NAAFI (WO 32/5498–501). There is another copy of the minutes of the Committee on Soldiers' and Sailors' Pay, 1918–19 (WO 32/4793).

WO 71 contains the files of the Judge Advocate General on courts martial proceedings. The series includes files on individuals who faced home and overseas Field General Courts Martial, notably those executed for military offences (WO 71/387–690). The files are arranged by name and date. In addition, there are files on two General Courts Martial (WO 71/1027–8).

WO 81/142–56 are the Judge Advocate General's Letter Books for the war period.

WO 83/20–33 comprise the Judge Advocate General's Minute Books for the war period.

WO 86/62–86 are the registers of District Courts Martial, giving in tabulated form the name, rank, regiment, place of trial, charge and sentence of those tried. They cover NCOs and other ranks. A total of 143,009 District Courts Martial were held during the course of the war. The registers comprise those courts martial held for charges home and abroad, 1913–14 (WO 86/62), those for charges at home, 1914–15 (WO 86/63–4), and those for home and abroad, 1915–19 (WO 86/65–86).

WO 90/6–8 are registers for General Courts Martial that took place abroad. These include officers as well as other ranks. A total of 6,542 General Courts Martial were held during the war. The registers comprise those for courts martial convened, 1900–17 (WO 90/6), those convened in India, 1879–1920 (WO 90/7), and those convened, 1917–43 (WO 90/8).

WO 92/3–4 are registers of General Courts Martial convened at home, 1899–1945.

WO 93 contains miscellaneous papers of the Judge Advocate General, including nominal rolls of courts martial for men of the Australian Imperial Force and Canadian Expeditionary Force, 1915–19 (WO 93/42–5); particulars of death sentences carried out between 1914 and 1918 (WO 93/49); extracts on disciplinary matters from the official post-war publication, *Statistics of the Military Effort of the British Empire* (WO 93/50–51); and general correspondence on instances of mutiny in army and RAF (WO 93/52).

WO 106/297 contains material on morale-building Royal visits to the British army in the field, 1914–18.

WO 141 contains, among the special series of War Office registered papers, more material on the Singapore mutiny in February 1915 (WO 141/7–8). There are also papers relating to other inquires including alleged corrupt practices in the British Remount Commission in Canada (WO 141/28); the failure of Colonel Malleson in field command in East Africa in 1916 (WO 141/62); charges brought against two officers (WO 141/63); the surrender of the 1st Battalion, Gordon Highlanders in August 1914 (WO 141/37–8); and an interview given by Major-General Charles Townshend, who had surrendered at Kut in 1916, to *The Times* after his release from Turkish imprisonment in 1918 (WO 141/64).

WO 158/969 has papers on the court of inquiry into indiscipline in the 6th Battalion, Royal Marines in North Russia, 1919.

WO 213/1–26 are Registers of Field General Courts Martial for more serious crimes, 1914–18, including officers as well as other ranks, and for Military Courts,

1914–18. A total of 154,711 Field General Courts Martial were held during the war, and 4,449 Military Courts, the latter for prisoners of war and civilians.

Losses, Veterans and Dependants

Questions of mortality and life expectancy provide a ready example of the difficulties of assessing war's true impact. Clearly, there was immense loss of life in the short term. In the long term, however, the war may not have made any substantial difference in demographic terms, and there is a considerable debate as to its impact upon civilian health. Indeed, the war cut across demographic trends in complicated ways. Precise figures of war losses are all but impossible to determine, especially when it is appreciated that there is a difference between war dead and war-related dead. There is also the even wider question of the possible demographic deficit arising from the longer-term implications of war and war-related deaths.

In the case of Britain, war dead numbered approximately 753,000, representing over 704,000 military deaths, over 32,000 naval deaths, over 14,000 merchant marine deaths, and just over 1,500 civilian deaths from German air or naval bombardment. It represented a loss of about 11.8 per cent of those mobilised and 6.3 per cent of males aged between 15 and 49. It has been argued that the effect was dysgenic, in that some sectors of society had volunteered in greater proportion to others, while many working-class men had been physically unfit for military service through the level of pre-war deprivation in urban areas. Moreover, officers suffered proportionally more dead than other ranks. Thus, there was an element of truth in the post-war concept of a 'lost generation' among the potential future socio-political elite, although the greater fertility among poorer classes and the greater availability of contraception to their social superiors equally affected the vitality of traditional elites.

While the war was obviously destructive of life, it also needs to be borne in mind that it contributed to advances in medicine. In 1914, for example, British military doctors were confronted with outbreaks of meningitis in tented camps. Trench warfare in the autumn introduced dangers from tetanus, gas gangrene infection and what became known as trench fever, caused by scratching of louse excreta. New antiseptics and anesthetics were developed and new methods for the control and prevention of diseases such as enteric, nephritis, malaria, dysentery, and typhus.

In Mesopotamia, the problems of 'deficiency diseases' such as scurvy advanced acceptance of the vitamin theory, propounded just prior to the war as an alternative to the erroneous bacteriological explanation for such disease. Blood transfusion became widely established as a routine surgical measure and innovations were made in the preliminary 'surgical toilet' of wounds. The perception of an increased incidence of heart disease among soldiers, a condition known as 'soldier's heart', similarly led to pioneering research work at Colchester and Hampstead hospitals.

There were particularly significant developments in terms of the production of artificial limbs. Far from being an invention of the Second World War, plastic surgery was first evolved by an ear, nose and throat surgeon, Harold Gillies, at the Queen's Hospital in Sidcup. In previous wars, there had usually been about five deaths to disease from every one in battle but, between 1914 and 1918, if the effects of the influenza pandemic of 1918 are excluded, the average was only one death from disease to 15 from battle. At the same time, however, it was the first war in which the wounded had a greater chance of living than dying from the effect of their wounds.

Overall, the demographic gain in Britain, as elsewhere, outweighed the demographic loss since the British population grew by some 2 million between 1911 and 1921, albeit with a reduced growth rate compared to that between 1901 and 1911. Female health particularly improved and infant mortality declined. Much was due to the improvement in the nutrition of mothers and children, enhanced concerns for infant and maternal welfare seen in better medical care, and increases in family income through separation allowances and wages keeping pace with inflation. Generally, the British working class was better fed and clothed during the war and it has been argued that these higher living standards were not eroded by post-war economic depression. Thus, the war did not substantially alter existing demographic trends and the loss of life was made good relatively quickly.

ADM 1 is a major source for naval casualty lists since there is one for virtually every ship lost or otherwise sustaining casualties. They include, for example, those from 1914 for HMS *Carmania*, HMS *Aboukir*, HMS *Cressy*, HMS *Hogue*, HMS *Hawke*, HMAS *Sydney*, and the battle off the Falkland Islands in December 1914 (ADM 1/8394/325 and 334, 8398/374 and 377, 8402/412, and 8405/459) as well as RNAS casualties in an armoured car action near Douai in September 1914 (ADM 1/8395/340); general tables of casualties between August and November 1914 (ADM 1/8403/429 and 433); and the question of the identification and disposal of bodies from the *Aboukir*, *Cressy* and *Hogue* washed up in Holland (ADM 1/8400/395). Similar information for 1915 losses include those of HMS *Agamemnon*, Submarine *E15*, HMS *Canopus*, HMS *Ocean*, HMS *Bacchante*, HMS *Lynx* (ADM 1/8413/57, 8419/107, 8418/90, 8419/111, 8420/115, and 8429/222 and 230); as well as naval casualties in the Expeditionary Force in Cameroon and in the landing operations at Gallipoli (ADM 1/8413/62 and 8421/135), and general casualty tables to October 1915 (ADM 1/8436/311B).

From 1916 casualty lists include those for HM Drifters *Freuchy* and *Morning Star* (ADM 1/8444/4) and for ships lost and engaged at Jutland (ADM 1/8457/114–18, 8458/122–32, 8459/133–40, 8460/151, and 8573/315), as well as the question of the disposal of corpses washed up in Norway and Sweden (ADM 1/8461/159 and 8476/299). The 1917 lists include those for HMS *Ben Machree* (ADM 1/8479/21) while there are lists of hospital ships lost to enemy action in 1917 (ADM 1/8485/79) and of all British and neutral vessels sunk or captured between August 1914 and July 1917 (ADM 1/8509/1). Casualty lists for 1918 include those of HMS *Raglan*, HM Monitor *M28*, HMS *Hazard*, HMS *Britannia*, which was torpedoed on 9 November 1918, and HM Yacht *Goissa* lost to a mine on 15 November (ADM 1/8513/32, 8514/38, 8542/285, and 8544/300). The question of the costs of burying the bodies of merchantmen washed ashore also came under scrutiny in April 1918 (ADM 1/8524/132). Total naval enlistments and casualties for the war were tabulated in April 1921 (ADM 1/8606/90).

ADM 101 contains a selection of Surgeon's Journals, consisting of daily logs recording cases with which naval surgeons dealt. Those for the period of the Great War (ADM 101/294–469) include establishments and units such as the Air Station on the Isle of Grain in 1914 (ADM 101/314); HM Aviation Service with the Expeditionary Force in 1914 (ADM 101/316); the RN Armoured Car Division, 1915 (ADM 101/316), the British Naval Mission to Serbia, 1915 (ADM 101/352–3); the RMA Heavy Howitzer Brigade, 1915 (ADM 101/370); RN Airship Detachment No 2, 1915 (ADM 101/371); RNAS Expeditionary Force in France, 1915 (ADM 101/372); RNAS No 5 Wing, France, 1916 (ADM 101/391); RMA Heavy Siege Train, Belgium, 1917 (ADM 101/400–401); Dunkirk Air Station, 1917 (ADM 101/441); Vendome Air Station, 1917 (ADM 101/444); and Malta Seaplane Base, 1918 (ADM 101/469).

The majority of logs, however, are for vessels including, for example, among those involved and taking casualties at Jutland in 1916, the battlecruiser HMS *Lion* (ADM 101/386), the battleship HMS *Warspite* (ADM 101/399), and the light cruiser HMS *Southampton* (ADM 101/396). Other vessels included are those of the Auxiliary Patrol of Armed Drifters, 1915 (ADM 101/331); vessels on the Tigris and Euphrates in Mesopotamia in 1916 (ADM 101/414); and the monitor HMS *Montagua*, 1917 (ADM 101/431).

ADM 104 contains Indices and Registers of Casualties on ships between 1914 and 1919. There are indices and registers of ships, 1910–18 (ADM 104/103–10); registers of reported deaths (ADM 104/122–5); and indices and registers of those killed and wounded, 1914–29 (ADM 104/140–42 and 145–9). In addition, there are General Notation Books of the Medical Department, 1911–20 (ADM 104/150–51).

ADM 116 contains some files on casualties in specific actions in 1916 including Jutland (ADM 116/1521–35), an action in the Dover Straits in February 1918 (ADM 116/1654), and the Zeebrugge raid in April 1918 (ADM 116/1655–6).

ADM 184/35 contains casualty lists for the RMLI, 1914–18, among the papers of the RM Plymouth Division.

ADM 242 contains Records of Naval Casualties, including a card index to Officers and Warrant Officers who died between 1914 and 1918 giving name, date, place and cause of death, naval memorial on which commemorated and, on occasions, the person informed of the death (ADM 242/1–5). There is a card index of HM ships lost (ADM 242/6) as well as a statistical casualty book, 1914–18 (ADM 242/11). All ranks who died are included on the War Graves Rolls (ADM 242/7–10), giving full name, rank, service number, ship's name, date and place of birth, cause of death, where buried, and next of kin.

AIR 1 contains much on accidents, crashes and casualties, 1916–18 (AIR 1/843–60, 865–6, 914–6, 960–69, 989–91 and 1022–3). There was an attempt to record all officers missing, those whose deaths were reported and also instances of reported burials (AIR 1/435), the material in question including information from Switzerland and RFC personnel held in Germany and Austria-Hungary as well as reports by post-war search parties (AIR 1/435/273/1–4, 7, and 9). There are even some examples of messages dropped by German aircraft notifying pilots captured or killed, 1916–17 (AIR 1/435/15/273/11). The series also includes a variety of other casualty returns and statistics (AIR 1/10/15/1/38, AIR 1/39/15/7, AIR 1/57/15/9/56–7, AIR 1/58/15/9/58–60, AIR 1/451/15/312/22 and 24, AIR 1/813/204/4/1255 Pts I and II, AIR 1/836/204/5/259 and 261, and AIR 1/2150), and lists of casualties, both civil and military, due to German air raids and naval bombardments of Britain during the war (AIR 1/604/16/15/235 and AIR 1/720/46/1). RNAS casualties, 1914–18, are also included (AIR 1/109/15/28 and 32) and those of Australian aircrew, 1917–18 (AIR 1/970/204/5/1103). There are also returns of crashed and lost machines (AIR 1/30/15/1/146, AIR 1/342/15/226/275, and AIR 1/822 and 828), which in the case of losses of DH4, DH9 and DH9a aircraft between July and November 1918 also include crews lost (AIR 1/162/15/124/8). There is also some material on German air losses in comparison to those of the British (AIR 1/8/15/1/10 and 12). Material from the RFC Record Office at Blandford includes reports on deaths and casualty returns (AIR 1/1939–41 and 1948).

AIR 2 has a list of Americans who died on active service while with the RFC and RAF together with other rolls of honour (AIR 2/219/323437/22); a list of those lost with HM Airship C27 when shot down by a German aeroplane in December 1917 (AIR 2/41/AIR 606427/1917); papers on the attendance of injured aviators at coroner's inquests and the Home Office decision not to waive such inquests into wartime aeroplane fatalities (AIR 2/6/86/4290 and 9/87/7694); and a committee study of the physiological effects of high flying, 1917–18 (AIR 2/11/87/14).

BT 333 contains Registers and Indices of Marriages and Deaths of Passengers and Seamen at sea. Those covering the war years (BT 333/60–74) include details of those lost on the *Lusitania* in 1915 (BT 333/64–5).

BT 334 contains Registers of Deceased (Merchant) Seamen. Those covering the war years (BT 334/62, 65, 67, 71, and 73) usually give name, age, rank or rating, nationality or place of birth, last place of abode, name of ship, official ship number, port of registry, net tonnage, and the date, place and cause of death. A remarks column will usually state whether the ship was sunk by enemy action or mine, or was missing.

CAB 1/27 includes a paper on the medical examination of demobilised soldiers.

CAB 19, containing papers on the Dardanelles and Mesopotamia Commissions, includes correspondence by the Mesopotamia Commissioners with three of the Surgeons General (CAB 19/10–11 and 16), as well as two volumes of appendices to a report on the campaign's medical arrangements (CAB 19/27).

CSC 5/93 includes papers on shell shock and the condition known as 'soldier's heart'.

DO 119/922–4 include medical reports on the overseas native labour contingents drawn from Swaziland and Bechuanaland.

FD 1/5349 includes the Army Medical Service's war history.

FD 2/1–5 contain the annual reports of the Medical Research Committee for the war years.

FD 4 contains a series of files on 'special projects', which include material on the prevention of cerebral spinal fever in the armed forces and military cerebral spinal cases (FD 4/3 and 50); dysentery in the Eastern Mediterranean and the Macedonian campaign (FD 4/4–7 and 40); war nephritis in the BEF in France and Flanders (FD 4/43); the condition known as 'soldier's heart' (FD 4/8); wartime medical problems in the Royal Navy (FD 4/17); war wounds in 1917 (FD 4/12); and 'Spanish' influenza among British troops in 1918 (FD 4/36).

HO 45 deals with the cremation of Indian soldiers who died in English hospitals, 1914–15, while the Indian Expeditionary Force was serving on the Western Front (HO 45/270222); and also the special treatment of soldiers who became insane as a result of war service (HO 45/356030).

IR 59/451, among selected death duty accounts, is that of Rupert Brooke.

MH 106 contains a representative selection of medical records originally brought together by the Medical Research Committee and the British Museum during and immediately after the war for use in statistical studies on the treatment of injuries received and diseases contracted by British troops. Covering all theatres, though mostly the Western Front, the material includes admission and discharge registers, operations books and X-ray registers from six general hospitals (MH 106/873–1389); a stationary hospital (MH 106/1390–1524); six casualty clearing stations (MH 106/279–785); a combined casualty clearing hospital (MH 106/812–72); a combined casualty clearing station (MH 106/798–811); five divisional field ambulances (MH 106/1–278); an ambulance train (MH 106/1961–2078); the hospital ship, *Assaye* (MH 106/1909–60); and four UK hospitals, namely the County of Middlesex War Hospital at Napsbury (MH 106/1525–87), Queen Alexandra's Military Hospital, Millbank (MH 106/1588–1794), Catterick Military Hospital (MH 106/1795–1886), and Craiglockhart Hospital (MH 106/1887–1908), which treated both Siegfried Sassoon and Wilfred Owen. In addition, there are Medical Board Reports for Catterick and Millbank (MH 106/2239–94), some other UK hospitals (MH 106/2212–38) and general hospitals (MH 106/2300–84).

There are also selected medical sheets illustrating the diversity of diseases, injuries and treatments, divided into diseases (MH 106/2079–107), including shell shock (MH 106/2101); and wounds (MH 106/2130–39). Selected medical cards and medical sheets relate to the Leicestershire Regiment (MH 106/2130–39 and 2158–73); Royal Field Artillery (MH 106/2140–57 and 2174–83); Grenadier Guards (MH 106/2184–95); Hussar regiments (MH 106/2196–2201); and RFC (MH 106/2202–6). The collection is completed by sample care sheets and registers (MH 106/2385), as well as some general information on the provenance and use of the collection (MH 106/2386–9).

MH 120 contains files of the Hospital Management Branch of the Ministry of Pensions from 1917 to 1953, when responsibility was passed to the Ministry of Health. They are concerned specifically with the accommodation of military pensioners, the Ministry of Pensions having assumed responsibility for the health, training and employment of discharged, disabled officers and men under the Naval and Military War Pensions (Transfer of Powers) Act, 1917. Previously, responsibility had been vested in the Statutory Committee of the Royal Patriotic Fund Corporation established under the Naval and Military War Pensions Act, 1915. Hospital accommodation varied from those run wholly by the Ministry to those leased or lent to it by organisations such as the Red Cross Society. By 1921 the Ministry was maintaining 14,000 beds in 67 establishments though this had declined to 1,850 beds in 10 hospitals by 1936. Many of the files relate to the Second World War, but the class includes material on a General Practitioners' Scheme for Ireland, 1918–34 (MH 120/10–16); the Lingfield Epileptic Colony in Surrey, 1917–18 (MH 120/17); and the administration of the Ministry's hospitals between 1917 and 1926 (MH 120/48–55). Training responsibility passed to the Ministry of Labour in 1919 and for peacetime death and disability pensions and treatment to the service ministries in 1921.

MT 9 contains the rolls of honour of the Mercantile Marine as a whole for 1916–20 (MT 9/1416 and 1471). There is a separate roll of those buried in Italy (MT 9/1538) and lists of deaths and burials in Turkey (MT 9/1411), as well as material on the recovery of effects of deceased seamen (MT 9/1444). There is also material on an inquiry into deaths by gas poisoning on the *War Cypress* in 1918 (MT 9/1225).

MT 23 covers shore accommodation in the Mediterranean for sick and wounded evacuated from the Dardanelles in 1915 (MT 23/465); and the transfer of casualties from the former liners converted to hospital ships, *Britannic* and *Mauretania*, at Italian ports in 1916 (MT 23/540).

MT 25 has the report of an Inter-departmental Committee on malaria, 1918 (MT 25/13), and material on the Admiralty's responsibility for the burial of merchant seamen lost through enemy action, 1917 (MT 25/7).

RG 35/45–69 is an incomplete series of French and Belgian death certificates for those British servicemen who died in hospitals or elsewhere outside immediate war zones between 1914 and 1920, including prisoners of war and internees whose deaths while in military or non-military hospitals in enemy and occupied territory were notified to the British authorities. They are in French or Flemish but are often informative. They are arranged alphabetically but certificates for surnames beginning with C, F, P, Q and X are missing. Certificates for unknown soldiers are to be found under U.

WO 32 has War Office observations on the report of the Mesopotamia Commission with respect to the care of the sick and wounded, 1917–18 (WO 32/5005), as well as material on the nutrition of the besieged garrison at Kut in 1916 (WO 32/5113), and health issues in Mesopotamia (WO 32/5114 and 5205). There is also a report by the Committee on Medical Establishments in France, 1917–18, the files also containing more reports on Mesopotamia (WO 32/4751–2). In addition, there are files on Sir William Lawrence's report to Kitchener on hospital provision for the Indian Expeditionary Force with the BEF, 1914–15 (WO 32/5110); control of malaria at Salonika, 1916–17 (WO 32/5112); dental treatment, 1915–17 (WO 32/5936–7); the purchase of cinchona bark and quinine from Java, 1917–18 (WO 32/18457); infectious diseases in the BEF, 1916–17, but also including the effects of mustard gas in 1917 (WO 32/5115); and the prevention of typhus, 1914–18 (WO 32/9797). A number of other files also consider the effects of gas including the first use of gas by the Germans on the Western Front (WO 32/4841, 5169, 5176, 5180, 5192, and 5951), one additionally reporting on civilian casualties as a result of enemy naval bombardment of east coast towns, 1914–15 (WO 32/5180).

There is also material on ascertaining the date of death for probate and insurance purposes (WO 32/5950); the shortening of the period of time for resolving issues connected to the estates of deceased soldiers and payment of the proceeds to relatives (WO 32/21089–90), as well as a narrative of the development of the War Office disposal of personal effects section (WO 32/9316) and its Casualties

(Officers) Branch (WO 32/9317). Other matters considered include the conveyance of the bodies of men who died of wounds, 1914–15 (WO 32/2742–4), and travelling facilities for relatives visiting the sick and wounded in hospitals at home and abroad, 1918 (WO 32/2749).

WO 33/859 has printed reports on the fate of officers and men lost at sea, 1918.

WO 106/1554 and 1556 contain reports on the medical services in the Mesopotamia campaign.

WO 141/29–33 contain material on the administration of medical services in the campaign in German East Africa.

WO 158 has papers relating to ambulance trains, 1914–17 (WO 158/8–11) and medical issues in the campaign in the Cameroons (WO 158/528). From the same campaign, there are returns of casualties of Europeans serving with the Nigeria Regiment and of Nigerian civil servants who also lost their lives (WO 158/542 and 546) as well as total Nigeria Regiment casualties (WO 158/571). In addition, there are histories of hospitals and reports on the work of bacteriological laboratories in Britain, 1914–18 (WO 158/797).

WO 159, containing papers of Kitchener's private office, includes reports by Arthur Lee, MP and Sir William Lawrence on the care of sick and wounded in France, 1914–15 (WO 159/16–17).

WO 161/28 has a report by the Senior Medical Officer with the British contingent of the Tsingtau Expeditionary Force in China, 1914.

WO 162/66–9 contain material on medical arrangements during the Gallipoli campaign, 1915.

WO 188/146 deals with research into the treatment of clothing with antiseptic substances to halt wound infection, 1916.

WO 900/51, among examples of documents subsequently destroyed, includes samples of certificates awarded for military service and disability, 1914–18.

ZLIB 10, containing material on transport in wartime, includes printed works on British ambulance trains in general (ZLIB 10/1) and that of the Great Western Railway in particular (ZLIB 10/6).

Yet, the impact of the war was also felt over a longer term, both through dependants left widows or orphans, and through prolongation or even delay of suffering. Over 192,000 widows' pensions had been granted by 1921, including provision for over 344,000 children. In 1921, some 1.1 million men were in receipt of disability pensions – 36,400 men being considered to have 100 per cent disability – but this figure had climbed to 2.4 million by 1929. There were still 3,000 limbless survivors of the war in Britain in 1977 and still 27,000 men living in receipt of disability pensions in 1980.

The sense of loss could also hit harder when those originally listed as missing were subsequently found to be dead, as with some 25 per cent of the 28,000 bodies of British soldiers found for the first time between 1921 and 1928, at which point the memorials to the missing in France and Flanders alone contained over 268,000 names. Bodies, indeed, are still regularly discovered in France and Flanders.

ACT 1 contains correspondence and papers relating to military and war pensions. It includes material on problems posed in terms of the Navy and Army Insurance Fund arising from the expansion of the forces (ACT 1/5); a special report by a Select Committee in 1915 on the effect of wartime disablement and sickness benefits on military and naval pensions (ACT 1/8); general correspondence on wartime military and naval aspects of the application of the 1911 National Insurance Act (ACT 1/14); and general correspondence and papers on war pensions and allowances, 1914–15 (ACT 1/62).

ADM 1 includes material on pensions and related issues. There is a copy of the Order in Council relating to the extension of the provisions of the Injuries in War (Compensation) Act to persons other than servicemen in May 1915 (ADM 1/8422/146); general material on pensions for wounded and injured warrant officers from January 1917 (ADM 1/8479/15); consideration of pay and sick leave entitlement among officers and nurses suffering from tuberculosis in September 1917 (ADM 1/8497/200); dependants' pensions (ADM 1/8499/216); a file on the Wills (Soldiers and Sailors) Act, 1918 (ADM 1/8502/236); and pensions for wounded or disabled officers (ADM 1/8539/249).

ADM 116/1340 has papers on naval disablement pensions, 1914–17.

AIR 1/25/15/1/119 deals with the appointment of the Military, Naval and Air Force Pensions Committee in 1919.

AIR 2 contains some material on pension and related issues including an individual case of injury pay in 1915 (AIR 2/941–2); papers on the War Pensions (Administrative Provisions) Act, 1919 (AIR 2/113/A 28647); and pension grants for deafness caused by wounds (AIR 2/129/22/Wounds/73).

AIR 5/545 contains the record of a conference on service and disablement pensions, 1919.

AO 27/2 has files on general enquiries relating to the Ministry of Pensions, 1916–27, among the registered files of the Exchequer and Audit Department.

AO 30 contains section reference files on a number of pensions-related matters, including eligibility for disablement awards, 1916–57 (AO 30/1) and for alternative war pensions arising from the Great War (AO 30/5). In addition, there are papers on an investigation into overpayment of war pensions in the Gold Coast (Ghana), 1929–32 (AO 30/7–8).

CAB 1/22 includes papers on separation allowances, January 1917.

CAB 27, comprising papers from various Cabinet Committees, includes papers and reports of the Committee on Disability Pensions from February 1920 (CAB 27/102) and June 1920 (CAB 21/215).

CAB 37, containing papers circulated to the Cabinet between 1880 and 1916, includes a report of the Pensions Committee from October 1916 (CAB 37/157/30).

FO 115/2212 covers issues relating to disabled servicemen in the United States, 1917.

HO 45/303622 deals with *projets de loi* on the wills of servicemen from the Channel Islands.

MT 6/2337/2 deals with allowances for the dependants of railwaymen killed in action.

MT 9 compares dependants' allowances of naval and merchant marine officers (MT 9/1208), and has consideration of the application of the Injuries in War (Compensation) Act to civil servants lost on HMS *Hampshire* in 1916 (MT 9/1074).

PIN 9 contains papers of the War Pensions Committees established under the War Pensions Act, 1921. These voluntary bodies included representatives of disabled and ex-servicemen, widows and dependants, local authorities, employers, employees and associations. They existed to make recommendations on local administration of war pensions, to hear complaints and to enquire into matters referred to them by the minister. They were empowered to appoint sub-committees and to undertake welfare work. Most of the series dates from the Second World War and after, but there is material on the constitution and function of the committees in the north of Scotland (PIN 9/13) and Sussex (PIN 9/43) going back to the mid 1920s, and material on the General Purposes Sub-committee of the Plymouth and District Committee (PIN 9/21), which also dates back to the mid 1920s.

PIN 15 contains the registered files of the Ministry of Pensions, established under the War Pensions Act, 1921 and the relevant Royal Warrant (for the army), Order in Council (for the Royal Navy) and Order by His Majesty (for the RAF). It is a very large and comprehensive collection. Legislation, related authorities to award pensions, appeals, final awards and entitlements are all covered (PIN 15/101–25, 375–84, 387–99, 422–5, 525–91, 652–4, 829–36, 1560–66, and 3914–62), while there is also a report on the work of the Ministry compiled in 1930 (PIN 15/65–70). There is also material on such issues as the administration of medical assessment boards (PIN 15/3–14 and 24–6); the Ministry's own clinics (PIN 15/130–37); local treatment by GPs (PIN 15/138–42); and some specific establishments such as Bellahouston Hospital in Glasgow, into which there was an official inquiry in 1921 (PIN 15/657–62), and St Dunston's (PIN 15/1054–61 and 3195).

The files also deal with the treatment of specific disabilities, injuries and illnesses including tuberculosis (PIN 15/27–32, 47–9, 1062–76, and 1480–89); malaria and other tropical diseases (PIN 15/50–52); neurasthenia (PIN 15/53–8); gas poisoning (PIN 15/126–9); venereal diseases (PIN 15/368–70); self-inflicted wounds (PIN 15/494); lunacy (PIN 15/862–911); and cancer (PIN 15/2034–6). There are also files on different categories of pensions and pensioners such as constant attendance allowances (PIN 15/39–46); amputees (PIN 15/62, 1835–7, and 3372–8); those who declined to have recommended operations (PIN 15/435–7); funeral expenses (PIN 15/1981–9); widows' alternative pensions (PIN 15/85–92); 'unmarried wives' (PIN 15/148–50); children and orphans (PIN 15/216–25 and 610–43); remarried widows (PIN 15/253–62); pensioners in prison (PIN 15/1018–32); suicides (PIN 15/807–11); deserters (PIN 15/145–6); pecuniary needs pensions (PIN 15/2064–117); the facially disfigured (PIN 15/1526); eye injuries (PIN 15/1418–21); and deserted or separated wives (PIN 15/1209–27).

Apart from the practical considerations of payments to British servicemen residing overseas (PIN 15/23 and 672–96), including the condition of those in the Irish Free State (PIN 15/757–8), there are files on pensions awarded to personnel of imperial and other contingents such as the Egyptian Labour Corps (PIN 15/765); West African Frontier Force (PIN 15/1040–44); King's African Rifles (PIN 15/1124–46); Rhodesian and South African units (PIN 15/1422–30 and 1433–41); British

West Indies Regiment (PIN 15/1771–84 and 2655–66); Maltese (Active Service) Battalion and Royal Malta Artillery (PIN 15/1814 and 2666); Indian Army Territorial and Auxiliary units (PIN 15/2613); and even secret service agents who worked for British Military Intelligence in German-occupied Belgium (PIN 15/1701–2). Purely British services, of course, are also naturally represented including 'Women's Corps' (PIN 15/418); nurses (PIN 15/478); members of the Mercantile Marine killed or injured whilst under Admiralty orders (PIN 15/1733–50); Reservists of all kinds (PIN 15/205–15); and British casualties of the fighting between Greek and allied forces at Athens in December 1916 (PIN 15/159). There is also material on the Guedella Committee on the Supply of Artificial Limbs in 1919 (PIN 15/63–4).

PIN 26 contains a sample of 22,756 files on individuals awarded (or refused) pensions from all services and from all causes including heart disease, gunshot wounds, pyrexia, malaria and other tropical diseases, rheumatism, and shell shock. It represents approximately 2 per cent of the pensions awarded in the London Region of the Ministry of Pensions, though this was the largest and most accessible holding and covered the South-east England as a whole under the decentralised system of administration created in May 1919. War Pensions staff selected every fiftieth file, from which the assumption must be that there were originally 1,137,800 million files for the region. One official survey in March 1930 suggested 1.6 million pensions or gratuities had been granted, so that the London Region represented some 60 per cent of the total awards. The series is arranged by type of pension and then alphabetically.

The first files are for all services and all ranks listed in order of date of termination of pension or death (PIN 26/1–203). The remaining files are listed by covering dates (PIN 26/204–22756) and represent army other ranks' disability pensions, some of which are out of alphabetical order (PIN 26/204–16683); navy disability pensions (PIN 26/16684–17178); widows' pensions listed by name of husband (PIN 26/17179–19523); alternative widows' pensions, also listed by name of husband (PIN 26/19524–720); mercantile marine death and disability pensions (PIN 26/19721–820); dependants' pensions, listed by name of dependant (PIN 26/19821–53); other ranks (DM series) (PIN 26/19854–923); officers (DO series) (PIN 26/19924–54); alternative disabled pensions (PIN 26/19955–84); nurses' disability pensions (PIN 26/19984–20286); overseas death and disability pensions (PIN 26/20287–21065); and officers' death and disability pensions (PIN 26/21066–22756).

PIN 38 comprises the records of the Ministry's Disablement Service Branch, primarily those establishments in which artificial limbs were fitted and where the supply, repair and renewal of such appliances took place. Specific establishments covered are Queen Mary's (Roehampton) Hospital (PIN 38/301–21); Dunston Hill Hospital (PIN 38/328–60); Queen Alexandra's Hospital, Cosham (PIN 38/3612–73); Queen Alexandra's Military Hospital (PIN 38/374–91); the Optical Appliance Branch (PIN 38/484); Limb Fitting Centres (PIN 38/404–8); and St David's House, Ealing (PIN 38/490), the latter closed for 75 years. There are files on the supply, repair, fitting, inspection, disposal and instruction in the use of artificial limbs (PIN 38/393–403, 409–34, 454–9, 470–78 and 481–2), as well as on the supply of hearing aids (PIN 38/449–52).

PIN 41 contains the papers of the Central Advisory Committee on War Pensions established by the 1921 Act, consisting of representatives of central and local government, ex-servicemen and the local War Pensions Committees. It did not meet between 1928 and the outbreak of the Second World War but was revived in November 1939. Its purpose was to consider any matters referred to it by the minister and at times determined by him. Proceedings from 1921 to 1927 can be found (PIN 41/1).

PIN 45/1–6 are selected payments files for pensions in relation to the Great War, covering the period from 1918 to 1971. They are closed for 75 years.

PIN 56 contains registered files relating to the War Pensions Committees. There is material on travelling and other expenses (PIN 56/1 and 6–7); the reorganisation of local committee areas between 1921 and 1937 (PIN 56/9–13), with additional material on reorganisation of the London, Scottish and South-western regions between 1921 and 1924 (PIN 56/37–41); the Area Advisory Committee for the Irish Republic, 1923–58 (PIN 56/14–15); the extension of the scheme to both the Isle of Man and Jersey (PIN 56/16–17 and 43); and the constitution of local committees generally (PIN 56/19–36 and 42), including draft circulars sent to county councils in 1916 (PIN 56/18).

PIN 67 contains policy files on war pension payments. These include consideration over a continuous period of time dating back to 1916 and 1917 of such issues as the disposal of the estates of deceased pensioners (PIN 67/2–6); the treatment of pensioners subsequently committed to prison (PIN 67/7–13); and institutionalised psychiatric cases (PIN 67/47–56). There is also material on pension savings schemes from 1936 (PIN 67/14).

PIN 82/1–183 comprises a sample of widows' and dependants' pensions for all services, representing perhaps 8 per cent of pensions awarded. It is arranged in alphabetical order by serviceman's name with details of regiment or ship and cause of death. Each of the files contains about 50 forms.

PMG 42 contains details of Invalid Officers' War Disability Temporary Retired Pay and Gratuities, 1917–19. The files give name, rank, address, date of warrant and amount paid with regard to army officers and nurses (PMG 42/1–12), Royal Navy and Royal Marines (PMG 42/13–14) and RAF (PMG 42/15–16), the office of Paymaster General being responsible for all service pay and pensions prior to the establishment of the Ministry of Pensions.

PMG 43/1–2 have details of Officers' Widows and Dependants' Special Grants and Supplementary Allowances, 1916–20, relating to Royal Navy, Royal Marines and RAF (PMG 43/1), and army (PMG 43/2). Details are given of name and address of claimant, rank and name of officer, date of birth, and payment. There is an index.

PMG 44/1–9 contain material on Deceased Officers' pensions paid to relatives, 1916–20. Both those for the army (PMG 44/1–7) and Royal Navy, Royal Marines and RAF (PMG 44/8–9) include name and address of claimant, rank and name of officer, date of birth and date of payment. Some volumes are indexed.

PMG 45/1–6 cover Officers' Widows' Pensions, 1917–19, with details of name and address of widow, officer's name, rank and date of birth, and date of payments.

PMG 46/1–4 comprise the files on Officers' Children's Allowances, 1916–20, listed initially in alphabetical order and then by chronological order of warrant. There are details of child or children's name, name, rank and regiment of father, record of payments, and who collected the money. Each volume is indexed.

PMG 47/1–3 have details of Missing Officers' Pensions to Relatives, 1915–20. The details included are name and address of relative receiving pension, relationship to missing officer, name and rank of officer, and dates of payment.

PMG 56/1–9 have the details of Naval Establishment Allowances, 1914–28, to widows, children and dependants of mercantile crew specially entered in Admiralty service and of other civilians killed in naval warlike operations, and of civilians incapacitated as a result of such operations.

PRO 10 has some material, among samples of documents later destroyed, relating to the work of the Ministry of Pensions, 1914–22 (PRO 10/321), including pensions documents which escaped destruction by being utilised by the War Office between 1923 and 1928 (PRO 10/1107–8).

WO 32 has material on pensions and other payments to members of the Zion Mule Corps, 1916–23 (WO 32/18541, 18543–6, and 18808–9). In addition, there is material on the classification of war wounds, 1917 (WO 32/2791); arrangements between the War Office and the Ministry of Pensions for medical treatment of invalid soldiers, 1918–20 (WO 32/4746); the wearing of uniform by blinded officers, 1917–18 (WO 32/3291); the legal interpretation of testamentary dispositions by servicemen (WO 32/11398–9); the wartime suspension of pensions' commutation (WO 32/11208); pensions of ex-servicemen who re-enlisted for war service (WO 32/11210–11); and the rates and conditions for disability pensions (WO 32/11209). There are also copies of wartime pensions legislation (WO 32/11204); and papers on application of the Injuries in War (Compensation) Act, 1914 (WO 32/12409–12) as well as provision for insuring contractors' employees serving with the BEF in 1914–15 (WO 32/12408).

Governments had been as careful to maintain surveillance of veterans as of civilians. In most cases, however, ex-servicemen were a force for conservatism in one way or another. The demobilisation disturbances in Britain in January 1919 had a limited political element linked to the possibility of service in Russia, but the great majority were related solely to demands to go home or to familiar grievances over food, compulsory church parades, and working hours. Those involved in the demobilisation disturbances wanted not only to leave the army but also to sever all contact with it. Thus, most British ex-servicemen were indifferent to attempts by some veterans' organisations to forge a radical political movement. Between November 1918 and May 1920, some 3.7 million men were demobilised from the army and 281,000 from the RAF.

Ex-servicemen certainly had grievances. The National Association of Discharged Sailors and Soldiers (NADSS), formed in Blackburn in September 1916; the National Federation of Discharged and Demobilised Sailors and Soldiers (NFDSS), formed in London in April 1917; and the Comrades of the Great War (CGW), formed in August 1917, were created as pressure groups in response to the government's ad hoc approach to such matters as pensions, rehabilitation and disabilities.

Both NADSS and NFDSS were mildly radical, loosely sympathising respectively with the Independent Labour and Liberal parties while CGW was a Conservative riposte. Far more radical was the Soldiers, Sailors and Airmens' Union (SSAU). Formed in January 1919 as an association of socialist servicemen, it had a strength of about 10,000. There were also two splinter groups from NFDSS, the National Union of Ex-servicemen (NUX), formed in May 1919; and the International Union of Ex-servicemen (IUX), formed in Glasgow the same month.

Much of the basis of veterans' grievances was removed by government concessions on pensions in August 1919, followed by preferential treatment at labour exchanges and official encouragement of assistance to ex-servicemen by voluntary agencies. By July 1921, NADSS, NFDSS and CGW, too, had combined in a new British Legion, which rejected political partisanship. By 1938, the Legion had just over 409,000 members, many of whom were disabled. While there was some thought of being a political pressure group, the Legion soon became effectively a charitable organisation. The Legion's first Poppy Day in November 1921 began the annual process of raising funds for ex-servicemen. Indeed, poppies became the biggest annual charity appeal in inter-war Britain, gross receipts rising to over £578,000 by 1938.

ADM 1 has details of the introduction of the King's certificate for discharged disabled sailors in 1922 (ADM 1/8630/144), and of Beatty's presentation of the 1914 Star to discharged sailors at Sheffield in July 1920 (ADM 1/8588/83).

AIR 2 also includes details of the King's certificate for discharged disabled officers and men (AIR 2/75/A 9366, 129/C 80837, and 131/CW 12799), as well as the report of the Lytton Committee on the employment of ex-servicemen in the civil service, 1920 (AIR 2/154/333071/20).

BT 13, containing papers of the Board's Establishment Department, deals with demobilisation (BT 13/75), but also the employment of disabled ex-servicemen on the railways (BT 13/76). They also contain statistics on disabled ex-servicemen (BT 13/86).

CAB 27, containing papers of various Cabinet Committees, includes papers and reports of the Committee on the Employment of Ex-servicemen on Housing Schemes, which met five times from January and February 1921, and which considered possible steps in the event of an unfavourable response from the building trade to a government proposal for employing 50,000 ex-servicemen on housing schemes. There are also minutes and papers of the two subsequent meetings of the Committee on Co-operation of Government Departments in the Employment of Ex-servicemen in the Building Industry from April and June 1921 (CAB 27/141). The papers of the Unemployment Committee between September 1920 and December 1922 also have some reference to the training of unskilled ex-servicemen as well as to emigration (CAB 27/114–19).

CUST 49/431 deals with the employment of disabled ex-servicemen.

LAB 2 has some material on the provision for disabled ex-servicemen, including the scheme for the National Roll, 1917; the Labour Resettlement Scheme, 1918; and the record of a conference between the Ministry and the Parliamentary Committee of Employers (LAB 2/229/1–3). There are papers on training for demobilised and disabled men, including minutes of the Labour Resettlement Committee and its sub-committees, 1918–19 (LAB 2/269/1–8).

MT 49/197, among papers of Sir Eric Geddes as Minister of Transport, deals with the King's National Roll, 1920–21.

NATS 1 has some material on the employment of disabled ex-servicemen by government departments (NATS 1/87), and on the appeal in 1918 by the CGW on behalf of disabled and discharged ex-servicemen faced with being combed out for further military service under the tightening of military service legislation (NATS 1/990).

PIN 15, containing the Ministry's registered files, sheds some light on ex-servicemen's grievances. There is material on unrest among ex-servicemen connected to the administration of labour exchanges, 1919–20 (PIN 15/421); conferences with servicemen's organisations and deputations to the minister or prime minister in 1920, 1929 and 1933 (PIN 15/482–3 and 791–2); as well as reports on the British Legion's annual conferences (PIN 15/718–25). In addition to the specific problem of the unemployed disabled, on which there was an interdepartmental committee in 1920–21 (PIN 15/33–8), there is also material on a scheme for disabled servicemen at a diamond cutting factory in Brighton (PIN 15/15) and the British Red Cross Emergency Help Committee for the Relief of Disabled Ex-servicemen in Distress (PIN 15/599–604). Other organisations or funds represented in the files are the Lord Kitchener National Memorial Fund (PIN 15/419) and the King's Fund for Disabled Ex-servicemen (PIN 15/3650–3 and 3882).

PT 1/89 has a report by Lord Lytton's committee on the employment of ex-servicemen, 1920–24.

TS 27/240 deals with legal issues arising from the administration by the Ministry of Pensions of the King's and Latham Funds for the assistance of officers and other war disabled, 1925.

WO 32 contains material on the Lord Kitchener National Memorial Fund, 1919–38, including its charter (WO 32/10812–15). There are also papers on wartime and post-war representations to the War Office by the NFDSS (WO 32/4794 and 11214). The employment of ex-servicemen in the immediate post-war period is covered by several files (WO 32/4223–6 and 4800).

One specific measure taken for the relief of British ex-servicemen was in land settlement schemes, initially seen as a response to the task of rehabilitating disabled veterans. Provision was made for three experimental domestic colonies by the Small Holdings and Allotments Act of 1916. The war ended, however, before any wider scheme had been implemented and it was killed off by financial retrenchment in 1921. Over the country as a whole, only some 24,000 candidates had been accepted by 1921, of whom only just over 9,000 had been allotted small holdings. By 1923 the total had risen to about 19,000 while, in Scotland, some 6,000 allotments were provided for ex-servicemen.

In Ireland, it was believed that local authorities in the south, which had become dominated by nationalists, could not be trusted to house ex-servicemen while state promotion of a scheme would give ex-servicemen a stake in the status quo. In the event, the scheme to provide small holdings or cottages was affected both by post-war financial retrenchment and the creation of the Free State in 1921. After negotiation with the Free State and the establishment of the Irish Soldiers' and Sailors' Land Trust in 1922–3, the scheme was limited to 3,672 dwellings, of which 2,626 were in southern Ireland and 1,046 in Ulster. With rent strikes in Eire and contradictory court decisions in both Eire and the North concerning the ability of the Trust to charge rents to ex-servicemen, the targets were only met in 1933. No further houses were built in the south after 1932, however, though building continued in Northern Ireland until 1952 and the Trust survived until 1987.

With the failure of the domestic settlement scheme, soldier settlement was promoted as an imperial policy. In April 1919 it was announced that free passage to the dominions would be granted for ex-servicemen and their dependants for a year from January 1920, the deadline subsequently extended to March 1923. In all, some 37,199 ex-servicemen accompanied by 48,828 dependants took up the free passage option, accounting for 12 per cent of British emigration to the empire between 1919 and 1922. The largest proportion went to Australia. Fears of dislocation after the war had prompted similar schemes within the dominions themselves.

AP 1–8 contain the papers of the Irish Soldiers' and Sailors' Land Trust as established by the Irish Land (Provision for Sailors and Soldiers) Act, 1919 and the Irish Free State (Consequential Provisions) Act, 1922. The Trust began functioning on 31 December 1922, with the five Trustees meeting for the first time on 22 January 1924. The Trust operated through headquarters in London and agencies in Belfast and Dublin. The papers include the minute books from 1924–87 (AP 4/1–80), of which only those prior to 1971 are open (AP 4/1–44); accounts to 1962 (AP 6/1–7); headquarters papers, including policy and staffing, to 1967 (AP 3/1–49); and registers of properties, 1923–7 (AP 5). The correspondence with Eire runs to 1985 (AP 1/1–254), and with Northern Ireland to 1987 (AP 2/1–83). In addition, there is miscellaneous correspondence and material from the Dublin agency office to 1976 (AP 7/1–530). Tenancy files (AP 7/1–19) are closed for 75 years but may be seen under conditions of privileged access, while the rest of the material includes tenancy administration records (AP 7/20–26), maps (AP 7/27–170 and 173–530), and photographs of properties (AP 7/171–2). There are also registers of documents to which the Trust set its seal, 1953–61 (AP 8/1–2). Local management of remaining southern properties passed to estate agents in 1975, and that of remaining northern properties to the Milibern Trust in 1987.

CAB 37, containing papers circulated to the Cabinet between 1880 and 1916, includes a report from the Cabinet Committee on Land Settlement for Sailors and Soldiers in March 1916 (CAB 37/144/75).

CO 537/1036 is a memorandum on overseas settlement, 1922.

CO 571/1–7 contain correspondence relating to immigration into the colonies and dominions, 1913–20.

CO 721/1–118 comprise correspondence of the Overseas Settlement Department of the Colonial Office, including that with the Dominions, on overseas settlement, 1919–25.

DO 57/1–189 comprise correspondence on overseas settlement, 1926–36, the Overseas Settlement Department being transferred from the Colonial Office to the Dominion Office.

RECO 1/683–90 deal with issues of post-war emigration.

Commemoration

The memory of the war dead served differing purposes in the former belligerents. In Britain, it has been argued that the symbolism of sacrifice was intended to inhibit serious criticism of post-war social and political structures, the annual rituals of commemoration reaffirming a national identity.

It should not be forgotten, however, that it was also an attempt to give meaning to mass death and its emotional traumas though clearly greater meaning was given to sacrifice through the shrines of national worship erected in each state. The 'silent cities' created by the Imperial War Graves Commission (IWGC) – a name assumed in May 1917 by an organisation which had originated as a Red Cross graves registration unit in March 1915 – were an unprecedented imposition of the authority of the empire and state over the rights of the citizens through the refusal to countenance repatriation of the dead. It made the collective cultural impact of the dead all the greater as did the uniformity of the cemeteries.

By 1930 some 891 British cemeteries had been completed on the Western Front with over 540,000 headstones. Large monuments also commemorated the missing, including the Menin Gate at Ypres, which was unveiled in July 1927, and that at Thiepval on the Somme, unveiled in August 1932. Similar cemeteries and memorials were constructed in Egypt, Gallipoli, Macedonia, Mesopotamia, and East Africa.

In Britain itself, there were memorials to the missing of the Royal Navy, Royal Air Force and the Merchant Navy, but there were also two national shrines, namely the Tomb of the Unknown Warrior in Westminster Abbey and the Cenotaph in Whitehall. The idea of the Cenotaph (literal Greek for empty tomb) originated in discussions as to a suitable saluting point in honour of the dead for the victory parade planned for 'Peace Day' on 19 July 1919. Originally just wood and plaster and designed by Sir Edwin Lutyens, the Cenotaph made a considerable impact. Almost immediately, there was considerable support for making it a permanent structure given the near universal belief that it represented a necessary and special point for commemoration, especially for those who could not afford to visit the resting places of their relatives abroad. Consequently, the Cenotaph was re-erected as a permanent shrine for Armistice Day in November 1920, some 400,000 people visiting it in just three days.

The Tomb of the Unknown Warrior also became a focus for pilgrimage in its own right. The concept originated as the suggestion of the Dean of Westminster in October 1920 as a result, in turn, of an idea put to him by the Reverend David Railton, MC. On 9 November 1920, therefore, four bodies of unidentified soldiers were exhumed from the main British battlefields in

France and Flanders and one selected. That chosen was transferred to England and interred in Westminster Abbey. Large crowds lined the route from Dover to London and at least 40,000 people passed through the Abbey on the first day alone.

Such national shrines were the focus for activity with the concomitant concept of Armistice Day. In Britain, Armistice Day was observed by the Silence. This originated with the suggestion of a former High Commissioner in South Africa, Sir Percy Fitzpatrick, based on the model of the three minutes' silence customarily observed in South Africa during the war at noon each day. Fitzpatrick saw it as a symbol of integration and unity, embracing the bereaved and veterans, but also providing a lesson for children for the future. Endorsed by the War Cabinet, it was publicised as a personal request by the King on 7 November for the first anniversary of the armistice in four days' time. Serving as both public and private commemoration, it was an immense success and was then made a central part of the unveiling of Cenotaph and the commitment of the body of the Unknown Warrior the following year.

ADM 1 contains relevant material including papers on the enlargement of the cemetery at Mudros to accommodate the dead from Gallipoli in July 1915 (ADM 1/8426/187); the letter of sympathy sent to bereaved next of kin by the First Lord on behalf of the King (ADM 1/8430/234); presentation of decorations to next of kin (ADM 1/8474/272); the gift of land for naval graves in Trinity Cemetery, Aberdeen (ADM 1/8503/253 and 8506/266); the gift of 100 guineas by an American firm as a tribute to the Fleet in January 1918 (ADM 1/8510/14); the appointment of a Standing Committee to consider allocation of badges, mottoes and war honours to ships and the creation of the Naval War Trophies Committee (ADM 1/8545/314 and 8572/304); arrangements for peace celebrations, the visit of the Fleet to Southend and Armistice Day in 1919 (ADM 1/8550/35 and 8572/305); the erection of naval war memorials, for which £40,000 was allocated in March 1921, including those to the Naval Staff Department and to Admiralty civil servants (ADM 1/8553/72, 8603/55, and 8606/86); registration of naval graves in Britain and the design of IWGC naval headstones (ADM 1/8576/340 and 8592/122); private memorials and reburials at Haslar cemetery (ADM 1/8604/69 and 8617/231); and visits by next of kin to war graves in Belgium and France (ADM 1/8611/154).

AIR 1 has material on the unveiling of the RNAS Memorial at Walmer, 1920 (AIR 1/95/15/9/260), as well as material on the Arras Memorial, 1930 (AIR 1/677/21/13/1891).

AIR 2 has papers dealing with RAF participation in the unveiling of the memorials to the missing at Arras and Thiepval in 1932 (AIR 2/9244); the memorial service for the RAF held at Westminster Abbey in 1919 (AIR 2/100/A 11798); instructions on the exhumation and reburial of bodies by the IWGC, 1918–21 (AIR 2/75/A 9020); the request by the IWGC for comment on the design of headstones, 1918–19 (AIR 2/98/D 15116); arrangements for cheap travel for relatives visiting war graves in Belgium and France, 1920–21 (AIR 2/152/299004/20); and the report by the RAF Memorial Fund on discussion with units on a suitable RAF memorial, 1918–19 (AIR 2/73/A 8633).

AIR 5/562 contains papers on the observation of Armistice Day, 1921.

CAB 21/160 deals with the observing of the first anniversary of the armistice in 1919.

CAB 27, comprising papers of various Cabinet Committees, includes minutes of four meetings of the Committee on Peace Celebrations, May–July 1919 (CAB 27/52); notes from the Committee on Armistice Anniversary, November 1919 (CAB 21/160); papers and a report of the Memorial Services Committee, dealing with the entombment of the Unknown Warrior and the unveiling of the Cenotaph, from October to November 1920 (CAB 27/99); and minutes of a meeting of the Committee on the Observation of Armistice Day from October 1921 (CAB 27/142).

CM 4 contains material on the maintenance of graves and cemeteries around the world. Most files date from after the Second World War, but one for Shotley in Suffolk begins in 1917 (CM 4/30).

CUST 49/420 deals with the Board's memorial service in 1918.

DSIR 4, comprising papers of the Building Materials Research Committee established in 1919 to investigate the suitability of various materials for post-war housing construction, also advised on the selection of stone for memorials. These included those of Haig, Beatty and Jellicoe (DSIR 4/1775 and 1777). Decay in the stonework of the Royal Naval Division's memorial was examined in 1939 (DSIR 4/1778) and the Committee assessed artificial stone for cemetery headstones in Egypt, 1938–9 (DSIR 4/2326). It also took samples from the memorial on the Sandon Estate in 1930 to determine the best material for preserving inscriptions (DSIR 4/1774).

ED 24, containing private office papers, includes correspondence on schools and Armistice Day (ED 24/2035) and schools and the peace celebrations in 1919 (ED 24/2036), as well as the compilation of local war records (ED 24/2038).

FO 141 has material on the establishment and maintenance of war graves and cemeteries in Egypt and Turkey (FO 141/501, 533, 560, 625, 661, 718, 722, 756, 771–2, 783), and Italy (FO 141/812). In addition, there are papers on the registration of graves of the Egyptian Labour Corps (FO 141/441), and on war memorials in Egypt (FO 141/510, 692 and 768).

FO 286 contains papers on the establishment and maintenance of the cemetery at Phalerum and the memorial at Piraeus for British and French servicemen killed during the allied attempt to seize Athens in December 1916 (FO 286/665–6, 674 and 710–12). There is also material on the dilapidation by 1926 of the war memorial at Doiran, which commemorated the dead of the Salonika campaign, and the proposed pilgrimage to war graves at both Salonika and Gallipoli in the same year (FO 286/969).

FO 686/99 deals with war graves in the Hejaz, 1921–4.

MEPO 2 deals with the visits to London of both the French prime minister, Clemenceau, and the allied commander-in-chief, Marshal Foch, in November 1918 (MEPO 2/1753), and of President Woodrow Wilson in December 1918 (MEPO 2/1760).

MT 9 deals with the care of mercantile marine graves by the IWGC (MT 9/1472) and the unveiling of the Merchant Navy Memorial, 1928 (MT 9/1847A). It also covers the issue of memorial plaques and scrolls (MT 9/1891), and mercantile marine participation in the procession on the Thames for the victory celebrations, 1919 (MT 9/1338).

T 220/43 includes, among papers of the Imperial and Foreign Division established in 1938, the charters of the IWGC, 1923–31.

TS 27/687 contains papers on the accumulation of endowment funds by the IWGC and the appointment of trustees to administer them, 1926.

WO 32 has much material of relevance including papers of a Cabinet Committee that advised the IWGC on the sites and designs of memorials in 1928 (WO 32/3136); of the Anglo-French Mixed Committee for the acquisition of land for cemeteries and memorials, 1919–23 (WO 32/5865); and of the National Committee for the Preservation of the Graves of British Soldiers in France (later the Prince of Wales's National Committee for the Preservation of British War Graves), 1915–16 (WO 32/5847–8 and 5850). There are also papers on the French legislation for the British acquisition of land for cemeteries, 1915–16 (WO 32/5846); the Anglo-French-German War Graves agreement, 1936 (WO 32/4377), on agreements with the Greek and Italian governments, 1918–19 (WO 32/5851–2); and with the United States for American cemeteries in Britain, 1918 (WO 32/5765–6). The files also include the constitution and charters of the IWGC, 1917–40 (WO 32/9433–40), details of the IWGC Endowment Fund Act, 1926 (WO 32/3146), and of the Treasury's agreement in 1916 to preserve British war graves in France in perpetuity (WO 32/5849). Questions of maintenance of war cemeteries are also covered including graves in Upper Silesia, Chatham, Palestine, Gallipoli and Yokohama (WO 32/3142–5, 3844, 4146–7 and 4843).

Land acquired elsewhere included that from the London Necropolis Company at Brookwood, Surrey, for the interment of soldiers who died of wounds, 1914–23 (WO 32/18165 and 18171–4); at Camberley for a war memorial, 1921–2 (WO 32/18175); at Chatham for an IWGC memorial to the Royal Navy, 1921–3 (WO 32/20465); at Aberdeen in 1915 (WO 32/5952); and for the burial of Mohammedans in Woking, 1914–16 (WO 32/18578–9). In the case of a Scots Guards cemetery at Bayonne, however, the sale of land was involved, 1933–8 (WO 32/13966–7). The question of national monuments on battlefields is also dealt with (WO 32/3133–4, and 4847–8), including the deliberations of Lord Midleton's Committee on National Monuments on Battlefields, 1921–32 (WO 32/3135 and 3137), and the suggestion that Ypres itself be preserved in its ruined state as a memorial and/or mausoleum (WO 32/5569 and 5583), an idea that did not commend itself to the Belgian government. British flags, however, were formally presented to both Amiens and Verdun to commemorate their wartime defence (WO 32/5575 and 5649).

Specific issues addressed were the message of sympathy sent by the King but drafted by Rudyard Kipling to the bereaved (WO 32/4841); the form of headstone for the graves of chaplains, 1918–21 (WO 32/5872); the design of commemorative plaques and scrolls for next of kin of the dead (WO 32/4677); and the form of the Royal letter, which accompanied such plaques and scrolls (WO 32/4842 and 5651). There was also discussion on a proposal by J. J. Calder to present Hill 60 at Ypres to the nation as a national memorial, 1927–30 (WO 32/3138), while a much later file concerns the erection of a Turkish memorial at Gallipoli, 1953–9 (WO 32/15147). The proposed reduction of the military presence on Armistice Day, 1936, is also considered (WO 32/4373), as is the 'holiday pay' of Royal Ordnance workers for the Armistice in 1918 (WO 32/3401), while there are papers on the victory parade and peace celebrations in both London and Paris, 1919 (WO 32/5238). The Victoria Cross was awarded to both the French and the American Unknown Warriors (WO 32/4996A and 5653). Another kind of commemoration is represented by the funeral arrangements in 1932 for Field Marshal Lord Plumer, popular wartime commander of Second Army (WO 32/14987).

WO 106/1450 has material from the Battle Exploits Memorials Committee, 1920.

WORK 20 contains, amongst correspondence and papers on statues and memorials in London, much material on wartime commemoration. There are papers on the erection and removal of the temporary wooden Cenotaph (WORK 20/1/2 and 226); and on the construction and unveiling of the permanent Cenotaph in 1920, which also contain additional material on the Tomb of the Unknown Warrior (WORK 20/1/3, 1/4, 8/5, and 139). Subsequent correspondence concerns such matters as the disposal of Cenotaph memorial cards, reproductions of the Cenotaph, lighting and barriers, the laying of wreaths and mementoes, and flags on the Cenotaph (WORK 20/143, 205–6, 255, and 305). The erection of battlefield memorials in Belgium, France and at Gallipoli is also covered (WORK 20/96). Other effectively national memorials were post-war statues of Nurse Cavell (WORK 20/128 and 250), Kitchener (WORK 20/108 and 154), Haig (WORK 20/185–6), Jellicoe and Beatty (WORK 20/207–8 and 229), Foch (WORK 20/193), and the memorial tablet to Asquith in Westminster Abbey (WORK 20/192). Lloyd George, however, did not get a statue until after the Second World War (WORK 20/273–5 and 310–12). There was also the Belgian National Memorial on the Victoria Embankment (WORK 20/131) and the national memorial to the Mercantile Marine on Tower Hill (WORK 20/177).

WORK 21 deals with national ceremonial. It includes material on the visit of President Woodrow Wilson to London and Manchester in 1918 (WORK 21/36/2); the peace celebrations in 1919 (WORK 21/74–5); and various aspects of the inter-war Armistice Days (WORK 21/58, 84 and 113–14).

While the national shrines provided a focus for commemoration at home, it was possible for some of the bereaved to visit the cemeteries and battlefields overseas. Indeed, there was to be an increasing number of sponsored pilgrimages to the battlefields after the war. At the purely local level, commemoration was principally accomplished by the erection of war memorials, which complemented the official face of national remembrance, and were the more essential as a visible representation of grief and a reminder of the dead entombed in foreign fields. The memorial movement had in essence begun during the war itself with the compilation of local rolls of honour and, often, the erection of street shrines. Most post-war memorials were the work of local committees. Sometimes, there was a choice made between a memorial and providing some form of community benefit such as a community hall. Some memorials, on the other hand, had no physical existence, being instead funds applied to a variety of individual or community purposes.

ADM 1/8579/10 deals with the unveiling of a memorial in Walsall to Ordinary Seaman Carless, VC in 1920.

WO 32 has a considerable amount of information on individual war memorials, mostly but not exclusively in Belgium and France. Those covered commemorate Indian units; the Salonika Expeditionary Force; Canadians and New Zealanders; 15 different divisions; four different brigades; seven different regiments; eight different battalions; an RE Tunnelling Company; the Tank Corps; the Cavalry; and the Church Army (WO 32/4375, 5125–6, 5854–64, 5866–96, and 5954). There is also material on a memorial window in St Andrew's Garrison Church, Aldershot, and the enlargement of the Chapel at the Royal Military College, Sandhurst, as a war memorial (WO 32/3829–30 and 3836–42).

WORK 20 has material on statues and memorials erected in London. Apart from the national monuments, there is material on a number of war memorials erected for individual services, regiments or corps including the Imperial Camel Corps (WORK 20/134), Civil Service Rifles (WORK 20/137), Guards (WORK 20/142 and 232), Submarine Service (WORK 20/141), Machine Gun Corps (WORK 20/146), Cavalry (WORK 20/147), Royal Artillery (WORK 20/151), Royal Naval Division (WORK 20/159 and 231), and the Rifle Brigade (WORK 20/174). There is also a file on a proposed fountain in front of the Royal Exchange to commemorate London troops generally (WORK 20/109).

ZLIB 10, containing material on war transport, includes the Rolls of Honour of the Great Western and Midland Railway Companies (ZLIB 10/15 and 23); details of the unveiling of the GWR war memorial and a memorial service for Midland employees (ZLIB 10/7 and 22); and details of the welcome home celebrations at the Albert Hall organised for its employees by the London Train, Bus and Tram Companies in June 1919 (ZLIB 10/41).

There were still other manifestations of commemoration to be found in museums. In November 1916, C. Reginald Grundy, editor of an art magazine, had suggested establishing local war museums in every major centre. The issue was raised in Parliament in February 1917, but appeared to receive little government support. Within a few weeks, however, the War Cabinet announced the creation of a National War Museum on 5 March 1917, partly because local museums were beginning to collect war material. The National War Museum, redesignated as the Imperial War Museum in January 1918 and initially opened at Crystal Palace in June 1920, was to have the priority in collecting trophies. The museum moved from Crystal Palace to South Kensington in 1924 and to its present site in Lambeth Road in 1936.

An intended feature of the Imperial War Museum was to display war art. Charles Masterman's War Propaganda Bureau at Wellington House, having formed a pictorial section in April 1916, started to sponsor official artists, the first of whom, Muirhead Bone, was appointed in July 1916. After Wellington House became part of the Ministry of Information, the latter's British War Memorials Committee continued to sponsor art. Some was envisaged as part of a London Hall of Remembrance but, when this was stillborn, the Imperial War Museum became the official repository.

Tanks and other war relics were also offloaded to local authorities by the War Office War Trophies Committee. Indeed, at least 262 'presentation tanks' were awarded to those British towns and villages in 1919 which had been successful in selling national war bonds or war savings certificates. Most went for scrap in the Second World War.

ADM 1 has some material on the Admiralty's relationship with war artists, including the extension of facilities to enable Muirhead Bone and Francis Dodd to make sketches of naval subjects in May 1917 (ADM 1/8487/85), and suitable artists and subjects for naval representation in the National War Museum (ADM 1/8501/234). There is also material on the proposal in 1920 for a permanent record of war films to be kept at the IWM (ADM 1/8595/159).

ADM 169, the registered files of the Greenwich Royal Naval Hospital, include material on arrangements to protect the Painted Hall, paintings and relics of Nelson from air raid damage (ADM 169/429 and 454).

AIR 1 deals with the manufacturer's supply of model aircraft to the National War Museum, 1917 (AIR 1/510/16/3/56), and has miscellaneous correspondence on war trophies, 1917–19 (AIR 1/1084/204/5/1714).

AIR 2 includes papers on the proposed establishment of war museums with particular reference to trophies secured by the Australian Imperial Force, 1917–19 (AIR 2/67/A 237); the appointment of RAF representatives to the trustees of the IWM, 1920–22 (AIR 2/156/370176/20); the proposal for its relocation to the former Bethlem Hospital in Lambeth, 1930–31 (AIR 2/1308); and the transfer of RAF records to the museum, 1933–9 (AIR 2/2538).

AR 1, containing correspondence and papers relating to the Wallace Collection, 1897–1979, includes several files relating to wartime conditions at the museum. Housed in London at Hertford House, Manchester Square, the collection of the 4th Marquess of Hertford and his son, Sir Richard Wallace, had been bequeathed to the nation by Lady Wallace in 1894 and opened to the public in 1900. Aspects highlighted are measures to safeguard the collection during air raids (AR 1/46, 60, 288, 445–7, and 450); closure and dismantling of the collection (AR 1/50–51 and 292); staffing implications of military service (AR 1/54, 58, 291 and 537); use of the building by Naval Intelligence and the Ministry of Munitions (AR 1/293, 449, 452, and 535), its suggested use as a military hospital (AR 1/587); and reinstallation of the Collection after the war (AR 1/295 and 453).

EN 1, containing records relating to the administration of the IWM, 1917–39, whose collections at that time related solely to the Great War, is retained at the Museum rather than the PRO. The files were stored and maintained centrally, reflecting the smaller size of the museum at that time. They are arranged alphabetically by subject, across a wide range, but very broadly fall into three main areas. Those on internal administration include committee papers, reports and other internal files, many relating to the various sites occupied by the museum and its departments. Those on collections, which at the time were organised across a number of 'sections' such as 'women's work', include papers on acquisitions and exhibitions, such as the extensive touring exhibitions organised before the museum had its own exhibition space at Crystal Palace in 1920. Those on external contacts include correspondence with government, the Commonwealth and other museums. A rough hand list of file titles is available but the records are not yet fully catalogued.

EN 2, a provisional series number, contains records from the separate file series relating to the RAF section of the museum, 1917–39.

EN 3, also a provisional series number, contains records from the Women's Work section of the museum, 1917–39.

FO 286 has information on exhibits being collected in Greece for the National War Museum (FO 286/659), including posters (FO 286/705).

TS 27, comprising miscellaneous registered files, has material on legal issues relating to the IWM, including discussion in 1920 of whether an Act of Parliament was required to appoint its trustees (TS 27/83); its proposed statutes and regulations, 1921 (TS 27/133A); and the copyright of photographs and pictures assigned to it, 1925 (TS 27/246). There is also a file on the alleged breach of copyright by the museum in showing overseas Lowell Thomas's film of the war in Palestine in 1923 (TS 27/192). An American journalist, Lowell Thomas, played a leading role in the establishment of the image of 'Lawrence of Arabia'.

WO 158/828 has correspondence on the presentation to the Tank Corps of the painting, 'A Tank in Action' by John Hassall in July 1918.

WORK 20 primarily includes material on the erection of statues and memorials in London. While not strictly a museum, there is also material on the wartime use of Trafalgar Square for temporary buildings erected by the YMCA, YWCA, Ministry of Labour, and as a WAAC recruitment office (WORK 20/3/4, 3/5, and 3/6).

4. War, State and Society

No STATE has yet been able to totally subordinate all civilian needs to those of the military in wartime. Wartime mobilisation, like 'universal conscription', therefore, is always necessarily partial. Nonetheless, the Great War witnessed increasing state control and intervention, even in a mature liberal democracy such as Britain. Precedents had also been established and many features of the wartime state between 1914 and 1918 would be reproduced during the Second World War. In the process, the war also impacted upon society, although to what extent this was lasting remains a matter of historical debate. Some socio-economic trends can be measured in modern states through the collection of statistics, but others must remain a matter of speculation. Indeed, the calculation of changes in perceptions and attitudes is essentially qualitative rather than quantitative and, therefore, problematic. Societies are not uniform and the effect of war will vary depending both upon the nature of a particular society, and also the intensity of its war experience.

The Growth of Government

The first indication of the enhancement of state power was the spate of emergency legislation enacted. The Defence of the Realm Act (DORA), which became law on 8 August 1914, gave government sweeping powers. Its provisions were extended on 18 August and 27 November 1914 and, again, in both 1915 and 1916.

The railways were swiftly taken under state control in August 1914 followed by shipyards. In the case of the railways, this did not mean nationalisation *per se* since the individual rail companies were guaranteed the same level of profits they had enjoyed in 1913 and, through the Railway Executive Committee, the rail system was pointedly administered not by the government but for the government. Indeed, since control was initially intended to last for just one week, this necessitated renewal of the requisition measure every seven days for the duration.

AN 1 contains the minutes of the Railway Executive Committee, 1914–18 (AN 1/1–5); the wartime minutes of the London, Brighton and South Coast Railway, 1916–18 (AN 1/7–9); and minutes of the General Managers' Representatives Sub-committee, 1917–18 (AN 1/10). Also covered are staff matters, including wartime allowances and bonuses (AN 1/17–18); and collision agreements and insurance against war risks (AN 1/19). In addition, there are Railway Executive Committee instructions, 1914–19 (AN 1/20–26); wartime circulars, 1916–18 (AN 1/30–32); other instructions from 1914 (AN 1/53); and a census of staff on controlled railways, 1918 (AN 1/37). Other matters covered include the supply of railway wagons and the control of coastal traffic, 1915–18 (AN 1/41–5). Minutes of Goods Managers' Meetings, 1914–18 (AN 1/46–52) are duplicated elsewhere [AN 1/46 in RAIL 1080].

BT 62/1–2 contain some material on the Railway Executive Committee and government control of wartime railways among the papers of the Controller of Trading Accounts.

HO 45/245940 deals with government control of railways in wartime.

MT 6 has much on aspects of government control of railways (MT 6/2335/9, 2361/11, 2368/3, 2435/29); allowances for dependants and war bonuses for railwaymen (MT 6/2337/2, 2361/3, 2366/5, 2430/10, 2437/6, 2445/7, 2454/10, 2471/13 and 2515/1); and wartime legislation as it affected railwaymen (MT 6/2419/1, 2424/3, 2436/53, 2440/2, 2461/20).

POWE 16/162 deals with the pooling of private coal wagons for use by railways, 1917.

WO 32 includes the regulations for the emergency control of the railways, 1914–19 (WO 32/5259), and the Orders in Council for the control of railways in Britain in 1914 and in Ireland in 1916 (WO 32/5291–2).

ZLIB 10 includes books on transport in wartime between 1861 and 1966, mostly relating to the two world wars. They include a general history of the railways in the war (ZLIB 10/2); the Great Western Railway's war record (ZLIB 10/10); and the GWR's general manager's report on the war experience, 1920 (ZLIB 10/11).

Of course, the near universal assumption in 1914 was that intervention would not be necessary for long. It should be noted, moreover, that the progressive extension of state intervention was largely in response to circumstances rather than as a result of any coherent plan. Indeed, DORA regulations were so carelessly defined that the government's lawyers had endless difficulties, especially in terms of compensation claims made in respect of requisitions.

ACT 1 deals with insurance cases arising from the Emergency Powers Act, 1914 as well as with the liability of insurance companies to pay death duties (ACT 1/39); and also contains a statistical examination of compensation settlements for owners of vessels lost on requisitioned service in 1917 (ACT 1/56).

AIR 2 deals with claims against the Ministry of Munitions arising from an embargo on cypress, which had been supplied to contractors as a substitute for spruce in aircraft construction (AIR 2/945–6). There is also material on the acquisition of land for aerodromes or other facilities such as that at Lympne (AIR 2/4316–9); Donibristle near Aberdour (AIR 2/3/87/523); Biggin Hill (AIR 2/10/87/8868);

Farnborough and Aldershot (AIR 2/13/Aldershot 8/758, 830, 955, 969, 993, and 10859); Malta (AIR 2/19/D. W. AIR/1049/18); Cranwell (AIR 2/19/D. W. AIR/10151/1918); Cardington (AIR 2/46/CinC AIR/4119/19); Halton (AIR 2/76/B5840 and B6132); and for night landing grounds for home defence (AIR 2/10/87/8948). Policy as regards retaining racecourses used for landing grounds after the cessation of hostilities is also covered (AIR 2/84/B5595).

CAB 16/31 has papers from the ad hoc committee of the Committee of Imperial Defence on Emergency Powers, 1914.

FO 141/471 deals with claims for compensation against the British military authorities presented to the British embassy and consulates in Egypt, 1915–24.

FO 286 has similar post-war claims relating to damage done by British military activities in Greece (FO 386/654 and 924).

HO 45 contains petitions of right claiming government compensation for various damages, requisitions, loss of vessels, etc. The class covers claims against the Admiralty (HO 45/309607, 312426, 319336, 323507, 325146, 331590, 331677, 343590, 345839, 358028, 361302, 362392, 365054, 370185, 374259, 375703, 378624, 378822, and 385624); Air Ministry (HO 45/385612 and 391053); Board of Trade (HO 45/378090); Food Controller or the Ministry of Food (HO 45/371190, 387075, 388677, and 393710); General Post Office (HO 45/380278); Ministry of Munitions (HO 45/307975, 314772, 330865, 335323, 344901, 348577, 354210, 357524, 358888, 361020, 362338, 362342, 364325, 365161, 366639, 368945, 369815, 369816, 371148, 372561, 372681, 377108, 377509, 378099, 378746, 379103, 379164, 379237, 379649, 380611, 382077, 383611, 383793, 384401, 384516, 385716, 386246, 387024, 387210, 389839, 391998, and 394155); Ministry of Shipping (HO 45/374259, 375145, 379630, 381545, 381602, 383546, 383622, 384262, and 389236); Royal Commission on Sugar Supply (HO 45/275404, 304011, and 321827); War Office (HO 45/274803, 274804, 279506, 306284, 308512, 309349, 309403, 311178, 311382, 312924, 322542, 323750, 333332, 345265, 348584, 351747, 357960, 363509, 367063, 369939, 372371, 372551, 372660, 373325, 373385, 373420, 373824, 373935, 378209, 378318, 379652, 383838, 384243, 385666, 385760, 386799, 386967, 387023, and 393965); and War Printing Office (HO 45/320972, 337753, and 3431130). There are also miscellaneous claims against railway legislation (HO 45/387521); and for the return of excess profits duty (HO 45/383074).

MT 9 includes the Royal Proclamation authorising the requisitioning of vessels in 1914 (MT 9/949); material on the requisitioning of vessels, 1916–17 (MT 9/1125); and a claim against the Ministry of Shipping, extending from 1917 to 1955 (MT 9/2399).

MT 25/3 includes material on the surrender of requisitioned shipping by the Admiralty and War Office in consequence of the extreme gravity of the tonnage situation arising from unrestricted submarine warfare in 1917.

NATS 1/146–212 deal with requisition of wartime premises by the Ministry.

POWE 16/141 covers a case brought before the War Compensation Court, 1917–21, over the wartime requisition of a mine.

PRO 10/475 contains specimens of Treasury documents later destroyed, mostly concerning immediate post-war claims on government including papers from the

War Compensation Court, Defence of the Realm Losses Commission, Defence of the Realm (Licensed Trade Claims) Commission, and Admiralty Transport Arbitration Board.

PT 1 contains the report of a Committee of Enquiry into the War Expansion of Public Departments, 1917 (PT 1/28). There is also material on its own staffing and accommodation, 1915–16 (PT 1/75).

T 80 contains papers dealing with post-war compensation, including the work of the Defence of the Realm Losses Commission, 1915–20 (T 80/1–4); Defence of the Realm (Licensed Trade Claims) Commission, 1915–20 (T 80/5); and War Compensation Court, 1920–28 (T 80/6–9).

TS 27 has case papers on a compensation claim for land acquired by the Ministry of Reconstruction in 1918 (TS 27/62); other land acquired under DORA regulations (TS 27/92 and 99); and on the question as to whether civilian staff who died with Lord Kitchener on HMS *Hampshire* in 1916 were covered under the War Compensation Act (TS 27/42).

TS 28/66 relates to a challenge in 1921 to the right of the Air Ministry to retain land originally acquired under DORA.

TS 32/16 are the papers relating to a claim by the Wick Harbour Trustees against the Admiralty for payment of wartime harbour dues, 1920–21.

TS 43/29–37 cover wartime legal issues relating to the War Office.

TS 44/1–5 have papers on wartime legal issues raised in connection with the Ministry of Munitions and its successors, 1915–25.

TS 46/5–8 contain material on City of London Corporation claims relating to the War Office acquisition of Deptford Cattle Market as a wartime supply depot, 1916–24.

WO 32 has some material on the results of wartime requisitions, including Belgian and French wartime and post-war claims for compensation as a result of requisitions by, injuries inflicted by, and damages done by British troops, 1915–24 (WO 32/14286–90). In addition, there are claims arising from the acquisition of land and the loss of rights of way on the Pinehurst estate, 1914–25, the site of the Royal Aircraft Factory, Farnborough (WO 32/18161–2, 18164 and 18166); claims by Great Burstead Parish Council and Barnet Urban District Council for compensation for the employment of their fire brigades during Zeppelin raids, 1916–17 (WO 32/11308–9); complaints of the encroachment of troops on the Basingstoke canal, 1914–17 (WO 32/18163); general land acquisition under DORA, 1917–18 (WO 32/2655–63, and 18548–50); the acquisition of land at Foulness Island, 1914–24 (WO 32/18284 and 18287); and the acquisition of land for the Chilwell National (Shell) Filling Factory, 1915–21 (WO 32/18331–4).

State intervention was most marked by the appearance of new government ministries, departments and agencies. More often than not, these appeared in the key areas such as food, manpower policy and munitions as a result of the incapacity of existing organisations in both public and private sectors to meet new demands. At the insistence of David Lloyd George, the Defence of the Realm (Amendment No 2) Act in March 1915 gave government powers over engineering, as a first step in placing the country on a total war footing: firms could now be forced to take government work if they had the necessary plant to do so. The perceived shell shortage in France and Flanders then enabled Lloyd George to wrest control of munitions from the War Office, the Ministry of Munitions appearing in May 1915 with its own sweeping powers under the Munitions of War Act to control all armaments factories as felt necessary. A merger of the War Office Armament Output Committee and the Treasury Munitions of War Committee, the Ministry of Munitions developed a highly innovative approach to the enforcement of what was perceived as best standard practice in such areas as managerial organisation, cost accounting, welfare provision for labour, electrification and automation. The ministry commandeered raw materials, centralised foreign purchases and dealt in the import market. There were eventually over 25,000 employees in 50 departments and, by 1918, the ministry directly managed 250 government factories and supervised another 20,000 'controlled' establishments.

CAB 1/34/2 has miscellaneous Ministry of Munitions papers.

CAB 17/141 deals with the transfer of the design of ammunition and weapons from the War Office to the Ministry of Munitions, 1916.

MT 6 contains copies of the Munitions of War legislation (MT 6/2419/1 and 2461/20).

MUN 5 contains records of the Historical Branch of the Ministry of Munitions and material collected for the ministry's official history. Matters covered include the organisation of supply prior to the ministry's creation, including papers of U. F. Wintour as Director of Army Contracts (MUN 5/5–10). There are other papers on the early period of the war (MUN 5/341), with historical notes (MUN 5/342–3). The wartime organisation of the ministry is also covered (MUN 5/10–48 and 344–6).

MUN 10 contains papers of Lloyd George as Minister of Munitions, 1915–16, including drafts and extracts from his post-war memoirs relating to the Ministry (MUN 10/31–9).

PRO 30/57/82, among Kitchener's papers, includes correspondence and reports on the early attempts to establish a munitions policy, 1914–15, prior to the establishment of the Ministry of Munitions.

WO 32 has material on the establishment of the Ministry of Munitions and the transfer to it of responsibilities from the War Office (WO 32/4956, 9282–5, and 9296). The files also deal with the post-war transfer of the Ministry's Contracts Branch to the War Office, 1919–20 (WO 32/17596), as well as resignations and appointments to the War Office Contracts Advisory Office (WO 32/17588). There is also material on the formation of the Mechanical Warfare Department of the Ministry of Munitions, 1917–18 (WO 32/9288). The 'shells scandal' in 1915, which prompted the creation of the Ministry, is reflected in Sir John French's memorandum on the supply of ammunition (WO 32/5155), and other reports from 1914–15 (WO 32/4952 and 5152).

WO 159/23 contains, among Kitchener's Private Office Papers, correspondence with Churchill in August 1914 on ammunition supplies for the army.

WO 79/73–85 comprise the private papers of Major-General Sir Stanley Von Donop, Master-General of the Ordnance at the time of the transfer of the manu-facturing functions of the War Office to the Ministry of Munitions. They include copies of Von Donop's diary of events between March 1915 and June 1916 dealing with munitions and the relationship of the War Office with the Ministry (WO 79/73, 77 and 82–3); correspondence, memoranda and notes by Von Donop on munitions supply, 1914–16, including criticisms of the Ministry of Munitions and refutation of criticisms of the War Office (WO 79/74 and 77–83); Cabinet and other papers on munitions supplied to Sir George Arthur for his biography of Kitchener in 1920 (WO 79/84); material on the production of high explosive shells (WO 79/84); post-war correspondence on the munitions controversy, including that relating to publication of Lloyd George's *War Memoirs* in 1933–34 (WO 79/75), and the War Office's refusal to permit Von Donop to publish in his own defence in 1919 (WO 79/74). There are also annotated extracts from *Hansard* concerning muni-tions, 1915–16 (WO 79/76); and notes on Von Donop's evidence to the Royal Commission on Private Manufacture and Trading in Arms, 1935 (WO 79/85).

After Lloyd George became prime minister, new ministries of Labour, Ship-ping, and Food were created together with a Department of National Service. In all, the number of national government employees in Britain almost doubled between 1911 and 1921. It should not be assumed, however, either that inter-vention had not occurred in these areas already, or that this automatically improved government administration. The Ministry of Shipping, for example, was merely an extension of a web of shipping controls established in 1915 and 1916 through agencies such as the Ship Licensing Committee, Requisitioning (Carriage of Foodstuffs) Committee and Shipping Control Committee: 6.2 million tons of privately-owned merchant shipping had already been requisi-tioned by December 1915. In terms of efficiency, the creation of both a Ministry of Labour and a Department of National Service, which became a full ministry in August 1917, further confused manpower and industrial relations policy since there was considerable duplication between them. Matters were further complicated by the establishment of the Ministry of Reconstruction in August 1917. Moreover, partial responsibility for labour relations was also vested in the Ministry of Munitions, the Admiralty, the War Office and the Board of Trade.

ADM 1/8504/255 deals with discussion in November 1917 of the relationship between the Admiralty and the proposed Air Ministry, the RAF incorporating the RNAS on its formation in April 1918.

ADM 116 contains papers on the appointment of the Shipping Controller in 1916–17 (ADM 116/1520); the creation of the Air Board (ADM 116/1559); and Admiralty organisational changes, 1917–18 (ADM 116/1584–85A).

AIR 1 has a variety of material on the creation of the Air Ministry in 1918, an Air Board having been established under the New Ministries Act in 1916 to organise the supply of aircraft. The Board was reconstituted with a minister at its head in January 1917, at which time manufacture and inspection passed to the Ministry of Munitions. The functions of the Air Board passed to an Air Council in January

1918 and this continued under the new Air Ministry. War Cabinet discussions on the formation of the Air Ministry in 1917 are included (AIR 1/22/15/1/115 and 2266/209/70/25); as well as the actual creation of the ministry and the reorganisation of the Air Board (AIR 1/38/15/1/248/2 and 256). Papers of Sir Hugh Trenchard included within the series similarly deal with the formation of the Air Ministry (AIR 1/718/29/9), and there is also more general material on the Ministry's creation (AIR 1/1061/204/5/1581). A report on the duties and functions of the Air Board and its relationship to Admiralty, War Office and Ministry of Munitions was prepared in February 1917 (AIR 1/2405/303/4/8). There is also a report on the advisory committee on the transfer of aeronautical supply to the Ministry of Munitions, 1916 (AIR 1/2623).

AIR 2 has more material on the transfer of the responsibility for aeronautical supply from the Air Board to the Ministry of Munitions (AIR 2/965), as well as the constitutions, powers and functions of the Air Board and the Air Council (AIR 2/74/A 8952, 104/A 15619, A 15623, 110/A 20031, and 2865).

CAB 1 includes a paper on the nationalisation of shipping, 1917 (CAB 1/23), and there is also a report by the Shipping Control Committee from March 1916 (CAB 1/17).

CAB 15, comprising chiefly the papers of the Committee of Imperial Defence's Committee on the Co-ordination of Departmental Action on the Outbreak of War, includes a series of reports on departmental experiences of the war compiled in 1919 as a means of informing the drafting of future War Books (CAB 15/6). Included are the War Trade Department, Restrictions of Enemy Supplies and War Trade Advisory Committee, Public Trustee's Office, Ministry of Munitions, Royal Mint, Board of Customs and Excise, Meteorological Office, Director of Public Prosecutions, Home Office, Department of the Government Chemist, Public Record Office, Royal Commission on Sugar Supply, Office of Works, Board of Agriculture and Fisheries, and National Health Insurance Committee, as well as a report on prisoners of war.

CAB 17, containing miscellaneous papers of the Committee of Imperial Defence, not only deals with measures taken on the opening of the war (CAB 17/102B), but the reorganisation of the Air Board in 1916 (CAB 17/135–6).

CAB 21/21 deals with the creation of the Air Ministry.

CO 537, comprising confidential correspondence, 1759–1965, includes pre-war papers on the actions to be taken by the Colonial Office on the outbreak of war (CO 537/357, 359, 366–7, 369–70, 372–3, 375–6); wartime staffing (CO 537/612); and suggested revisions to the War Book, 1916–19 (CO 537/607 and 618–19).

LAB 2 contains a copy of the legislation for new ministries, together with a note on the functions of the Ministry of Reconstruction (LAB 2/15); a memorandum on the creation of the Ministry of Labour and its functions, 1917–18 (LAB 2/18–19); and files on the transfer of various powers and duties to the Ministry from the Board of Trade (LAB 2/2192–3). Preparation of the Ministry's War Book in 1919–20 is also covered (LAB 2/2187).

MAF 60/1–6 contains a history of the Ministry of Food, 1917–21. Established in 1917 it took over the control of oil and fats from the Ministry of Munitions, that of cheese and frozen fish from the Board of Trade, that of food preservation from the Board of Agriculture, that of food economy campaigns from the War Savings Committee, and that of oats from the War Office. It also absorbed various ad hoc bodies and purchased most imported foodstuffs as well as home produced meat and potatoes. It organised rationing and price controls. A Food Council was established in September 1918 to consider general questions of food policy. After the war it took on more responsibilities though its activities were steadily eroded by the end of wartime controls.

MT 9/1620 has material on the creation of the Ministry of Shipping, 1916.

MT 25/86–7 contain both an incomplete draft and the final report compiled in 1921 on the control of shipping by the Ministry of Shipping, 1914–18.

PIN 15, containing registered files of the Ministry of Pensions, its predecessors and successors, includes material on the wartime origin, creation and role of the Ministry (PIN 15/336–7, 1393–6 and 2601), as well as its early work in 1917 (PIN 15/1165).

WO 32 contains material on the creation of a new wartime Department for the Surveyor General of Supply in 1917 (WO 32/17589–90) and the post-war establishment of the Ministry of Supply in 1919 (WO 32/17591, 17593, and 17628–9). There is also information on the transfer of powers over recruiting from the War Office to the Ministry of National Service, 1917–18 (WO 32/9286–7, and 9292).

The most marked change from the situation prior to December 1916 was Lloyd George's determination to strengthen central control over departments. Interestingly, however, the Treasury lost much of its former centralising influence. One reason was simply the exigencies of war: Lloyd George, while still Chancellor, told the War Office in October 1914 that it did not need to seek Treasury approval for war purchases. A second reason was that many of the new ministries were never subjected to Treasury control, establishing legislation giving them control over their own staffs. Generally, too, there was a movement of businessmen into government. In the long term, however, this represented only a temporary overturning of traditional orthodox Treasury control, the prevailing Civil Service view being that the wartime creations resulted in extravagance and inefficiency.

CSC 4/50 contains annual reports of the Civil Service Commissioners, 1913–20.

CSC 5/78 deals with loan of staff to the War Office.

CUST 49/397 contains material on the committee on wartime expansion in public departments.

MAF 39/149 deals with wartime staffing matters.

MAF 42/14 contains more information on wartime staffing.

MAF 47/1 also deals with wartime staffing.

MAF 60 has further material on staffing (MAF 60/184, and 270–98).

T 176/4, among the papers Sir Otto Niemeyer, Principal at the Treasury, 1912–19, has a copy of the Treasury's war history compiled in 1924–5.

Wartime Treasury correspondence with other government departments or agencies includes that with the Admiralty (**T 5/41–54**); Foreign Office (**T 12/33–41**); War

Office (**T** 24/49–59); Central Control Board (**T** 112/1); Civil Service Commission (**T** 113/1); Development Commission (**T** 115/1); Board of Education (**T** 116/1); Ministry of Food (**T** 117/1), Friendly Societies (**T** 118/1); India Office (**T** 120/1); Ministry of Information (**T** 121/1); Insurance Commission (**T** 123/1); Ministry of Labour (**T** 126/1); local authorities (**T** 127/1); Local Government Board (**T** 128/1–2); the Mint (**T** 130/1–2); Ministry of Munitions (**T** 132/1–10); Ministries of National Service and Reconstruction (**T** 134/1); Ministry of Pensions (**T** 136/1–2); Ministry of Shipping (**T** 140/1–3); Board of Trade (**T** 142/1–7); and Charity Commissioners (**T** 157/1).

T 114/1–5 deserves special mention since it includes out-letters to temporary wartime commissions and committees including the Air Board, American Dollar Securities Committee, Ministry of Blockade, Defence of the Realm Losses Commission, Committee for Relief in Europe, Food Production Department of the Ministry of Food, Foreign Trade Department, Imperial War Graves Commission, Imperial War Museum, Military Service (Civil Liabilities) Committee, National Savings Committee, National War Aims Committee, Overseas Prize Disposal Committee, Prisoners of War Department, Prize Claims Committee, Railway Executive Committee, Commission Internationale de Revitaillement, Reparation Commission of the Ministry of Reconstruction, Restriction of Enemy Supplies Department, Russian Accounts and Russian Liquidation Committees, Scottish War Savings Committee, Ministry of Shipping, Sugar Supply Commission, War Pensions Statuary Committee, War Trade Department, and Wheat Supplies Commission.

War Finance

Financial policy proved a particular problem when the costs of war escalated alarmingly, the initial assumption being that war costs could be recouped through post-war reparations. In addition, Britain was largely bankrolling her Entente partners. As a consequence, whereas British governments had spent only about one eighth of the national income prior to the war, the percentage of national income spent by government rose to, and remained over, 50 per cent in 1916.

Even in peacetime, only a portion of public expenditure could be realistically covered by taxation revenue, whether direct or indirect, with the remainder coming from government borrowing. The standard rate of British income tax was increased from 1s 2d in the pound to 3s 6d in September 1915 and to 6s 0d in the pound in April 1918 and there were new taxes such as excess profits duty. The war imposed a degree of equality, not least through the increase in the numbers paying income tax from 1.5 million in 1914, when the starting point was annual income of £160, to 7.7 million by 1918, the threshold being lowered to £130 in 1916. Indirect taxation also increased dramatically on commodities such as beer, spirits, tobacco, matches, sugar, cocoa, coffee and motor vehicles.

Yet, peacetime patterns were largely maintained in the sense that Britain raised only between 23 and 26 per cent of wartime public expenditure from taxation. Printing more money and borrowing, therefore, remained the principal means of war finance. This was achieved through selling war bonds, three war loans being floated between October 1917 and September 1918.

Inflationary pressures were considerable, the rise in the circulation of paper currency between 1913 and 1918 being 1,154 per cent, the one pound note or 'Bradbury' (named after the Bank of England official who signed them) and ten shilling note making their first appearance. Since more paper money did not mean more goods to purchase, despite varying degrees of control, prices rose.

As might be expected, the volume of export trade declined with the balance of trade deficit reaching £784 million by 1918, of which £602 million was with the United States. Conceivably, invisibles reduced this to a deficit of about £275 million, but the level of British investment overseas fell dramatically through liquidation of assets to meet war costs. Initially, Britain used its gold reserves to purchase war needs. As these reserves were depleted, so it acquired dollar-denominated securities, which could be liquidated in the United States without further increasing negative trade balances either through dollar exchange or as collateral for loans. Britain owed J. P. Morgan & Co. of New York $400 billion alone by June 1917, having acted as banker for its allies largely on the strength of American loans.

Britain had to pay for purchases with dollars, yet also needed to maintain the value of the pound against the dollar in order to keep down the price of imports, but the pound came under increasing pressure. The process culminated in a major sterling crisis in December 1916. At times during the next few months, Britain occasionally had barely more than a week's money in hand to meet American interest payments. By July 1917 Britain had reached the point at which no more actual gold could be sent to the United States without destroying the whole basis of British credit. Subsequently, in February 1918, the British Treasury had to accept the subrogation of the rights of its collateral to the United States.

ADM 116 contains correspondence and cables on gold shipments to the United States (ADM 116/1690–91), and on economies in expenditure, 1916 (ADM 116/1495–6).

ADM 137 also contains material on bullion shipments with correspondence between the Admiralty and the Bank of England, 1915–19 (ADM 137/696), and shipments of Russian bullion from Archangel in 1914 (ADM 137/1916). There is also material on the Government War Insurance Scheme (ADM 137/2744–9).

ADM 181/100 are papers for the Navy Estimates for 1915–17.

ADM 268/36 contains papers of the Ad-hoc Committee on War Bonuses and War Increased Awards for Admiralty Staff, 1917.

AIR 1 has a little material on war-related finance including the Air Board and Air Ministry Appropriation Account (AIR 1/2324/223/42/1); reports by the House of Commons on National Expenditure, 1915–19 (AIR 1/2411/303/4/26); and a report on the Finance Branch of the Explosives Department of the Ministry of Munitions from August 1915 (AIR 1/2413/303/10).

AIR 2 has details of the opening of a War Savings Association in the Air Ministry (AIR 2/67/A 505), and the gift by the Maharaja of Bikaner of 300,000 rupees in 1918 for the purchase of aircraft and tanks (AIR 2/81/B 3924).

AO 27/1 and **3** contain registered files of the Exchequer and Audit Department dealing with appropriation accounts and financial matters connected to the Air Ministry.

BT 13/59 deals with war risks insurance, 1914.

CAB 1, the miscellaneous papers collected by Sir James Masterton-Smith, includes a report compiled in January 1915 on financial affairs since the beginning of the war (CAB 1/11); a report on Britain's economic position vis-à-vis that of the Dominions in February 1917 (CAB 1/23); and a report by Andrew Bonar Law on war finance, April 1917 (CAB 1/24).

CAB 17, among the miscellaneous papers of the Committee of Imperial Defence, reveals immediate pre-war ideas on policy towards war finance and war risks insurance, 1904–14 (CAB 17/80–3). There is also material on the CID's Finance Committee, 1916 (CAB 17/145); and correspondence and papers of the Committee on the Co-ordination of the Military and Financial Effort, 1916 (CAB 17/159).

CAB 27, containing papers of various ad hoc Cabinet Committees, includes some relating to the Co-ordination of Military and Financial Effort Committee in 1916 (CAB 27/4).

CAB 37, containing copies of the papers circulated to the Cabinet between 1880 and 1916, includes two relating to the Cabinet Finance Committee in 1915–16 (CAB 37/136/39 and 151/5), as well as rather more relating to the Cabinet Committee on the Co-ordination of Military and Financial Effort in 1916 (CAB 37/141/38, 142/11, and 145/20, and 35–6).

CHAR 3/83–4 deal with wartime legislation, principally the War Charities Act, 1916, which prohibited the operation of all but registered war charities. War charities were defined as funds, institutions or associations whose charitable object was connected to the relief of participants and victims of the war, but not where such object was subsidiary to the principal purposes of the charity.

CHAR 4 contains registers of war charities arranged by region, and including the name, location and purpose of each charity, and the name of committee members (CHAR 4/1–4). Files also deal with those charities exempted from registration (CHAR 4/15–22), and with those refused registration (CHAR 4/23). An index is available (CHAR 4/24). Over 18,000 new charities sprang up during the war.

CUST 44/21 contains the annual reports of the Board of Customs and Excise, 1910–20.

CUST 49/367, 374 and **416** deal with exemptions from customs duty on entertainment for wounded soldiers, at Pembrey explosives factory, and on tobacco for soldiers on YMCA premises.

HO 45 deals with the Jersey War Loan, 1915–18 (HO 45/278293); lotteries and newspaper competitions for war savings certificates, 1915–19, and official views on the premium bond scheme advocated by Horatio Bottomley (HO 45/298101). There are also records of the War Charities Committee, 1916 (HO 45/308566).

IR 73 contains the papers of Sir Richard Hopkins, chairman of the Board of Inland Revenue, 1916–21, including material on excess profits duty from 1915–18 (IR 73/10–15 and 17), and the ministry levy in 1917 (IR 73/16).

IR 74 contains Private Office memoranda, dealing with such issues as wartime income tax (IR 74/33, 46, and 105); excess profits duty (IR 74/70, 227–8, 235, and 237); the ministry levy (IR 74/226, 229); and the proposals for the 'conscription of wealth' in 1917 (IR 74/17).

MEPO 3/2437 has material on the application of the War Charities Act, 1916, among the correspondence and papers of the Commissioner's Office.

MT 6 deals with Treasury concerns at the free conveyance of 'comforts' destined for Canadian troops, and compensation for railwaymen killed in air raids (MT 6/2468/10, and 2471/13).

MT 9 deals with the sale of war savings certificates by officers of the mercantile marine, 1918 (MT 9/1347); but also has a body of material on war risks insurance covering such categories as fishing vessels, merchant seamen, cargoes, merchant fleet auxiliaries, general losses, and missing vessels (MT 9/965, 998, 980, 1079, 1123, and 1163). The Government Scheme, 1914–15, is also generally covered (MT 9/1026).

MUN 4/7066 contains the minutes of the Munitions Expenditure Emergency Standing Committee.

NSC 1/1–6 contain the wartime minutes of the National Savings Committee, including its Publicity, Finance and Women's Sub-committees and its Central Advisory Committee.

NSC 2/1–3 have annual reports for the war years.

NSC 3/1–2 have copies of the Committee's two wartime in-house magazines, *War Savings* and *The Silver Bullet*.

NSC 5/1–8 contain wartime posters.

NSC 7 has the overall history of the Committee's war efforts (NSC 7/1–2), with material on its Scottish Savings Committee (NSC 7/10). Wartime campaigns promoting war loans, and specific efforts such as Tank Week, War Weapons Week and Businessman's Week are also detailed (NSC 7/35–6, and 38–9).

PRO 10/316 includes a report on the work of the American Dollar Securities Committee, 1916–22, by its chairman, Sir William Gibbs Turpin, as well as other material relating to the committee.

T 1 contains the papers of the Treasury Board including correspondence, appointments, policy papers, reports, draft minutes, estimates, and proposals of various kinds. The arrangement is complicated and records are located by consulting the subject registers (T 108) and the 'name' registers (T 2), divided alphabetically into 'individuals' and 'public offices'. A rough handwritten manuscript register (T 108/27) specifically covers matters arising from the war. The latter index is divided broadly by file category as follows: American and Foreign Securities Questions, American Securities Questions, Conscientious Objection, Exchange Affairs, Financial Questions, Hambro's Transactions, Military Services Civil

Liabilities Department, Miscellaneous, Morgan & Co., Mortgages and Debts, National Relief Fund, Pre and Post Moratorium Bills, Remittances Abroad for Investment, Trading with the Enemy, Trading with the Enemy – Banking Questions, Transmission of Money to and from Enemy Countries, War Propaganda Bureau, and War Trade Department. There are also separate indices for files dealing with Belgium, Denmark, France, Germany, Italy, Norway, Romania, Russia, and the United States.

The name registers for the war years cover 1914 (T 2/466–9); 1915 (T 2/470–3); 1916 (T 2/474–8); 1917 (T 2/479–83); and 1918 (T 2/484–9). Once an original paper number is found from T 2 or T 108, it should be located in the skeleton registers in T 3, which enables associated papers to be traced in succeeding files. Registers covering the war years (T 3/103–7), in turn, guide the reader to the correct pieces to order from T 1 for 1914 (T 1/11599–720); 1915 (T 1/11721–891); 1916 (T 1/11892–12023); 1917 (T 1/12024–123); and 1918 (T 1/12124–267).

T 170/1–144 contain the papers of Sir John Bradbury, Joint Permanent Secretary to the Treasury, 1913–19, and chief financial adviser to the government during the war. They include much on the financial side of the war, such as a report on the financial situation arising from the outbreak of war (T 170/26); material on successive war loans (T 170/31–4, 70–71, 75–8, 97, and 114); specimens of the new one pound note (the 'Bradbury') and papers on its introduction (T 170/35–61); papers on allied finances (T 170/68–9, and 102); Bradbury's 1915 extensive memorandum on war finance (T 170/83–8); material on American loans and the position of the pound in relation to the dollar (T 170/62–3, 91–2, 95, 101, 104, and 109) as well as the final report of the American Dollar Securities Committee in June 1919 (T 170/130); papers on the National Savings Committee and the Scottish War Savings Committee (T 170/116 and 138); and wartime taxation (T 170/107, and 119–20). Bradbury's papers also concern such issues as war profiteering (T 170/105), and the medical treatment of soldiers after their discharge (T 170/74).

T 172 contains miscellaneous papers prepared in the Chancellor of the Exchequer's Office on a variety of issues. They include reports of wartime deputations received and conferences attended by Treasury representatives (T 172/141, 199–251, 485–507, and 833–47); papers on war insurance and war risks (T 172/157 and 189); material on war loans (T 172/684–763); papers on various war savings campaigns including War Weapons Week, Businessman's Week and Feed the Guns; as well as material on local savings campaigns in Newport and Plymouth (T 172/342, 366, 623, and 771). The financial implications of wartime diplomatic agreements are also dealt with (T 172/380–94, and 676–83), while the papers of Sir Samuel Hardman Lever as assistant commissioner for finance in the United States from February 1917 to November 1918 deal with financial aspects of the relationship with the United States (T 172/420–60).

T 176, containing the Niemeyer papers, covers gold shipments to the United States (T 176/1A), as well as financial agreements on war debts (T 176/1B).

T 203/1 contains the minutes of the Treasury's Expenditure Emergency Standing Committee, 1917–19.

T 204/1–5 and **7** have the minutes of the Naval Expenditure Emergency Standing Committee, 1914–19.

T 253 contains papers concerning the British Government's Foreign Accounts with J. P. Morgan & Co. of New York, primarily in the form of itemised statements of account. The account was opened in 1915 to liquidate American dollar securities held by British subjects or companies and acquired by or deposited on loan with the Treasury. The scheme was controlled by the American Dollar Securities Committee from December 1915 onwards and was intended to improve and maintain the value of the pound in relation to the dollar. Executive work in connection with the deposit of securities on loan was carried out by the National Debt Office. Acquisition and loan work ceased by April 1919, although the administration of the scheme continued into the post-war years. The series covers the years 1915–17 (T 253/1), and for 1919–24 (T 253/3), the accounts for 1917–19 (T 253/2) being missing.

T 254/1 contains the weekly returns of currency in circulation between 1914 and 1919, as well as certificates of currency recalled for cancellation, with summarised issue accounts and balance sheets.

T 255 contains the Russian Accounts comprising the Russian Liquidation Committee journal, 1918–33 (T 255/1), the Russian Account Committee ledgers and journals, 1919–28 (T 255/2–3), and ledgers and correspondence of the Agent of the Imperial Russian Treasury, 1915–16 (T 255/4–5). Established in June 1918 the Russian Liquidation Committee of the Treasury was intended to supervise the liquidation of goods ordered in Britain on the account of the Russian Imperial government, and to examine the position after liquidation. The Russian Accounts Committee of the Ministry of Munitions replaced it in 1919. The papers detail the sums due to the British government and others from the pre-revolution Russian authorities and the post-1917 White authorities in Russia and the Baltic states in respect of goods supplied and service rendered during the war and during the period of allied intervention in Russia from 1918–20.

TS 27, containing miscellaneous registered papers, deals with legal issues arising from some aspects of war finance, including Scottish investments in War Loan Stock at the Bank of England in 1917 (TS 27/53); and the Russian Liquidation Committee (TS 27/68).

WO 32 has material on the Treasury's dealings with the War Office (WO 32/11278–81, and 11286), including papers on the decision to empower the Secretary of State for War to authorise urgent expenditure without Treasury authorisation in 1915 (WO 32/11279). There are also the five reports of the Select Committee on National Expenditure, 1917–20, with observations by the Army Council (WO 32/11289–302); reports of discussions of the presentation of formal estimates during the war, 1917–18 (WO 32/11282–3); and reports of the Special Committee on Army Paymasters' Outstanding Accounts, 1916–17 (WO 32/11312–18). Expenditure on stores for the Royal Engineers came under the scrutiny of the Scott Moncrieff Committee in 1916 (WO 32/5156). There is also information on financial assistance to war costs derived from Indian revenues (WO 32/2765–6).

WO 33 contains the reports of the Treasury Standing (or Colwyn) Committee on the Co-ordination of Departmental Action on Contracts, 1918 (WO 33/859); the Interim Report of the Committee on War Office Expenditure, 1916 (WO 33/751); and reports on army expenditure, 1914–22 (WO 33/761, and 932).

War and Industrial Mobilisation

One measure of the transition to modern, industrialised 'total' war was that it became as important to out-produce as to out-fight an opponent. No belligerent, however, was prepared for the demands that the war would make, as epitomised by the 'shell shortage' most soon experienced. Generally, production levels fell through economic dislocation, resulting from trade disruption, shortages of raw materials, and manpower problems though the effects varied from industry to industry. Inevitably, the concentration on war production involved a reduction in consumer production while the drift of labour to war production generally altered regional employment patterns. War also naturally tended to strengthen larger production units at the expense of smaller ones.

One crucial sector was obviously munitions. Although Britain faced an early shell shortage, shortfalls were the product of the extraordinary additional orders placed with private firms by government in 1914 without regard for capacity, rather than of unrealistic expectations on the part of industry itself. Yet, from a situation in which only 500,000 shells were produced in 1914, the British armaments industry produced 76.2 million shells in 1917. Similarly, Britain had no real airframe or aero engine industry in 1914 but, in 1918, produced over 22,000 aero engines and 32,000 aircraft.

Certain sectors of the economy were obviously stimulated by the particular demands of modern war. In turn, pre-war trends could be further distorted by new demand. Thus, coal, shipping and heavy industry, all previously in decline, were revitalised. Some industries contracted, either through the decline in exports such as the cotton and wool trades, or through having little protection against recruitment, such as the building and paper trades. However, the war also stimulated the growth of industries little established before the war such as scientific instrument making. The loss of German imports of optical instruments, for example, seriously affected production of such vital equipment as range finders, prompting the Ministry of Munitions to provide British firms with capital investment and scientific and technical assistance sufficient to boost production. The loss of such state investment at the end of the war, however, almost destroyed the industry. Not all state intervention produced satisfactory results: government investment in production of soluble cellulose acetate, the weather-proofing applied to the linen fabric used for aircraft skins, resulted in a financial scandal.

ADM 1 deals with the locating of the Naval Cordite Factory at Holton Heath near Poole in February 1915 (ADM 1/8412/47); as well as munitions supply from Brazilian sources in July 1915 (ADM 1/8428/214); and general munitions production in 1915 (ADM 1/8432/260). Royal Dockyards were not regarded as controlled establishments under the Munitions of War Act (ADM 1/8447/25), but there was a naval representative on the Ordnance Board, when it was reconstituted as a committee of the Ministry of Munitions in March 1916 (ADM 1/8451/58). The series also deals with the organisation of the Controlling Department on Shipbuilding (ADM 1/8488/104) and Lord Curzon's Committee on Increased

Mercantile Shipbuilding in August 1917 (ADM 1/8493/164). In addition, there is a report on the empire's oil situation, September 1918 (ADM 1/8537/240).

ADM 116, groups of 'case' papers collected by the Admiralty Secretariat, contain material on the Royal Navy's own cordite factories (ADM 116/1449 and 1452), and upon merchant ship construction, 1917–18 (ADM 116/1608–9).

AIR 1, comprising material collected by the Air Historical Branch, contains much information on aircraft production including figures for the quarterly production of aircraft and engines (AIR 1/9/15/1/30); statements of the number of aircraft supplied to other countries between 1916 and 1918 including Belgium, Brazil, Chile, France, Greece, Japan, Norway, Romania and Russia (AIR 1/39); as well as aircraft presented by the Patriotic League of Britons Overseas (AIR 1/113/15/39/33), and the Dominions (AIR 1/142/15/40/314). There are engine returns for the BEF in March 1915 and weekly returns for 1918 (AIR 1/826/204/5/132 and AIR 1/947–51); files on the scarcity of aero engines in December 1916 (AIR 1/731/176/6/14); the construction programme for 1917 (AIR 1/149/15/93); and the aeronautical supply position that September (AIR 1/719/35/6).

   Among files dealing with the Admiralty, there is one on the Joint Army and Navy Aeronautical Purchasing Commission in Paris, 1915–16 (AIR 1/630/17/122/23), and others on the work of the British Aviation Commission in Paris, 1916 (AIR 1/884–5), while one box deals with the work of the RAF's Paris Representative of the British Aviation Supplies Department, 1916–18 (AIR 1/2002). Another large body of material on aircraft production (AIR 1/2301–9) includes output reports for airframes and engines for the war as a whole (AIR 1/2302/215/400); correspondence of the Department of Aircraft Production, 1914–18 (AIR 1/2302/215/12); minutes of the Directorate of Aircraft Equipment (AIR 1/2303); and details on the work of local wartime munitions committees (AIR 1/2306/215/22). In addition, there are some copies of the *Ministry of Munitions Journal* (AIR 1/2324/223/46/1 and 4), and some minutes of the War Cabinet's War Priorities Committee, 1917–18 (AIR 1/678/21/13/2102).

AIR 2, the registered files of the Air Ministry, include the minutes of the first 45 meetings of the Aircraft Supply Committee, 1917–18 (AIR 2/995), as well as files on the supply of material required for aircraft manufacture. There is, for example, information on the substitution of other woods and even papier maché for spruce (AIR 2/55/AB 275/7442 and 7553); reports on trading in duralumin by Vickers Ltd (AIR 2/723); and complaints by the Associated Rubber Manufacturers Ltd regarding rubmetal (AIR 2/994). There are also reports on aeroplane and engine contracts in 1916 (AIR 2/124/B 10984); and policy on the filming of magneto manufacture at the British Thompson Houston Works in 1918 (AIR 2/76/B 136).

AVIA 13/1212 contains the papers of the Burbridge Commission into the organisation and management of the Royal Aircraft Factory, Farnborough, 1914–16. Established as the Balloon Equipment Store at Woolwich Arsenal in 1878, it was renamed the Balloon Factory in 1892. Moving to Farnborough in 1905, it became the Royal Aircraft Factory in 1912, but was confined to research and development in 1916 following considerable criticism of its products. Generally, the Factory trailed behind the Germans in technical efficiency, not least engine development.

BT 5/120–14 contain the wartime minutes of the Board of Trade.

BT 13 contains a few papers of some of the Board of Trade's wartime committees including the Coal Exports Committee, 1916 (BT 13/68); Tramways Committee and Chemical Products Committee, 1917 (BT 13/82); and reports of the Shipping and Shipbuilding Committee, 1918 (BT 13/86); Electric Power Supply Committee and Non-Ferrous Metals Trade Committee, 1918 (BT 13/87). It also includes the minutes of the third meeting of the Munitions of War Committee in 1915 (BT 13/62). In addition, there is material on prospects for coal, iron and steel after the war (BT 13/76); gas supply for traction and paper control (BT 13/85); and alcohol as motor fuel (BT 13/90).

BT 7 contains the correspondence and papers of the Cotton Control Board, 1917–19. Established in Manchester in June 1917, the Board took eight censuses of the cotton industry between October 1917 and January 1919, detailing the number of firms, bales and yarn in stock, bales consumed, and number of looms and spindles running. There are the census returns (BT 7/1–28); minutes of the Board's sub-committees, 1917–19 (BT 7/29); ledgers showing firms' financial dealings with the Board (BT 7/33–44); notes on its Contraband Committee (BT 7/47); and an account of the work of the Board in 1917 (BT 7/48). The Board continued in existence after 1919 as the Cotton Reconstruction Board.

BT 55 contains the records of wartime committees of the Board of Trade. These are listed as a whole (BT 55/1), and comprise papers of the Commercial and Industrial Policy Committee, 1916 (BT 55/8–13); the Electrical Trades Committee, 1916–17 (BT 55/20–21); the Engineering Industries Committee, 1916–17, and the Engineering Trades (New Industries) Committee, 1918 (BT 55/22–4); the Financial Facilities for Trade Committee, 1916 (BT 55/32); the Glassware Trade Committee, 1916–18 (BT 55/37); the Iron and Steel Industries Committee, 1916–17 (BT 55/38–41); the Standing Council on Post-war Priority, 1918–19 (BT 55/50); the Committee on the Post-war Position of the Sulphuric Acid and Fertiliser Trades, 1917 (BT 55/55); the Shipping and Ship Building Committees, 1916–17 (BT 55/112–13); the Textile Industries Committee, 1914–17, and the Trade Relations Committee, 1916 (BT 55/115–21). Papers of the post-war Toy Committee contain a report on the toy trade since the outbreak of war in 1914, compiled in 1922 (BT 55/80).

BT 62/1–26, containing papers of the Controller of Trading Accounts, have some material on zinc purchases in 1918, with papers of the Advisory Committee on the Zinc Concentrates Contract of the same year (BT 62/9).

BT 66 contains the papers of the Optical Munitions, Glassware and Potash Branches of the Ministry of Munitions. Originally dealt with by a division of the Munitions Supply Department in June 1915, optical munitions became the responsibility of a separate Optical Munitions Branch in July 1916. It was transferred in turn to the American and Transport Department in October 1916 as the Optical Munitions and Glassware Branch. The Potash Production Branch was added in June 1917 with both branches then passing to the Ministry's Materials Group in August 1917. Responsibility for the two branches passed to the Board of Trade in June 1919. Papers of the Optical Munitions and Glassware Branch, 1915–20 (BT 66/1–7) include a history of the branch, while there are also papers of the Potash Production Board, 1916–19 (BT 66/8–14).

BT 198/1–4 contain the minutes and papers of the 'morning meetings' of the Board of Trade, 1917–19, involving the President, secretaries and principal departmental heads. In 1919 the meetings were formalised as the Board of Trade Council.

CAB 1 contains miscellaneous papers of the Assistant Secretary of the Ministry of Munitions, Sir James Masterton-Smith, 1917–19 (CAB 1/34). Other papers cover shipbuilding in March 1916 and February 1917, as well as the possible nationalisation of shipping (CAB 1/15, 22 and 23); the possible reorganisation of the Ministry of Munitions in March 1916 (CAB 1/16); steel production in April 1916 (CAB 1/17); arms output and production switches from February 1916 (CAB 1/15); the metal situation in 1916 (CAB 1/17); and collieries and coal production in January 1917 (CAB 1/22). In addition, there is a variety of material on allied and neutral munitions output (CAB 1/15, 18, 20, and 21).

CAB 15/6 contains minutes and papers of the War Priorities Committee, 1917–18, and of its Permanent Sub-committee, Permanent (Labour) Sub-committee, and Works Construction Sub-committee. The committee worked under the auspices of the Committee on the Co-ordination of Departmental Action, itself a pre-war standing committee of the Committee of Imperial Defence.

CAB 17 deals with coal supplies and shipping shortages in 1916 (CAB 17/140 and 165–6), as well as production difficulties generally in providing war equipment (CAB 17/169–70).

CAB 21 contains papers on issues considered by the War Cabinet and Cabinet. There is more material on the War Priorities Committee in 1918 (CAB 21/118). Other papers address the finishing of textiles in 1917 (CAB 21/30); a number of aspects of ship building (CAB 21/32–6), including labour supply; railway facilities at ports (CAB 21/39); port development in Ireland and Scotland (CAB 21/79); French steel capacity (CAB 21/115); the co-ordination of allied purchases in the United States (CAB 21/123); consideration of copper and lead purchases in Australia in 1918 by a Cabinet Committee on Australian Purchases (CAB 21/111); petroleum supplies and saltpetre supplies (CAB 21/119–20). A paper by Waldorf Astor in 1917 deals with the redistillation of portable spirits for use in the munitions industry (CAB 21/28).

CAB 27/10 contains papers of the Cabinet Committee on Allocation of Guns, established in October 1917, and which held four meetings between then and December, to determine allocation priorities in relation to competing demands by the British army and those of allied governments.

CAB 40 contains the main papers of the Cabinet War Priorities Committee, 1917–18. Established in September 1917 under the chairmanship of Jan Smuts to report on conditions in the aircraft industry, it was reconstituted as a standing committee on all aspects of munitions production. It operated through various inter-departmental boards or sub-committees dealing with particular commodities. In all, there were 21 meetings. Its functions are outlined (CAB 40/1), while there are minutes of the Committee (CAB 40/2–3), and papers of the Information, Works Construction, General Services, Machine Tools and Ball Bearings, Permanent, Explosives and Chemicals, Oxygen and Carbide Allocation, Timber Allocation, Linen and Fabric, Non Ferrous (Metals) Materials, and Steel sub-committees (CAB 40/4–34). The series also deals with a variety of strategic commodities and products such as nitrate of soda, flax, oats, electrical power, dyestuffs, mineral oil, Nissen huts, bomb proof shelters, agricultural machinery, and rubber as well as issues such as works construction, transport, and labour (CAB 40/35–121). Other files deal with services provided by various companies and works construction projects (CAB 40/122–71). The Committee was dissolved in December 1918.

CUST 49/351 deals with oil fuel control in 1915.

CO 537, containing Colonial Office confidential correspondence, includes material on ammunition contracts placed in Canada (CO 537/1124), as well as the importation of nickel from Canada (CO 537/1125), and of copper and lead from Australia (CO 537/1137).

DSIR 8 contains the papers of the Fuel Research Board, established in February 1917 to investigate the long-term adequacy and the efficient utilisation of coal resources. It was an initiative on the part of a Sub-committee on Coal Conservation of the Reconstruction Committee, in co-operation with the British Association's Committee on Fuel Economy. In March 1917 the board undertook a survey of coal resources and experimental investigations into more economical and efficient means of preparing coal and its by-products. The Survey Department, however, was not established to sift through the data collected until 1919, when a Fuel Research Station was also created. The series includes the constitution and terms of reference of the board (DSIR 8/1), and a proposal in 1915 that the British Association Fuel Economy Committee constitute a standing committee on fuel (DSIR 8/15). The Irish Peat Enquiry of 1917 is considered (DSIR 8/18–19), while gas standards research, 1917–18, is also detailed (DSIR 8/20).

DSIR 36 has material on wartime manufacturing and resources, including a memoir by Dr P. G. H. Boswell on sand resources for glass making, and reports on glass works (DSIR 36/1 and 19); a report by the Department's Advisory Council on raw materials, 1916, together with statistics on zinc production (DSIR 36/73–4); a survey of world production of tungsten ores, 1914–16 (DSIR 36/186); reports by the Ministry of Munitions on the manufacture of sulphuric acid, June 1917, and on oil fuel supplies from home sources, 1918 (DSIR 36/1639 and 1642); and reports on the synthetic manufacture of glycerine from 1916 and on the production of cerium from May 1918 (DSIR 36/2655 and 2657).

DSIR 37 contains files of various departments of the Ministry of Munitions passed to the Department of Scientific and Industrial Research when it was established in 1919. Among them are records of the Explosives Supply Department (DSIR 37/15–22), created in June 1915 to supervise all contracts for high explosives, the organisation of state manufacture in national factories, and the holding, accounting and transit arrangements for high explosive supplies. Largely technical records, they include material on TNT (DSIR 37/15). There are also files of the Nitrogen Production Committee (DSIR 37/23–140), created in June 1916, to examine the military, agricultural and industrial requirements of Britain and the empire including details of a conference between the Faraday Society and the Munitions Invention Department on synthetic production (DSIR 37/23); the Germans' Haber process for the production of ammonia (DSIR 37/68); reports on American processes (DSIR 37/111–15); visits to French factories including those producing TNT (DSIR 37/116–18); and patent specifications (DSIR 37/119–39). The Chemical Waste Products Committee was established in 1918 to examine the use of unutilised chemical waste (DSIR 37/224–7).

HO 45/266710 deals with the supply of Indian saltpetre for explosives factories, 1914–16.

MT 9 deals with the supply of coal to France, 1916 (MT 9/1060), and has returns of shipbuilding construction, 1915–17 (MT 9/1106).

MT 23/449, among papers of the Admiralty Transport Department, deals with the conveyance of war materiel destined for the French Ministry of Munitions from Newhaven to Boulogne, 1915.

MT 25/1–88, comprising the correspondence of the Ministry of Shipping, 1917–21, include material on accelerated shipbuilding in 1917 (MT 25/1); timber shipments (MT 25/8); fuel oil reserves, 1916–18 (MT 25/20); and coal shipments (MT 25/58).

MUN 1/1–24 contain the daily records of the Munitions Council, 1917–21, including duplicated daily confidential reports sent to members of the Council and the ministry's heads of department, précis of important letters, notes on committees and boards, summaries of labour returns from national factories, and statistics of employment and unemployment. Established in August 1917 to replace less effective weekly and fortnightly meetings of heads of departments, the Council was intended to aid and advise the Minister and to co-ordinate the work of over 50 departments organised into 10 groups, each group supervised by a member of the Council. Initially the groups were Finance (Finance and Contracts Departments), Design (Design, Inventions and Inspection Departments), Steel and Iron (Munitions Supply Department), Materials (Munitions Supply and American and Transport Departments), Explosives (Factories, Trench Warfare Supply and Explosives Departments), Projectiles (Factories, Trench Warfare Supply and Explosives Supply Departments), Guns (Factories, Trench Warfare Supply and Explosive Supply Departments), Engines (Mechanical and Engine, and Aircraft Production Departments), Labour (Labour Department), and the Secretariat.

In November 1917 a Requirements and Statistics Group was formed from within the Secretariat, embracing the new North American Department. In January 1918, the Projectiles and Guns Groups were merged in an Ordnance Group. The Engines Group was then sub-divided in February 1918 and an Air Group created in April 1918. In July 1918 the rest of the Engines Group was combined with parts of the Trench Warfare Supply and Inventions Departments to form a Warfare Group. The Master General of the Ordnance joined the Council in October 1918 as representative of the War Office, an additional member having been added in April to sit as the minister's representative on the Inter-allied Munitions Council in Paris.

MUN 2 contains records of the Department of Requirements and Statistics including bound and printed weekly reports of contracts placed, deliveries made, labour returns, orders in hand, and area organisation. Preliminary typescript volumes for July 1915 to July 1916 contain the first 23 reports (MUN 2/1A). Indices to most reports, and reports numbers 19–224, covering the period from November 1915 to December 1919, are included (MUN 2/1B–20). There are also bound collections of off prints from report numbers 15–17, arranged by subject (MUN 2/21–34). Originally part of the Secretariat, the Department became independent of it in November 1917 as a separate Group represented on the Munitions Council.

MUN 3 contains specimens of documents destroyed after the war which had passed through the various registries of the ministry including that at Whitehall Gardens (Labour), Whitehall Place (Supply), Storeys Gate (Explosives) and King Charles Street (Trench Warfare). There are account books and other financial records from the Rochdale National Shell Factory (MUN 3/1–19), and examples of orders placed with American companies (MUN 3/20–32). Supply records generally are included (MUN 3/33–156), including orders placed in Switzerland and Canada, dealings with National and Trade Filling Factories and National Factories, liaison with the Shipping Controller and internal transport of munitions. Specimens include contract records (MUN 3/157–65), and inspection records (MUN 3/166–72). Labour records (MUN 3/173–215) include files on individual munitions workers, complaints of unfair dismissal and claims for exemption from military service. Examples of correspondence with firms (MUN 3/216–96) include issues such as hours of employment, and Sunday and public holiday labour.

Local records (MUN 3/297–313), which mostly relate to Essex, Norfolk, Suffolk, Ipswich and Norwich, include claims for exemption from military service and lists and indices of men released or exempted. Miscellaneous specimens include enquiries deemed to be of minor importance (MUN 3/314–31). The winding up of the Ministry, which became the Disposal and Liquidation Commission in 1921, is reflected (MUN 3/332–462), including financial records (MUN 3/332–49), factory records such as wage rolls (MUN 3/350–62), disposal records for surplus material (MUN 3/363–4), minor establishment records (MUN 3/365–6), sales records (MUN 3/367–72), and papers on disposal of surplus stores in France and Belgium (MUN 3/373–462).

MUN 4/1–3380 contain the Central Registry records of the Ministry grouped according to the following subject headings: administration, Admiralty, aero supplies, aircraft ammunition, Air Force, air raids, aluminium, American Expeditionary Force, anti-aircraft guns, appointments, area organisation, Australia, Belgium, brass, Brazil, Canada, canteens, chemicals (including gas) and chemical warfare, claims and losses, claims under Workmen's Compensation Act, coal and coke, colonies, Commission Internationale de Revitaillement, communications, complaints and representations, contracts, controlled establishments, copper, demobilisation and reconstruction, Denmark, Department of Munitions Requirements and Statistics, design, DG of Munitions Supply, DG of Ordnance Supply, disposal of surplus government property, Egypt, electrical supply, establishments, explosives, fertilisers, finance, flax, food, forage, France, fuses, Germany, glassware, Greece, grenades, guns, gun ammunition, gun ammunition filling, Holland, honours and awards, India, inland transportation, inspection, intelligence, Inter-allied Munitions Board, Inter-allied Munitions Council, instructions and suggestions, Ireland, iron and steel, Italy, Japan, labour, land and property, lead, legal cases, liquidation and contracts, machine guns, machinery and plant, machine tools, manganese, mechanical transport, mechanical warfare, metals and raw materials, Minister for Munitions, Munitions Council, munitions – general, National Factories, New Zealand, nickel, Norway, offers of personal service, optical munitions, Ordnance Committee, Ordnance factories, organisation, parliament and general, petroleum products and fats, pistols, Poland, Portugal, potash, priorities, propellants, protection of vulnerable points, publications, publicity, railway material, railway traffic, records, regulations, research, returns and routine reports, rifles, Romania, Russia, Russia – liquidation of contracts, salvage, scrap, security, Serbia, shell manufacture, shipping, ship freight and other charges, small arms, small arms ammunition, Spain, staff, statistics, storage, stores, Sweden, Switzerland, timber, tin and tin plate, trade, trade control, transport, trench warfare, USA, War Cabinet, War Office, war trade, welfare, health and housing, wolfram and tungsten, works, and zinc.

As well as those culled from the various registries, the series includes the papers of a number of senior administrators in the Ministry including Andrew Weir, later Lord Inverforth, who was Surveyor General of Supplies at the War Office and, later, Minister of Munitions.

MUN 5, containing the records of the Historical Branch, has files on a number of specific matters including labour (MUN 5/48–102 and 346–53), finance (MUN 5/102–8 and 353–5), contracts (MUN 5/109–13 and 355–7), industrial and commercial control (MUN 5/113–17), design (MUN 5/120–21 and 359), inspection (MUN 5/122 and 359), supply (MUN 5/122–41 and 360–62), external production (MUN 5/141–77 and 362–72), guns (MUN 5/177–9 and 373–4), gun ammunition (MUN 5/179–88 and 374–7), small arms and small arms ammunition (MUN 5/188–91 and 377–8), explosives (MUN 5/191–5 and 378–82), trench warfare supplies (MUN 5/195–9 and 382–7), machine tools (MUN 5/199–201 and 387–8), metals (MUN 5/201–8 and 388–9), other stores (MUN 5/208–16 and 389–93), and transportation (MUN 5/216–18 and 393), as well as a number of 'unregistered papers' (MUN 5/219A–321A). There are also reports on visits to gun ammunition filling factories in France (MUN 5/395).

MUN 7 are records transferred to the War Office in 1923, relating to the Departments of Explosives Supply and Munitions Inspection, and munitions design. General papers on explosives supply can be found (MUN 7/1–74 and 539–58), with papers on contracts (MUN 7/75–234). Acetone supplies are dealt with (MUN 7/234–45) as well as other propellants (MUN 7/246–52), non-ferrous metals (MUN 7/395), and the Wool Purchase Scheme, 1916 (MUN 7/473–537). Inspection matters are covered (MUN 7/345–94, 397–428, 439–48, and 456–63), and design issues likewise (MUN 7/335–44, 429–38, 449–555 and 559). In addition, there are papers on the explosives factory at Gretna (MUN 7/253–72), and of the Director-General of Factories (MUN 7/396). There is also material on the Raw Materials and Salvage Sections of the War Office Contracts Branch (MUN 7/464–72 and 538).

MUN 9/1–30 contain various papers relating to Lloyd George as Minister of Munitions, including records of a conference held with tool manufacturers, and an interview between Lloyd George and Sir John French in September 1915.

POWE 16 deals with the supply of British coal to Belgium, France, Italy, Norway and Portugal, 1916–21 (POWE 16/526–7, 535).

POWE 22/5 contains details of oil boring agreements between various companies and the Ministry of Munitions.

POWE 26 contains the papers of the Board of Trade Departmental Committee on Coal, 1916–17 (POWE 26/3–7); minutes of the Advisory Board on Coal, 1917–19 (POWE 26/11); and reports of meetings between the Coal Controller and district committees, 1917–19 (POWE 26/13). In addition, there is a report of a departmental committee appointed by the Board of Trade in 1917 to enquire into the post-war position of non-ferrous metals (POWE 26/9).

POWE 33 deals with petroleum supplies in general, 1916–17 (POWE 33/1–4), but also has minutes of the Petroleum Pool Board and details of the Pool Board Scheme (POWE 33/6, 129–31 and 1997). There is also material on the work of the Petrol Control Committee, 1916–18 (POWE 33/1987–97) including the results of a census in 1916 on fuel stocks, consumption and the requirements for motor spirit

(POWE 33/1994); and a conference on the control of petroleum from March 1916 (POWE 33/1986). In addition to a report on the work of the Petrol Control Committee (POWE 33/1995), there is also a report on the work of the Munitions Mineral Oil Production Department, 1917–19 (POWE 33/133).

PREM 1/6 is concerned with the enquiry report into the wartime financial dealings and methods of the British Cellulose Company, 1918–19.

PRO 10 contains specimens of documents later destroyed. Some relate to the Ministry of Munitions and the Disposal and Liquidation Commission (PRO 10/47 102–7, 282–3, 436–41 and 1392). Examples from wartime emergency departments of the Board of Trade can be found (PRO 10/84–98) (though some have been lost subsequently), including the Petrol and Paper Control Departments and the Tramway Committee, while those relating to the Timber Supply Department include a file with original letters on the Swedish and Norwegian timber trades, 1917–18 (PRO 10/97–8). Also represented is the Committee on Work of National Importance, 1916–19 (PRO 10/114), and the Cotton Control Board, including a report of the Cotton Inquiry Tribunal of October 1918 as well as copies of the *Board of Trade Journal and Commercial Gazette* (PRO 10/115). Material from other Board of Trade emergency departments can also be found (PRO 10/991–6 and 1109).

SUPP 2/23–7 contain the wartime balance sheets of the Royal Ordnance Factories.

SUPP 5, comprising Headquarters and Factory Records, contains material principally on the Royal Gunpowder Factory at Waltham Abbey and Woolwich Arsenal. Included are statistical summaries and production returns from Woolwich (SUPP 5/62–3, 185); records of experiments (including photographs) at Waltham Abbey (SUPP 5/653–4, 664, 862, 930–1, 933, 935 and 1061); material on wages and costs at Waltham Abbey (SUPP 5/428, 678); experiments at other factories at Gretna, Marlows Cordite Drying Stores, Oldbury, Penrhyndeudraeth, and Queen's Ferry (SUPP 5/930, 1158–63, 1166–74, and 1202–9); reports from both Woolwich and Waltham Abbey (SUPP 5/1053, and 1225–6), and a cordite factory at Aruuankadu (SUPP 5/427); records of contracts and purchases (SUPP 5/928–9); building work and fire regulations at Woolwich (SUPP 5/978 and 1047–8); material on the design and construction of ordnance factories (SUPP 5/1050); and the use of Chiselhurst Caves for munitions storage (SUPP 5/1041–6).

SUPP 6 contains various minutes, reports and memoranda relating to the Ordnance Board, 1914–15 (SUPP 6/184–9), and its successor, the Ordnance Committee, 1915–18 (SUPP 6/200–235, 254–67, and 287–9). Other committees covered are the Royal Artillery Committee (SUPP 6/546, 554, and 568–9); the Trench Warfare Section of the Ordnance Committee and the Trench Warfare Committee (SUPP 6/509, 603–8); the Royal Small Arms Factory Committee on Production (SUPP 6/661); the Anti-aircraft Equipment Committee (SUPP 6/602); and the Small Arms Section of the Ministry of Munitions Design Committee and the Small Arms Committee (SUPP 6/660 and 664). Other reports include those on various explosive propellants including enemy bullets (SUPP 6/621, 624, 641); war materials (SUPP 6/642); and schedule of approved anti-aircraft guns and electric lights for air defence (SUPP 6/645).

SUPP 10 are the papers of Kenneth B. Quinan, the American manager of the Cape Explosives Factory in South Africa, upon whose expertise the government drew from 1915–19 in designing and erecting explosive factories as Director of Factories in the Explosives Supply Department of the Ministry of Munitions. A large part of the series (SUPP 10/1–107) contains plans, designs, reports and papers on the factories established at Avonmouth (SUPP 10/1–10), Billingham (SUPP 10/11–14, and 73–4), Gretna (SUPP 10/15–42), Hanbury (SUPP 10/43–52), Longwith (SUPP 10/57), Misk (SUPP 10/58), Oldbury (SUPP 10/59–68), Pembrey (SUPP 10/69–72), Penrhyndeudraeth (SUPP 10/73–4), Queen's Ferry (SUPP 10/75–100), Rainham (SUPP 10/101), Sandycroft (SUPP 10/103–5), and Swindon (SUPP 10/73–4). Overseas plants at Hopewell in Virginia, Renfrew in Canada and Toulouse are also covered (SUPP 10/53–5, 102, and 106–7). Statistics on production and the costs of production are included (SUPP 10/222–76), while Quinan's miscellaneous correspondence (SUPP 10/209–21, and 277–300), has some post-war reports on war material from the occupied zone of Germany.

SUPP 12/1 contains the papers of Sir Eric Geddes as Deputy Director of Munitions Supply from July 1915 to August 1916, including some correspondence with Lloyd George.

WO 32 contains minutes of conferences between the British, French, Italian and Russian governments on munitions supply, 1916 (WO 32/5089) as well as papers on the Canadian contribution to the gun ammunition programme, 1917 (WO 32/5159). It also deals with complaints of slow deliveries of gas shells and mortar bombs, 1916–17 (WO 32/5175), and the transfer of engineering responsibilities in National Shipyards from the War Office to the Admiralty, 1918 (WO 32/5106).

WO 142, containing papers of the various manifestations of the Chemical Warfare Department of the Ministry of Munitions, has reports on the production of gas and/or smoke shells at the Stratford Naval Filling Factory, 1915–18 (WO 142/213–19); HM Factories at Avonmouth and Sutton Oak, the latter also dealing with TNT (WO 142/225–35); Blackley Mustard Gas Plant (WO 142/236); the Allhusen Works at Gateshead (WO 142/237); the Nobel Explosives Company Factory, Ardeer (WO 142/220); HM Cylinder Department at Himley in Staffordshire (WO 142/253); and Middlewich in Cheshire (WO 142/276). Gun ammunition filling reports cover the National Filling Factories at Banbury, Hereford, and Chittening, and HM Factory, Walthamstow (WO 142/274 and 276), while there is also material on the flame projector works at Wembley (WO 142/25). There are also reports on the production of gas masks and their components at Greenwich, Stamford Hill, Nottingham, Stanstead House, Fairfax Hall at Harringay, Batavia Mills and Holloway Mills, the Green Walk Anti-Gas Mask Factory at Tottenham, and the Crowndale Works at Camden (WO 142/259–63).

WO 188/3 deals with factories producing anti-gas respirators, 1918.

WORK 52/1 contains the works contract precedent book maintained by the Directorate of Army Contracts, 1914–38, including entries of contracts for building work, specifications, estimates, details of Treasury decisions, compensation and damage claims and other matters.

The need to ensure war-related production inevitably gave government a greater role in determining manpower policies. The introduction of such policies was not always easy given the prevailing assumptions in 1914 that the war would be short, and the failure in consequence to control the movement of skilled manpower into the armed forces. The net effect was to compel the search for alternative sources of labour such as the unskilled and women. The introduction of new sources of labour then raised the difficulties of dilution, whereby the restrictive practices of the pre-war skilled unions had to be tackled head on. The British government, however, fought shy of compulsory labour direction and a voluntary national registration programme was introduced in June 1915. In theory, the introduction of military conscription was an important step towards proper manpower planning through the ability to manipulate exemptions, and a Manpower Distribution Board was established in August 1916. The board's attempts to co-ordinate policy, however, were resisted by both War Office and Ministry of Munitions. The board was replaced by the Department of National Service in December 1916. The resulting National Service Scheme to release young and fit men from industry, by providing substitutes from non-essential work, was again voluntary when introduced in February 1917. Moreover, while the government used its powers under DORA to prevent non-essential industries from hiring men between the ages of 18 and 60, it shrank from compelling them to disgorge those already so employed.

A War Cabinet Committee on Manpower was finally established on 6 December 1917. This finally effected a coherent manpower policy, subordinating military demands to an overall assessment of priorities: merchant ship building and the production of aircraft, tanks, iron ore, food and timber all took precedence over army manpower.

ADM 1/8540/263 has material on the release of miners from the armed forces in October, 1918.

AIR 1/1287–8 cover RFC personnel requirements, 1916–17.

AIR 2 has a little material on manpower including points put to the Manpower Distribution Board by the Air Board in 1916 (AIR 2/47/AB 127/4); and a 1918 report on British manpower by a representative of the French Ministry of War with comments by the Chief of the Air Staff (AIR 2/82/B 4540).

BT 13/60 deals with labour requirements in arms factories, 1914.

BT 15 contains material on supply of labour to arms factories, 1914 (BT 15/60), and has some papers of the Manpower Distribution Board, 1916 (BT 15/72).

CAB 1/19 has papers on the establishment of the Manpower Distribution Board (CAB 1/19), as well as other reports on manpower issues in 1915–17 (CAB 1/12, and 21–5). There is also an amended paper of the Cabinet Committee on Manpower from September 1915 (CAB 1/42).

CAB 17 includes some material on manpower, containing memoranda and correspondence on the supply of labour and from the Manpower Distribution Board, both from 1916 (CAB 17/153–4 and 156–7).

CAB 21, containing papers on issues considered by the War Cabinet and Cabinet, include files on a manpower conference in 1917 (CAB 21/23); and a report by the Director General on National Service, 1917 (CAB 21/24).

CAB 27 contains material from the four meetings of the War Cabinet Manpower Committee, 1917–18 (CAB 27/14), established in December 1917, and the earlier Cabinet Committee on the Size of the Army in 1916 (CAB 27/3).

CAB 37, containing copies of papers circulated to the Cabinet between 1880 and 1916, includes two reports from an earlier Cabinet Manpower Committee in 1915 (CAB 37/133/20 and 134/3).

CUST 49/386 has material on the issue of an 'Industrial Army'.

HO 45 contains some files relating to the National Registration Act in 1915 (HO 45/286162) and the subsequent Committee on National Registration, 1916–17 (HO 45/339302).

MT 9/1084 deals with manpower requirements for the Mercantile Marine, 1917.

NATS 1 contains the records of the Ministry of National Service. The ministry had eight internal divisions: Secretariat, Finance Department, Statistics Department, Trade Exemptions Department, Labour Supply Department, Recruiting Department, Registration or Recording Department, and the Women's Work Department. The divisions were overseen by the minister and departmental heads sitting on the National Service Council. From November 1917 there were also 10 separate regional headquarters further sub-divided into areas with regional directors supervising deputy directors of recruiting, commissioners of medical services, and deputy controllers of registration and of statistics.

There are papers from the ministry's Finance and Organisation Branch (NATS 1/1–212), and from its Recording Department (NATS 1/377–401). Policy and co-ordination files (NATS 1/213–376), include records of the Manpower Distribution Board (NATS 1/326–7), the National Service Council (NATS 1/337–52) and reports on various manpower conferences with trade unions and other organisations (NATS 1/356–76). Among the latter can be found files on labour dilution (NATS 1/231), and consideration of those manpower planning proposals that might cause labour unrest (NATS 1/232). Files on labour supply policy (NATS 1/402–76) include the reports of regional committees dealing with the discharge of munitions workers (NATS 1/432–43), and more files on dilution (NATS 1/444, 453–4 and 456). These can be supplemented by the records of the Labour Supply Department (NATS 1/477–710), which include material on Controlled Establishments (NATS 1/614–21), Trade Committees (NATS 1/581–603 and 622–49) and part-time labour (NATS 1/680–704). The War Work Voluntary Scheme is especially well represented (NATS 1/488–90, 492–7, 499–503, 507, 514, 516, 519, and 556–9). There are also the records of the Secretariat (NATS 1/1063–1114).

PRO 10 includes specimens of Ministry of National Service documents destroyed (PRO 10/49–53) as well as others, which escaped destruction by transfer to the Ministry of Pensions (PRO 10/1107–8). Further specimens (PRO 10/474) have since been lost.

PRO 30/57/73–4, among Kitchener's Papers, include material on the early attempts to determine manpower policy in 1914–16.

T 172 contains papers of the Treasury's Intelligence Department relating to unemployment issues in 1914–15 (T 172/165–78 and 191–8).

Labour

Determining manpower policies, in turn, led to direct involvement in labour relations. War, of course, distorted the normal working of the labour market, effectively restructuring it in complex ways. Clearly, there were winners and losers. The most obvious winners were likely to be those involved in war production, some businessmen and traders. The likely losers were those in non-essential employment, those on fixed incomes and marginal groups such as the elderly. In the process, socio-economic differentials were likely to be narrowed, but older inequalities would remain alongside newer divisions thrown up by war. Differentials between the skilled and unskilled were certainly eroded since labour rather than skill was what was predominantly required.

Through the need of the state to ensure war production, the position of labour within society generally improved in the short term, not least through the increase in trade union membership and the establishment of larger unions through wartime amalgamation. Generally the war resulted in lower working hours and higher wages. What mattered, however, to the individual was the actual purchasing power of wages in relation to wartime inflation, and the amount of disposable income available. Inflation did not affect all commodities uniformly, food and clothing prices rising far faster than those for fuel. Yet, an average increase in retail prices of perhaps 25 to 30 per cent a year still represented a considerable break from the pre-war experience of increases of only 1 or 2 per cent a year.

All statistics, however, need to be treated with care because averages tend to hide considerable differences between one industry and another, and there could be wide variations even within the same industry. Wage data is equally difficult to calculate given the additional complication of piece-rates, time-rates, bonuses, overtime payments and other variations. Moreover, wartime gains were not always sustained.

The first substantial state intervention in the labour market was an agreement on dilution. The Crayford Agreement was directly negotiated in November 1914 between the Engineering Employers Federation and the unions. In March 1915, however, the government itself negotiated the Shells and Fuses Agreement in March 1915 to speed dilution. Following the recommendations of the Board of Trade's Committee on Production, the so-called Treasury Agreements were then reached with 35 unions to prevent workers taking advantage of their strengthened position: they outlawed strikes, introduced more flexible working practices, permitted dilution on war work, and referred industrial disputes to official arbitration. Under the first agreement, employers had promised not to use dilution as a means of reducing employment or wages after the war and, by the second, promised restraint of business profits.

These voluntary agreements were incorporated in the statutory provisions of the Munitions of War Act in June 1915, clause VII of which effectively tied workers to their place of employment, by preventing them from working for six weeks unless they obtained a leaving certificate from an employer first. While there was some resentment among workers that the legislation might be used to impose working conditions upon men, it provided for appeals to a munitions tribunal although only 26 per cent of appeals made by workers were successful. The Trade Card scheme introduced in late 1916 to exempt workers in war industries from conscription made the unions themselves responsible for determining exemption. Extended from engineering to other skilled unions, however, it was not actually put into effect since it was recognised as unworkable when unskilled workers were just as needed for war production.

Rising food prices, high rents, restricted labour mobility and wartime profiteering, however, all contributed to growing discontent on the factory floor which could not be controlled by the union hierarchies. The increasing significance of shop floor collective action organised by shop stewards was enhanced by the proliferation of government departments in the running of the economy, since there was little overall co-ordination and employers were generally encouraged to buy their way out of difficulties. Generally, the government learned to tread warily in the case of large-scale disputes enjoying popular local support. Like employers, unions increasingly viewed the intervention of the state in industrial relations as something to be avoided. Thus, in 1917, the proposals of the Committee on Relations between Employers and Employed, popularly known as the Whitley Committee, to establish widespread joint employer–labour consultative procedures, were ignored by both sides of industry.

Overall, Britain had by far the worst rate of militancy of any belligerent, with longer strikes and from an earlier date than elsewhere. However, there was far less militancy than during the peacetime industrial unrest of the period between 1910 and 1914: over 8,000 awards made by arbitration tribunals during the war were accepted without protest.

ADM 1 deals with proposed action against 'trade agitators' under DORA provisions in October 1915 (ADM 1/8436/331A), while there is also material on the establishment of the Shipyard Labour Board and the organisation and control of shipyards and marine engineering shops in February 1917 (ADM 1/8480/30 and 33). There are also papers on Shipyard Labour from May 1918 (ADM 1/8525/140). The grievances of carpenters and shipwrights in dockyards came under consideration in August 1917 (ADM 1/8497/196), while there had been a strike in Malta's dockyard in May 1917 (ADM 1/8500/221). When Arab and Somali workmen had declined to work on HMS *Dartmouth* in Simonstown, South Africa, in November 1914, permission had been sought to flog them (ADM 1/8404/450). There is also material on the use of civilian workmen behind the lines on the Western Front (ADM 1/8516/66).

ADM 116, the 'case' papers of the Admiralty Secretariat, includes material on labour problems at Rosyth Dockyard in 1916 (ADM 116/1545); the Shipyard Labour Department (ADM 116/1583); and skilled labour generally (ADM 116/1599B and 1743).

AIR 1 contains a little information on labour matters including notes by Colonel W. Sefton Brancker on his speech to employees of the Royal Aircraft Factory engaged in an industrial dispute in December 1914 (AIR 1/408/15/231/50); and a file on labour disputes involving aerodrome works and services, 1917–18 (AIR 1/2422/305/18/21).

AIR 2/1527–8 deal with wage clauses on contracts and contracts procedures, 1917–18.

BT 13 contains papers of the Committee on Trade Relations After the War, 1916 (BT 13/66), and the Coal Mines Contract Agreement, 1917 (BT 13/77).

CAB 1 addresses the issues of dilution on the Clyde and Tyne in March 1916 (CAB 1/17), as well as the application of the Munitions of War Act to Admiralty contractors (CAB 1/16–17).

CAB 21/29 deals with the Co-operative Movement, 1917.

DSIR 36/3 includes the results of enquiries made in 1915 into labour and trade difficulties in the glass industry.

HO 45 deals with Munitions of War Tribunals, 1915–16 (HO 45/290314) and the issue of whether or not 'peaceful persuasion' breached DORA regulations and therefore permitted the arrest of pickets outside munitions factories (HO 45/308532). The railway strike of September 1918 is also covered (HO 45/346578). There is also material on the Shop Committee in 1915 and a report on retail trades (HO 45/276947).

LAB 2 is a major source on wartime labour, the 'A' files, for example, dealing with Munitions Tribunals (LAB 2/51–6 and 65–6), including tables showing the results of cases dealt with between 1915 and 1918 by both central and local tribunals (LAB 2/65/1–2 and 66/1). Other 'A' files cover such general matters as the relationship between employers and employees, 1917 (LAB 2/11); draft amendments to the Munitions of War Act, 1918 (LAB 2/18–19); deputations and resolutions of the TUC Parliamentary Committee, 1917 (LAB 2/218/15); the creation of works' committees (LAB 2/254/11); labour unrest in 1917 (LAB 2/254/3–13), including reports to the commission of enquiry into the unrest from different areas (LAB 2/253/8); and disputes and 'sympathetic' disputes in the public services, 1918 (LAB 2/427/3–4).

Some specific matters covered include proceedings of a conference on hours and wages in shrapnel forging at the Vickers Naval Construction Works, 1917 (LAB 2/166/27); shipyard labour, 1917 (LAB 2/242/17); wages agreements for woodworkers in the aircraft industry, 1916–17 (LAB/254/2); labour unrest at the Hotchkiss factory in Coventry, 1917 (LAB 2/254/6); and the engineers' strike, 1917 (LAB 2/254/13). Intelligence Division files include material on 'Ca', 'Canny' and 'Stay' in strikes in South Wales, 1916–19 (LAB 2/544/13). There are also 'WA' (Waged Agreement) and 'IR' files, which give a great deal of information on arbitration in particular disputes in such trades and industries as the building trade (LAB 2/4–8); boot and shoe trade (LAB 2/26–7); shipbuilding (LAB 2/36–9); iron and steel (LAB 2/40–46); engineering, shipbuilding and boilermaking (LAB 2/70–72); brass (LAB 2/73–4); mining (LAB 2/76–8); gas (LAB 2/80–84); painting and decorating (LAB 2/90–93); tramways (LAB 2/99–101); engineering (LAB 2/103–18); docks (LAB 2/120–22); railways (LAB 2/153–4); electrical engineering (LAB 2/157–60); steel (LAB 2/165–7); aircraft manufacturing (LAB 2/185–6); general labouring (LAB 2/193–7); and munitions (LAB 2/243–55 and 420–27).

Individual files themselves deal with such issues as representations by the

Rushden branch of the National Union of Boot and Shoe Operatives on behalf of workers cutting boots for the Serbian army in 1915 (LAB 2/26/15), and there are similar arbitration awards for others cutting boots for the Russian and Italian armies in 1916 (LAB 2/26/26–30 and 40). Examples from other industries or trades include the case brought by the Boilermakers against the Manchester Ship Canal Company, demanding parity with Merseyside wage rates in 1917 (LAB 2/71/19); the dispute between the National Woodworkers Aircraft Committee and the Ministry of Munitions on payment by results at the Aintree National Factory in 1918 (LAB 2/246/8); the threatened general stoppage by the Amalgamated Society of Engineers over the extension of bonuses to piece-rate workers in 1917 (LAB 2/247/8); the dispute over Sunday pay between the Scottish Oil Mineral Association and the Scottish Oil Workers Association, 1916–17 (LAB 2/2191); and a report for the War Cabinet on the labour situation at Cubitt and Siemens Brothers in Woolwich, 1918 (LAB 2/252/2). There is also a history of the Labour Section of the Ministry of Munitions compiled in 1920–21 (LAB 2/2194).

LAB 10 contains papers of the Industrial Relations Department of the Ministry of Labour, including a record of conferences held between the ministry and various labour organisations, 1917–21 (LAB 10/399), and the minutes of the Fair Wages Advisory Council, 1900–32 (LAB 10/650). Correspondence with Joint Industrial Councils, which cover the war years, include those of the London Cabinetmakers Conciliation Board (LAB 10/870); Local Authorities Non-Trading Services (Manual Workers); (LAB 10/880); Road Transport (LAB 10/882), Tramways (LAB 10/884); and Glass Manufacturing (LAB 10/885).

LAB 11 contains the records of trade boards established by the Board of Trade in 1909 and taken over by the ministry in 1917, which were originally intended to set minimum wage rates for specific industries. Those covering firms representative of specific trades for the war years are of the Paper Box, Tin Box, and Tailoring Trades (LAB 11/1577–9); Paper Box, Sugar Confectionery, and Cocoa Trades (LAB 11/1920–22); and Shirtmaking (LAB 11/2264).

LAB 34/14–18 contain the Trades Dispute Records Books for the war years, yielding analysis of returns of strikes and lockouts by industry, location and occupation with details of the number of workers affected, the period covered by the disputes, the causes and the outcome.

LAB 35 contains the minutes of trade boards, supplementing the information on individual firms found in LAB 11. Those relating to specific trades covering the war years are for Chain making (LAB 35/74–5); Hollow Ware (LAB 35/148); Lace Furnishing (LAB 35/166); Paper Boxes (LAB 35/223–4); Shirtmaking (LAB 35/332 and 340); Sugar Confectionery (LAB 35/349–50); Tailoring (LAB 35/356); and Tin Boxes (LAB 35/357).

LAB 98 contains records of the Statistical Department, responsibility for compilation of statistics being transferred from the Board of Trade in January 1917. Dealing with such matters as wage rates and hours of work, they are arranged by industry. Those covering the war years are for Non-ferrous Metals (LAB 98/6); Wool (LAB 98/8); Other Textiles (LAB 98/9); Tailoring, Boots and Shoes (LAB 98/10); Cocoa and Sugar Confectionery (LAB 98/13); and Retail Distribution (LAB 98/30).

MT 6/2468/9 includes the Board of Trade's views on War Office proposals raised in the War Cabinet Labour Committee, 1917.

MT 9/1083 deals with the labour available for shipbuilding and vacant berths for merchant seamen, December 1916.

MT 23 has a report on the South Wales coal strike, 1915 (MT 23/385); and material on whether men working in the port of Bristol were entitled to two days' leave in lieu of a deferred bank holiday (MT 23/813).

MT 25/6 contains a report on dock labour, 1917.

PT 1 has material on War Bonus Petitions from its staff, which led to the Murray Committee on the work of the Office, 1917–18 (PT 1/226–30). There is also the report of the Murray Committee itself (PT 1/37).

Women

It is well known that there were substantial increases in the number of women in employment during the war. Traditionally, of course, it has been said that this wartime participation enhanced the status of women to the extent that they received the vote in 1918. Generalisations about the perceptions of women, however, are extremely difficult and much rests on the assessment of whether women had a greater role both inside and outside the home after 1918, whether they valued themselves more highly, and how far they achieved greater opportunities for personal freedom. It also needs to be borne in mind that contemporaries had a different perception of emancipation than is now common: in 1914 it simply meant equal rights in the public sphere and not the wider autonomy now implied.

Initially, middle- and upper-class women responded to appeals to undertake voluntary efforts, such as assisting the 200,000 Belgian refugees who reached Britain in the autumn of 1914. This was an acceptable extension of traditional social service and a variety of support groups and comforts funds for refugees, servicemen, prisoners and those working-class women laid off in 1914 were created. Upper- and middle-class women also undertook the morality patrols by the Women's Police Service and the Women's Patrols Committee of the National Union of Women Workers in the vicinity of army camps, an activity then extended to factories by agreement with the Ministry of Munitions in July 1915.

Quasi-military organisations such as the Women's Emergency Corps and the Women's Volunteer Reserve were also created under the patronage of titled women. Traditionally, indeed, the British army had only employed women as nurses prior to 1914 and this pattern was continued by Queen Alexandra's Imperial Military Nursing Service (QAIMNS); the Territorial Force Nursing Service (TFNS); the Voluntary Aid Detachments (VADs), formed in 1909 and containing both men and women; and the aristocratic First Aid Nursing Yeomanry (FANY), formed in 1907.

There was considerable reluctance to use women in any other capacity, but their work in the munitions industry forced the army to reconsider. In April 1915, therefore, the Army Council authorised the employment of women as cooks and waitresses in Britain in Lady Londonderry's Women's Legion, which received official recognition in February 1916. It eventually numbered some 6,000 women. If women could replace men at home, then there was no logical reason why they should not do so overseas and, in March 1917, the first cooks of the new Women's Army Auxiliary Corps (WAAC) arrived in France. Unlike civilian volunteers such as the VADs and FANYs, the 41,000 women who served in the WAAC – renamed Queen Mary's Army Auxiliary Corps (QMAAC) on 9 April 1918 – were mostly working or lower middle class. Consequently, there was a tendency to view them as lacking the more altruistic patriotic motivations perceived in their social superiors. Indeed, the WAAC quickly earned a totally unjustified reputation for immorality. The corps was disbanded in May 1920, not being revived until the creation of the Auxiliary Territorial Service (ATS) in 1938. A Women's Royal Naval Service (WRNS) also came into existence in January 1918, having been approved in November 1917 after representations by Lady Rocksavage. It was followed by the Women's Royal Air Force (WRAF) in April 1918, but neither WRAF nor WRNS attracted quite the same hostility as the WAAC. From 10,000 members in April 1918, the WRAF grew to some 24,659 officers and airwomen by December 1918. The WRNS was wound up in October 1919, having mustered 438 officers and 5,054 ratings at peak strength.

ADM 1 deals with the introduction of women clerks and other female workers to the Navy in June 1915 (ADM 1/8425/181); but it also contains papers on Queen Alexandra's Royal Naval Nursing Service (QARNNS) from January 1917 (ADM 1/8479/14); the formation of the WRNS (ADM 1/8506/264, 8507/277–8 and 8508/281); and WRNS representation on courts of inquiry involving members of the corps (ADM 1/8533/220). There are also minutes and papers of the Co-ordinating Committee on Women's Corps (ADM 1/8507/278 and 8523/120). In 1921 former members of the WRNS were permitted to wear uniform when selling poppies in Trafalgar Square (ADM 1/8615/197), while special consideration was given to engraving WRNS medals in 1922 (ADM 1/8628/127).

ADM 104 contains records of nurses of the QARNNS and its reserve of civilian nurses enlisted for wartime service only. Details of QARNNS nursing sisters are arranged by date of appointment, the records including date of birth, date of entry and discharge, next of kin, annual report marks, sick leave, comments on character and ability, training qualifications and medal awards (ADM 104/161). There are also records of those signed up for wartime service in the QARNNS Reserve (ADM 104/162–5). The series also contains the nursing sisters' and wardmasters' establishment book, 1912–27, with details of names, ranks, dates of appointment, and date and reason for discharge and an index to establishments, whether hospital or barracks (ADM 104/96).

ADM 116 deals with the creation of the WRNS among the case papers of the Admiralty Secretariat (ADM 116/3739–41), while also containing further material on the WRNS in 1919 (ADM 116/1917–18), and on its organisation, uniform and allowances (ADM 116/3455).

ADM 318/1–556 comprise the personal files of officers commissioned in the WRNS, 1917–19, with the exception of those who resigned for personal reasons during 1918.

ADM 321/1–2 are manuscript registers of WRNS officers' appointments and promotions, 1917–19.

ADM 336/1–22 contain the ratings' registers of the WRNS, 1918–19, arranged alphabetically by official number (G1 to G6923) in 22 microfilmed volumes.

AIR 1 contains material on the case of the Hon. Violet Douglas-Pennant, dismissed as Commandant of the WRAF in 1918, which continued to reverberate until 1936 (AIR 1/2313/221/49). In addition, there are details of the constitution of and regulations for the WRAF (AIR 1/619/16/15/347); and a general file on the WRAF which includes information on pay, 1917–18 (AIR 1/106/15/9/284).

AIR 2 has more material on Violet Douglas-Pennant (AIR 2/11889–908). In addition, there are files on labour substitution of servicemen in all theatres in 1917 by women and coloured labourers (AIR 2/943); the creation of the WRAF (AIR 2/93/CW 1528, 94/CW 5788 and CW 12318); the authority for recruiting the WRNS, WRAF and QMAAC (AIR 2/70/A 6347); the establishment of an RAF nursing service (AIR 2/93/CW 66031); minutes of a joint committee of the Air Board and the Ministry of Munitions on training women for the RFC (AIR 2/11/87/Instruction/404); minutes of a conference between representatives of the QMAAC, WRNS, WRAF and the Ministry of Labour on women's recruitment in 1918 (AIR 2/93/CW 1898); and papers on the demobilisation of the WRAF (AIR 2/122/B 9511).

AIR 10, comprising Air Ministry publications, includes the constitution and regulations of the WRAF (AIR 10/4); and details on the voluntary transfer of personnel from the WRNS, WAAC and Women's Legion Motor Drivers to the WRAF (AIR 10/18).

AIR 80/1–268 contain the Airwomen's Records of the WRAF, 1917–18. No officers' files have survived. The record sheets vary, but can include physical description and details of how and where women were employed. They include both 'Mobile' and 'Immobile' members, the former being full-time members of the service who lived in camp or nearby accommodation and the latter part-time staff who resided at home.

HO 45 deals with women's police and women's patrols, 1914–18 (HO 45/309485), and is also concerned with members of the WAAC absent without leave, 1918 (HO 45/356503).

MEPO 2, comprising the general correspondence and papers of the Commissioner's Office, has some material on women's police. Women's patrols are covered as well as an enquiry on their functions received from New Zealand (MEPO 2/1608 and 1684), while there is also a file on the appropriateness of members of the patrols giving evidence in cases concerning gross indecency in Hyde Park in 1916 and their role in controlling prostitution in parks and open spaces (MEPO 2/1708 and 1720). There is also material on the London Women's Patrol Committee (MEPO 2/1710 and 1748). Absentees from the WAAC are also covered (MEPO 2/1743).

MEPO 13/56–6 have two photographs of women police in 1918, including one of them chasing boys bathing in the Serpentine in Hyde Park.

MH 106 contains selected wartime medical sheets of servicemen and women, illustrating the diversity of diseases contracted, injuries received and treatments prescribed, together with medical cards relating to individuals. Material on women's services includes individuals who served in VADs, the Scottish Women's Hospital, Women's League, WRNS, QMAAC, and as Nursing Sisters (MH 106/2207–11).

NATS 1 contains a number of files relating to women's services including memoranda on women's patrols by Miss V. Markham, as well as material on a proposed National Corps of Women Workers (NATS 1/272); material on the WAAC, including the problem of too many women employed in the cotton trade enlisting in it, publicity generally, a recruiting campaign in Wales and the early history of the WAAC (NATS 1/1268, 1273, 1279, 1286, and 1299–301). There is also material on the WRAF (NATS 1/1280); the WRNS (NATS 1/1304); VADs (NATS 1/1283); and volunteer female motor drivers (NATS 1/1292).

TS 28/3 contains papers on the House of Lords Select Committee on the WRAF, 1919–20, and its investigation of the dismissal of Violet Douglas-Pennant as Commandant and of her allegations of immorality in the force.

WO 32 has material on the War Office's Committee on the Supply of Nurses, 1916–17 (WO 32/9342–4), while it also deals with the creation of the Duchess of Westminster's hospital in France in 1914 (WO 32/11226). There are also papers on the introduction of female labour into all army units serving at home in 1917 (WO 32/5530); the decision as to whether women served on a civil or military basis (WO 32/5253); recruitment, pay and conditions of women taking over army duties, 1916–17 (WO 32/5250–51); rates of pay for female forage guards, 1917–18 (WO 32/5531); women's entitlement to disablement compensation (WO 32/5255); administrative support for the women's services (WO 32/5254); and proposals on the uniforms and badges for those women holding the equivalent of commissioned rank (WO 32/5252). A somewhat minor issue was the design of a cap badge for women members of the Navy and Army Canteen Board, forerunner of the NAAFI (WO 32/5503), while there is also material on the post-war formation of an association for wartime commissioned women, 1919–20 (WO 32/13950).

WO 95/84–5 comprise the unit war diaries of the WAAC and QMAAC attached to the BEF in France.

WO 145/1 includes a register of nurses who were recipients of the Royal Red Cross.

WO 162, containing the papers of the Adjutant General's Department, includes an incomplete nominal roll of the WAAC (WO 162/16); a list of women drivers employed by the Corps (WO 162/62); and recommendations for honours and awards (WO 162/65). In addition, however, there is much material on women's service in the army generally, including the report of the Women's Services Committee, chaired by Sir George Newman, in 1916 (WO 162/30). Records of conferences include that held on women's military employment in January 1917 (WO 162/31–4); meetings of the Co-ordinating Conferences on Women's Corps, 1918–19 (WO 162/40); a conference on the WAAC in June 1917 (WO 162/56); and a conference with the Ministry of Labour on the QMAAC (WO 162/42). There is also general correspondence on women's employment (WO 162/37); and on the employment of VADs (WO 162/36).

Material on recruitment covers that for women workers to be attached to the American Expeditionary Force (WO 162/34) and the RFC (WO 162/60); as well as more general recruiting of the WAAC and QMAAC (WO 162/45, 48 and 55); and transfer of personnel to the WRNS and WRAF (WO 162/44). Conditions in France for the WAAC, including hostels and accommodation, and various visits to WAAC and QMAAC units are also covered (WO 162/39, 47, and 63–4). There is also material on the discharge and demobilisation of members of the QMAAC and on possible post-war overseas resettlement (WO 162/51 and 53–4), including a report on the Women War Workers' Resettlement Committee, November 1918 (WO 162/41).

WO 329, comprising the medal rolls for the First World War, includes those awarded women who served in the QAIMNS and its Reserve, TFNS, VADs, WAAC, and the British and French Red Cross organisations.

WO 398/1–240 contain the microfilmed records of the members of the WAAC and QMAAC, 1917–20.

WO 399/1–15792 comprise nursing service records of the TFNS and QAIMNS, 1902–22, from the correspondence files of the Directorates of Army Medical Services and Territorial Force. The files are arranged alphabetically but split between the 2/ series, which primarily concern the QAIMNS, and the 9/ series, originally opened for Territorial correspondence generally, but which concerns only the TFNS.

Primarily, it was entry to the war economy by working-class women rather than voluntary activity on the part of middle- and upper-class women which, at least in theory, provided the greatest opportunity to change the perception of women's role in society.

Women had largely ceased to be a significant element in the British pre-war agricultural labour force. Accordingly, there was a quasi-military aspect to the attempt to recruit more women to undertake agricultural work. Women's War Agricultural Committees were established to draw up a voluntary register of women willing to work on the land but the results were limited. The same was true of the Board of Agriculture's Women's National Land Service Corps of February 1916, although efforts were supplemented by private organisations such as the Women's Defence Relief Corps, the Women's Legion Agricultural Branch and the Women's Farm and Garden Union.

In March 1917 a new Women's Land Army emerged, with the intention of providing a permanent skilled and mobile female labour force for work on farms and in forestry, although a separate Women's Forestry Corps continued to be administered by the Board of Trade. Significantly, Land Army members, numbering only about 16,000 by September 1918, were paid less than unskilled male agricultural labourers, although an elaborate welfare network was created for them.

BT 71/3 contains some material on women's work on timber production among the papers of the Timber Supply Department, 1917–19.

MAF 42 contains papers on the Women's Land Army, Women's Legion Agricultural Section, and Women's War Agricultural Committees (MAF 42/8), the work of which was co-ordinated by the Women's Branch of the Food Production Department established in January 1917. There are also papers on the appointment of the Cripps Committee and its report in 1918 (MAF 42/15), and the transfer of responsibility for dealing with the Federation of Women's Institutes to the Board of Agriculture, 1917–19 (MAF 42/17), the central administration of the WI having been transferred to the Women's Branch of the Food Production Deportment from the Agricultural Organisation Society in October 1917. The WI returned to self-government under the financial auspices of the Development Commission in 1919.

MAF 59/1–3 contain records of the Women's Land Army, including details of Women's County Committees, a handbook, and miscellaneous articles and photographs.

NATS 1 has some material on women agricultural workers, including the Scottish Women's Land Army Scheme in 1918 (NATS 1/560–64 and 1203), the recruiting campaign for the Women's Agricultural Volunteers in Wales (NATS 1/1279), and the Women's Land Army generally (NATS 1/1308 and 1319). There is also discussion of the transfer of women from munitions work to agricultural work in 1918 (NATS 1/549–50).

Before the war the most common employment for women had been in domestic service. Relatively large numbers had also been employed in millinery, dressmaking, pottery, weaving and light industrial work in the North and Midlands. Many women were employed casually in terms of 'sweated trades', child minding, taking in washing and in agricultural work, but such 'invisible' employment was not recorded in the census returns. About 90 per cent of the women employed before the war were single and overwhelmingly working class.

In the first 12 months, while some 400,000 women came into employment, so did a million men since the first recourse of employers was to unemployed men. Moreover, women had been worse hit than men by the initial increase in unemployment, with possibly 44.4 per cent of the female labour force out of work in September 1914. Positive recruitment of women came only after the establishment of the Ministry of Munitions and, especially, after the introduction of conscription in January 1916. Thus, in incorporating re-employment, official statistics tend to imply a larger increase in women's employment than was actually the case. Moreover, increases of women employed in some areas resulted from decreases elsewhere, as better pay available in war industries lured women from traditional and 'invisible' employment.

Figures vary but the number of women in paid employment may have risen from 5.9 million to 7.3 million, representing a wartime increase of 1.4 million. Particularly large increases were recorded in transport, commerce and administration, where women were far more acceptable. In fact, approximately half of the women brought into employment to substitute for men in uniform were employed in commerce rather than industrial occupations. Indeed, the number of women employed in industry increased only from 2.1 million to 2.9 million, representing an increase from 26.1 per cent of the total labour force to 36.1 per cent. The majority of the 'new' women who entered employment during the war were either working-class women entering the work force earlier than might have been the case previously, or married women returning to employment.

Wartime propaganda exaggerated the extent of dilution, especially in the munitions industry, as did the greater visibility of women in public transport. Unions and employers alike resisted dilution and women were employed for very specific functions. In practical terms, dilution was not substitution *per se*, but a reorganisation of working practices so that the unskilled could perform more tasks. Women's war work certainly did not mean equal pay, which government and unions alike had resisted. Indeed, while a Ministry of Munitions circular, L2, of October 1915 appeared to suggest that women should get the same pay as men, this was only a requirement where women did not require supervision. Only in munitions work did women's pay keep pace with inflation, but it was still less than that of men.

At the end of the war, the numbers of women employed in industry began to decline rapidly. Some 750,000 women were made redundant by the end of 1918 alone and two thirds of those who had entered employment during the war had left it by 1920. The decline was even greater in more traditional areas such as the textile industry and domestic service. By contrast, the number of women increased in newer industries such as chemicals and light engineering. To some extent, women also maintained their wartime position in white collar work, although here, too, there was competition from ex-servicemen.

It was assumed that women would return to the home and wartime regulations were changed so that women visiting labour exchanges would find it difficult to insist on industrial or even office employment on pain of losing unemployment benefit and there was considerable government propaganda to reinforce the desirability of domesticity and the concept of a marriage bar. Moreover, the achievement of the franchise tended to fragment the women's movement and left women without an effective political voice. Even the extension of the franchise can be seen as a war measure rather than a women's measure. The argument for electoral reform was the potential disenfranchisement of men, who had lost their residence qualification of 12 months' continuous occupation through service overseas; the need to reward those without the vote who had fought for their country; and the need to allow all those who had contributed to the victory to determine the future. The eventual legislation enfranchised some 7 million women over the age of 30 in 1918, who were either ratepayers or married to ratepayers. With some 5 million or so women over the age of 21 excluded from the new franchise, the terms ensured that women would not be a majority of the electorate.

ACT 1 contains table of sickness experienced among women, 1916–17 (ACT 1/9); and considers the provision of allowances to women before and after confinement in the light of an inquiry by the War Cabinet Committee on Women in Industry, 1918 (ACT 1/65). In addition, there is a report by the Ministry of Reconstruction on the financial aspects of a proposed scheme of pensions for mothers (ACT 1/66).

AIR 2 has some material on the wider employment of female labour including a report on women in London factories, 1916–17 (AIR 2/10/87/9035), and material on the engagement of women as factory examiners (AIR 2/11/87/ID/192).

CUST 49/408 includes, among the board's registered papers, the report of a committee on female substitution, 1915–17.

FD 4/16 is concerned with labour wastage among women munitions workers.

HO 45/300791 deals with the appointment of women factory inspectors, 1915–18.

HO 185/258, among the papers of the Ministry of Munitions Control Board (Liquor Traffic) and State Management Districts Central Office, has the minutes of the Women's Advisory Committee and Women's Service Committee.

KV 1/50, a report by the H Branch (Organisation and Administration) of MI5 prepared in 1921, includes a supplement on women's work for the bureau.

LAB 2 has much material on the employment of women, particularly in relation to trades and industrial disputes. The 'A' files include general information, for example, on women's wages in munitions factories in 1918 and the proceedings of a conference between the Ministry of Labour and the Joint Committee of Women's Trade Unions in the same year (LAB 2/426/2). The 'WA' and 'IR' files dealing with disputes in different industries and trades include, for example, files on the National Union of Boot and Shoe Operatives' case against the Federated Association of Manufacturers over the employment of women in 1915 (LAB 2/26/18); a dispute in the Humber Brass and Copper Works, Hull, in 1916 on the employment of women for work usually done by men and boys (LAB 2/73/17); and another in the aircraft woodworking industry, 1917–18, in which the Amalgamated Society of Engineers similarly objected to women undertaking the work of skilled men (LAB 2/246/5). Women's wages in Admiralty firms are also covered (LAB 2/249/3); as well as wage orders and regulations for women in controlled and uncontrolled firms producing munitions, 1917–18 (LAB 2/243/12–14).

LAB 5 contains the papers of the War Cabinet Committee on Women in Industry and of its Physiological Sub-committee, 1917–19. They include verbatim reports of meetings between October 1918 and February 1919; charts showing comparisons between men and women in industry; reports on the women's welfare organisation at Messrs Armstrong, Whitworth & Co.; and the working of the block system at the London Omnibus Co. (LAB 5/1). There are reports of the Physiological Sub-committee in October and November 1918 (LAB 5/2); and the printed report of the Committee, including appendices and summaries of evidence (Cmd. 135 and 167) (LAB 5/3). In addition, there is a draft memorandum on hours of employment of women and young persons in wartime factories dating from November 1917 (LAB 5/4).

LAB 15, the records of the Ministry's Factory Department and Inspectorate, contains a memorandum of guidance to local committees and local advisory committees for the inspection of lodgings arising from the work of the Board of Trade Advisory Committee on Women's War Employment (Industrial), 1916 (LAB 15/93). In addition, there is a report of a conference of employers, operatives and inspectors on the substitution of female for male labour in the bleaching, dyeing and printing works of Messrs J. Jackson, 1916 (LAB 15/94); reports, including statistics on the increase in women's employment, 1916–18 (LAB 15/96); and another copy of the draft memorandum on the hours of employment for women and young persons in war factories (LAB 15/96).

MT 6 contains material on female labour on the Glasgow and South Western Railway, 1915–17 (MT 6/2454/12); and also deals with women tramway drivers, 1915–18 (MT 6/250/1).

MT 9 has material on the inquiry by the British Legion in 1931 on the role played by British women during the war (MT 9/2049), and a roll of honour of women who died while serving with the mercantile marine (MT 9/1589).

MT 23/652 deals with war bonuses paid to temporary women clerks in the Admiralty's Transport Department, 1916.

MUN 3, containing specimens of documents subsequently destroyed, includes material on the loan of exhibits and photographs for an exhibition of women's war work (MUN 3/273–6). They include examples from Messrs Smith and Coventry Ltd of Manchester, machine tool makers, from March 1917 to June 1919 (MUN 3/273); Messrs Mellor, Bronley & Co., engineers from Leicester, May 1917 (MUN 3/275); and Messrs G. Beaton & Co., engineers from West London, also dating from May 1917 (MUN 3/276).

MUN 4, comprising the records of the Central Registry of the Ministry of Munitions, has no specific records group covering women's experience, but contains much of value. Wage rates for women, for example, are considered (MUN 4/126, 3896, 3914, and 2020); as well as maximum working hours (MUN 4/534). There is more general material (MUN 4/3646), and the report of the Women's Employment Committee (MUN 4/6361).

MUN 5, containing the records of the Ministry of Munitions' Historical Branch, includes considerable information on women among the files dealing with labour generally (MUN 5/48–102 and 346–53). Particularly useful material (MUN 5/81–9) includes such items as a memorandum on the post-war regulation of women's wages by the Industrial Group of Reconstruction Sub-committee on Women's Employment, March 1917 (MUN 5/81); the awards of arbitration tribunals on women's wages (MUN 5/82 and 89); press statements on women's wages (MUN 5/83); minutes of the War Cabinet's Committee on Women in Industry (MUN 5/84–5) and its Physiological Sub-committee (MUN 5/87); and another copy of the final report of the War Cabinet Committee on Women in Industry (MUN 5/89).

NATS 1 contains a wide ranging selection of material on women's war work (especially NATS 1/1267–320), some of which has already been mentioned in the context of women's services and agriculture. In addition, files cover such issues as the proposed National Corps of Women Workers (NATS 1/1270); women's dock labour in Newhaven (NATS 1/1274); provision of female labour in support of the American Expeditionary Force in France (NATS 1/1277); women's welfare while accommodated in camps (NATS 1/1312); and the work of the Women's Section of the National Service Department, which includes examples of posters (NATS 1/1318). There is also a report on female substitution by HM Inspector of Factories covering the period from June to December 1917 (NATS 1/985); and a file on the employment of women by the National Gas Council (NATS 1/1171).

RECO 1 contains papers of the Women's Housing Sub-committee of the ministry's Advisory Council (RECO 1/618–38), and the report of the Women's Employment Committee (RECO 1/885).

SUPP 5/861, amid records relating to the Royal Arsenal, Woolwich and the Royal Gunpowder Factory, Waltham Abbey, has photographs of women war workers at Waltham Abbey.

T 172/273 includes, among miscellaneous papers prepared in the office of the Chancellor of Exchequer, material on a conference on Women's War Savings, 1916.

WO 142/263 includes a report compiled in 1918 on the work of women in the Anti-Gas Department at Porton Down among the records of the Chemical Warfare Department of the Ministry of Munitions.

Food Supply

While labour disputes and strikes might take on an increasingly political hue as the war progressed, most were essentially about the relationship between wages and prices, especially the price of food. In this respect, as might be expected, urban areas were more vulnerable than rural areas, especially through the migration of additional population attracted by wartime employment opportunities. Accordingly, prices were likely to increase at a greater rate in major urban centres than elsewhere.

British agriculture faced many difficulties, with farms expected to produce more food with fewer workers and fewer horses. Farmers themselves, however, tended not to enlist and skilled agricultural workers enjoyed a degree of protectionism, with the result that it was mostly the unskilled whose labour was lost. Conceivably, the agricultural labour force declined by only a tenth by the end of 1916 rather than the third usually assumed. In addition to women, school children, soldiers and prisoners of war made up some of the deficiency.

ADM 1/8400/893 deals with remuneration for Boy Scouts undertaking wartime duties, 1914.

ED 10/73–5 deal with contributions of school children to the war effort in 1917–18 through the collection of fruit, horse chestnuts and waste paper.

ED 11/78 and **142** deal with the employment of children in agriculture.

ED 12/14–16 and **26** deal with schools assisting in growing food and cutting wood.

ED 24/2031–2 deal with children's collection of chestnuts and acorns.

HO 45 deals with the use of prisoners of war in agriculture, 1916–18 (HO 45/340700), and the sale of horses from agricultural holdings, 1917–18 (HO 45/347571). The efforts of reformatory and industrial schools to increase food production, 1917–19, are also covered (HO 45/326192).

MAF 62/1–5A contain the records of the Agricultural Wages Board, 1917–18, including wage regulations and district wage committees.

NATS 1 contains papers on Harvest Camps, 1917–18 (NATS 1/650–79), and on the use of Boy Scouts for agricultural and other labour (NATS 1/705–10). There is also discussion of the state of agricultural employment in 1918 (NATS 1/241), and discussion of the use of prisoners of war, together with papers of the Ministry's Prisoner of War Employment Committee (NATS 1/567–71 and 1331).

Britain needed to import about 60 per cent of its food requirements in 1914, including 80 per cent of the wheat upon which much of the population depended as a staple. Initially, however, in common with the 'business as usual' approach, there was little intervention in agriculture, although controls were introduced to secure the continued importation of commodities such as sugar, grains and meat. Nonetheless, other interventionist policies were rejected, including a suggestion by the Milner Committee to encourage more domestic cereal production through guaranteeing minimum prices for wheat in August 1915, and the proposal for a compulsory plough policy in March 1916.

The poor North American wheat harvest in 1916 forced a re-evaluation and a Food Production Department of the Board of Agriculture was instituted in January 1917. Subsequently, the Corn Production Act of August 1917 guaranteed minimum prices for wheat, oats and potatoes to encourage investment by farmers, as well as guaranteeing minimum wages through an Agricultural Wages Board. The opposition to ploughing pasture, however, was considerable at a time when livestock prices were rising, and farmers were often tempted to plough poorer soils which had little yield. In some cases, farmers could not respond to the government directives channelled to them through the County Agricultural Executive Committees, which had been formed in 1915, if the resources to meet them were lacking. Nonetheless, under what now became a compulsory plough policy, an additional 2.1 million acres were cultivated. By 1918, the wheat and potato crops were 40 per cent above pre-war averages and reliance upon imports was reduced.

Yet, the achievement was modest: it has been calculated that the percentage of home grown food increased by barely 1 per cent. Britain could feed itself for an additional 30 days a year by 1918, domestic grain output now satisfying 16 weeks of the year's need. Nonetheless, the essential stability in production meant that the calorie level of the average British diet had declined by only 3 per cent, although the protein intake had declined by 6 per cent.

AIR 2/76/B 301 deals with the work of the Canadian Forestry Corps on behalf of the RFC.

BT 13 contains papers of the Board of Trade's Establishment Department but go beyond staffing matters to cover the responsibilities of the Board as a whole. Files covering the war years have considerable information on meat imports, particularly from Argentina and Australia (BT 13/59–63, 65, 67, 69, 72, 80–81, 86, and 91). Some files also cover timber supplies and related products such as paper and wood pulp (BT 13/79, 84–5, 89–90), and cotton supplies (BT 13/65). Shipments of both meat and dairy produce from New Zealand from 1915–19 are also covered (BT 13/79 and 90) as well as a horse census in 1917 (BT 13/79). There are some papers of the Fish Oil Committee, 1916 (BT 13/69) and on the fish purchase scheme, 1916 (BT 13/71).

BT 55/29–31 contain the papers of the Flax Control Board of the Board of Agriculture, established in December 1917 to promote the cultivation of 10,000 acres of flax fibre. The Flax Production Branch succeeded the Board in the management of the scheme and took over responsibility for those organisations previously responsible for flax production such as the British Flax and Hemp Growers Society, which had operated under the auspices of the Development Commission with the assistance of the War Office. A Central Committee of Flax Production also assisted in the board's work. The papers include flax and flax seed orders, and flax supplies from Ireland and East Africa. In addition, they include papers of the board's Advisory Committees at Leslie, Yeovil, Selby, Spalding and Peterborough (BT 55/30). The branch was wound up in 1921.

BT 62/1–26 contain papers of the Controller of Trading Accounts of Board of Trade's Finance Department. The Controller was appointed in 1918 to administer accounts of trading services controlled by the Board during the war and, later, those transferred to the Board to be liquidated after the war. The appointment was discontinued in 1930. Among the papers are those of the Flax Seed Advisory Committee, 1918 (BT 62/3); files on fish and oil purchases from Scandinavia (BT 62/1, 12); and financial accounts of the Home Grown Timber Committee (BT 62/6).

BT 71 contains the papers of the Home Grown Timber Committee of the Board of Agriculture, 1915–17, the Timber Supply Department of the Board of Trade, 1917–18, and the latter's successor, the Timber Disposal Department. Established in November 1915, the Home Grown Timber Committee was intended to increase timber supplies for military needs. Originally involved in the purchase of woods and the erection of sawmills, it was given compulsory powers to acquire standing timber in April 1916. It was absorbed by the Directorate of Timber Supplies in March 1917, passing to the control of the Board of Trade in May 1917, being eventually wound up in 1922. Mostly the papers relate to labour questions, including the work of the Canadian Lumbermen's Battalion and the Canadian Forestry Corps as well as American, Portuguese and female labour (BT 71/1–4). Contracts negotiated for the purchase and sale of home grown timber are also included (BT 71/5–20). A history of the branch appears (BT 71/2), and notes on wartime timber supply compiled by C. W. Bird (BT 71/21).

CAB 1 includes material on the purchase of Dutch agricultural produce in 1916 (CAB 1/18); as well as information on food supplies in Egypt and the Sudan (CAB 1/22); and Colombian meat supplies (CAB 1/20).

CAB 17 contains miscellaneous correspondence on agriculture in 1916 (CAB 17/171), and correspondence with Lord Rhondda on food supply in 1918 (CAB 17/198).

CAB 21 contains material on the Cabinet Timber Supplies Committee established in May 1917 (CAB 21/80); a report of the Forestry Sub-committee of the Reconstruction Committee, 1917 (CAB 21/82); and a report on the use of wild birds' eggs (CAB 21/85).

CAB 27/11 has papers of the Cabinet's Committee on the Dutch Agricultural Agreement, 1917.

DSIR 36/2410 contains a report by the Royal Society Food (War) Committee on the availability and suitability of fatty acids for dietary use, May–September 1918.

MAF 10 contains Corn Returns, comprising weekly wartime inspection returns

(MAF 10/172–81), abstracts (MAF 10/254–8), and Factors' Corn Returns with summaries of dealers' transactions (MAF 10/309).

MAF 36 deals with commercial controls. Those records relating to the war years are for the Fertiliser Committee, 1915–17 (MAF 36/58–64), and the Seeds Advisory Committee, 1917–22 (MAF 36/223).

MAF 39 includes a variety of material on the workings of the Board of Agriculture during the war (MAF 39/5, and 10–11). In addition, there is a summary of emergency legislation (MAF 39/6); a history of the Food Production Department, 1917–19 (MAF 39/12); material on County and War Agricultural Committees (MAF 39/13 and 23); and on other departments and committees (MAF 39/24 and 64). Wartime departmental reorganisation is covered (MAF 39/42 and 94), as well as relations with the Treasury (MAF 39/168–79, and 188–90); reconstruction issues (MAF 39/327–8); and the work of the Board's permanent secretary from 1917–19, Sir A. D. Hall (MAF 39/89).

MAF 42 contains the records of the Board of Agriculture's Food Production Department. Policy making was assisted by the Advisory Committee of Food Production with executive functions discharged by County Agricultural Executive Committees appointed jointly by the President of the Board of Agriculture and advisory War Agricultural Committees. The papers include memoranda and circulars (MAF 42/1–7); material relating to the Milner Committee on food production, 1915 (MAF 42/9); departmental notes on food production (MAF 42/10); tractor purchases from the United States (MAF 42/11); internal staffing and organisational matters (MAF 42/12 and 14); and the opposition to ploughing across footpaths in Lincolnshire and Rutland (MAF 42/13). The Food Production Department was wound up in March 1919.

MAF 48 contains correspondence and papers on land issues. Orders for cultivation under DORA and the Corn Production Act are included (MAF 48/219–30) as well as further material on the Corn Production Act, including issues of compensation and revocation (MAF 48/231–6).

MAF 53/7–8 have papers on wartime deputations to the President of the Board of Agriculture, 1917–18.

MAF 60/1–577 contain the papers of the wartime Ministry of Food. Historical and documentary files compiled for the ministry's official history on commodities and costings are included (MAF 60/7–52). The papers of the ministry's permanent secretary from 1917–18, U. F. Wintour (MAF 60/53–86) include memoranda, material on the Inter-allied Food Council, military rations, and fodder for racehorses. In addition to Cabinet memoranda on food issues included among Wintour's papers, other Cabinet papers once in the custody of Lachlan MacLean are also in the series (MAF 60/87–92 and 113–14), as well as further material on the Inter-allied Food Council (MAF 60/149). There is a wealth of material on specific commodities such as eggs and poultry (MAF 60/137); potatoes (MAF 60/176, 357–8); dates (MAF 60/190); and milk (MAF 60/448). Committee papers (MAF 60/313–51, 360–61, 366–71, 570, and 575) include those of the Agricultural Costings Committee, Butter and Cheese Imports Committee, Fish Friers Trade Advisory Committee, Imports Board Shipping Committee, East India Tanned Kip Committee, Leather Supplies Committee, Feeding Stuffs Board, National Kitchens

Advisory Committee, Woollen Trade Committee, Rabbits, Game and Poultry Committee, and Milk Advisory Committee. Statistics, reports and other papers on the food situation can also be found (MAF 60/189, 562, and 565–6).

PRO 30/30/4–5, among some of Lord Milner's wartime papers, contain material on the Milner Committee on the Home Production of Food, 1915.

WORK 6/188/2–191/7 contain material on various schemes for flax growing, including the acquisition of premises for flax factories, 1918–20.

Coupled with the attempt to increase food production was the effort to control consumption. It had been assumed that ensuring a constant supply of food would stabilise prices, but this did not prove the case. A price spiral began almost at once from a combination of financial dislocation and panic buying: wheat prices were up by 80 per cent and meat prices by 40 per cent during the first 12 months of the war. Shipping shortages further drove up prices and, as prices rose, so it fuelled demands for increased wages. Self-regulation of business was much preferred to price fixing, and a modest public education programme and encouragement of allotments was preferred to either wage increases or rationing. Covert purchases by the Grain Supplies Committee were partly intended to arrest high prices by releasing grain on the market at less than cost price, but this became known to the private sector in March 1915 and the policy had to be abandoned in the face of strike action by wheat merchants. Public dissatisfaction resulted in the establishment of the Royal Commission on Wheat in October 1916 to control all grain purchasing abroad as the Royal Commission on Sugar Supplies had been doing for the sugar trade since August 1914. Both the wheat and sugar commissions were finally wound up in 1921.

BT 13 contains the 1917 report of a departmental committee on the causes of price rises since the outbreak of war (BT 13/73); as well as an earlier report of the Retail Coal Prices Committee, 1915 (BT 13/61); and material on the coal economy campaign, 1918 (BT 13/91)

CAB 1 includes a paper on the introduction of compulsory rationing dating from February 1918, as well as material on food supplies, and a report of the Ministry of Munitions Food Investigation Committee, January 1918 (CAB 1/26). An earlier report is concerned with the carriage of brewing materials and beer by rail in January 1917 (CAB 1/22).

CAB 21 contains the compulsory rationing scheme considered by the War Cabinet in 1917 (CAB 21/84); a report on a conference on food prices (CAB 21/86); and one on coal shortages among London's poor (CAB 21/87).

CO 537, comprising confidential correspondence, includes material on the proposed establishment of the International Food Board in 1917 (CO 537/1127); and on the wartime purchase of wool from South Africa (CO 537/1128–33), and of wool and wheat from Australia (CO 537/1135 and 1138). It also deals with the prohibition on the export of sugar in 1914 (CO 537/588).

FO 115 deals with purchase of meat and wool in the United States (FO 115/1919–20 and 2003–7).

LAB 2/274/1 is concerned with the retail price of food on 1 October 1918 and the increases in working-class expenditure since 1914 represented by it.

MAF 60 includes material on the Royal Commission on Wheat Supplies among Wintour's papers (MAF 60/61). There are also further papers on the Commission (MAF 60/427B–427D and 577), as well as papers on the Royal Commission on Sugar Supply (MAF 60/142). Wheat supplies, including the purchase of wheat from Australia, are dealt with (MAF 60/128 and 133), and sugar supply (MAF 60/141). There are also several files dealing with prices and subsidies (MAF 60/104–7, 159, and 258–66) as well as papers of the Inter-departmental Committee on Reduction of Food Prices, 1917–19 (MAF 60/146). Concerns at links between prices and industrial unrest are illustrated (MAF 60/372).

MT 9, the papers of the Board of Trade's Marine Department, includes material on the origins of the Wheat Commission (MT 9/1120); and shipments of wheat and flour from the United States in 1915 (MT 9/1001).

MT 23/651 contains, among papers of the Admiralty Transport Department, a letter from the National Association of Flour Importers on comparative ocean freight rates for carrying wheat and flour, 1916.

PRO 30/68 contains the papers of Sir Alan Garrett Anderson, vice chairman of the Royal Commission on Wheat Supplies. They include papers relating to the Royal Commission, including the purchase of Australian wheat, correspondence with the Food Controller, and estimated wheat and grain requirements (PRO 30/68/1–9). There are also further papers on wheat and the Royal Society Food (War) Committee, as well as a copy of the final commission report in 1921 (PRO 30/68/12–15). Anderson's role as representative of the Wheat Commission on the Balfour Mission to the United States from April to June 1917 is well represented (PRO 30/68/10–11), as is the work of the Food Council and material on coffee imports and bread prices in industrial areas (PRO 30/68/16–20).

T 172/339 contains Treasury papers on sugar supply in 1916.

Three months after the establishment of the Wheat Commission, Lord Devonport was appointed as first Food Controller of the new Ministry of Food. Devonport extended the food economy campaign and prepared for the introduction of rationing, the two themes being linked by encouragement of a voluntary rationing scheme in February 1917. Under continuing pressure, not least from the socialist War Emergency Workers' National Committee (WEWNC), his successor, Lord Rhondda, who had been given wider powers, introduced a bread subsidy in September 1917, together with a relaxation on brewing restrictions and a range of price controls.

It was intended to bring in sugar rationing in the autumn of 1917, but difficulties were encountered in establishing a workable system. Price controls also proved unpopular when they were set higher than the public wished, while some overseas traders took commodities to other markets. The only solution was compulsory rationing, a policy long advocated by the ministry's second permanent secretary, William Beveridge. Prompted by some local authorities taking matters into their own hands, nation-wide sugar rationing was introduced on 31 December 1917 followed by meat and fats in London and the home counties in February 1918. Rationing was then extended nation-wide in April. Local authorities were also tasked with ensuring priority supplies of food and milk for nursing mothers and children under five. Rationing achieved not so much a general reduction but a levelling of consumption. The result of the government's food policies overall, however, was that there was no serious food shortage and the supply of energy in the national diet remained adequate throughout the war.

BT 13 contains a few papers on the Tobacco and Matches Control Board (BT 13/90), while tobacco purchases are also covered (BT 13/86).

BT 72 contains papers of the Tobacco and Matches Control Board, 1917–19. Established by orders of June and September 1917, it administered restrictions on the importation, distribution and sale of tobacco and matches before being dissolved in 1919. There are statistical tables, memoranda and circulars, some dating back to 1916 (BT 72/1–2). A manuscript index to the papers originally held by the Board can be found elsewhere (BT 13/95/38633).

HO 45 deals with aspects of the rationing of meat and sugar (HO 45/314869 and 347805), and restrictions on the sale of sweets and ice cream at places of amusement after 8 p.m. (HO 45/335313).

MAF 60 contains a considerable amount of material on control of food and rationing. A history of rationing compiled in 1920 by Beveridge is to be found (MAF 60/108–9) and histories of the control of various commodities (MAF 60/456–76 and 573–4). Beveridge's diary as permanent secretary is included (MAF 60/302) and earlier papers of the Food Controller (MAF 60/127). The work of the local Food Control Committees is included (MAF 60/147, 236–9 and 428–33) with sample material from those at Crewe, Liverpool, Midhurst, Preston and Sawbridgeworth. General material on rationing includes ration scales (MAF 60/185–6, 195–203, 215–34, 242–5, and 554–60) and papers of the Committee on Rationing and Distribution (MAF 60/360).

MT 6/2459/3 deals with paper economy in 1917.

MT 9/1359 is concerned with the issue of ration books to merchant seamen, 1918–19.

NSC 7/37 deals with the promotion of the Food Control Campaign in 1916–17.

Social Values and Leisure

Apart from changing patterns of employment and consumption, war was also likely to change individuals' normal patterns of behaviour in varying ways. As suggested by the establishment of female morality police, wartime sexual mores in particular were often those which most concerned contemporaries. Prostitution and venereal disease were understandably of perennial concern to the military authorities, the WAAC and 'munitionettes' equally arousing fears that women would embrace male characteristics such as drunkenness and predatory sexual conduct. Contemporary perceptions did not necessarily correspond with reality. Nonetheless, there was a perceived change in attitudes among women as evidenced by the appearance in female fashion of shorter hairstyles, more make-up, lighter fabrics and shorter skirts. More women had also taken up smoking and alcohol although, in the case of alcohol, this went against a more general trend.

Inevitably, the increase in state intervention also affected individuals to a far greater extent than before, and in many different ways. At a minor level, the British experienced greater control of licensing laws in 1914, the average closing hour of public houses being brought forward from 12.30 a.m. to 10 p.m. Similarly, British summer time was introduced in May 1916. In fact general alcohol consumption was already in decline before the war and complete state purchase of the liquor trade was not implemented, but an estimated 95 per cent of the British population were affected in some way by the licensing activities of the Central Control Board (Liquor Traffic) by 1918. Licensed premises were actually taken over by the state in Enfield Lock, Carlisle and Gretna: these state-owned public houses were only sold off in the 1970s and licensing laws only relaxed in 1985. DORA's many restrictions included prohibition on public clocks chiming between sunset and sunrise, on whistling for taxi cabs between 10 p.m. and 7 a.m. and on loitering under railway arches.

Public leisure was also inevitably affected by war, although initially racing and football continued until 1915. Racing in particular lobbied vigorously for resumption through Lord Derby, Secretary of State for War, 1916–18. The University Boat Race was abandoned in 1915 and the Whitsun and August Bank Holidays cancelled in 1916. The holiday trade, however, survived remarkably well, the cancellation of bank holidays not lessening holiday crowds at seaside resorts.

Attendance at the infant cinema, dominated by American imports, increased in Britain up to around 20 million a week, embracing both middle and upper class audiences for the first time. In the same way, theatres which had been primarily frequented by the middle and upper class became popular with the working class. Music halls also remained immensely popular. Museum and gallery going also continued to the extent that the closure of those in London in 1916, largely as an economy measure, was partially rescinded though objects of major value were removed to other parts of the country as a precaution against air raids. Nevertheless, licensing restrictions and the imposition of more taxes upon places of entertainment in May 1916 had some effect on leisure patterns, the additional 2d on cinema tickets up to 1s 2d and 1d on seats up to 6d pushing the wealthier patrons into cheaper seats and pricing out many working-class patrons.

Escapism doubtless had a significant role in the determination to maintain leisure pursuits, but some feared cultural pollution from the measurable increases in dancing with American jazz and ragtime the basis for the development of popular new dances such as the foxtrot and the Charleston. Moreover, the cinema was blamed for the increase in juvenile delinquency, particularly among those aged 11 to 13. The National Council of Public Morals pointed more to the social and economic pressures of the war and, certainly, the absence of fathers on military service and the disruption of family life generally played its part. In fact, 'ordinary' crime declined, but there were new crimes such as failure to observe the blackout as well as increased fraud and profiteering. Like other statistics, however, crime figures are open to differing interpretations, especially when it was by no means the case that all crime was recorded.

ADM 1 contains evidence of restrictions such as the order that blinds be drawn in railway carriages at night, 1914 (ADM 1/8398/381); the prohibition of liquor in dockyards in December 1915 (ADM 1/8442/357); and the sea travel restrictions placed on women and children in the light of German unrestricted submarine warfare (ADM 1/8476/305 and 8516/63). There is a copy of the British Summer Time (Daylight Saving) Act, 1916 (ADM 1/8455/99), and consideration of the application of the entertainment tax to places of entertainment within barracks in May 1916 (ADM 1/8456/107).

AIR 1/721/46/4 and **6** deal with lighting restrictions, 1914–18.

AIR 2/85/B 6443 deals with the Summer Time Act and the intention to establish common time between all three services.

CAB 1/18 includes a paper on the postponement of elections until the end of the war.

CAB 21/113 contains a file on the campaign to resume horse-racing, 1918.

CUST 49/351 deals with oil fuel controls in 1915.

ED 11 deals with the effects of summer time on schools, 1916 (ED 11/29), and juvenile delinquency, 1914–17 (ED 11/114).

HO 45 deals with DORA regulations generally (HO 45/228849); licensing hours and liquor control (HO 45/258927, 264063, 271126, 276372); fire prevention and restrictions on fireworks (HO 45/260259); speed restrictions after dark and lighting restrictions (HO 45/269033, 300000, 302000, 305545, 321933, 371825); petrol restrictions (HO 45/310839); public meetings (HO 45/311932); the imposition of entertainment tax in co-operation with police and local authorities, 1916–19 (HO 45/311549); summer time (HO45/312364, 312899, and 357138); and early closing restrictions (HO 45/321012, 322255, and 330810).

Courts martial generally under DORA are covered (HO 45/271164), as well as powers to stop and search vehicles on public highways (HO 45/260888). Venereal disease among 'camp followers' is addressed (HO 45/251861) and, more generally (HO 45/307990 and 359931). The perceived increase in juvenile delinquency and other crime is also considered (HO 45/301145). Children committed to reformatories while their fathers were absent on war service and the role of reformatory schools in wartime generally are discussed (HO 45/260199 and 349984). Restrictions on the supply of cocaine and opium are also dealt with (HO 45/312966), while fraudulent claims by munitions workers for subsistence allowances feature (HO 45/357517). The suspension of jury service in wartime is also covered (HO 45/312306).

HO 185/1–353 contain the papers of the Central Control Board (Liquor Traffic) and the State Management Districts Central Office at Carlisle. Initially established to manage public houses in Carlisle in June 1915, it extended its reach to the surrounding area in 1916 and also to many other areas including Enfield Lock and Chepstow National Shipyard. Included are minutes; managers' reports; orders on liquor control; papers on opening hours (HO 185/239 and 257); reports on drinking by women and young people (HO 185/238); reports of beer consumption and brewing; reports of Chief Constables on the working of orders (HO 185/259–61); files on individual properties; papers on the canteen at Dormanstown Steel and Iron Works (HO 185/350); and compensation issues. The series includes a report on the overall working of liquor control, 1916–18 (HO 185/227); and the papers of Lord d'Abernon as the board's head, 1916–19 (HO 185/262–73, 353).

HO 190 contains the papers of the Carlisle District Office of the Central Control Board (Liquor Traffic). Files include papers on the purchase of raw materials; coffee carts for HM forces (HO 190/424–5); managers' reports; reports of the Public Houses Committee; trading accounts; the resistance of the Carlisle Licensed Victuallers' Association to government control (HO 190/482); minutes of the Local Advisory Committee; valuations; correspondence with the Chief Constable; reports and statistics on drunkenness (HO 190/822, and 1128–30); and the visit of HM King George V to Carlisle in May 1917 (HO 190/854). There are also files on individual properties managed by the Carlisle Office. Since state ownership of these properties extended well beyond the war, the majority (HO 190/948–1127, 1132–47, and 1238 onwards) are subject to the 75 year rule.

HO 358 has the minutes and papers of the Central Conference of Chief Constables, established in March 1918 as a result of increasing wartime demands upon policing. It met thereafter in May and November annually. The first wartime meetings are covered in HO 358/2.

MEPO 1/68 contains Out-letters from the Commissioner between April and December 1914.

MEPO 2, comprising general correspondence and papers of the Commissioner's Office, has much of interest relating to wartime policing in the metropolis. Matters covered include protection of reservoirs (MEPO 2/1611); liquor restrictions in theatres and evasions of liquor controls (MEPO 2/1620 and 1694); enforcement of shop closing orders (MEPO 2/1706); and considerable material on the duties of the Special Constabulary, particularly with reference to lighting restrictions (MEPO 2/1623–46). There is miscellaneous correspondence on such issues as horse-racing (MEPO 2/1679); indecency in cinemas, and the perceived effect of cinema on juveniles (MEPO 2/1691 and 1696); juvenile delinquency generally (MEPO 2/1699); drugging of soldiers on leave (MEPO 2/1698); disorderly houses (MEPO 2/1714); strike picketing (MEPO 2/1719); the withdrawal from sale of games of Crown and Anchor at the request of the War Office in 1917 (MEPO 2/1731); and investigation of unregistered war charities, including 'The Red Star Society' and 'Tubs for Tommies' (MEPO 2/1729 and 1732).

MEPO 3 consists of 'special series' of correspondence and papers. They include files on riots at the Brotherhood Church in Southgate Road in 1917 (MEPO 3/150); fraudulent collections for the so-called Queen Alexandra's Field Forge Fund (MEPO 3/252); the prohibition of women suffering from venereal disease from intercourse with members of the armed forces (MEPO 3/2434); and general policing (MEPO 3/2457)

MEPO 6/26–30 contain the registers of Habitual Criminals for the war years.

MEPO 20/1 is the register of murders and violent deaths covering the years 1912–17.

PREM 1/2 contains protests from Lord Derby and the National Workmen's Council on the continuing prohibition of horse-racing, 1917–18.

T 172/292–3 contain material on the imposition of entertainment tax in 1916.

TS 27/46 contains papers on the claim by a brewery against the government's acquisition of the Ordnance Arms at Enfield Lock, 1916–18.

WO 32 includes some files on the application of DORA, including amendments to the right of trial by jury, 1915 (WO 32/5526), and the recognition of the uniforms of specified boys' organisations as 'public non-military' (WO 32/5494–6). The preoccupation of the military authorities with the threat posed by venereal disease is also much in evidence (WO 32/4745, 5597, and 11401–4), the extension of DORA regulations to cover the post-demobilisation period attracting particular criticism from women's organisations (WO 32/11403).

State Welfare

If there was greater regulation of individual's lives, there were also potential longer-term benefits in the shift in emphasis from pre-war laissez-faire attitudes to an acknowledgement that government should provide, not only the resources for, but control over the provision of services previously left to charitable organisations. A kind of 'moral economy' dictated that sacrifice required, firstly, a measure of control over profits and perceived inequalities and, secondly, an appropriate reward rather than simply a restoration of the pre-war status quo. In the process, there was a certain paradox in that the kind of changes anticipated required a continuing role on the part of the state when, after the experience of war, many people wanted a diminution of state intervention.

The Factory Acts were waived for the duration, but the Health of Munitions Workers Committee of the Ministry of Munitions was empowered to inspect working premises. Over 900 factory canteens were established from the proceeds of the excess profits tax. The ministry also set up cloakrooms, washing facilities and day nurseries, of which 28 were in existence in 1917–18. It led the way in providing facilities for its own employees and spent some £4.3 million on housing for its workers, building 10,000 permanent homes on 38 sites such as the Well Hall estate in Woolwich and at Gretna in Dumfries.

Many of these changes were of direct benefit to women for, not only had they become more visible in industrial employment, but clearly ran the risks of TNT poisoning, from which 109 women died during the war, and of industrial accidents. An explosion at the national filling factory at Barnbow killed 35 women in December 1916 while many women were among the 69 fatalities in an explosion at Silvertown in East London in January 1917 and 35 women died in another at Chilwell in July 1918.

ADM 1/8507/273 contains the enquiry report on the massive explosion at Halifax, Nova Scotia, in December 1917 caused by the collision of SS *Mont Blanc* and SS *Imo*.

CAB 1 contains a number of reports considered by the Cabinet, including those on explosions at munitions factories at West Gorton in February 1916 (CAB 1/15), Woolwich in March 1916 (CAB 1/16), Faversham in April 1916 (CAB 1/17), and Pitsea and Wigan in May 1916 (CAB 1/18). There was also an explosion at an arms dump in Rouen in April 1916 (CAB 1/17).

CN 1/29 contains photographs of Halifax dockyard after the explosion in December 1917.

EF 2/3 contains reports by the Explosives Inspectorate of accidents on government property, 1917–18.

EF 5/18–20 contain reports by the Explosives Inspectorate on the Royal Gunpowder Factory at Waltham Abbey, 1878–1940, and on Government War Factories, 1914–18.

FD 4/13 contains reports on the diet of war workers, 1918.

HO 45 covers explosions or fires at wartime munitions factories including those at Bradford, Faversham, Ardeer, Heckmondwike and Morecambe (HO 45/104216, 109118, 249623, 271759, 271823, and 350619). The series also contains the proceedings of the committee on the explosion at Chilwell Munitions Factory, 1918 (HO 45/364648). Licensing of explosives factories is also covered (HO 45/298413).

LAB 14 contains health, safety and welfare records, some being transferred from the Home Office in 1940. They include the Munitions of War general order, 1916 (LAB 14/9); papers on the case of the ministry versus Mackey & Monks Ltd, 1917 (LAB 14/200); and the welfare order relating to Tin or Terne Plate Factories, 1917 (LAB 14/202). There are also minutes of the Chief Inspector of Factories' Work Committee, 1918 (LAB 14/15 and 19), and material on the end of emergency restrictions in National Shell Factories in 1918–19 (LAB 14/23 and 36).

LAB 15 contains records of the Factory Department and Inspectorate. General memoranda for 1915 are included (LAB 15/12) and the records of conferences of superintending inspectors, 1913–19 (LAB 15/65). Orders in force under both DORA and the Factories Act between 1917 and 1919 are detailed (LAB 15/102). In addition, there are papers of the inspectors' conference held on 8 February 1918 dealing with such issues as wartime hours of employment, village and rural industries, munitions tribunal fines, and standards for the future (LAB 15/105).

MT 6/2434/15 deals with the concerns of the Ministry of Munitions to suppress flashes from trolley wheels on electric railways.

MT 25/53 has details of the post-war sale of Chepstow National Shipyard.

POWE 26 covers DORA restrictions under Lighting, Heating and Power Emergency Orders as well as Fuel Wood and Household Fuel and Lighting Orders, 1916–19 (POWE 26/8 and 16).

POWE 33/5 has minutes of the Petroleum Ration Committee, 1917–18.

SUPP 5 deals with opening hours of public houses in the vicinity of Woolwich Arsenal in 1915 (SUPP 5/1049), and contains papers of the Committee on the Health of Munitions Workers, 1915–16 (SUPP 5/1051). Ignitions in the cordite presses at the Royal Gunpowder Factory, Waltham Abbey, in 1916–17 are covered (SUPP 5/331), and a report on the explosion at Messrs Kynoch in Durban, South Africa in 1916 can also be found (SUPP 5/333).

SUPP 28 includes general reference card material on accidents (SUPP 28/1–2), but also the results of the Home Office enquiry into the TNT explosion at the Hooley Hill Rubber and Chemical Company factory in June 1917 (SUPP 28/350–54).

TS 32, containing registered files dealing with Admiralty matters, includes more material on the post-war sale of the wartime housing and other buildings constructed at Chepstow National Shipyard (TS 32/31 and 52).

WO 32/18667 deals with the conveyance of explosives on passenger trains, 1914–15.

WORK 6 contains papers on the reconstruction, 1917–30, of part of the area destroyed by the explosion at Silvertown in 1917 (WORK 6/362/9); and the post-war transfer of responsibility for Ministry of Munitions housing estates and properties at the Chepstow National Shipyard to the Commissioner of Works (WORK 6/394/1 and 396/1).

Local authorities were encouraged to maintain milk supplies for mothers and babies and, in 1916, women working in the production of TNT were provided with a free daily pint of milk in the (mistaken) belief that it nullified its toxicity. The permissive Notification of Births Act (1907) was also amended in July 1915 to require compulsory registration of births within 36 hours, thus providing local authorities with information on which to act to ensure child health. Midwifery training also came under greater scrutiny with amendments to the Midwives Act (1902) in 1916 and the Maternity and Child Welfare Act in August 1918 required local authorities to establish formal committees to provide services for mothers and infants under five. The Rents and Mortgage Interest (Rent Restriction) Act of December 1915, though frequently evaded, was an attempt to control wartime rent increases, while problems with evictions experienced where there was a change of landlords subsequently brought the Increase of Rents and Mortgages (Amendment) Act in April 1918. It might also be noted that, while one of the few rights of British servicemen was to refuse inoculation, there was an official campaign in 1914 to persuade men to be vaccinated before going overseas. When too many declined, the concession was withdrawn by means of refusing leave to those not inoculated. Similarly, there was an official campaign to persuade younger recruits not to start smoking on health grounds.

BT 13/73 contains material on the legislation to restrict increases of rent and mortgage interest.

DV 1, comprising papers of the Central Midwives Board, includes the minutes of the Board, 1914–20 (DV1/6–8); the minutes of the Board's committees, 1912–18 (DV1/30–31).

DV 2/7–11 contain the Board's annual reports, 1914–18.

FD 4/11 contains reports on TNT poisoning.

HO 45 deals with powers taken to prevent creditors treating debtors too harshly in wartime (HO 45/262091), and with official concerns at the campaign by the British Union for the Abolition of Vivisection to encourage troops not be inoculated (HO 45/273078).

POWE 16 has material on the regulation of coal supplies and of coal prices under the Price of Coal (Limitation) Act 1915 (POWE 16/176), together with colliery trading accounts under the regulations (POWE 16/177).

POWE 26/2 is also concerned with the Price of Coal (Limitation) Act.

In educational terms, it had been intended to bring forward new legislation had not the war broken out in 1914, since there was a general consensus on the need to improve education further in view of the greater efficiency of German schools. Greater numbers of working-class children attended fee-paying secondary schools during the war, but, by 1917, an estimated 600,000 children had also left school early to take up wartime employment. A new Education Act was passed in 1918 but, with the onset of post-war economic difficulties, the continuation classes envisaged for those between the ages of 14 and 18 never materialised. The number of free places at secondary schools remained limited and there was no acceptance of the principle of universal secondary education.

ED 10 contains material on the 1918 Education Act (ED 10/21), and the views of the Board of Education on reconstruction issues (ED 10/77). Wartime supply of coal for schools is covered (ED 10/72), and that of books and stationery (ED 10/83–5). Supply of teachers is also covered (ED 10/76, 79–80 and 82).

ED 11/275 has material on problems arising from and compensation for the military occupation of schools.

ED 12 has more material on the supply of teachers (ED 12/20–21 and 27), while petrol licences and the issue of cheaper rail fares for teachers are dealt with (ED 12/24 and 28–30), and more on military occupation of schools (ED 12/22 and 31).

ED 24 has more on military occupation of schools (ED 24/1623–4 and 1627–3), and material on war insurance issues (ED 24/1625).

It had been intended to continue some wartime controls into peacetime Britain and some of the new ministries survived the end of the war, such as those of Pensions and Labour, to be joined by new ministries of Health and Transport in 1919. The reassertion of Treasury controls over departmental staffing and public expenditure, however, effectively rendered much of the impact of war on central government null and void. State munitions factories and shipyards were generally sold off though the railways continued to be regulated under the Railways Act (1921), the 120 or more pre-war rail companies being amalgamated into just four large concerns. Lloyd George had hoped that, in the interests of British industrial competitiveness, the co-operative spirit of the Whitley Councils would be continued. Trade unions and employers alike, however, urged restoration of pre-war practices. Indeed, 'Whitleyism' survived primarily only in newer industries.

Ration coupons expired in May 1919 and food controls lapsed by 1920, although both were reintroduced amid the post-war price boom. Government expenditure, however, continued to grow with the continued acceptance of the assumption of the war years that the state should take a more pro-active role in social policies and provide more services for the citizen. Thus, rent controls were retained and there were extensions in unemployment insurance and other health insurance benefits. On the other hand, the wage controls introduced for munitions workers in 1916 and agricultural workers in 1917, outlining a minimum wage, lasted only for 18 months after the war, the Cabinet accepting but never implementing the principle of a minimum wage.

Much else was also curtailed by post-war economic retrenchment, not least expectations of housing construction. Wartime plans for a Ministry of Health did come to fruition, but without control over some areas of health provision, such as the factory inspectorate, and with wide powers left in the hands of local authorities. There was post-war legislation on transport, land acquisition, forestry, electricity supply and industrial courts, but it was less than had been intended. The Ministry of Reconstruction, itself established in 1917, was dissolved in 1923.

While it was the reduction of government expenditure that chiefly accounted for the effective end of reconstruction by 1921, reconstruction itself was a term open to differing interpretations. For some, it implied transformation, but for others it meant the restoration of the pre-war status quo. Nevertheless, many of those involved in reconstruction planning would re-emerge during the Second World War.

ADM 1 has some material on reconstruction including reports by the Reconstruction Committee on legislation arising from the war (ADM 1/8480/32), and upon naval demobilisation (ADM 1/8500/222, 8540/260 and 8546/321). There is also the interim report of the Legal Committee on the Termination of War Legislation, April 1918 (ADM 1/8521/108); the report of a sub-committee on the legal aspects of reconstruction from July 1918 (ADM 1/8532/213); and material on the application of the Whitley report to the civil service (ADM 1/8560/158).

ADM 116 contains wartime discussion on changes to the Representation of the People Act, 1916–18 (ADM 116/1498); as well as papers on the construction of Rosyth 'Garden City', 1914–22 (ADM 116/2160–72), including the problem of housing shortages (ADM 116/2164 and 2170). There is also material on the Reconstruction Committee, 1917–19, and Reconstruction Sub-committee, 1918 (ADM 116/1636 and 1745–62); and on demobilisation procedures (ADM 116/1821).

ADM 137 has material on both reconstruction and demobilisation, including the minutes and sub-committee minutes of the Admiralty Reconstruction Committee (ADM 137/3944–8), and papers on demobilisation arrangements (ADM 137/3949–55).

ADM 197 contain papers of the Admiralty's Whitley Councils including the creation of the organisation, 1919–25 (ADM 197/1–3); proceedings, minutes, notes and agendas, 1919–23 (ADM 197/4–5, 36, 43 and 103); and minutes of the Admiralty Industrial Council, 1919–21 (ADM 197/66), which includes a statement from 1915 on petitions received from civilian employees.

ADM 212/165 deals with the demobilisation of Admiralty departments, 1918–19.

AIR 1 has a little material on demobilisation and related issues, 1918–19 (AIR 1/65/15/9/93 and 2423/305/18/40–1), with specific information on the demobilisation of men of the Royal Defence Corps employed by the RFC and RAF (AIR 1/1190/204/5/2596).

AIR 2 contains consideration by the Demobilisation Committee on the post-war disposal of RAF stores originally obtained from the army (AIR 2/89/D 9186), and papers on the formation of the Air Ministry's Departmental Whitley Council (AIR 2/113/A 30986).

AIR 31/1 has the proceedings of the Air Ministry's Departmental Whitley Committee, 1919–20.

BT 13 contains some material on Reconstruction Committees, 1916–18 (BT 13/69, 76–7, and 91), and a report on Land Acquisition for Public Purposes in 1918 (BT 13/84).

BT 67/1 contains a variety of papers later passed to the Board of Trade from the Ministry of Reconstruction, including some dealing with railways, conservation of resources, excess profits duty, and the post-war steel industry.

CAB 21 contains a selection of files on issues dealt with by the War Cabinet and Cabinet. Among them are files dealing with the Reconstruction Committee as reconstituted in February 1917 (CAB 21/72–3, 82), including the report of its Sub-committee on the suggested formation of the Ministry of Health in 1917 (CAB 21/72). The functions of the Cabinet Committee were subsumed by the establishment of the Ministry of Reconstruction in August 1917. There is also an early report considering the effect of demobilisation on the labour market from April 1915 (CAB 1/12).

CAB 26/1 comprises the minutes and papers of the Cabinet Home Affairs Committee, 1918–19. Established by the Home Secretary in July 1918, it was intended to consider significant domestic questions requiring inter-departmental co-operation. Among those general administrative issues dealt with was the process of demobilisation. Subsequently, the committee reviewed forthcoming legislation and became a standing committee on domestic issues in 1922.

CAB 27 contains papers of both the Cabinet Disposal of Surplus Government Property Committee, established in October 1918 and which met three times (CAB 27/47); and of the 43 meetings of the Cabinet Demobilisation Committee, established in October 1918 (CAB 27/42–3). In addition, there are papers of the latter's Unemployment Donation Sub-committee (CAB 27/48); and the Co-ordination of Demobilisation Section of the War Cabinet, which itself met six times in 1919 (CAB 27/49).

CAB 33 has the minutes and registered files on the War Cabinet Post War Priority and Demobilisation Committees. Established in July 1918 under the chairmanship of Jan Smuts, the Post War Priority Committee was intended to consider post-war priorities and the problems involved in the removal of wartime controls over materials, manufactures and production. The Post War Priority Committee was dissolved in December 1918, when its functions were taken over by the Demobilisation Committee. Almost immediately, the functions of the Demobilisation Committee, itself established in October 1918, were taken over by the Co-ordination of Demobilisation Section of the War Cabinet, chaired by Sir Eric Geddes.

The series includes files on imports and exports (CAB 33/4), vocational training (CAB 33/5) and the cancellation of allied demands for war materials (CAB 33/6). There are papers on the constitution, functions and resolutions of the Post War Priority Committee (CAB 33/8–10). There are also the minutes and circulated papers of the Post War Priority Committee, its Standing Committee on Post War Priority, and the General Purposes Committee of the Standing Committee, and its Permanent (Labour) and Demobilisation Permanent Sub-committees; as well as those of the Demobilisation Committee, its Permanent Sub-committee, and its Standing Council (CAB 33/2–3 and 12–26). In addition, there are notes of the meeting between representatives of the Co-ordination of Demobilisation Section and the Board of Trade in January 1919 (CAB 33/1).

CAB 37, containing copies of papers circulated to the Cabinet between 1880 and 1916, includes reports from the Cabinet Reconstruction Committee established in March 1916 (CAB 37/145/13, 149/4, 6, 8, 9 and 14, 150/14, and 161).

DO 119/913–4 have material on the demobilisation of the 1st Rhodesian Regiment.

DSIR 4/1 deals with the formation of the Building Materials Research Committee of the Department of Scientific and Industrial Research in 1919, tasked with examining the suitability of building materials and methods of construction for use in new housing after the war.

HLG 29/115 is a file on the introduction of the Ministry of Health Bill, 1918.

HO 45/356778 contains the report of the Royal Commission on Proportional Representation, 1918.

LAB 2 has some material on the application of the Whitley recommendations to government industrial establishments and departments (LAB 2/639–41), as well as industrial reaction to the publication of the Whitley report, 1917–18 (LAB 2/229/7–8).

LCO 3 contains the records of Ministry of Reconstruction Committees. Agenda, minutes and circulated papers of the Acquisition and Valuation of Land Committee between 1917 and 1919, dealing with the acquisition of land for public purposes, can be found (LCO 3/1–27 and 3/34–9). There is similar material for its sub-committees, namely the Land Committee (Compensation) (LCO 3/28–33) and Land Transfer Sub-committee, (LCO 3/40–45).

MAF 48/242–4 also contains reports by the Acquisition and Valuation of Land Committee of the Ministry of Reconstruction.

MT 9, comprising papers of the Board of Trade's Marine Department, includes an enquiry by the Chamber of Shipping in 1916 on post-war shipbuilding policy (MT 9/1048); the report of an Advisory Committee on post-war trade, 1916 (MT 9/1030); consideration by the Ministry of Reconstruction of post-war shipping controls, 1916–17 (MT 9/1122); and similar consideration of post-war shipping by the Imperial War Conference in 1918 (MT 9/1213).

MT 25, the papers of the Ministry of Shipping, includes a report of the sub-committee on the termination of DORA regulations, 1918 (MT 25/12); and proceedings and reports of the Imperial War Conference on demobilisation, the Demobilisation Committee, and the Empire Demobilisation Committee, all also from 1918 (MT 25/16–18). There is also material on Australian demobilisation (MT 25/26).

MT 49/1–94 comprise the correspondence and papers of Sir Eric Geddes as Minister without Portfolio and Minister of Transport in implementing the Railways Act, 1921, returning the railways to private ownership but now consolidated into four regional companies compared to the 123 which had existed in 1914.

MUN 4/5358 contains the minutes and papers of the Heath Committee in March 1919 on the application of the Whitley report to the non-industrial civil service.

PREM 1/1 contains correspondence on the proposed establishment of the Ministry of Health, 1917–18.

PRO 30/30/8 is a speech by Lord Milner as Secretary of State for War on demobilisation in 1918.

PRO 30/68/22 has, among the papers of Sir Alan Garrett Anderson, the report of the Committee on Demobilisation and Reconstruction as presented to the Munitions Council in October 1918.

PT 1/40 has the minutes of the Office's Whitley Council, 1919–36.

RECO 1 contains the records of the Ministry of Reconstruction and the two Reconstruction Committees of the Cabinet which preceded it, as well as committees and sub-committees. The first Cabinet Reconstruction Committee had sub-committees on Commercial and Industrial Policy, Demobilisation of the Army, Acquisition of Powers, and Forestry. The second Reconstruction Committee formed further sub-committees on the Acquisition and Valuation of Land, Adult Education, Civil War Workers, Local Government, and Machinery of Government. There was a short-lived Wages and Employment Panel as well as a panel on housing, while the Ministry's Advisory Council and Women's Advisory Committee also established their own sub-committees. The interests of the ministry ranged across such areas as agriculture, mining, employers, housing, rents, industry and trade, and industrial recovery.

Papers of ministry committees and sub-committees represented include those of the Acquisition of Powers Sub-committee (RECO 1/91–131); Advisory Committee for the Disposal of Surplus Government Property (RECO 1/132–216); Forestry Sub-committee (RECO 1/222–51); Central Materials Supply Committee (RECO 1/357–409); Finance Sub-committee (RECO 1/410–62); Housing (Financial Assistance) Committee (RECO 1/639–43); Committee on the Increases of Rent Act (RECO 1/644–54); Reconstruction Committee (RECO 1/655–58); Adult Education Committee (RECO 1/669–79 and 886–901); Storage and Transit Committee (RECO 1/680–82); Surplus Government Property Advisory Council (RECO 1/820–31); Local Government Committee (RECO 1/902–38); Machinery of Government Committee (RECO 1/964); committees dealing with post-war problems (RECO 1/705–819); and other miscellaneous committees (RECO 1/252–70). Specific issues addressed include shipping (RECO 1/271–334); housing (RECO 1/463–617); and physical training (RECO 1/691–704).

Papers of the War Cabinet are to be found in RECO 1/853–61, and of the Imperial War Conference, 1917–18, in RECO 1/839–46. Material on the Road Transport Board is to be found in RECO 1/862–4. Circulars to County Councils on rural development with replies and reports from counties are located in RECO 1/939–63, and a report of the Board of Trade Committee on Electrical Power Supply at RECO 1/884. The various pamphlets on reconstruction problems published during and immediately after the war and related correspondence can be found in RECO 1/865–83. The minutes and papers of the Roberts Committee on the Whitley report's application to the civil service in 1918 are RECO 1/659. Also included is material on the Army Demobilisation Committee (RECO 1/832–8) and the War Cabinet Co-ordination of Demobilisation Section (RECO 1/847–52).

SUPP 3/68 deals with the abrogation of restrictive conditions of sale on those national factories erected during the war.

SUPP 6/662 deals with the application of the Whitley report to Government Factories.

T 275 contains the post-war papers of the National Whitley Council. They include, however, some wartime material including draft civil service schemes (T 275/58), and the report of an Inter-departmental Committee on the application of the Whitley recommendations to government, 1918–19 (T 275/59). Established initially as a sub-committee of the Reconstruction Committee under the chairmanship of J. H. Whitley, MP in 1916, the report appeared in six parts between 1917 and 1918, making recommendations for the improvement of employer-labour relations through establishing national joint councils, district councils and works committees. An inter-departmental committee established by the War Cabinet in 1918 under the Minister of Labour, G. H. Roberts, considered the application of the recommendations to government, recommending joint consultative councils within government industrial establishments. A sub-committee under Sir Thomas Heath considered the application of the report to the non-industrial civil service, reporting in March 1919. This, in turn, was followed by a provisional joint committee in April and May 1919 to consider its application to the administrative departments. The Civil Service National Whitley Council then met for the first time in July 1919.

WO 32 has more material from the Acquisition and Valuation of Land Committee of the Ministry of Reconstruction, 1917–19 (WO 32/18551); as well as on the creation of a National Salvage Department in 1918 (WO 32/9294), the disposal of surplus transportation material in 1918–19 (WO 32/5148), and the earlier establishment of a field salvage organisation in 1917 (WO 32/5160). The establishment of the War Office Whitley Council is also represented (WO 32/9320). There is also a variety of material on the initially troubled demobilisation process including preliminary consideration of demobilisation by War Office, Ministry of Labour and Ministry of Reconstruction, 1917 (WO 32/5239–41); reports on its progress, 1918–19 (WO 32/5242 and 5248); problems involved (WO 32/5244, 5490, and 6262); repatriation of Dominion forces (WO 32/5243); its consequences for the strength of the army (WO 32/5245); and the question of demobilisation disturbances (WO 32/11337).

WO 106 has material on demobilisation among the papers of the Director of Military Operations, including a report of the interim War Office committee on demobilisation in 1917 (WO 106/344), and a conference at the War Office in December 1918 (WO 106/345).

WO 107/69–74, among the papers of the Quartermaster-General's Department, include material on the work of the Salvage Directorate, 1917–19.

The Management of Morale

What drove the tentative beginnings of 'war welfare' was the recognition that the maintenance of national morale was a crucial component in national survival. Successful political leadership in wartime therefore required astute manipulation of public opinion. While liberal democracies like Britain entered the war with greater legitimacy in the eyes of their population than more coercive political systems, much still depended upon the ability and authority of politicians.

In dealing with public opinion and what might be termed home management, political leaderships were conscious of a range of potential weapons enabling them to influence wartime public opinion. Initially, there was often more than sufficient support for the war in the major belligerent states, the appeal to patriotic nationalism being reinforced by the shared values, political and cultural forms, symbols and rituals which underpinned the concept of nation and state. As a result, there was almost a process of 'self-mobilisation' and attempts to manipulate the public were often indirect and even superficial.

As the war continued, however, governments were increasingly concerned to maintain the national will to win. Indeed, it has been argued that, in the face of growing war weariness and the revolution in Russia, there was a concerted attempt to 'remobilise' public opinion in 1917, as characterised in Britain by the establishment of the National War Aims Committee (NWAC). Generally, the state sought to project ideals of duty, sacrifice and solidarity within the civilian population while, at the same time, dealing with perceived injustices undermining civilian resolve such as war profiteering and shirking.

HO 139/35 includes some material on the NWAC.

PRO 10/801–3, among examples of material subsequently destroyed, include papers of the NWAC.

T 102 contains the official records of the NWAC, including general correspondence (T 102/1–15); minutes and papers (T 102/16); the organisation of events by its Meetings Department (T 102/17–18); its accounts (T 102/19); schedules of approved literature (T 102/20); lists of speakers and of meeting places (T 102/21); and speakers' reports (T 102/22–6).

In seeking to stimulate or revive national morale and damage that of the enemy, whether external or internal, propaganda was the most obvious tool. Propaganda could also embrace the efforts of a range of official and unofficial groups and organisations, including the church, and extend into the classroom, and into popular leisure pastimes such as the infant cinema, the gramophone and the music hall.

It could involve use of a variety of popular forms from graphic art, such as pictorial postcards and cartoons, to souvenirs. In Britain, mediums for propaganda included porcelain figures of Kitchener, china plates with illustrations of other national figures, as well as the crested china busts, binoculars, artillery, shells and tanks produced by the Goss factory in Stoke-on-Trent and similar firms. War-related jigsaw puzzles, parlour games, and toy soldiers all fulfilled similar purposes for children throughout Europe.

Official propaganda agencies such as Charles Masterman's War Propaganda Bureau at Wellington House in London's Buckingham Gate found little difficulty in persuading writers, artists and intellectuals to produce material for them. Among many, Wellington House enlisted Gilbert Murray, Rudyard Kipling, Sir Arthur Conan Doyle, Thomas Hardy, Arnold Bennett, John Galsworthy and H. G. Wells. John Buchan became head of the Department of Information, which succeeded Wellington House in December 1916, also taking over the responsibilities of the Neutral Press Committee established in September 1914 and the News Department of the Foreign Office. It became the Ministry of Information in March 1918, although the Department's Political Intelligence Bureau was transferred to the Foreign Office and its Enemy Propaganda Bureau now reported direct to the War Cabinet as the autonomous Department of Propaganda in Enemy Countries. The ministry was dissolved in November 1918.

The general tendency of a patriotic press to play the game with respect to domestic news consumption meant that most British government propaganda was targeted at opinion overseas. Using German atrocities, Wellington House and the Department of Information, first sought to undermine German efforts to influence neutral opinion, not least in the United States. In many ways, the Germans themselves did much to make the work of British propagandists easier. In October 1915, for example, they executed the British nurse, Edith Cavell, for helping allied servicemen to escape from Belgium to the Netherlands. In July 1916 they also executed Captain Charles Fryatt of the British steamer, *Brussels*, for trying to ram a U-boat attacking his vessel. Much was also made of a German firm issuing commemorative medals on the sinking of the *Lusitania* by *U-20* in May 1915 with the loss of 128 Americans among the 1,198 who died. Only too real was the genocide inflicted upon the Armenian population by the Turks in 1915, an estimated 1.5 million people dying as a result of massacre, deportation, starvation and disease.

Subsequently, and especially after the United States entered the war, British propaganda was targeted on opinion in Austria-Hungary and Germany. By this time, Lloyd George had succumbed to demands for a more overtly active propaganda arm and had turned the machine over to the press barons, Beaverbrook and Northcliffe. One result was the establishment of Northcliffe's Enemy Propaganda Bureau, which was served by a number of opponents of the preservation of Austro-Hungarian rule.

ADM 1 has material on the Navy's handling of the press and propaganda generally, including a conference between the First Lord and press representatives on naval aspects of the war in April 1916 (ADM 1/8455/91); the appointment of war correspondents to the Dardanelles (ADM 1/8427/205); the appointment of Buchan and the formation of the Department of Public Information (ADM 1/8462/170); the collection of information by war correspondents (ADM 1/8467/220); a conference on increasing publicity for the service in January 1918 (ADM 1/8514/41); the formation of a Press Panel authorised to enter restricted areas in March 1918 (ADM 1/8518/75), and of subsequent local panels at naval bases (ADM 1/8525/140). There are also the rules for visits by writers and journalists to the Grand Fleet issued in August 1918 (ADM 1/8533/223). The return of Fryatt's body to Britain in July 1919 is also covered (ADM 1/8563/207).

ADM 116 deals with the making of the propaganda film, *Britain Prepared*, in 1915 (ADM 116/1447); and the German allegations of misuse of British hospital ships (ADM 116/1395–8).

AIR 1 contains some information on propaganda including wartime press stories on British air services (AIR 1/9/15/1/21); the policy of the Propaganda Section of the Air Intelligence Directorate on its formation in 1918 (AIR 1/30/15/1/155/1–3); the propaganda use of aircraft on the Western Front; and the effect of air-dropped propaganda over Constantinople between August and October 1918 (AIR 1/32/15/1/176 and 187). There is also earlier material from 1917 on cinema propaganda for the RFC (AIR 1/129/15/40/203); as well as notes on the production of propaganda from April 1918 (AIR 1/344/15/226/290); and the consideration of air-dropped propaganda by the Supreme War Council in 1918 (AIR 1/2296/209/ 77/20). While files on aerial photography primarily relate to that undertaken for military purposes, there is one on cinematograph photography dating from October 1917 (AIR 1/898/204/5/738). A visit of press representatives to the Western Front in March 1915 is also covered (AIR 1/943/204/5/982). There is a sample of a leaflet dropped during a reprisal raid following the sinking of the hospital ship, *Asturias*, in March 1917 (AIR 1/115/15/39/66).

AIR 2 has material on propaganda leaflets dropped from aircraft and from kites (AIR 2/48/AIR 492 and RU 7867); and propaganda in connection with the RAF Pigeon Service (AIR 2/95/D 3095); as well as papers on the wider work of the latter (AIR 2/95/D 12946). There is a file on procedures for RFC and RAF press announcements, 1917–19 (AIR 2/102/A 14429). There are also reports and details of conferences of the British War Mission (AIR 2/85/B 6086), which disseminated propaganda in enemy countries.

BT 13 includes a paper on the Board of Trade's representative at a conference dealing with the use of the cinema for official propaganda, 1918 (BT 13/83), and a report on the British War Mission in the United States (BT 13/76).

CAB 1/26 includes a paper on British and allied propaganda in Germany in June 1918.

CAB 17/196 is a report by the Committee of Imperial Defence on the 'Propaganda Library', 1917.

CAB 21 contains a memorandum by Buchan on the formation of the Department of Information in 1917 (CAB 21/37); a report of a conference on the issuing of official communications from the same year (CAB 21/38); and a 1918 report on the Official Press Bureau's experience of war intended to inform the compilation of a future War Book (CAB 21/93). There is also material on the British War Mission to the United States (CAB 21/53–4).

CAB 27 includes files on the Cabinet Committee on Overlapping in the Production and Distribution of Propaganda, which met four times in November 1917 (CAB 27/17); the Cabinet Press Advisory Committee, which met six times between October 1917 and January 1918 (CAB 27/18); and the Cabinet Committee on Review of the Foreign Press, which met just once in November 1917 (CAB 27/19).

CO 537, comprising confidential papers of the Colonial Office, includes some material on propaganda, including papers of the Policy Committee of the British War Mission, 1918 (CO 537/1009); propaganda on peace policy, 1918 (CO 537/1012); the winding up of the Ministry of Information (CO 537/1014); and a proposed propaganda mission by South African 'Dutchmen' to neutral Holland in 1915 (CO 537/1190).

CUST 49/448 deals with the return of Edith Cavell's body to England in 1919.

ED 10/81 deals with the disclosure of military information by teachers, 1917.

ED 12/25 has material on the use of technical schools to assist in munitions production.

ED 24 deals with a number of war-related matters including the presentation of war issues (ED 24/1891); the role of rural teachers in war work (ED 24/596); and the use of teachers for recruiting purposes (ED 24/1565–6).

FO 96/205–12, among Miscellaneous Papers of the Foreign Office, contain the correspondence, papers and pamphlets of Arnold Toynbee relating to Turkish atrocities in Armenia, 1915–16, including Toynbee's correspondence with the Armenian Refugees Committee (FO 96/205); his correspondence with Lord Bryce, 1915–17 (FO 96/206–7); original documents (FO 96/208–10); and printed pamphlets (FO 96/212).

FO 115, containing correspondence relating to the United States, not unexpectedly includes much information on the perception of the war in the American press (FO 115/1836–7 and 1961–3); the effects of British propaganda (FO 115/2028, 2185–6, and 2434–6); the competing propaganda of the Germans (FO 115/1905, 2060, and 2229); and the *Lusitania* (FO 115/2085). There is also material on the Armenian atrocities (FO 115/1852).

FO 141/663 deals with propaganda to counter the influence of the Turanian movement in Egypt, 1916–19.

FO 170, comprising the records of the British embassy and consular offices in Italy, has a number of files on wartime propaganda (FO 170/1061 and 1145–6).

FO 195, the papers of the British embassy and consular offices in Turkey, has material between the outbreak of the war in August 1914 and Turkish entry into the war in November 1914 on the non-publication of allied war news in the Baghdad press (FO 195/2460/5024), and pro-German war news published in the Adrianople press (FO 195/2460/5064).

FO 286, comprising embassy and consular records from Greece, includes material on the distribution of film propaganda, 1917–18 (FO 286/650); payments to Mr Saxton Hibber for propaganda work as well as a propaganda pamphlet in Greek (FO 286/657); consideration of another propaganda leaflet (FO 386/665); paper allocation for such leaflets (FO 386/669); and general allied propaganda (FO 286/670).

FO 371, the papers of the Foreign Office's Political Department, includes material on propaganda abroad and the monitoring of general war news by the News Department, 1914–15 (FO 371/2208–21). There is also the material collected after the war through searching the Turkish archives for evidence of the Armenian genocide (FO 371/4221 and 9158). Reference to the series is by means of a card index in the Search Room and numerical registers covering the period from 1906–20 (FO 662).

FO 395 contains the records of the News Department of the Foreign Office established in 1914 to collect information from the foreign press, supply information to and to monitor the domestic press, and to carry out propaganda abroad. It lost its propaganda functions to the Department of Information in 1917, but retained a censorship role. The files for 1916–18 are arranged by region, covering Africa (FO 395/1, 64 and 162–3); the United States and America generally (FO 395/1–12, 65–86, 211–30, and 248–55); the Balkans (FO 395/13–15, 87–9, and 164–6); Belgium (FO 395/15, 90, and 167); Egypt (FO 395/16); the Far East (FO 395/16–18, 91–3, and 168–72); France (FO 395/18–19, 94–6, and 173–4); Italy (FO 395/20–21, 97–9, and 175–6); the Netherlands (FO 395/22–4, 100–104, and 177–80); Russia (FO 395/25–6, 105–10, and 181–5); Scandinavia (FO 395/27–9, 111–16, and 186–93); Spain and Portugal (FO 395/30–32, 117–22, and 194–7); and Switzerland (FO 395/33–5, 123–8, and 198–210). General and miscellaneous matters are also covered (FO 395/36–56, 129–52, and 231–47). There is a card index in the Search Room and registers are also available (FO 566 and 662).

FO 800/208–9, among private papers relating to Secretaries of State for Foreign Affairs, include material on the British War Mission to the United States, 1917, in the papers of Arthur Balfour.

HO 45 deals with the return of Edith Cavell's body to Britain (HO 45/302577), and also that of Fryatt (HO 45/382997).

HW 3 has considerable material on one of the most effective of all propaganda campaigns, namely the exploitation of Room 40's interception and decryption of the Zimmermann telegram, made public in January 1917. Instructions from Arthur Zimmermann of the German Foreign Ministry to the German ambassador in Mexico to offer an alliance, with Mexico being promised the return of those territories it had lost to the United States in 1848, played an important role in preparing the United States for its entry to the war as an associated power of the Entente. The series includes the German code book used to encode the telegram; a later account by Nigel de Grey of how he deciphered the telegram; exchanges relating to the affair between the Admiralty and the British naval attaché in Washington; US diplomatic reactions; official and other press announcements by Germany and Mexico; and papers by Clarke on the aftermath of the affair (HW 3/176–80 and 182).

HW 7/8 includes an account of the Zimmermann affair among official histories of intelligence organisations compiled by various officers.

INF 4/1–11 contain papers on wartime information and propaganda directed at neutral and allied countries, which were collected in 1938–39 to inform an official history of the Ministry of Information and also by way of preparation for another war. Most were obtained from Sir Robert Donald, wartime editor of the *Daily Chronicle*. They include material on the War Office Cinematograph Committee and film censorship; Press Bureau instructions; a report of the War Propaganda Bureau, 1915–16; reports on propaganda efforts in Scandinavia, Switzerland and Latin America; papers on the News Section of the Department of Information; dissemination of reports and propaganda by the Admiralty and MI7, located in the War Office Directorate of Military Operations; a paper by H. G. Wells on the principles of propaganda; and a paper by Masterman on the operations of Wellington House dating from 1917.

MT 9, comprising papers of the Board of Trade's Marine Department, has files on Charles Fryatt, including compensation for his widow and dependants and a memorial to him (MT 9/1058 and 1066). The series also includes material on the *Lusitania* including post-war suggestions for the disposal of the surplus from the disaster fund and the possibility of salvage (MT 9/1718, 2749, and 2853).

MT 25 includes material on German allegations of misuse of hospital ships by the Entente, 1917 (MT 25/9), and on British efforts to counter enemy propaganda in Italy, 1918 (MT 25/23). There is also notification of Northcliffe's appointment and authority as head of the British War Mission in the United States, 1917 (MT 25/22). In addition, there is yet more material on the transportation of the remains of Edith Cavell and her re-interment in England (MT 25/32).

PRO 10/101 contains examples of documents later destroyed from the Ministry of Information.

T 1, containing papers and correspondence of the Treasury Board, includes material on the War Propaganda Bureau, including staffing matters, salaries, translation costs, lists of staff, reports, and files on foreign exhibitions. Guidance on how to locate the files, which are listed in T 108/27, is given above under the War Finance Section of this chapter.

T 172/546 includes material on German propaganda in Italy, 1917.

TS 27, containing miscellaneous registered files, has material on the claims of the Spanish Marconi Company against the Foreign Office regarding wartime dissemination of wireless news in Spanish (TS 27/57B, 64B, and 75–6); as well as on the legal issues raised by the agreement between Reuters and the Ministry of Information in 1918 (TS 27/66).

TS 32/72 has papers on the legal issues involved in the Admiralty's co-operation with British Instructional Films, 1927–30, to produce its 'reconstruction' of the Gallipoli campaign.

WO 32 has a number of files on aspects of propaganda including details of the post-war investigation into Fryatt's execution (WO 32/5608–10), and the arrangements for the funeral procession of Nurse Cavell in 1919 (WO 32/4846). There is material on the transfer of the Ministry of Information's Intelligence Department to the Foreign Office in 1918 (WO 32/5755); the proceedings of an allied propaganda conference in 1918 (WO 32/5756); and examples of propaganda leaflets dropped from the air over enemy lines, 1916–18 (WO 32/5140–43).

WO 106 has files on Italian propaganda (WO 106/817), but also propaganda aimed at Czechs and other 'oppressed nationalities' within the Austro-Hungarian empire, 1918 (WO 106/824–5).

WO 153/1348 is a map illustrating the distribution of British propaganda by continent, 1917.

WO 161/78 contains the report of the Committee on Alleged German Outrages, May 1915, chaired by a former British ambassador to Washington, Lord Bryce, and consciously intended to influence opinion in the United States.

Censorship, of course, was applied by all belligerents although this was initially military rather than political censorship. In Britain, where Fleet Street alone produced 326 daily, weekly or monthly titles, DORA gave the government sweeping powers in this regard. In fact, newspaper proprietors and editors themselves operated a self-censorship far more effective than that of the Official Press Bureau established in June 1915. Indeed, the latter was small and concentrated largely on a few newspapers believed to have particular significance in opinion-forming. Overall, censorship appears to have had little effect in changing the ways in which the British press operated and was far less significant than reductions in advertising revenues and increases in the price of paper.

ADM 1 has some material on censorship. The public availability of the *Navy List* was suspended in January 1915 (ADM 1/8410/27), but resumed in November 1918 (ADM 1/8544/302). Similarly, the *Naval Review* was censored in June 1915 and suspended in October (ADM 1/8423/157). Not surprisingly, the public sale of Admiralty Charts was also restricted in October 1915 (ADM 1/8437/312). There was concern at a misleading report in the *Daily Mail* in July 1917 of an explosion on HMS *Vanguard* (ADM 1/8492/153).

ADM 116 contains material on the censorship of inland telegraphs and postal packets, 1914–16 (ADM 116/1319A); the interception and use of German Atlantic submarine telegraph cables (ADM 116/1371); and on Russian cables (ADM 116/1568–9).

ADM 137 has some material of relevance, including reports by the Admiralty's Chief Censor on the German press and the output of German wireless stations, 1917–18 (ADM 137/4792–8), copies of the *Cable Censor's Handbook* (ADM 137/2980–82), and general material on censorship (ADM 137/1952).

AIR 1/32/15/1/182 is concerned with the censorship of RAF magazines, August–November 1918.

AIR 2 includes arrangements for preventing the movement overseas of technical papers on aeronautical matters by the scientist, Percy Houseman, in 1917–18 (AIR 2/84/A 46867), and also a confidential notice issued to the press in 1918 asking them to refrain from mentioning by name RFC officers who performed acts of gallantry (AIR 2/120/B 8114).

CAB 1/21 includes a paper on the treatment of German and Austro-Hungarian peace offers in December 1916 by the British press.

CAB 17/91–2 reveal, among miscellaneous papers of the Committee of Imperial Defence, immediate pre-war considerations on press, cable and wireless censorship, 1905–13.

CAB 27/13 contains material on the Cabinet Committee on the Export of Printed Material, established in September 1917 to consider regulations governing the export of printed material to foreign countries. It met three times between its formation and January 1918.

CO 537, comprising confidential correspondence of the Colonial Office, 1759–1965, includes immediate pre-war material on the measures to be taken to censor press, post, and telegraphic communications, 1909–13 (CO 537/354, 365, 377, and 380), and on the wartime safeguarding of ciphers (CO 537/593, 600, 602, and 605–6). It also deals with censorship problems arising in the relationship with the United States in 1916 (CO 537/608).

DEFE 1 contains the papers of the Postal and Telegraph Censorship Department from the Second World War. It includes, however, two copies of a report on cable censorship, 1914–19 (DEFE 1/130 and 402), and a report on postal censorship, 1914–19 (DEFE 1/131), both compiled in 1921.

DO 119/888, among papers of the British High Commissioner in South Africa, contains information on the censorship of letters passing between Germany and Austria-Hungary and German colonies in Africa, 1914.

FO 115, comprising general correspondence relating to the United States, has a number of files dealing with censorship issues between 1914 and 1918 (FO 115/1870–71, 2030–33, 2191–3, and 2360–61).

FO 141 has some material on censorship in the records of the British embassy and consulates in Egypt, 1916–18 (FO 141/664); as well as a file on the particular issue of *The Times* printing an article in 1917 on 'The Clean Fighting Turk'; and the work of the Military Press Bureau, 1916 (FO 141/598).

FO 382, while primarily concerned with the enforcement of the economic blockade on the Central Powers, includes material on censorship (FO 382/2505–23), and the control of mails (FO 382/1766–80, and 2106–13).

FO 395, the records of the Foreign Office's Political Department, has material on censorship issues, 1916–18 (FO 395/57–63, 153–61, and 256–65).

HCA 61/2 deals with a dispute between the Newspaper Proprietors Association and the Admiralty Registrar of the Probate, Divorce and Admiralty Division of the High Court of Justice, 1914–15, over the alleged privileged prize advertising accorded to *The Times*.

HO 45 deals with the suppression of *The Globe* in 1915 (HO 45/303412), and has leaflets submitted to the Official Press Bureau prior to publication, 1917–19 (HO 45/352206).

HO 139/1–55 contain the general correspondence of the Official Press Bureau. Files have miscellaneous contents ranging over such issues as the Antwerp operation in 1914; film censorship; postal and cable censorship; confidential notices to the press; reference to official photographs; the loss of HMS *Audacious* in 1914, which was concealed from the British public; the Dardanelles campaign; Serbia;

the fall of Kut; publication of casualty figures; British War Mission propaganda in enemy countries; and selected confidential letters sent to editors. There are also files recording the issue of D, E and G Notices (HO 139/43–9), including those relating to Ireland. The Bureau was wound up in April 1919.

HO 144 contains some files removed from HO 45 and closed for 100 years on censorship by the Press Bureau (HO 144/1667), and censorship of correspondence (HO 144/1560–62).

HW 3/13 has correspondence of W. F. Clarke between 1918 and 1957 relating to press stories and publications which compromised the wartime work of the Admiralty's Room 40.

KV 1/73–4 contain reports on wartime postal censorship compiled in April 1919 by the Testing Department (MI9c). Initially, there was some opposition to opening civilian mail, but the Cabinet authorised its extension from mail emanating from enemy states to embrace neutrals such as the United States in May 1915 and China in September 1915, as well as to Ireland in April 1916. The reports include some photographs of intercepted letters containing secret messages, and of chemical testers at work.

MEPO 3/2590 contains material on *The Continental Times*, a pro-German newspaper published in Berlin intended for the consumption of Americans living in Europe.

PRO 10 contains examples of material later destroyed. That relating to the Official Press Bureau (PRO 10/497–50) includes confidential print on the economic situation in Germany and Austria-Hungary.

WO 32 has some material on the wartime role of MI7b, the military press control and propaganda section of the General Staff, 1917–20 (WO 32/9297, and 9302–4). In addition, there is a draft amendment to DORA regulations to facilitate the prosecution of press offences, 1915 (WO 32/4893). There was anxiety at the possible publication of any use of explosive (dum dum) bullets in 1915 (WO 32/5187), while concern at publication of details of air operations surfaced in 1918 (WO 32/9295), and of gas warfare even after the war in 1919 (WO 32/5181–2). The censorship of diplomatic and consular correspondence is also covered (WO 32/4894), while there are reports on the censorship of cables, 1914–16 (WO 32/4895), and on censorship as an instrument of trade control, 1918–19 (WO 32/9542).

WO 106 contains the *Cable Censors' Handbook* and lists compiled by MI8 of enemy traders and agents, 1917 (WO 106/295), and a report on wartime cable censorship from 1919 (WO 106/5984).

WO 158/963 deals with the censorship and publicity organisation at GHQ, BEF and Army HQs, 1918–19.

Aliens and the Enemy Within

Like the press, the British public actually needed little tuition in anti-German sentiment and the pre-war spy scare persisted until at least 1915. Increasingly, the public demanded internment of aliens and subjected actual or supposed

Germans to harassment after such events as air raids on London. There were at least seven deaths in East End riots in May 1915 following the loss of the *Lusitania*, and even dachshunds were stoned in the streets on occasions. There were also large-scale demonstrations against enemy aliens in a number of cities in 1918. One prominent victim of hysteria was the First Sea Lord, Prince Louis of Battenberg, hounded from office in October 1914, after which the family name was changed to Mountbatten. Jews also came under physical attack in East London in 1917 in the belief that they were evading conscription.

The existence of such popular anti-German sentiment did not lessen the possibility that there might be German spies at work and that resident or refugee aliens might also pose a danger to the state. Amid the pre-war spy panics of Edwardian Britain, the Secret Service Bureau had been formed in 1909, its Home Department operating under the auspices of the War Office and its Foreign Department under the Admiralty. Part of the Directorate of Military Operations, the Home Department (MO5) became MI5 or the Security Service in 1916. The Foreign Department was to become MI6 or the Secret Intelligence Service. Twenty-one members of a German spy ring were arrested on 4 August 1914 and, ultimately, 12 were executed.

ADM 1 deals with the employment of aliens on British trawlers and also has a report on passenger traffic in fishing craft between Britain and Holland in December 1914 (ADM 1/8407/482) as well as the appropriate treatment for vessels with carrier pigeons on board found in restricted areas (ADM 1/8392/294). There is also material on the prevention of espionage by those impersonating officers in August 1915 (ADM 1/8429/221); the repatriation of two suspect Austrian subjects in December 1915 (ADM 1/8441/352); and police and Home Office circulars on the notification of any escape and recapture of enemy POWs held in Britain (ADM 1/8506/265). Consideration was given, however, to employing German POWs in the docks (ADM 1/8489/109). The series also contains material on the relinquishing of German titles by Prince Louis of Battenberg in June 1917 (ADM 1/8490/132).

ADM 131/119–20 deal with measures taken to prevent sabotage and spying and to apprehend suspected agents in the Plymouth Command, 1914–18.

ADM 137 has copies of intercepted letters which passed to and from German POWs at the Donnington Hall POW Camp and the United States (ADM 137/3855), and digests of papers on aliens, censorship, passports and naturalisation issues (ADM 137/4180–81). There is also material on German agents in Latin America (ADM 137/2828); and on alien pilots in east coast ports (ADM 137/1881).

ADM 178/99 contains material on the case in 1915 of an American citizen of German extraction, Gustave Triest, who posed as an officer of the Royal Naval Reserve and was charged with spying. Pronounced to be of unsound mind, he was released to the custody of his father.

AIR 1 deals with the prohibitions placed on pigeon owners in September 1914 (AIR 1/140/15/40/301); and has copies of *Home Defence Intelligence Summaries*, *Home Forces Intelligence Circulars* and *Weekly Intelligence Summaries* of GHQ Britain on aliens and other similar matters (AIR 1/20/3/1, 550–60, and 2104).

CAB 1/26 includes the report of the Aliens Committee in February 1918.

CAB 17, comprising miscellaneous papers of the Committee of Imperial Defence, includes some of the immediate pre-war considerations of future policy on the treatment of aliens, 1909–13 (CAB 17/90), as well as early wartime policy embracing the Aliens Restriction Order, 1915 (CAB 17/112), and the dangers posed by carrier pigeons (CAB 17/103).

CAB 21/20 deals with the Titles Deprivation Bill, 1917.

CO 537, which contains confidential correspondence of the Colonial Office, includes material on the internment of German and Austro-Hungarian reservists in 1914 (CO 537/586–7); the Afrikaner revolt in South Africa in 1914–15, including the death of the former Boer commando leader, Koos De la Rey (CO 537/564–8 and 570); fears of Indian sedition in Kenya in 1916 (CO 537/775); and disorder in Ceylon, 1916–18 (CO 537/675–9). The series also deals with the application of DORA in the colonies (CO 537/1121) and the employment of non-British subjects in government offices (CO 537/613).

DO 119, the papers of the British High Commission in South Africa, deals with the Afrikaner revolt (DO 119/899, 902 and 921); but also the native uprising in Nyasaland in 1915 (DO 119/905), and native unrest in Bechuanaland in 1917 (DO 119/927).

DPP 1 contains case papers relating to serious wartime offences by named individuals. Two files relate to charges for treason (DPP 1/24 and 30); five to charges under the Official Secrets Act (DPP 1/25–8 and 37); two to murder (DPP 1/45 and 49) including the Voisin case (DPP 1/49); three to charges under DORA (DPP 1/29 and 33–4), including the first German agent to be executed, Karl Lody (DPP 1/29); 12 to espionage charges (DPP 1/31, 35–6, 38–42, 44–5, and 47–8), including a Dutchman, Leonard Vieyra (DPP 1/47); and one to charges under the Army Act (DPP 1/51).

DPP 4 contains transcripts of proceedings in selected criminal trials. Three files relate to a case of bribery connected to army canteens in 1914 (DPP 4/42–4), while one relates to the Voisin case (DPP 1/53), and one to charges under the Official Secrets Act (DPP 4/49) relating to the spy, Olsson (also covered by DPP 1/37).

ED 11 includes material on dealing with Belgian refugee children and teachers, 1914–17 (ED 11/29), as well as Belgian refugees in general (ED 11/23).

ED 91/48 deals with Belgian refugee children in Welsh schools, 1915–16.

FO 115 has some material on the activities of German agents in the United States (FO 115/1904, 1958–9, and 2011–12), as well as Hindu agitators (FO 115/2234–7).

FO 141/574 deals with registration of aliens in Egypt, 1917–19.

FO 286 has material on the Austro-German espionage bureau in Switzerland (FO 286/650), and the activities of enemy agents in Greece (FO 286/678).

HO 45 is a major source for issues concerning public security. The dangers from spies and agents are covered (HO 45/254753, 255584, 267450, 333624, and 355539), of which one file (HO 45/333624) is concerned with the possible deliberate spread of animal diseases. Alien matters, including restriction orders, registration, movements, deportation, curfews, employment, and changes of name are covered (HO 45/254772, 255987, 256000, 257118, 258157, 258926, 266937, 270427, 272042, 276355, 276521, 277334, 277601, 278281, 278567, 278944, 307293, 309317, 310716, 317072, 317810, 320732, 322712, 323249, 326287, 326555, 330000, 335981, 337399, 338498, 347079, 347254, 355329, 360702, 365520, and 371591).

Internment is also covered (HO 45/255193, 269116, 291742, and 329066), the two latter files being concerned with the use of Aylesbury Inebriates Reformatory as an internment camp, and the diet of internees. Prisoners of war held in Britain are dealt with (HO 45/255562, 274861, 327753, 328584, 342181, 345466, and 350150); as well as citizens of friendly or allied powers (HO 45/262173, 264909, 269510, 269578, 272533, 276100, 281476, 303789, 304395, 307823, 317810, 318095, 330094, 333037, 333052, 343995, 344662, 349367, 352661, 356918, and 368063). These files include discussion of their liability to military service in Britain and the sometimes difficult judgements concerning potential allies such as Poles, Czechs and Alsatians or British subjects married to aliens.

The question of Belgian refugees is raised (HO 45/261921, 268174, 299216, 332274, and 344019), and the specific issue of the employment of aliens in munitions factories is also considered (HO 45/311425). Anti-German riots and the alleged maltreatment of German women and children are similarly covered (HO 45/270000 and 298199). MI5's appreciation of police assistance during the war is expressed (HO 45/357291). Offering rewards for information on hostile vessels is covered (HO 45/276081), and the use of Boy Scouts to help guard public property (HO 45/258763).

HO 144 contains material removed from HO 45 due to its sensitivity. Files relating to the internment of Peter Petroff, later a Soviet minister, are open (HO 144/17485–7). There is also a list of interned enemy aliens, 1914–18 (HO 144/11720), but the remaining files in this series are closed for 100 years. They include lists of aliens deemed friendly to whom certificates were issued by the Polish Information Committee for the Treatment of Poles of German or Austro-Hungarian Nationality (HO 144/22260); material on the repatriation, deportation and treatment of Russian citizens (HO 144/3339 and 22524); the relinquishing of German titles by the Royal Family (HO 144/22945); the internment of a German industrialist, Erich Gerbel, subsequently allowed to stay due to his value to British industry (HO 144/20602); the cases of Horst von der Goltz and George Tchiterine (HO 144/2158 and 21710); lists of aliens tried for wartime offences (HO 144/22261); and general files on control of aliens (HO 144/21594, 22253, 22262, and 22938). There is another file on Karl Lody (HO 144/3324), and another on the Voisin murder case (HO 144/2183).

HO 162/28–81 are the out-letters relating to the registration of aliens, 1914–18.

KV 1 contains reports compiled in 1921 by H Branch (Organisation and Administration) Branch of MI5 at the direction of the Committee of Imperial Defence as contributions towards future War Books. There are a few pre-war items, but most relate to the First World War. These include the list of those arrested in August 1914 (KV 1/7). There are also analyses of the reports (KV 1/11–12 and 69–70) and an index (KV 1/68). A Branch (Alien War Service), which supervised aliens employed on war service, is covered (KV 1/13–14), the branch being effectively the former Labour Intelligence Division of the Ministry of Munitions, which had processed all aliens working in munitions factories since December 1916 as well as investigating industrial unrest on the Clyde. D Branch (Imperial Overseas Special Intelligence Bureau) supervised operations in the Eastern Mediterranean and Cyprus, the branch having been established in September 1916 to co-ordinate counter-espionage measures throughout the empire (KV 1/15–19). E Branch (Control of Ports and Frontiers) was regarded as the front line in detecting enemy agents (KV 1/20–34). Instructions to port officers are included (KV 1/71), and the Port Officers' Guide, containing descriptions of suspect individuals, firms, ships and publications (KV 1/72). The work of F Branch (Prevention of Espionage) is also covered (KV 1/35–8), as well as reports on the wartime work of G Branch (Investigation of Espionage) (KV 1/41–8); and of H Branch itself (KV 1/49–63). The latter include the only surviving copy from 1918 of one of the 21 volumes of the official Black List of suspects (KV 1/61), and an example of a monthly report from June 1918 (KV 1/51). Additional material on control of aliens includes papers considered by a CID Sub-committee on Aliens in Wartime (KV 1/65–7), some dealing specifically with Belgian refugees. Reports on the work of the Testing Department (KV 1/74) include accounts of the detection of the German agents, Anton Küepferle and George Bacon, through discovery of secret messages written in lemon juice and socks impregnated with secret ink respectively.

KV 2 contains the personal files of convicted spies. They include the Dutchman, Vieyra (KV 2/3), and the American, George Bacon (KV 2/4–5). The files on Mata Hari include photographs (KV 2/1–2).

KV 3 has the only two surviving subject files from the period, dealing with counter-espionage laws in foreign states, 1905–17 (KV 3/1), and invisible ink and secret writing, 1917–19 (KV 3/2).

MEPO 3, the special series of correspondence from the Commissioner's Office, has some material on alien control (MEPO 3/2435 and 2446), as well as a file on Margueritte Gertrude McLeod, aka Mata Hari, executed for espionage by the French in 1917 (MEPO 3/2444).

MH 8 comprises the records of the War Refugees Committee, originally a voluntary committee to administer relief from public funds. Responsibility for its work was taken over by the Local Government Board in September 1914, the board encouraging the formation of local committees but retaining direct control of a clothing department and of arrangements for leave for Belgian soldiers coming to Britain, and for repatriation. Apart from general correspondence (MH 8/1), there are also general record books, minute books and financial accounts (MH 8/14–38). Material on Belgian refugees includes individual cards (MH 8/6 and 39–93), while there is also coverage of Serbian refugees (MH 8/4–5 and 11–13). Various applications, allocation cases and hostel lists are also included (MH 8/8–10), together with material on the National Food Fund (MH 8/2–3), and correspondence with the Local Government Board (MH 8/7). The committee continued to function until 1916, when alternative arrangements were made through the British consul general in Rotterdam.

MT 9/1008 deals with the employment of aliens in shipping company offices, 1915.

MT 25/2 includes instructions on precautions to be taken in foreign ports against sabotage by German agents, 1917.

PREM 1/3 is concerned with the stripping of British Orders of Chivalry from aliens including, of course, enemy royalty, 1916–18.

PRO 10/48 and **339** contain specimens of records subsequently destroyed pertaining to the War Refugees Department of the Local Government Board, 1917–19. An additional file (PRO 10/340) has since been lost.

PRO 30/57/75 contains correspondence relating to the discussion of enemy aliens in the Committee of Imperial Defence in 1914 among Kitchener's papers as Secretary of State for War.

PT 1/35 deals with the requirement for the Office's staff to take the oath of allegiance under DORA regulations.

TS 27, containing miscellaneous registered files, includes material on whether two foreign-born Privy Councillors, Sir Edgar Speyer and Sir Ernest Cassell, should be allowed to remain members, 1915–16 (TS 27/36); the question of breach of DORA regulations by neutral aliens on neutral ships in British ports, 1916 (TS 27/47); and the legality of the seizure of the British property and holdings of the King of Bulgaria, 1916–22 (TS 27/48 and 71); as well as the Titles Deprivation Act, 1917 (TS 27/60).

WO 32 has some material of relevance, including the consideration given to the court martial of Albert Meyer as a German spy, 1915–16 (WO 32/3903); the case of Franz Rintelen, a German naval officer who organised an espionage and subversion network in the United States (WO 32/15541–2 and 15544); and the post-war request by the German embassy for the exhumation and reburial of the body of Lody, 1936–7 (WO 32/4159–61). One aspect of anti-German feeling is reflected in the discussion of the wartime discontinuance of the Prussian eagle from the badge of the 14th King's Hussars (WO 32/2902–5). The arrest and internment of aliens in 1914–15 is also covered (WO 32/5364, 5368, and 5370), a particular concern being that, if released to return home, many would be liable to military service (WO 32/5372). In 1915 there was a conference on the control of passenger traffic between Britain and the continental ports (WO 32/4892).

WO 71, among the records of the Judge Advocate General's Department, contains the general courts martial proceedings for four executed wartime German spies (WO 71/1237–9), including Karl Lody (WO 71/1236). There are also papers on the general courts martial of three other civilians prosecuted either for attempting to communicate with the enemy or supplying information to the enemy in 1915 (WO 71/1312–13).

WO 94/103 has material relating to German spies held in the Tower of London, including those executed, 1914–18, from the records of the Constable's Office.

WO 106/262 deals with the native revolt in Nyasaland, 1916.

WO 141 contains, among registered papers previously closed, files on espionage cases brought against 16 individuals (WO 141/1–3, 61 and 83) including Küepferle (WO 141/1) and Bacon (WO 141/3). There are also details of charges brought against the former German consul at Sunderland under DORA regulations, and the British consul at Dunkirk as a result of allegations by a number of MPs (WO 141/1). There is yet another file on Karl Lody (WO 141/82).

WO 158/989 is an *Intelligence Circular* on alleged enemy signalling from Britain, 1916.

WO 900/45–6, among specimens of documents later destroyed, contain a list of German subjects interned as POWs, 1915–16.

Understandably, governments were also sensitive to the possibility of anti-war opposition within Britain itself and surveillance of actual and potential dissidents was common under the additional wartime powers taken by the state. The military authorities were sufficiently worried by the prospect of 'British Bolshevism' to recast home defence plans in 1917–18. By 1917, MI5 had 250,000 report cards and 27,000 personal files on potential dissidents, well in excess of the 70,000 or so resident aliens in Britain. The head of Special Branch, Sir Basil Thomson, began a series of fortnightly reports on pacifism, revolutionary organisations in the United Kingdom and morale abroad in early 1918. Becoming weekly reports in April 1919, they continued until at least October 1924. In fact, Thomson's own assessment was that the risk of revolution was slight.

The expectation of many European socialists that war could be prevented through international solidarity had been frustrated in 1914. In every belligerent, the majority of socialists supported their national war efforts, arguing that the war was one of defence and liberty in which the working class had as much interest in victory as anyone else.

The Labour Party was split, with Ramsay MacDonald resigning as chairman of the Parliamentary Labour Party (PLP) in opposition to the war. Most members of MacDonald's Independent Labour Party (ILP) followed a similar anti-war course. Opposition to the war, however, remained a minority activity though support for a negotiated peace gained considerable ground by early 1917. Negotiated peace had become a metaphor for wider opposition to the war and there was something of a revival of the pre-war hopes of international solidarity among socialists. In the event, however, this proved illusory.

In the meantime, dissenters were frequently prosecuted. The leaders of the Clyde Workers Committee, for example, were deported from the Clyde in March 1915 and one Clydeside socialist leader imprisoned for incitement to sedition. The suffragette, Alice Wheeldon, and three fellow conspirators received 22 years imprisonment in total in 1917 for a bizarre plot to poison Lloyd George and the Labour member of the War Cabinet, Arthur Henderson. The philosopher, Bertrand Russell, was fined £100 in June 1916 for anti-conscription activities and, in May 1918, was given six months' imprisonment for alleging that American troops would be used as strike breakers in Britain. Two other leading British pacifists, Clifford Allen and E. D. Morel, were also imprisoned at varying times.

Pacifism had suffered something of a blow in August 1914 when the chairman of the Peace Society, J. A. Pease, chose not to resign from Asquith's Cabinet. New politically motivated groups soon emerged, however: a junior minister who did resign, Charles Trevelyan, formed the Union of Democratic Control (UDC) with MacDonald, Norman Angell and Morel on 5 August 1914.

The UDC had about 10,000 members at peak strength. Conscription was the major issue for the British peace movement and the No Conscription Fellowship (NCF) was formed by Fenner Brockway and Allen on 3 December 1914. It had 61 branches by November 1915. Pacifism, however, made little impact. Indeed, what was of far more concern for the government than pacifism was the Metropolitan Police pay strike in August 1918.

CO 537, containing confidential correspondence, includes material on the activities of the Roman Catholic Archbishop, Daniel Mannix, who led opposition to conscription in two successive referenda in Australia in October 1916 and December 1917 (CO 537/1141, 1143–4, and 1146–7).

DPP 1/50 has the case papers for the prosecution of Alice Wheeldon and her fellow conspirators.

HO 45, as with aliens, is an important source for domestic opposition to the war. Anti-recruiting and anti-conscription activities are considered (HO 45/263275, 278537, and 307402), with campaigns by the socialist journals, *Tribunal* and *Labour Leader* (HO 45/316469). The treatment of conscientious objectors who refused to work while in prison is also covered (HO 45/343652 and 348601). The court martial of James Duckers, chairman of 'The Stop the War Committee' is dealt with (HO 45/311118), while there are also separate files on the pacifist activities of Philip Snowden and his wife (HO 45/312987), and Norman Angell (HO 45/328752). Material on the suppression of Christobel Pankhurst's *Britannia* is included (HO 45/303883); with further material on *Labour Leader* and the *Independent Labour Party Press* (HO 45/297549); and leaflets seized under DORA regulations (HO 45/356800). Prohibition on the publication of the proceedings of secret Parliamentary sessions is covered (HO 45/314696); and the exclusion of the public from any court hearings dealing with infringement of DORA regulations (HO 45/302677). Policing matters generally are also included (HO 45/273421, 319389, 333647, and 357291).

HO 144 also deals with perceived domestic threats. The file on Alice Wheeldon is open (HO 144/13338), but all other files are closed for 100 years. Policing matters are covered (HO 144/10128) including the Metropolitan Police Strike (HO 144/3469). There are files on conscientious objection (HO 144/5802 and 21081), and specific files on the pacifist activities of Fenner Brockway (HO 144/17490), Arthur Creech Jones (HO 144/10311), and Stephen Hobhouse (HO 144/22259). Another file relates to the case of two of the 'Beeston Brethren', sentenced to six months for incitement to civil disaffection (HO 144/20903). Examples of seditious literature are also included (HO 144/1579).

MEPO 3/257A and **B** deal with the Metropolitan Police strike in 1918.

NATS 1/244 deals with the possible relationship between the anti-recruiting movement and labour unrest.

PRO 10/802, among examples of material subsequently destroyed, includes a packet of pamphlets seized from the offices of the NCF in November 1917.

PRO 30/69 are the papers of James Ramsay MacDonald, subsequently British prime minister in 1924 and from 1929 to 1935. There is considerable material on his opposition to the war. The series includes MacDonald's personal correspondence from the war years (PRO 30/69/736–40); political and party correspondence (PRO 30/69/1158–62); 'political public' correspondence (PRO 30/69/1423–7); general war correspondence (PRO 30/69/1237–8); correspondence from the general public (PRO 30/69/1454); and political constituency correspondence (PRO 30/69/1700–703). Specific issues such as food prices; the outbreak of the war; war relief; the impact of war upon trades; attacks on MacDonald by the press and by Horatio Bottomley; MacDonald's expulsion from the Moray Golf Club; and his attempt to join an ambulance corps in 1914 are also to be found (PRO 30/69/1231–3, 1235–6, 1239–43, and 1456). Labour and ILP affairs, as well as relations with international socialist organisations are covered (PRO 30/69/1234, 1245–9, 1252, 1352–3, and 1394). These include minutes of the British Section of the International Socialist Bureau (PRO 30/69/1246), and correspondence with the Australian Labour Party concerning Australia's two wartime conscription referenda (PRO 30/69/1248). Aspects of wartime pacifism and peace proposals are also dealt with (PRO 30/69/1244 and 1250–51). MacDonald's wartime speeches, parliamentary questions and publications appear (PRO 30/69/1041, 1044, 1069, 1393, 1395, 1590, 1626 and 1816), including contributions to the *UDC Journal* and *Labour Leader*. Some miscellaneous souvenirs from 1914–15 are also included (PRO 30/69/1455).

TS 27/39 deals with the legality of prohibiting a proposed public meeting by the British Stop the War Committee in Trafalgar Square on 23 April 1916.

WO 32/5719 gives consideration to the prosecution of George Lansbury in 1920 for the alleged attempted conversion of British servicemen held prisoner by the Bolsheviks as a result of the allied intervention in Russia.

WO 106/332–42 consist of reports and correspondence held by the War Office Directorate of Military Operations on 'Universities and the War, 1914–18' including material from Oxbridge and other institutions in England, Wales, Scotland and Ireland.

The greatest wartime challenge to the authority of the British government was arguably the Easter Rising in Dublin in April 1916. The Home Rule bill had been put on the statute book in September 1914 but its operation suspended for the duration. The pro-Union Ulster Volunteer Force (UVF) had largely enlisted in the British army as the 36th (Ulster) Division. By contrast, the nationalist Irish Volunteers had split. While the majority became John Redmond's National Volunteers, from which some enlisted in the 10th (Irish) Division, a rump of 13,000 or so, still called the Irish Volunteers, followed the leadership of Eoin MacNeill and opposed assisting the British. Plans for an insurrection begun by the Irish Republican Brotherhood (IRB) in 1915 depended upon both the participation of the Irish Volunteers and also German assistance. The former British diplomat and Irish Protestant nationalist, Sir Roger Casement, went to Germany, but recruited only 55 men for his 'Irish Brigade' among Irish prisoners of war held by the Germans. He did secure a vague declaration of support, but the Germans sent only an arms shipment in April 1916 on a merchant ship intercepted by the Royal Navy and scuttled by the crew.

Casement himself was arrested after landing at Tralee Bay from the *U-19* on 21 April 1916. The rising itself on Easter Monday, 24 April 1916, was staged by fewer than 2,000 men and women drawn from the more radical sections of the Irish Volunteers, led by Patrick Pearse, and James Connolly's Irish Citizen Army. Some 258 civilians, 132 soldiers and police, and 64 rebels died before the self-proclaimed Provisional Government of the Irish Republic surrendered on 29 April 1916. Fifteen of those captured were subsequently shot between 3 and 12 May before United States pressure halted the executions, while Casement was hanged in August 1916. The rising forced the British government to recognise the likelihood of partition, the Ulster Unionists rejecting the solution of a whole-island scheme for autonomy, dominion-status and a restored Irish parliament recommended by an Irish Convention, which sat between July 1917 and March 1918. The executions swayed public opinion in Ireland itself, the nationalist Sinn Féin winning five by-elections in 1917 and 1918 and 73 seats at the general election in 1918. Subsequently, of course, the Anglo-Irish War of 1919–21 led to partition and the emergence of the Irish Free State in the south.

ADM 1/8503/244 contains reports and telegrams on the Easter Rising.

ADM 137/1187 contains material on Sinn Féin in 1916.

ADM 223/671 is listed as 'Irish papers, 1914–18' among the collection of the Naval Intelligence Division, but they have been retained by the Department and are not available to researchers.

BT 13/71 contains material on civil servants suspended from duty as a result of suspicion of involvement in the Easter Rising.

BT 15/68 includes a report on the rebel occupation of the Dublin Mercantile Office and damage to its furnishings.

CAB 1, the miscellaneous Cabinet papers collected by Sir James Masterton-Smith, includes reports on police unrest in Dublin in October 1916 (CAB 1/20); on the application of the Representation of the People Bill to Ireland (CAB 1/25); and on both the impact of Irish and Catholic opinion on American attitudes to Britain, and also the discussion of the extension of the Military Service Bill to Ireland in 1918 (CAB 1/26). There is also consideration of a plea for a conciliatory policy in Ireland from December 1916 (CAB 1/21).

CAB 27/46 contains material of the Cabinet Committee on the Government of Ireland Amendment Bill, established under the chairmanship of Walter Long in April 1918 to consider new Home Rule legislation. It met five times between April and June 1918.

CO 903 contains Confidential Print relating to Ireland from 1885 to 1919, dealing with criminal and political activities. It includes extracts from police reports, proceedings of assizes, judges' addresses to juries, and returns of strength of the rival volunteer forces for 1914 (CO 903/18) and in five yearly volumes for the period 1915–19 (CO 903/19). Within the latter can be found the text of the proclamation of an Irish Republic by Pearse and Connolly and Intelligence Notes giving a daily account of the events in Dublin in 1916.

CO 904 contains the surviving records of the Irish administration in Dublin Castle from 1795 onwards, including memoranda on nationalist movements, accounts of judicial proceedings, censorship matters, seizures of seditious literature, and police and military reports. Files deal with the United Irish League, 1905–20 (CO 904/21); and Sinn Féin, 1907–21, including copies of the proclamation of the Easter Rising, reports from government agents, and correspondence on the Home Rule, Sinn Féin and INV Conventions in 1917 (CO 904/23). There are reports on civil servants suspected of sympathising with Sinn Féin, 1916–17 (CO 904/25–6 and 224); material on illegal arms importation (CO 904/28–9); compensation claims for destruction of property in 1916 (CO 904/46–47A); précis and reports of police and military intelligence information (CO 904/94–107, 120, and 157); correspondence and reports on censorship and seizures of literature (CO 904/160–61, and 164–7); correspondence on wartime judicial proceedings (CO 904/32, 122, and 169); correspondence between the Foreign Office and the British Embassy in Washington on Irish affairs (CO 904/184); material on the duties of the Royal Irish Constabulary (RIC) in wartime (CO 904/174, 187, and 223); and an alphabetical list of internees and deportees, 1917–20 (CO 904/186). There are also alphabetically arranged files containing intelligence information on leading nationalists (CO 904/193–216), including Eamon De Valera (CO 904/199) and Casement (CO 904/195).

CO 906 has a few relevant wartime files among the papers of the Irish Office, dealing with the RIC's wartime duties (CO 906/35) and the arrest of James Cotter under DORA regulations (CO 906/37), as well as papers on the provision of wartime allotments (CO 906/36).

DPP 1/32 contains the case papers for Private Joseph Dowling, charged with assisting the enemy by joining Casement's German Irish Brigade having been arrested on landing from a U-boat in Galway in May 1918, to ascertain the likelihood of another rebellion. Dowling received a sentence of penal servitude for life.

DPP 4/46 contains transcripts of the proceedings at the trial of Casement for treason.

FO 115/2072–4 deal with the question of Ireland in relation to opinion in the United States.

HO 45 includes material relating to the report of the Royal Commission into the Easter Rising (HO 45/10974 and 312350). Also included is the report of the Royal Commission on the death of an anti-war campaigner, Francis Sheehy-Skeffington, and two journalists (HO 45/317388); together with details of the court martial of Captain J. C. Bowen-Colthurst, who was responsible for their summary executions (HO 45/10842).

HO 144 contains a variety of material on Casement including trial papers and other correspondence from 1916–20, such as a post-mortem for evidence of homosexual activities, and pleas for clemency received from prominent figures such as George Bernard Shaw and Arthur Conan Doyle (HO 144/1636–7); and later correspondence on his diaries and eventual reburial, 1922–59 (HO 144/23414–509). Among papers in this series closed for 100 years are files on arms smuggling to Ireland from the United States (HO 144/1652); the transfer of Irish prisoners to English gaols and hunger strikes (HO 144/22523); the case of Captain Bowen-Colthurst (HO 144/21349); the activities of Countess Markievicz, the former

Constance Gore-Booth, who had married a Polish Count and was a somewhat exotic member of the Citizen Army (HO 144/1580); De Valera's imprisonment and subsequent escape (HO 144/10309); and the internment of Mrs Sheehy-Skeffington (HO 144/1584). There is also a file on Private Dowling (HO 144/3444) and files on an individual, Robert Brennan, reprieved for armed revolt (HO 144/11681), and the internment of Darrell Figgis (HO 144/4481).

HO 161/1–5 are the notorious diaries of Casement covering years between 1901 and 1911 when he was British consul in the Congo and Brazil. Found in his London lodgings after his arrest, they were not used at the trial, but made available to individuals such as the American Ambassador to demonstrate Casement's homosexual activities and general depravity.

HO 184 contains records of the RIC for the war period, including records of service (HO 184/35–6); returns (HO 184/57–9); constabulary lists (H0184/101–3 and 242); circulars by the Inspector General and branches (HO 184/119, and 121–4); and attestation papers (HO 184/237).

J 17/662 has the depositions to the High Court with respect to the proceedings against Casement. J 93/3 contains the shorthand notes of Casement's trial, and J 130/119 the trial notes made by Lord Chief Justice Reading.

KB 12/217 is the indictment file for Casement.

KV 2, containing personal files on convicted spies, includes material on Casement's activities, 1914–16 (KV 2/6–10), and on those of De Valera from 1915 onwards (KV 2/514–5).

MEPO 2/10659–74 comprises recently released material on Casement, including his activities immediately prior to his arrest; earlier enquiries to trace his movements; the attempted establishment of the Irish Brigade; Casement's involvement in German arms smuggling; Casement's imprisonment, trial and execution; German maps found in his possession; and the notorious diaries. There is also material on Sinn Féin (MEPO 2/10664); Daniel Bailey, arrested with Casement but against whom no evidence of treason was offered (MEPO 2/10668); Robert Montieth, an associate of Casement wanted for treason (MEPO 2/10669); and press cuttings on the Easter Rising (MEPO 2/10674).

NATS 1/245–67 contain the papers of the Irish National Recruiting Committee, 1917–18, while NATS 1/40 has material on voluntary recruitment in Ireland.

NSC 7/13 contains the papers of the Ulster Savings Committee, 1917–19.

PCOM 9/2315–40 are files relating to Casement's imprisonment in Brixton, execution, and eventual reburial.

PREM 1 contains correspondence with Lord Curzon on the situation in Ireland, 1916–18 (PREM 1/231); the proceedings of the Irish Convention, 1917–18, and correspondence on it with constitutional nationalists, including John Redmond (PREM 1/233–5). Military preparations on the part of Sinn Féin in 1917 are also covered (PREM 1/232).

PRO 30/57/60, among Kitchener's papers as Secretary of State for War, is a file on Irish affairs in 1914.

PRO 30/67 comprises the papers of St John Brodrick, later Earl of Midleton, a former Secretary of State for War and for India, and a leading southern Unionist. It has material on wartime recruitment in Ireland (PRO 30/67/29); the Easter Rising, including a contemporary account (PRO 30/67/31); correspondence on Irish affairs with Lloyd George and Curzon, 1917 (PRO 30/67/33); considerable material on the Irish Convention, 1917 (PRO 30/67/33–6); and southern Unionism, including the troubled affairs of the Irish Unionist Alliance, 1918–19 (PRO 30/67/38–40).

PRO 30/89/11 and **16** contain ephemera relating to the Easter Rising retained by William Evelyn Wylie, later Irish Attorney General, but then a lieutenant in the Trinity College OTC and a prosecuting officer at the trials of the leading rebels. The OTC defended Trinity College and other parts of Dublin.

TS 21/69 covers the agreement to pay Alderman James Kelly of Dublin a sum of £3,250 for claims arising from his false arrest during the Easter Rising.

WO 32 contains a variety of Irish material. It has reports and summaries of operations during the Easter Rising (WO 32/4307, 9510, 9523–4, 9568, and 9575), including one on the work of members of the Dublin University OTC (WO 32/9576), the claims of Alderman Kelly (WO 32/9506), and even the naval response (WO 32/9526). The casualties inflicted by the rebels (WO 32/9525) and the legal position of those rebels apprehended under DORA are also covered (WO 32/9571). Additionally, there is information on general wartime security measures (WO 32/5527, 9507, 9512–15, 9569, and 9574), as well as the defence of Ireland (WO 32/9508–9 and 9876).

WO 33/882 has the printed instructions for the CinC, Ireland, 1918.

WO 35 comprises military papers relating to Ireland from 1775–1923. Issues addressed include military and other regulations applied in Ireland under DORA, ranging from prosecutions for selling petrol without licences to prohibitions on meetings and the banning of J. B. Houston, a socialist speaker, from entering Ireland (WO 35/56B, and 61–5). Material on the Easter Rising includes military and police reports, the courts martial of captured rebels, the Sheehy-Skeffington case, the operational orders of the 59th Division, compensation grants to the dependants of those members of the Dublin Battalion of the VTC killed by rebels, applications for souvenirs, and burial fees for civilians killed (WO 35/67–9). There are also lists of civilians prosecuted between 1916 and 1920 (WO 35/94–105), listed by case numbers with an index (WO 35/120) and a register of cases tried (WO 35/132). In addition, there are details of the exhibits presented to the court martial of Countess Markievicz (WO 35/210–11).

WO 71 comprising the courts martial records of the Judge Advocate General's Department, has those of the field general courts martial for armed rebellion of the 15 leading rebels apprehended and subsequently executed in 1916 (WO 71/344–58).

WO 93/16–17, among the miscellaneous records of the Judge Advocate General's Department, contain proclamations and orders issued in Ireland under martial law provisions, 1916–17.

WO 94/104 contains two documents relating to Casement's initial imprisonment in the Tower of London among the papers of the Constable of the Tower.

WO 141 contains the special series of registered War Office papers previously closed. Included are files on the situation in Ireland in 1914 (WO 141/4); material on a paid organiser spreading pro-German ideas, 1915–16 (WO 141/5–6); Casement's attempts to recruit a German Irish Brigade, the case of Private Dowling, and the trials of other members (WO 141/3, 9, 15, 36, and 65–75); compensation for the dependants of persons killed in Dublin in 1916 (WO 141/16–18); petitions from prisoners taken in 1916 (WO 141/24–5); and disposal of those women arrested in 1916, only a few being detained and only Markievicz tried (WO 141/19–20). Recently released are files relating to the shooting of civilians by troops in Dublin (WO 141/21–3), but others remain closed for 100 years including one on courts martial in 1917 (WO 141/27).

Other First World War Record Sources in the UK

Bodleian Library
Department of Special Collections and Western Manuscripts, Broad Street,
  Oxford, OX1 3BG
Tel: 01865 277158
Fax: 01865 277102
Email: *western.manuscripts@bodley.ox.ac.uk*
Web: www.bodley.ox.ac.uk

Collections include those of Herbert Asquith, H. A. L. Fisher, and Lord Milner

British Library
96 Euston Road, London, NW1 2DB
Tel: 020 7412 7676
Fax: 020 7412 7609
Email: *reader-services-enquiries@bl.uk*
Web: www.bl.uk

Collections include those of Arthur Balfour, John Burns, Sir John Jellicoe, and Lord Northcliffe

Churchill College, Cambridge
Director of Archives, Churchill Archives Centre, Cambridge, CB3 ODS
Tel: 01223 336087
Fax: 01223 336135
Email: *archives@chu.cam.ac.uk*
Web: www.chu.cam.ac.uk/archives

Collections include those of Sir Winston Churchill, Lord Esher, Sir Maurice Hankey, Reginald McKenna, and Sir Henry Rawlinson

House of Lords Record Office
Clerk of the Records, House of Lords, London, SW1A OPW
Tel: 020 7219 3074
Fax: 020 7219 2570
Email: *hlro@parliament.uk*
Web: www.parliament.uk

Collections include those of Lord Beaverbrook, Andrew Bonar Law, Herbert Samuel, and David Lloyd George

Imperial War Museum

Keeper of the Department of Documents, Lambeth Road, London, SE1 6HZ
Tel: 020 7416 5221/2/3
Fax: 020 7416 5374
Email: docs@iwm.org.uk
Web: www.iwm.org.uk

Collections include those of J. H. Boraston, Sir John French, Sir Henry Horne, Sir Ivor Maxse, Sir Horace Smith-Dorrien, and Sir Henry Wilson, as well as many ordinary servicemen

Leeds University Library

Brotherton Library, University of Leeds, LS2 9JT
Tel: 0113 343 5513
Fax: 0113 233 5561
Email: library@library.leeds.ac.uk
Web: www.leeds.ac.uk/library/spcoll/liddle

The Liddle collection contains documents relating to over 4,000 ordinary servicemen and women in the Great War

Liddell Hart Centre for Military Archives

King's College, Strand, London, WC2R 2LS
Tel: 020 7848 2187
Fax: 020 7848 2760
Email: SHS.4719@mail.kcl.ac.uk
Web: www.kcl.ac.uk/lhcma

Collections include those of Sir Edmund Allenby, Sir Sydney Clive, Sir James Edmonds, Sir Ian Hamilton, Sir Lancelot Kiggell, Sir Frederick Maurice, Sir William Robertson, Sir Ernest Swinton, and Sir Edward Spears

National Army Museum

Department of Archives, Photographs, Film and Sound, Royal Hospital Road, Chelsea, London, SW3 4HT
Tel: 020 7730 0717
Email: apfs@national-army-museum.ac.uk
Web: www.national-army-museum.ac.uk

Collections include those of Sir Henry Rawlinson and many ordinary servicemen

National Library of Scotland

Department of Manuscripts, George IV Bridge, Edinburgh, EH1 1EW
Tel: 0131 466 2812
Fax: 0131 466 2811
Email: mss@nls.uk
Web: www.nls.uk

Collections include those of John Buchan, Sir Douglas Haig, and R. B. Haldane

National Maritime Museum

Manuscripts Section, Centre for Research, Romney Road, Greenwich,
   London, SE10 9NF
Tel: 020 8312 6712
Email: LXVeri@nmm.ac.uk
Web: www.nmm.ac.uk

Collections include that of Sir David Beatty

Public Record Office of Northern Ireland

66 Balmoral Avenue, Belfast, BT9 6NY
Tel: 02890 255905
Fax: 02890 255999
Email: proni@dcalni.gov.uk
Web: www.proni.nics.gov.uk

Collections include that of Sir Edward Carson

Two additional websites of great value in locating archives are those of the Historical Manuscripts Commission (www.hmc.gov.uk)) and the PRO-sponsored Access to Archives site (www.a2a.pro.gov.uk)

Further Reading

General

Ian F. W. Beckett, *The Great War, 1914–1918* (London, 2001)

John Bourne, *Britain and the Great War, 1914–18* (London, 1989)

Hugh Cecil and Peter Liddle, eds, *Facing Armageddon: The First World War Experienced* (London, 1996)

Stephen Constantine, Maurice Kirby and Mary Rose, eds, *The First World War in British History* (London, 1998)

Sir Michael Howard, *The First World War* (Oxford, 2002)

Keith Jeffery, *Ireland and the Great War* (Cambridge, 2000)

Peter Liddle, ed., *Home Fires and Foreign Fields: British Social and Military Experience in the First World War* (London, 1985)

Catriona Macdonald and E. W. McFarland, eds, *Scotland and the Great War* (East Linton, 1999)

Hew Strachan, ed., *The Oxford Illustrated History of the First World War* (Oxford, 1998)

Hew Strachan, *The First World War: Volume I To Arms* (Oxford, 2001)

John Turner, ed., *Britain and the First World War* (London, 1988)

Trevor Wilson, *The Myriad Faces of War: Britain and the Great War* (London, 1978)

Sir Llewellyn Woodward, *Great Britain and the War of 1914–18* (London, 1967)

The Higher Direction of the War

Manfred Boemeke, Gerald Feldman and Elisabeth Glaser, eds, *The Treaty of Versailles: A Reassessment after 75 Years* (Cambridge, 1998)

R. E. Bunselmeyer, *The Cost of War, 1914–19: British Economic War Aims and the Origins of Reparation* (Hamden, CT, 1975)

Kathleen Burk, *Britain, America and the Sinews of War, 1914–18* (Boston, MA, 1985)

Kenneth Calder, *Britain and the Origins of the New Europe, 1914–18* (Cambridge, 1976)

Michael Dockrill and David French, eds, *Strategy and Intelligence: British Policy and Intelligence during the First World War* (London, 1996)

Michael Dockrill and J. D. Goold, *Peace Without Promise: Britain and the Peace Conference, 1919–23* (London, 1981)

David Dutton, *The Politics of Diplomacy: Britain and France in the Balkans in the First World War* (London, 1998)

George Egerton, *Britain and the Creation of the League of Nations: Strategy, Politics and International Organisation, 1914–19* (Chapel Hill, NC, 1978)

R. J. W. Evans and Hartmut Pogge von Strandmann, eds, *The Coming of the First World War*, 2nd edn (Oxford, 1990)

David French, *British Economic and Strategic Planning, 1905–15* (London, 1982)

David French, *British Strategy and War Aims, 1914–16* (London, 1986)

David French, *The Strategy of the Lloyd George Coalition, 1916–18* (Oxford, 1995)

Erik Goldstein, *Winning the Peace: British Diplomatic Strategy, Peace Planning and the Paris Peace Conference, 1916–20* (Oxford, 1991)

Paul Guinn, *British Strategy and Politics, 1914–18* (Oxford, 19765)

Cameron Hazlehurst, *Politicians at War* (London, 1971)

Matthew Hughes, *Allenby and British Strategy in the Middle East, 1917–19* (London, 1999)

Barry Hunt and Adrian Preston, eds, *War Aims and Strategic Policy in the Great War* (London, 1977)

Lorna Jaffe, *The Decision to Disarm Germany: British Policy towards Post-war German Disarmament, 1914–19* (Boston, MA, 1985)

Antony Lentin, *Lloyd George, Woodrow Wilson and the Guilt of Germany* (Leicester, 1984)

Antony Lentin, *The Versailles Peace Settlement: Peacemaking with Germany* (London, 1991)

W. Roger Louis, *Great Britain and Germany's Lost Colonies, 1914–18* (Oxford, 1967)

Keith Neilson, *Strategy and Supply: The Anglo-Russian Alliance, 1914–17* (London, 1984)

Harold Nelson, *Land and Power: British and Allied Policy on Germany's Frontiers, 1916–19* (London, 1963)

William Philpott, *Anglo-French Relations and Strategy on the Western Front, 1914–18* (Basingstoke, 1996)

V. H. Rothwell, *British War Aims and Peace Diplomacy, 1914–18* (Oxford, 1971)

Alan Sharp, *The Versailles Settlement: Peacekeeping in Paris, 1919* (London, 1991)

Zara Steiner, *Britain and the Origins of the First World War* (London, 1977)

David Stevenson, *The First World War and International Politics* (Oxford, 1988)

John Turner, *British Politics and the Great War: Coalition and Conflict, 1915–18* (New Haven, CT, 1992)

Keith Wilson, ed., *Decisions for War 1914* (London, 1995)

New Ways of War

Shelford Bidwell and Dominick Graham, *Firepower: British Army Weapons and Theories of War, 1904–45* (London, 1982)

Brian Bond, ed., *The First World War and British Military History* (Oxford, 1991)

Brian Bond, ed., *Look to Your Front: Studies in the First World War* (Staplehurst, 1999)

Brian Bond and Nigel Cave, eds, *Haig: A Reappraisal 70 Years On* (Barnsley, 1999)

Ian Malcom Brown, *British Logistics on the Western Front, 1914–19* (Westport, CT, 1998)

Anthony Bruce, *The Last Crusade: The Palestinian Campaign in the First World War* (London, 2002)

Malcolm Cooper, *The Birth of Independent Air Power* (London, 1986)

Paul Davis, *Ends and Means: The British Mesopotamian Campaign and Commission* (Cranbury, NJ, 1994)

James Goldrick, *The King's Ships Were at Sea* (Annapolis, MD, 1984)

Andrew Gordon, *The Rules of the Game: Jutland and British Naval Command* (London, 1996)

Paddy Griffith, *Battle Tactics on the Western Front: The British Army's Art of Attack, 1916–18* (New Haven, CT, 1994)

Paddy Griffith, ed., *British Fighting Methods in the Great War* (London, 1996)

L. F. Haber, *The Poisonous Cloud: Chemical Warfare in the First World War* (Oxford, 1986)

Paul Halpern, *A Naval History of World War I* (Annapolis, MD, 1994)

Paul Harris, *Men, Ideas and Tanks: British Military Thought and Armoured Forces, 1903–19* (Manchester, 1995)

Paul Harris and Niall Barr, *Amiens to the Armistice: The BEF in the Hundred Days Campaign* (London, 1998)

Guy Hartcup, *The War of Invention: Scientific Developments, 1914–18* (London, 1988)

Paul Kennedy, ed., *The War Plans of the Great Powers, 1880–1914* (London, 1979)

Lee Kennett, *The First Air War, 1914–18* (New York, 1991)

Arthur Marder, *From the Dreadnought to Scapa Flow: The Royal Navy in the Fisher Era, 1904–1919*, 5 volumes (Oxford, 1961–70)

Allan Millett and Williamson Murray, eds, *Military Effectiveness: The First World War* (Boston, MA, 1988)

John Morrow, *The Great War in the Air: Military Aviation from 1909 to 1921* (Washington DC, 1993)

Michael Occleshaw, *Armoured Against Fate: Intelligence in the First World War* (London, 1989)

Robin Prior and Trevor Wilson, *Command on the Western Front: The Military Career of Sir Henry Rawlinson, 1914–18* (Oxford, 1992)

Robin Prior and Trevor Wilson, *Passchendaele in Perspective* (New Haven, CT, 1997)

Gary Sheffield, *Forgotten Victory: The First World War, Myths and Realities* (London, 2001)

Tim Travers, *The Killing Ground: The British Army, the Western Front and the Emergence of Modern Warfare, 1900–18* (London, 1987)

Tim Travers, *How the War Was Won: Command and Technology in the British Army on the Western Front, 1917–18* (London, 1992)

Tim Travers, *Gallipoli 1915* (Stroud, 2001)

David Woodward, *Lloyd George and the Generals* (Newark, NJ, 1983)

The Nation in Arms

R. J. Q. Adams and P. F. Poirier, *The Conscription Controversy in Great Britain, 1900–18* (London, 1987)

Ian F. W. Beckett, *The Amateur Military Tradition, 1558–1945* (Manchester, 1991)

Ian F. W. Beckett and Keith Simpson, eds, *A Nation in Arms: A Social Study of the British Army in the First World War* (Manchester, 1985)

Derek Boorman, *At the Going Down of the Sun: British First World War Memorials* (York, 1988)

Joanna Bourke, *Dismembering the Male: Bodies, Britain and the Great War* (London, 1996)

Roger Chickering and Stig Förster, eds, *Great War, Total War: Combat and Mobilisation on the Western Front, 1914–18* (Cambridge, 2000)

Mark Connelly, *The Great War: Memory and Ritual* (Woodbridge, 2002)

Gloden Dallas and Douglas Gill, *The Unknown Army: Mutinies in the British Army in World War One* (London, 1985)

Kent Fedorowich, *Unfit for Heroes: Reconstruction and Soldier Settlement in the Empire between the Wars* (Manchester, 1995)

John Fuller, *Troop Morale and Popular Culture in the British and Dominion Armies, 1914–18* (Cambridge, 1990)

Angela Gaffney, *Aftermath: Remembering the Great War in Wales* (Cardiff, 1998)

Adrian Gregory, *The Silence of Memory: Armistice Day, 1919–46* (Oxford, 1994)

Keith Grieves, *The Politics of Manpower, 1914–18* (Manchester, 1988)

John Horne, ed., *State, Society and Mobilisation in Europe during the First World War* (Cambridge, 1997)

Gaynor Kavanagh, *Museums and the First World War: A Social History* (Leicester, 1994)

T. C. Kennedy, *The Hound of Conscience: A History of the No-Conscription Fellowship* (Fayetteville, AK, 1981)

Alex King, *Memorials of the Great War in Britain: The Symbolism and Politics of Remembrance* (Oxford, 1998)

Leah Leneman, *Fit for Heroes: Land Settlement in Scotland after World War I* (Aberdeen, 1989)

David Lloyd, *Battlefield Tourism: Pilgrimage and the Commemoration of the Great War in Britain, Australia and Canada, 1919–39* (Oxford, 1998)

Philip Longworth, *The Unending Vigil* (London, 1967)

Geoffrey Moorhouse, *Hell's Foundations: A Town, Its Myths and Gallipoli*, 2nd edn (London, 1993)

Gerald Oram, *Worthless Men: Race, Eugenics and the Death Penalty in the British Army during the First World War* (London, 1998)

J. M. Osborne, *The Voluntary Recruiting Movement in Britain, 1914–16* (New York, 1982)

Julian Putkowski and Julian Sykes, *Shot at Dawn* (Barnsley, 1989)

John Rae, *Conscience and Politics: The British Government and the Conscientious Objector to Military Service, 1916–19* (Oxford, 1970)

Andrew Rothstein, *The Soldiers' Strikes of 1919* (London, 1980)

Gary Sheffield, *Leadership in the Trenches: Officer–Man Relations, Morale and Discipline in the British Army in the Era of the First World War* (London, 2000)

Peter Simkins, *Kitchener's Army: The Raising of the New Armies, 1914–16* (Manchester, 1988)

Stephen Ward, ed., *The War Generation: Veterans of the First World War* (Port Washington, NY, 1975)

Jay Winter, ed., *Sites of Memory, Sites of Mourning: The Great War in European Cultural History* (Cambridge, 1995)

War, State and Society

R. J. Q. Adams, *Arms and the Wizard: Lloyd George and the Ministry of Munitions* (London, 1978)

L. Margaret Barnett, *British Food Policy during the First World War* (Boston, MA, 1985)

Rosa Maria Bracco, *Merchants of Hope: British Middlebrow Writers and the First World War, 1919–39* (Providence, RI, 1993)

Gail Braybon, *Women Workers in the First World War* (London, 1981)

Gail Braybon and Penny Summerfield, *Out of the Cage: Women's Experiences in Two World Wars* (London, 1987)

Kathleen Burk, ed., *War and the State: The Transformation of British Government, 1914–18* (London, 1982)

Julia Bush, *Behind the Lines: East London Labour, 1914–18* (London, 1984)

Adrian Caesar, *Taking It Like a Man: Suffering, Sexuality and the War Poets* (Manchester, 1993)

Peter Calahan, *Belgian Refugee Relief in England during the Great War* (New York, 1982)

Jane Carmichael, *First World War Photographers* (London, 1989)

Hugh Cecil, *The Flower of Battle: British Fiction Writers of the First World War* (London, 1995)

L. J. Collins, *Theatre at War, 1914–18* (London, 1998)

Gerrard De Groot, *Blighty: British Society in the Era of the Great War* (London, 1996)

Peter Dewey, *British Agriculture in the First World War* (London, 1989)

Peter Dewey, *War and Progress: Britain, 1914–45* (London, 1997)

Deborah Dwork, *War is Good for Babies and Other Young Children* (London, 1987)

John Ferguson, *The Arts in Britain in World War I* (London, 1980)

Niall Ferguson, *The Pity of War* (London, 1998)

Frank Field, *British and French Writers of the First World War* (Cambridge, 1991)

John Horne, *Labour at War: France and Britain, 1914–18* (Oxford, 1991)

Samuel Hynes, *A War Imagined: The First World War and English Culture* (London, 1990)

Paul Johnson, *Land Fit for Heroes: The Planning of British Reconstruction, 1916–19* (Chicago, 1968)

Ross McKibbin, *The Evolution of the Labour Party, 1910–24* (Oxford, 1974)

Arthur Marwick, *Women at War, 1914–18* (London, 1977)

Arthur Marwick, *The Deluge: British Society and the First World War*, 2nd edn (London, 1991)

Gary Messinger, *British Propaganda and the State in the First World War* (Manchester, 1992)

Alan Milward, *The Economic Effects of Two World Wars on Britain* (London, 1970)

Avner Offer, *The First World War: An Agrarian Interpretation* (Oxford, 1989)

John Onions, *English Fiction and Drama of the Great War, 1918–29* (Basingstoke, 1990)

L. F. Orbach, *Homes for Heroes: A Study of the Evolution of British Public Housing, 1915–21* (London, 1977)

Panikos Panayi, *The Enemy in Our Midst: Germans in Britain during the First World War* (New York, 1991)

Michael Paris, ed., *The First World War and Popular Cinema, 1914 to the Present* (Edinburgh, 1999)

Martin Pugh, *Electoral Reform in War and Peace, 1906–18* (London, 1978)

Martin Pugh, *Women's Suffrage in Britain, 1867–1928* (London, 1980)

Martin Pugh, *Women and the Women's Movement in Britain, 1914–59* (London, 1992)

Nicholas Reeves, *Official British Film Propaganda during the First World War* (London, 1986)

Keith Robbins, *The Abolition of War: the Peace Movement on Britain, 1914–18* (Cardiff, 1976)

Aviel Roshwald and Richard Stites, eds, *European Culture in the Great War* (Cambridge, 1999)

G. R. Rubin, *War, Law and Labour: The Munitions Acts, State Regulation and the Unions* (Oxford, 1987)

G. R. Rubin, *Private Property, Government Requisition and the Constitution, 1914–27* (London, 1994)

Michael Sanders and Philip Taylor, *British Propaganda during the First World War, 1914–18* (London, 1982)

Marvin Schwartz, *The Union of Democratic Control in British Politics during the First World War* (Oxford, 1971)

Stuart Sillars, *Art and Survival in First World War Britain* (New York, 1987)

M. Swenarton, *Home Fit for Heroes: The Politics and Architecture of Early State Housing in Britain* (London, 1981)

Duncan Tanner, *Political Change and the Labour Party, 1900–18* (Cambridge, 1990)

Deborah Thom, *Nice Girls and Rude Girls: Women Workers in World War I* (London, 2000)

Bernard Waites, *A Class Society at War: England, 1914–18* (Leamington Spa, 1987)

Stuart Wallace, *War and the Image of Germany: British Academics, 1914–18* (Edinburgh, 1988)

Alan Wilkinson, *The Church of England and the First World War* (London, 1978)

Trevor Wilson, *The Downfall of the Liberal Party, 1914–35* (London, 1966)

Jay Winter, *The Great War and the British People* (London, 1985)

Jay Winter and Jean-Louis Robert, eds, *Capital Cities: London, Paris, Berlin 1914–18* (Cambridge, 1997)

Jay Winter and Richard Wall, eds, *The Upheaval of War: Family, Work and Welfare in Europe, 1914–18* (Cambridge, 1988)

Angela Woollacott, *On Her Their Lives Depend: Munitions Workers in the Great War* (Berkeley, CA, 1994)

Chris Wrigley, *David Lloyd George and the British Labour Movement* (Hassocks, 1976)

Chris Wrigley, ed., *A History of British Industrial Relations, 1914–39* (Brighton, 1987)

Index

Aberdeen, 166, 168
Aberdour, 41, 174
Aden, 78–80
Admiralty, 5, 7, 10–11, 14–15, 17–18, 29, 39, 41,
    43–5, 47–8, 50, 60, 77, 84, 89–90, 92–3,
    95–8, 100, 123, 139, 146–7, 155, 161, 166,
    171, 175–6, 178–80, 182, 188, 193, 196,
    200–201, 210, 217, 224, 226–7, 235–7, 240
Awards Council, 41
Board of, 98, 100
Board of Invention and Research, 39–42
    Aeroplane Sub-committee, 42
Committees,
    Landships, 60
    Maintenance, 98
    Naval Clasps (1919), 132
    Naval War Trophies, 166
    Reconstruction, 226
    Shell (1917–18), 100
    War Bonuses, 182
Compass Observatory, 43
Departments,
    Air, 102
    Anti-Submarine Warfare, 93
    Materials, 93, 99
    Medical, 152
    Naval Staff, 166
    Shipbuilding (Controlling), 187
    Shipyard Labour, 200
    Transport, 54, 78, 127, 192, 211
    War, 98
Divisions,
    Anti-Submarine, 94
    Intelligence, 47–50, 94, 171, 248
    Plans, 99
    Trade, 84, 90, 94, 99
Engineering Laboratory, 40, 43
Experimental Station, 41
Experimental Works, 41, 43
Industrial Council, 227
Naval War Staff, 99
Prize Branch, 85
Research Laboratory, 41
Room 40, 15, 47–51, 235, 239
Transports Arbitration Board, 176
War Room, 100

Whitley Council, 226–7
Adrianople, 234
Adriatic, 16–17, 49, 114
Aegean, 95, 114
Aerial bombing, 111–17
Aerial photography, 42, 59, 66, 105–7, 233
Aerial reconnaissance, 105–7
Aeronautical Control Committee, 30
Aeronautical Research Council, 43
Afghanistan, 29
Afghan War, Third (1919), 29
Afrikaner Rebellion (1914), 22, 78, 241
Agricultural Wages Board, 212–13
Agriculture, viii, 207–8, 212–18
Board of, 126, 179–80, 207–8, 213–15
    Boards,
        Flax Control, 213–14
        Flax Production, 214
    Committees,
        Advisory, 214
        Flax Production, 212
        County Agricultural Executive, 213, 215
        County and War Agricultural, 215
        Fertiliser, 215
        Flax Seed Advisory, 214
        Home Grown Timber, 214
        Seeds Advisory, 215
    Departments,
        Finance, 214
        Food Production, 213, 215
        Timber Disposal, 214
        Timber Supply, 214
    Directorates,
        Timber Supplies, 214
Aintree, 202
Air 'aces', 107–8
Air Board, 45, 108, 110, 115, 137, 178–9, 181–2,
    197, 205
Air Council, 42, 110, 178–9
Aircraft,
    BE1, 110
    BE2, 111
    BE2c, 108, 110
    BE9, 111
    Bristol, 110
    Bristol Fighter, 109

Cierva, 110
De Havilland, 110
  DH4, 108, 152
  DH9, 152
  DH9a, 152
FE2, 108, 110
FE4, 109–10
FE8, 108, 110
Fairey Seaplane, 103
Gotha GIV, 112, 115
Hamble, 110
Handley Page, 108, 110, 114
HRE2, 110
RE8, 106, 110
SE5, 108, 110
Sopwith, 108, 110
  Camel, 102
  Pup, 102
Short, 110
Spad, 108
Sueter-Sopwith, 103
Tarrant, 42
TE1, 109
Vickers Vimy, 115
Aircraft carriers, 101–4, 117
Aircraft Constructors, British Society of, 43
Aircraft design, 42–3, 47
Aircraft Landing Places, Inter-departmental
  Committee on (1914), 111
Air Inventions Committee, 39, 42–3, 45, 61
Air Ministry, 43, 110–12, 117, 175–6, 178–9,
  182–3
  Appropriation Account, 182
  Committees,
    Aeronautics (Advisory), 42–3, 45, 106–7,
      111, 116
      Aerodynamics Sub-committee, 45
    Aircraft Development, 42
    Aircraft Supply, 188
  Departments,
    Aircraft Production, 188
  Directorates,
    Aircraft Equipment, 188
    Intelligence, 233
  Propaganda Section, 233
  Technical Branch, 42
  Whitley Council, 227
Air operations, 66, 102–18
Air Organisation, Committee on, 108
Air policy, 5, 11, 108, 114
Air Progress Committee, 108
Air raid precautions, 112–17
Air raids, 103–4, 106, 111–17, 150, 153, 171, 176,
  193, 240
  Committee (1917), 113
  Home Defence Against, Committee on
    (1917), 113
Air Raid Scheme, 116
Airships, 43, 102–4, 113, 152
  No 2, 103
  No 3, 103

No 4, 103
No 5, 103
No 7, 103
No 8, 103
C5A, 103
C26, 137
C27, 103, 153
NS11, 103
SS20, 103
SS22, 103
SS23, 103
SS24, 103
SS36, 103
SS40, 103
Aisne, Battle of the (1914), 52, 54, 106
Albania, 9, 75
Albert, King, 55
Aldeburgh, 113
Aldershot, 170, 175
Aleppo, 25
Alexandretta, 70
Alexandria, 70
Alien Masters Committee, 84
Aliens, 240–45
Allen, Clifford, 245–6
Allenby, Sir Edmund, 70, 105, 254
Allenstein, 34
Allhusen Works, 196
Allied Blockade Committee, 11, 85, 91
Allied Economic Conference (1916), 23
Allied Military Committee, 37
Allied Mission to Russia, 18
Allied Naval Council, 11
Allied Petroleum Conference (1918), 15
Allied Purchasing Commission, 11
Allied Supreme Council of Supply and Relief, 15
Alsace-Lorraine, 27–8, 242
Amalgamated Society of Engineers, 202, 210
Amanulla, Amir, 29
Ambulance,
  Trains, 154, 156
  Units, 140
American Civil War (1861–5), 83, 92
American Dollar Securities Committee, 181,
  184–6
American Expeditionary Force (AEF), 15–16, 27,
  56, 125, 148, 193, 206, 211, 245
Amery, Leopold, 23
Amiens, 168
  Battle of (1918), 56, 60
Anatolia, 74
Anderson, Sir Alan Garrett, 217, 229
Angell, Norman, 245–6
Anglicans, 131
Anglo-American Recruiting Convention, 125
Anglo-American War (1812–14), 83
Anglo-Austrian Mixed Arbitration Tribunal, 32
Anglo-Bulgarian Mixed Arbitration Tribunal,
  32–3
Anglo-French,
  Conferences, 12, 17

Mixed Committee (1919–23), 168
Naval agreements, 11
Anglo-French-German War Graves Agreement
(1936), 168
Anglo-French-Russian agreements, 15–16
Anglo-German Mixed Arbitration Tribunal, 33
Anglo-Hungarian Mixed Arbitration Tribunal, 33
Anglo-Irish War (1919–21), 248
Anglo-Persian Oil Company, 65
Anglo-Russian,
Armoured Car Unit, 52
Convention (1907), 18
Naval agreement (1914), 1, 17
Angola, 78
Anley, General, 64
Antarctic, 139
Anti-aircraft,
Defence, 40–41, 43, 112–13, 195
Equipment Committee, 195
Anti-German disturbances, 240, 242
Anti-submarine,
Committees, 41
Warfare, 92–6, 103
Antwerp, Siege of (1914), 52–4, 81, 131, 139,
141, 238
Anzacs, 23, 55, 57, 70, 72, 147
Aqaba, 107
Arabia, 29, 70, 144
Arab,
Bureau, 67–9
Legion, 70
Levy Corps, 144
Revolt (1916), 65, 67–9, 71
Arabs, 10, 29, 34, 70, 200
Archangel, 17–19, 95–6, 182
Allied High Commission, 19
Ardeer, 196, 223
Argentina, 49, 213
Armenia, 10, 34,
Genocide, 232, 234–5
Refugee Committee, 234
Armistice, 25–7, 84
Commissions, 26–7, 35
Day, 165–9
Armoured cars, 52, 60, 66, 77, 132–4, 152
Armstrong Whitworth, Messrs, 113, 210
Army,
Annual Acts, 129, 145, 241
Canteen Committee, 148
Council, 55–6, 58, 75, 126, 142, 186, 203
Medal Office, 143
Medical Service, 119, 153, 207
Postal Services, 56, 142
Records Office, 143
Reserve, 121
Service Corps (ASC), 55, 142
Arras, 166
Battle of (1917), 54, 56
Arthur, Sir George, 7, 69, 178
Artificial limbs, 151, 159
Artillery, 57, 59, 61–2, 75, 105–7

Aruuankadu, 195
Asiatic Petroleum Company, 85
Asquith, Herbert, 1–3, 5, 7–8, 10–11, 14, 16, 39,
66, 68, 141, 169, 245, 253
Associated Rubber Manufacturers, Messrs, 188
Astor, Waldorf, 190
Athens, 13–14, 51, 71, 87, 159, 167
Atlantic, 92, 96
Aubers Ridge, Battle of (1915), 52, 56–7, 105
Australia, 22–5, 31–2, 48, 76, 164, 190–91, 193,
213, 216–17, 229, 246–7
Flying Corps, 109, 153
Labour Party, 247
South, 24
Western, 24
Australian and New Zealand Army Corps *see*
Anzacs
Australian Imperial Force (AIF), 22, 25, 52, 125,
148–9, 171
Electrical and Mining Company, 57
Austria, 26–7, 30–31, 34–7, 90
Austria-Hungary, vii–viii, 9–10, 12, 14–15, 25–6,
28, 30, 32, 76, 131, 139, 152, 232, 237–9,
241–2
Army, 48, 50, 73, 75–6
Navy, 48
Auxiliary Territorial Service (ATS), 204
Avonmouth, 196
Aylesbury, 242
Azameken, 80
Ayas Bay, 69

Babington Smith, Sir Henry, 85
Bacon, George, 243–4
Baghdad, 36, 66, 68, 70, 73, 142, 234
Bagot, Commander W. T., 26
Bahamas, 24
Bailey, Daniel, 250
Baird, J. L., 110, 137
Baker, Professor H. B., 64
Baku, 21
Balfour,
Arthur, 2–3, 14, 235, 253
Declaration (1917), 12
Mission, 217
Balkans, 11–12, 14–15, 38, 49, 73–6, 88, 139,
235
Balkan Wars (1912–13), 105
Ball,
Captain Albert, 136
Captain J. J., 73
Balls, Captain W. C., 64
Balloons, 40, 42–3, 74, 92, 102–5, 108, 136
Baltic, 18, 20, 101
States, 20, 84, 186
Banbury, 196
Bank Holidays, 203, 219
Barbados, 24
Barnbow, 222
Barnet, 176
Barrow, Sir Edmund, 67

Barry, 83
Basingstoke, 176
Basra, 66, 73
Batavia Mills, 196
Battenberg, Prince Louis of, 240
Battle Exploits Memorial Committee, 169
Bavaria, 37
Bayonne, 168
Beaton & Co., Messrs G., 211
Beatty, Sir David, 103, 162, 167, 169, 255
Beaverbrook, Lord, 232, 254
Bechuanaland, 153, 241
Bedford, 104
'Beeston Brethren', 246
Belfast, 164
Belfort, 112
Belgian Relief Commission, 12, 89
Belgium, 1, 9–10, 14, 16, 26–8, 30–31, 36–8,
　　50–52, 54–8, 90, 106, 109, 112, 118–20,
　　139, 144, 152, 155, 159, 166, 168–70, 176,
　　185, 188, 193–4, 232, 235
　Air Force, 109
　Army, 27, 53, 78–80, 243
　Congo, 250
　National Memorial, 169
　Refugees, 203, 241–3
Bellahouston Hospital, 158
Beneš, Eduard, 35
Bennett, Arnold, 232
Berlin, 10, 48–9, 239
Bermondt-Avalov, Pavel, 21
Bermuda, 24, 79
　Contingent, 138
Bertie, Sir Francis, 14, 19
Beveridge, William, 217–18
Biggin Hill, 174
Bight, German, 101
Bikaner, Maharaja of, 183
Billingham, 196
Birch, Frank, 50
Bird, C. W., 214
Birdwood, Sir William, 72
Blackburn, 161
Blackley Mustard Gas Plant, 196
Blackout, 220–21
Black Sea, 18, 20–21, 34, 100
Black Watch, 1st Battalion, 141
Blair, Colonel, 20
Blandford, 153
Blockade,
　Allied Economic, viii, 31, 37, 83–91, 238
　Ministry of, 86–9, 91, 181
　　General Black List Committee, 91
　　Finance Section, 89
　　War Trade Intelligence Department, 86,
　　　88, 90–91
　　War Trade Statistical Department, 86, 91
Bluff, The, 54
Blythe, F., 116
Boilermakers' Union, 202
Bolsheviks, 17–21, 29, 138, 142, 245, 247

Bombardment of East Coast, German, 48, 81,
　　104–5, 116, 150, 153, 155
Bombers, 42, 112–17
Bombs, 43, 74, 112–17
Bomb sights, 40–41
Bonar Law, Andrew, 2–3, 183, 254
Bone, Muirhead, 170–71
Boraston, J. H., 254
Borkum, 103
Boscombe, 64
Boswell, Dr P. G. H., 191
Bottomley, Horatio, 183, 247
Boulogne, 117, 192
　Conference (1916), 16
Bowen-Colthurst, Captain J. C., 249
Boyle, Lt. Col. J. W., 20
'Bradbury', viii, 182, 185
Bradbury, Sir John, 35–6, 185
Bradford, 223
Bramshott, 140
Brancker, W. Sefton, 108, 200
Brazil, 9, 36, 49, 91, 187–8, 193, 250
Brennan, Robert, 250
Brest Litovsk, Treaty of (1918), 17
Brighton, 163
Bristol, 203
Britannia, 246
British Aeroplane Company, 47
British Air Mission,
　Russia, 20
　Washington, 11
British American Tobacco, 85
British armies of occupation,
　Constantinople, 29, 32, 37, 118–19
　Pay of, 31
　Rhineland, 16, 29, 31, 37–8, 55, 118–19
British Army *see* British Expeditionary Force
　(BEF)
British Association, 191
　Fuel Economy Committee, 191
British Aviation Commission, 188
British Aviation Supplies Department, 188
British Chamber of Commerce in Belgium, 30
British Chemical Manufacturers, Association of,
　61
British Chemical Mission, 61, 64
British Cellulose Company, 195
British Expeditionary Force (BEF), 1–3, 8, 15–17,
　　22, 27, 37, 48, 52–9, 80, 108–9, 121–2,
　　124, 128–9, 140, 145, 148–50, 152, 154–5,
　　161, 176, 188, 190, 206, 251–2
　GHQ, 49, 53, 55–8, 60, 64, 75, 239
　Central Laboratory, 62–3
　Explosive Supplies Directorate, 63
　Gas Services Directorate, 63–4
　Inspector-General of Communications, 56
　Intelligence Branch, 48, 51
　Service Records of, 141–4
　Works Directorate, 56
　First Army, 53, 55–6
　Second Army, 55–6, 59, 169

Third Army, 54–6, 106
Fourth Army, 54–6
Fifth Army, 54–6, 120
IV Corps, 54
XIV Corps, 55, 69
Tank Corps, 62, 64
Cavalry Division, 105
2nd Mounted Division, 82
Armoured Car Division, 60
Guards Division, 55, 170
4th Division, 54
6th Division, 54, 82
7th Division, 54, 130
8th Division, 82
10th Division, 247
24th Division, 57
25th Division, 127
36th Division, 247
59th Division, 251
63rd Division *see* Royal Naval Division
201st Brigade, 148
202nd Brigade, 148
British Fishing Vessels War Risks Insurance
    Association, 30
British Flax and Hemp Growers Association,
    214
British Gas Warfare Mission, 63
British Hay Traders' Association, 127
British Honduras, 24
British Instructional Films, 236
British Intelligence Missions,
    Petrograd, 21
British Legion, 162–3, 211
British Military Missions
    Adriatic, 75
    Allied Armies of the Orient, 16
    Baltic, 20
    Bucharest, 16
    Czechoslovakia, 16
    French Army, 16
    Italy, 75–6
    Klagenfurt, 37
    Makran, 16
    Murmansk, 19
    Poland, 16, 20
    Portuguese Expeditionary Force, 16–17, 58
    Romania, 21
    Rome, 13, 16
    Russia, 17, 20
    Salonika, 16
    Serbia, 16, 75
    Siberia, 19–21
    South Russia, 20–21
    Vladivostock, 18
    Washington, 15–16, 140
British Museum, 154
British Naval Missions
    Greece, 11, 13
    Russia, 17
    Serbia, 152
British Phosphate Commission, 32

British Red Cross Emergency Help Committee,
    163
British Remount Commission, 149
British Restitution Service, 30
British Spas War Disablement Committee, 127
British Summer Time, vii, 219–20
British Supply Missions,
    Russia, 19
British Thompson, Messrs, 188
British Union for the Abolition of Vivisection,
    225
British War Mission, 233–6, 239
    Policy Committee, 234
British West Indies Regiment, 159
Brixton, 250
Broad Fourteens, 93
Brockway, Fenner, 246
Brodrick, St John *see* Midleton, Lord
Brooke, Rupert, 154
Brooke-Popham, Air Vice Marshal, 108–10, 115
Brookwood, 168
'Brotherhood Church', 221
Brown, Captain R. A., 136
Bruges, 114
Brussels, 114
Bryce, Lord, 234, 237
    Committee on Alleged German Outrages
        (1915), 237
Buchan, John, 232–3, 254
Buckingham Incendiary Bullet, 42
Buckingham Palace, 132
Bulgaria, 9–10, 25, 27, 30–31, 34, 36–8, 73,
    75–6, 90, 244
Bullion shipments, 182, 185
Burbridge Commission, 188
Burge, Lieutenant M. R. K., 50
Burma, 79
Burney Scheme, 103
Burnham Committee, 141
Burns, John, 253
Burstead, Great, 176
Burton-on-Trent, 112–13, 115
Businessman's Week, 184–5
Byrne, Colonel F., 18

Cabinet, vii, 1–3, 6, 8, 23, 87, 124, 215, 245
    Committees,
        Aerial Operations (1917), 116
        Air Organisation (1917), 111
        Air Policy (1917), 111
        Air Raids (1917), 116
        Aliens (1918), 241
        Allocation of Guns (1917), 190
        Armistice Anniversary (1919), 167
        Australian Purchases (1918), 190
        Belgian Imports and Exports (1915), 7
        British Desiderata in Turkey in Asia (1915),
            12, 16
        Control of Industry (1915), 7
        Co-ordination of Military and Financial
            Effort (1916), 183

Demobilisation (1918), 227–9
Disability Pensions (1920), 157
Disposal of Surplus Government Property
    (1918), 227
Domestic Questions (1916)
Drink (1915), 7
Dutch Agricultural Agreement (1917), 87,
    214
Eastern (1918), 67
Economic Defence and Development
    (1918), 86–7
Economic Offensive (1918), 86–7
Egyptian Administration (1917), 67
Elections (1918), 6
Employment of Ex-servicemen in the
    Building Industry (1921), 162
Employment of Ex-servicemen on Housing
    Schemes (1921), 162
Export of Printed Material, 238
Finance (1915–16), 183
Food Prices (1915), 7
German Reparations (1921), 31–2
Government of Ireland Amendment Bill
    (1918), 248
Home Affairs (1918–19), 227
Inter-Ally Council (1918), 12
Joint War-Air (1916), 108–9, 111
League of Nations (1918), 31
Manpower (1915), 197–8
Meat Supplies after War (1916), 7
Memorial Services (1920), 167
Mesopotamia Administration (1917), 67
Middle East (1918), 67
Naval, Military and Air Force Pay (191), 147
Northern Neutrals (1917), 87
Observation of Armistice Day (1921), 167
Official War Histories (1922–3), 119
Overlapping in Production and
    Distribution of Propaganda (1917), 234
Pay of the Army of Occupation (1919), 31
Peace (1916–20), 12
Peace Celebrations (1919), 167
Pensions (1916), 157
Press Advisory (1917–18), 234
Prevention and Relief of Distress (1915), 7
Prohibited and Restricted Imports (1917),
    86
Prohibition of Imports (1917), 87
Proxy Voting (1916), 7
Reconstruction (1916–18), 191, 214, 226,
    228–30
    Sub-committees,
        Acquisition and Valuation of Land, 229
        Acquisition of Powers, 229
        Adult Education, 229
        Civil War Workers, 229
        Commercial and Industrial Policy, 229
        Demobilisation of the Army, 229–30
        Forestry, 229
        Local Government, 229
        Machinery of Government, 229

        Wages and Employment Panel, 229
    Recruiting (1915), 125
    Release of Long-range Guns (1917), 101
    Registration (1916), 7
    Research (1918), 43–4
    Restrictions of Imports (1917), 86–7
    Retrenchment (1915), 7
    Review of the Foreign Press (1917), 234
    Size of the Army (1916), 124, 198
    Soldiers' and Sailors' Pay (1917–19), 147,
        149
    South Wales Coal Mines (1916), 7
    Terms of Peace (1917), 12
    Timber Supplies (1917), 214
    Unemployment (1920–22), 162
    War Priorities (1917–18), 190–91
Sub-committees,
    Forestry, 214
    Official Histories (1929–39), 119
    Unemployment Donation (1918–19), 227
    War Policy (1915), 7
Government, 2–8
Office, 5–6, 61
    Eastern Reports, 6, 67
    Empire and Africa Reports, 6
    Foreign Reports, 6
    Historical Section, 57, 118–20
    Western and General Reports, 6
Secretariat, vii, 3, 7
Cairo, 70
    Brothel riots (1915), 147
Calais, 55
    Conference
        (1915), 11
        (1917), 4–5
Calder, J. J., 168
Calico Printers Association, 85
Calthrop, E. R., 109
Camberley, 168
Cambrai, Battle of (1917), 53–4, 56–7, 60, 64,
    106
Cambridge University, 247
Camden, 196
Cameroon, 29, 76, 78–80, 84, 96, 118, 151, 156
Camouflage, 40–41, 44, 93
Campbell,
    Captain, 106
    J. M., 40
Caprivi Strip, 78
Canada, 22–5, 110, 124, 137, 149, 170, 191, 193,
    196, 223
    Air Force, 42
    Expeditionary Force (CEF), 22, 25, 54–5, 57,
        59, 139, 149, 184
        Cavalry Brigade, 53
        Princess Patricia's Light Infantry, 128
    Forestry Corps, 213–14
    Lumbermen's Battalion, 214
Cannock Chase, 63
Cape of Good Hope, 24
Caporetto, Battle of (1917), 4, 73, 75

Cardington, 43, 61, 104, 110, 175
Carless VC, Ordinary Seaman, 169
Carlisle, 219–21
    Licensed Victuallers' Association, 221
Carson, Sir Edward, 3, 87, 255
Casement, Sir Roger, 247, 249–52
Caspian, 10, 18, 20
Cassell, Sir Ernest, 244
Catterick Military Hospital, 154
Caucasus, 10, 20–21, 29
Cavalry, 62
Cavan, Lieutenant-General the Earl of, 55, 69, 74
Cavell, Nurse Edith, 169, 232, 234–6
Cecil, Viscount, 14
Cenotaph, The, 165–7, 169
Censorship, 236–9, 246–7, 249
Central Control Board (Liquor Traffic), 181, 210, 219–21
    Carlisle District Office, 221
        Local Advisory Committee, 221
        Public House Committee, 221
    State Management Districts Central Office, 210, 220
    Women's Advisory Committee, 210
    Women's Service Committee, 210
Central Flying School, 109, 135, 137
Central Medical War Committee, 126
Central Powers, 9–11, 28, 51, 73, 83–4, 86, 91, 238
Ceuta, 12
Ceylon, 24, 79, 241
    Defence Force, 77
Champagne, 50
Chadwych-Healey, Captain, 54
Chanak, 29, 37
Channel,
    English, 92, 96
    Islands, 86, 157
    Ports, 53, 56, 112
    Tunnel, 81
Chantilly Conference
    (1915), 11, 16, 54
    (1916), 11, 16, 54
Charity Commission, 181
Charteris, John, 118
Chatham, 113, 168
Chepstow National Shipyard, 221, 223–4
Cheshire Regiment, 13th Battalion, 125
Chief Constables, 221
    Central Conference, 221
Children, 156, 158, 160–61, 205, 210, 212, 218, 220–22, 224–5, 241–2
Chile, 49–50, 188
Chilwell National (Shell) Filling Factory, 176, 222–3
China, 9, 22, 76–8, 91, 144, 156, 239
    Labour Corps, 128
Chiselhurst Caves, 195
Chittening, 196
Church Army, 145, 170

Churchill, Winston, 1–2, 9, 39, 49, 60, 68, 101, 141, 177, 253
Cinema *see* Films
City and Guilds College, 40
Civil Service Commission, 180–81
Civil Service Rifles, 170
Clarke,
    George, 40
    W. F., 49–50, 235, 239
Clemenceau, Georges, 16, 27, 167
Clive, Brigadier-General G. Sydney, 54, 254
Clyde, 201, 245
    Workers Committee, 245
Coal Controller, 194
Coal Mines Contract Agreement (1917), 201
Coast defence, 80–83, 129, 133
    Range Finding, Committee on, 82
Coast Guard, 81, 132, 134
Coates, Major, 40
Colchester, 150
Cole, R. A. M., 64
Cologne, 112, 114
Colombia, 214
Colonial defence, 77
Colonial Office, 10, 24, 78, 89–90, 119, 164–5, 179, 191, 234, 238, 241
    Overseas Settlement Department, 164–5
    Prisoner of War Department, 138, 181
Colonies, 22–5, 164
Commemoration, vii, 165–72
Committee of Imperial Defence (CID), 2, 5–8, 12, 48, 51, 53, 77, 81–2, 86–7, 101, 104, 110–11, 116, 118, 183, 233, 238, 241, 244
    Ad-hoc committees,
        Arms Traffic (1917), 86
        Emergency Powers (1914), 175
        Instructions for Shipping (1914), 86
        London in Wartime, 82
        Seizing Enemy Vessels in Neutral Ports, 86
        Supplies in War (1914), 86
    Committees,
        Air, 110
        Colonial Defence, 77
        Co-ordination of Departmental Action (1914), 5, 179, 190
        Emergency, 82
        Finance, 183
        Home Ports Defence, 81–2
        Overseas Defence, 77
        Territorial Changes (1916–17), 12
    Sub-committees,
        Aliens in Wartime, 243
        Asiatic Turkey (1915), 67
        Civil Population and Hostile Landing, 82
        Enemy Personnel, 49
        Mesopotamia (1915), 67
        Questions of Principle (1915), 87
        Trade Co-ordination (1915), 87
        Trading with the Enemy, 90
        Transfer of Enemy Vessels (1916), 87
Commons, House of, 67, 182

Select Committee on Military Service, 126
Select Committee on National Expenditure, 182, 186
Communism, vii
Compensation claims, 30–31, 35–7, 105, 115–17, 174–6, 184, 193, 196, 215, 225, 251
Comrades of the Great War (CGW), 161–3
Conan Doyle, Sir Arthur, 232, 249
Confederacy, 83
Conference of Ambassadors, 31, 33–4
Connaught Rangers, 141
　5th Battalion, 141
Connolly, James, 248
Conscientious objection, 123, 125–8, 184, 246
Conscription, 22, 121, 123–4, 126–8, 130–31, 143, 173, 197, 208, 240, 245–7
Conservative Party *see* Unionist Party
Constantine, King, 13
Constantinople, 29, 31–2, 34, 38, 70, 74, 118–19, 233
Contraband Committee, 84
Convoys, 92–4, 96, 102
Co-operative Movement, 201
Coplans, Professor Miles, 76
Corfu, 73, 75
Corn Production Act (1917), 213, 215
Corn Returns, 214–15
Coronel, Battle of (1914), 50, 97–8
Costa Rica, 9
Cotter, James, 249
Cotton Control Board, 189, 195
　Contraband Committee, 189
Cotton Inquiry Tribunal, 195
Cotton Reconstruction Board, 189
Council of Four, 27, 32–4
Council of Heads of Government, 31
Council of Ten, 27
Council of War, 5
County Territorial Associations (CTAs), 122, 129, 142
Courts Martial, 94, 100, 126, 128, 145–50, 220, 244, 249, 251–2
Coventry, 201
Cowans, General Sir John, 142
Craiglockhart Hospital, 154
Cranwell, 175
Crayford Agreement (1914), 199
Creech Jones, Arthur, 246
Crete, 13, 218
Crewe, Lord, 87
Crime, 220–22
Crimean War (1854–6), 72
Cripps Committee, 208
Cromarty Defence Committee, 82
Crookes, Sir William, 42
Crystal Palace, 52, 170–71
Ctesiphon, Battle of (1915), 72
Cuba, 9, 36
Cubitt and Siemens Brothers, Messrs, 202
Cuffley, 113, 116
Culley, Lieutenant S. D., 114

Cunard, Messrs, 93
Cunliffe-Owen, Major-General, 68
Curtis and Harvey, Messrs, 47
Curzon, Lord, 250–51
　Committee, 187–8
Customs and Excise, Board of, 90, 167, 179, 183
Cuxhaven, 102–3
Cyprus, 24, 31, 243
Cyrenaica, 70
Czech Legion, 17, 20
Czechoslovakia, 16–17, 28, 35–6, 144, 237, 242

D'Abernon, Lord, 221
Daily Chronicle, 236
Daily Mail, 237
Dalmatia, 33
Damascus, 25, 65
D'Annunzio, Gabriele, 37
Danube, 18
Dardanelles, 2–3, 8–9, 62, 65–73, 98, 101–2, 140, 155, 233, 238
　Commission (1916), 66–9, 72, 153
　Committee (1915), 2–3, 5–6, 68
Dar es Salaam, 77, 80
Darfur, 79
Darling Committee (1919–23), 148
Davies,
　Major David, 17
　O. C. M., 64
Dawes, Charles, 34
Dawes Scheme (1924), 34, 36
Dazzle painting, 41, 93, 96
Deal, 81, 133
Debenham Committee, 55
De Bettignies, Mademoiselle, 140
Decorations *see* Medals
De Croy, Prince and Princess, 140
Defence of the Realm Act (DORA), 85, 173–4, 176, 200–201, 215, 219–20, 222–3, 229, 237, 239, 241, 244, 246, 249, 251
Defence of the Realm Losses Commission, 176, 181
Defence of the Realm (Licensed Trade Claims) Commission, 176
De Grey, Nigel, 235
De La Rey, Koos, 22, 241
Demobilisation, 29, 127, 143, 153, 161–2, 193, 205, 226–31
Denikin, General, 18, 21
Denmark, 83, 88, 94, 136, 185, 193
Department of Scientific and Industrial Research (DSIR), 40, 44–6, 191
　Advisory Committee on Raw Materials, 191
　Building Materials Research Committee, 167, 228
Dependants, 156–61, 174
Deptford, 176
Derby, 113, 115
　Lord, 108, 219, 222
　Scheme, 124, 130
Dering, Sir Herbert, 14

Desertion, 145–6, 148, 158
Detention of Neutral Shipping, Committee on, 84
De Valera, Eamon, 249–50
Development Commission, 181, 208, 214
Devonport, 99
    Lord, 217
De Wet, Christiaan, 22
Dilution and substitution, 197–9, 201, 209–11
Disabilities *see* War disabilities
Discipline, 145–50, 161, 230
Diseases, 150–51, 153–5, 158–9, 206, 220–22, 224–5
Disposal and Liquidation Commission, 193, 195
Distribution of Prize Money, Committee on, 85
Dobson & Crowther, Messrs, 127
Dodd, Francis, 171
Dogger Bank, Battle of the (1915), 97, 101
Doiran, 167
Dominion Office, 119, 165
    Overseas Settlement Department, 165
Dominions, 22–5, 36, 52, 71, 77, 125, 128–9, 136, 138, 140, 164, 183, 188, 230
Donald, Sir Robert, 236
Donibristle, 174
Donnington Hall, 240
Doran, Major-General B. J. C., 142
Dormanstown, 221
Douai, 151
Douglas, Major-General Sir W., 142
Douglas-Pennant, Hon. Violet, 205–6
Doullens Conference (1918), 4–5, 7–8, 54
Dover, 83, 92, 99, 101, 113, 115, 152
Dowling, Private Joseph, 249–50, 252
Dreyer Fire Control System, 40, 97
Dublin, 164, 247–8, 251–2
    Mercantile Office, 248
Duckers, James, 246
Duff, Sir Beauchamp, 67
Dum-dum bullets, 61–2, 239
Dundonald, Lord, 65
Dunkirk, 55, 60, 102–3, 115, 132, 136, 152, 244
Dunning, Commander E. H., 102
Dunster Force, 21
Dunston Hill Hospital, 159
Durban, 224
Dusseldorf, 112, 114
Dvina River Force, 18–19, 21
Dyett, Sub Lieutenant, 146

East African Expeditionary Force, 79
    2nd East African Division, 80
East African Frontier Force, 79
East Anglia, 80, 113
'Easterners', 8–10
Eastern Front, 21, 27, 117
Eastern Mission, 33
Easter Rising (1916), 247–52
Edmonds, Sir James, 118–19, 254
Education,
    Board of, 2, 44, 181, 225

Act (1918), 225
Egerton, Major-General, 68
Egypt, 19, 22, 26, 29, 32, 49–50, 54, 65–74, 95, 117, 139, 144, 147, 165, 167, 175, 193, 214, 234–5, 238, 241
    Military Press Bureau, 238
    National Bank, 31
    Survey of, 73
    War Trade Department, 85
Egyptian Expeditionary Force, 66, 68, 70, 722
Egyptian Labour Corps, 68, 158, 167
Ekaterinburg, 19
Elles, General Hugh, 64
Elope Force, 21
Emden, 103
Emergency Powers Act (1914), 174
Emigration schemes, 164–5
Empire Demobilisation Committee, 229
Enemy Debts Committee, 85
Enemy Exports Committee, 84
Enfield Lock, 219, 221–2
Engineering Employers Federation, 199
England, 90, 123, 166, 236, 247
    Bank of, 182, 186
Entebbe, 80
Entente, 4, 9–11, 16–17, 26–8, 51–2, 83, 92, 181, 235–6
Esher, Lord, 7, 253
Essen, 39
Essex, 193
Estonia, 21
Etaples, 117, 145
Euphrates, 66, 152
Ewing, Sir Alfred, 47
Excess Profits Duty, 175, 184, 227
Executions, 145–6, 148–9
Exemption, 123, 125–9, 193
Explosions, 222–4
Explosives, 44, 46–7
    Inspectorate, 223
Ex-servicemen, 161–5
    Emigration schemes, 164–5
    Resettlement schemes, 163–5

Factory Acts, 222–3
Fair Wages Advisory Council, 202
Faisal, Emir, 69
Falklands, the, 24, 140
    Battle of (1914), 50, 97, 100, 151
Falls, Cyril, 54
Faraday Society, 191
Farnborough, 39, 43, 106, 109–10, 175, 176, 188
Faroes, 91
Fascism, vii
Faversham, 116, 223
Federated Association of Manufacturers, 210
Festubert, Battle of (1915), 52, 56
Fiennes, Lady, 140
Fifty Year Rule, 118
Figgis, Darrell, 250

Fiji, 22, 24
Filgate, Captain T. W., 140
Films, 171–2, 188, 232–3, 235–6, 238
Finland, 31
First Aid Nursing Yeomanry (FANY), 203–4
Firth of Forth, 83, 92, 95
Fisher,
    H. A. L., 253
    Admiral Lord, 2, 5, 68, 95, 101
    Lord, 39
Fish Purchase Scheme, 213
Fitzclarence VC, Brigadier-General C., 142
Fitzpatrick, Sir Percy, 166
Fiume, 37
Flame throwers, 59, 61
Flanders, 4, 52–6, 75, 80, 122, 154, 156, 166, 177
Flers-Courcelette, Battle of (1916), 60
Foch, Ferdinand, 4, 7–8, 11, 16–17, 27, 53, 167, 169
Folkestone, 112
Food, Ministry of, 126, 175, 178–81, 215–16
    Committees,
        Agricultural Costings, 215
        Butter and Cheese Imports, 215
        East India Tanned Kip, 215
        Feeding Stuffs, 215
        Fish Friers Trade Advisory, 215
        Imports Board Shipping, 215
        Leather Supplies, 215
        Milk Advisory, 216
        National Kitchens Advisory, 215–16
        Rabbits, Game and Poultry, 216
        Rationing and Distribution, 218
        Woollen Trade, 216
    Departments
        Food Production, 181, 207–8
            Women's Branch, 207–8
Food Control Campaign, 218
Food Control Committees, 218
Food Controller, 175, 217–18
Food Council, 217
Food supply, 212–18
Foreign Office, 1, 10, 13–14, 19, 28, 31, 50, 68, 87, 89–90, 119, 138, 180, 234, 249
    Committees,
        Contraband, 91
        Enemy Exports, 91
        Russia, 67
    Departments,
        Commercial, 13
        Consular, 13
        Contraband, 88
        Foreign Trade, 88, 181
        Overseas Trade, 89
        News, 232, 235
        Political, 13–14, 19, 68, 78, 235, 238
        Political Intelligence (PID), 13, 28, 31–3
        Prisoners of War and Aliens, 138–9
        Russian Claims, 31
        War, 14, 19, 68, 78
Foreign Policy, British, 9–21

Foulkes, Brigadier-General C. H., 64
Foulness, 176
'Fourteen Points', 28
France, vii, 1, 4, 9–11, 13–17, 21, 25–9, 36, 49, 51, 54–6, 60–62, 64, 75–6, 80, 82–3, 85, 87–8, 90, 92, 106–7, 112, 115, 118–20, 122, 125–6, 128–9, 131, 139–40, 144, 152, 154–6, 166, 168–70, 176–7, 185, 188, 190–94, 196, 206–7, 211, 235
    Air Force, 109, 114–15
    Army, 4, 16–17, 27, 50, 52–3, 56, 58, 63, 72, 80, 104
    Balloon Defence Scheme, 104
    General Headquarters (GQG), 17
    Military Mission to Hejaz, 68
    Ministry of Munitions, 40, 192
    Ministry of War, 197
Fraser,
    Commander B., 21
    T., 68
French,
    Sir John, 3–4, 8, 56, 63, 82, 140, 177, 194, 254
    Captain the Hon. J. R. L., 142
Friedrichshafen, 114
Friendly Societies, 181
Froude Tank Fund, 44
Fryatt, Captain Charles, 232–3, 235–6
Fuel Research Board, 191

Galicia, 33
Gallipoli, 23, 65–73, 82, 117, 119–20, 131, 136–8, 140, 142, 151, 156, 165–9, 236
    Anzac Cove, 65, 131
    Brighton Beach, 73
    Cape Helles, 65
    Ocean Beach, 73
    Suvla Bay, 65–6, 71, 73
    V Beach, 73
    Y Beach, 68
Galsworthy, John, 232
Galway, 249
Gardiner, Captain W. C., 61
Gas, 19, 37, 42, 59–65, 155, 158, 193, 196
Gateshead, 196
Gaza, 107
Geddes, Sir Eric, 55, 98, 163, 196, 228–9
General Post Office, 175
George V, King, 6, 14, 57, 89, 112, 129, 132, 139, 146, 148–9, 166, 168, 221
German East Africa, 22–3, 29, 60, 76–80, 118–19, 149, 156, 165
German War Documents Project (GWDP), 15
German South-West Africa, 23, 29, 76–80, 91
Germany, vii–viii, 1, 9–10, 12, 14–17, 19–20, 26–38, 46, 48–51, 56, 83–4, 86, 88–9, 91, 96, 105, 111–12, 114–15, 117, 119–20, 131, 136, 139, 141, 152, 185, 187, 191, 193, 225, 232–7, 239–44, 247, 249–50, 252
    Air Force, 107, 109, 111–17, 119, 143, 152–3, 188, 220

Army, 4, 20, 26, 37–8, 49–62, 72–3, 76,
    80–81, 106, 142, 155
Colonies, 24, 29, 32, 36, 76–80, 238
Foreign Ministry, 15, 235
Navy, 48, 50, 91–6, 100–102, 105, 244
    East Asian Squadron, 101
    High Seas Fleet, 26, 28, 34, 36, 48, 97,
        104
    Mutinies (1918), 100
    Spring Offensive (1918), 4, 52–3, 56, 120
Weimar Republic, 32, 35
Gerrard, H., 41
Ghadarites, 148
Ghent, 112–13, 140
Gibraltar, 12, 24, 79, 92, 96
Gillies, Harold, 151
Girouard, Sir Percy, 55
Givenchy, Battle of (1915), 52
Glasgow, 158, 162
Globe, The, 238
Gold Coast, 24, 157
Goltz, Horst von der, 242
Goodall, Stanley, 41
Goodwin Whiffen, Major G., 54
Goole, 113
Gordon Highlanders, 1st Battalion, 149
Gosport, 41
Goss, Messrs, 232
Gough, Sir Hubert, 20
Government Chemist, 45, 179
Government Code and Cipher School, 49–50
Grain, Isle of, 152
Grain Supply Committee, 216
Great Lakes, African, 76–7, 91
Greco-Turkish War (1920–21), 34, 37
Greece, 9, 11–13, 15, 28, 30–31, 34, 36, 50, 69,
    74–5, 91, 96, 125–6, 138, 144, 168, 172,
    175, 188, 193, 235, 241
    Army, 16, 159
Greene, Sir W. Graham, 46
Greenwich, 171, 196
Gregory, Squadron Commander, 60
Grenadier Guards, 154
Gretna, 194–6, 219, 222
Grey, Sir Edward, 1, 14, 19
Grimsby, 113
Groningen, 131
Grundy, C. Reginald, 170
Guatemala, 9
Guedella Committee (1919), 159
Gush, Engineering Commander, 40

Haber process, 37, 46, 191
Habsburgs, 29
Hague,
    Conference (1929–30), 36
    Conventions, 111, 141
Haig, Sir Douglas, 3–4, 8–9, 17, 53–6, 111,
    118–19, 142, 167, 169, 254
Haiti, 9
Haking, Sir Richard, 27, 118

Haldane,
    J. S., Dr, 64
    Richard Burdon, 2, 254
Halifax (Nova Scotia), 223
Hall, Sir A. D., 215
Halton, 175
Hambro,
    Lady, 49
    Messrs, 184
Hamilton, Sir Ian, 69, 254
Hampstead, 150
Hanbury, 196
Hanbury-Williams, General, 20
Hankey, Maurice, 2–3, 5, 7, 34, 39, 60, 68, 95,
    253
Hanlon Field, 63
Hardy, Thomas, 232
Harington, General Sir Charles, 32
Harker, Dr J. A., 46
Harmonsworth, Cecil, 88
Harringay, 196
Hartlepool, 83, 104–5
Harvest Camps, 212
Harwich, 26, 41–2
Haslar, 41, 166
Hassall, John, 172
Hatton Sproule, Lieutenant Colonel Harry, 140
Hawkcraig, 41–2
Hay, Captain, 64
Hazelton, Major G., 47
Headlam, General, 119
Heald, C. B., 118
Health, 150–51, 222–5
    Ministry of, 154, 225–9
Heath, Sir Thomas, 230
    Committee (1919), 229–30
Heckmondwike, 223
Hejaz, 65, 67–9, 71–3, 107, 167
Heligoland Bight, 97, 101
Henderson,
    Arthur, 2–3, 121, 245
    Sir David, 108
Hereford, 196
Herschell, Lord, 49
Hertford, Marquess of, 171
Hertford House, 171
Hewitt, Group Captain Ludlow, 106
Hibber, Saxton, 235
Hickman, Major-General, 62
High Court of Justice, 89, 238
    Probate, Divorce and Admiralty Division, 89,
        238
Hill 60, 168
Himley, 196
Hindus, 241
Hobhouse, Stephen, 246
Hogarth, Dr, 118
Holland, Lieutenant Colonel G., 54
Holloway Mills, 196
Holton Heath, 187
Home defence, 80–83, 113–14, 240

Home forces, 82–3
Home Office, 89–90, 153, 179, 223–4
    Shop Committee, 201
    Trading with the Enemy Department, 89
Honduras, 9
Hong Kong, 24, 79–80
Honourable Artillery Company (HAC), 142
Hooley Hill, 224
Hooper, Captain H. B., 139
Hope, Captain Herbert, 48
Hopewell (Virginia), 196
Hopkins, Sir Richard, 184
Horne, Sir Henry, 254
Horse racing, 127, 219–20, 222
Hospitals, 150–51, 154–5, 158–9, 206
Hospital ships, 36, 98, 101, 151, 154–5, 233, 236
    Assaye, 154
    Asturias, 233
    Britannic, 155
    Mauretania, 155
    Ophelia, 98, 101
Hotchkiss, Messrs, 201
Houlthurst, 114
Houseman, Percy, 237
Housing, 222, 224, 228, 230
Houston, J. B., 251
Howden, 104
Hughes, W. M., 31
Hull, 113, 115, 210
'Hundred Days' (1918), 52, 56, 64
Hungary, 26–7, 31, 36–8
Hussar Regiments, 154
    14th Hussars, 244
Hussein, Sherif, 69
Hyde Park, 205
Hydrophones, 41–2, 47, 93
Hythe, 62, 117

Iceland, 91
Imber Court, 43
Imperial Camel Corps, 170
Imperial Institute, 45
Imperial Trust, 44
Imperial War Cabinet, 23
    Committee on Indemnity (1918), 31–2
Imperial War Conference (1917), 23–5, 229–30
Imperial War Graves Commission (IWGC),
    165–8, 181
    Endowment Fund Act (1926), 168
Imperial War Museum (IWM), 170–72, 181
    RAF Section, 171
    Women's Work Section, 172
Incendiary bullets, 42
Income tax, 181–2, 184
Independent Labour Party (ILP) *see* Labour
    Party, Independent
India, 22–3, 29, 77–80, 124, 130, 149, 191, 193
    Army, 22, 55, 66, 79–80, 124, 140
        Corps on Western Front, 54–8, 154–5
        Territorial and Auxiliary Forces, 159
        2/4th Cavalry, 140

5th (Native) Light Infantry, 148–9
23rd Sikh Pioneers, 142
Government of, 66
North-West Frontier, 77, 79
Office, 90, 181
Survey of, 72
Industrial disputes, 200–203, 210, 221, 243
Industrial research, 44–6, 191
Industrial safety, 222–4
Industry, viii, 187–96, 200–203, 208–12, 222–4
    Aircraft, 43, 110, 127, 188, 190, 193, 201–2,
        210
    Boilermaking, 202
    Boots and shoes, 201–2, 210
    Brass, 201
    Cabinetmaking, 202
    Calico, 127
    Chainmaking, 202
    Chemical, 61, 63, 189, 209
    Coal, 189–90, 192–4, 201, 203
    Confectionery, 202
    Copper, 190–91, 193
    Cotton, 45, 187, 189, 195, 206
    Electrical, 189–90, 193, 201
    Engineering, 189, 200–202, 209, 211
    Glass, 189, 193, 201–2
    Iron, 45, 189, 193, 197, 201
    Lead, 190–91, 193
    Motor, 45
    Munitions *see* Munitions
    Non-ferrous metals, 189–90, 194, 202
    Oil and petroleum, 188, 190–95, 202
    Optical glass, 45–6, 187, 189, 191, 193
    Paper, 127, 187, 189, 202, 218
    Potash, 189, 193
    Rubber, 190
    Scientific instruments, 45, 187
    Shipbuilding, 41–3, 97, 187–90, 192–3, 197,
        201, 203, 228–9
    Silk, 127
    Steel, 189–90, 193, 201, 227
    Textiles, 190, 202
    Tin, 193, 202, 223
    Toy, 189
    Tramways, 201–2
    Wool, 45, 187, 202
Influenza pandemic, 151, 154
Information,
    Department of, 232–3, 235
        Enemy Propaganda Bureau, 232
        News Section, 236
        Political Intelligence Bureau, 232
    Ministry of, 170, 181, 232, 234, 236
        British War Memorials Committee, 170
        Intelligence Department, 236
Injuries in War (Compensation) Acts, 157–8, 161
Inland Revenue, Board of, 184
Inoculation and vaccination, 224–5
Insurance Claims, Committee on, 105
Insurance Commission, 181
Intelligence, 14–15, 21, 38, 47–51, 57, 71, 75, 80,

86–9, 94, 99, 118, 140, 159, 193, 235, 248–9
Intercepts and decrypts, 19, 26, 47–51, 235, 237–9
Inter-Allied,
    Armistice Commission, 27
    Aviation Committee, 108
    Commissions of Control, 34, 36–8
    Committees,
        Anti-aircraft, 12
        Tanks, 12
        Trade, 11
    Council, 11
    Food Council, 215
    Munitions Board, 193
    Munitions Council, 192–3
    Naval Commission of Control, 29
International Food Board, 216
International Red Cross, 62
International Shipping Committee, 96
International Socialist Bureau, 247
International Union of Ex-servicemen (IUX), 162
Internment, 52–3, 131, 136–9, 141, 242, 244–5, 249
Intervention, state, 173–81, 187, 199–200, 218–31
Invasion fears, 80–83, 122
Inventions, 39–47
    Awards Committees, 40–42, 47
Ipswich, 193
Iraq, 29, 38, 51, 70
Ireland, 29, 31, 54, 123–4, 127–8, 155, 163–4, 190, 193, 214, 239, 247–52
    Northern, 164
'Irish Brigade', German, 247, 249–50, 252
Irish Citizen Army, 248, 250
Irish Convention, 248, 250–51
Irish Free State, 158, 160, 164, 248
    (Consequential Provisions) Act, 164
Irish Home Rule, 247–9
Irish Land (Provisions for Sailors and Soldiers) Act (1919), 164
Irish National Recruiting Committee, 127, 250
Irish National Volunteers (INV), 247, 249
Irish Peat Enquiry, 191
Irish Republican Brotherhood (IRB), 247
Irish Soldiers' and Sailors' Land Trust, 164
Irish Unionist Alliance, 251
Irish Volunteers, 123, 247–8
Islam, 33
Italo-Turkish War (1911–12), 105
Italy, vii, 4, 9, 11–15, 22, 25–8, 34, 36, 38, 65, 68, 74, 76, 88, 104, 107, 118–19, 125–6, 131, 137–9, 144, 155, 168, 185, 193–4, 196, 234–7
    Asiago Front, 76
    Air Force, 110
    Army, 4, 51, 63, 73–6, 202
    British Army in, 74–6
    Navy, 94
    Piave Front, 76, 107

Jabotinsky, M., 128
Jackson, Messrs J., 210
Jamaica, 24
Japan, 9, 11–13, 17, 21, 24–5, 27, 34, 77, 91, 101, 131, 144, 188, 193
Java, 155
Jeddah Agency, 68–9
Jellicoe, Sir John, 103, 167, 169, 253
Jersey, 125, 160
    Insular Defence Corps, 125
    War Loan, 183
Jerusalem, 65
Jeudwine, General, 119
Jewish War Services Committee, 127
Joffre, Joseph, 17
Joint Army and Navy Aeronautical Purchasing Committee, 188
Joint Committee of Women's Trade Unions, 210
Joint Industrial Councils, 202
Joint Naval and Military Committee (1916), 53
Jones,
    Clement, 23
    Lieutenant H. A., 53
Jordan, Sir John, 13
Jutland, Battle of (1916), 48, 97–101, 103, 117–18, 131, 151–2

Kantara, 70
Karl, Emperor, 26
Kelly, Alderman James, 251
Kemal, Mustapha, 27, 29
Kensington, South, 124, 170
Kent, Colonel A. E., 64
Kenya, 24, 141, 241
Kerr, Lord Mark, 73
Keyes,
    Commander Adrian, 68
    Admiral Sir Roger, 101
Keynes, J. M., 34
Kiachow, 33
Kiel, 103
Kiggell, Sir Lancelot, 254
King's African Rifles, 78–9, 158
    1/2nd Battalion, 142
King's Certificate, 162
King's Fund, 163
King's Proctor, 91
King's Royal Rifle Corps (KRRC),
    2nd Battalion, 141
    16th Battalion, 141
Kipling, Rudyard, 168, 232
Kirke, Colonel Walter, 51
Kitchener, Lord, 2–3, 7–9, 11, 15, 19, 50, 54, 58, 63, 69, 74, 78, 80, 122–3, 127, 129, 135, 142, 155–6, 169, 176–8, 198, 232, 244, 250
    National Memorial Fund, 163
Klagenfurt, 34, 37
Knox, Sir Alfred, 17, 19–21
Kolchak, Admiral, 20
Krupps, 39
Küepferle, Anton, 243–4

Kut, Siege of (1915–16), 66, 69–70, 72, 142,
    149, 155, 239
Kynoch, Messrs, 224

La Becqe, 54
Labour, viii, 187, 190, 193–4, 196–203, 207–12
    Corps, 56
    Ministry of, 155, 162, 172, 178–9, 181, 201–2,
        205–6, 210, 225, 230
        Factory Department and Inspectorate, 210,
            223
            Chief Inspector of Factories' Work
                Committee, 223
        Industrial Relations Department, 202
        Intelligence Division, 201
        Labour Resettlement Committee, 163
        Statistical Department, 202
    Party, 2–3, 121, 162, 245, 247
        Independent (ILP), 245–7
    Resettlement Scheme, 162–3
Labour Leader, 245–6
Lambeth, 170–71
Lancashire Fusiliers, 1st Battalion, 140
Lancaster Illumination Scheme, 43
Lancers, 9th, 141
Langemarck, 59
Langley, Sir W., 13
Lansbury, George, 247
Lansdowne, Lord, 3
Larkhill, 103
Latham Fund, 163
Latvia, 21
Lausanne,
    Conference (1932), 34
    Treaty of (1922–3), 27, 29, 32, 34
Lawrence,
    T. E., 65, 68–9, 71, 172
    Sir William, 155–6
Lawson, Lieutenant-General H. M., 128–9
League of Nations, 28–9
Leake VC, Captain Martin, 140
Lebanon, 70
Le Cateau, Battle of (1914), 52, 54
Lee,
    MP, Arthur, 156
    Captain H. E., 19
    Commander, 147
Leefe Robinson, Lieutenant W., 113–14
Leek Silk Manufacturers and Dyers Standing
    Joint Committee, 127
Leete, Alfred, 127
Leicester, 211
Leicestershire Regiment, 154
Leipzig, 35–6
    Exhibition, 85
Leisure, 219–22
Leslie, 214
Le Touquet, 147
Lettow Vorbeck, Paul von, 80
Lever, Sir Samuel Hardman, 185
Liberal Party, 2–3, 162

Liberia, 9, 36
Libya, 65, 142
Licensing laws, 219–21, 223
Lille, 136
Limb Fitting Centres, 159
Limburg, 33
Lincolnshire, 215
Lindley, Sir Francis, 19
Lindops, Lieutenant V. S. E., 136
Lingfield Epileptic Colony, 155
Lithuania, 36
Liverpool, 41, 127, 218
    Cotton Association, 85
    Steamship Owners Association, 96
Lloyd George, David, 2–4, 7–9, 14, 27–8, 35, 39,
        52, 116, 119, 141, 169, 176–8, 180, 194,
        196, 225, 232, 245, 251, 254
Local Government Board, 126, 181, 243–4
    War Refugees Committee, 243–4
Locker-Lampson, Lieutenant Commander O., 60
Lodge, Sir Oliver, 41–2
Lody, Karl, 241–2, 244
London, 27, 82, 104, 112–13, 115–17, 126, 142,
        161, 164, 167, 169–72, 209, 211, 216,
        218–19, 222, 232, 240
    Chamber of Commerce, 85
    City of, Corporation, 176
    Conference on Reparations (1924), 32
    Declaration of,
        (1909), 83
        (1914), 9, 11–12
    Fire Brigade, 116
    Necropolis Company, 168
    Omnibus Company, 210
    Tower of, 244, 251
    Treaty of
        (1839), 1
        (1915), 12
Londonderry, Lady, 204
London Gazette, 136, 144
Long, Walter, 248
Longwith, 195
Loos, Battle of (1915), 52, 54, 56–7, 106
Lords, House of, 83, 206
Lorrraine, Sir Percy, 14, 35, 49
Lovat Scouts, 129
Lovett Evans, Sir Charles, 64
Lowestoft, 105, 113
Lucas, Commander, 29
Lutyens, Sir Edwin, 165
Luxeuil, 112, 114
Luxemburg, 33
Lydd, 103
Lympne, 174
Lys, Battle of the (1918), 54–5, 57
Lytton Committee (1920), 162–3

MacDonald, Ramsay, 245–7
MacDonogh, Sir George, 51
Macedonia, 9, 74, 118, 153–4, 165
Machine guns, 59, 61–2, 193

Madsen, 61
Machine Gun Corps, 59, 62, 170
    Heavy Branch, 62, 64, 130
Mackenzie-Kennedy, Major-General E. C. W., 142
Mackey & Monks, Messrs, 223
Mackinder, Sir Halford, 19
MacLean, Lachlan, 215
MacNeill, Eoin, 247
'Mad Mullah', 79
Madrid, 14, 49, 51
Mahan, Alfred Thayer, 96
Malleson, Colonel, 149
Malta, 22, 24, 31, 79, 101, 152, 175, 200
    Active Service Battalion, 159
    Mining Company, 143
    Royal Malta Artillery, 159
Man, Isle of, 125, 160
Mance, Sir Henry Osborne, 35, 54
Manchester, 169, 189, 211
    Calico Printers' Association, 127
    Gorton, 223
    Ship Canal Company, 202
Mannix, Archbishop Daniel, 246
Manpower Distribution Board, 197–8
Manpower Policy, 123, 128–9, 196–8
Manston, 108
Marne, Battle of the (1914), 54, 109
Mapplebeck, Captain W., 136
Maps, 20–21, 33, 37, 56–8, 64, 69, 71–3, 75–6,
    80, 107, 117, 237, 250
Marara, 70
Marconi Company, 236
Margate, 105, 115, 132
Marienwerder, 34
Markham, Miss V., 206
Markievicz, Countess, 249–52
Marlows Cordite Drying Stores, 195
Masterman, Charles, 170, 232, 236
Masterton-Smith, Sir James, 5, 12, 18, 31, 66,
    86, 101, 115, 124, 183, 190, 248
Mata Hari *see* McLeod, Margueritte
Maternity and Child Welfare Act (1918), 224
Maude, Lieutenant-General Sir Stanley, 142
Maurice, Sir Frederick, 254
    Affair (1918), 4, 7
Mauritius, 22, 79
Maxse, Sir Ivor, 254
Maxwell, Sir John, 69
McCudden, Captain J. B., 136
McKenna, Reginald, 3, 9, 253
McLeod, Margueritte, 243
Mecca, 66
Medal and Clasps Tribunal, 142
Medal Committee, War Workers', 139
Medals and decorations, 119, 131–3, 135–44,
    206–7
    African General Service Medal, 141
    Air Force Cross, 131, 137
    Air Force Medal, 131, 137
    Albert Medal, 136, 139
    Allied Subjects Medal, 143

Bronze Medal for Saving Life at Sea, 139
Conspicuous Gallantry Medal, 131, 133
Distinguished Conduct Medal, 144
Distinguished Flying Cross, 131, 137
Distinguished Flying Medal, 137
Distinguished Service Cross, 132, 137, 140
Distinguished Service Medal, 131, 133
Distinguished Service Order, 137, 140, 144
Khedive's Sudan Medal, 141
Mentions in despatches, 132–3, 141, 144
Mercantile Marine War Medal, 132, 138–9
Meritorious Service Medal, 141
Military Cross, 140, 144
Military Medal, 140
Order of the British Empire, 133, 138, 140
Order of St Michael and St George, 140
Naval Meritorious Service Medal, 133
Royal Red Cross, 206
Silver Medal for Saving Life at Sea, 139
Silver War Badge, 137, 139, 143
Territorial Force War Medal, 143
Victoria Cross, 131–2, 135–7, 140–42, 169
Victory Medal, 133, 139–40, 143–4
War Medal, British, 133, 137, 139, 143
War Service Badges, 126, 131
1914 Star, 132–3, 140, 143
1914–15 Star, 133, 137, 143
Medical Board, 154
Medical Research Committee, 153–4
Medicine, 118–19, 150–51, 153–6
Mediterranean, 11, 49, 69, 71, 73, 92–4, 97,
    153–5, 243
    Expeditionary Force (MEF), 62, 70, 130
    GHQ, 70–72
Mellor, Bronley & Co., Messrs, 211
Memel, 36
Memorials *see* War Memorials
Menin Gate, 165
Mercantile Marine *see* Merchant Navy
Mercantile Marine Vessels, Committee on
    (1917), 93
Mercantile Marine Service Association, 30
Merchant Navy, 118, 126, 131–2, 138–9, 148,
    151–3, 155, 159, 165, 167, 169, 184, 198,
    203, 211, 218
    Reserve, 133
Merseyside, 202
Mesopotamia, 17, 22, 49, 66–72, 107, 117, 137,
    140, 150, 152, 155–6, 165
    Commission, 66–7, 69–70, 153, 155
    Expeditionary Force, 70
    GHQ, 49, 65, 72
    Tigris Corps, 72
Messines, Battle of (1917), 54, 56–7, 64, 106
Meteorological Office, 179
Meteren, 54
Metropolitan Police, 221–2
    Strike, 246
Mexico, 49, 235
Meyer, Albert, 244
Michelin School of Bombing, 115

Middle East, vii, 11, 19, 65–7, 69–71, 76, 137
Middlesex,
  County War Hospital, 154
  Regiment, 25th Battalion, 19
Middlewich, 196
Midhurst, 218
Midleton, Lord, 7, 54, 127, 251
Midleton Committee on National Monuments
  on Battlefields, 168
Midwives Board, Central, 224
Milford Haven, 83
Milibern Trust, 164
Military, Naval and Air Force Pensions
  Committee (1919), 157
Military Service Acts, 124–5, 128–30
  (1916), 123, 126, 129
  (1918), 123, 248
Military Service (Civil Liabilities) Committee,
  181, 184–5
Military Service Conventions, 125–6
Millar, Signalman, 131
Millbank, 63–4, 154
Million Fund, 44–5
Milne,
  Sir Berkeley, 100
  Sir George, 74
Milner,
  Lord, 4, 7, 12, 35, 54, 69, 86, 229, 253
  Committee, 213, 215–16
Mines,
  Land, 56–8
  Sea, 40, 42, 66, 83, 92–6, 99, 101, 139
Misk,196
Mixed Arbitration Tribunals, 32–3
Mobilisation,
  Industrial, 187–98
  Military, 55, 130, 135
Mohammedans, 168
Moir, Ernest, 46
Moltke, Helmuth von, 53
Mombassa, 80
Mons, Battle of (1914), 52, 54, 56, 59, 109
Montagu Stuart-Wortley, Major-General the
  Hon. E. J., 142
Monteith, Robert, 250
Montenegro, 9, 144
Moore-Brabazon, J. T. C., 59, 106
Morale,
  National, viii, 231–9
  Service, 145–50
Morality, 203, 205–6, 218–22
Moray Golf Club, 247
Morel, E. D., 245
Morocco, 14, 50
Morecambe, 223
Morgan & Co, J. P., 182, 185–6
Mosul, 25
Moulton, Lord, 46
Mount Sorel, 54
Mudros, 70, 140, 166
Mullion, 103

Munitions, 18, 40, 75, 118–19, 177–8, 187,
  192–6, 201, 208–12, 223
Ministry of, 39–40, 46–7, 64, 171, 174–9,
  181, 187–97, 202–3, 205, 208–12, 224
  Boards,
    Potash Production, 189
  Branches,
    Contracts, 177, 192
    Finance, 182
    Historical, 177, 194, 211
    Optical Munitions, 189
    Optical Munitions and Glassware, 189
    Potash Production, 189
  Committees,
    Demobilisation and Reconstruction, 229
    Food Investigation, 216
    Health of Munitions Workers, 222–3
    Russian Accounts, 186
  Council, 192–3, 229
  Departments,
    Aircraft Production, 46, 192
    American and Transport, 189, 192
    Chemical Warfare, 62–3, 196, 212
    Design, 63
      Chemical Advisory Committee, 63
      Small Arms Section, 195
    Explosives Supply, 46, 182, 191–2, 194,
      196
    Factories, 192
    Inspection, 192, 194
    Labour, 192, 202
    Mechanical and Engine, 192
    Mechanical Warfare, 177
    Mineral Oil Production, 195
    Munitions Inventions (MID), 39, 43–4,
      46–7, 191–2
      Chemical Inventions Committee, 61
      Chemical Research Section, 61
      Chemical Waste Products Committee,
        46, 191
      Nitrogen Products Committee, 46, 191
    North American, 192
    Supply, 189, 192
    Trench Warfare, 40, 63, 192
      Chemical Advisory Committee, 63
      Chemical Warfare Committee, 63
    Trench Warfare Supply, 192
  Directorates
    Munitions Supply, 193
    Ordnance Supply, 193
  Divisions,
    Labour Intelligence, 242
  Groups,
    Air, 192
    Design, 63, 192
    Engines, 192
    Explosives, 63, 192
    Finance, 192
    Guns, 192
    Industrial (Reconstruction), 211
    Labour, 192

Materials, 192
Ordnance, 192
Requirements and Statistics, 192
Steel and Iron, 192
Warfare, 192
Secretariat, 192
Munitions of War Acts, 177, 187, 199, 201
Munitions of War Committee, 189
Murmansk, 17–20
Murray,
Sir Archibald, 55, 68, 70
Gilbert, 232
Colonel R. E., 78
Murray Committee, 203
Museums, 170–72, 219
Mutinies, 146, 148–9

Nairobi, 80
Napoleonic Wars, 121, 131
Napsbury, 154
Natal, 24
National Association of Discharged and
Demobilised Sailors and Soldiers (NADSS),
161–2
National Association of Flour Importers, 217
National Association of Master Bakers and
Confectioners, 127
National Committee for the Preservation of the
British War Graves, 168
National Council of Public Morals, 219–20
National Debt Office, 186
National factories, 192–3, 195–6, 202, 222–3,
230
National Federation of Discharged and
Demobilised Sailors and Soldiers (NFDSS),
161–3
National Gas Council, 211
National Health Insurance Committee, 179
National Insurance Act (1911), 157
Nationalism, 22–3, 28–9, 37, 123, 247–52
National Organisation of Fish, Poultry, Game
and Rabbit Traders, 127
National Physical Laboratory, 43–6
National Registration Act, 198
National Relief Fund, 185
National Reserve, 123, 129
National Roll, King's, 162–3
National Savings Committee, 181, 184–5
National Service, Ministry of, 130, 175, 178,
180–81, 197–8
Finance Department, 198
Labour Supply Department, 198
Medical Department, 127
Prisoners of War Employment Committee,
213
Recruiting Department, 127, 198
Registration Department, 198
Secretariat, 198
Statistics Department, 198
Trade Exemptions Department, 127, 198
Women's Work Department, 198, 211

National Service Council, 198
National Service Scheme, 197
National Shipyards, 196, 221
National Union of Boot and Shoe Operatives,
202, 210
National Union of Ex-servicemen (NUX), 162
National Union of Women Workers, 203
National War Aims Committee, 181, 231
National War Museum *see* Imperial War
Museum
National Workmens' Council, 221
Native Labour Corps, 22–3, 68, 78, 80, 128,
143, 153, 158, 167
Nauru, 32
Naval Aircraft Works, 43, 61, 110
Naval Airship Works, 104
Naval and Military War Pensions Act,
(1915), 154
(1917), 154
Naval aviation, 101–4
Naval Convention, Allied (1915), 11
Naval Marriages Act (1915), 131
Naval Review, 237
Navy and Army Canteen Board, 146–9, 206
Navy and Army Insurance Fund, 157
Navy, Army and Air Force Institute (NAAFI),
149, 206
Navy List, 134, 237
Neale Aerial Warship, 42–4
Neilson, Captain, 20
Nekl, 68
Nelson, Admiral Lord, 171
Nepal, 144
Netheravon, 109
Netherlands, 11, 14, 35, 50–53, 83–4, 88–9, 91,
95, 109, 113, 131–2, 136–7, 139, 141, 151,
193, 214, 232, 234–5, 240
Neuilly, Treaty of (1919), 27, 32, 36
Neumann, Karl, 36
Neutral Press Committee, 232
Neutrals, 14, 83–4, 86–7, 236, 239
Neuve Chapelle, Battle of (1915), 52, 56–7
New Armies, 65, 80, 122, 124–5, 128–30, 135,
141, 143
Newcastle, 113
New Europe Group, 28
Newfoundland, 22, 24
Regiment, Royal, 25
Newhaven, 45, 211
New Hebrides, 33
Newman, Sir George, 206
New Ministries Act (1916), 178
Newspaper Proprietors Association, 238
Newport, 185
New South Wales, 24
New York, 182, 186
New Zealand, 22–5, 32, 36, 76, 129, 170, 193,
205, 213
Division, 57, 125
Western Pacific Expeditionary Force, 79–80
Nicaragua, 9

Nicholas II, Tsar, 19–20
Nicholson, Lord, 121
Niemeyer, Sir Otto, 35, 180, 185
Nigeria, 24, 141
    Regiment, 156
Nightingale, Major Guy, 140
Nissen, Major P. N., 47
    Huts, 47, 190
Nivelle, Robert, 4, 17
Nixon, General Sir John, 67, 142
Nobel Explosives Company, 196
No Conscription Fellowship (NCF), 246
Nore, The, 100
Norfolk, 193
Northern Barrage, 95
Northcliffe, Lord, 232, 236, 253
North Sea, 83, 92, 96
Norway, 83–4, 88–9, 93, 151, 185, 188, 193–5
Norwich, 193
Notification of Births Act (1907), 224
Nottingham, 196
Novorossiisk, 17
Nurses, 140, 159–60, 203–4, 206–7
Nyasaland, 24, 241, 244

Oberdorf, 115, 136
O'Caffrey, Lieutenant P. M. C., 49
Ocean Island, 32
Ockleford, Lieutenant, 70
Officers' Training Corps (OTC),
    Dublin University, 251
    Inns of Court, 129
    Trinity College, 251
Official Histories, vii, 11, 15, 18, 50, 53–4, 67–8,
    72, 74, 78, 95, 97, 99, 101, 105, 117–20
Official Secrets Act, 241
Oldbury, 195–6
Oliphant, Lancelot, 1
Olsson case, 241
Orders in Council, 83–4, 87
Ordnance,
    Board, 187, 195
    Committee, 193
        Trench Warfare Section, 195
Orfordness, 43, 61, 115
Orkneys, 3, 83
Orlando, Vittorio, 27
Ormsby-Gore, Captain, 67
Ostend, 53, 60, 100, 103, 106
'Otters', 40, 93
Owen, Wilfred, 142, 154
Overseas Prize Disposal Committee, 84, 89, 181
Oxford, 109
    University, 247

Pacific, 11, 24, 32, 76, 79
Pacifism, 245–7
Palestine, 12, 29, 65–71, 73, 107, 117, 128, 168
    Exploration Fund, 73
Panama, 9, 84, 144
Pan-Islamism, 79

Pankhurst, Christobel, 246
Papal States, 15
Parachutes, 43, 107, 109
    Calthrop, 109–10
    Spencer, 109
Paravanes, 92–4
Pares, Professor Bernard, 18, 20
Paris, 13–14, 23, 27–9, 37, 112–13, 169, 188, 192
    Economic Conference (1916), 23
    Peace Conference (1919), 23–5, 27–38
        British Delegation, 29–30, 33–5, 37
        British Empire Delegation, 23, 25
Paris Plage, 147
Parker,
    Dr L. H., 64
    VC, Lance Corporal, 131
Parkeston Quay, 41
Parliamentary Committees,
    Air, 115
    Employers, 162
    Recruiting, 129
Passchendaele see Ypres, Third Battle of
Patriotic League of Britons Overseas, 188
Patsig, Helmut, 36
Pay, 131, 137, 139, 147, 205–6
Paymaster General, 160
Peace,
    Celebrations, 165–7, 169
    Offers, 12, 15
    Settlement, 25–38
    Society, 245
Pearse, Patrick, 248
Pease, J. A., 245
Peel, Lord, 84
Peking, 13, 51
Pembrey Explosives Factory, 183, 196
Penrhyndeudraeth, 195–6
Pensions, 35–6, 127, 156–61, 180–81, 198
    Ministry of, 144, 154–5, 157–9, 161, 225
        Disablement Service Branch, 159
        Hospital Management Branch, 154
        London Region, 159
        Optical Appliance Branch, 159
Persia, 14, 17, 20–21, 29, 69–70, 72, 79,
    118–19, 144
    Committee, 67
    South Persia Rifles, 143
Persian Gulf, 65
Pétain, Philippe, 4, 17, 111
Peterborough, 214
Petroff, Peter, 242
Petrograd, 18–19, 21, 51
    Conference (1917), 12
Petroleum Rationing Committee, 223
Phalerum, 167
Photographs, 7, 18–19, 42, 54, 57–9, 66, 68,
    72–3, 76, 78–9, 95, 100–101, 103–4, 106–7,
    109, 113, 115, 195, 205, 208, 211–12, 223,
    238, 243
Pilcher, Major-General T. D., 142
Pilckem, 59

Pinehurst, 176
Piraeus, 13, 167
Pitsea, 223
Plebiscites, 34
Plesetskaya, 21
Plumer, Sir Herbert, 169
Plymouth, 81, 84, 92–3, 98–9, 102, 158, 185,
    240
Pohl, Admiral von, 101
Poland, 16, 28, 144, 193, 242
Police, 125, 220–22, 246
Poole, 187
    Major-General F. C., 19–20
Poppy Day, 162, 204
Portchester, 95, 101
Porton Down, 62–5, 212
Portsmouth, 100–101
Portugal, 9, 14, 16, 34, 78–9, 88, 139, 144,
    193–4, 214, 235
    Expeditionary Force, 16–17, 52, 55, 57–8
Portuguese East Africa, 80
Potter's Bar, 116
Poulsen Wireless Telegraph Company, 47
Power, Lieutenant, 61
Press, 14, 232–9, 247
    Bureau, Official, 69, 90, 96, 116, 236–9
    Panel, 232
Preston, 218
Price of Coal (Limitation) Act (1915), 225
Prices, 182, 199–200, 213, 216–17, 219, 224–5,
    247
Prime Minister's Committee (1918), 6
Prisoners of war, 20–21, 27, 78, 80, 93, 127,
    131–2, 136, 138–43, 145, 147, 179, 212–13,
    240, 242, 245, 247
    Committee on the Treatment by the Enemy
        of British, 139, 142
    Information Bureau, 143
Privy Council, 86, 90, 244
    Advisory Council, 44–5
        Applications Committee, 44
    Committee for Scientific and Industrial
        Research, 44–6
Prize Claims Committee, 181
Prize courts, 84, 89, 91
Prize money, 66, 84–5, 91
Propaganda, 108, 209, 231–9
    Leaflets, 233, 235–6
Public Prosecutions, Director of, 179
Public Record Office, 179
Public Records Act
    (1958), vii, 118
    (1967), viii, 118
Public Trustee Office, 31, 85, 90, 179, 203, 244
    Investment Advisory Committee, 90
    Trading with the Enemy Department, 31, 90
    Whitley Council, 229
Pulham, 103–4

Q-ships, 92–4, 98, 132
'Queen Alexandra's Field Forge Fund', 221

Queen Alexandra's Hospital (Cosham), 159
Queen Alexandra's Imperial Military Nursing
    Service (QAIMNS), 203
Queen Alexandra's Military Hospital, 154, 159
Queen Alexandra's Royal Naval Nursing Service
    (QARNNS), 204
Queen's Ferry, 195–6
Queen Mary's Army Auxiliary Corps (QMAAC),
    204–7
Queen Mary's (Roehampton) Hospital, 159
Queensland, 24
Quinan, Kenneth B., 195–6

Radio Research Establishment, 43
Railton, Rev. David, 165
Railway Executive Committee, 173–4, 181
    General Managers' Representative
        Sub-committee, 174
    Good Managers' Meetings, 174
Railways, 53–5, 57, 75, 79, 116, 158, 170, 173–4,
    184, 193, 201, 211, 223–5, 227
    Glasgow and South Western, 211
    Great Western, 156, 170, 174
    London, Brighton and South Coast, 174
    Midland, 170
Railways Act (1921), 225, 229
Rainham, 196
Ramsgate, 113, 117, 132
Rapallo Conference (1917), 4
Rationing, 216–18, 223, 226
Rawlinson, Sir Henry, 54, 253–4
Reading, 108
    Lord Chief Justice, 250
Reconstruction, 37–8, 193, 226–31
    Ministry of, 176, 178–9, 181, 209, 226
        Advisory Council, 211, 229
            Women's Housing Sub-committee, 211
        Committees,
            Acquisition and Valuation of Land, 228,
                230
            Adult Education, 229
            Central Materials Supply, 229
            Disposal of Surplus Government
                Property Advisory, 229
            Increases of Rent, 229
            Local Government, 229
            Machinery of Government, 229
            Reconstruction, 229
            Storage and Transit, 229
            Women's Advisory, 229
        Sub-committees,
            Acquisition of Powers, 229
            Finance, 229
            Forestry, 229
            Housing, 229
        Surplus Government Property Advisory
            Council, 229
Recruitment, 121–30
Red Cross, 207
    Graves Registration Unit, 165
    Society, 154

Redmond, John, 247, 250
Red Sea, 84, 131
'Red Star Society', 221
Refugees, 203, 234, 241–3
Relief in Europe, Committee for, 181
Renfrew (Canada), 196
Rents and Mortgage Interest (Rent Restriction)
 Act (1915), 224
Rents and Mortgages (Amendment) Act (1918),
 224
Reparations, 29–32, 34–6, 105, 115
 Commission, 31, 34–5, 96, 181
  Committee of Experts, 34
  London Committee, 35–6
Representation of the People Act (1918), 126,
 137, 226, 248
Requisitioning (Carriage of Foodstuffs)
 Committee, 178
Requisitions, 174–6
Reserve Battalion, 15th (Overseas), 128
Resettlement schemes, 163–5
Restriction of Enemy Supplies, Committee on,
 84, 179, 181
Retail trades, 201
Reuters, 236
Revitaillement, Commission Internationale de,
 18, 181, 193
Rheims, Battle of (1918), 56
Rhine, 26
Rhineland, 16, 29, 31, 34, 37–8, 114, 118–19
Rhodesia, North and South, 78
 1st Rhodesian Regiment, 228
Rhodesians, 22, 158
Rhodes Moorhouse VC, Lieutenant, 136
Rhondda, Lord, 214, 217
Richthofen, Manfred von, 136
Rifle Brigade, 170
Rintelen, Franz, 244
Road Transport Board, 230
Roberts,
 Field Marshal Lord, 57
 G. H., 230
Robertson, Sir William, 3–5, 7–9, 68, 254
Rochdale National Shell Factory, 193
Rocksavage, Lady, 204
Roehampton, 136, 159
Roman Catholics, 123, 246, 248
 Chaplains, 146
Romania, 9, 14, 16, 20, 36–7, 60, 74, 144, 185,
 188, 193
Rome, 12–13, 51, 68, 87
Room 40 *see under* Admiralty
Rosyth, 101, 200,
 'Garden City', 226
Rotterdam, 35, 91, 243
Rouen, 223
Rowan, Major C., 21
Royal Aircraft Factory, 39, 43, 45, 107, 109–110,
 176, 188, 200
Royal Air Force (RAF), 18, 21, 30, 77, 108,
 110–12, 114–16, 124, 130, 135–8, 143, 147–9,

153, 158, 160–61, 165–6, 171, 178, 188, 193,
 227, 233, 237
Independent Force (IAF), 112, 114–15, 148
 No 3 Wing, 114
 No 9 Wing, 114
Memorial Fund, 166
Pigeon Service, 233
Service records of, 136–8
Staff College, 110, 115, 136
Royal Airship Works, 43, 104
Royal Armament Research and Development
 Establishment, 44
Royal Army Clothing Department, 55
Royal Army Medical College,
 Anti-Gas Department, 63–4
Royal Army Medical Corps (RAMC), 63, 128–9,
 148
Royal Army Ordnance Corps (RAOC), 56
Royal Army Veterinary Corps (RAVC), 56
Royal Arsenal *see* Woolwich
Royal Artillery (RA), 59, 65, 170
 Committee, 195
 Experimental Battery, 63
Royal Australian Navy, 98, 146
Royal Commissions,
 Awards for Inventors (1919–37), 47
 Compensation for Suffering and Damage by
  Enemy Action (1921), 30
 Easter Rising (1916), 249
 Private Manufacture and Trading in Arms
  (1935), 178
 Proportional Representation (1918), 228
 Sugar Supply (1914), 175, 179, 181, 216–17
 Wheat Supplies (1916), 181, 216–17
Royal Defence Corps, 129, 227
Royal Engineers (RE), 56, 73, 140, 186
 Experimental Company, 63
 Experimental (Chemical Warfare) Stations,
  62–3
 Special Brigade, 62–4
 Special Gas Companies, 62
 Tunnelling Company, 170
 6th Field Survey Company, 76
 7th Field Survey Company, 73
Royal Exchange, 170
Royal Field Artillery (RFA), 70, 154
Royal Fleet Auxiliaries, 122
Royal Flying Corps (RFC), 49, 60, 68, 70, 74,
 77, 105–11, 122, 124, 130, 135–8, 141, 143,
 152, 154, 197, 206, 213, 227, 232, 237
 Administration and Command, Committee
  on (1916), 108
 Administration Wing, 108
 Air Operations Directorate, 108
 Record Office, 153
 Service records of, 136–8
 Alexandria Seaplane Squadron, 66
 HQ, Middle East, 66
 8 Brigade, 114–15
 No 5 Group, 135
 No 5 Wing, 113

No 41 Wing, 115
No 4 Squadron, 111
No 10 Squadron, 108
Royal Fusiliers, 128
Royal Garrison Artillery (RGA), 117
Royal Gunpowder Factory *see* Waltham Abbey
Royal Hampshire Regiment, 1/7th Battalion, 142
Royal Institute of British Architects, 117
Royal Irish Constabulary (RIC), 249–50
Royal Marines (RM), 124, 133–5, 147, 160
  Band, 133
  Chatham Division, 81, 132–3
  Depot, 133
  Divisional Train, 133
  Engineers, 133
  Labour Corps, 133
  Medical Unit, 133
  Ordnance Company, 133
  Plymouth Division, 81, 132–3, 152
  Portsmouth Division, 81, 132–3, 146
    Portsmouth Battalion, 132
  Special Home Coast Defence Units, 133
  Special Reserve, 135
  Submarine Miners, 146
  5th Battalion, 81
  6th Battalion, 149
Royal Marine Artillery (RMA), 132–3
  Anti-aircraft Brigades, 53
  Heavy Howitzer Brigade, 152
  Heavy Siege Train, 152
  Portsmouth Division, 81
  Siege Brigades, 52
  Special Service Brigade, 53, 133
Royal Marine Light Infantry (RMLI), 131–2, 146, 152
Royal Military College, Sandhurst, 170
Royal Military Police, 56
Royal Mint, 179, 181
Royal Munster Fusiliers,
  1st Battalion, 140
  2nd Battalion, 140
Royal Naval Air Service (RNAS), 60, 66, 76–8, 81, 102–3, 108–9, 111–15, 122–4, 132–8, 146, 152–3, 166, 178
  Armoured cars, 60, 132–4, 151
  Armoured trains, 53
  Expeditionary Force, 152
  Laboratory, 124
  Meteorological Service, 124
  Service records of, 136–8
  No 5 Wing, 152
Royal Naval Division, 53, 66, 122–3, 128, 135, 139, 141, 146, 167, 170
Royal Naval Hospital, Greenwich, 171
Royal Naval Reserve (RNR), 122–3, 126, 132–5, 146, 240
  Service records of, 135, 138
  Trawler Section (RNR)(T), 122, 146
Royal Naval Scientific Service, 41
Royal Naval Volunteer Reserve (RNVR), 49, 122, 132–5

Anti-Aircraft Corps, 113–14, 117, 123, 135
Birmingham Electrical Volunteers, 135
Bristol Division, 135
Clyde Division, 135
Crystal Palace Division, 135
London Division, 135
Mersey Division, 135
Mine Clearance Service, 135
Motor Boat Reserve, 135
Service records of, 135
Shore Wireless Service, 135
Tyne Division, 135
Wales Division, 135
Royal Navy (RN), 9, 44, 49, 83, 91–104, 121–2, 131, 133–4, 146, 154, 158, 160, 165, 168, 204, 233, 247
  Airship Service, 102–3
    Airship Detachment No 2, 152
  Armoured cars, 60, 66, 77, 152
  Auxiliary Patrol, 99, 152
  Cordite factories, 187–8
  Dover Patrol, 99
  Grand Fleet, 97–9, 103, 132, 147, 233
  Grisney Patrol, 100
  Naval Brigades, 52–3, 123, 131
  Service records of, 132–4
  Special Service Squadrons, 52
  5th Destroyer Flotilla, 99–100
Royal Norfolk Regiment, 1/4th Battalion, 148
Royal Northumberland Fusiliers, 1/2nd Battalion, 142
Royal Ordnance, 168, 195
Royal Patriotic Fund Corporation, 154
Royal Small Arms Factory, Committee on Production, 195
Royal Society, 39
  Food War Committee, 214, 217
  Physiology War Committee, 63
Rufigi Delta, 77
Ruhleben, 139
Runciman, Walter, 9
Russell, Bertrand, 245
Russia, vii, 1, 3, 7, 9–12, 15, 17–21, 28–9, 48, 50–52, 60, 65, 83, 88, 96, 125–8, 132–4, 137, 139, 144, 161, 182, 185–6, 188, 193, 196, 231, 235, 237, 242, 247
  Allied intervention in, 17–21, 142
  Army, 63, 69, 202
  Aviation Corps, 109–10
  Committee (1918), 20
  North, 17–21, 140, 142, 149
  South, 17–18, 20–21
Russian Supplies Committee (1915–18), 18
Rutherford, Sir Ernest, 41–2
Rutland, 215
  Lieutenant F. J., 136

St Andrew's Ambulance Association, 128
St David's House, Ealing, 159
St Dunston's, 158
St Eloi, 54

St Germain, Treaty of (1919), 27, 32-3, 35
St Ildephonse, 36
St Ingbert, 114
St John's Ambulance Association, 128
St Julien, 105
St Nazaire, 139
St Quentin, 106
Salisbury, Lord, 7
Salonika, 9, 16, 22, 25, 50, 73-6, 155, 167, 170
   Army, British, 74-6
   Mission, 13
Salvage, 193-4, 230-31
Samoa, 36, 79-80
Samson, Commander G. R., 66, 114
Samuel, Herbert, 254
Sanders, Liman von, 37, 68, 72
Sandon, 167
Sandycroft, 196
San Remo, 28
Sassoon, Siegfried, 154
Sawbridgeworth, 218
Saxe-Coburg-Gotha, House of, 112
Scandinavia, 14, 88, 91-2, 139, 214, 235-6
Scapa Flow, 26, 35
Scarborough, 104-5
Schleswig, 34
Schlieffen, Alfred von, 53
Schlieffen Plan, 53
Schools, 167, 212-13, 220, 225, 232, 234, 241
Science and war, 39-47
Scotland, 31, 105, 123, 158, 160, 163, 186, 190, 247
Scots Guards, 168
Scott, Percy, 40
Scottish Horse, 129
Scottish Oil Mineral Association, 202
Scottish Oil Workers Association, 202
Scottish Rifles, 11th Battalion, 141
Scottish War Savings Committee, 181, 184-5
Scottish Women's Hospital, 206
Scottish Women's Land Army Scheme, 208
Scott Moncrieff Committee, 186
Scout Movement, 212, 242
Seaplanes, 102-4, 152
Secret agents, 49, 51, 107, 109, 159, 240-44
Secret Service, 49-50, 210, 239-40, 242-3
Selby, 214
Senussi, 26, 65, 68, 70, 138, 142
Separation allowances, 36, 125, 151, 157
Serbia, 9, 16, 73-6, 144, 193, 238, 243
   Army, 74-5, 202
Serbs, Croats and Slovenes, Kingdom of, 34, 37
Service records, 132-8, 140-44, 204-5, 207
Sèvres, Treaty of (1920), 27-8, 34
Seychelles, 22, 77
Shackleton, Sir Ernest, 20, 139
Shandon, 41
Shaw, George Bernard, 249
Sheehy-Skeffington, Francis, 249-51
Sheffield, 115, 162
Shells and Fuses Agreement (1915), 199

Shell shock, 145, 153-4, 159
Shell shortage, 2, 177-8
Sherwood Foresters, 141
Shetland Royal Naval Reserve, 122
Ship Licensing Committee, 178
Shipping,
   Chamber of, 228
   Control Committee, 178-9
   Controller, 96, 178, 193
   Merchant, 83-4, 92-6
   Ministry of, 19, 78, 96, 175, 178, 180-81, 192, 229
   Neutral, 83-4, 87-9
Ships,
   HMS Aboukir, 93-5, 151
   HMS Agamemnon, 151
   HMS Amphitrite, 146
   SS April, 93
   HMS Argus, 102-4, 117
   HMS Ariadne, 100
   HMS Ark Royal, 102
   Assaye, 154
   Asturias, 233
   HMS Audacious, 96, 238
   HMS Avenger, 100
   HMS Bacchante, 151
   HMS Ben Machree, 151
   HMS Birmingham, 92
   SS Boldwell, 95
   SMS Breslau, 66, 97, 99-100
   HMS Britannia, 151
   RMS Britannic, 155
   SS Brussels, 232
   HMS Campania, 102-4
   HMS Canopus, 151
   HMS Cardiff, 49
   HMS Carmania, 151
   HMS Comely Bank, 103
   HMS Commonwealth, 49
   HMS Cressy, 93-5, 151
   HMS Dartmouth, 200
   HMS Dreadnought, 97
   HMS Eagle, 104, 147
   SMS Emden, 96-7, 100
   Ems, 93
   HMS Engadine, 103
   HMS Formidable, 94-5, 98
   HMD Freuchy, 151
   HMS Furious, 102, 104
   HMS Glasgow, 50
   SS Glitra, 92
   HMS Glorious, 103
   SMS Goeben, 66, 97, 99-100
   HMY Goissa, 151
   HMS Hampshire, 3, 50, 93-5, 158, 176
   Hare, 148
   HMS Hawke, 151
   HMS Hazard, 151
   HMS Hermes, 102-3
   HMS Hogue, 93-5, 151
   SS Imo, 223

HMS *Invincible*, 98
Kamerun, 84
SMS *Karlsruhe*, 94
Kursk, 148
SMS *Königsberg*, 76–8
HMS *Leviathan*, 146
HMS *Lion*, 152
RMS *Lusitania*, 93–5, 139, 153, 232, 234, 236, 240
HMS *Lynx*, 151
SMS *Magdeburg*, 48
HMS *Mary Rose*, 97
RMS *Mauretania*, 155
HMS *Montagua*, 152
SS *Mont Blanc*, 223
HMD *Morning Star*, 151
HMS *Natal*, 100
HMS *Nubian*, 99
HMS *Ocean*, 151
Ophelia, 98, 101
HMT *Osiris II*, 146
SS *Otaki*, 132
HMS *Queen Elizabeth*, 99
HMS *Pargust*, 132
HMS *Pasley*, 94
HMS *Pathfinder*, 92, 98
HMS *Raglan*, 151
HMS *Repulse*, 103
SS *River Clyde*, 73
HMS *Royal George*, 146
HMS *Satellite*, 146
Sophie Busse, 87
HMS *Southampton*, 146, 152
HMS *Strongbow*, 97
HMAS *Sydney*, 97, 151
HMS *Tara*, 142
Telconia, 48
HMS *Terror*, 99
HMS *Teutonic*, 100, 146
HMS *Topaze*, 146
HMS *Triumph*, 101
HMS *Vanguard*, 237
HMS *Vernon* (Establishment), 95, 100
HMS *Vindictive*, 104
HMS *Vindex*, 101–2
War Cypress, 155
HMS *Warspite*, 152
SS *Woodfield*, 138
HMS *Zubian*, 99
HMS *Zulu*, 99
HM Monitor *M28*, 151
Ships' logs, 98
Shipyard Labour Board, 200
Shoeburyness, 64, 117
Sholto Douglas, Wing Commander W., 106
Short Brothers, Messrs, 43
Shotley, 167
Siam, 9, 16, 144
Siberia, 18–21
Sidcup, 151
Siege Committee, 62

Silesia, 31, 34, 37, 168
Silvertown, 222, 224
Simonstown, 77, 200
Sinai, 65, 73
Singapore, 79
    Mutiny (1915), 148–9
Singapore and Penang Volunteer Force, 77
Sinn Féin, 248–50
Slavo-British Legion,
    1st Battalion, 19, 21
    2nd Battalion, 21
Slessor, Sir John, 104, 106
Slovenia, 34
Small Arms Committee, 195
Small Holdings and Allotments Act (1916), 163
Smith, J., 116
Smith and Coventry, Messrs, 211
Smith Dorrien, Sir Horace, 54, 79, 254
Smuts, Jan, 23, 35, 79, 111–12, 116, 190
    Committee (1917), 112
Snowden, Philip, 246
Soissons, Battle of (1918), 54, 56
Soldiers' and Sailors' Committees, 148
'Soldiers' Heart', 150, 153–4
Soldiers, Sailors and Airmens' Union (SSAU), 162
Somaliland, 24, 79, 200
Somerset Light Infantry, 1st Battalion, 141
Somme, Battle of the (1916), 3, 52, 54, 56–8, 60, 106, 165
Sonar, 39
Sopron, 34
Sopwith Aviation, 47
Sorlavala, 21
Sound ranging, 43, 61
South Africa, 22–4, 29, 35, 76–9, 84, 124, 136, 147, 158, 166, 195, 200, 216, 224, 234, 238, 241
    Aviation Corps, 109, 138
    1st Mounted Brigade, 80
South African War (1899–1902), 22, 83
Southampton, 148
Southend, 166
South Shields, 83
Spain, 14–15, 49–50, 84, 88–9, 96, 139, 193, 235–6
Spalding, 214
Spears, Brigadier-General E. L., 21, 254
Special Branch, 245
Special constables 125
Special Commissions (Dardanelles and Mesopotamia) Act (1916), 66
Special Reserve, 121, 138, 141, 143
    Officers, 143
Spee, Maximilian von, 101
Speyer, Sir Edgar, 244
Spies *see* Secret agents
Sport, 127, 219–20
Spring Rice, Sir Cecil, 14
Stamford Hill, 196
Standard Oil Company, 36

Standing Committee on Metallurgy, 46
Stanstead House, 196
Stern, Lieutenant Colonel S., 64
Stevenston, 83
Stewart, MP, Gershom, 54, 125
Stock Exchange, 85
Stockholm, 14
Stoke-on-Trent, 232
Stokes mortar, 40
Stonehenge, 109
Stopford, Lieutenant-General Sir Frederick, 142
'Stop the War Committee', 245–6
Straits Settlements, 24, 77, 79–80
Strategic bombing, 105, 111–17
Strategy, British, 8–21
Stratford Naval Filling Factory, 196
Stuart VC, Lieutenant, 132
Submarine cables, 48, 237
Submarines, 40–41, 49, 91–6, 139, 170, 220
    E15, 151
    G4, 93
    G9, 94
    G11, 49
Sudan, 51, 78–9, 214
Sueter, Commodore Murray, 102–3, 146–7
Suez Canal, 65, 70–71, 73
Suffolk, 193
Sugar *see under* Royal Commissions
Sumner,
    Lord, 30, 33
    Captain P. H., 106
Sunderland, 244
Superior Blockade Committee, 85
Supply, Ministry of, 180
Supreme Economic Council, 33, 35, 85
Supreme War Council (SWC), 4, 11–12, 15–17,
    33, 233
    Executive War Board, 12
    Military Representatives, 11–12, 17
Sutton Oak, 196
Swaziland, 153
Sweden, 49, 83, 88, 151, 193, 195
Swindon, 196
Swinton, Ernest, 60, 254
Switzerland, 14, 50, 83, 88, 91, 136, 139, 141,
    152, 193, 235–6
Sykes,
    Sir Frederick, 107
    Sir Mark, 14
Syren Lake Force, 21
Syria, 31, 35, 67, 69–73

Tanganyika Motorboat Expedition, 78, 147
Tank,
    Board, 64
    Committee, 64
    Corps, 61–2, 64, 170, 172
    Week, 184
Tanks, 60–62, 64–5, 69, 106, 117, 146, 170,
    183, 197
    Training Centres, 82

Taxation, 181–6, 220, 222
Taylor, Isaac, 47
Tchiterine, George, 242
Tehran, 14
Termination of War Legislation, Legal
    Committee on, 226
Territorial Force (TF), 54, 121–2, 124, 129–30,
    141, 143–4
    Nursing Service (TFNS), 203, 207
Thames, 113, 168
    Tunnels, 116
Thiepval, 165–6
Thomas, Lowell, 172
Thomson,
    Sir Basil, 245
    Sir William, 20, 70, 74
Thirty Year Rule, vii, 118
Tiflis, 51
Tigris, 25, 66, 73, 152
Timber supply, 188, 193, 195, 197, 207, 213–14
Times, The, 149, 238
Titles Deprivation Act (1917), 241, 244
TNT, 44, 46, 191, 196, 222, 224
Tobacco and Matches Control Board, 218
Togoland, 29, 33, 76, 79–80, 118
Tokyo, 51
Tondern, 102–3
Torpedoes, 40, 93–6, 101
Tottenham, 196
Toulouse, 196
Towell, Lieutenant, 59
Tower Hill, 169
Townshend, Major-General Sir Charles, 68, 72,
    142, 149
Toynbee, Arnold, 234
Trade, Board of, 9, 30, 85, 90, 138, 175, 178–81,
    188–9, 194–5, 202, 207, 214, 227–8, 233
    Committees,
        Chemical Products, 189
        Coal, 194
        Coal Exports, 189
        Commercial and Industrial Policy, 189
        Electric Power Supply, 189, 230
        Electrical Trades, 189
        Engineering Industries, 189
        Engineering Trades (New Industries), 189
        Financial Facilities for Trade, 189
        Fish Oil, 213
        Glassware Trade, 189
        Iron and Steel Industries, 189
        Non-Ferrous Metals Trade, 189
        Petrol Control, 194–5
        Post-War Position of Non-Ferrous Metals,
            194
        Post-War Position of Sulphuric Acid and
            Fertiliser Trades, 189
        Post-War Priority, 189
        Production, 199
        Retail Coal Prices, 216
        Shipping and Shipbuilding, 189
        Trade Relations after the War, 201

Textile Industries, 189
Toy, 189
Trade Relations, 189
Tramways, 189, 195
Women's War Employment (Industrial),
210
Zinc Concentration Contract, 189
Council, 189
Departments,
Enemy Debts Clearing Office, 30–31, 90
Marine Insurance Committee, 31
Treaty Execution Committee, 31
Enemy Property Branch, 85
Establishment, 124, 213
Export Licensing, 86
Marine, 89, 96, 217, 228, 236
Petrol Control, 195
Paper Control, 195
Reparation Claims, 30, 105, 115
Solicitor's, 86
Timber Supply, 195, 207
War Trade, 85–8, 179, 181, 185
Petroleum Pool Board, 194
Trade boards, 202
Trade Card Scheme, 200
Trade Clearing House, 88, 91
Trades unions, 199–203, 209–10
Congress (TUC), 201
Trade with the Enemy, Inter-departmental
Committee on, 86
Trading Accounts, Controller of, 189
Trading with the Enemy (Amendment) Act
(1914), 85, 90
Trafalgar Square, 172, 204, 247
Tralee Bay, 247
Trans-caspia, 17, 29
Trans-caucasia, 18
Transjordan, 29, 73
Transport, 54–5, 57, 139–40, 173–4, 193, 209–11,
230
Ministry of, 163, 225, 229
Trans-Siberian Railway, 17
Transvaal, 24
Treasury, 18, 36, 86–7, 89–90, 127, 168, 175,
180–82, 184–6, 196, 198, 217
Agreements, 199
Board, 184, 236
Committees,
Munitions of War, 177
Russian Accounts, 181, 185
Russian Liquidation, 181, 185
War Office Expenditure, 186
War Trade Advisory, 85–7, 179
Departments,
Intelligence, 198
Divisions,
Imperial and Foreign, 168
Standing Committees
Co-ordination of Departmental Action on
Contracts, 186
Expenditure Emergency, 185

Munitions Expenditure Emergency, 185
Naval Expenditure Emergency, 185
Trench warfare, 59–60, 63, 193
Committee, 195
Trenchard, Sir Hugh, 107–8, 114–15, 179
Trevelyan, Charles, 245
Trianon, Treaty of (1920), 27, 32–3
Tribunals, 123, 126, 201
Appeal, 126
Central, 126
Glasgow, 127
Local, 126
Middlesex Appeal, 126
Munitions, 201, 223
Special, 126
Veterinary, 126
Triest, Gustav, 240
Tripolitania, 26
Trowbridge, Rear Admiral, 100
Tsingtau, 76–9, 101, 156
'Tubs for Tommies', 221
Tudor-Hart, P., 40, 95
Turkey, vii, 9–10, 12, 14–15, 22, 25–31, 34–5,
37–8, 49, 65–74, 91, 120, 131, 136, 138–9,
141, 149, 155, 167–8, 232, 234–5
Army, 70, 132
Fifth Army, 68
VIII Corps, 73
Turner, Brigadier-General A. J. 20
Turpin, Sir William Gibbs, 184
Tyne, 113, 201
Tynemouth, 83

U-Boats, 26, 36, 92–6, 104, 232, 249
U–8, 93
U–9, 93
U–12, 93
U–15, 92
U–17, 92
U–19, 247
U–20, 94
U–21, 91
U–35, 142
U–39, 94
U–48, 94
Uganda, 24
Ukraine, 17
Ulster, 164, 248
Savings Committee, 250
Volunteer Force (UVF), 123, 247
Unionist Party, 2–3, 162
Union of Democratic Control (UDC), 28, 245–7
United Irish League, 249
United States, vii, 9–17, 27–8, 32, 36, 43, 46,
49–50, 63, 83–4, 87–9, 92, 95, 101, 119,
125–8, 136, 139, 144, 153, 157, 168–9, 182,
185–6, 190, 193, 213–17, 232–40, 244,
248–9
American Ambulance Unit, 143
Army *see* American Expeditionary Force (AEF)
Army Air Service, 109–10

Chemical Warfare Service, 63
Federal Bureau of Investigation (FBI), 85
Naval Consulting Board, 40
Navy, 41
Universities and the war, 247
University College, London, 63
Unknown Warrior, Tomb of the, 165–7, 169
Uskub, 74
Uxbridge, 42

V2 rocket, 104
Vatican, 14
Vendome, 103, 152
Venice, 114
Venizelos, Eleutherios, 13
Verdun, 140, 168
  Battle of (1916),109
Versailles, 4, 37
  Treaty of (1919), 23, 27–38, 105
Veterans *see* Ex-servicemen
Vickers, Messrs, 188, 201
Victoria, 24
Victoria Embankment, 169
Vienna, 10
Vieyra, Leonard, 241, 243
Villiers, E. C., 40
Vimy Ridge, Battle of (1917), 23, 54, 56–7
Vittorio Veneto, Battle of (1918), 25, 75
Vladivostock, 17–19
  Allied High Commission, 19
Voisin case, 241–2
Volklingen, 114
Voluntary Aid Detachments (VADs), 203–4,
  206–7
Voluntary enlistment, 121–3, 125–8, 130–31
Volunteer Force, 122, 142
  Motor, 129
Volunteer Training Corps (VTC), 81, 122,
  124–5, 127, 129, 142
  Central Association, 125
  Dublin Battalion, 251
Von Donop, Sir Stanley, 58, 178

Wages, 199–203, 207–12, 226
Wales, 90, 123, 206, 208, 241, 247
  South, 201, 203
Wallace, Sir Richard, 171
Wallace Collection, 171
Walmer, 166
Walsall, 112, 169
Waltham Abbey, 195, 212, 223–4
Walthamstow, 196
Walworth, 143
War aims, 9–21, 24–5
War artists, 170–72
War bonds, 171, 182,
War Book, 5, 90, 179, 234, 242
War Cabinet, 3–8, 15, 23, 31, 51, 68, 87, 97,
  108, 166, 170, 179, 193, 202, 216, 230, 245
  Committees,
    Air Raid Policy (1917–18), 113

Demobilisation (1918), 227–8
Labour, 202
Manpower (1917–18), 197–8
Post-War Priority (1918), 227–8
War Priorities (1917–18), 188, 190–91
Women in Industry (1918), 209, 211
  Physiological Sub-committee, 210–11
Co-ordination of Demobilisation Section, 228,
  230
Department of Propaganda in Enemy
  Countries, 232
Eastern Reports, 67
Historical Section, 120
War casualties, 52, 69, 80, 104–5, 112–13,
  115–16, 143, 150–56, 206, 211, 239
War cemeteries *see* War graves
War charities, 183, 221
  Act (1916), 183–4
  Committee, 183
War Committee, 3, 5–7, 68, 87
War Compensation Court, 175–6
War costs, 33–4, 36,
War Council, 2, 5–7, 60, 65
War crimes, viii, 29, 35–7, 69, 80, 138, 232–7
Ward, MP, John, 19
War diaries, 53, 55–6, 64, 70–71, 74–5, 79–80,
  82, 108, 111, 206
War disabilities, 143–4, 156–63
Wareham, 82
War Emergency Workers' National Committee
  (WEWNC), 217
War Expansion of Public Departments,
  Committee on, 176
War finance, 181–6
War graves, 152, 156, 165–9
War insurance, 182–5
War loans, 182–3, 185–6
War memorials, 165–70
Warneford VC, Flight Sub-Lieutenant Rex,
  113–14, 136, 140
War Office, 3, 14, 45–6, 50, 54–6, 63–4, 70, 75,
  80, 90, 108–9, 119–20, 122–3, 125, 129,
  140, 144, 148–9, 155, 161, 163, 175–80, 186,
  192–4, 196–7, 202, 214, 221, 236, 240
Branches,
  Casualties (Officers), 156
  Mobilisation, 130
  Statistics, 130
Bureaux,
  Information on POWs, 131
Committees,
  Armament Output, 177
  Battle Honours, 119–20
  Battle Nomenclature, 119–20
  Cinematograph, 236
  Demobilisation, 231
  Medical Establishments (1917–18), 155
  Paymasters' Outstanding Accounts, 186
  Supply of Nurses, 206
  War Trophies, 170
  Women's Services, 206

Departments,
- Adjutant General's, 128, 130, 142, 206
- Central, 143
- Military Secretary's, 144
- Quartermaster-General's, 56, 71, 75, 79, 82, 142, 231
- Surveyor General's, 180, 194

Directorates,
- Air Organisation, 109
- Army Contracts, 177, 196
- Military Aeronautics, 108–9
- Military Intelligence (DMI), 50–51
  - MI2, 51
  - MI5, 210, 240, 242–3, 245
  - MI6, 51, 240
  - MI7, 236
  - MI7b, 239
  - MI8, 239
  - MI9c, 239, 243
- Military Operations (DMO), 16, 55, 230–31, 236, 247
  - MO2 (c), 57
- Ordnance, Master-General of, 58, 64–5, 178, 192
- Prisoners of War, 142
- Salvage, 230–31
- Works, 75

Experimental Ground, 65

Offices,
- Contracts, 194
- Contracts Advisory, 177

Sections,
- Raw Materials and Salvage, 194

Whitley Council, 230

War Pensions *see also* Pensions
- Central Advisory Committee on, 159–60

War Pensions Act (1921), 158

War Pensions (Administrative Provisions) Act (1919), 157

War Pensions Committees, 158, 160
- London, 160
- Plymouth, 158
- Scotland, 158, 160
- South West, 160
- Sussex, 158

War Pensions Statuary Committee, 181

War Policy Committee (1917), 4, 6

War Printing Office, 175

War Propaganda Bureau *see* Wellington House

War savings, 183–5, 212, 250
- Committee, 180

War service, 130–44

War Weapons Week, 184–5

War widows, 156–61

War Work Voluntary Scheme, 198

Washington, 11, 14, 48, 51, 235, 237, 249

Waterlow, Sir P., 33

Wedgwood MP, Commander Josiah, 67

Wei hai Wei, 78

Weir,
- Andrew, 194

Sir William, 42

Weizmann, Chaim, 40

Wejh, 68

Welfare, State, viii, 222–31

'Welsh Army Corps', 123

Wellington House, 170, 185, 232, 236

Wells, H. G., 232, 236

Wembley, 62–3, 196
- Pyrotechnics Laboratory, 63

Wesleyans, 131

West Africa, 24, 78, 80

West African Expeditionary Force, 79

West African Frontier Force, 78, 158

Western Front, 2, 8, 22, 27, 39, 51–61, 65, 107–8, 110–11, 114, 117–20, 124, 137, 147, 154–5, 165, 200, 233

'Westerners', 8–10

West Indies, 22, 24, 159

Westminster,
- Abbey, 165–6, 169
- Duchess of, 206

Wheat *see under* Royal Commissions

Wheeldon, Alice, 245–6

Whitby, 104–5

Whitehall, 165

Whitley,
- Committee, 200, 228, 230
- Councils, 225–30
- J. H., 230

Wick Harbour Trustees, 176

Widows *see* War widows

Wigan, 223

Wilhelm II, Kaiser, 26, 35–6
- Canal, 103

Williams VC, Seaman, 132

Willows, Ernest, 47

Wills (Soldiers and Sailors) Act (1918), 157

Wilson,
- Sir Henry, 4, 8, 10, 16, 254
- Woodrow, President, 27–8, 33, 35, 61, 167, 169

Wiltshire Regiment, 3rd Battalion, 141

Windsor, House of, 112

Wingate, Sir Reginald, 68–9

Wintour, U. F., 177, 215, 217

Wireless, 40, 47–9, 106

Woking, 168

Women, viii, 95, 159, 172, 198, 203–12, 214, 218–22, 224, 242
- Service records of, 204–5, 207

Women War Workers' Resettlement Committee, 207

Women Workers, National Corps of, 206, 211

Women's
- Agricultural Volunteers, 208
- Army Auxiliary Corps (WAAC), 172, 204–7, 218
- Corps, Co-ordinating Committee on, 204, 206
- County Committees, 208
- Defence Relief Corps, 207
- Emergency Corps, 203

Employment Committee, 211
Farm and Garden Union, 207
Forestry Corps, 207
Institute (WI), 208
Land Army, 207–8
Legion, 204–5, 207
    Agricultural Branch, 207
National Land Service Corps, 207
Patrols, 203, 205
Police Service, 203, 205
Royal Air Force (WRAF), 204–7
Royal Naval Service (WRNS), 204–7
Volunteer Reserve, 203
War Agricultural Committees, 207
War Savings, 212
Wood, Albert Beaumont, 41
Woodward, Major E. M., 70
Wool (Dorset), 82
Wool Purchase Scheme, 194
Woolwich, 39, 43–4, 46–7, 116, 188, 195, 202,
    212, 222–3
Worcestershire Regiment, 141
Workmen's Compensation Act, 193
Work of National Importance, Committee on, 195
Works, Office of, 179, 224
World War, Second, vii, 104, 110, 118, 121, 137,
    143, 151, 154, 158, 160, 167, 169, 173, 226,
    238
Wylie, William Evelyn, 251

X Committee (1918), 4, 6

Yarde-Buller, Brigadier-General H., 58
Yarmouth, Great, 105, 112
Yokohama, 168
Young Men's Christian Association (YMCA),
    143, 145, 172, 183
Young Women's Christian Association (YWCA),
    172
Ypres, 140, 165, 168
    First Battle of (1914), 52, 54, 56, 142
    Second Battle of (1915), 54, 56, 59, 105
    Third Battle of (1917), 4, 6, 52, 54, 56–7,
        118–19
Yugoslavia *see* Serbs, Croats and Slovenes,
    Kingdom of

Zanzibar Carrier Corps, 143
Zeebrugge, 53, 99–101, 106, 114–15
    Raid (1918), 100–101, 132, 152
Zeppelins, 50, 102, 111–16, 140, 176
    L15, 116
    L21, 114
    L31, 114
    L33, 116
    L49, 115
    L70, 116
    LZ77, 114, 116
Zierikzee, 113
Zimmermann, Arthur, 235
    Telegram (1917), 235
Zionism, 10, 29, 33, 40, 70
Zion Mule Corps, 71, 143, 161